Fodor's 90
Caribbean

D0595389

Fodor's Travel Publications, Inc.
New York and London

Fodor's Caribbean

Editors: Jacqueline Russell, Christopher Billy, Vernon Nahrgang
Area Editor: Honey Naylor
Editorial Contributors: Carmen Anthony, Pamela Bloom, John DeMers, Dan Dignam, John English, Ian Glass, David Grambs, Sandra Hart, Joan Iaconetti, Regina McGee, Carolyn Price, Mark Rowland
Research: Todd Whitley
Art Director: Fabrizio La Rocca
Cartographer: David Lindroth
Illustrator: Karl Tanner
Cover Photograph: Tsuneo Nakamura/Four by Five

Design: Vignelli Associates

Special Sales

Contents

Maps and Plans

Foreword

This is an exciting time for Fodor's, as we continue our ambitious program to rewrite, reformat, and redesign all 140 of our guides. Here are just a few of the new features:

★ Brand-new computer-generated maps locating all the top attractions, hotels, restaurants, and shops

★ A unique system of numbers and legends to help readers move effortlessly between text and maps

★ A new star rating system for hotels and restaurants

★ Stamped, self-addressed postcards, bound into every guide, give readers a chance to help evaluate hotels and restaurants

★ Complete page redesign for instant retrieval of information

★ FODOR'S CHOICE—Our favorite museums, beaches, cafés, romantic hideaways, festivals, and more

★ HIGHLIGHTS—An insider's look at the most important developments in tourism during the past year

★ TIME OUT—The best and most convenient lunch stops along exploring routes

★ A mini-journal for travelers to keep track of their own itineraries and addresses

We would like to thank all the island tourist boards and Jose DeJesus at American Airlines for their help and support.

While every care has been taken to assure the accuracy of the information in this guide, the passage of time will always bring change, and consequently, the publisher cannot accept responsibility for errors that may occur.

All prices and opening times quoted here are based on information available to us at press time. Hours and admission fees may change, however, and the prudent traveler will avoid inconvenience by calling ahead.

Fodor's wants to hear about your travel experiences, both pleasant and unpleasant. When a hotel or restaurant fails to live up to its billing, let us know and we will investigate the complaint and revise our entries where the facts warrant it.

Send your letters to the editors of Fodor's Travel Publications, 201 E. 50th Street, New York, NY 10022.

Highlights '90 and Fodor's Choice

Highlights '90

The Caribbean tourism scene was thrown into a tailspin during the 1988–89 winter season when machinists from **Eastern Airlines**—the second leading carrier to the region—went on strike; the airline's bankruptcy soon followed in March 1989. Almost all of Eastern's planes were immediately grounded, leaving many Caribbean nations devastated, at least initially, by the loss of tourist trade. Perhaps the hardest hit was the U.S. Virgin Islands, which at the time of the strike was losing tourism revenue at the rate of $4.9 million a week.

American Airlines, Pan American World Airways, and most flag carriers, including **Air Jamaica** and Trinidad's **BWIA International,** were quick to step up their service to the Caribbean. Eastern's absence, however, as the leader in low-cost airfares drove prices up measurably.

Continental moved into the Caribbean in December 1988, just three months before Eastern's bankruptcy, with flights to Aruba, Dominican Republic, Jamaica, and St. Maarten from its $250 million hub in Newark, New Jersey. No other major carrier flies to these destinations from Newark.

American increased its service to most Caribbean islands in the immediate wake of Eastern's bankruptcy. But its most significant expansion came in April 1989, when American added 11 flights daily out of Miami, which was previously one of Eastern's last remaining strongholds into the Caribbean. American's new destinations out of Miami—added to San Juan, Puerto Rico, and Santo Domingo, Dominican Republic—were Montego Bay and Kingston, Jamaica; Port-au-Prince, Haiti; and Puerto Plata, Dominican Republic. Also expanded was service out of San Juan—the site of American's Caribbean hub. The complete expansion added a total of 3,219 extra seats daily into the Caribbean for American.

In June 1988, **TWA** added express service from San Juan to St. Croix, St. John, and St. Thomas in the U.S. Virgin Islands. TWA flights from New York, St. Louis, and Miami connect with **Virgin Islands Seaplane Shuttle,** whose 17-seat jet prop Grumman Mallard amphibious aircraft depart six times daily from San Juan to the U.S. Virgin Islands.

On the waterways, the super-deluxe, all-suite *Seabourn Pride* made her maiden voyage in December 1988. The nine-deck, 212-passenger vessel, with whirlpools, sauna, and Nautilus, calls at various ports in the Caribbean. Sitmar Cruises merged with Princess Cruises, and there are now eight ships flying the Princess banner.

Columbus sailed through the Caribbean in 1492 and again in 1493, and in commemoration of those voyages, several islands will be having 500th anniversary celebrations. Columbus's ship was blown ashore on the Dominican Republic's Amber Coast in 1492, and there will be island-wide festivities in rememberance of that mishap in 1992. Other islands will be celebrating their "discovery" that year, too. Puerto Rico's anniversary celebration will take place in 1993, and there is major construction throughout the island in preparation for the party.

Anguilla Anguilla is quickly becoming the trendy spot in the Caribbean. The **Rendezvous Bay Hotel,** the island's oldest hotel, is busily constructing new units and plans to have 27 new rooms open by 1990. **Cap Juluca,** a glamorous Moroccan-style resort, continues to add such luxe touches as a free-form swimming pool and additional tennis courts.

Aruba Aruba, one of the fastest growing tourist destinations in the Caribbean, is experiencing more hotel growth than any other Caribbean island. In the interest of developing its accommodations, the Aruban government sent out feelers to dozens of hotel companies, expecting only two or three to respond. Unfortunately, eight companies answered the call with properties so large they will almost triple Aruba's hotel room count by the time they are completed. As a result, downtown Oranjestad and Palm Beach to its north look more like a construction site than one of the region's hottest vacation spots. The projects are very closely regulated by the government, however, and when they are completed by the end of 1991, Aruba should return to its former serene self.

Shortage of labor could prove to be a problem in Aruba, however, since there are about 12,000 too few employees to work in these new hotels. So don't be surprised if those fresh towels don't make it to your room on time.

Aruba now welcomes a daily **Continental** flight from Newark. Also, after a two-year rift caused by Aruba's campaign for independence from the Netherlands Antilles, **ALM Antillean Airlines** resumed service to Aruba from Miami and New York in mid-1988. **Air Aruba** added more flights for interisland connections, as well, making island hopping much easier.

The people of Aruba also elected a new government last year, and the People's Electoral Movement has now replaced the People's Party of Aruba. The change, however, has had absolutely no bearing on the island's tourism industry.

Barbados To complement its cruise attractions, Barbados opened a $2 million cruise passenger center—the **Carlisle Bay Center**—in July 1988. The center is located about a half mile south of Bridgetown Harbour, within walking distance. Carlisle is a day-use facility, with duty-free shops, restaurants, a swimming pool (most likely put in at the hoteliers' request to keep cruisers off the hotel beaches), and water-sport facilities.

Sky Tours Ltd.—another new tourist attraction on Barbados—started operations in mid-1988. Sky Tours' 10 passenger Cessna 402 aircraft give tourists a bird's-eye view of the island. The 30-minute ride takes off from Grantley Adams International Airport. Sky Tours is an adventurous diversion but is definitely not for the weak of stomach.

Bonaire The tiny island of Bonaire, primarily a dive destination, does not have much of a tourism industry to speak of but did make some changes last year to upgrade its hotel accommodations. **Captain Don's Habitat** added four cottage rooms, eight beachfront villa units, and a 40-room two-story structure on the beach, more than doubling Don's room count. **Sand Dollar Condominium and Beach Club** added 30 rooms in January 1989, as well as a pool and tennis courts. Also in the works for Sand Dollar is a casino and a shopping center.

Cayman Islands Although Hurricane Gilbert passed through the Cayman Islands, there was very little damage reported, aside from broken windows. The biggest news in the Caymans last year was the ground-breaking of the 306-room **Radisson Grand Cayman**—the largest hotel on the three-island British colony. At press time, the $40 million resort was scheduled for completion in December 1989. The 35-room **Coconut Harbor Resort** also opened its doors in George Town during the 1988–89 winter season. The resort offers a complete dive shop—a must in the Caymans—an open-air bar, and air-conditioned rooms.

A new ferry was introduced on Grand Cayman in 1989. The ferry, which runs between Grand Pavilion and Rum Point, cuts travel time between the two points from one hour by car to about 15 minutes by boat. Round-trip tickets on the boat, which operates Monday–Saturday, go for $12.

Curaçao Curaçao has spent the last year improving its cruise attractions and chasing down new cruise lines. Unfortunately, the attractions have come on line faster than the new cruise lines. Still, cruise business is on the upswing on Curaçao. **Costa Cruise Lines** and **Chandris Fantasy Cruises** operate weekly calls at Curaçao, and **Regency Cruise Lines** also started regular calls there in the fall of 1988.

Private investors have been working on the restoration of **Porto Paseo,** a section of Otrobanda just outside the cruise terminal. When completed, Porto Paseo will include a restaurant overlooking the harbor, an open-air dining terrace facing the cruise terminal entrance, a Mediterranean-style bistro, a coffee shop, an antiques shop specializing in European and Antillean pieces, a souvenir shop with works by local artists and artisans, a tourist information office, and a museum on the history of Otrobanda. The entire project will not be completed until 1993, but Porto Paseo will be opened in stages over the next few years.

An island nightlife center—something Curaçao was in dire need of—was also scheduled for completion by December 1989 at the **Rif Fort Arches.** Rif Fort includes an entertainment center, a seafood restaurant, a West Indian restaurant, a casino, a nightclub, a bar on top of the fort, an English pub, and souvenir shops. Across the harbor, the **Waterfort Arches,** which houses a group of shops and boutiques, was recently renovated. Both forts were built in 1828 by the Dutch to protect the harbor entrance to Willemstad.

The government of Curaçao has also invested $1.2 million in a plan to increase the number of beaches—another commodity sorely lacking here. One new beach was added outside the **Princess Beach Hotel.** Two larger beaches are also in the planning stages behind the Waterfort and Rif Fort arches.

Dominica On Dominica, plans are underway to expand little **Canefield Airport** and add lights to accommodate night landings. No completion date has been set. The **Anchorage Hotel** has added a squash court to its facilities, and the **Castle Comfort** guest house has added five rooms to its comfortable accommodations. The **Fort Young Hotel,** virtually demolished by a 1980 hurricane, was scheduled to reopen in 1988 but at press time renovation was still underway. Built on the site of an 18th-century fort, the upscale facility will have 50 rooms and suites, a swimming pool, and a dining room with an orchestra and dance floor.

Dominican Republic In the Dominican Republic, facilities continue to spring up on the island's Amber Coast. In Playa Dorada, **Heavens** is an earthly resort featuring a glitzy disco and a wealth of water-sport clinics. The **Radisson Puerta Plata,** opened in 1988, is a luxury resort with rooms and suites in two-story pastel-color villas, all with remote control TV and minibars. The **Playa Chiquita** in Sosúa is an all-suites resort replete with kitchenettes and wet bars inside and a swim-up bar outside in the free-form pool. Also in Sosúa, the **Sir Francis Drake** is an inexpensive all-suites facility with a restaurant and pool with swim-up bar. The moderately priced **Cofresi Beach Resort** is an all-inclusive resort in a dramatic setting hard by the Atlantic reefs. On the windsurfing beach at Cabarate, the **Punta Goleta Beach Resort** continues to expand and will ultimately have about 1,800 rooms and suites. The **Playa Dorada Hotel,** in Playa Dorada, is no longer affiliated with Holiday Inn.

Grenada In 1988, construction was completed on the first phase of **Camerhogne Park,** a recreation and conference center at Grand Anse Bay, where many of the hotels and resorts are located. The park, designed primarily for the use of visiting cruise-ship passengers, has picnic tables, locker and shower facilities, food concessions, and a jetty for water taxis.

Government approval was finally given, after two years of deliberation, on Grenada's **port expansion** and **harbor renovation.** The $5 million project includes construction of a new port on St. George's Esplanade coast, the dredging of Carenage Harbour, and the building of a coastal road between the two ports. Also included is a new $3 million duty-free shopping complex. The project is ongoing and should be completed by the end of 1990. The new port will decongest traffic at the cruise port, since all commercial ships will be rerouted to a separate pier.

The Moorings, a Florida-based hotel and yacht charter company, bought Grenada's 20-suite **Secret Harbour** resort in Lanse aux Epines in March 1989. After a $14 million renovation, the property will become Moorings' base in the southeastern Caribbean for its combination land/yacht vacation packages. The project is scheduled for completion by the end of 1991, but the property will be open in various stages of completion.

Grenada's sister island, Carriacou, welcomed its first new hotel in about 10 years last year. The 18-unit **Cassada Bay** offers its guests free ferry service to neighboring islands for snorkeling and spelunking.

BWIA International brought daily flights to Grenada for the first time from New York in the summer of 1989. Previously, there were only three flights a week to the island aboard BWIA.

Jamaica The last year in Jamaica's tourism industry proved that bad things do come in threes. First, the island was hit with Hurricane Gilbert in September 1988; then the tourism season was slightly interrupted by the country's national elections; and finally, Jamaica, like most other destinations, felt the sting of Eastern's bankruptcy.

Like an unwelcome guest, **Hurricane Gilbert** swooped into Jamaica virtually unannounced, ransacked the island, and left its dazed residents to clean up the mess, uncertain of what the future held for tourism. While many media reports of the widespread damage were greatly exaggerated, the people of Jamaica, almost all of whom depend on tourism for their livelihoods, were devastated by the two months following the hurricane. Many of the resorts, however, actually improved their appearances and facilities after the hurricane. Hotel owners took advantage of the down time following the hurricane to make repairs and embark on some long-standing improvement projects. Damage to the hotels and tourism facilities totalled $350 million officially, but it was reported that many hoteliers padded their insurance claims to make the extra funds available for the improvements as well as the repairs.

Another dilemma hit Jamaica in the form of its **national elections,** which have a history of violence. (The last election, in 1980, left 750 people dead and crushed the island's tourism industry for years.) The February 1989 elections, however, were relatively peaceful. Only one death and few outbreaks of violence were reported when Michael Manley, the social democratic leader of the People's National Party, swept to victory over incumbent Edward Seaga's Jamaica Labour Party. There was some apprehension that because of Manley's history of overspending on social programs and his bent toward public ownership during his last reign in the 1970s, Jamaica's economy and its tourism industry were in for some big changes. But during his first few months in office, Manley appeared to have moved more toward the political center and tourism has followed much the same road it had traversed under Seaga's rule.

Jamaica's **cruise facilities** were expanded in October 1988, when two berths were added to the Montego Bay cruise port. A new passenger terminal is still, at press time, under construction at Ocho Rios. Both projects cost the government more than $15 million.

Martinique   Martinique's popular Fort-de-France steak house **Le Coq Hardi** is expanding to make room for the crowds that flock in. **Ti Sable at Anse-d'Arlet** opened in March 1988 to take its place in the restaurant lineup, and a new chef has been lined up at the **Cul-de-Sac,** in Port de Plaisance. In Pointe du Bout, the **PLM Azur-Carayou** has added a snack bar on the beach.

Montserrat   On Montserrat, the **Belham Valley Hotel and Restaurant** has been under new management since mid-1988. The restaurant is now open for lunch as well as dinner. The new owners have retained some of the popular items from the old menu and added new touches of their own. **Cynthie's, Lett's,** and **Teacher Jim's** have all closed, but the **Emerald Cafe** is a new gem on the dining scene. There are white embroidered linens on inside tables, a sparkling terrace with umbrella tables, and a fine selection of wines and liqueurs to complement the island specialties and homemade pastries.

In late 1988 the **Anchorage Hotel** on Antigua was acquired by Divi Resorts. At press time the hotel was to be closed during its facelift; it's set to reopen by 1990. The New Horizons Hotel is now the all-inclusive **Pineapple Beach Club.** The erstwhile Lobster Pot Restaurant at the Siboney Beach Club is now the **Coconut Grove,** and a few steps along the beach, **Jean-Michel's** at the Antigua Village is no more.

Nevis   On Nevis, the **Cliffdweller's Hotel** has closed.

Puerto Rico   The biggest splash in the Caribbean is the marina that opened in late 1988 on the east coast of Puerto Rico. It is the Caribbean's largest marina, accommodating 800 boats and cruise ships, and is part of the $300 million **Puerto del Rey Marina and Beach Resort** now under development near Pajardo. The resort will consist of a 325-room hotel, 255 condo units, an 18-hole championship golf course, and tennis and beach clubs.

Puerto Rico is gearing up for a major celebration in 1993 (many islands have their plans set for 1992) to commemorate the 500th anniversary of the arrival of Christopher Columbus. In preparation for the party many new hotels and developments are under way.

In San Juan, the Radisson Hotel Corporation put $18 million into renovation of the former Normandie, which was built in 1938 in the shape of the famous French ocean liner of that name. The 200-room property opened in late 1988 as the **Radisson Normandie.**

The 676-room **Caribe Hilton International** has entered the second phase of a $40 million renovation and expansion program that is scheduled for completion in 1989. The first stage, completed in September 1988, included an 800-car parking garage, expansion and redecoration of reception areas, new restaurants, and conference space. Plans for the second stage include a free-form swimming pool with waterfalls, slides, and a Jacuzzi that will accommodate 30 people; redecoration of the remaining guest rooms; and the refurbishment of La Rotisserie restaurant.

Puerto Rico Industrial Development Co. (PRIDCO), owner of the **Condado Beach Hotel,** is investing $2.5 million in renovation of the property's west wing, including redecorating of guest rooms and installation of a casino on the lobby level.

The **Condado Plaza Hotel & Casino** is undergoing an ambitious 6½-year, $36 million capital improvement program that includes the addition of about 65 new suites with Jacuzzis and kitchens. The hotel's sixth restaurant, Tony Roma's, opened in 1988 on the ground floor of the Laguna Wing.

Also in San Juan, **Howard Johnson's** is in the final phase of a multimillion dollar, three-year renovation program. Rooms have been refurbished, corridors and conference facilities upgraded, and the penthouse swimming pool area has been landscaped and redecorated. A 40-room executive section on the top two floors is complete; each floor has a business center, with work space, lounge, and bar. Plans are underway to add a casino, 70 rooms and 80 suites, and to renovate the restaurant and cocktail lounge.

Under new management since March, **Holiday Inn & Casino** on 4 acres of beachfront in Isla Verde. Normandie Hotel Corp. and E.C.E.G.E. Development plan to open a $100 million, 230-room hotel at the Luis Muñoz Marín International Airport. Construction began in early 1988, with an opening set for 1991. Negotiations are underway with international hotel companies for management of the property.

"Out on the island," as they say in Puerto Rico, there is yet more activity. A million-dollar renovation at **Palmas del Mar** in Humacao has been completed on the rooms and on suites at the **Candelero Hotel** and **Palmas Inn and Villas** in the Club Cala time-sharing program. In addition, the **Fair Lakes Village** project is under construction through the PDM Corporation. Its 58 villas will be situated on five fingers of land jutting into a lake next to a golf course and a beach. The **Ritz-Carlton Hotel Co.** plans to build a 475-room hotel at Palmas del Mar. Ground was broken in early 1989 for the $125 million resort. The opening is planned for March 1991.

The Pratt Hotel Corp., in partnership with Mamanaco Universal, is reopening the former Dorado del Mar in 1990 as the **Sands Hotel & Casino & Country Club.** Work began on the property in late 1987, and the cost of the renovation is $60 million. The resort will offer 108 villas as well as tennis facilities, a swimming pool, and an 18-hole championship golf course.

The H.I. Development Corporation, owner and operator of the Ponce Holiday Inn, is building three new hotels with a total of 532 rooms. Construction has begun on the Isla Verde property and on a 150-room Holiday Inn in Mayaguez. The existing property in Ponce has been redecorated and a $400,000 disco has opened. An $8 million, 122-room **Days Inn Ponce Resort** is scheduled to open in Ponce in 1988. In Ponce's historic district, the 80-room **Malia Hotel** has completed redecorating public areas and guest rooms. PRIDCO has begun construction of a $20 million, 250-room **Hilton International** in Ponce. Located on La Guancha beach, the property will have a casino and a pool, as well as guest access to a municipal golf course on adjoining land. Opening is set for 1990.

In Rio Grande the 550-room **Bahia Bay Plantation** was scheduled to reopen in late 1989, with an 18-hole golf course, a convention center, deluxe sports facilities, and a bird sanctuary. On the west coast, the **Mayaguez Hilton International** has entered the final phase of a $6 million facelift with the opening of a new casino. The 150-room hotel now sports two floors for executive check-ins and meetings, and all of the hotel's 145 guest rooms and five suites have been redecorated.

Three new paradors opened in 1988, bringing the total number of the Puerto Rico Tourism Company's *paradores puertorriquenos* to 17. In keeping with government guidelines, each of the paradors is located near a tourist attraction, and each has a restaurant offering typical Puerto Rican fare. The $400,000 **Parador Casa Grande** in Utaudo has 20 suites with balconies, a swimming pool, and a restaurant. It's located on the grounds of a former coffee plantation, with lush trails beckoning hikers to explore the surrounding mountains. In Aquadilla, **Hacienda El Pedre-**

gal is a 20-room country inn with spectacular views of the Atlantic Ocean. **La Familia,** in the boating center of Fujardo, has 21 rooms, a swimming pool, solarium, restaurant, and cocktail lounge. There are five more paradors in the planning stages.

St. Lucia On St. Lucia, the **Dasheen Resort** has closed. Also on St. Lucia, **Cunard La Toc** and **Cunard La Toc Suites** are now operated as separate hotels, although guests enjoy facilities of both. Having undergone a $15 million renovation, the Cariblue is now called **Le Sport** and billed as "The Body Holiday," with all manner of pampering and fitness facilities. **Windjammer Landing,** a development of two- and three-bedroom luxury villas, was set to open in March 1989.

St. Martin/ On St. Maarten, the new **St. Maarten Limousine Service** offers
St. Maarten transportation to and from Princess Juliana International Airport with rates ranging from $30 to $65 one-way. If you're headed for the **Oyster Pond Yacht Club,** you'll find it all spruced up after a 1988 face-lift. **Punta Venezia** is the latest addition to the posh villas of Point Pirouetta. At press time, 120 of the projected units of the plush **La Plage at the Royal Islander Club** on Maho Bay were open. On the French side, St. Martin, **Hovea** is a small, very French guest house (just eight rooms) not far from Marigot. The Nettle Bay area is experiencing a building boom. In the spring of 1988, 35 units of the **Maeva Beach Residence** opened. The beachside Maeva is comprised of modern studios and suites with all-electric kitchens.

St. Vincent and St. Vincent and the Grenadines are hard at work updating
the Grenadines airport facilities. Under construction and pegged for a late 1989 opening is a new $9.6 million airport on Bequia, the closest of the Grenadines to the main island. There is also ongoing construction on roads and electricity on the seven uninhabited islands in the hopes of attracting hotel development. Night lighting has also been added to the airport at Canouan.

The St. Vincent government also offered a 15-year tax exemption for new hotel projects, hoping to lure prospective hoteliers to their island.

Turks and **Leeward Development** of villas and condominiums is well un-
Caicos Islands derway on Provo, with manicured lawns, good roads, and the Leeward Restaurant already open. Work continues on the **Sheraton Hotel,** also on Provo, but as yet no opening date has been set. Construction is also underway on a **Ramada Hotel & Casino** in Provo, which is set to open in early 1990.

Fodor's Choice

No two people will agree on what makes a perfect vacation, but it's fun and helpful to know what others think. We hope you'll have the chance to experience some of Fodor's Choices yourself while visiting the Caribbean. For detailed information about each entry, refer to the appropriate chapter in this guidebook.

Scenic Views

El Yunque Rain Forest, Puerto Rico

Grand Etang, Grenada

The Pitons (Petit and Gros), St. Lucia

Brimstone Hill, St. Kitts

Mountain Top, St. Thomas

Governor's Coach ride (on the Catadupa Choo Choo) out of Montego Bay into the Jamaica mountains

Beaches

Magens Bay, St. Thomas, U.S. Virgin Islands

Negril, Jamaica

Seven Mile Beach, Grand Cayman

Shoal Bay, Anguilla

Petite Anse, Diamant, Martinique

Trunk Bay, St. John, U.S. Virgin Islands

Most of Antigua's 365 beaches

Diving/Snorkeling

Palm Beach, Aruba

Buck Island Reef, St. Croix, U.S. Virgin Islands

Cayman Islands (all three of them)

Barbados' coral reef off the west coast

Virgin Gorda, British Virgin Islands

Turks and Caicos Islands' reefs

Golf

Tryall Golf, Tennis and Beach Club, Jamaica

Mahogany Run, St. Thomas, U.S. Virgin Islands

Casa de Campo, Dominican Republic

Hyatt Dorado Beach, Puerto Rico

Mount Irvine, Tobago

Britannia Golf Course, Grand Cayman (played with a Jack Nicklaus–designed ball that goes half the normal distance)

Fishing

The waters around . . .

Little Cayman

La Romana, Dominican Republic

Puerto Rico

Caicos Island

Port Antonio, Jamaica

U.S. Virgin Islands

Parks and Gardens

St. John, U.S. Virgin Islands, national park

Parc Naturel, Basse-Terre, Guadeloupe

Washington/Slagbaai National Park, Bonaire

Andromeda Gardens, Barbados

Carinosa Gardens, Ocho Rios, Jamaica

Morne Trois Pitons National Park, Dominica

Shopping

Willemstad, Curaçao

Charlotte Amalie, St. Thomas, U.S. Virgin Islands

Philipsburg, Sint Maarten

George Town, Grand Cayman

St. George's, Grenada (if just for those incredible spices)

Old San Juan, Puerto Rico

Casinos

The Alhambra, Aruba

Curaçao Caribbean Hotel and Casino, Curaçaò

El Embajador, Santo Domingo, Dominican Republic

Treasure Island Hotel and Casino, St. Maarten

Cerromar Beach, Dorado, San Juan, Puerto Rico

St. James Club, Antigua

Nightlife and Bars

The Hideaway, Trinidad

Silver's Country and Western, Treasure Island Beach Hotel, Grand Cayman

Hedonism II, Negril, Jamaica

Condado Beach Hotel, San Juan, Puerto Rico

Le Club disco, Mullet Bay, Sint Maarten

Yesterdays, St. Thomas, U.S. Virgin Islands

Hotels

Castelets, St. Barthélemy (*Very Expensive*)

Malliouhana, Mead's Bay, Anguilla (*Very Expensive*)

Sandy Lane, Barbados (*Very Expensive*)

Trident Villas and Hotel, Port Antonio, Jamaica (*Very Expensive*)

Hotel Santo Domingo, Santo Domingo, Dominican Republic (*Expensive*)

Mullet Bay Resort and Casino, Sint Maarten (*Expensive*)

Ramada Hotel El Convento, San Juan, Puerto Rico (*Expensive*)

Stouffer Grand Beach Resort, St. Thomas, U.S. Virgin Islands (*Expensive*)

Restaurants

Admiral's Inn, Antigua (*Expensive*)

Bistro Le Clochard, Curaçao (*Expensive*)

Coccoloba Plantation, Anguilla (*Expensive*)

Grand Old House, Grand Cayman (*Expensive*)

La Belle France, Anse Marcel, St. Martin (*Expensive*)

La Cage aux Folles, St. James, Barbados (*Expensive*)

La Canne à Sucre, Point-à-Pitre, Guadeloupe (*Expensive*)

Le Lafayette, Fort-de-France, Martinique (*Expensive*)

Getaways

Mustique, The Grenadines (where you can rent Princess Margaret's house)

Southern Cross Club, Little Cayman

Captain's Quarters, Saba

Peter Island Hotel and Yacht Harbour, British Virgin Islands

Jumby Bay, Long Island, off Antigua

Golden Lemon, Dieppe Bay, St. Kitts

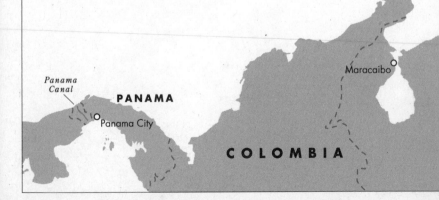

The Caribbean

Miami

Havana

THE BAHAMAS

Cuba

Turks and Caicos Islands

Little Cayman

Cayman Brac

Grand Cayman

Montego Bay

GREATER

Haiti

Hispaniola

Jamaica

Caribbean

Panama Canal

PANAMA

Panama City

Maracaibo

COLOMBIA

0   200 miles

0   300 km

N

ATLANTIC OCEAN

Dominican
Republic

LEEWARD ISLANDS

St. John
St. Thomas
San Juan
Virgin Gorda
Tortola
Anguilla
St. Barthélemy

Santo
Domingo

St. Maarten/
St. Martin
St. Eustatius
Saba
Barbuda

St.
Croix

Puerto
Rico

Antigua

St. Kitts
Nevis
Montserrat

A N T I L L E S

Marie
Galante

Guadeloupe

WINDWARD ISLANDS

Dominica

Martinique

Sea

St. Lucia

St. Vincent

Barbados

The
Grenadines

Aruba

Bonaire

Grenada

Curaçao

Tobago

L E S S E R   A N T I L L E S

Trinidad

Caracas

VENEZUELA

World Time Zones

MONDAY
SUNDAY

International Date Line

+12 +13

-9

+12

+11

-10

-11

-10

3

7

4

5 -8

6

8

10

11

12

9

14 15

13

17 16

18

19 22

20

21 23

24

-4

-3

-5 -4

-7

-6

-5

-4

-3

25

+11   +12 -   -11   -10   -9   -8   -7   -6   -5   -4   -3   -2

Numbers below vertical bands relate each zone to Greenwich Mean Time (0 hrs.).
Local times may differ, as indicated by lightface numbers on the map.

Algiers, **29**	Berlin, **34**	Delhi, **48**	Istanbul, **40**
Anchorage, **3**	Bogotá, **19**	Denver, **8**	Jerusalem, **42**
Athens, **41**	Budapest, **37**	Djakarta, **53**	Johannesburg, **44**
Auckland, **1**	Buenos Aires, **24**	Dublin, **26**	Lima, **20**
Baghdad, **46**	Caracas, **22**	Edmonton, **7**	Lisbon, **28**
Bangkok, **50**	Chicago, **9**	Hong Kong, **56**	London (Greenwich), **27**
Beijing, **54**	Copenhagen, **33**	Honolulu, **2**	Los Angeles, **6**
	Dallas, **10**		Madrid, **38**
			Manila, **57**

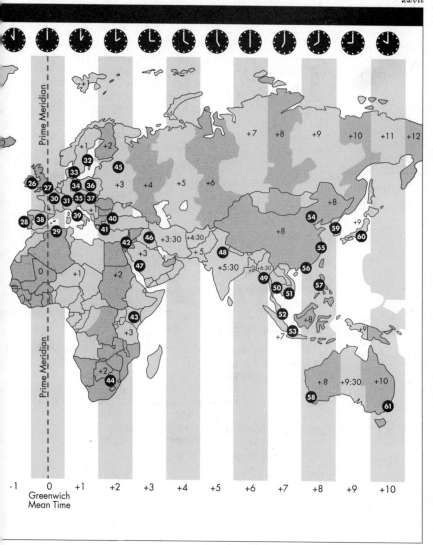

-1   0   +1   +2   +3   +4   +5   +6   +7   +8   +9   +10

Greenwich
Mean Time

Introduction

I f you have seen one island you have by no means seen them all. Tiny 5-square-mile Saba has less in common with the vast 19,000-square-mile Dominican Republic than Butte, Montana, has with Biloxi, Mississippi. Butte and Biloxi, however different in terrain and traits, sit in the same country and the citizenry speak more or less the same language. Saba, which is Dutch, and the Dominican Republic, whose roots are in Spain, simply sit in the same sea.

The Caribbean has towering volcanic islands, such as Saba; islands with forests, such as Dominica and Guadeloupe; and some islands, notably Puerto Rico, that boast both rain forests and deserts. Glittering discos, casinos, and dazzling nightlife can be found on islands like Aruba and the Dominican Republic, and throughout the region there are isolated cays (pronounced *keys*) with only sand, sea, sun, lizards, and mosquitoes. Some islands, St. Kitts among them, have ancient forts to view, while Puerto Rico and the Caicos islands have caverns and caves to explore. There are also places like Grand Turk where the only notable sights to see are beneath the translucent sea.

Different though they are in many ways, the islands are stylistically similar. The style-setter is the tropical climate. Year-round summertime temperatures and a plethora of beaches on which to bask produce a pace that's known throughout the region as "island time." Only the trade winds move swiftly. Operating on island time means, "I'll get to it when the spirit moves me." You may hate it, or you may become addicted to it and not be able to peel yourself off the beach and return home.

The similarities are also attributable to the history of the region. The Arawaks paddled up from South America and populated the islands more than 1,000 years ago. In the early 14th century, the cannibalistic Caribs, who gave the area its name, arrived, probably from Brazil, then polished off the peaceful Arawaks and managed, for a time at least, to scare the living daylights out of the Europeans who sailed through in search of gold. (The original name of the Caribs was Galibi, a word the Spanish corrupted to *Canibal*—the origin of the word "cannibal.") Christopher Columbus made four voyages through the region between 1492 and 1503, christening the islands while dodging the Carib arrows. He landed on or sailed past all of the Greater Antilles and virtually all of the eastern Caribbean islands.

From the 16th century until the early 19th century, the Dutch, Danes, Swedes, English, French, Irish, and Spanish fought bitterly for control of the islands. Some islands have almost as many battle sites as sand flies. Having gained control of the islands and annihilated the Caribs, the Europeans established vast sugar plantations and brought in Africans to work the fields. With the abolition of slavery in the mid-19th century, Asians were imported as indentured laborers. Today, the Caribbean population is a rich gumbo of numerous nationalities, including Americans and Canadians who have retired to and invested in the islands.

It must be remembered that the Caribbean, like the European continent, is made up of individual countries, replete with customs, immigration officials, and, in some instances, political difficulties. Most of the islands/nations have opted for independence; others retain their ties to the mother country. They are developing nations, and many have severe economic and unemployment problems.

Virtually all of the islands depend upon tourism, which is an industry that moves on island time. Human nature being such as it is, many islanders are resentful of their dependency on tourist dollars. Like as not, the person who serves you has stood in a long line, vying with other anxious applicants for the few available jobs. After serving your meals and cleaning your luxurious room, he or she returns to a tiny shack knowing full well that in less than a week you will have shelled out more than an islander makes in a month. If you encounter fewer smiling faces than you anticipated, consider chalking it up to your perceived great wealth and life of leisure.

Mother Nature has endowed most of these islands with the proverbial sun-kissed beaches, swaying palms, and year-round summer. These pleasures notwithstanding, there are some who deem it overrated. They object to encountering resentment when all they seek is a pleasant vacation for which they have paid dearly. Some feel rather keenly that they'd always like hot water—or at least *some* water—when they turn on the shower; in even the most luxurious resorts there are times when things simply don't work, and that's a fact of Caribbean life. And other visitors simply have no patience for island time.

On the other hand, there are those who travel to the Caribbean year after year. Some return to the same familiar hotel on the same familiar beach on the same familiar island, while the more adventurous try to sample as much as this smorgasbord has to offer.

Defining the Caribbean

The Caribbean Sea, an area of more than a million square miles, stretches south of Florida down to the coast of Venezuela. In the northern Caribbean are the **Greater Antilles**—the islands closest to the United States—comprised of Cuba, the Cayman Islands, Jamaica, Haiti, the Dominican Republic, and Puerto Rico. (Due to the political unrest in Haiti and Cuba, they are not included in this book.) The

Lesser Antilles—greater in number but smaller in size than the Greater Antilles—are divided into three groups: The Leewards and the Windwards in the eastern Caribbean, and the islands in the southern Caribbean. The eastern Caribbean islands, from the Virgin Islands in the north all the way south to Grenada, form an arc between the Atlantic Ocean and the Caribbean Sea. Islands in the Leeward chain in order of appearance are the U.S. and British Virgin Islands, Anguilla, St. Maarten/St. Martin, St. Barthélemy, Saba, St. Eustatius, St. Kitts, Nevis, Antigua, Barbuda, Montserrat, and Guadeloupe; the Windwards are comprised of Dominica, Martinique, St. Lucia, Barbados, St. Vincent and the Grenadines, and Grenada. In the southern Caribbean, off the coast of Venezuela, Trinidad and Tobago are anchored in the east, while Aruba, Bonaire, and Curaçao (known as the ABC islands) bathe in the western waters. The Turks and Caicos Islands, which lie in the Atlantic Ocean between Florida and the north coast of Hispaniola (Haiti and the Dominican Republic), are part of the Bahamas but are included in this book because of their proximity to and affinity with the Caribbean islands.

When to Go?

"The Season" in the Caribbean traditionally coincides with winter in North America—that is, roughly, from mid-December till mid-April. But, contrary to common North American belief, the islands are not completely deserted during the summer. That's the time when the islanders themselves and many Europeans travel in the region. While the climate varies less than 10° between summer and winter, many hotels slash prices 30% or more in the summer. And Mother Nature is at her glamourous best then, with brilliant flamboyant trees, as well as other spectacular tropical plants that bloom from summer till fall.

You will find it easier to rent a car and to make hotel and restaurant reservations in summer; easier, that is, if the facilities are open. Many hotels and restaurants close during August and September or have limited facilities; some are also closed in October. They close to renovate, to rest . . . and to wait out the season for hurricanes and tropical depressions, which are most likely to occur between June and October. These storms, as Jamaica discovered when Hurricane Gilbert swept through in mid-September 1988, can wreak havoc.

Finding Your Own Place in the Sun

The glory of the Caribbean, aside from the guaranteed qualities of warm sun and warm sea, is that no one island is exactly like another, so that they cater to a variety of tastes. What follows is a list of the Caribbean islands broken down by their specialties. You might visit **Martinique**, for example, for its natural beauty and its cuisine. **Guadeloupe**, on the other hand, is better visited for its diving and nightlife.

Luxury Resorts A wealth of posh resorts await those who seek comfort in the lap of luxury. **Anguilla**, rapidly becoming one of the Caribbean's most popular destinations, has the dazzling Malliouhana, the Coccoloba, and the Moroccan-style Cap Juluca. **Antigua's** elegant Curtain Bluff has a long list of well-heeled repeat guests. On **St. Lucia**, the deluxe lodgings are Cunard La Toc and La Toc Villas. On Dutch **St. Maarten**, La Samanna is a favorite hideaway of the rich and/or famous, and on French **St. Martin** La Belle Creole is a re-creation of a Mediterranean village, replete with a village square and opulent villas. For the ultimate in luxurious privacy, the **British Virgin Islands** has the Peter Island Resort and Yacht Club on its own 1,300-acre private island. Castelets on **St. Barts** draws worldly personalities to its intimate setting. And Caneel Bay Resort on **St. John, U.S. Virgin Islands,** which has six beaches, takes up 170 acres of the Virgin Islands National Park.

Casinos and Nightlife You can flirt with Lady Luck until the wee small hours in the dazzling casinos of Santo Domingo, **Dominican Republic;** San Juan, **Puerto Rico;** St. Maarten; and Curaçao. **Aruba** is loaded with lively night places, and San Juan's glittering floor shows are legendary. The merengue, born in the **Dominican Republic,** is exuberantly danced everywhere on the island. Both **Guadeloupe** and **Martinique** claim to have begun the beguine, and on both islands it is danced with great gusto.

Getting Away from It All If you're looking to back out of the fast lane, you can park at one of the secluded, Spartan mountain lodges on **Dominica,** which is one of the friendliest islands in the Caribbean. Or opt for the quiet grandeur of a renovated sugar plantation on **Nevis**, where you can feast in an elegant dining room or enjoy a barbecue on the beach. Tranquil **Anguilla,** with soft white beaches nudged by gin-clear water, offers posh resorts as well as small, inexpensive, locally owned lodgings. From the low-key **Turks and Caicos Islands,** which lie in stunning blue-green waters, you can boat to more than a score of isolated cays where the term "low key" sounds too fast-paced. **St. Kitts** is another peaceful green oasis with lovely beaches and upscale accommodations in the bargain. **St. Lucia** offers a plethora of places, from the simple to the simply elegant, for "liming" (we call it "hanging out"), the local favorite pastime. On tiny **Saba** there is little to do but tuck into a small guest house, admire the lush beauty of the island, and chat with the friendly Sabans. Nearby **St. Eustatius** is another friendly, laid-back island, as is **Montserrat.**

Foreign Culture

African **Trinidad** moves with the rhythm of Calypso and is the stomping ground of a flat-out, free-wheeling Carnival that rivals the pre-Lenten celebrations in Rio and New Orleans. The Trinidadians, whose African heritage has been augmented by many Asian races, have built up the most prosperous commercial center in the Caribbean. Politically volatile Haiti is not included in this book, but exotic and unique Haitian artwork is prominently displayed throughout the Caribbean.

British **St. Kitts** is known as the Mother Colony of the West Indies; it was from here that British colonists were dispatched in the 17th century to settle Antigua, Barbuda, Tortola, and Montserrat. If you're a history buff, you won't want to miss Nelson's Dockyard at **Antigua's** English Harbour or the hunkering fortress of Brimstone Hill on St. Kitts. Sports fans who understand the intricacies of cricket can watch matches between **Nevis** and St. Kitts teams. And the waters around Antigua and the **British Virgin Islands** are a mecca for serious sailors.

Dutch **Saba, St. Eustatius, St. Maarten, Bonaire,** and **Curaçao** all fly the Dutch flag, but there the similarity ends. Saba is a tiny volcanic island known for its beauty, its friendly inhabitants, and its gingerbread-trimmed houses. Curaçao's colorful waterfront shops and restaurants are reminiscent of Amsterdam. Quiet St. Eustatius—affectionately called Statia—has well-preserved historical sites and is famed for being the first foreign nation to salute the new American flag in 1776. The main streets of Philipsburg, the capital of St. Maarten, are lined with colorful Dutch colonial buildings replete with fretwork and verandas. It's also popular for its duty-free shops. Bonaire is best known for its excellent scuba diving.

French **Martinique, Guadeloupe, St. Martin,** and **St. Barthélemy** (often called St. Barts or St. Barths) comprise the French West Indies. The language, the currency, the cuisine (the most imaginative in the Caribbean), the culture, and the style are *très* French. St. Barts is the quietest, Martinique the liveliest, St. Martin the friendliest, and Guadeloupe the lushest. And as an extra added attraction, you can wing over from Guadeloupe to see what life is like on the offshore islands of Les Saintes, Marie Galante, or Désirade.

Spanish In the **Dominican Republic,** which occupies the eastern two-thirds of the island of Hispaniola, the language and culture are decidedly Spanish. The Colonial Zone of Santo Domingo is site of the oldest city in the Western Hemisphere, and its restored buildings reflect the 15th-century

Columbus period. One also gets a sense of the past in **Puerto Rico's** Old San Juan, with its narrow cobblestone streets and filigreed iron balconies. The well-preserved town was founded by Ponce de León in the 16th century.

The Beauties of Nature **Dominica,** laced with rivers and streams, is a ruggedly beautiful island with arguably the lushest, most untamed vegetation in the Caribbean. **Puerto Rico's** luxuriant 28,000-acre El Yunque is the largest rain forest in the U. S. Forestry system. Little **Saba** is awash with giant vegetation, and the island's Mt. Scenery is justly named. **Guadeloupe's** 74,000-square-mile Natural Park boasts dramatic waterfalls, cool pools, and miles of hiking trails. Majestic Mt. Pelée, a not entirely dormant volcano, towers over **Martinique's** rain forest; on **St. Eustatius,** adventurers can crawl down into a jungle cradled within a volcanic crater; and on **St. Lucia** you can drive right through a volcano.

The Lure of History **Antigua's** well-preserved Nelson's Dockyard is a must for history aficionados. The ancient colonial zones of both Santo Domingo, **Dominican Republic,** and Old San Juan, **Puerto Rico,** should also be high on your "history" list. The Historical Society in **St. Eustatius** (Statia) publishes an excellent walking tour of sites to be seen. Brimstone Hill on **St. Kitts** is a well-maintained fortress with several museums full of military memorabilia. **Nevis** has many sugar mills restored as comfortable hotels. Port Royal, outside Kingston, **Jamaica,** was a pirates' stronghold until an earthquake shook things up in 1692.

Cuisine The cuisine on **Martinique** and **Guadeloupe** is a marvelous marriage of Creole cooking and classic French dishes; you'll find much of the same on the other French islands of **St. Martin** and **St. Barts.** You'll also find a fine selection of French wines in the French West Indies. **Grenada,** the spice island, has an abundance of seafood available and an incredible variety of vegetables.

Music Calypso was born in **Trinidad; Jamaica** is the home of reggae; the **Dominican Republic** gave the world the merengue; and both **Martinique** and **Guadeloupe** claim to be the cradle of the beguine. The music of **Barbados** ranges from the Crop Over Festival (late June–early August) to the hottest jazz. Steel drums, limbo dancers, and jump-ups are ubiquitous in the Caribbean. Jump-up? Simple. You hear the music, jump up, and begin to dance.

Diving Jacques Cousteau named Pigeon Island, off the west coast of **Guadeloupe,** one of the 10 best dive sites in the world. The Wall off Grand Turks in the **Turks and Caicos Islands** is a sheer drop of 7,000 feet and has long been known by scuba divers. The eruption of Mt. Pelée at 8 AM on May 8, 1902, on **Martinique** resulted in the sinking of several ships. **St. Eustatius** boasts an undersea "supermarket" of ships, as well as entire 18th-century warehouses, somewhat the worse for wear, below the surface of Orange Bay. The waters surrounding all three of the **Cayman Islands** are acclaimed by experts, who make similar pilgrimages to **Bonaire**'s 50 spectacular sites.

Boating **Guadeloupe**'s Port de Plaisance and the marinas on Tortola in the **British Virgin Islands, St. Vincent and the Grenadines,** and St. Thomas in the **U. S. Virgin Islands** are the starting points for some of the Caribbean's finest sailing. Yachtsmen also favor the waters around **Antigua** and put in regularly at Nelson's Dockyard, which hosts a colorful regatta in late April or early May.

Golfing According to those who have played it, the course at Casa de Campo in the **Dominican Republic** is one of the best in the Caribbean. That island also has a Robert Trent Jones course on the Amber Coast at Playa Dorada. Golfers on St. Thomas, **U. S. Virgin Islands,** play the spectacular Mahogany Run. There are superb courses in **Puerto Rico,** including four shared by the Hyatt Dorado and the Hyatt Regency Cerromar. **Jamaica** has nine courses, with Tryall west of Montego Bay rated among the top.

Day Trips There are many day trips from St. Martin/St. Maarten. **Saba** is just 28 miles away; **St. Eustatius** is another 10 miles south; and **Anguilla,** the new "in" place in the Caribbean, is just a 15-minute boat ride away from St. Martin/St. Maarten. **Nevis** is a mere 2 miles south of **St. Kitts,** while **Dominica** sits about halfway between **Martinique** and **Guadeloupe. Barbuda,** 30 miles from **Antigua,** is noted for hunting and diving. **Les Saintes, Désirade,** and **Marie Galante** are easily accessible from Guadeloupe. Islands like these are small enough to explore in a day, and so seductive that you'll probably insist upon returning.

Water Sports

Sunbathing

Before abandoning yourself to the pleasures of the tropics, you would be well advised to take precautions against the ravages of its equatorial sun. Be sure to use a sunscreen with a high sun protection factor, or SPF (an SPF of under 15 offers little protection); if you're engaging in water sports, be sure the sunscreen is waterproof. At this latitude, the safest hours for sunbathing are 4–6 PM, but even during these hours it is wise to limit exposure during your first few days to short intervals of 15–20 minutes. Keep your system plied with fruit juices and water; avoid coffee, tea, and alcohol, which have a dehydrating effect on the body.

Touring the island in an open jeep or dangling an arm out a car window can also expose you to sunburn, so be sure to use sunscreen. If you have permed or color-treated hair, you may wish to use a sun-protective gel to keep it from becoming brittle; if you have a bald head, apply sunscreen. While snorkeling, *always* wear a T-shirt and apply sunscreen to protect the top and backs of your thighs from "duck burn."

Swimming

Any resort you visit is likely to offer a variety of swimming experiences, depending on which side of the island you choose.

The calm, leeward Caribbean side of most islands has the safest and most popular beaches for swimming. There are no big waves, there is little undertow, and the saltwater—which buoys the swimmer or snorkeler—makes staying afloat almost effortless.

The windward, or Atlantic, side of the islands, however, is a different story: Even strong, experienced swimmers should exercise caution here. The ocean waves are tremendously powerful and can be rough to the point of being dangerous; unseen currents, strong undertows, and uneven, rocky bottoms may scuttle the novice. Some beaches post signs or flags daily to alert swimmers to the water conditions. Pay attention to them! Where there are no flags, limit your water sports to wading and sunbathing.

Swimmers on these islands must also be aware of underwater rocks, reefs, shells, and sea urchins—small, spike-covered creatures whose spines, while not fatal, can cause very painful punctures if you step on them, even through snorkel fins. Moray eels, which are harmless unless provoked, almost never leave the crevices they live in. But don't *ever* poke at one, or even point closely at them—they're lightning-fast and may mistake your finger for a predator. It's possible to receive a minor cut while swimming and not feel it until you're out of the water, so make a habit of checking yourself over after leaving the beach. If you do get a small cut from a broken glass or shell, clean it immediately with soap and water.

Nike, Inc. now manufactures an athletic shoe for wear in water sports. The Aqua Sock, a lightweight slip-on shoe with a waffle rubber outsole and Spandex mesh upper, offers protection from rocky beaches and underwater hazards such as coral and broken shells, and cushions the foot against the impact of windsurfing. It floats, is unaffected by salt and chlorine, and dries quickly.

How much truth is there to the old saw that you should wait an hour after eating before going for a swim? According to Mark Pitman, MD, Chief of Sports Medicine at the Hospital for Joint Diseases in New York City, blood travels from the muscles to the intestines after a meal to absorb the digesting food. This leaves the muscles "cold" and more likely to cramp. It is safe to float or dogpaddle after a light lunch, but save the Olympic lap-swimming for later.

Never dive, particularly from a boat or cliff, without checking the depth of the water and the bottom conditions. And even when the Caribbean is mirror-calm, never run blindly into the water, even if the beach is familiar. Changes in the tide can turn what was a sandy bottom yesterday into a collection of broken shells today.

Few beaches or pools in the Caribbean—even those at the best hotels—are protected by lifeguards, so you and your children swim at your own risk.

Sharks More than a decade after the release of the film *Jaws*, shark phobia endures. Sharks *are* among the fish that populate Caribbean waters; they can swim in water as shallow as three feet and are attracted by the splashing of swimmers. But there are only about a dozen shark attacks reported each year worldwide, and most of these take place off the coasts of California and Florida. You are unlikely to see a shark while swimming or diving in the Caribbean, especially if you spot dolphins nearby. The dolphin is a natural enemy of the shark, and will attack its most vulnerable points—the gills and the tip of the nose—so sharks steer clear of them.

Snorkeling

Snorkeling requires no special skills, and most hotels that rent equipment have a staff member or, at the very least, a booklet offering instruction in snorkeling basics.

As with any water sport, it's never a good idea to snorkel alone, especially if you're out of shape. You don't have to be a great swimmer to snorkel, but occasionally currents come up that require stamina.

The four dimensions as we know them seem altered underwater. Time seems to slow and stand still, so wear a water-resistant watch and let someone on land know when to expect you back. Your sense of direction may also fail you when you're submerged. Many a vacationer has ended up half a mile or more from shore—which isn't a disaster unless you're already tired, chilly, and it's starting to get dark.

Remember that taking souvenirs—shells, pieces of coral, interesting rocks—is forbidden. Many reefs are legally protected marine parks, where removal of living shells is prohibited because it upsets the ecology. Because it is impossible to tell a living shell from a dead one, the wisest course is simply not to remove any. Needless to say, underwater is also not the place to discard your cigarette packs, gum wrappers, or any other litter.

Good snorkel equipment isn't cheap, and you may not like the sport once you've tried it, so get some experience with rented equipment, which is always inexpensive, before investing in quality mask, fins, and snorkel. The best prices for gear, as you might imagine, are not to be found at sea-side resorts.

Scuba Diving

Diving is America's fastest-growing sport. While scuba (which stands for self-contained underwater breathing apparatus) looks and is surprisingly simple, *phone your physician before your vacation and make sure that you have no condition that should prevent you from diving!* Possibilities include common colds and other nasal infections, which can be worsened by diving, and ear infections, which can be worsened and cause underwater vertigo as well. Asthmatics can usually dive safely but must have their doctor's okay. A full checkup is an excellent idea, especially if you're over 30. Since it can be dangerous to travel on a plane after diving, you should schedule both your diving courses and travel plans accordingly.

At depths of below 30 feet, all sorts of physiological and chemical changes take place in the body in response to an increase in water pressure, so learning to dive with a reputable instructor is a must. Nitrogen, for example, which ordinarily escapes from the body through respiration, forms bubbles in the diver's bloodstream. If the diver resurfaces at a rate of more than one foot per second, these nitrogen bubbles may accumulate; the severe joint pains caused by this process are known as "the bends." If the nitrogen bubbles travel to your heart or brain, the result can be fatal.

In addition to training you how to resurface slowly enough, a qualified instructor can teach you to read "dive tables," the charts that calculate how long you can safely stay at certain depths. Many instructors supplement these charts with underwater computers that continuously monitor nitrogen, depth, and other information.

The ideal way to learn this sport is to take a resort course once you've arrived at your Caribbean destination. The course will usually consist of two to three hours of instruction on land, with time spent in a swimming pool or waist-deep water to get used to the mouthpiece and hose (known as the regulator) and the mask. A shallow 20-foot dive from a boat or beach, closely supervised by the instructor, follows.

Successful completion of this introductory course may prompt you to earn a certification card—often called a C-card—from one of the major accredited diving organizations: NADI (National Association of Diving Instructors), CMAS (Confederation Mondiale des Activities Subaquatiques, which translates into World Underwater Federation), NASE (National Association of Scuba Educators), or PADI (Professional Association of Diving Instructors). PADI offers a free list of training facilities; write PADI for information (Box 24011, Santa Ana, CA 92799).

The more advanced Openwater I certification course takes five or six sessions—once a day at a beach hotel, or once a week at a YMCA or school pool back home. You must be able to swim a certain distance to qualify, even if it's dog-paddling. The course requires about 20 hours of classroom work, followed by a written test covering use of dive gear, basic skills and safety measures, and basic rescue techniques. Underwater skills are also practiced and tested.

A certification course will keep you very busy and pleasantly tired for most of your vacation. If your travel plans include a great deal of sightseeing as well, you'll have little time left to relax. You may wish to complete the classroom instruction and basic skills training at your hometown YMCA, for example, then do your five required open-water dives on vacation.

Unfortunately, there are a few disreputable individuals who may try to assure you that they can teach you everything you need to know about diving even though they aren't certified instructors. DON'T BELIEVE IT! Reputable diving shops proudly display their association with the organizations mentioned above. If you have any doubt, ask to see evidence of accreditation. Legitimate instructors will happily show you their credentials and will insist on seeing *your* C-card before a dive.

Keep in mind that your presence can easily damage the delicate underwater ecology. By standing on the bottom you can break fragile coral that took centuries to grow. Many reefs are legally protected marine parks; spearfishing or taking living shells and coral is rude and destructive, and often strictly prohibited. When in doubt, remember the diver's caveat: "Take only pictures, leave only bubbles."

Snuba

Not quite ready for scuba diving? Not to worry. For those kept from diving by poor health or claustrophobia, there is snuba, a combination of snorkeling and scuba diving. The snuba system consists of an inflatable raft that supports a tank of compressed air and a 20-foot air hose for one or two persons. The raft not only warns boats of your presence, but also provides a convenient resting place when you're tired. (There is even a clear window in the raft so you can still have an underwater view while taking a break.) The rental cost is approximately $25 an hour, and it takes only about an hour to become a certified snuba user.

Caribbean snuba outlets include **Virgin Island Diving Schools,** St. Thomas (tel. 809/774–8687); **SNUBA of St. Thomas** (tel. 800/524–7389 or 809/774–2775); **Pineapple Beach Club Resort,** Antigua (tel. 809/463–2006); and **SNUBA of St. John,** U.S. Virgin Islands (tel. 809/776–6922).

At press time, eight additional Caribbean islands were slated to get snuba equipment: Aruba, Barbados, Curaçao, Grand Cayman, Saba, St. Croix, St. Maarten, and Tortola. Check with your travel agent or the tourism board of the island you plan to visit for availability and information.

Waterskiing

Some large hotels have their own waterskiing concessions, with special boats, equipment, and instructors. Many beaches (especially those in Barbados), however, are patrolled by private individuals who own boats and several sizes of skis; they will offer their services through a hotel or directly to vacationers, or can be hailed like taxis. Ask your hotel staff or other guests about their experiences with these entrepreneurs. Be *sure* they provide life vests and at least two people in the boat: one to drive and one to watch the skier at all times.

Windsurfing

Windsurfing is as strenuous as it is exciting, so it is perhaps not the sport to try on your first day out, unless you're already in excellent shape. As with most water sports, it is essential to windsurf with someone else around who can watch you and go for help if necessary.

Always wear a life vest and preferably a diveskin to protect your own skin from the sun. Avoid suntan oil that could make your feet slippery and interfere with your ability to stand on the board. Nike, Inc. now makes athletic shoes specifically for wear in water sports (*see* Swimming, above).

Sailing

Whether you charter a yacht with crew, or captain a boat yourself, the waters of the Caribbean—especially those around the Virgin Islands and the Grenadines—are excellent for sailing, and the many secluded bays and inlets provide ideal spots to drop anchor and picnic or explore. Like hotel rates, charter prices are lower during the off-season.

St. Thomas, U.S. Virgin Islands, and Tortola and Virgin Gorda in the British Virgin Islands do most of the charter and marina business. In St. Thomas, contact the **Virgin Island Charter Yacht League** (tel. 809/774–3944). In Tortola, **The Moorings** (tel. 809/494–2332); in Virgin Gorda, **North South Yacht Charters** (tel. 809/495–5421). The cost of chartering a yacht ranges from $100 to $250 a day per person (all-inclusive, with meals and drinks).

Sailing out of Grenada through the Grenadines is also recommended and many charters are available. From Guadeloupe, you can sail to Dominica and Antigua and anchor at the Isles of Marie Galante and Les Saintes.

1 Essential Information

Before You Go

Government Tourist Offices

Each of the various tourist boards listed below is a good source of general information on the particular island (or islands) it represents. Call or write for free brochures with histories, listings of hotels, restaurants, sights and stores, and up-to-date calendars of events. The **Caribbean Tourism Association** (20 E. 46th St., New York, NY 10017, tel. 212/682–0435) is another resource, especially for information on the islands that don't have tourist offices in the United States. In addition, the names and addresses of tourist boards located on the islands themselves appear under *Tourist Information Services* in each individual island chapter.

Anguilla   **Anguilla Tourist Office. In the United States:** 1208 Washington Drive, Centerport, NY 11721, tel. 212/869–0402 or 516/673–0150.
In the United Kingdom: c/o Windotels, Suite 21, College House, 29–31 Wright's Lane, Kensington W8 5SH, tel. 01/730–7144.

Antigua and Barbuda   **Antigua and Barbuda Department of Tourism. In the United States:** 610 5th Avenue, Suite 311, New York, NY 10020, tel. 212/541–4117; 121 SE 1st Street, Suite 508, Miami, FL 33131, tel. 305/381–6762.
In Canada: 60 St. Clair Avenue E, Suite 205, Toronto, Ont. M4T 1N5, tel. 416/961–3085.
In the United Kingdom: 15 Thayer Street, London W1M 5LD, tel. 01/486–7073.

Aruba   **Aruba Tourist Authority. In the United States:** 1270 Avenue of the Americas, Suite 2212, New York, NY 10020, tel. 212/246–3030; Box 776, Streamwood, IL 60107, tel. 312/337–1716; Box 012348, Miami, FL 33101, tel. 305/326–7280.
In Canada: 1801 Eglinton Avenue W, Suite 109, Toronto, Ont. M6E 2H7, tel. 416/782–9954.

Barbados   **Barbados Board of Tourism. In the United States:** 800 2nd Avenue, New York, NY 10017, tel. 212/986–6516; 3440 Wilshire Boulevard, Suite 1215, Los Angeles, CA 90010, tel. 213/380–2198.
In Canada: 20 Queen Street W, Suite 1508, Toronto, Ont. M5H 3R3, tel. 416/979–2137; 615 Dorchester West Boulevard, Suite 960, Montreal, P.Q. H3B 1P5, tel. 514/861–0085.
In the United Kingdom: 263 Tottenham Court Road, London q(2)W1P 9AA, tel. 01/636–9448 or 01/636–9449.

Bonaire   **Bonaire Government Tourist Office. In the United States:** 275 7th Avenue, New York, NY 10001, tel. 212/242–7707.
In Canada: 815 A Queen Street E, Toronto, Ont. M4M 1H8, tel. 416/465–2958.

British Virgin Islands   **British Virgin Islands Tourist Board. In the United States:** 370 Lexington Avenue, New York, NY 10017, tel. 212/696–0400.
In Canada: (no mailing address), tel. 416/283–2235.
In the United Kingdom: c/o Wingjet Ltd., 26 Hockerill Street, Bishop's Stortford, Hertfordshire CM23 2DW, tel. 279/506747.

Cayman Islands   **Cayman Islands Tourist Board. In the United States:** 420 Lexington Avenue, Suite 2733, New York, NY 10170, tel. 212/682–

5582; c/o One Magnificent Mile, 980 North Michigan Avenue, Suite 1260, Chicago, IL 60611, tel. 312/944–5602; 9794 Forest Lane, Suite 569, Dallas, TX 75243, tel. 817/430–4221; Two Memorial City Plaza, 820 Gessner, Suite 170, Houston, TX 77024, tel. 713/461–1317; 3440 Wilshire Boulevard, Suite 1202, Los Angeles, CA 90010, tel. 213/738–1969; 250 Catalonia Avenue, Suite 401, Coral Cables, FL 33134, tel. 305/444–6551.
In Canada: 234 Eglinton Avenue E, Suite 306, Toronto, Ont. M4P 1K5, tel. 416/485–1550.
In the United Kingdom: Trevor House, 100 Brompton Road, London SW3 1EX, tel. 01/581–9960.

Curaçao **Curaçao Tourist Board. In the United States:** 400 Madison Avenue, Suite 311, New York, NY 10017, tel. 212/751–8266.

Dominica **Caribbean Tourism Organization. In the United States:** 20 East 46th Street, 4th floor, New York, NY 10017, tel. 212/682–0435.
In the United Kingdom: c/o Dominica High Commission, 1 Collingham Gardens, London SW5 0HW, tel. 01/370–5194 or 01/373–8743.

Dominican **Dominican Republic Tourist Office. In the United States:** 485
Republic Madison Avenue, New York, NY 10022, tel. 212/826–0750.
In Canada: 29 Bellair Street, Toronto, Ont. M5R 2C8, tel. 416/928–9188.

Grenada **Grenada Tourist Office. In the United States:** 141 East 44th Street, New York, NY 10017, tel. 212/687–9554 or 800/638–0852.
In Canada: 439 University Avenue, Suite 820, Toronto, Ont. M5G 1Y8, tel. 416/595–1339.
In the United Kingdom: c/o Grenada High Commission, 1 Collingham Gardens, Earls Court, London SW5 0HW, tel. 01/370–5164.

Guadeloupe **French West Indies Tourist Board. In the United States:** 628 5th Avenue, New York, NY 10020, tel. 212/757–1125; French Government Tourist Office, 9454 Wilshire Boulevard, Beverly Hills, CA 90212, tel. 213/272–2661; French Government Tourist Office, 645 North Michigan Avenue, Chicago, IL 60611, tel. 312/337–6301; French Government Tourist Office, 103 World Trade Center, Dallas, TX 75258, tel. 214/742–7011; 1 Hallidie Plaza, Suite 250, San Francisco, CA 94102, tel. 415/986–4161.
In Canada: French Government Tourist Office, 1981 Avenue, McGill College, Suite 490, Montreal, P.Q. H3A 2W9, tel. 514/288–4264; French Government Tourist Office, 1 Dundas Street W, Suite 2405, Toronto, Ont. M5G 1Z3, tel. 416/593–4717.
In the United Kingdom: c/o French Government Tourist Office, 178 Piccadilly, London W1V 0AL, tel. 01/499–6911.

Jamaica **Jamaica Tourist Board. In the United States:** 866 2nd Avenue, New York, NY 10017, tel. 212/688–7650 or 800/223–5225; 36 South Wabash Avenue, Suite 1210, Chicago, IL 60603, tel. 312/346–1546; 1320 South Dixie Highway, Coral Gables, FL 33146, tel. 305/665–0557; 8411 Preston Road, Suite 605, LB31, Dallas, TX 75225, tel. 214/361–8778; 3440 Wilshire Boulevard, Suite 1207, Los Angeles, CA 90010, tel. 213/384–1123.
In Canada: 1 Eglinton Avenue E, Suite 616, Toronto, Ont. M4P 3A1, tel. 416/482–7850.
In the United Kingdom: Jamaica House, 63 St. James's Street, London SW1A 1LY, tel. 01/493–3647.

Martinique	**French West Indies Tourist Board. In the United States:** 610 5th Avenue, New York, NY 10020, tel. 212/757–1125; French Government Tourist Office, 9454 Wilshire Boulevard, Beverly Hills, CA 90212, tel. 213/272–2661; French Government Tourist Office, 645 North Michigan Avenue, Chicago, IL 60611, tel. 312/337–6301; French Government Tourist Office, 103 World Trade Center, Dallas, TX 75258, tel. 214/720–4010; 1 Hallidie Plaza, Suite 250, San Francisco, CA 94102, tel. 415/986–4161. **In Canada:** French Government Tourist Office, 1981 Avenue, McGill College, Suite 490, Montreal, P.Q. H3A 2W9, tel. 514/288–4264; French Government Tourist Office, 1 Dundas Street W, Suite 2405, Toronto, Ont. M5G 1Z3, tel. 416/593–4717. **In the United Kingdom:** c/o French Government Tourist Office, 178 Piccadilly, London W1V 0AL, tel. 01/499–6911.
Montserrat	**Montserrat Tourist Board. In the United States:** 110 East 59th Street, New York, NY 10022, tel. 212/752–8660.
Nevis	**St. Kitts-Nevis Tourist Board. In the United States:** 414 East 75th Street, New York, NY 10021, tel. 212/535–1234. **In Canada:** 11 Yorkville Avenue, Suite 508, Toronto, Ont. M4W 1L3, tel. 416/921–7717.
Puerto Rico	**Puerto Rico Tourism Company. In the United States:** 575 5th Avenue, 23rd floor, New York, NY 10017, tel. 212/599–6262 or 800/223–6530. **In Canada:** c/o Puerto Rico Tourism Information Company, 11 Yorkville Avenue, Suite 1003, Toronto, Ont. M4W 1L3, tel. 416/925–5587.
Saba	**Caribbean Tourism Association. In the United States:** 20 East 46th Street, New York, NY 10017, tel. 212/682–0435.
St. Barthélemy	**French West Indies Tourist Board. In the United States:** 610 5th Ave., New York, NY 10020, tel. 212/757–1125; French Government Tourist Office, 9454 Wilshire Boulevard, Beverly Hills, CA 90212, tel. 213/272–2661; French Government Tourist Office, 645 North Michigan Avenue, Chicago, IL 60611, tel. 312/337–6301; French Government Tourist Office, 103 World Trade Center, Dallas, TX 75258, tel. 214/742–7011; 1 Hallidie Plaza, Suite 250, San Francisco, CA 94102, tel. 415/986–4161. **In Canada:** French Government Tourist Office, 1981 Avenue, McGill College, Suite 490, Montreal, P.Q. H3A 2W9, tel. 514/288–4264; French Government Tourist Office, 1 Dundas Street W, Suite 2405, Toronto, Ont. M5G 1Z3, tel. 416/593–4717. **In the United Kingdom:** c/o French Government Tourist Office, 178 Piccadilly, London W1V 0AL, 01/499–6911.
St. Eustatius	**Caribbean Tourism Association. In the United States:** 20 East 46th Street, New York, NY 10017, tel. 212/682–0435.
St. Kitts	**St. Kitts-Nevis Tourist Board. In the United States:** 414 East 75th Street, New York, NY 10021, tel. 212/535–1234. **In Canada:** 11 Yorkville Avenue, Suite 508, Toronto, Ont. M4W 1L3, tel. 416/921–7717.
St. Lucia	**St. Lucia Tourist Board. In the United States:** 820 2nd Ave., 9th floor, New York, NY 10017, tel. 212/867–2950 or 800/456–3984. **In Canada:** 151 Bloor Street W, Suite 425, Toronto, Ont. M5S 1S4, tel. 416/961–5606. **In the United Kingdom:** 10 Kensington Court, London W8 5DL, tel. 01/937–1969.

St. Martin/ St. Maarten	**St. Martin Tourist Office. In the United States:** c/o Mallory Factor, 275 7th Avenue, 19th floor, New York, NY 10001, tel. 212/989-0000. **In Canada:** 243 Ellerslie Avenue, Willowdale, Ont. M2N 1Y5, tel. 416/223-3501.
St. Vincent and the Grenadines	**St. Vincent and the Grenadines Tourist Office. In the United States:** 801 2nd Avenue, New York, NY 10017, tel. 212/687-4981; 14347 Hay Meadow Circle, Dallas, TX 75240, tel. 214/239-6451. **In Canada:** 100 University Avenue, Suite 504, Toronto, Ont. M5J 1V6, tel. 416/971-9666 or 416/971-9667. **In the United Kingdom:** 10 Kensington Court, London W8 5DL, tel. 01/937-6570.
Trinidad and Tobago	**Trinidad and Tobago Tourist Board. In the United States:** 118-35 Queens Boulevard, 15th floor, Forest Hills, NY 11375, tel. 718/575-3909; 330 Biscayne Boulevard, Miami, FL 33132, tel. 305/370-2056. **In Canada:** c/o Trinidad and Tobago Tourism Development Authority, 40 Holly Street, Suite 102, Toronto, Ont. M4S 3C3, tel. 416/367-0390 or 800/268-8986. **In the United Kingdom:** 48 Leicester Square, London WC2 H7LT, tel. 01/839-7155.
Turks and Caicos	**Turks and Caicos Islands Tourist Board. In the United States:** For general information contact the **Caribbean Tourism Association,** 20 East 46th Street, New York, NY 10017, tel. 212/682-0435. **In the United Kingdom:** c/o West India Committee, 48 Albemarle Street, London W1X 4AR, tel. 01/629-6353.
U.S. Virgin Islands	**U.S. Virgin Islands Tourist Information Office. In the United States:** 1270 Avenue of the Americas, New York, NY 10020, tel. 212/582-4520. **In the United Kingdom:** 25 Bedford Square, London WC1B 3JA, tel. 01/637-8481.

Tour Groups

A good number of the islands are little more than a few miles wide, so there is little call for traditional escorted tours in the Caribbean. The primary options here are air/hotel packages (*see* Package Deals for Independent Travelers, below) and cruise tours (*see* Cruises, below). Cruise tours function somewhat like escorted programs, shuttling groups from island to island and arranging transportation when the sights are far apart. Both types of package mix and match Caribbean Islands in seemingly infinite varieties. If you don't see the particular itinerary you had your heart set on, tell your travel agent or tour operator to keep looking; odds are it exists somewhere.

When considering a tour, be sure to find out (1) exactly what expenses are included—particularly tips, taxes, side trips, additional meals, and entertainment; (2) ratings of all hotels on the itinerary and the facilities they offer; (3) cancellation policies for both you and the tour operator; (4) the number of travelers in your group; and (5) if you are traveling alone, the cost of the single supplement. Most tour operators request that bookings be made through a travel agent—in most cases there is no additional charge for doing so.

General-Interest **American Express Vacations** (Box 5014, Atlanta, GA, tel. 800/
Tours 241–1700) offers a host of both escorted and independent packages. Trips range anywhere from 3 to 21 days in length to any
one island location in the Caribbean. **Horizon Tours** (1010 Ver-
mont Ave., Suite 202, Washington, DC 20005, tel. 202/393–
8390 or 800/525–7760) serves as many as 45 different Caribbean
locations while smaller operations like **Bonaire Enterprises**
(Box 775, Morgan, NJ 08879, tel. 800/526–2370) provide a welcome alternative: The company confines all business to Bonaire
alone.

Vacation packages need not drain your bank account—**Tour-
Scan, Inc.** (Box 2367, Darien, Connecticut 06820, tel. 203/655–
8091 or 800/962–2080) gathers and computerizes up to 11,000
deals each season, and boasts an average $300–$400 savings
per traveler, while exacting no club fee.

Other major operators include **Certified Tours** (Box 1525, Fort
Lauderdale, FL, tel. 800/872–7786), **GWV International** (300
1st Ave., Needham, MA 02194, tel. 800/225–5498), and **Caval-
cade Tours** (450 Harmon Meadow Blvd., Secaucus, NJ 07092,
tel. 800/521–2319).

Special-Interest The **Smithsonian Associates Travel Program** (1100 Jefferson
Tours Dr., SW, Washington, DC 20560, tel. 202/357–4700) offers
Culture/Arts many educational and research programs around the world.
New last year was a close look at the culture and customs
of Jamaica.

Diving **Aqua Adventures** (114 E. 32nd St., Suite 501, New York, NY
10016, tel. 212/686–6210 or 800/654–7537) offers scuba packages at some 68 or so diving resorts in the Caribbean. **Sea
Safaris Travel** (3770 Highland Ave., Suite 102, Manhattan
Beach, CA 90266, tel. 213/546–2464, 800/821–6670, or 800/262–
6670 in CA) specializes in Cayman Islands dive packages.

Environmentalist **Oceanic Society Expeditions** (Fort Mason Center, Bldg. E, San
Francisco, CA 94123, tel. 415/441–1106) is a nonprofit environmental group with a variety of research and preservation
projects open to public participation. One program charts sections of coral reef and takes a census of underwater life in the
West Indies; in another, participants swim with dolphins. No
special skills are necessary, just good swimming ability.

Equestrian **Fits Equestrian** (2011 Alamo Pintado Rd., Solvang, CA 93463,
tel. 805/688–9494) tours Jamaica on horseback, with optional
polo lessons and instructions for beginners and experienced
riders.

Honeymoon Many hotels and most Caribbean tour operators (*see* Package
Deals for Independent Travelers, below) have pampering honeymoon packages, with special suites, free champagne, and
other options.

Natural History **Questers Worldwide Nature Tours** (257 Park Ave. S, New York,
NY 10010, tel. 212/673–3120) focuses on the flora and fauna of
Trinidad and Tobago. Rain-forest, beach, and swamp environ-
ments are explored with an experienced naturalist. **Oceanic
Society Expeditions** (*see* above) explores the island and marine
ecology of St. Vincent and St. Lucia. Day trips include opportunities to search for whales and dolphins.

Singles **Singleworld** (Box 1999, Rye, NY 10580, tel. 914/967–3334 or 800/223–6490) offers packages strictly for singles, organized by two age groups: "under 35" and "all ages."

Club Med (tel. 800/258–2633) offers a number of all-inclusive packages at several locations throughout the Caribbean.

Package Deals for Independent Travelers

Most packages include air transportation, accommodations, and transfers to and from your hotel. Some add meals and sightseeing, and make local representatives available to answer questions and offer advice. The travel section of a local newspaper and a good travel agent are your best sources for shopping around.

The number of Caribbean packages is truly overwhelming; the following is a small sampling of typically reliable packagers. **American Airlines Fly AAway Vacations** (tel. 800/854–TOUR), **American Express Vacations** (tel. 800/241–1700), **Cayman Airtours** (tel. 800/247–2966), **Continental Airlines' Grand Destinations** (tel. 800/634–5555), and **GoGo Tours** (68 offices across the country; if you can't find one near you, call GoGo's headquarters at tel. 201/934–3500). **Thomson Vacations** and **Travel Impressions** only work through travel agents; your agent should have information on their deals.

Leeward Islands Air Transport (LIAT, tel. 809/462–0700), which has its headquarters at Antigua's V. C. Bird International Airport, offers a *21-day Explorer* ticket and a *30-day Super Caribbean Explorer* ticket, both of which allow unlimited onward stopovers (no backtracking except to transfer). The Explorer is valid only from July 1 through August 31 and December 15 through January 31. The cost is $169 in summer, $199 in winter. This ticket is sold worldwide, *except in the Caribbean.* The 30-day Super Caribbean Explorer is available year-round for $357 and can be purchased in Antigua and Barbuda, Anguilla, Barbados, the British Virgin Islands, Caracas, Dominica, Guadeloupe, Guyana, Grenada, Martinique, Montserrat, Nevis, St. Eustatius, St. Kitts, St. Lucia, St. Vincent and the Grenadines, San Juan, Trinidad and Tobago, and the U.S. Virgin Islands. There are no refunds; a $20 charge is assessed for a change in routing; and the tickets are valid only on LIAT flights. Both tickets are very good options if you plan to do extensive island-hopping.

Tips for British Travelers

Tourist Information There is no general office for the Caribbean in the United Kingdom, but a number of different islands have their own tourist information offices (*see* Government Tourist Offices, above).

Passports and Visas *See* the Before You Go section in each island chapter for specific passport and visa requirements. Some islands require passports, others do not but may require a "British Visitor's" passport, generally available from the post office.

Customs Exact customs regulations vary slightly from island to island, but in general, the restrictions apply to alcohol and cigarettes only. Travelers are allowed to bring in 200 cigarettes, 1 liter of alcohol over 22% by volume (most spirits), or 2 bottles of wine.

Returning to the United Kingdom, if you are 17 or over, you may take home: (1) 200 cigarettes or 100 cigarillos or 50 cigars or 250 grams of tobacco; (2) 2 liters of table wine and (a) 1 liter of alcohol over 22% by volume (most spirits), (b) 2 liters of alcohol under 22% by volume (fortified or sparkling wine), or (c) 2 more liters of table wine; (3) 50 grams of perfume and ¼ liter of toilet water; and (4) other goods up to a value of £32.

Insurance We recommend that to cover health and motoring mishaps, you insure yourself with **Europ Assistance** (252 High St., Croydon, Surrey CR0 1NF, tel. 01/680–1234).

It is also wise to take out insurance to cover the loss of luggage (although check that such loss isn't already covered in any existing homeowner's policies you may have). Trip-cancellation insurance is another wise buy. **The Association of British Insurers** (Aldermary House, Queen St., London EC4N 1TT, tel. 01/248–4477) will give comprehensive advice on all aspects of vacation insurance.

Tour Operators Here is just a selection of companies offering packages to the Caribbean. Also, contact your travel agent for the latest information:

Caribbean Connection (Concorde House, Forest St., Chester CH1 1QR, tel. 0244/41131) has a 70-page catalogue devoted to Caribbean Holidays, with a number of special deals, including Supersavers, and Second Week Free offers.

Kuoni Travel (Kuoni House, Dorking, Surrey RH5 4AZ, tel. 0306/740500) specializes in "Caribbean Multi-Centre Holidays," which allow you to mix and match your stays on different islands. Prices start at £936 for a week.

Sovereign Worldwide (Trafalgar House, 2 Chalk Hill Rd., London W6 8DN, tel. 01/748–4495) offers a variety of packages with special offers, including "2 Centre" vacations, combining stays on two separate islands, and special "2 for 1" and "3 for 2" offers, giving you an extra week or two for free. Price range from £499 to $1,099 for one week.

Tradewinds Faraway Holidays (Station House, 81/83 Fulham High St., London SW6 3JP, tel. 01/731–8000) has trips to a number of islands, ranging from £648 to £1692 for seven nights.

Airlines and Airfares **British Airways** and **British West Indian Airways** are the only airlines with direct flights from London to the Caribbean. APEX fares range from £464 low season to £545 high season. It is always worth checking the small ads in *Time Out* magazine or the Sunday papers for cheaper charter flights. You may be able to pick up something for rock-bottom prices, but you should be prepared to be flexible about your dates of travel, and you should book as early as possible.

Festivals and Seasonal Events

January **Antigua:** The first week in January brings international tennis tournaments, clinics, and friendly and not-so-friendly matches for an official Tennis Week.

Aruba: The New Year takes off with midnight fireworks, and, on earth, groups of singers stroll from house to house with musical greetings.

Curaçao: Marking the first of the Carnival seasons to hit the Caribbean, the Curaçao Carnival creates its own blend of music, dance, and costumed parade from January to February.

Dominican Republic: Duarte's Birthday is held on January 26 in celebration of the founding father.

Grenada: There's a New Year Fiesta and yacht race, highlighted by the "Around Grenada" sailing contest. An annual Game Fishing Tournament is held in mid-January, with serious fishermen vying for sailfish, marlin, yellowfin, and tuna.

Guadeloupe: Carnival celebrations begin on a Sunday in January and continue until Lent.

St. Barthélemy: The Annual St. Bart's Music Festival, held from January 30 to February 5, imports an international collection of soloists and musicians. Artists perform four musical concerts at L'Orient; and there are additional dance performances in Gustavia.

St. Lucia: Food vendors sell local delicacies, bands play, and masqueraders come down from the countryside to show off their dancing skills during New Year's Fiesta on January 1 and 2.

February **Aruba:** From mid- to late February, Carnival hits Aruba. The entire island participates in dancing street parades, musical contests, and the election of Carnival Queen. The culmination is a Grand Parade that begins at noon on the Sunday preceding Lent.

Barbados: The Holetown Festival commemorates the first settlement of Barbados on February 17, 1627, with a week of fairs, street markets, and medieval revelry. Fifteenth- and 16th-century religious chorales echo throughout the village churches against the backdrop of an unmistakably modern beat resounding across the fairgrounds.

Bonaire: Bonaire drinks and feasts its way through Carnival in the month of February.

Dominican Republic: A nationwide Carnival takes place during the third week of the month, followed by National Independence Day on February 27.

Guadeloupe: Carnival continues in Guadeloupe as a pre-Lenten fantasy culminating on Ash Wednesday. On Shrove Tuesday, or "Mardi Gras," the peak of Carnival frenzy, a parade of floats and costumed red devils and diablesses flood the streets of Pointe-à-Pitre. Last but not least, Ash Wednesday arrives and commands an all black-and-white dress code for the revelers. "King Carnival" burns on his funeral pyre, rum flows, and the dancing climbs to a fevered pitch.

Martinique: One of the biggest and best Carnivals offers six weeks of *zouks* (all-night revelries). Wheeled carnival floats, ranging from the grotesque and the extravagant to the naive, sometimes carry more than 50 revelers, an orchestra with massive amplification, and a delirious multitude of costumed dancers at its heels. When the processions break up at sunset, the revelers split into small groups and dance until dawn. Burlesque marriages, burning effigies, and devils in red with tridents in tow are all part of the Mardi Gras scene.

St. Barthélemy: A smaller-scale Mardi Gras takes to the streets of St. Barthélemy.

St. Lucia: This island's riotous version of Carnival merrymaking precedes Independence Day on February 22, which itself remains the biggest celebration of the year. The Carnival features a Kiddies Carnival where schools and children's groups compete against one another in costumed themes. Also, a predawn jump-up called *J'Ouvert* winds through the streets of

Castries, then climaxes with the "Last Lap"—a parade renowned for its magnificent array of colorful dress.

St. Martin/St. Maarten: During Carnival, which continues until Ash Wednesday, all business stops for five days. The celebration peaks on Shrove Tuesday, when dancing fills the streets of Marigot and Grand Case. The Dutch version of Carnival comes at Eastertime. Also, look for the St. Maarten/Heineken Regatta, an annual weekend of yacht races and soirees, in the early part of the month.

Trinidad and Tobago: During Carnival, adults and children alike are swept up in the excitement of "Playing Mas"—the state of surrendering completely to the rapture of fantastic spectacle, parades, music, and dancing. For those who feel the urge, places in a genuine "mas' band" can be purchased (long in advance) for fees that vary according to the prestige of the group and the intricacy of the costumes.

March **Curaçao:** The Curaçao Regatta is an open race for all types of boats.

Montserrat: St. Patrick's Day (March 17) is celebrated here on the "Emerald Isle" with great gusto; Montserrat claims a substantial citizenry of Irish descent.

St. Barthélemy: The St. Barts Cooking School manages three one-week cooking courses sponsored by Chef Hubert, the owner of a restaurant at the Hotel Manapany in Paris.

Trinidad and Tobago: Usually observed on a Sunday in March or April (consult the island tourist office for confirmation of dates), Phaguah celebrates the triumph of good over evil. Hindus observe a daylong agenda of prayer and fasting as well as singing, dancing, drumming, and a fair share of good-natured dousing of your neighbor with *aheer*, a vermillion dye.

April **Antigua:** In mid-month, Windsurfing Antigua Week takes off with nine days of sailing and endless parties. Immediately following comes International Sailing Week, when over 300 yachts from the four corners of the globe converge in Antigua for the Caribbean's greatest regatta and nonstop parties.

Barbados: The Oistins Fish Festival is a two-day affair held every Easter to honor the local fishing industry: Fishing competitions, boat races, street entertainment, and open-air bazaars abound. Steel bands and food stalls make the events all the more lively, and spectators can mingle with the thronging crowds of Bajans on the beaches, in the marketplace, and in the quaint rum shops that line the roadside. An exhibition by the Coast Guard rounds out the activities.

Bonaire: The Queen's Birthday on April 30 is an annual open-to-all celebration of Her Royal Majesty's "official birthday," and the lieutenant governor invites everyone on the island (including visitors) to his home for a cocktail reception.

British Virgin Islands: Virgin Gorda Festival and the Spring Regatta.

Cayman Islands: Grand Cayman Carnival comes first to Grand Cayman (Batabano) and then to Cayman Brac a week later (Brachanal).

Grenada: The Grenada Easter Regatta includes a week of both interisland and local races.

Guadeloupe: Easter Monday is a public holiday here. Families picnic on beaches and riverbanks. Soccer games between Guadeloupe and Martinique remain the year's classic sports events.

Jamaica: Negril Reggae Festival is a popular musical event.

Puerto Rico: Citron Harvest Festival.

St. Barthélemy: Local handicrafts are put on display and sold during St. Barts Arts, Crafts, and Products Week.

St. Martin/St. Maarten: For 15 days around Easter, the Dutch side celebrates its Carnival when "King Moumou" and "Queen of the Carnival" are elected. Visitors can count on numerous beauty contests, food competitions, musical concerts including calypso, parades, "jump-ups," floats, steel bands, string bands, and bright, fanciful costumes.

U.S. Virgin Islands: At Carnival time residents compete for the title of Calypso King. In addition, St. Thomas holds the International Rolex Cup Regatta—a three-day schedule of yacht racing and social events.

May **Anguilla:** Boat racing is the national sport in Anguilla, and the most important competitions take place on Anguilla Day (May 30).

Barbados: The Barbados Jazz Festival is a two-day event held at the end of the month. Performances of original compositions and traditional jazz take place in several locations in Bridgetown.

Puerto Rico: A 16th-century Dominican convent in San Juan is the setting for a week of music and dance performances known as *Semana de la Danza*.

St. Lucia: Just about every type of competition that can be held on or in water constitutes the week-long "Aqua Action" festival on Whitsun (Pentecost) weekend—canoe racing, Sunfish sailing, windsurfing, sport fishing, waterskiing, and a nonmariners race. At the end of the month, local fishermen decorate their boats and the whole island feasts on St. Peter's Day.

St. Martin/St. Maarten: The Historical and Cultural foundations organize the St. Martin Food Festival in May. All segments of society take part, contributing many of the dishes, desserts, liquors, and crafts; older citizens dress in their traditional garb. Entertainment includes steel bands and "old-time" band music.

Turks and Caicos Islands: At the end of May, the Annual South Caicos Regatta features local catboat and powerboat races, dances, and entertainment.

June **Aruba:** The Aruba High Winds Windsurfing Tournament features half a dozen different races, including one to Venezuela and back. But the real highlight of the season is the Aruba Jazz and Latin Music Festival, held in Oranjestad early in the month. Well-known entertainers offer Latin, pop, jazz, and salsa music at Mansur stadium. Soloists have included Ruben Blades, Wynton Marsalis, Wilfrido Vargas, and Diane Schuur.

Bonaire: Dia de San Juan (June 24) and Dia de San Pedro (June 28) recall folkloric traditions of music and dance in the villages of Bonaire.

British Virgin Islands: The U.S. and British Virgin Islands share the Hook In & Hold On Boardsailing Regatta in June and July.

Cayman Islands: The Cayman Islands host Million Dollar Month, a series of saltwater fishing contests with huge cash prizes.

Dominican Republic: Puerto Plata presents a Windsurfing International Tournament the second week in June.

Puerto Rico: From all over the world, orchestras, choruses, and choirs converge on San Juan for Festival Casals.

U.S. Virgin Islands: From June to July, the Hook In & Hold On

Boardsailing Regatta challenges competitors from around the world to a race between the U.S. and British Virgin Islands.

July   **Antigua:** Antigua's Carnival in late July lasts 10 days, during which a queen is crowned, calypso and steel bands compete, and the streets are full of floats and dancing celebrants in colorful costume.

Barbados: Cutting across July and August, the Crop Over Festival is a monthlong cheer for the end of the sugarcane harvest. Tents ring with the fierce battle of Calypsonians for the coveted Calypso Monarch award, and the air is redolent with smells of Bajan cooking during the massive "Bridgetown Market" street fair. The "Cohobblopot" blends drama, dance, and music with the crowning of the king and queen of costume bands, and both the King of Calypso and the Clown Prince are crowned on the night of "Pic-O-de-Crop Show." Finally, "Kadooment Day"—a national holiday—closes the show, but not before fireworks fill the sky and costumed bands fill the streets with pulsating Caribbean rhythms.

Dominican Republic: In the third week in July Santo Domingo cuts loose with the immensely popular Merengue Festival. During this 10-day party that rivals the best of the Caribbean Carnivals in overall gaiety and gastronomic splendor, outdoor bands and orchestras play on the Malecón, and all the hotel chefs proudly present their best.

French West Indies: Bastille Day (July 14).

Martinique: The Festival of Fort-de-France, which lasts the entire month, features theater, art, music, and dance performances from all over the world. Look for the Tour de la Martinique in mid-month—an annual island bike race registering international contestants.

Saba: Carnival is celebrated with picnics, sporting events, entertainment, and various recreational activities.

St. Martin/St. Maarten: Schoelcher Day honors Victor Schoelcher, the French parliamentarian who led the campaign against slavery. Look for boat races in Grand Case featuring the beautiful Anguillan sailing boats.

U.S. Virgin Islands: Besides a Fourth of July celebration, the islands mark the anniversary of the July 3, 1848, abolition of slavery.

August   **Anguilla:** The beginning of August is Carnival time in Anguilla. Street dancing, Calypso competitions, Carnival Queen Coronation, the Prince and Princess Show, and nightly entertainment are all featured alongside sumptious beach barbecues serving local lobster, chicken, and a vast array of fresh grilled fish.

Barbados: Once an end-of-August celebration, Crop Over has expanded into a whole month's worth of folk fests. With the sugarcane harvest complete, the islanders party with total abandon. Kadooment Day, the first Monday in August, tops it all off with dance jams and, for the children, a costume parade christened Kiddies Kadooment.

Grenada: Catch the ample street selections of food and craft exhibits during Rainbow City Festival on August 4 and 5. The first weekend in August is the annual Carriacou Regatta, which takes place on this offshore island some 16 miles to the north, a week of racing and partying. Then in mid-August the official Carnival takes off with steel-band and calypso music galore.

Guadeloupe: In imitation of the celebrated French "Tour de

France," Guadeloupe has its own "Tour de la Guadeloupe": an exciting 10-day race in early August featuring teams from many countries. Nine grueling itineraries cover the whole island. The famous Fête des Cuisinières (Festival of Cooks) held on August 11 is a true Guadeloupe original. This is both a religious and gastronomic occasion, with some 100 women chefs in Creole dress honoring St. Laurent, the patron saint of cooks. Each chef carries her finest dishes, decorated with flowers, to the Pointe-à-Pitre Cathedral to celebrate High Mass. Following the Mass, there's an all-day feast at the Ecole Amédée Fengarol with feasting, singing, and dancing. Tickets are in great demand; a limited number are available from the Tourist Office.

Jamaica: The August Reggae Sunsplash International Music Festival is getting hotter every year. The best, brightest, and newest of the Caribbean reggae stars gather to perform in open-air concerts in Kingston and MoBay.

Martinique: The annual Tour de Yoles Rontes is a point-to-point race for yawls held in early August.

St. Barthélemy: The Festival de la Saint Barthélemy on August 24 marks the feast day of the patron saint of St. Barts. The feast of St. Louis on August 25 is commemorated in Corrossol by a fishing festival with dances and windsurfing contests.

St. Lucia: Members of La Rose Flower Society parade the streets dressed as kings and queens, princes and princesses, even doctors and nurses, for the Feast of St. Rose de Lima.

Turks and Caicos Islands: In early August, Provo Days gear up with a slew of activities: sailing races, regattas, parties, parades, dances, and a Miss Inter-Island/Miss Universe representative beauty contest. The Turks and Caicos Billfish Tournament is held at Turtle Cove Marina on Provo.

September   **Martinique:** Bridge devotees enjoy the Bridge Tournament in mid-September.

St. Barthélemy: The Fête du Vent on September 1 and 2, is celebrated with fishing contests and dances in L'Orient.

Trinidad and Tobago: Hosein is a Muslim religious festival, which, though solemn, is never lacking in color or imagination. Celebrants parade through the streets singing, beating drums, and carrying *tadgeahs* (large, exquisitely colored mosque-like models).

October   **Bonaire:** The annual Sailing Regatta is mid-October, with much ado about boats.

Cayman Islands: Pirate's Week finds Caymanians dressed as rogues and wenches and out to capture first a local galleon, and then the local governor. There's a mock battle, and the day ends in parties and parades.

Curaçao: One of the more uncommon musical events is the World Troubador Festival.

Dominican Republic: Puerto Plata has started its own Merengue Festival in the second week of October.

St. Vincent and the Grenadines: Independence Day is October 27.

Trinidad and Tobago: In October or November of each year, the Hindus create a Festival of Lights to pay tribute to the goddess Lakshmi. The devout scatter thousands of little earthenware lamps all over the cities and villages, in their homes and temples alike. At night, the result is an enchanted spectacle. Another highlight of the month is Trinidad's Pan Jazz Festival, during which leading pannists (players of metal drums, called *pans*) from North and South America converge in Port of Spain.

U.S. Virgin Islands: Hurricane Thanksgiving Day is the day when islanders give thanks for something they didn't get.

November   **Aruba:** In addition to the International Theatre Festival this month, Aruba sponsors the International Fishing Tournament on the first weekend in November.

Barbados: Residents show off their music, singing, dancing, acting, and writing talents during National Independence Festival of the Creative Arts. Shows lead all the way up to Independence Day on November 30.

Martinique: If you want to try a Semi-Marathon, Martinique invites you to a 22-kilometer race starting in Fort-de-France on November 25.

St. Martin/St. Maarten: On Concordia Day, parades and a joint ceremony by French and Dutch officials at the obelisk Border Monument commemorate the long-standing peaceful coexistence between both countries. This is also "St. Martin's Day" and the official beginning of "the season."

December   **Anguilla:** Separation Day is a day of patriotic festivities.

Barbados: The first weekend of December marks the annual Run Barbados International Road Race Series. The 26-mile, 385-yard marathon course (42,195 meters) over paved roads alongside the seashore and the 10K in and around Bridgetown attracts competitors from around the world. Among the top prizes for overseas entrants are airfare and hotel accommodations for the next year's race!

French West Indies: From Christmas to New Year's is Reveillon season, marked by special menus and dances at hotels and restaurants.

Guadeloupe: On Young Saints Day costumed children parade through the streets carrying toys.

Martinique: The town of Robert on the Atlantic coast (about a half-hour drive from Fort-de-France) holds the annual Nautique du Robert, a festival of the sea. On alternate years, Fort-de-France hosts either an International Jazz Festival or an International Guitar Festival, the latter with classes and concerts from world-famous guitarists. This is always held the first two weeks in December.

Nevis-St. Kitts: Carnival Week.

Puerto Rico: Although they hold a White Christmas Festival in Puerto Rico, you have little reason to fear snow in the Caribbean.

St. Barthélemy: The Route du Rose, a transatlantic regatta of Tall Ships that sets sail from St-Tropez in early November, arrives at St. Barts and there are many festivities to celebrate the finale.

St. Lucia: St. Lucia National Day is an island-wide celebration in honor of the island's patron saint.

When to Go

The Caribbean "season" has traditionally been a winter one, usually extending from December 15 to April 14. The winter months are the most fashionable, the most expensive, and the most popular for cruising or lazing on the beaches, far from the icy north, and most hotels are heavily booked at this time. You have to make your reservations at least two or three months in advance for the very best places. Hotel prices are at their highest during the winter months; the 20–40% drop in rates for "summer" (after April 15) is one of the chief advantages of off-season summer travel. Cruise prices also rise and fall with the seasons. Saving money isn't the only reason to visit the Caribbean during the off-season. Temperatures in summer are virtually the same as in winter. Some restaurants close and many hotels offer limited facilities, but reservations are easy to get, even at top establishments, and you'll have the beaches virtually to yourselves. Couples will enjoy relative solitude off-season, but singles in search of partners should visit during the high season, or choose a resort that enjoys a high occupancy rate year-round.

The flamboyant flowering trees are at their height of glory in summer, and so are most of the flowers and shrubs of the West Indies. The water is clearer for snorkeling and smoother in May, June, and July for sailing in the Virgin Islands and the Grenadines.

The Caribbean climate approaches the ideal of perpetual June. Average year-round temperature for the region is 78° to 85°. The extremes of temperature are 65° low, 95° high, but as everyone knows, it's the humidity, not the heat, that makes you suffer, especially when the two go hand in hand. You can count on downtown shopping areas being hot at midday any time of the year, but air-conditioning provides some respite. Stay near beaches, where water and trade winds can keep you cool, and shop early or late in the day.

High places can be cool, particularly when the Christmas winds hit Caribbean peaks (they come in late November and last through January), but a sweater is sufficient for protection from the trade winds.

Since most Caribbean islands are mountainous (notable exceptions being the Caymans, Aruba, Bonaire, and Curaçao), the altitude always offers an escape from the latitude. Kingston (Jamaica), Port of Spain (Trinidad), and Fort-de-France (Martinique) are three cities that swelter in summer, but climb 1,000 feet or so and everything is fine.

Hurricanes occasionally sweep through the Caribbean, and officials on many islands are unfortunately not well equipped to provide locals, much less tourists, with much warning. It's best to check the news daily and try to keep abreast of brewing tropical storms by reading stateside papers when available. The rainy season, which usually refers to the fall months, consists mostly of brief showers interspersed with sunshine. You can watch the clouds come over, feel the rain, and remain on your lounge chair for the sun to dry you off. A spell of overcast days is "unusual weather," as everyone will tell you.

Generally speaking, there's more planned entertainment in the winter months. The peak of local excitement on many islands, most notably Trinidad, St. Vincent, and the French West Indies, is Carnival.

Climate What follows are the average daily maximum and minimum temperatures for the Caribbean islands.

Current weather information on 500 cities in the United States and around the world is only a phone call away. To obtain the **Weather Trak** telephone number for your area, call 800/247–

Caribbean Temperature Chart

ISLAND	JANUARY / FEBRUARY	MARCH / APRIL	MAY / JUNE	JULY / AUGUST	SEPTEMBER / OCTOBER	NOVEMBER / DECEMBER
Anguilla	26.5°C – 21.5°C	29.0°C – 25°C	30.5°C – 26.0°C	31.5°C – 27.0°C	30.5°C – 26.0°C	29.5°C – 25.0°C
	79.7°F – 70.7°F	84.2°F – 86.0°F	87.0°F – 78.8°F	89.0°F – 80.6°F	87.0°F – 78.8°F	85.1°F – 86.0°F
Antigua	27.0°C – 22.0°C	28.0°C – 22.5°C	29.0°C – 24.5°C	30.0°C – 25.0°C	30.0°C – 24.0°C	28.5°C – 23.5°C
	81.0°F – 72.0°F	83.0°F – 73.0°F	85.0°F – 76.5°F	86.0°F – 77.0°F	86.0°F – 76.0°F	84.0°F – 75.0°F
Aruba	29.0°C – 23.0°C	30.5°C – 23.0°C	31.0°C – 24.0°C	32.0°C – 25.5°C	32.5°C – 26.5°C	30.5°C – 24.0°C
	85.0°F – 74.0°F	87.0°F – 74.0°F	88.0°F – 76.0°F	90.0°F – 78.0°F	91.0°F – 79.5°F	87.0°F – 76.0°F
Barbados	28.0°C – 21.0°C	29.5°C – 21.5°C	31.0°C – 23.0°C	30.5°C – 23.0°C	30.5°C – 23.0°C	31.0°C – 21.5°C
	83.0°F – 70.0°F	85.5°F – 71.0°F	88.0°F – 74.0°F	87.0°F – 74.0°F	87.0°F – 74.0°F	88.0°F – 74.0°F
Bonaire	specific monthly temperatures not available (25.5°C – 32.0°C year round)					
	specific monthly temperatures not available (78.0°F – 90.0°F year round)					
British Virgin Islands	specific monthly temperatures not available (24.0°C – 30.0°C year round)					
	specific monthly temperatures not available (76.0°F – 86.0°F year round)					
Cayman Islands	30.5°C – 18.5°C	31.5°C – 16.0°C	32.5°C – 21.0°C	32.5°C – 22.5°C	33.0°C – 22.0°C	31.0°C – 17.0°C
	87.0°F – 66.0°F	89.0°F – 61.0°F	91.0°F – 70.0°F	91.0°F – 73.0°F	92.0°F – 72.0°F	88.0°F – 63.0°F
Curaçao	28.5°C – 23.5°C	29.5°C – 23.5°C	30.5°C – 25.5°C	31.0°C – 25.5°C	31.5°C – 26.0°C	29.5°C – 24.0°C
	84.0°F – 75.0°F	85.5°F – 75.0°F	87.0°F – 78.0°F	88.0°F – 78.0°F	89.0°F – 79.0°F	85.5°F – 76.0°C
Dominica	specific monthly temperatures not available (23.5°C – 32.0°C year round)					
	specific monthly temperatures not available (75.0°F – 90.0°F year round)					
Dominican Republic	29.0°C – 19.0°C	29.0°C – 20.0°C	30.5°C – 22.0°C	31.0°C – 22.5°C	31.0°C – 22.0°C	29.5°C – 20.5°C
	85.0°F – 67.0°F	85.0°F – 68.5°F	87.0°F – 72.0°F	88.0°F – 73.0°F	88.0°F – 72.0°F	85.5°F – 69.0°F
Grenada	29.0°C – 24.0°C	29.0°C – 24.5°C	30.0°C – 25.5°C	30.0°C – 25.0°C	29.0°C – 24.5°C	29.5°C – 24.5°C
	85.0°F – 76.0°F	85.0°F – 76.5°F	86.0°F – 78.0°F	86.0°F – 77.0°F	87.0°F – 76.5°F	85.5°F – 76.5°F
Guadeloupe	28.0°C – 19.0°C	29.0°C – 20.0°C	30.5°C – 22.5°C	31.0°C – 23.0°C	31.0°C – 22.0°C	29.0°C – 20.5°C
	83.0°F – 67.0°F	85.0°F – 68.5°F	87.0°F – 73.0°F	88.0°F – 74.0°F	88.0°F – 72.0°F	85.0°F – 69.0°F
Haiti	29.0°C – 17.5°C	30.0°C – 18.5°C	30.5°C – 20.0°C	32.0°C – 21.0°C	30.5°C – 20.5°C	28.5°C – 18.5°C
	85.0°F – 64.0°F	86.0°F – 66.0°F	87.0°F – 68.0°F	90.0°F – 70.0°F	87.0°F – 69.0°F	84.0°F – 66.0°F

Location						
Jamaica	30.0°C – 19.0°C / 86.0°F – 67.0°F	30.5°C – 20.5°C / 87.0°F – 69.0°F	31.5°C – 22.5°C / 89.0°F – 73.0°F	32.0°C – 23.0°C / 90.0°F – 74.0°F	31.5°C – 23.0°C / 89.0°F – 73.0°F	31.0°C – 21.5°C / 88.0°F – 71.0°F
Martinique	28.5°C – 21.0°C / 84.0°F – 70.0°F	29.5°C – 21.5°C / 85.5°F – 71.0°F	30.5°C – 23.0°C / 87.0°F – 73.0°F	30.5°C – 23.0°C / 87.0°F – 74.0°F	31.0°C – 23.0°C / 88.0°F – 74.0°F	29.5°C – 22.0°C / 88.5°F – 72.0°F
Montserrat	28.0°C – 21.0°C / 83.0°F – 70.0°F	29.5°C – 21.5°C / 85.5°F – 71.0°F	31.0°C – 23.5°C / 88.0°F – 75.0°F	31.0°C – 24.0°C / 88.0°F – 76.0°F	31.5°C – 23.5°C / 89.0°F – 74.0°F	28.5°C – 22.5°C / 84.0°F – 73.0°F
Nevis	27.0°C – 21.5°C / 81.0°F – 71.0°F	28.0°C – 22.5°C / 83.0°F – 73.0°F	29.0°C – 24.0°C / 85.0°F – 76.0°F	30.0°C – 24.0°C / 86.0°F – 76.0°F	29.5°C – 24.0°C / 88.5°F – 76.0°F	28.5°C – 23.0°C / 84.0°F – 73.0°F
Puerto Rico	28.0°C – 22.0°C / 83.0°F – 72.0°F	28.5°C – 22.5°C / 84.0°F – 73.0°F	31.5°C – 24.5°C / 87.0°F – 76.5°F	31.0°C – 25.5°C / 88.0°F – 78.0°F	31.0°C – 24.0°C / 88.0°F – 76.0°F	29.5°C – 23.0°C / 85.5°F – 74.0°F
Saba	specific monthly temperatures not available (24.0°C – 28.5°C year round) specific monthly temperatures not available (76.0°F – 84.0°F year round)					
St. Barthelemy	25.0°C / 77.0°F	26.0°C / 78.0°F	27.0°C / 80.0°F	27.0°C / 80.0°F	27.0°C / 80.0°F	26.0°C / 78.0°F
St. Eustatius	29.0°C – 22.5°C / 85.0°F – 73.0°F	30.0°C – 23.0°C / 86.0°F – 74.0°F	31.0°C – 23.5°C / 88.0°F – 75.0°F	32.0°C – 24.0°C / 90.0°F – 76.0°F	32.0°C – 24.0°C / 90.0°F – 76.0°F	30.0°C – 23.5°C / 86.5°F – 75.0°F
St. Kitts	27.0°C – 21.5°C / 81.0°F – 68.0°F	28.0°C – 23.0°C / 83.0°F – 74.0°F	29.0°C – 24.0°C / 85.0°F – 76.0°F	25.0°C – 24.0°C / 86.0°F – 76.0°F	29.5°C – 24.0°C / 85.5°F – 76.0°F	28.5°C – 24.0°C / 84.0°F – 75.5°F
St. Lucia	27.0°C – 20.0°C / 81.0°F – 68.0°F	28.0°C – 21.0°C / 83.0°F – 70.0°F	29.0°C – 22.0°C / 85.0°F – 72.0°F	29.5°C – 22.0°C / 85.5°F – 72.0°F	29.5°C – 22.0°C / 85.5°F – 72.0°F	28.0°C – 21.5°C / 83.0°F – 71.0°F
St. Martin / St. Maarten	27.5°C – 22.0°C / 82.0°F – 72.0°F	29.0°C – 22.5°C / 85.0°F – 73.0°F	29.5°C – 23.5°C / 85.5°F – 75.0°F	30.5°C – 24.0°C / 87.0°F – 76.0°F	30.5°C – 24.0°C / 87.0°F – 75.0°F	28.0°C – 22.0°C / 83.0°F – 72.0°F
St. Vincent and the Grenadines	29.0°C – 22.0°C / 85.0°F – 72.0°F	29.5°C – 23.0°C / 85.5°F – 74.0°F	29.5°C – 23.0°C / 85.5°F – 74.0°F	25.0°C – 24.0°C / 86.0°F – 76.0°F	30.5°C – 24.0°C / 87.0°F – 75.0°F	29.5°C – 23.5°C / 85.5°F – 75.0°F
Trinidad and Tobago	31.0°C – 20.0°C / 88.0°F – 69.0°F	32.0°C – 20.5°C / 90.0°F – 69.0°F	32.0°C – 22.0°C / 90.0°F – 72.0°F	31.0°C – 22.0°C / 88.0°F – 72.0°F	32.0°C – 22.0°C / 90.0°F – 72.0°F	31.5°C – 21.5°C / 89.0°F – 71.0°F
Turks and Caicos Islands	27.0°C – 21.0°C / 81.0°F – 70.0°F	28.5°C – 22.5°C / 84.0°F – 73.0°F	30.5°C – 24.5°C / 87.0°F – 76.5°F	31.5°C – 25.5°C / 89.0°F – 78.0°F	31.0°C – 24.5°C / 88.0°F – 76.5°F	28.5°C – 23.5°C / 84.0°F – 73.0°F
U.S. Virgin Islands	25.0°C – 23.0°C / 86.0°F – 74.0°F	30.5°C – 21.5°C / 87.0°F – 71.0°F	31.0°C – 24.0°C / 88.0°F – 75.0°F	35.0°C – 25.0°C / 95.0°F – 77.0°F	33.0°C – 24.5°C / 92.0°F – 76.0°F	25.0°C – 22.0°C / 86.0°F – 72.0°F

3282. The local number plays a taped message that tells you to dial the three-digit access code for the destination you're interested in. The code is either the area code (in the United States) or the first three letters of the foreign city. For a list of all access codes, send a stamped, self-addressed envelope to Cities, Box 7000, Dallas, TX 75209. For further information, phone 214/869–3035 or 800/247–3282.

What to Pack

Pack light because baggage carts are scarce at airports and luggage restrictions are tight.

Clothing Dress on the islands is light and casual. Bring loose-fitting clothes made of natural fabrics to see you through days of heat and high humidity. Take a coverup for the beaches, not only to protect you from the sun, but also to wear to and from your hotel room. Bathing suits and immodest attire are frowned upon off the beach on many islands. A sun hat is advisable, but there's no need to pack one because inexpensive straw hats are available everywhere. For shopping and sightseeing, bring walking shorts, jeans, T-shirts, long-sleeve cotton shirts, slacks, and sundresses. Air-conditioning in hotels and restaurants often borders on the glacial, so bring a sweater or jacket for dining out. Evening wear is casual; jacket and tie is rarely required.

Miscellaneous It's advisable to wear a hat and sun-block lotion while sightseeing. Bring a spare pair of eyeglasses and sunglasses and an adequate supply of any prescription drugs you may need. You can probably find what you need in the pharmacies, but you may need a local doctor's prescription. Although you'll want an umbrella during the rainy season, you can pick up inexpensive ones locally. Leave the plastic or nylon raincoats at home; the high humidity makes them extremely uncomfortable. Bring suntan lotions and film from home in abundant supply; they're much more expensive in the islands. It's wise, too, to bring insect repellent, especially if you plan to walk through rain forests or visit during the rainy season.

Carry-on Luggage Passengers on U.S. airlines are limited to two carry-on bags. For a bag you wish to store under the seat, the maximum dimensions are 9″ × 14″ × 22″. For bags that can be hung in a closet or on a luggage rack, the maximum dimensions are 4″ × 23″ × 45″. For bags you wish to store in an overhead bin, the maximum dimensions are 10″ × 14″ × 36″. Any item that exceeds the specified dimensions may be rejected as a carryon and taken as checked baggage. Keep in mind that an airline can adapt the rules to circumstances, so on an especially crowded flight don't be surprised if you are allowed only one carry-on bag.

In addition to the two carryons, you may bring aboard a handbag (pocketbook or purse); an overcoat or wrap; an umbrella; a camera; a reasonable amount of reading material; an infant bag; crutches, cane, braces, or other prosthetic device; and an infant/child safety seat.

Foreign airlines have slightly different policies. They generally allow only one piece of carry-on luggage in tourist class, in addition to handbags and bags filled with duty-free goods. Passengers in first and business class are also allowed to carry on one garment bag. It is best to call your airline to find out its current policy.

Checked Luggage Luggage allowances vary slightly from airline to airline. Many carriers allow three checked pieces; some allow only two. It is best to check before you go. In all cases, check-in luggage cannot weigh more than 70 pounds per piece or be larger than 62 inches (length + width + height).

Taking Money Abroad

Traveler's checks and all major U.S. credit cards are widely accepted in the Caribbean. U.S. dollars are also widely accepted in most of the islands. The large hotels, restaurants, and department stores accept credit cards readily, but some of the smaller restaurants and shops operate on a cash-only basis. There may even be some room for bargaining when paying with U.S. dollars.

Although you won't get as good an exchange rate at home as abroad, it's wise to change a small amount of money into the local currency before you go to avoid long lines at airport currency-exchange booths. Some U.S. banks will change your money. If your local bank can't provide this service, you can exchange money through **Deak International.** To find the office nearest you, contact Deak (630 5th Ave., New York, NY 10011, tel. 212/635–0515).

For safety, it's always wise to carry traveler's checks. The most widely recognized are **American Express, Barclays, Thomas Cook,** and those issued through such major commercial banks as **Citibank** and **Bank of America.** Some banks will issue the checks free to established customers, but most charge a 1% commission fee. Buy some of the traveler's checks in small denominations to cash toward the end of your trip. This will save your having to cash a large check and ending up with more foreign currency than you need. You can also buy traveler's checks in the currency of some of the islands, a good idea if the dollar is dropping in relation to the local currency. The value of some currencies changes with great frequency and very radically; some are subject to inflation, others to devaluation, while still others float with the U.S. dollar. Remember to take the addresses of offices in the islands where you can get refunds for lost or stolen traveler's checks.

Banks and government-approved exchange houses give the best rates; hotels will also change currency, but generally at lower rates.

Getting Money from Home

There are at least three ways to get money from home:

1) Have it sent through a large commercial bank with a branch on the island where you're staying. The only drawback is that you must have an account with the bank; if not, you will have to go through your own bank and the process will be slower and more expensive.

2) Have it sent through **American Express.** If you are a cardholder, you can cash a personal check or a counter check at an American Express office for up to $1,000; $200 will be in cash

and $800 in traveler's checks. There is a 1% commission on the traveler's checks. You can also get money through **American Express MoneyGram.** Through this service, you can receive up to $5,000 cash. It works this way: You call home and ask someone to go to an American Express office or an American Express MoneyGram agent located in a retail outlet and fill out an American Express MoneyGram. It can be paid for with cash or any major credit card. The person making the payment is given a reference number and telephones you with that number. The American Express MoneyGram agent calls an 800 number and authorizes the transfer of funds to an American Express office or participating agency in the islands. In most cases, the money is available immediately on a 24-hour basis. You pick it up by showing identification and giving the reference number. Fees vary according to the amount of money sent. For sending $300, the fee is $22; for $5,000, $150. For the American Express MoneyGram location nearest your home, and to find out where the service is available in the islands, call 800/543–4080. You do not have to be a cardholder to use this service.

3) Have it sent through **Western Union** (tel. 800/325–6000). If you have a MasterCard or Visa, you can have money sent for any amount up to your credit limit. If not, have someone take cash or a certified cashier's check to a Western Union office. The money will be delivered in two business days to a bank near where you're staying. Fees vary with the amount of money sent and its destination. For Puerto Rico and the U.S. Virgin Islands, the rate is $47 for $1,000 and $37 for $500. For other destinations in the Caribbean, the fees average $69 for $1,000 and $59 for $500. Add $4 if you use credit cards.

Cash Machines   Virtually all U.S. banks now belong to a network of Automatic Teller Machines (ATMs) that dispense cash 24 hours a day. There are eight major networks in the United States, and some banks belong to more than one. In the past year, two of the largest systems, Cirrus, which is owned by MasterCard, and Plus, which is affiliated with Visa, have extended their service to U.S. territories and to foreign cities that attract large numbers of tourist and business travelers. The Plus system, for example, already has outlets in Puerto Rico and the U.S. Virgin Islands and may be expanding to other islands in the Caribbean. Each network has a toll-free number you can call to locate its machines in a given city. The Cirrus number is 800/424–7787; the Plus number is 800/843–7587. Note that these cash cards are not issued automatically; they must be requested at your specific branch.

Cards issued by Visa, American Express, and MasterCard can also be used in ATMs, but the fees are usually higher than the fees on bank cards (and there is a daily interest charge on the loan). All three companies issue directories that list the national and international outlets that accept their cards. You can pick up a Visa or MasterCard directory at your local bank. For an American Express directory, call 800/CASH–NOW (this number can also be used for general inquiries). Contact your bank for information on fees and the amount of cash you can withdraw on any given day. Although each bank individually charges for taking money with the card, using your American Express, Visa, or MasterCard at an ATM can be cheaper than exchanging money in a bank because of variations in exchange rates.

Traveling with Film

If your camera is new, shoot and develop a few rolls before you leave home. Pack some lens tissue and an extra battery for your built-in light meter. Invest about $10 in a skylight filter and screw it onto the front of your lens. It will protect the lens and also reduce haze.

Film doesn't like hot weather. If you're driving in summer, don't store film in the glove compartment or on the shelf under the rear window. Put it behind the front seat on the floor, on the side opposite the exhaust pipe.

On a plane trip, never pack unprocessed film in check-in luggage; if your bags get X-rayed, you can say good-bye to your pictures. Always carry undeveloped film with you through security, and ask to have it inspected by hand. (It helps to isolate your film in a plastic bag, ready for quick inspection.) Inspectors at American airports are required by law to honor requests for hand inspection; abroad, you'll have to depend on the kindness of strangers.

The old airport scanning machines—still in use in some countries—use heavy doses of radiation that can turn a family portrait into an early morning fog. The newer models—used in all U.S. airports—are safe for anything from five to 500 scans, depending on the speed of your film. The effects are cumulative; you can put the same roll of film through several scans without worry. After five scans, though, you're asking for trouble.

If your film gets fogged and you want an explanation, send it to the **National Association of Photographic Manufacturers** (600 Mamaroneck Ave., Harrison, NY 10528). They will try to determine what went wrong. The service is free.

Staying Healthy

Few real hazards threaten the health of a visitor to the Caribbean. Poisonous snakes are hard to find, and the small lizards that seem to have overrun the islands are harmless. The worst problem may well be a tiny predator, the "no see'um," a small sand fly that tends to appear after a rain, near wet or swampy ground, and around sunset. If you feel particularly vulnerable to insect bites, bring along a good repellent.

The worst problem tends to be sunburn or sunstroke. Even people who are not normally bothered by strong sun should head into this area with a long-sleeve shirt, a hat, and long pants or a beach wrap. These are essential for a day on a boat but are also advisable for midday at the beach. Also carry some sun-block lotion for nose, ears, and other sensitive areas such as eyelids, ankles, etc. Be sure to drink enough liquids. Above all, limit your sun time for the first few days until you become used to the heat.

Since health standards vary from island to island, it's best to inquire about the island you plan to visit before you go. No special shots are required for most destinations in the Caribbean; where they are, we have made note of it in the individual chapters. If you have a health problem that might require purchasing prescription drugs while in the Caribbean, have your doctor write a prescription using the drug's generic name; brand names can vary widely from island to island.

The International Association for Medical Assistance to Travelers (IAMAT) is a worldwide organization offering a list of approved English-speaking doctors whose training meets British and American standards. Contact IAMAT for a list of physicians and clinics in the Caribbean that belong to this network. **In the United States:** 736 Center Street, Lewiston, NY 14092, tel. 716/754–4883. **In Canada:** 40 Regal Road, Guelph, Ontario N1K 1B7. **In Europe:** Gotthardstrasse 17, 6300 Zug, Switzerland. Membership is free.

Insurance

Travelers may seek insurance coverage in three areas: health and accident, lost luggage, and trip cancellation. Your first step is to review your existing health and home-owner policies. Some health insurance plans cover health expenses incurred while traveling, some home-owner policies cover luggage theft, and some major medical plans cover emergency transportation.

Health and Accident
Several companies offer coverage designed to supplement existing health insurance for travelers:

Carefree Travel Insurance (Box 310, 120 Mineola Blvd., Mineola, NY 11501, tel. 516/294–0220 or 800/645–2424) provides coverage for medical evacuation. It also offers 24-hour medical advice by phone, will help find English-speaking medical and legal assistance anywhere in the world, and offers direct payment to hospitals for emergency medical care.
Wallach and Company, Inc. (243 Church St., NW, Suite 100D, Vienna, VA 22180, tel. 703/281–9500 or 800/237–6615) offers comprehensive medical coverage, including emergency evacuation for international trips of 10–90 days.
International SOS Insurance (Box 11568, Philadelphia, PA 19116, tel. 215/244–1500 or 800/523–8930) does not offer medical insurance but provides medical evacuation and repatriation services.
Travel Guard International, underwritten by Cygna (1100 Centerpoint Dr., Stevens Point, WI 54481, tel. 715/345–0505 or 800/782–5151), offers medical insurance, with coverage for emergency evacuation when Travel Guard's representatives in the United States say it is necessary.

Lost Luggage
Luggage loss is usually covered as part of a comprehensive travel insurance package that includes personal accident, trip cancellation, and sometimes default and bankruptcy insurance. Several companies offer comprehensive policies:

Access America, Inc., a subsidiary of Blue Cross–Blue Shield (600 3rd Ave., Box 807, New York, NY 10163, tel. 212/490–5345 or 800/284–8300).
Near Services (1900 N. MacArthur Blvd., Suite 210, Oklahoma City, OK 73127, tel. 800/654–6700 or in Oklahoma City, 405/949–2500).
Travel Guard International (*see* Health and Accident Insurance, above).
Carefree Travel Insurance (*see* Health and Accident Insurance, above).

Luggage Insurance
Airlines are responsible for lost or damaged property only up to $1,250 per passenger on domestic flights, and $9.07 per

pound ($20 per kilo) for checked baggage on international flights, and up to $400 per passenger for unchecked baggage on international flights. If you're carrying valuables, either take them with you on the airplane or purchase additional insurance for lost luggage. Some airlines will issue additional insurance when you check in, but many do not. Rates are $1 for every $100 valuation, with a maximum of $400 valuation per passenger. Hand luggage is not included.

Insurance for lost, damaged, or stolen luggage is available through travel agents or directly through various insurance companies. Two companies that issue luggage insurance are **Tele-Trip** (3201 Farnam St., Omaha, NE 68131, tel. 800/228–9792), a subsidiary of Mutual of Omaha, and **The Travelers Insurance Co.** (Ticket and Travel Plans Dept., 1 Tower Sq., Hartford, CT 06183, tel. 201/277–2318 or 800/243–3174). Tele-Trip, which operates sales booths at airports and also issues policies through travel agents, insures checked luggage for up to 180 days and for $500–$3,000 valuation. For one–three days, the rate for a $500 valuation is $8.25; for 180 days, $100. The Travelers Insurance Co. insures checked or hand luggage for $500–$2,000 valuation per person, also for a maximum of 180 days. Rates for up to five days for $500 valuation are $10; for 180 days, $85. Both companies offer the same rates on domestic and international flights. Check the travel pages of your local newspaper for the names of other companies that insure luggage.

Before you go, itemize the contents of each bag in case you need to file an insurance claim. Be certain to put your home address on each piece of luggage, including carry-on bags. If your luggage is stolen and later recovered, the airline must deliver the luggage to your home free of charge.

Trip Cancellation Flight insurance is often included in the price of a ticket when paid for with an American Express, Visa, or other major credit and charge cards. It is usually included in combination travel insurance packages available from most tour operators, travel agents, and insurance agents.

Student and Youth Travel

The **International Student Identity Card (ISIC)** entitles students to special fares on local transportation and discounts at museums, theaters, sports events, and many other attractions. If purchased in the United States, the $10 ISIC also includes $2,000 in emergency medical insurance, plus $100 a day for up to 60 days of hospital coverage. Apply to the **Council on International Educational Exchange (CIEE)** (205 E. 42nd St., New York, NY 10017, tel. 212/661–1450). In Canada, the ISIC is available for C$7.50 from the Federation of Students–Services (171 College St., Toronto, Ont. M5T 1P7).

Council Travel, a CIEE subsidiary, is the foremost U.S. student travel agency, specializing in low-cost charters and serving as the exclusive U.S. agent for many student airfare bargains and student tours. (CIEE's 80-page *Student Travel Catalog* and "Council Charter" brochure are available free from any Council Travel office in the United States; enclose $1 postage if ordering by mail.) In addition to the CIEE headquarters at 205 East 42nd Street and a branch office at 35 West 8th Street in New York City (tel. 212/254–2525), there are

Council Travel offices in Amherst, MA; Austin; Berkeley; Boston; Cambridge; Chicago; Dallas; La Jolla; Long Beach; Los Angeles; Portland, OR; Providence; San Diego; San Francisco; and Seattle.

The **Educational Travel Center** (438 N. Frances St., Madison, WI 55703, tel. 608/256–5551) is another student travel specialist worth contacting for information on student tours, bargain fares, and bookings.

Students who would like to work abroad should contact **CIEE's Work Abroad Department** (205 E. 42nd St., New York, NY 10017). The council arranges various types of paid and voluntary work experiences overseas for up to six months. CIEE also sponsors study programs in Latin America and publishes many books of interest to the student traveler: these include *Work, Study, Travel Abroad; The Whole World Handbook* ($8.95 plus $1 postage) and *Volunteer! The Comprehensive Guide to Voluntary Service in the U.S. and Abroad* ($4.95 plus $1 postage).

The Information Center at the **Institute of International Education** (809 UN Plaza, New York, NY 10017, tel. 212/984–5413) has reference books, foreign university catalogues, study-abroad brochures, and other materials that may be consulted by students and nonstudents alike, free of charge. The Information Center is open weekdays 10–4. For a current list of IIE publications, prices, and ordering information, write to Institute of International Education Books at the above address. Books must be purchased by mail or in person; telephone orders are not accepted. General information on IIE programs and services is available from the institute's regional offices in Atlanta, Chicago, Denver, Houston, San Francisco, and Washington, DC.

Traveling with Children

Publications   *Family Travel Times* is an 8- to 12-page newsletter published 10 times a year by **TWYCH** (Travel with Your Children, 80 8th Ave., New York, NY 10011, tel. 212/206–0688). The $35 yearly subscription includes access to back issues and twice-weekly opportunities to call in for specific information. Send $1 for a sample issue. The September issue is always devoted entirely to the Caribbean.

Great Vacations with Your Kids, by Dorothy Jordan (founder of TWYCH) and Marjorie Cohen, offers complete advice on planning a trip with children (toddlers to teens) and details everything from city vacations to adventure vacations to child-care resources ($9.95, E.P. Dutton, 2 Park Ave., New York, NY 10016, tel. 212/725–1818).

"Kids and Teens in Flight" and **"Fly Rights"** are U.S. Department of Transportation brochures with information on special services for young travelers. To order free copies, call 202/366–2220.

Accommodations   In addition to offering family discounts and special rates for
Hotels   children (for example, some large hotel chains do not charge extra for children under 12 if they stay in their parents' room), many hotels and resorts arrange for baby-sitting services and run a variety of special children's programs. The following list is representative of the kinds of services and activities offered by some of the major chains and resorts. It is by no means ex-

haustive. If you are going to be traveling with your children, be sure to check with your travel agent for more information or ask hotel representatives about children's programs when you are making reservations.

In **Puerto Rico,** the **Hyatt Regency Cerroman Beach** and the **Hyatt Dorado Beach Hotel** operate a complimentary camp for children age 5–12 all summer and at Christmastime. One of the camp's main attractions is a meandering, free-form freshwater pool with waterfalls, bridges, and a 187-foot water slide. The camp's staff includes bilingual college-age counselors. For more information, call 800/233–1234. The **El San Juan** in Puerto Rico (tel. 800/468–2818) has a program for children in the same age group that features swimnastics, treasure hunts, beach walks, exercise classes, tennis, and an always-open game room.

Superclub's Boscobel Beach in **Jamaica** (tel. 800/858–8009) is an all-inclusive resort that specializes in traveling families. Seven-night packages are in the $1,000-per-person range, and two children under 14 are allowed to stay free if they occupy the same room as their parents. A small army of SuperNannies is on hand to take charge. The activities are scheduled in half-hour periods so that children can drop in and out. For younger children there are morning "Mousercises," a petting zoo, shell hunts, and craft classes; for teens, "Coke-tail" parties at a disco and "No-Talent" shows. The classes in the Jamaican patois are popular with all ages.

Casa de Campo in the **Dominican Republic** (tel. 800/223–6620) has a fully operational summer camp that children can attend on a day-by-day basis. The program includes lessons in sailing, tennis, golf, painting, and pottery as well as bike races, donkey polo, and softball and soccer games. "Campers" are divided into two groups—age 5–8 and 9–12. On **St. Thomas** in the U.S. Virgin Islands the **Stouffer Grand Resort** (tel. 800/233–4935) has half-day and full-day programs for children age 3–12. In addition to supervising volleyball matches, arts and crafts classes, water games, and iguana hunts, the staff arranges outings to the Coral World Marine Life Park and Observatory. **Club Med** has recently added Mini Club programs for children to their regular roster of activities at resorts in the **Dominican Republic** and **St. Lucia.** Designed for children age 2–11 and scheduled from 9 AM to 9 PM, the fully supervised Mini Club activities include tennis, waterskiing, sailing, scuba diving in a pool, costume parties, and painting and pottery classes. For more information, call 800/CLUB–MED.

Villa Rentals **At Home Abroad, Inc.** (405 E. 56th St., Suite 6H, New York, NY 10022, tel. 212/421–9165).
Villas International (71 W. 23rd St., New York, NY 10010, tel. 212/929–7585 or 800/221–2260).
Hideaway International (Box 1270, Littleton, MA 01460, tel. 508/486–8955).
Villas and Apartments Abroad (420 Madison Ave., Room 305, New York, NY 10017, tel. 212/759–1025).

Home Exchange See *Home Exchanging: A Complete Sourcebook for Travelers at Home or Abroad,* by James Dearing ($9.95, Globe Pequot Press, Box Q, Chester, CT 06412, tel. 800/243–0495 or 800/962–0973 in CT).

Getting There All children, including infants, must have a passport for foreign travel; family passports are no longer issued. (For more information, *see* the Passports and Visas sections in the individual chapters.)

On international flights, children under age 2 not occupying a seat pay 10% of adult fare; on domestic flights, they travel free. Various discounts apply to children age 2–12. Reserve a seat behind the bulkhead of the plane, which offers more legroom and can usually fit a bassinet (supplied by the airline). At the same time, inquire about special children's meals or snacks, which are offered by most airlines. (See "TWYCH's Airline Guide" in the February 1988 issue of *Family Travel Times* for a rundown on children's services furnished by 46 airlines; an update is planned for February 1990.) Ask your airline in advance if you can bring aboard your child's car seat. (For the pamphlet *Child/Infant Safety Seats Acceptable for Use in Aircraft*, contact the Community and Consumer Liaison Division, APA-200, Federal Aviation Administration, Washington, DC 20591, tel. 202/267–3479.)

Hints for Disabled Travelers

The **Information Center for Individuals with Disabilities** (Fort Point Place, 1st floor, 27–43 Wormwood St., Boston, MA 02217, tel. 617/727–5540) offers useful problem-solving assistance, including lists of travel agents who specialize in tours for the disabled.

Moss Rehabilitation Hospital Travel Information Service (12th St. and Tabor Rd., Philadelphia, PA 19141, tel. 215/329–5715) provides information on tourist sights, transportation, and accommodations in destinations around the world. The fee is $5 for up to three destinations. Allow one month for delivery.

Mobility International (Box 3551, Eugene, OR 97403, tel. 503/343–1284) is a membership organization with a $20 annual fee offering information on accommodations, organized study, and so forth around the world.

The **Society for the Advancement of Travel for the Handicapped** (26 Court St., Penthouse Suite, Brooklyn, NY 11242, tel. 718/858–5483) offers access information. Annual membership costs $40, $25 for senior travelers and students. Send $2 and a stamped, self-addressed envelope for a list of tour operators who arrange travel for the disabled.

Travel Industry and Disabled Exchange (TIDE, 5435 Donna Ave., Tarzana, CA 91356, tel. 818/343–6339) is an industry-based organization with a $15-per-person annual membership fee. Members receive a quarterly newsletter and information on travel agencies and tours.

Publications *The Itinerary* (Box 1084, Bayonne, NJ 07002, tel. 201/858–3400) is a bimonthly travel magazine for the disabled. Call for a subscription; it's not available in stores.

Twin Peaks Press publishes a number of useful resources: *Travel for the Disabled* ($9.95), *Directory of Travel Agencies for the Disabled* ($12.95), and *Wheelchair Vagabond* ($9.95 paperback, $14.95 hardcover). Order through your local bookstore or directly from the publisher (Twin Peaks Press, Box 129, Vancouver, WA 98666, tel. 206/694–2462).

Access to the World: A Travel Guide for the Handicapped, by Louise Weiss, is a well-known and trusted guidebook that has recently been updated (Henry Holt & Co., $12.45).

Access Travel, published by the U.S. Office of Consumer Affairs, is a free brochure that lists design features, facilities, and services for the handicapped at 519 airport terminals in 62 countries. To order, contact the Consumer Information Center (Pueblo, CO 81009, tel. 800/948–3334).

"Fly Rights," a free U.S. Department of Transportation brochure, offers airline access information for the handicapped. To order, call 202/366–2220.

Accommodations In the more popular destinations throughout the Caribbean, the specific needs of the disabled are now often being taken into consideration when new hotels are built or existing properties are renovated. A number of cruise ships, such as the *QE II* and the Norwegian Caribbean Line's *Seward,* have also recently adapted some of their cabins to meet the needs of disabled passengers. To make sure that a given establishment provides adequate access, ask about specific facilities when making a reservation or consider booking through a travel agent who specializes in travel for the disabled (*see* above).

The **Divi Hotel** company, which has nine properties throughout the Caribbean, runs one of the best dive programs for the disabled at its resort in **Bonaire.** The facility is equipped with ramps, guest rooms and bathrooms can accommodate wheelchairs, and the staff is specially trained to assist disabled divers. For more information, call 800/367–3484.

Hints for Older Travelers

The **American Association of Retired Persons** (AARP, 1990 K St., NW, Washington, DC 20049, tel. 202/872–4700) has two programs for independent travelers: (1) *The Purchase Privilege Program,* which offers discounts on hotels, airfare, car rentals, and sightseeing; and (2) the *AARP Motoring Plan,* which furnishes emergency aid (road service) and trip-routing information for an annual fee of $33.95 per person or married couple. The AARP also arranges group tours through two companies: **Olson-Travelworld** (5855 Green Valley Circle, Culver City, CA 90230, tel. 800/227–7737) and **RFD, Inc.** (4401 W. 110th St., Overland Park, KS 66211, tel. 800/448–7010). AARP members must be at least 50 years old. Annual dues are $5 per person or per couple.

If you're planning to use an AARP or other senior-citizen identification card to obtain a reduced hotel rate, mention it at the time you make your reservation rather than when you check out. At restaurants, show your card to the maître d' before you're seated; discounts may be limited to certain set menus, days, or hours. Your AARP card will identify you as a retired person but will not ensure a discount in all hotels and restaurants. When renting a car, remember that economy cars, priced at promotional rates, may cost less than the cars that are available with your ID card.

The **National Council of Senior Citizens** (925 15th St., NW, Washington, DC 20005, tel. 202/347–8800) is a nonprofit advocacy group with some 4,000 local clubs across the country. Annual membership is $10 per person or $14 per couple. Members receive a monthly newspaper with travel information and an ID for reduced rates on hotels and car rentals.

Mature Outlook (6001 N. Clarke St., Chicago, IL 60660, tel. 800/336–6330), a subsidiary of Sears, Roebuck, & Co., is a travel club for people over 50 years of age, offering hotel discounts and a bimonthly newsletter. Annual membership is $9.95 per person or couple. Instant membership is available at participating Holiday Inns.

Elderhostel (80 Boylston St., Suite 400, Boston, MA 02116, tel. 617/426–7788) is an innovative program for people 60 or over (only one member of a traveling couple has to qualify). Participants live in dormitories on some 1,200 campuses around the world. Mornings are devoted to lectures and seminars, afternoons to sightseeing and field trips. The fee for a trip includes room, board, tuition (in the United States and Canada) and round-trip transportation (overseas). Special scholarships in the United States and Canada are available for those who qualify financially.

Publications *Travel Tips for Senior Citizens* (U.S. Dept. of State Publication 8970, revised Sept. 1987) is available for $1 from the Superintendent of Documents (U.S. Government Printing Office, Washington, DC 20402, tel. 202/783–3238).

The International Health Guide for Senior Citizen Travelers, by Dr. W. Robert Lang, MD, is available for $4.95, and *The Senior Citizens Guide to Budget Travel in the United States and Canada,* by Paige Palmer, is available for $3.95, plus $1 for shipping from Pilot Books (103 Cooper St., Babylon, NY 11702, tel. 516/422–2225).

The Discount Guide for Travelers over 55, by Caroline and Walter Weintz, lists helpful addresses, package tours, reduced rate car rentals, etc., in the United States and abroad. To order, send $7.95 to NAL/Cash Sales (Bergenfield Order Dept., 120 Woodbine St., Bergenfield, NJ 07021, tel. 800/526–0275).

"Fly Rights" (tel. 202/366–2220), a free brochure published by the U.S. Department of Transportation, offers information on airline services available to elderly passengers.

Further Reading

Caribbean Style (Crown Publishers) is a coffee-table book with magnificent photographs of the interiors and exteriors of homes and buildings in the Caribbean. The collection runs the gamut from splendid plantations to ramshackle shanties.

Don't Stop the Carnival, by Herman Wouk, is a hilarious novel about a New York press agent who left his old life behind and bought a resort hotel in the Caribbean. The novel is slightly dated, but the vicissitudes of the hero are acknowledged by everyone who has ever tried to run a hotel in the islands. It is a marvelous romp through the region.

If you want to familiarize yourself with the sights, smells, and sounds of the West Indies, pick up Jamaica Kincaid's *Annie John,* a richly textured, coming-of-age novel about a girl growing up on the island of Antigua. *At The Bottom Of The River,* also by Kincaid, is a collection of short stories that depicts the mysteries and manners of a world replete with merengue music, bay rum, and blooming red hibiscus in the dreams and reminiscences of a young adult.

Michelle Cliff is the author of *The Land of Look Behind, Claiming an Identity They Taught Me to Despise*, and, most recently, *No Telephone to Heaven*, a structurally daring, often violent novel set in Jamaica—a landscape of wild bamboo and jasmine, populated by refugees moving through the outskirts of Kingston.

Another notable chronicle of Caribbean life and customs is the provocative *Wide Sargasso Sea*, by Jean Rhys. Published in 1968, its imaginative construction still entices the reader into a world of exotic, haunting beauty that Rhys herself encountered growing up on the Windward Islands of the West Indies.

James Michener's Caribbean saga, which was untitled at presstime, will be out in December 1989. Michener headquartered himself in Coral Gables, Florida, to facilitate his 10 extensive research expeditions through the Caribbean region, and he has publicly expressed both the dramatic assets and liabilities inherent to a culture so rich in diversity.

If you're interested in probing this very issue more deeply, head for V. S. Naipaul. *Guerrillas*, *The Loss of El Dorado*, and *The Enigma of Arrival* all examine the multicultural origins of Caribbean society, and the complexities of colonization, enslavement, and economic dispossession.

Staying in the Caribbean

Dining

For the longest time, cuisine in the Caribbean was thought the weakest part of many an island vacation. In recent years, however, island visitors have come to realize that most of what they had been eating and complaining about was not Caribbean at all—just poorly prepared Continental fare with a papaya slice or banana leaf for garnish.

The cuisine of the islands is difficult to pin down because of the region's history as a colonial battleground and ethnic melting pot. The gracefully sauced French presentations of Martinique, for example, are far removed from the hearty Spanish casseroles of Puerto Rico, and even farther removed from the pungent curries of Trinidad.

The one quality that best defines Caribbean-style cooking has to be its essential spiciness. While reminiscent of Tex-Mex and Cajun, Caribbean cuisine is more varied and more subtle than its love of peppers implies. There is also the seafood that is unique and abundant to the region. Caribbean lobster, closer in comparison to crawfish than to Maine lobster, have no claws and tend to be much tougher than the New England variety.

Another local favorite is conch, biologically quite close to landloving escargots. Conch chowder, conch fritters, conch salad, conch cocktail—no island menu would be complete without at least a half dozen conch dishes.

For many vacationers, much of the Caribbean experience has to do with the consumption of frothy blended fruit drinks, whose main and potent ingredient is Caribbean rum. Whether you are staying in a super-deluxe resort or a small locally operated guest house, you will find that rum flows as freely as water.

After each restaurant review, we have indicated only when reservations are necessary or suggested. Since dining is usually casual throughout the region, we have mentioned attire only when formal wear is needed.

Lodging

Plan ahead and reserve a room well before you travel to the Caribbean. If you have reservations but expect to arrive later than 5 or 6 PM, advise the hotel, inn, or guest house in advance. Some places will not, unless so advised, hold your reservations after 6 PM. Also, during high season be sure to find out what the rate quoted includes—European Plan (EP: no meals), American Plan (AP: three meals), or Modified American Plan (MAP: two meals); use of sporting facilities and equipment; airport transfers; and the like. Be sure to bring your deposit receipt with you in case any questions arise when you arrive at your hotel.

An American Plan may be ideal for travelers on a budget who don't want to worry about additional expenses; but travelers who enjoy a different dining experience each night will prefer to book rooms on a European Plan. Since many hotels insist on a Modified American Plan (breakfast and dinner), particularly during the high season, find out whether you can exchange dinners for lunch.

Decide whether you want a hotel on the leeward (calm water, good for snorkeling) or windward (waves, good for surfing) side of the island. Decide, too, whether you want to pay the extra price for a room overlooking the ocean or pool. Beachcombers will want to know how close the property is to a beach; at some hotels you can walk barefoot from your room onto the sand; others are across a road or a 10-minute drive away.

Nighttime entertainment is alfresco in the Caribbean, so if you go to sleep early or are a light sleeper, ask for a room that doesn't overlook the dance floor.

Air-conditioning is not a necessity on all islands, most of which are cooled by trade winds; but an air conditioner can be a plus if you enjoy an afternoon snooze. Breezes are stronger in second-floor rooms, particularly corner rooms, which enjoy cross ventilation.

Given the vast differences in standards and accommodations in the various islands covered in this book, it would be impossible (and misleading) to establish uniform categories such as deluxe, first class, etc. Instead, we have used categories to indicate price rather than quality. Prices are intended as a guideline only. The larger resort hotels with the greater number of facilities are, naturally, going to be more expensive, but the Caribbean is full of smaller places that make up in charm, individuality, and price for what they lack in activities—and the activity is generally available on a pay-per-use basis everywhere.

Credit Cards

The following credit card abbreviations have been used: AE, American Express; CB, Carte Blanche; DC, Diners Club; MC,

MasterCard; V, Visa. It's a good idea to call ahead to check current credit card policies.

Electrical Current

110 and 120 volts A.C. is the general rule throughout the Caribbean, but there are a number of exceptions. To be sure, check with your hotel when making reservations.

Cruises

Cruising the Caribbean is perhaps the most relaxed and convenient way to tour this beautiful part of the world. A cruise offers all the benefits of island-hopping without the inconvenience. For example, a cruise passenger packs and unpacks only once and is not bound by flight schedules, tour-bus schedules, and "non schedules" of fellow travelers.

Cruise ships usually call at several Caribbean ports on a single voyage. Thus, a cruise passenger experiences and savors the mix of nationalities and cultures of the Caribbean, as well as the variety of sightseeing opportunities, the geographic and topographic characteristics, and the ambience of each of the islands. A cruise passenger tries out each island on his or her cruise itinerary and has the opportunity to select favorites for in-depth discovery on a later visit.

As a vacation, a cruise offers total peace of mind. All important decisions are made long before boarding the ship. For example, the itinerary is set in advance, and the costs are known ahead of time and are all-inclusive. There is no additional charge for accommodations, entertainment, or recreational activities. All meals are included, and (surprise!) there are no prices on the menu. A cruise ship is a floating Caribbean resort; each passenger gets to know the cruise staff and sits back and relaxes while he or she enjoys the consistency of service and experience.

Fly-and-Cruise

Several cruise lines offer attractive fly-and-cruise options, which give passengers the option of flying first to a warm-weather port like Miami or San Juan and boarding the ship there. The airfare is built into the rate, so the cost of the total package is usually higher than the cost of cruise-only packages that cover comparable distances at sea. In most cases, however, the air-plus-cruise rate will be lower than round-trip airfare to the ship's pier.

When to Go

Cruise ships sail the Caribbean year-round—the waters are almost always calm, and the prevailing breezes keep temperatures fairly steady. Tropical storms are most likely in September, October, and November, but modern navigational equipment warns ships of impending foul weather, and, if necessary, cruise lines vary their itineraries to avoid storms.

Cruises are in high demand—and therefore also higher priced—during the standard vacation times in midsummer to early fall and around Easter. Some very good bargains are usually

Caribbean Cruises

Class/Ship	Number of passengers	Length (days)	Alternate lengths (segments) available	Departs from	Anguilla	Antigua	Aruba	Barbados	Bonaire	BVI	Cayman Islands
CHANDRIS FANTASY CRUISES											
Amerikanis	614	7	6, 8	San Juan		●		●			
Azur	648	7	6, 8	San Juan				●			
MV Horizon	2,000	8		San Juan		●		●			
Victoria	540	8		San Juan				●			
COMMODORE CRUISE LINE											
The Caribe	1,100	7		Miami							●
COSTA CRUISES											
CarlaCosta	800	7		San Juan							
CostaRiviera	1,000	7		Ft. Lauderdale							
Daphne	400	7		San Juan		●		●			
CUNARD											
Countess	750	7	3,4,14	San Juan		●					
Princess	750	8	7,10,11,17,18	Ft. Lauderdale					●		
Queen Elizabeth II	1,900	10	11	NYC				●			
Sagafjord	588	12	10,11,12,13,16	Ft. Lauderdale		●		●			
Vistafjord	736	13	16	NYC		●		●		●	
HOLLAND AMERICA											
M.S. Westerdam	1,100	10		NYC		●					
Neeuw Amsterdam	1,200	7		Tampa							●
Noordam	1,200	7		Ft. Lauderdale						●	
Rotterdam	1,114	10		Ft. Lauderdale		●		●			
NORWEGIAN CRUISE LINES											
Norway	1,774	7		Miami							
Skyward	728	7		San Juan				●			
Starward	758	7		San Juan		●		●			
Sunward II	676		3,4	Miami							●
OCEAN CRUISE LINES											
Ocean Islander	250	7		Barbados				●			
PRINCESS CRUISES											
Dawn Princess	925	7		San Juan				●			
Pacific Princess	626	7		San Juan				●			
Sky Princess	1,202	10		Ft. Lauderdale				●			
Star Princess	1,470	7		Ft. Lauderdale				●			
ROYAL CARIBBEAN CRUISE LINE											
Song of America Western	1,390	7		Miami							●
Sun Viking	726	7	8,10	San Juan				●			
SEABOURNE CRUISE LINE											
Seabourne Pride	212	7	14	Ft. Lauderdale							
SUN LINE CRUISES											
Stella Solaris	650	12	14	Ft. Lauderdale				●			

Curaçao	Dominica	Dominican Rep.	Grenada	Guadeloupe	Jamaica	Martinique	Montserrat	Nevis	Puerto Rico	Saba	St. Barthelemy	St. Eustatius	St. Kitts	St. Lucia	St. Martin	St. Vincent & the Grenadines	Trinidad/Tobago	Turks & Caicos	USVI		Bermuda	Mexico
				•										•	•				•			
						•						•	•						•			
						•			•					•					•			•
			•			•			•					•					•			•
		•			•				•										•			•
•			•			•			•										•			
																			•			•
						•			•					•	•				•			
				•					•					•	•				•			
				•															•			•
				•		•			•						•				•			
				•															•		•	
									•										•		•	
					•																	•
									•										•			
				•											•				•			
						•			•					•	•				•			
					•				•						•				•			
						•									•							
						•										•	•		•			
						•										•	•		•			
						•												•	•			
		•				•			•										•			
				•																		•
					•				•			•		•					•			
	•	•												•					•			
			•															•	•			•

available during the immediate post-vacation periods such as fall to mid-December, early spring, and the first few weeks after the Christmas and New Year's holidays. Christmas sailings are usually quite full and are priced at a premium.

Choosing a Cabin

Write to the cruise line or ask your travel agent for a ship's plan. This elaborate layout, with all cabin numbers noted, may seem overwhelming at first, but closer inspection will show you all facilities available on all decks (the higher the deck, the higher the prices). Outside cabins have dramatic portholes that contribute to the romance of cruising, but even if they aren't sealed shut, most provide no more than a view of the surrounding deck. Inside cabins are less expensive, but check the plan—you don't want to be over the kitchen, over the engine room, or next to the elevators if you want quiet. Then check on the facilities offered. Those prone to motion sickness would do best in a cabin at midship, on one of the lower decks. Cabins in the center of the ship are the most stable, and the higher you go, the more motion you'll experience. Look over the less-expensive cabins that have upper and lower berths, those that have bathtubs in addition to showers, and the luxury suites, which can still provide all the accoutrements of a voyage across the sea.

Tipping

Even though some of the liners advertise a no-tipping policy, be aware that most of the ship's service personnel depend on tips for their livelihood. There is no hard-and-fast rule about who gets what, but if you think of services rendered on board as you would at resort hotels, bars, and restaurants, you'll come close. It is customary to tip the cabin steward, the dining-room waiter, the maître d', the wine steward, and the bartender. Gratuities to other ship's personnel are usually given the night before the voyage ends.

Shore Excursions

Tour options are typically posted on the bulletin board near the purser's office a day before arrival at your port of call. If the ship is in port for a full day, you might choose to join a tour offered by one of the local tour companies or to rent a car and explore on your own (*see* Guided Tours and Getting Around sections of the individual island chapters).

Cruise Lines

To find out which ships are sailing where and when they depart, contact the **Caribbean Tourism Association** (20 E. 46th St., New York, NY 10017, tel. 212/682–0435). The CTA carries up-to-date information about cruise lines that sail to its member nations. Travel agencies are also a good source; they stock brochures and catalogues issued by most of the major lines and usually have the latest information about prices, departure dates, and itineraries. The **Cruise Lines International Association** publishes a useful pamphlet entitled *Answers to the Most Asked Questions about Cruising;* to order a copy send a stamped, self-addressed envelope to CLIA (17 Battery Pl., Suite 631, New York, NY 10004).

The accompanying chart gives the names and ports of call of all of the individual cruise ships run by the companies given in the following list. Use the addresses and phone numbers listed below to contact the individual lines for more information.

American Canadian Caribbean Line (Box 368, Warren, RI 02885, tel. 800/556–7450).

Bermuda Star Line (1086 Teaneck Rd., Teaneck, NJ 07666, tel. 800/237–5361).

Carnival Cruise Lines (5225 N.W. 87th Ave., Miami, FL 33178, tel. 800/432–5424).

Chandris Fantasy Cruises (900 3rd Ave., New York, NY 10022, tel. 212/750–0044, 800/621–3446, or 800/432–4132 in FL).

Clipper Cruise Line (7711 Bonhomme Ave., St. Louis, MO 63105, tel. 800/325–0010).

Commodore Cruise Line (1007 North America Way, Miami, FL 33132, tel. 800/327–5617 or 800/432–6793 in FL).

Costa Cruises (World Trade Center, 80 S.W. 8th St., Miami, FL 33130, tel. 305/358–7325).

Cunard (555 5th Ave., New York, NY 10017, tel. 800/854–0500).

Holland America (300 Elliot Ave. W, Seattle, WA 98119, tel. 206/281–3535).

Norwegian Cruise Lines (2 Alhambra Plaza, Coral Gables, FL 33134, tel. 305/447–9660 or 800/327–3090).

Ocean Cruise Lines (1510 S.E. 17th St., Ft. Lauderdale, FL 33316, tel. 305/764–3500, 800/556–8850 on the East Coast, or 800/338–1700 on the West Coast).

Ocean Quest International (512 S. Peters St., New Orleans, LA 70130, tel. 800/338–3483).

Princess Cruises (10100 Santa Monica Blvd., Los Angeles, CA 90067, tel. 212/553–1666, 800/421–0422, or 800/421–0880).

Royal Caribbean Cruise Line (903 South America Way, Miami, FL 33132, tel. 305/379–2601 or 800/327–6700).

Royal Viking Line (95 Merrick Way, Coral Gables, FL 33134, tel. 305/447–9660 or 800/422–8000).

Seabourn Cruise Line (55 Francisco St., San Francisco, CA 94133, tel. 415/391–7444 or 800/351–9595; 800/527–0999 in Canada).

Sun Line Cruises (1 Rockefeller Plaza, New York, NY 10020, tel. 212/397–6400 or 800/468–6400).

Windjammer Barefoot Cruises (Box 120, Miami Beach, FL 33119, tel. 305/432–3364 or 800/327–2601; in Canada 800/233–2603).

2   Anguilla

by Honey Naylor

The author of
Fodor's Pocket
New Orleans,
Honey Naylor
has contributed to
various other
Fodor's guides.
Her featured
articles have
appeared in
Travel & Leisure,
USA Today, New
Orleans
Magazine,
Travel-Holiday,
and other
national
publications.

At first glance, Anguilla's (which rhymes with vanilla) charms may be difficult to detect. It is not a particularly pretty island. There are no lush rain forests or majestic mountains. The highest point on the island rises a dizzying 213 feet above sea level. It's a dry limestone isle with a thin covering of soil over the rock and has neither streams nor rivers, only saline ponds used for salt production. And there isn't a whole lot to do here. You won't find glittering casinos, dance-till-dawn discos, knock-your-socks-off nightclubs, world famous historic sites, or duty-free shops stuffed with irresistible buys. Nevertheless, this long, skinny, eel-shape island just 20 minutes from the bustle of St. Martin-Sint Maarten's resorts and casinos has debuted and become a very popular, and so far unspoiled, princess at the Caribbean ball.

Anguilla's beauty is apt to be found in its 30 beaches surrounded by gin-clear waters and coral reefs. Peace, quiet, and pampering account for the island's growing popularity among travelers searching for a Caribbean getaway. You can swim, do some diving, practice your backhand, catch up on your reading, compare the relative merits of the beaches, or just find one that suits you and sink down on it to worship the sun.

This is the most northerly of the Leeward Islands, lying between the Caribbean Sea and the Atlantic Ocean. Stretching from northeast to southwest, it's about 16 miles long and only 3 miles across at its widest point. The keen eye of Christopher Columbus seems not to have spotted this island. Anguilla means eel in Italian, but the Spanish *anguila* or French *anguille* (both of which also mean eel) may have been the original name. New archaeological evidence shows that the island was inhabited as many as 2,000 years ago by Indians who named the island Malliouhana, a more mellifluous title that's been adopted by some of the island's shops and resorts.

In 1631, the Dutch built a fort here and maintained it for several years, but no one has been able to locate it today. English settlers from St. Kitts colonized the island in 1650. And, despite a brief period of independence with St. Kitts-Nevis in the 1960s, Anguilla has remained a British Colony ever since the 17th century.

There were the obligatory Caribbean battles between the English and the French, and in 1688 the island was attacked by a party of "wild Irishmen," some of whom settled on the island. But Anguilla's primary discontent was over its status vis-à-vis the other British colonies, particularly St. Kitts. In the 18th century, Anguilla, as part of the Leeward Islands, was administered by British officials in Antigua. In 1816, Britain split the Leeward Islands into two groups, one of them comprised of Anguilla, St. Kitts, Nevis, and the British Virgin Islands administered by a magistrate in St. Kitts. For more than 150 years thereafter various island units and federations were formed and disbanded, with Anguilla all the while simmering over its subordinate status and enforced union with St. Kitts. Anguillians twice petitioned for direct rule from Britain, and twice were ignored. In 1967, when St. Kitts, Nevis, and Anguilla became an Associated State, the mouse roared, kicked St. Kitts policemen off the island, held a self-rule referendum, and for two years conducted its own affairs. In 1968, a senior British official arrived and remained for a year working with the Anguilla Council. A second referendum in 1969 confirmed the desire of the Anguillians to remain apart from St. Kitts-Nevis and the following month a British "peacekeeping force" parachuted down to the island, where it was greeted with flowers, fluttering Union Jacks, and friendly smiles. When the paratroopers were not working on their tans, they helped a team of royal engineers improve the port and build roads and schools. Today Anguilla elects a House of Assembly and its own leader to handle internal affairs, while a British governor is responsible for public service, the police, and judiciary and external affairs.

The territory of Anguilla includes a few offshore islets or cays, such as Scrub Island to the east, Dog Island, Prickly Pear Cays, Sandy Island, and Sombrero Island. The island's population numbers about 7,500, predominantly of African descent but also including descendants of Europeans, especially Irish. Historically, because the limestone land was hardly fit for agriculture, Anguillians have had to seek work on neighboring islands. Until recently, the primary means of employment were fishing and boat building. Today, tourism has become the growth industry of the island's stable economy. But the government is determined to keep Anguilla's tourism growing at a slow and cautious pace to protect the island's natural resources and beauty. New hotels, scattered throughout the islands, are being kept small, select, and casino-free, and promotion of the island emphasizes its quality service, serene surroundings, and friendly people.

Before You Go

Tourist Information Contact the **Anguilla Tourist Information Office** (c/o Medhurst & Assoc., 271 Main St., Northport, NY 11768, tel. 212/869–0402, 516/261–1234, or 800/553–4939). In the United Kingdom, contact the **Anguilla Tourist Office** (College House, Suite 19, 29-31 Wright's La., Kensington, London W8 5SH, tel. 01/937–7725). You can also get information directly from the island by writing or calling the **Anguilla Tourist Office** (The Valley, Anguilla, British West Indies, tel. 809/497–2759). Reservations can be made through **International Travel Resorts, Inc.** (25 W. 39th St., New York, NY 10018, tel. 212/840–6636 or 800/223–9815).

Arriving and Departing
By Plane **American Airlines** (tel. 800/433–7300) has nonstop flights from the United States to its hub in San Juan. The airline's **American Eagle** flies twice weekly to Anguilla, the first flight connecting with East Coast and Canadian flights, the second with those from the Midwest and West. **Windward Islands Airways** (Winair) (tel. 809/775–0183) wings in daily from St. Thomas and from St. Maarten's Juliana Airport. **Air BVI** (tel. 809/774–6500) flies in from St. Thomas and San Juan three times a week, and **LIAT** (tel. 809/465–2286) comes in from St. Kitts and Antigua. **Air Anguilla** (tel. 809/497–2643) has regularly scheduled daily flights from St. Thomas, St. Maarten, and Tortola. It also provides air-taxi service on request from neighboring islands, as does **Tyden Air** (tel. 809/497–2719).

From the Airport At **Wallblake Airport** you'll find taxis lined up to meet the planes. A trip from the airport to Sandy Ground will cost about $7. Fares, which are government-regulated, should be listed in brochures the drivers carry. If you are traveling in a group, the

Anguilla

0 |——————————————| 4 miles
0 |——————————————| 6 km

N

Flat Cap Point

⑦ ⑧ ⑨

Crocus Bay ⑩ ❶

Sandy Island

North Hill

Road Bay Sandy Ground

Wallblake Airport

⑪ ⑫ ⑬ ⑭ ⑮ ⑯

Sandy Ground ④

Long Bay

⑰ ⑱

Meads Bay

㉓ ㉔ ㉕

㉘ ㉙

㉚ ㉛

Little Harbour

Barnes Bay

⑲ ⑳

West End

Maunday's Bay

Rendezvous Bay ㉖ ㉗

Blowing Point Harbour

❺

㉑ ㉒ Cove Bay

Shoal Bay West

Anguillita Island

Exploring
Blowing Point
Harbour, **5**
The Fountain, **2**
Sandy Ground, **4**
Sandy Hill Bay, **3**
Wallblake House, **1**

Dining
Anguilla Great
House, **23**
Aquarium, **15**
Ario's, **28**
The Barrel Stay, **11**
Cinnamon Reef Beach
Cub, **30**

Coccoloba
Plantation, **19**
Cross Roads, **7**
Hibernia, **12**
Johnno's, **15**

Lucy's Harbour View
Restaurant, **29**
Malliouhana, **17**
Pappagallo, **26**
Pepper Pot, **8**
Pimm's, **21**
Riviera Bar &
Restaurant, **13**
Roy's, **10**

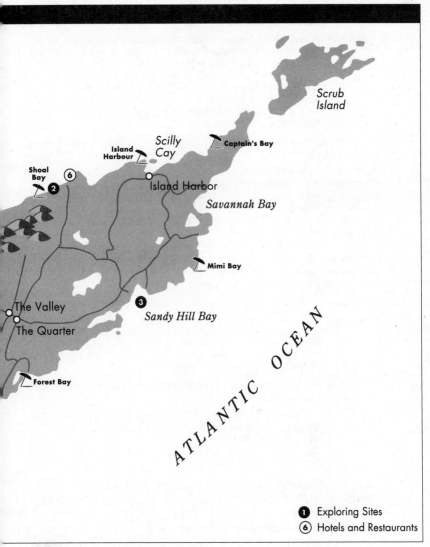

Scrub
Island

Scilly
Cay

Island
Harbour

Captain's Bay

Shoal
Bay

6

2

Island Harbor

Savannah Bay

Mimi Bay

The Valley

3

Sandy Hill Bay

The Quarter

ATLANTIC OCEAN

Forest Bay

1 Exploring Sites
6 Hotels and Restaurants

fares apply to the first two people; each additional passenger adds $2 to the total.

By Boat A ferry-boat journey across the water from Marigot on St. Martin several times a day between 7:30 AM and 5:30 PM. You pay the $8 one-way fare on board. Don't buy a round-trip ticket, which restricts you to the boat on which you bought the ticket. In the evenings, the boats leave at 7 PM and 10:45 PM. The trip takes about 30 rough minutes, and if you're inclined toward seasickness, it's a good idea to take motion-sickness medication before boarding.

Taxis are always waiting to pick passengers up at the Blowing Point landing.

Passports and Visas U. S. and Canadian citizens need proof of identity. A passport is preferred (even one that's expired, but not more than five years ago). A photo ID, along with a birth certificate (original with raised seal), a voter's registration card, or a driver's license is also acceptable. Visitor's passes are valid for stays of up to three months. British citizens must have a passport. All visitors must also have a return or ongoing ticket.

Customs and Duties You may bring in duty-free one carton of cigarettes or cigars, a reasonable personal supply of tobacco, one bottle of liquor, and perfume for personal use.

Language English, with a West Indian lilt, is spoken on Anguilla.

Precautions The manchineel tree, which bears a resemblance to an apple tree, shades many beaches. The tree bears poisonous fruit and the sap from the tree causes painful blisters, so avoid sitting beneath the tree, because even dew or raindrops falling from the leaves can blister your skin.

Be *sure* to take along a can of insect repellent—mosquitoes are all over the place.

Anguilla is a quiet, relatively safe island, but there's no point in tempting fate by leaving your valuables unattended in your hotel room or on the beach.

Staying in Anguilla

Important Addresses **Tourist Information:** The **Anguilla Tourist Office** (The Secretariat, The Valley, tel. 809/497–2759) is open weekdays 8–noon and 1–4.

Emergencies **Police** and **Fire:** 809/497–2333.

Hospital: There is a 24-hour emergency room at **The Cottage Hospital** (The Valley, tel. 809/497–2551).

Ambulance: 809/497–2637 or 809/497–2551.

Pharmacies: The **Government Pharmacy** (The Valley, tel. 809/497–2551) is located in the Cottage Hospital. The **Paramount Pharmacy** (Waterswamp, tel. 809/497–2366) is open Monday–Saturday 8:30 AM–8:30 PM and has a 24-hour emergency service.

Currency Legal tender here is the Eastern Caribbean dollar (E.C.), but U.S. dollars are widely accepted. (You'll usually get change in E.C.s). The E.C. is fairly stable relative to the dollar, hovering between E.C.$2.60 and $2.70 to U.S.$1. Credit cards are not widely accepted, but some places accept personal and traveler's checks. Be sure to carry lots of small bills; change for a $20 bill is often difficult to obtain.

Taxes and Service Charges The government imposes an 8% tax on accommodations. The departure tax is $5 at the airport, $1.15 by boat.

A 10% service charge is added to all hotel bills and most restaurant bills. If you're not certain about the restaurant service charge, ask. If you are particularly pleased with the service, you can certainly leave a little extra. Tip taxi drivers 10% of the fare.

Guided Tours A round-the-island tour by taxi will take about 2½ hours and will cost $40 for one or two people, $5 for each additional passenger.

Bennie Tours (Blowing Point, tel. 809/497–2788), **Bertram's Tour and Taxi Service** (The Valley, tel. 809/497–2256), and **Malliouhana Travel and Tours** (The Valley, tel. 809/497–2431) all put together personalized package tours on and around the island.

Getting Around *Taxis* Taxi rates are regulated by the government and there are fixed fares from point to point. Posted rates are for one to two people; each additional person pays $2. The fare from the airport to hotels ranges from $8 to $15, from Blowing Point Landing $11 to $12.50.

Rental Cars This is your best bet for maximum mobility, if you're comfortable driving on the left. For the most part, Anguilla's roads are narrow paved two-laners, and some of the ritziest hotels are only reachable on ghastly dirt roads. Watch out for the four-legged critters that amble across the road, and observe the 30 mph speed limit. To rent a car you'll need a valid driver's license and a local license, which can be obtained for $10 at any of the car rental agencies. Among the agencies are **Bennie & Sons (Avis)** (tel. 809/497–2221 or 800/331–2112), **Budget** (tel. 809/497–2217 or 800/527–0700), **Connors (National)** (tel. 809/497–6433 or 800/328–4567), and **Island Car Rental** (tel. 809/497–2804).

Telephones and Mail To call Anguilla from the United States, dial area code 809 + 497 + the local four-digit number. International direct-dial is available on the island. **Cable & Wireless** (Wallblake Rd., tel. 809/497–2210) is open weekdays 8–6, Saturday 9–1, Sunday and holidays 10–2. A pay phone is accessible 24 hours a day for credit card and collect calls. To make a local call on the island, dial the four-digit number.

Airmail letters to the United States cost E.C. .60; postcards E.C. .25.

Opening and Closing Times Banks are open Monday–Thursday 8–1; Friday 8–1 and 3–5. Shopping hours are variable. No two shops seem to have the same hours. Your best bet is to call the shop you're interested in, or ask at the tourist office for opening and closing times.

Beaches

The island's big attractions are its beaches. All are free to the public and all are white sand. Nude bathing is a no-no, but nevertheless not uncommon. Most of the island's beaches are on coral reefs that are great for snorkeling though not for swimming.

One of the prettiest beaches in the Caribbean, **Shoal Bay,** is a 2-mile L-shape beach of talcum-soft white sand. There are beach chairs, umbrellas, a backdrop of seagrape and coconut trees, and for seafood and tropical drinks there's Trader Vic's, Uncle Ernie, and the Round Rock (*see* Dining, below). Souvenir shops for T-shirts, suntan lotion, and the like abound. Head to Shoal Bay for good snorkeling in the offshore coral reefs, and visit the water-sports center to arrange diving, sailing, and fishing trips.

Rendezvous Bay is 1½ miles of pearl-white sand. Here the water is calm, and there's a great view of St. Martin. The Anguilla Great House's open-air beach bar is handy for snacks and Happy Jacks (rum punches).

One of the most popular beaches, wide, mile-long **Maunday's Bay** is known for good swimming and snorkeling. Rent watersport gear at Tropical Watersports. Try Pimm's at Cap Juluca for fine food and drink (*see* Dining, below).

Adjacent to Maunday's Bay, **Shoal Bay West** is a pleasant beach with a backdrop of Cove Castles, a set of futuristic villas where Chuck Norris has a home. The snorkeling is best in the area of the Oasis restaurant. Comb this beach for lovely conch shells as well.

Barnes Bay is a superb spot for windsurfing and snorkeling. The elegant Coccoloba Plantation perches above and offers a poolside bar. In high season this beach can get a bit crowded with day-trippers from St. Martin.

The clear blue waters of **Road Bay** beach are usually dotted with yachts. The Mariner Hotel, several restaurants (*see* Lodging, below), a water-sport center, and lots of windsurfing and waterskiing activity make this an active commercial area. The snorkeling is not very good here but do visit this bay for its glorious sunsets.

Sandy Island, nestled in coral reefs about 2 miles offshore from Road Bay, is a tiny speck of sand and sea, equipped with a beach boutique, beach bar and restaurant, and free use of snorkeling gear and underwater cameras. The *Shauna* (tel. 809/497–6395 or 809/497–6845) will ferry you there from Sandy Ground.

Island Harbor, another busy beach, is shaded by coconut trees and lined with colorful fishing boats. Depart from here for **Scilly Cay,** a 3-minute motorboat ride away. You can get snorkeling equipment on the ferrying motorboat, but at times the waters are too rough to see much. On Scilly Cay there is a beach bar that serves drinks and grilled lobster and seafood.

The good news and the bad news about **Cove Bay** is the same—it's virtually deserted. There are no restaurants or bars, just calm waters, coconut trees, and a talcum-powder-soft sand that stretches down to Maunday's Bay.

Mimi Bay is a difficult-to-reach, isolated, half-mile beach east of Sea Feathers. But the trip is worth it. When the surf is not too rough the barrier reef makes for great snorkeling.

Also not far from Sea Feathers is **Sandy Hill,** a base for fishermen. Here you can buy fresh fish and lobster right off the boats and snorkel in the warm waters. Don't plan to sunbathe—the beach is quite narrow here.

The reward for traveling along an inhospitable dirt road via four-wheel drive is complete isolation at **Captain's Bay** on the northeastern end of the island. The surf slaps the sands with a vengeance and the undertow is quite strong here. Wading is the safest water sport.

Exploring Anguilla

Numbers in the margin correspond with points of interest on the Anguilla map.

Make your first stop on the island the Tourist Office in the Valley. Here you can pick up a large, colorful map of the island with splashy pictures of Anguilla's beaches. The island is sprinkled with salt ponds and small villages, the most important of which is The Valley, where administrative offices, banks, a few boutiques, guest houses, eateries, and markets are located. But there is little to see in Anguilla except for the beaches and the resorts. Take a look at the island's historic house, and then go beachcombing.

❶ Wallblake House is a plantation house that was built around 1787 by Will Blake (Wallblake is probably a corruption of his name). Legends of murders, invasions by the French in 1796, and high living surround the house. Now owned and actively used by the Catholic Church, the plantation has spacious rooms, some with tray ceilings edged with handsome carving. The long, narrow pantry with red and black baked brick tiles is now being converted to a kitchen. On the grounds there is an ancient vaulted stone cistern and an outbuilding called the Bakery (which wasn't used for breadmaking but for baking turkeys and hams). The oven measures 12 feet across, and rises 3 feet up through a stepped chimney. *Cross Roads. Call Father John, tel. 809/497–2405, to make an appointment to tour the plantation.*

If you follow the road west toward the Cottage Hospital, you'll come to a dirt road that leads to **Crocus Bay** and several strips of white-sand beaches.

❷ Four miles northeast of The Valley on the main road, as you approach the coast at **Shoal Bay,** you'll pass near **The Fountain,** where Arawak petroglyphs have been discovered. Presently closed to the public, the area is being researched by the Anguilla Archaeological and Historical Society. The AAHS (tel. 809/497–2767) plans to open a museum in the former Customs House in The Valley.

Two miles farther east, the fishing village of **Island Harbour** nestles in its sheltered cove.

Follow rutted dirt roads from Island Harbour to the easternmost tip of the island. You'll pass Captain's Bay, with its isolated beach, on the north coast, on the way to the aptly named **Scrub Island** and **Little Scrub Island** off the eastern tip of the island.

❸ You can also choose to bypass the east end of the island because there isn't much to see there. From Island Harbour, a paved road leads south, skirts Savannah Bay on the southeast coast, and continues to **Sandy Hill Bay.** If you're an aficionado of ruined forts, there's one here you might want to explore.

Four miles down the coast, beyond the Long Salt Pond, is **Forest Bay,** a fit place for scuba diving. South of Forest Bay lies **Little Harbour,** with a lovely horseshoe-shape bay and the splendid **Cinnamon Reef Beach Club.**

From Forest Bay, follow the paved road past Wallblake Airport, just outside The Valley, and turn left on the main road. In **4** 4 miles you'll come to **Sandy Ground,** one of the most active and most developed of the island's beaches. It is home to the **Mariners Hotel, Tamariand Water Sports** dive shop, a commercial pier, and several small guest houses and restaurants. The *Shauna* departs from here for Sandy Island 2 miles offshore.

5 Farther down the south coast is **Blowing Point Harbour,** where you'll have docked if you arrived by ferry from Marigot in St. Martin.

Time Out If you plan to picnic (on the beach or in your room), try the **Fat Cat** (George Hill, tel. 809/497–2307) for escargots to go, as well as take-out quiche, soups, chili, chicken, and conch dishes. **Amy's Bakery** (Blowing Point, tel. 809/497–6775) turns out homemade pies, cakes, tarts, cookies, and breads.

The main paved road travels down more or less the center of the island, which at this northwest end is quite narrow. Teethjarring dirt roads lead to the coasts, the beaches, and some of the best resorts on the island.

On the south coast, west of Blowing Point, is the crescent-shape home of **Rendezvous Bay,** the island's first hotel, built in 1959. The white sand drifts down the coastline to **Cove Bay,** a pretty coconut palm-fringed beach.

Maunday's Bay, on the extreme southwest coast, is the home of **Cap Juluca,** a stunning resort that looks as if it had been plucked out of Marrakech.

On the opposite side of the island is **Coccoloba Plantation,** one of the most dazzling resorts in the Caribbean, overlooking the white sands of **Barnes Bay.** A five-minute walk from Barnes Bay is **Meads Bay,** and **Long Bay** is farther to the north.

Participant Sports

Bicycling There are plenty of flat stretches, making wheeling pretty easy. Bikes can be rented at **Island Car Rental** (Airport Rd., tel. 809/497–2723).

Boating Sunfish and Hobie Cats are available at **Tropical Watersports** (tel. 809/497–6666 or 809/497–6779). *Sundancer,* a 30-foot powerboat, is available for charters at **Tamariand Water Sports.** (809/497–2020). Sailboats and speedboats can be rented at **Sandy Island Enterprises** (tel. 809/497–6395).

Deep-Sea Fishing Albacore, dolphin, and kingfish are among the sea creatures angled after off Anguilla's shores. Trips can be arranged through **Tropical Watersports.** Fishing tackle, diving gear, and other sports equipment is available at the **Tackle Box Sports Center** (The Valley, tel. 809/497–2896).

Fitness Lest you go flabby lolling around on the beach, you can get out the exercise equipment, aerobics, and martial arts instruction at **Island Gym** (Long Ground, tel. 809/497–2363).

Jogging There are miles and miles of broad, flat beaches. Just pick one out and jog away.

Tennis For professional instruction, contact Carl Gavine at **Coccoloba** (tel. 809/497–6871), where there are two lighted courts. There are two courts at the **Carimar Beach Club** (tel. 809/497–6881), three championship courts at **Malliouhana** (tel. 809/497–6111), two Deco Turf tournament courts at **Cinnamon Reef** (tel. 809/497–2727), and six courts at **Fountain Beach and Tennis Club** (tel. 809/497–6395).

Sea Excursions Picnic, swimming, and diving excursions to Prickly Pear, Sandy Island, and Scilly Cay are available through **Sandy Island Enterprises** (tel. 809/497–6395) and **Tropical Watersports** (tel. 809/497–6666 or 809/497–6779).

Water Sports The major resorts offer complimentary Windsurfers, paddle-boats, and waterskis to their guests. If your hotel has no water-sports facilities you can get in gear at **Tropical Watersports** (Maunday's Bay, tel. 809/497–6666 or 809/497–6779) or **Tamariand Water Sports** (Sandy Ground, tel. 809/497–2020).

Tamariand Watersports has PADI instructors, short resort courses, and more than a dozen dive sites.

Shopping

Shopping tips are readily available in *Anguilla Life* and *What to Do in Anguilla*, but you have to be a really dedicated shopper to peel yourself off the beach and poke around in Anguilla's few shops.

Good Buys *Resort Wear and Jewelry* Head for **La Romana** (Malliouhana, tel. 809/497–6111), cloned from the St. Martin and St. Barts boutiques; **Whispers** (Cap Juluca, tel. 809/497–6666); and **Sunshine Shop** (South Hill, tel. 809/497–2149) for island cotton pareos, silkscreened items, cotton resort wear, and hand-painted wood items from Haiti.

Native Crafts **Lismaca Boutique** (The Valley, no phone) carries locally designed and made embroidered and crocheted dresses, shawls, separates, and even men's suits. **The Valley Gap** (Shoal Bay Beach, tel. 809/497–2754) has local crafts, T-shirts, and swimwear. **Vanhelle Boutique** (Sandy Ground, tel. 809/497–2965) carries gift items, as well as Brazilian swimsuits for men and women. The **Anguilla Arts and Crafts Center** (The Valley, no phone) has a wide selection of island crafts. The **Local Gift Shop** (The Quarter, no phone) has shells, handmade baskets, wood dolls, hand-crocheted mats, lace tablecloths and bedspreads.

Dining

Anguilla's eateries range from the exotic to down-home seaside shacks. Call ahead—in the winter to make a reservation, and in the summer to see if it's open.

The most highly recommended restaurants are indicated by a star ★.

Category	Cost*
Expensive	over $30

Moderate	$20–$30
Inexpensive	under $20

per person, excluding drinks, service, and sales tax (8%)

The Barrel Stay. The eclectic menu in this thatched-roof beachside eatery includes Hawaiian ham steak, red snapper Portuguese (in a sauce of tomatoes, onions, and green peppers), and French ice cream. Dinner is by candlelight. *Sandy Ground, tel. 809/497–2831. Reservations suggested in season. AE. Expensive.*

★ **Cinnamon Reef Beach Club.** Out on the stylish terra-cotta-tile terrace, begin with snails served in their shells in light garlic butter or chilled jumbo shrimp with cocktail sauce. You can order a soup sampler, which is a serving of two of the soups: black bean, chilled cream of pumpkin, or Anguillian goat soups. Shrimp baked with garlic butter and stuffed with homemade breadcrumbs and herbs, steak au poivre, and chicken Florentine are among the main dishes. Try the banana pudding cream pie or hot butterscotch sundae for dessert. On Friday nights enjoy a "jump-up" with steel band and barbecue. *Little Harbour, tel. 809/497–2727. Reservations advised. AE, MC, V. Expensive.*

Coccoloba Plantation. Dining is either indoors or on a lovely terrace overlooking the sea. Executive Chef Eric Scuiller, who trained at the Ecole Hôtellerie Chaptal in Brittany, presents an à la carte menu of Continental cuisine with a focus on fish. Main dishes include monkfish pan-fried with Virginia bacon and braised cabbage, grilled swordfish with diced tomato and sweet basil, breast of chicken with orange-ginger sauce, and duckling broiled with lime sauce. Don't miss the lobster Coccoloba. Lunch is a poolside buffet of salads, sandwiches, burgers, fish, cold meats, and homemade desserts. *Barnes Bay, tel. 809/497–6871. Reservations required in high season. AE, DC, MC, V. Expensive.*

Malliouhana. Sparkling crystal, fine china, romantic lighting, and sterling silver domed platters make even a lowly hamburger seem elegant. Jo Rostang, owner-chef of La Bonne Auberge in Antibes, created the menu and is still the consulting chef. Not surprisingly, the cuisine is haute French. Fresh salmon in a croissant pastry and spit-roasted duck or chicken are among the choices. The wine cellar contains about 35,000 bottles. During high season the restaurant is reserved for guests. *Mead's Bay, tel. 809/497–2731. Reservations imperative. No credit cards. Expensive.*

Pappagallo. As you might surmise from the name, this is an Italian restaurant. The chef, Rudy Ninghini, is from Bologna's La Panoramica Restaurant. Everything here is fresh, from the homemade pasta to the Italian vegetables from owner Giorgio Piazzi's garden. Genovese pasta al pesto and scottata (thinly sliced filet mignon with arugula and Parmesan cheese) are among the specialties. There is a waterfront terrace and an indoor dining room, where the Mayoumba Folkloric Group performs on Thursdays (when there's a $40 prix-fixe dinner). *Cul de Sac Hotel, tel. 809/497–6461. Reservations advised. AE, MC, V. Expensive.*

Pimm's. More dramatic than this there isn't. You expect Rudolph Valentino to sweep in beneath the domes, arches, and billowing canvas of this Arabian Nights tent. For starters, try the fresh lobster gazpacho soup chilled with avocado mousse.

For the main course there is fish pot-au-feu, fresh local fish cooked in its own juices with white wine; Pimm's grouper with leeks in a light vermouth sauce; Juluca Conch, slices of conch in a puff pastry with banana and curry sauce. You can end things lightly with lemon mousse, or succumb to the Devil Made Me Do It white and dark chocolate in mint sauce. *Cap Juluca, Maunday's Bay, tel. 809/497–6666. Reservations required. AE, MC, V. Expensive.*

Anguilla Great House. At lunch, this open-air beach bar serves light fare: salads, burgers, and sandwiches. Dinner is more serious, with veal cordon bleu, curried lamb, curried goat, West Indian–style snapper, pepper steak, ginger chicken, and lobster topped with cream sauce. *Rendezvous Bay, tel. 809/497–6061. Reservations accepted. AE, MC, V. Moderate.*

Arlo's. Pasta, pizza, and other simple fare is served in this Italian-American restaurant beside the sea. The large bar is a popular gathering place, with animated conversation lasting long into the evening. *South Hill, tel. 809/497–6810. Reservations suggested. No credit cards. Moderate.*

★ **Hibernia.** A French restaurant in the flower-fringed courtyard of Syd-An's Apartments. Nouvelle cuisine is beautifully presented at the six tables covered with black-and-white checked cloths. Begin with cream of vegetable soup and warm salad with chicken liver and grapefruit. For entrees, try the medallions of beef in red mustard sauce, breast of chicken with tomato and basil, and grilled lobster. Check out the T-shirts for sale; they're probably the best on the island. *Sandy Ground, tel. 809/497–3180. Reservations suggested in high season. No credit cards. Closed Tues. in high season. Moderate.*

★ **Lucy's Harbour View Restaurant.** Passing through a swinging wood gate you'll step up to a terrace restaurant with a splendid sea view. The specialty is "Lucy's delicious whole red snapper," but there is a wide selection here, including several curried and Creole dishes, such as conch and goat. Be sure to try Lucy's sautéed potatoes. Live music Wednesdays and Fridays. *South Hill, tel. 809/497–6253. Reservations accepted. No credit cards. Closed Sun. Moderate.*

Riviera Bar & Restaurant. A beachside bistro serving French and Creole specialties with an Oriental accent. A four-course lobster meal is featured, and the fish soup à la Provençale is highly recommended. Sushi, sashimi, and oysters sautéed in soy sauce and sake are also among the eclectic offerings. There's a very happy Happy Hour from 6 to 7 daily. Live entertainment is featured frequently in season. *Sandy Ground, tel. 809/497–2833. Reservations accepted. AE, V. Moderate.*

★ **Aquarium.** An upstairs terrace all gussied up with gingerbread trim, bright blue walls, and red cloths. The lunch menu lists sandwiches and burgers. Stewed lobster, curried chicken, barbecued chicken, and mutton stew are offered at night. This is a popular spot with locals. *South Hill, tel. 809/497–2720. Reservations accepted. No credit cards. Closed Sun. Inexpensive.*

Cross Roads. Millie Philip's roadside bar features hearty breakfasts and, at lunch, seafood salads, fish, and chicken. Hearty fare at low prices. *Wallblake, tel. 809/497–2581. Reservations accepted. No credit cards. Inexpensive.*

Johnno's. This is *the* place to be on Sunday afternoons for barbecue and music by the island band AngVibes, but grilled or barbecued lobster, chicken, and fish are good anytime. *Sandy Ground, tel. 809/497–2728. No reservations. No credit cards. Inexpensive.*

Pepper Pot. Cora Richardson's small eatery in the center of town offers roti aficionados their favorite dish, made of boneless chicken, tanias, celery, pepper, onion, garlic, and local peas—a full meal in itself—for E.C. $5. Dumpling dinners, lobster, whelk, and conch are also good choices. *The Valley, tel. 809/497-2328. Reservations accepted. No credit cards. Inexpensive.*

★ **Roy's.** An Anguillian mainstay, Roy and Mandy Bosson's pub is a spacious covered deck. One of the island's best buys, it features Roy's fish and chips, cold English beer, pork fricassee, and a wonderful rich chocolate rum cake. Sunday lunch special is roast beef and Yorkshire pudding. A faithful clientele gathers in the lively bar. *Crocus Bay, tel. 809/497-2470. Reservations accepted. No credit cards. Closed Mon. and Sat. lunch. Inexpensive.*

Lodging

Anguilla has a wide range of accommodations. There are grand and glorious resorts; apartments and villas from the deluxe to the simple; and small locally owned guest houses where you can get a real taste of life on Anguilla. When you call to reserve a room in a resort, be sure to inquire about special packages.

The most highly recommended lodgings are indicated by a star ★.

Category	Cost*
Very Expensive	over $250
Expensive	$180–$250
Moderate	$80–$180
Inexpensive	under $80

* *All prices are for a standard double room for two, excluding 8% tax and a 10% service charge.*

Hotels   **Cap Juluca.** Once you get past the potholed road leading to this luxurious, whitewashed Moorish resort with its domes, arches, low walls, and private courtyards, you'll be rewarded with a pampering touch. The still-developing property, situated on 179 acres and a lovely white beach, has five villas with such luxe touches as huge marble baths and sunken double tubs in private walled gardens, rooftop solariums with refrigerators and built-in barbecues, and Continental breakfast brought to your terrace. Ceiling fans whir over spacious rooms and suites with king-size platform beds. (All rooms are also fully air-conditioned.) The resort will eventually have 66 rooms, a free-form pool, more tennis courts with a clubhouse, and a section of private villas, each with its own pool. *Box 240, Maunday's Bay, tel. 809/497-6666/6779 or 800/235-3505. 18 rooms, including 3 suites. Facilities: restaurant, bar, boutique, room service, laundry service, library, VCRs and cassettes for rent, 2 tennis courts, water-sports center. No credit cards (personal checks accepted upon prior arrangement). Very Expensive.*

★ **Cinnamon Reef Beach Club.** Low-key luxury in these recently redecorated villas with vast expanses of terra-cotta tile, polished wood, and handsome upholstered bamboo furniture. Each villa is split level, with living room, raised bedroom (two double beds), dressing room, sunken shower, patio, and hammock. Each has a built-in hairdryer and minibar. Most of the villas are beachfront; five are tucked up on a bluff. Two villas, each with two beachfront and two garden suites (the latter with kitchenettes), can be converted into two-bedroom houses for families. (During the winter, children under 12 are not allowed.) This is a fun, friendly place with a gracious staff and lots of repeat guests. A calypso combo plays nightly and the Friday night barbecue is an island favorite. Meal plans and packages are available. *Box 141, Little Harbour, tel. 809/497–2727, 800/223–1108, or 416/485–8724 in Canada. 18 rooms. Facilities: restaurant, lounge, pool, 2 tennis courts, room service, turndown service, all water sports. AE, MC, V. Very Expensive.*

★ **Coccoloba Plantation.** E. David Brewer, who has been at the helm of Jumby Bay and some of the Rockresorts, is now the managing director of this stunning property. The reception area in the great house is an enormous room with soaring ceiling, sofas upholstered in vivid fabrics, and handsome artwork. Guests stay in oceanfront villas, done in orange or magenta, each with a step-up bedroom, oversize marble bath, and gingerbread-trim patio. All rooms and suites are air-conditioned, with ceiling fans, glass-top coffee tables, personal safe-deposit box, built-in hairdryer, amenity packages, and one-time complimentary fully stocked refrigerator and minibar. Some suites have Jacuzzis, but most baths have showers only. Complimentary early morning coffee and afternoon tea are served. The tennis program is directed by Peter Burwash International Pro Carl Gavine. A tennis package is one of several special packages available. *Box 332, Barnes Bay, tel. 809/497–6871, 800/351–5656, or 800/468–0023 in Canada. 51 units. Facilities: restaurant, 2 bars, concierge, boutique, 2 tennis courts, 2 pools, Jacuzzi, TV/reading room, sauna, massage, exercise rooms, water-sports center. AE, DC, MC, V. Very Expensive.*

★ **Malliouhana.** Brick steps lead to a broad, airy reception area with high ceilings, splashing fountain, and Haitian prints. Accommodations range from deluxe double rooms to super-deluxe suites. All are stunning, with miles of white tile, king-size platform beds or canopied king-size or twin beds, balconies, Haitian prints, minibars, oversize tubs in marble baths, ceiling fans (as well as air-conditioning). The hotel sits on a bluff overlooking the beach and a secluded cove. The resort also provides excursions to Sandy Island, which is excellent for snorkeling. It is necessary to reserve well in advance. *Box 173, Meads Bay, tel. 809/497–6111 or 212/696–1323. 52 rooms and suites. Facilities: restaurant, bar, boutique, beauty salon, concierge, 3 pools, 4 lighted tennis courts, Nautilus-equipped exercise room, massage room, water-sport center. No credit cards. Very Expensive.*

Anguilla Great House. On Rendezvous Bay, these five one-story white West Indian bungalows feature chaise longues on verandas with vine-covered trellises. Each of the five units has five rooms with connecting doors to make up two-bedroom suites. Lush fabrics, antique reproductions, and marble baths with enormous showers evoke an earlier era. When complete, the hotel will have 65 rooms and a great house with a formal dining room. *Box 157, Rendezvous Bay, tel. 809/497–6061 or 800/223–0079. 25 rooms. Facilities: restaurant, gym. AE. Expensive–Very Expensive.*

The Mariners. West Indian–style cottages are set in lush landscaped gardens overlooking the harbor at Road Bay. Accommodations vary considerably, ranging from deluxe two-bedroom, two-bath cottages with full kitchens to small rooms with twin beds, minibars, and miniscule shower baths. Charter the Mariner's Boston whaler for picnics, snorkeling, and fishing trips. The Thursday night barbecue and Saturday West Indian night in the beachfront restaurant are popular island events. *Box 139, Sandy Ground, tel. 809/497–2671, 809/497–2815, or 800/223–0079. 53 rooms and suites. Facilities: restaurant, bar, boutique, pool, lighted tennis court, water-sport center. AE, MC, V. Expensive–Very Expensive.*

Shoal Bay Villas. On 2 splendid miles of sand, these fan-cooled units include studio, one-bedroom, and two-bedroom suites, all with modern Italian furnishings and kitchens. Happy Jack's Beach Bar and open-air restaurant is a pleasant spot for breakfast, lunch, and dinner. All water sports can be arranged. Children are not allowed during the winter. *Box 61, Shoal Bay, tel. 809/497–2051; 212/535–9530 in NY; 416/283–2621 in Canada. 13 units. Facilities: restaurant, bar. AE, MC, V. Expensive–Very Expensive.*

Cul de Sac. The inn sits on a small manmade beach. All accommodations are spacious studios or one-bedroom suites. There is a glassed-in pool, and Pappagallo's restaurant is the scene each Thursday night of the lively Mayoumba Folkloric show. *Box 173, Shaddick Point, tel. 809/497–6461 or 212/696–1323. 12 suites. Facilities: restaurant, lounge, pool, water-sports center. AE, MC, V. Moderate.*

Rendezvous Bay Hotel. Anguilla's first hotel sits amid 60 acres of coconut groves and fine white sand. The water here is as clear as Perrier. The main building is low and rose-colored, with a broad front patio, tile floors, and wicker chairs. The rooms are clean and simple, with one double and one single bed and a private shower bath. Ask for room No. 1 if you're traveling with your family—a king-bed room adjoins a twin-bed room with a connecting marble bath. Twenty-seven four-room villas are under construction. Each will have a living room, bedroom, upstairs dining room, bath, and terrace. There's to be a broad covered terrace, where, according to the owner, "you can sit outside in a hurricane." *Box 31, Rendezvous Bay, tel. 809/497–6549; 201/738–0246 or 800/223–9815 in USA; 800/468–0023 in Canada. 20 rooms. Facilities: restaurant, lounge, game and TV room, 2 tennis courts, water-sport center. No credit cards. Moderate.*

★ **Inter-Island Hotel.** The West Indian cottage is modestly furnished (no air-conditioning) with wicker and rattan, and the hotel has some rooms with balconies. Most rooms have refrigerators and shower baths. There are also two small one-bedroom apartments, each with a separate entrance on the ground floor. A homey dining room serves hearty breakfasts and fine West Indian dinners. *Box 194, The Valley, tel. 809/497–6259 or 800/ 223–9815; 800/468–0023 in Canada. 12 rooms. Facilities: restaurant, bar/nightclub, TV lounge, transportation to beach ½ mi away. No credit cards. Inexpensive.*

Home and Apartment Rentals The Tourist Office has a complete listing of vacation rentals. You can also contact **Sunshine Villas** (Box 142, Blowing Point, tel. 809/497–6149) or **Property Real Estate Management Services** (Box 256, George Hill, tel. 809/497–2596). Housekeeping accommodations are plentiful and well-organized. The following are recommended:

Cove Castles Villa Resort. A sumptuously decorated, well-equipped, and very private compound along the beach of Shoal Bay West. Very elegant. *Shoal Bay West, Box 248, tel. 809/497–6801 or 800/223–9815; in Canada, 800/468–0023. 4 3-bedroom villas. Facilities: restaurant. No credit cards. Very Expensive.*

★ **Carimar Beach Club.** This is the place for travelers seeking a quiet beach retreat. To ensure privacy, each villa is in a separate building. The location is sparkling Meads Bay, adjacent to the Malliouhana. There's one three-bedroom apartment, all others are two-bedrooms; accommodations are sumptuous but not air-conditioned. *Box 327, The Valley, tel. 809/497–6881 or 800/223–5581. 24 rooms. Facilities: laundry, 2 tennis courts, water-sports center. AE, MC, V. Very Expensive.*

Sea Grape Beach Club. Also on Meads Bay, these luxurious 2,000-square-foot two-bedroom condos are laid out on five levels. Each unit features acres of glass affording spectacular views, enormous closets, three baths, king-size beds, elegant furnishings, and spacious, very private decks. *Box 65, The Valley, tel. 809/497–6433, 809/497–6541, or 800/223–9815. 10 condos. Facilities: restaurant, bar, 2 tennis courts, satellite TV, water-sports center. No credit cards. Very Expensive.*

★ **Easy Corner Villas.** These one-, two-, and three-bedroom apartments with kitchens are furnished right down to microwaves. Only three of the units are air-conditioned; all have only shower baths. No. 10 is a deluxe two-bedroom villa. Not located on the beach, but on a bluff overlooking Road Bay, this is a good buy for families. *Box 65, South Hill, tel. 809/497–6433, 809/497–6541, or 800/223–8815. 17 units. AE, MC, V. Moderate.*

Rainbow Reef. David and Charlotte Berglund's secluded units are set on three dramatic seaside acres. A gazebo, with beach furniture and barbecue facilities, perches right over the beach. Each self-contained villa has two bedrooms, fully equipped kitchen, spacious dining and living area, and a large gallery overlooking the sea. *Box 130, Sea Feather Bay, tel. 809/497–2817 or 312/325–2299. 4 units. No credit cards. Moderate.*

★ **La Sirena.** Overlooking busy Meads Bay, this secluded complex has two- and three-bedroom apartments done in handsome upholstered rattan furnishings with queen-size beds, terra-cotta tile floors, and modern, fully equipped kitchens. Each unit is fan-cooled. A good buy, but children under 12 are not welcome. *Box 200, The Valley, tel. 809/497–6827 or 800/223–9815; 800/468–0023 in Canada. 5 units. Facilities: pool, picnic and snorkeling equipment. No credit cards. Moderate.*

★ **Skiffles Villas.** These self-catering villas, perched on a hill overlooking Road Bay, are usually booked a year in advance. The one-, two-, and three-bedroom apartments have fully equipped kitchens, floor-to-ceiling windows, and pleasant porches. *Box 82, Lower South Hill, tel. 809/497–6110, 219/642–4855, or 219/642–4445. 5 units. Facilities: pool. No credit cards. Moderate.*

Nightlife

The **Mayoumba Folkloric Group** performs song-and-dance skits depicting Antillian and Caribbean culture, replete with African drums and a string band. They entertain every Thursday at the Cul de Sac's **Pappagallo** restaurant (tel. 809/497–6461). Be on the lookout for Bankie Banx, Anguilla's own reggae superstar. He has his own group called New Generations. Other local groups include Keith Gumbs and The Mellow Tones;

Spracker, an excellent guitarist; and Dumpa, who plays a steel pan. Steel Vibrations, a pan band, often entertains at barbecues and West Indian evenings. The big beat of North Sound Brass International is popular for dancing.

The **Cinnamon Reef** (tel. 809/497–2850) has popular Friday evening poolside barbecues and nightly live entertainment. The **Mariners** (tel. 809/497–2671) has regularly scheduled Thursday night barbecues and Saturday night West Indian parties, both with live entertainment by local groups.

During high season, **Pimm's** (Cap Juluca, tel. 809/497–6666) has soothing dance music after dinner. Things are pretty loose and lively at **Johnno's** (tel. 809/497–2728), with alfresco dancing on weekends. The **Dragon's Disco** (no phone) is a hot spot on weekends. On Sunday evenings you can find Sleepy and the All Stars, a popular string and scratch band, waking things up at the **Round Rock** (tel. 809/497–2076). The **Coconut Paradise** restaurant (Island Harbour, tel. 809/497–4454) has nightly entertainment ranging from disco to limbo.

3 Antigua

One could spend an entire year exploring all Antigua's (An-tee-ga) beaches; the island has some 365 of them, many with snow-white sand. All the beaches are public, and many are backed by lavish resorts offering sailing, diving, windsurfing, and snorkeling.

Antigua, largest of the British Leeward Islands, is where Lord Horatio Nelson headquartered for his forays into the Caribbean to do battle with the French and pirates in the late 18th century. There is still a decidedly British atmosphere on the island, with Olde-English publick houses that will raise the spirits of Anglophiles.

Visitors with a taste for history will enjoy exploring English Harbour and its carefully restored Nelson's Dockyard, as well as an 18th-century Royal Naval base, old forts, historic churches, and tiny villages. Hikers will want to spend hours viewing a tropical rain forest, lush with pineapples, banana trees, and mangoes. Those of an archaeological bent will head for the megaliths of Greencastle to seek out some 30 excavations of ancient Indian sites.

About 4,000 years ago, Antigua was home to a people called Siboney. They disappeared mysteriously, and the island remained uninhabited for about 1,000 years. When Columbus happened on the 108-square-mile island in 1493, the Arawaks had set up housekeeping. The English took up residency 130 years later in 1623. Then a sequence of bloody battles involving the Caribs, the Dutch, the French, and the English began. Slaves had been imported from Africa to work the sugar plantations by the time the French ceded the island to the English in 1667. On November 1, 1981, Antigua, with its sister island Barbuda (30 miles to the north), achieved full independence.

The combined population of the two islands is about 80,000, only 1,200 of whom live on Barbuda. Having survived a battered childhood, Antigua and Barbuda are currently experiencing the growing pains typical of a newly created nation. Tourism is the main industry here—there has been a recent building boom in tourism properties, with the construction of condominiums and the extensive renovation and expansion of the major hotels—and the government is seeking to broaden its monetary resources by reintroducing agriculture and manufacturing into the economy.

Before You Go

Tourist Information Contact the **Antigua and Barbuda Tourist Offices** in the United States (610 5th Ave., Suite 311, New York, NY 10020, tel. 212/541–4117), in Canada (60 St. Clair Ave., Suite 205, Toronto, Ont. MT4 1N5, Canada, tel. 416/961–3085), and in the United Kingdom (Antigua House, 15 Thayer St., London WI, England, tel. 01/486–7073).

You could try to contact the island directly (Box 373, St. John's, Antigua, tel. 809/462–0480); however, letters have been known to float around for three months before delivery, and the phone system is maddening.

Arriving and Departing By Plane **American** (tel. 800/433–7300) and **BWIA** (tel. 800/327–7401) have direct service from New York, BWIA from Miami. BWIA also flies from San Juan and Toronto, **Air Canada** (tel. 800/422–6232) from Toronto, **British Airways** (tel. 800/247–9297) from

London, and **Lufthansa** (tel. 800/645–3880) from Frankfurt. **LIAT** (tel. 809/462–0701) has daily flights from Antigua to Barbuda, 15 minutes away, as well as to down-island destinations.

V. C. Bird International Airport is, on a much smaller scale, to the Caribbean what O'Hare is to the Midwest. When several wide-bodies are sitting on the runway at the same time, all waiting to be cleared for takeoff, things can get a bit congested.

From the Airport Taxis meet every flight, and drivers will offer to guide you around the island. The taxis are unmetered, but rates are posted at the airport and drivers are required to carry a rate card with them. The fixed rate from the airport to St. John's is $6; from St. John's to Nelson's Dockyard, $34.

Passports and Visas U.S. and Canadian citizens need only proof of identity. A passport is best, but a birth certificate (an original, not a photocopy) or a voter's registration card will do. A driver's license is *not* sufficient. British citizens need a passport. All visitors must present a return or ongoing ticket.

Customs and Duties Visitors may bring in 200 cigarettes, one quart of liquor, and six ounces of perfume, plus any personal items.

Language Antigua's official language is English.

Precautions Some beaches are shaded by manchineel trees, whose leaves and applelike fruit are poisonous to touch. Most of the trees are posted with warning signs and should be avoided; even raindrops falling from them can cause painful blisters. If you should come in contact with one, rinse the affected area and contact a doctor.

Incidents of petty theft here are increasing. Leave your valuables in the hotel safe-deposit box; don't leave them unattended in your room or on the beach. Also, the streets of St. John's are fairly deserted at night, so it's not a good idea to wander out alone.

Staying in Antigua

Important Addresses Tourist Information: The **Antigua and Barbuda Department of Tourism** (Thames and Long Sts., St. John's, tel. 809/462–0480) is open Monday–Thursday 8–4:30, Friday 8–3. The **Antigua Hotels Association** (Long St., St. John's, tel. 809/462–3702) can also provide assistance.

Emergencies **Police** (tel. 809/462–0125), **Fire** (tel. 809/462–0044), and **Ambulance** (tel. 809/462–0251).

Hospital: There is a 24-hour emergency room at the 210-bed **Holberton Hospital** (Hospital Rd., St. John's, tel. 809/462–0251/2/3).

Pharmacies: Joseph's Pharmacy (Redcliffe St., St. John's, tel. 809/462–1025) and **Health Pharmacy** (Redcliffe St., St. John's, tel. 809/462–1255).

Currency Local currency is the Eastern Caribbean dollar (E.C.$), often called beewees. The E.C. is tied to the U.S. dollar and fluctuates only slightly. Figure about E.C.$2.60 to U.S.$1. American dollars are readily accepted, although you will usually receive change in beewees. Be sure you understand which currency is being used, since most places quote prices in E.C. dollars. Most hotels, restaurants, and duty-free shops take major credit cards, and all accept traveler's checks. It's a good idea

Antigua (and Barbuda)

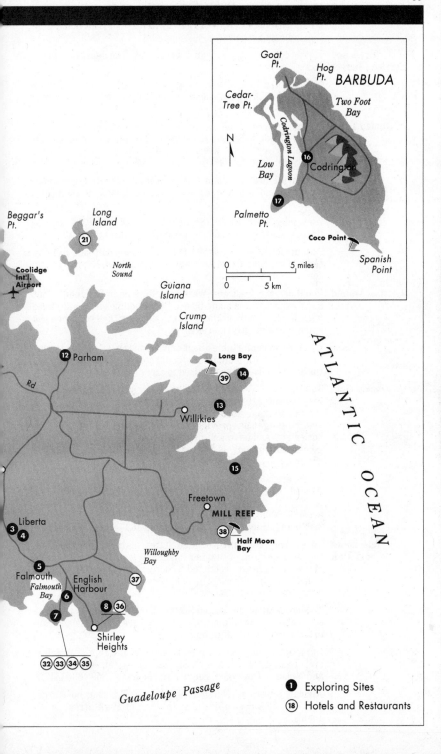

Goat Pt.
Hog Pt.
BARBUDA
Cedar-Tree Pt.
Two Foot Bay
Codrington Lagoon
⓰ Codrington
N
Low Bay
⓱
Palmetto Pt.
Coco Point
Spanish Point

0   5 miles
0   5 km

Beggar's Pt.
Long Island
㉑
North Sound
Coolidge Int'l. Airport
Guiana Island
Crump Island
ⓛ Parham
Rd
Long Bay
㊴ ⓮
�513
○ Willikies
ⓛ15
○ Freetown
MILL REEF
㊳
Half Moon Bay

A T L A N T I C   O C E A N

❸ Liberta
❹
Willoughby Bay
❺ Falmouth
Falmouth Bay
English Harbour
㊲
❻
❽ ㊱
❼
○ Shirley Heights
㉜㉝㉞㉟

Guadeloupe Passage

❶ Exploring Sites
⑱ Hotels and Restaurants

to inquire at the Tourist Office or your hotel about current credit card policy. Note: Prices quoted are in U.S. dollars unless indicated otherwise.

Taxes and Service Charges Hotels collect a 7% government room tax. The departure tax is $8.

Hotels add a 10% service charge to your bill. In restaurants, a 10% service charge is usually added to your bill. Taxi drivers expect a 10% tip.

Guided Tours All **taxi** drivers double as guides, and you can arrange an island tour with one for about $20 an hour. The most reliable and informed driver/guides are at **Capital Car Rental** (High St., St. John's, tel. 809/462–0863).

Bryson's Travel (St. John's, tel. 809/462–0223) offers personalized tours of the island, as well as cruises and deep-sea fishing trips.

Alexander, Parrish Ltd. (St. John's, tel. 809/462–0387) specializes in island tours and can also arrange overnight stays.

Antours (St. John's, tel. 809/462–4788) gives half- and full-day tours of the island. Antours is also the **American Express** representative on the island.

Getting Around
Buses You'll see the East and West Bus Stations in St. John's, but don't expect to see many buses. Bus schedules here epitomize what is called "island time," which is to say they roll when the spirit (infrequently) moves them.

Taxis If you're uncomfortable about driving on the left, a taxi is your best bet. Taxis are unmetered, but rates are fixed from here to there, and drivers are required to carry a rate card at all times.

Rental Cars To rent a car, you'll need a valid driver's license and a temporary permit ($10), which is available through the rental agent. Rentals average about $35–$40 per day, with unlimited mileage. Most agencies provide both automatic and stick shift, and both right- and left-hand-drive vehicles. If you plan on driving, be careful! Not only is driving on the left, but Antiguan roads are generally unmarked and full of potholes.

Jeeps are also available from most of the rental agencies. Among the agencies are **Budget** (St. John's, tel. 809/462–3009 or 800/527–0700), **National** (St. John's, tel. 809/462–2113 or 800/468–0008), **Carib Car Rentals** (St. John's, tel. 809/462–2062), and **Antours** (St. John's, tel. 809/462–4788).

Telephones and Mail To call Antigua from the United States, dial area code 809, then the local seven-digit number (and cross your fingers for luck). Many numbers are restricted from receiving incoming international calls. In addition, the telephone system is primitive, and even local connections crackle.

To place a call in the United States, dial 1, the appropriate area code, and the seven-digit number. To place an intraisland call, dial the local seven-digit number.

In an emergency, you can make calls from Cable & Wireless (WI) Ltd. (42–44 St. Mary's St., St. John's, tel. 809/462–9840, and Nelson's Dockyard, English Harbour, tel. 809/463–1517).

Airmail letters to North America cost E.C.60¢; postcards, E.C.40¢. The post office is at the foot of High Street in St. John's.

Opening and Closing Times In general, shops are open Monday–Saturday 8:30 AM–noon and 1–4 PM. Some close at noon on Thursdays and Saturdays. Duty-free shops that cater to tourists often have flexible hours. Banks are open Monday–Wednesday 8 AM–2 PM, Thursday 8 AM–1 PM, Friday 8 AM–1 PM and 3–5 PM.

Beaches

All of Antigua's beaches are public, and many are dotted with resorts that provide water-sports equipment rentals and a place to grab a cool drink. For more information regarding beachfront hotels, *see* Lodging, below.

Antigua A large coconut grove adds to the tropical beauty of **Carlisle Bay,** a long snow-white beach over which the estimable Curtain Bluff resort sits. Standing on the bluff of this peninsula, you can see the almost blinding blue waters of the Atlantic Ocean drifting into the Caribbean Sea.

Curtain Bluff's other beach, **Morris Bay,** has superb water for swimming, snorkeling, and sailing, as well as a long strip of white-gold sand that is ideal for sun worshiping.

Dickenson Bay has a lengthy stretch of powder-soft white sand and a host of hotels (the Siboney, the Anchorage, and Halcyon Cove) that cater to water-sports enthusiasts.

Long Bay, on the far eastern coast, has coral reefs in water so shallow that you can actually walk out to them. Here is a lovely beach, and the Long Bay Hotel.

Half Moon Bay (home of Half Moon Bay Hotel), a ¾-mile crescent of shell-pink sand, is a great place for snorkeling and windsurfing. The hotel will let you borrow gear with a refundable deposit.

Five Islands has four secluded beaches of fine tan sand and coral reefs for snorkeling. The Hawksbill Hotel is nearby.

Lignumvitae Bay, south of the Jolly Beach Hotel on the north coast, is a beautiful beach at the edge of a saltwater swamp.

Johnsons Point is a deliciously deserted beach of bleached white sand on the southwest coast.

The white sand of **Runaway Beach** is home to the Barrymore Beach Hotel and the Runaway Beach Hotel and so can get crowded. Refresh yourself with hot dogs and beer at the Barrymore's Satay Hut.

Barbuda **Cocoa Point,** on Barbuda, is an uncrowded 8-mile stretch of white sand. Barbuda is great for scuba-diving, with dozens of shipwrecks off its coasts.

Exploring Antigua

Numbers in the margin correspond with points of interest on the Antigua map.

St. John's The capital city of **St. John's,** home to some 35,000 people (near-
❶ ly half the island's population), lies at sea level on the northwest coast of the island. The city has seen better days, but it is currently having a face-lift and there are some notable sights to

see. First, be sure to stop in at the **Tourist Bureau** (corner of Long and Thames Sts.) for maps and information.

Cross Long Street and walk one block to Church Street. Those with a serious interest in archaeology will enjoy the historical displays of the **Museum of Antigua and Barbuda** whose exhibits trace the islands' history. The colonial building that houses the museum is the former courthouse, which dates from 1750. *Church and Market sts., tel. 809/463–1060. Admission free. Open weekdays 10–4, Sat. 10–1.*

Walk two blocks east on Church Street to **St. John's Cathedral.** The Anglican church sits on a hilltop, surrounded by its churchyard. At the south gate, there are figures of St. John the Baptist and St. John the Divine, said to have been taken from one of Napoleon's ships and brought to Antigua. The original church on this site was built in 1681 and replaced by a stone building in 1745. An earthquake destroyed that church in 1843, and the present building dates from 1845. With an eye to future earthquakes, the parishioners had the interior completely encased in pitch pine, hoping to forestall heavy damage. The church was elevated to the status of cathedral in 1848. *Between Long and Newcastle Sts., tel. 809/461–0082. Admission free.*

Recross Long Street, walk one block, and turn left on High Street. At the end of High Street, you'll see the **Cenotaph,** which honors Antiguans who lost their lives in World Wars I and II.

Trek seven blocks to the **Westerby Memorial,** which was erected in 1888 in memory of the Moravian Bishop George Westerby. One block south of the memorial is **Heritage Quay** (pronounced Key), a new multimillion-dollar complex, which opened some of its 40 shops in summer 1988. The complex, when completed, will include a 28-unit condominium/hotel, casino, supper club, 200-seat theater, shopping arcade, and food court. As soon as the construction of a new 500-foot pier and 200-foot causeway is completed, cruise-ship passengers will be able to disembark in the middle of Heritage Quay.

Redcliffe Quay, just south of Heritage Quay, is an attractive waterfront marketplace with shops, restaurants, and boutiques. Long ago on this site, slaves were held captive prior to being sold.

Time Out Stop for a pizza and a tall, cool one at the **Big Banana Holding Co.** (Redcliffe Quay, tel. 809/462–2621).

At the far south end of town, where Market Street forks into Valley Road and All Saints Road, a whole lot of haggling goes on every Friday and Saturday during the day when locals jam the public **marketplace** to buy and sell fruits, vegetables, fish, and spices. Be sure to ask before you aim a camera and expect the subject of your shot to ask for a tip.

Elsewhere on the Island After touring Fort James, we will divide the island into two more tours. First, we'll take in English Harbour and Nelson's Dockyard on the south coast, returning to St. John's along the Caribbean (western) coast. Then we'll travel to the eastern side of the island for sights ranging from historical churches to Devil's Bridge.

It's a good idea to wear a swimsuit under your clothes while you're sightseeing—one of the sights to strike your fancy may be an enticing, secluded beach. Be sure to bring your camera along. There are some picture-perfect spots around the island.

Fort James Follow Fort Road northwest out of town. In 2 miles, you'll come
2 to **Fort James**, named after King James II. The fort was constructed between 1704 and 1739 as a lookout point for the city and St. John's Harbour. The ramparts overlooking the small islands in the bay are in ruins, but 10 cannons still point out to sea. If you continue on this road, you'll come to Dickenson Bay, with its string of smart, expensive resorts.

English Harbour Take All Saints Road south out of St. John's. Eight miles out of
3 town—almost to the south coast—is **Liberta**, one of the first settlements founded by freed slaves. East of the village, on
4 Monk's Hill, is the site of **Fort George**, built in 1669. The fort wouldn't be of much help to anybody these days, but among the ruins, you can make out the sites for its 32 cannons, its water cisterns, the base of the old flagstaff, and some of the original buildings.

5 **Falmouth**, 1½ miles farther south, sits on a lovely bay, backed by former sugar plantations and sugar mills. **St. George's Church** dates from the late 18th and early 19th centuries. It was a church for the military in Nelson's time, and it has been restored and is now used for Sunday worship. **St. Paul's Church,** close by, was rebuilt on the site of a church once used by troops during the Nelson period.

6 **English Harbour** lies on the coast, just south of Falmouth. This is the most famous of Antigua's attractions. In 1671, the governor of the Leeward Islands wrote to the Council for Foreign Plantations in London pointing out the advantages of this landlocked harbor, and by 1704, English Harbour was in regular use as a garrisoned station.

In 1784, 26-year-old Horatio Nelson sailed in on HMS *Boreas* to serve as captain and second in command of the Leeward Island Station; he made frequent stops there for a period of three years. Under his command was the captain of HMS *Pegasus*, Prince William Henry, Duke of Clarence, who was to ascend the throne of England as William IV. The prince was Nelson's close friend and acted as best man when Nelson married the young widow Fannie Nisbet on Nevis in 1787.

The Royal Navy abandoned the station early in this century, and it fell into a state of decay. The Society of the Friends of English Harbour began restoring it in 1951, and on Dockyard
7 Day, November 14, 1961, **Nelson's Dockyard** was opened with much fanfare.

Nelson's Dockyard is to the Caribbean very much what Williamsburg, Virginia, is to the United States. Within the compound there are crafts shops, hotels, and restaurants. It is a hub for oceangoing yachts, and there is an abundance of activity here. (It serves as headquarters for the annual Sailing Week Regatta.) The dockyard's former lumber and supply store is now the beautifully restored and very British **Copper and Lumber Store Hotel.** Another fine hostelry, the **Admiral's Inn,** started out as a warehouse, built of bricks that had been used as ballast in British ships.

The **Admiral's House Museum** has several rooms displaying ship models, a model of English Harbour, silver trophies, maps, prints, and Nelson's very own telescope and tea caddy. *English Harbour, no phone. Admission: $2 per vehicle. Open daily 8–6.*

On a ridge overlooking the dockyard is **Clarence House** (tel. 809/463–1026), built in 1787 and once the home of the Duke of Clarence. Princess Margaret and Lord Snowdon spent part of their honeymoon here in 1960, and Queen Elizabeth and Prince Philip have dined here. It is now used by the governor-general; visits are possible when he is not in residence. Slip a tip to the caretaker, who'll give you a fascinating tour; the place is worth a visit.

⑧ As you leave the dockyard, turn right at the crossroads in English Harbour and drive up to **Shirley Heights** for a spectacular view of English Harbour. The heights are named for General William Henry Shirley, who fortified the harbour in 1787.

Time Out Cool off with yachtsmen, locals, and tourists at **Pizza of Paradise** (English Harbour, tel. 809/463–1194).

⑨ Drive back up to Liberta. Four and a half miles north of town, opposite the Catholic church, turn left and head southwest on **Fig Tree Drive.** (Forget about plucking figs; *fig* is the Antiguan word for banana.) This drive takes you through the rain forest, which is rich in mangoes, pineapples, and banana trees. This is also the hilliest part of the island—**Boggy Peak**, to the west, is the highest point, rising to 1,319 feet. Fig Tree Drive runs into **⑩** Old Road, which leads down to **Curtain Bluff,** an unforgettable sight. On this peninsula, between Carlisle Bay and Morris Bay, the Atlantic Ocean meets the Caribbean Sea, resulting in wonderful color contrasts in the water.

From here, the main road sweeps along the southwest coast, where there are lovely beaches and spectacular views. The road then veers off to the northeast and goes through the villages of Bolans and Jennings.

⑪ From Jennings, a road turns right to the **Megaliths of Greencastle Hill,** an arduous climb away. Some say the megaliths were set up by humans for the worship of the sun and moon; others believe they are nothing more than unusual geological formations.

The East End St. John's is 6 miles northeast of Jennings. To explore the other half of the island, take Parham Road east out of St. John's. Three and a half miles to the east, you'll see on your left the now-defunct sugar refinery. Drive 2 miles farther and turn left on the side road that leads 1¼ miles to the settlement of **⑫** **Parham. St. Peter's Church,** built in 1840 by Thomas Weekes, an English architect, is an octagonal Italianate building whose facade was once richly decorated with stucco, though it suffered considerable damage during the earthquake of 1843.

Backtrack and continue east for about three-quarters of a mile, to a fork in the road. One branch veers in a southeasterly direction toward Half Moon Bay and the other continues toward the northeast coast. The latter route runs through the villages of **⑬** Pares and Willikies to **Indian Town,** a national park, where archaeological digs have revealed evidence of Carib occupation.

⑭ Six miles farther south along the coast is **Devil's Bridge,** a natural formation sculpted by the crashing breakers of the Atlantic at Indian Creek. Surf gushes out through blowholes that were carved by the breakers.

If you take the southeast fork outside of Parham, you'll travel 9 miles to Half Moon Bay. Just before the coast is the village of **Freetown** and the **Mill Reef area,** where many pre-Columbian discoveries have been made.

⑮ **Harmony Hall,** northeast of Freetown, is a new art gallery that opened in December 1988. A sister to the Jamaican gallery near Ocho Rios, Harmony Hall is built on the foundation of a 17th-century sugar-plantation great house. Artist Graham Davis and Peter and Annabella Proudlock, who founded the Jamaican gallery, teamed up with local entrepreneur Geoffrey Pidduck to create an Antiguan art gallery specializing in high-quality West Indian art. A large gallery is used for one-man shows, and another exhibition hall displays watercolors. *Brown's Mill Bay, tel. 809/463–2057. Open daily 10–6.*

Barbuda Thirty miles due north of Antigua is Barbuda—all 62 square
⑯ miles of it. Almost all the island's 1,200 people live in **Codrington.** Barbuda's 8-mile **Cocoa Beach** lures beachcombers, and the island is ringed by wrecks and reef, which makes it a great draw for divers and snorkelers.

⑰ The sole historic ruin here is **Martello Tower,** which is believed to have been a lighthouse built by the Spaniards before the English occupied the island. LIAT (*see* Before You Go, above) has regularly scheduled daily flights from Antigua; air and boat charters are also available (contact the Tourist Board).

Participant Sports

Almost all the resort hotels can come up with fins and masks, Windsurfers, Sunfish, glass-bottom boats, catamarans, and other water-related gear (*see* Lodging, below).

Boating **Wadadli Watersports** (tel. 809/462–4101 or 4100) rents catamarans and other crafts. Sunfish and rowboats are available through the **Catamaran Hotel** (tel. 809/463–1036). Check yacht charters through **Nicholson Yacht Charters** (tel. 800/662–6066).

Fitness Center The **Benair Fitness Club** (Country Club Rd., Hodges Bay, tel. 809/462–1540) has fitness equipment, Jacuzzi, aerobic classes, and a juice bar.

Golf There is an 18-hole course at **Cedar Valley Golf Club** (tel. 809/ 462–0161), and a nine-hole course at **Half Moon Bay Hotel** (tel. 809/463–2101).

Hiking There are no organized hiking trips, but you can trek up 687-foot Monk's Hill, tackle Boggy Peak's slopes, or climb up Greencastle Hill to see the megaliths *(see* Exploring, above).

Horseback Riding Guided trail rides can be arranged through **Wadadli Stables** (tel. 809/461–2721) and **The Reliable Stable** (tel. 809/461–4086).

Sailing The **Antigua School of Sailing** (tel. 809/462–2026) offers short resort courses.

Scuba Diving With all the wrecks and reefs, there are lots of undersea sights to see. Contact **Dive Antigua** (tel. 809/462–0256) or **Aquanaut**

Dive Center (tel. 809/463–1024 or 809/463–1113). Dive packages are offered by the **Runaway Beach Club** (tel. 809/462–1318).

Sea Excursions **Miguel's Holiday Adventures** (tel. 809/461–0458 or 0361) will run you over to Prickly Pear Island for picnicking, snorkeling, fishing, and waterskiing, and they'll furnish the equipment. **Wadadli Watersports** (tel. 809/462–4101 or 4100) makes trips to Bird Island and Barbuda that include soft drinks and barbecue on the beach. The *Jolly Roger* (tel. 809/462–2064) has a "fun cruise," complete with "pirate" crew, limbo dancing, walking the plank, and other pranks. *Paradise I* (tel. 809/462–4158) is a 45-foot Beneteau yacht that offers day cruises with fishing, snorkeling, and lunch, as well as evening cocktail cruises. The *Falcon* (tel. 809/462–4792) is an elegant catamaran schooner that cruises to Bird Island and Barbuda for swimming, snorkeling, and barbecue; it also makes sunset cruises.

Tennis The **Temo Sports Complex** (Falmouth Bay, tel. 809/463–1781) has floodlit courts, glass-backed squash courts, showers, sports shop, and snack bars. There are also five lighted courts at the **St. James Club,** five courts at the **Half Moon Club,** four Har-Tru and one grass court at **Curtain Bluff,** and three courts at the **Anchorage Hotel** (*see* Lodging, below).

Waterskiing Rentals are available at **Wadadli Watersports** (tel. 809/462–4101 or 4100).

Windsurfing **Patrick's Windsurfing School** (tel. 809/462–3094) offers courses and rentals. Rentals are also available at **Wadadli Watersports** (tel. 809/462–4101 or 4100) and **Hodges Bay Club** (tel. 809/462–2300).

Spectator Sports

For information about sports events, contact **Antigua Sports and Games** (tel. 809/462–1925).

Cricket Practically the only thing most Americans know about this game is that there's something called a "sticky wicket." Here, as in Britain and all the West Indies, the game is a national passion. Youngsters play on makeshift pitches, which apparently compare to sandlots, and international matches are fought out in the stadium on Independence Avenue, St. John's (*see* Exploring, above).

Shopping

Antigua's duty-free shops are the reason so many cruise ships call here. Bargains can be found in perfumes, liqueurs and liquor (including, of course, Antiguan rum), jewelry, china, and crystal. As for local items, look for straw hats, baskets, batik, pottery, and hand-printed cotton clothing.

Shopping Areas **Redcliffe Quay** and **Heritage Quay,** both in St. John's, are waterfront festival markets with boutiques, restaurants, snack bars, and stores. The main tourist shops in St. John's are along **St. Mary's, High,** and **Long streets.**

Good Buys
China and Crystal **Specialty Shoppe** (St. Mary's St., tel. 809/462–1198), **The Scent Shop** (High St., tel. 809/462–0303), and **Norma's Duty-Free Shop** (Heritage Quay Shopping Center and Halcyon Cove Hotel, tel. 809/462–0172) have wares that make impressive presents for the people back home.

Jewelry Hans Smit is **The Goldsmitty** (Redcliffe Quay, tel. 809/462–4601), creating original 14K and 18K gold rings, necklaces, earrings, and cuff links. **Colombian Emeralds** (Redcliffe Quay, tel. 809/462–2086) is the largest retailer of Colombian emeralds in the world. Jewelry bargains are also at **Norma's Duty-Free Shop** (Heritage Quay Shopping Center and the Halcyon Cove Hotel, tel. 809/462–0172).

Liquor and **The Warehouse** (St. Mary's St., tel. 809/462–0495) and **Manuel** *Liqueurs* **Diaz Liquor Store** (Long and Market sts., tel. 809/462–0440) should whet your appetite.

Native Crafts Hand-printed fabrics with original designs by George Kelsick are at **Kel-Print** (St. Mary's St., tel. 809/462–2189). Antiguan-made pottery is at **The Pottery Shop** (Redcliffe Quay, tel. 809/462–4219). **Things Antiguan** (Redcliffe Quay, tel. 809/462–1567) is a source for Antiguan crafts. Antigua's calypsonian King Short Shirt sells his records as well as food and T-shirts at **Shorty's** (Dickenson Bay, tel. 809/462–2393). Records and tapes of calypso, carnival sounds, steel bands, reggae, and rock are at **Tower Marketing** (Church and St. Thomas sts., tel. 809/462–0180). Hand-crafted island jewelry is at **Gift to Nelson** (Nelson's Dockyard, no phone). **CoCo Shop** (St. Mary's St., tel. 809/462–1128) specializes in things made in Antigua: Antiguan Frangipani perfume, pottery, sea-island cottons, batiks, and hand-crafted jewelry. **Serendipity** (Redcliffe Quay, tel. 809/462–2026) has Montserrat cotton clothing, shawls, tablecloths, character dolls, and imported British clothing. **A Thousand Flowers** (Redcliffe Quay, tel. 809/462–4264) carries batiks, sarongs, lava wraps, and swimwear. **The Map Shop** (St. Mary's St., tel. 809/462–3993) has a wonderful collection of antique maps, books about the sea, prints, maps of the West Indies, and charts of the Caribbean. The works of local artists are at **The Art Gallery** (St. Mary's St., tel. 809/462–3027) and **Harmony Hall** (Brown's Mill Bay, tel. 809/463–2057).

Perfume **CoCo Shop** (St. Mary's St., tel. 809/462–1128), **The Scent Shop** (High St., tel. 809/462–0303), and **Norma's Duty-Free Shop** (Heritage Quay Shopping Center and Halcyon Cove Hotel, tel. 809/462–0172) carry choice selections of perfumes and other scented niceties.

Dining

The focus, naturally, is on fresh-caught fish and lobster, but Antigua offers sophisticated Continental and American dining as well. Because of its British heritage, Antigua tends to be a bit more formal in dressing for dinner. There are a few places, which will be noted, that require both jacket and tie. You don't need to don white tie and tails, but you'll be more comfortable if you're rather well turned out for dining.

Most menu prices are listed in E.C. dollars; some are listed in both E.C. and U.S. dollars. Be sure to check in advance if credit cards are accepted and ask in which currency the prices are quoted. Dinner reservations are often needed during the high season.

The most highly recommended restaurants are indicated by a star ★.

Category	Cost*
Very Expensive	over $35
Expensive	$20–$35
Moderate	$13–$20
Inexpensive	under $13

per person, excluding drinks, service, and sales tax (7%)

Admiral's Inn. The inn's brick building dates from 1788, and dining is either on the terrace or in a cozy room, where old wood tables are carved with two centuries of names. Lobster, seafood, and steak are the specialties. Lobster thermidor is excellent; so are the rum punches. *Nelson's Dockyard, tel. 809/463-1027. Reservations required. No credit cards. Expensive.*

Cacubi Room. Candlelight and crisp white napery enhance the elegant mood in the Blue Waters Hotel's air-conditioned restaurant. For openers, try the homemade liver pâté marinated in brandy and flavored with herbs. The chef's special creation is Flying Fish Cavalier (two fillets cooked in white wine and herbs, served in a cream sauce flavored with Cavalier rum and sprinkled with butter-fried coconut). This restaurant is famed for its flambéed desserts—try the pineapple flambé or crepes Suzette. Liqueurs and cigars are brought to your table after your meal. *Blue Waters Hotel, Boon Pt., tel. 809/462-0290. Jackets required. Reservations suggested. AE, MC, V. Expensive.*

★ **Clouds.** The elegantly decorated terrace sits high on a hill, overlooking Halcyon Cove and Dickenson Bay. Chef Julian Waters turns out starters such as melon glazed with ginger and honey, accompanied by grape and red wine sorbet. Soups include chilled zucchini and carrot. Among the entrées are pan-fried medallions of venison, noisettes of lamb, and breast of chicken filled with duck and pistachio-nut mousse, accompanied by herb butter and avocado. For dessert, try the fresh strawberry parfait. *Halcyon Cove Beach Resort, tel. 809/462-0256. Jacket and the required. Reservations required. AE, MC, V. Closed Sun. Expensive.*

Coconut Grove. Adjacent to the Siboney Beach Club, this is everybody's idea of casual beachfront dining. The covered terrace is so close to the beach you could build sandcastles; unfortunately, you may have time to build a community of castles before you're served. Still, the setting is pleasant and the place is very popular. The Continental menu includes French onion soup and gazpacho for appetizers. Tropical Chicken Coconut Grove is breast of chicken sautéed with tropical fruit, laced with Grand Marnier, and served in a coconut shell. The wine list is extensive. *Dickenson Bay, tel. 809/462-1538. AE. Moderate.*

Colombo's. The Sardinians who run this restaurant make every effort to please, and they do. The thatch-roof patio is evocative of the South Seas, and the full Italian menu includes homemade pastas, veal scaloppine, tournedos, and lobster Mornay. *Galleon Beach Club, English Harbour, tel. 809/463-1081. Reservations suggested. No credit cards. Closed Sept. Moderate.*

★ **Shirley Heights Lookout.** This restaurant is in part of an 18th-century fortification, and the view of English Harbour below is breathtaking. There's a breezy pub downstairs that opens onto the lookout point, and upstairs, a cozy, windowed room with hardwood floors and beamed ceilings. Pub offerings include burgers, sandwiches, and barbecue, while the upstairs room serves the likes of pumpkin soup and lobster in lime sauce. There's a barbecue livened by island music from a steel band every Sunday. *Shirley Heights, tel. 809/463–1785. Reservations required in season. AE, MC, V. Moderate.*

★ **The Dolphin.** In this miniature estate house is one of the best places on the island to sample local dishes. Specialties include conch, piquant pepperpot, and fish and chips. *All Saints' Rd., about 1 mi outside St. John's, tel. 809/462–1183. No credit cards. Closed Sun. Inexpensive.*

Lodging

Antigua's beaches are decorated with an assortment of resorts, ranging from the spectacular to small and self-catering homes away from home. Those seeking active nightlife and opportunities for meeting other island guests will want to stay in one of hotels in Dickenson Bay, where properties are close together, which makes for lots of beach action, and St. John's is just a five-minute cab ride away. The resorts scattered elsewhere on the island tend to cater more to honeymooners and to those who seek some seclusion. Most hotels offer the MAP, and due to distances to town, most guests take advantage of it. Therefore, unless otherwise noted, our price categories include breakfast and dinner.

The most highly recommended lodgings are indicated by a star ★.

Category	Cost*
Very Expensive	over $190
Expensive	$150–$190
Moderate	$125–$150
Inexpensive	under $125

All prices are for a standard double room for two, excluding 7% tax and a 10% service charge.

★ **Blue Waters Beach Hotel.** Luscious lime-colored buildings are set in a tropical garden along two white-sand beaches. Accommodations are in air-conditioned rooms or two- and three-bedroom villas, all of which are beachfront with balconies or patios. *Box 256, St. John's, tel. 809/462–0290 or 800/ 372–1323; in UK 01/367–5175. 67 rooms. MAP or EP available. Facilities: 2 restaurants, 2 bars, pool, 1 lighted tennis court, gift shop, water-sports center. AE, MC, V. Very Expensive.*

★ **Curtain Bluff.** It's difficult not to go overboard about this resort. A long avenue of trees leads out onto the peninsula where the hotel is bordered by the Atlantic Ocean on one side, the Caribbean Sea on the other; two white-sand beaches beckon below the bluff. Deluxe beachfront rooms and suites have cedar ceilings with whirring fans, marble baths, private balconies, and chaises longues. Owner Howard Hulford is a connoisseur of wine, and his collection makes up the hotel's 50,000-bottle wine cellar. His villa overlooking the waters is the ritzy locale of weekly cocktail parties and of anniversary parties honoring guests who are visiting the hotel for the 10th or 20th time. The hotel has a dive boat, sailboats, Windsurfers, and facilities for a host of water-related activities. Curtain Bluff comes highly recommended, although it is not for the budget conscious. *Box 288, St. John's, tel. 809/463–1115 or in NY, 212/289–8888. 60 rooms and suites. Facilities: restaurant, lounge, 4 tennis courts, pro shop, croquet, putting green, water-sports center. No credit cards. Closed Sept. Very Expensive.*

★ **Halcyon Cove Beach Resort and Casino.** Things are chic in this Dickenson Bay hotel. Luxury accommodations, all with air-conditioning and private balcony or patio, are scattered around the courtyard pool or on the beach. A water-sports center offers excursions on a glass-bottom boat and waterskiing, in addition to the other usual water sports. In the evening, you can go for a spin in the casino or around the dance floor. *Box 251, St. John's, tel. 809/462–0256 or 800/223–1588. 135 rooms. Facilities: 4 restaurants, 3 bars, room service, pool, 4 lighted tennis courts, casino, boutiques, water-sports center. AE, DC, MC, V. Very Expensive.*

Half Moon Bay. This two-story hotel sits on a lovely horseshoe bay on the southeastern tip of the island. Its reception area is an open breezeway with tile floors and wood rafters. All the rooms are oceanfront; the white sand beach, lined with tall palms, is literally a step away. Each room has either a balcony or a patio; standard rooms have half-tubs with showers. Suites have minifridges and lounge areas, and there is a two-bedroom cottage with a kitchen. There are no air-conditioning, phones, or TVs. Lunch is served by the free-form pool, and tea is served each afternoon. All water sports are free to guests. *Box 144, St. John's, tel. 809/463–2101 or 800/223–6510. 100 rooms. Facilities: 2 restaurants, 2 bars, pool, 5 tennis courts (1 lighted) with a pro, 9-hole golf course, water-sports center. AE. Very Expensive.*

★ **Hawksbill Beach Hotel.** The Hawksbill, on 37 acres on the Five Islands peninsula, boasts no fewer than four beaches of fine tan sand. Accommodations are in a luxurious two-story, three-bedroom West Indian Great House, with king-size beds, tile floors, wicker furniture, and kitchenette/bar. Other accommodations are in deluxe cottages facing the sea and smaller cottages nestled in the garden. Gentlemen are requested not to wear short sleeves into the dining room after 7 PM; children under age 8 are not welcome here. Water sports are complimentary except for a small charge for waterskiing. *Box 108, St. John's, tel. 809/462–0301 or 800/327–6511; in Canada, 416/622–8813). 75 rooms. Facilities: 2 restaurants, 2 bars, pool, tennis court, boutique, water-sports center. AE, DC, MC, V. Very Expensive.*

★ **Hodges Bay Club.** Opposite Prickly Pear Island, on a great snorkeling beach, are Hodges Bay's luxury one- and two-bedroom condominium villas. All villas have fully equipped kitchens, king-size beds, two balconies, and daily maid service. All bedrooms are air-conditioned and each has a private bath. *Box 1237, St. John's, tel. 809/462–2300 or 800/223–5581; in NY 212/535–9530). 26 suites. Facilities: restaurant, pool, 2 tennis courts, water-sports center. AE, DC, MC, V. Very Expensive.*

★ **Jumby Bay.** Ten minutes by launch from Antigua lies this 350-acre private island. Luxurious informality might characterize the ambience here. Accommodations are in junior suites located either in a multiunit facility or in cottages, both set amid quiet, sandy beaches and miles of walking trails. All meals are included in the rates, along with bar drinks, house wines, bicycles, tennis, water sports, and the ferry to and from Antigua. The management believes that children under age 8 would not be comfortable here. *Box 243, St. John's, tel. 809/462-6000 or 800/437-0049. 38 suites. Facilities: 2 restaurants, 3 bars, tennis, bicycles, sailboats, water-sports center. No credit cards. Very Expensive.*

Pineapple Beach Club (formerly the New Horizons). A broad stone walk leads directly from the reception area to the beach of this all-inclusive (meals, drinks, gratuities, sports, you name it) resort. The fan-cooled beachfront doubles have private terraces and shower-baths. There are no phones or TVs. Garden-view rooms are air-conditioned. The pool and the windsurfing school are located on Long Bay's white-sand beach. Live entertainment is offered nightly. *Box 54, St. John's, tel. 809/463-2006 or 800/223-9815; in Canada, 800/468-0023. 97 rooms. Facilities: restaurant, bar, pool, 2 tennis courts. AE, DC, MC, V. Very Expensive.*

St. James Club. London's St. James Club opened this resort in what was once a Holiday Inn facility. It sits on 100 acres of lush landscaping, and the spacious reception area has Haitian prints and well-placed conversation areas. The rooms are decorated in soft pastels, with two double beds and private balcony. Exquisite canopy beds and fridges are in the one-bedroom, two-bath suites and villas. The hotel is fully air-conditioned. A scuba school, a private yacht club and marina, Saturday-night barbecues, and soft white beaches complete the St. James's offerings. *Box 63, St. John's, tel. 809/463-1113 or in NY, 212/308-3330. 105 rooms. Facilities: 3 restaurants, 3 bars, 24-hr room service, casino, nightclub/disco, croquet, 2 pools (1 saltwater), 7 lighted tennis courts, gym, riding stable, water-sports center. AE, DC, MC, V. Very Expensive.*

Galley Bay Surf Club. This is a quiet and peaceful getaway in a tropical setting between a white beach and a blue lagoon. Beachfront villas have king-size beds, ceiling fans, showers, upscale tropical decor, and, of course, the beach. Rooms in Gauguin Village, a group of thatch-roof Tahitian-style cottages on the lagoon, are simply furnished (twin beds), and while each has a private patio, you have to walk across it to get to the bath. *Box 305, St. John's, tel. 809/462-0302 or 800/223-5581; in NY, 212/535-9530. 30 rooms. Facilities: restaurant, bar, tennis court, horseback riding, water-sports center. AE, MC, V. Expensive–Very Expensive.*

★ **Siboney Beach Club.** Ann and Tony Johnson's all-suites beach club on Dickenson Bay is a gem that's set in a tropical garden smack on the beach. Each suite is done in tropical decor, with rattan furnishings and colorful island prints. Guests can choose between air-conditioned or fan-cooled bedrooms and king-size or twin beds. Just off the living area, there's a private balcony or patio, each framed by palm fronds and tropical plants. There are fully equipped Pullman kitchens, which you can either use or seal off behind louvered panels and forget about while you dine at the Coconut Grove adjacent to the reception area. The staff here is especially friendly and helpful. *Box 222, St. John's, tel. 809/462-0806 or 800/533-0234. 12 suites. Facilities: restaurant, bar, pool. AE, MC, V. Expensive–Very Expensive.*

★ **Copper and Lumber Store Hotel.** The former supply store in Nelson's Dockyard has been transformed into a very British inn, with old brick, hardwood floors, Oriental rugs, and old English prints and maps. Stairs lead up to Old World suites with kitchens, each decorated differently but all with period furnishings, antique washstands, secretaries, and four-poster and canopy beds. If you're an Anglophile, you won't want to go home. *Box 184, St. John's, tel. 809/463–1058. 14 suites. Facilities: restaurant/pub. AE, MC, V. Moderate–Expensive.*

Callaloo Beach Hotel. Nick Fuller's place on Morris Bay is set on 37 acres with 1,600 feet of white-gold sand. Each of the twin-bedded rooms has Spanish tile floors, beamed ceilings, rattan furnishings, private bath, and veranda. The atmosphere is very laid back. *Box 676, St. John's, tel. 809/463–1110. 16 rooms. Facilities: restaurant, bar. AE, MC, V. Moderate.*

Jolly Beach Resort. This sprawling, Spanish-style stucco hotel is the largest in the eastern Caribbean. It's set on 38 tropical acres, with 1½ miles of beach at Lignumvitae Bay. The accommodations range from tiny functional rooms to villas. There's free waterskiing, windsurfing, and paddle- or sailboats. This is the place for jolly, energetic folks. *Box 744, St. John's, tel. 809/462–0061 or 800/321–1055; in FL, 800/432–6083; in Canada, 800/368–6669. 500 rooms. Facilities: 3 restaurants, 4 bars, disco, pool, 8 tennis courts, movie room, shops, car rental desk, water-sports center. AE, MC, V. Moderate.*

★ **Admiral's Inn.** Built in the 18th century of old brick that had been used as ballast for sailing vessels, this English inn in Nelson's Dockyard once housed engineers' offices and a warehouse. If you're looking for glitz and glamour, head for Dickenson Bay. The rooms are simple (some are air-conditioned, some have ceiling fans), and bathrooms have only showers. A complimentary boat runs you to the beach at Freeman's Bay, where you have free use of sailboats. *Box 713, St. John's, tel. 809/463–1027 or 800/223–5695; in NY, 212/725–5880; in Canada, 416/447–2335; in the United Kingdom, 01/387–1555. 14 rooms. Facilities: restaurant, pub. No credit cards. Inexpensive.*

Nightlife

Most of Antigua's evening entertainment centers on the resort hotels, which feature calypso singers, steel bands, limbo dancers, and folkloric groups on a regular basis. Check with the Tourist Board for up-to-date information.

Shirley Heights Lookout (Shirley Heights, tel. 809/463–1785) does Sunday-afternoon barbecues that continue into the night with music and dancing. It's a favorite local spot on Sunday night.

Casinos There are three hotel casinos, which request "reasonable attire," open from early evening until 4 AM. Slot machines and gaming tables attract gamblers to the **Halcyon Cove Resort** (Dickenson Bay, tel. 809/462–0256), the **Royal Antiguan** (Deep Bay, tel. 809/462–3733), and the **Flamingo** (Michaels Mount, tel. 809/462–1266). The **St. James Club** (Mamora Bay, tel. 809/463–1113) has a private casino.

Discos **Tropix** (Redcliffe Quay, St. John's, tel. 809/462–2317) is an informal spot that draws young locals, and **Chips** (Halcyon Cove Beach Resort, tel. 809/462–0256) is a new hot spot that attracts both tourists and locals.

4 Aruba

by Pamela Bloom

Pamela Bloom writes on pop music and the cabaret scene for the New York weekly Seven Days. *She also writes monthly book reviews and travel pieces for* Taxi *magazine.*

Imagine Aruba as one big Love Boat cruise. All of its 14 hotels sit side by side down one major strip along the southwestern shore, with restaurants, exotic boutiques, fiery floor shows, and glitzy casinos right on their premises so you don't even have to step outside. Nearly every night there are wild theme parties, Carnaval blasts, treasure hunts, beachside barbecues, and fish fries with steel bands and limbo dancers. Every Tuesday evening year-round, Arubans celebrate the Bonbini ("Welcome" in the Native Papiamento dialect) with arts and crafts and musical and dancing shows in the courtyard of Oranjestad's Fort Zoutman.

The "A" in the ABC Islands, Aruba is a small island—12 miles long and approximately 70 square miles. The national anthem proclaims, "the greatness of our people is their great cordiality," and this is no exaggeration. Once a member of the Netherlands Antilles, Aruba became an independent entity within the Netherlands in 1986, with its own royally appointed governor, a democratic government, and a 21-member elected parliament. Long secure in a solid economy, with good education, housing, and health care, the island's population of about 65,000 actually regards tourists as welcome guests. Waiters serve you with smiles and solid eye contact, English is spoken everywhere, and hotel hospitality directors appear delighted to serve your special needs. Good direct air service from the United States (*see* Arriving and Departing, below) makes Aruba an excellent choice for even a short vacation.

The island's distinctive beauty lies in its countryside—an almost extraterrestial landscape full of rocky deserts, cactus jungles, secluded coves, and aquamarine vistas with crashing waves. With its low humidity and average temperatures of 82° F, Aruba has the climate of a paradise; rain comes mostly during November. Many of the same tourists return year after year, and many hotels honor long-time customers with special plaques and presentations.

Before You Go

Tourist Information Contact the **Aruba Tourism Authority,** 1270 Avenue of the Americas, Suite 2212, New York, NY 10020, tel. 212/246–3030 or 800/TO–ARUBA, telex 668–688; in Miami, Box 012348, Miami, FL 33101, tel. 305/326–7280; in Canada, 1801 Englinton W. Street, 3118, Toronto, Ontario, M6E2H7, tel. 416/782–9954.

Arriving and Departing *By Plane* Flights leave daily to Aruba from both New York's JFK International and Miami's International airports, with easy connections from most American cities. From New York, **American Airlines** (tel. 800/433–7300) has one nonstop daily flight to Aruba. From Miami, **ALM** (tel. 800/327–7230) flies nonstop to Aruba. **Continental Airlines** (tel. 800/525–0280) flies nonstop daily from Newark, NJ. From Toronto and Montreal, you can fly to Aruba on American Airlines via San Juan. American also has connecting flights from several U.S. cities via San Juan.

Passports and Visas U.S. and Canadian residents need show proof only of identity—a valid passport, birth certificate, naturalization certificate, green card, valid nonquota immigration visa, or a valid voter's registration card. All other nationalities must submit a valid passport.

Aruba

California Pt.

B.A. Beach

9

Malmok Beach

Altovista

Fisherman's Hut

10

Palm Beach

Bushiribana

8

11 **12**

13 – 20

Noord

Eagle Beach

23

21

24

22

25

26

Manchebo Beach

27

Paradera

Santa Cruz

2

Druif
Bay

Oranjestad

1

Reina Beatrix
International
Airport

Balashi

28 – 36

37

N

| 0 | | 4 miles |
| 0 | | 6 km |

Exploring

Bushiribana Gold
Mine, **4**

California Lighthouse, **9**

Frenchman's Pass, **3**

Guadirikiri/Fountein
Caves, **7**

Hooiberg (Haystack
Hill), **2**

Natural Bridge, **8**

Oranjestad, **1**

Savaneta, **6**

Spanish Lagoon, **5**

Dining

Bali Floating
Restaurant, **33**

Bon Appetit, **14**

Boonoonoonous, **34**

Brisas del Mar, **38**

Buccaneer
Restaurant, **35**

Cattle Baron, **22**

Chez Mathilde, **29**

La Dolce Vita, **30**

Old Cunucu House, **15**

The Old Mill, **13**

La Paloma, **11**

Papagayo, **36**

Papiamento, **31**

Talk of the Town
Restaurant, **32**

La Taurina, **37**

Twinklebone's House
of Roastbeef, **12**

Lodging

Americana Aruba
Hotel & Casino, **16**

Aruba Beach Club, **25**

Aruba Concorde Hotel
& Casino, **17**

Aruba Palm Beach
Hotel and Casino, **18**

Atlantis Hotel &
Villas, **10**

Best Western Talk of
the Town Resort, **26**

● Exploring Sites

⑩ Hotels and Restaurants

Caribbean Sea

○ Andicouri

Arikok

Boca Prince

○ Miralamar

❼

Yamanota

❸

❹

Spanish Lagoon

❺

Boca Grandi

Bachelor's Beach

Colorado Pt.

Savaneta

San Nicolas

○ Seroe Colorado

❻ ㊳

Baby Beach

Bushiri Beach
Resort, **28**

Casa del Mar
Beach Resort, **27**

Divi Divi Beach
Resort, **23**

Golden Tulip Aruba
Caribbean Resort &
Casino, **19**

Playa Linda Beach
Resort, **20**

La Quinta Beach
Resort, **21**

Tamarijn Beach
Resort, **24**

Customs and Duties Besides articles for personal use, persons over 18 are allowed one-fifth of liquor and 200 cigarettes, 50 cigars, 250 grams of tobacco, and 2 liters each of alcohol and wine.

Precautions Aruba is a party island, but only up to a point. A police dog sniffs for drugs at the airport.

The strong tradewinds are a relief in the subtropical climate, but don't hang your bathing suit on a balcony—it will probably blow away. And help Arubans conserve water and energy. Turn off air-conditioning when you leave your room and keep your faucets turned off.

Staying in Aruba

Important Addresses **Tourist Information:** The **Aruba Tourism Authority** (L.G. Smith Blvd. 172, Box 1019, tel. 297/8–23777) has free brochures and guides who are ready to answer any questions.

Emergencies **Police:** (tel. 24555). **Hospital:** Horaceo Oduber (tel. 24300). **Pharmacy:** Botica del Pueblo (tel. 21253).

Currency Arubans happily accepts U.S. dollars virtually everywhere, so there's no real need to exchange money, except for necessary pocket change (cigarettes, soda machines, or pay phones). The currency used, however, is the Aruban florin (AFl), which at press time, exchanged to the U.S. dollar at AFl for 1.68 for cash and, AFl 1.79 for traveler's checks, and to the Canadian dollar at AFl 1.30. Major credit cards and travelers checks are widely accepted, but you will probably be asked to show identification when cashing a traveler's check. Prices quoted here are in U.S. dollars unless otherwise noted.

Taxes and Service Charges Hotels collect a 5% government tax. The departure tax is $9.50. Hotels add an 11% service charge on rooms and a 15% service charge on food and beverages; restaurants usually add a 15% service charge to your bill.

Guided Tours *Orientation* It's easy to rent a car, jeep, or motorbike in Aruba and go exploring—most of the highways are in excellent condition—but guided tours save time and energy. **De Palm Tours** (L. G. Smith Blvd. 142, Box 656, tel. 297/8–24545 or 297/8–24400; telex 5049 DPALM B+NA Cable DPTOURS; has a near-monopoly on the Aruban sightseeing business; reservations may be made through its general office or at its hotel branches. The basic 2½-hour tour hits the high spots of the island. Wear tennis or hiking shoes (there'll be optional climbing) and note that the air-conditioned bus can get cold. The tour, which begins at 9:30 AM, picks you up in your lobby and costs $12.50 per person.

Special-Interest **Corvalou Tours** offers unusual excursions for specialized interests. The Archeological/Geological Tour involves a four- to six-hour field trip through Aruba's past, including the huge monoliths and rugged, desolate north coast. Also available are architectural, bird-watching, and botanical tours. The fee for all tours is $40 per person, $70 per couple, with special prices for parties of five or more. Contact the Aruba Tourism Authority (*see* Important Addresses and Numbers, above) for arrangements.

For a three-in-one tour of prehistoric Indian cultures, volcanic formations, and natural wildlife, contact archeologist E. Boerstra of **Marlin Booster Tracking, Inc.** at Charlie's Bar (tel.

297/8–45086). The fee for a six-hour tour is $30 per person, including cold picnic lunch and beverages. Tours can be given in English, Dutch, German, and French.

Hikers will enjoy a guided three-hour trip to remote sites of unusual natural beauty, accessible only on foot. The fee is $25 per person, including refreshments and transportation; a minimum of four people is required. Contact **Windsurfing Aruba** (tel. 297/8–21036) or **De Palm Tours** (tel. 297/8–24545).

Boat Cruises If you try a cruise around the island, know that trimarans are much smoother than three-sail boats; people with queasy stomachs will be helped by lemon or lime candy, but avoid going on an empty stomach.

Midnight cruises, though stunning, are appreciated most by honeymooners. Prices run about $20 per person. Contact **Pelican Watersports** (tel. 297/8–24739) or De Palm Tours (tel. 297/8–24545).

Three-hour trimaran cruises with an hour's stop for swimming and snorkeling run daily; fee is $17.50 per person. On Monday, Wednesday, Friday, and Saturday, enjoy two-hour sunset cruises, including snacks and drinks, for $20 per person. Pelican Watersports (tel. 297/8–24739).

You can swim, sunbathe, and snorkel on a Fun Cruise on a 51-foot catamaran to the west coast of Oranjestad and to De Palm's privately owned coral island. The fee of $38.50 per person includes games and a treasure hunt. Contact De Palm Tours (tel. 297/8–24545).

On a sunset cruise to the soft white sands of Surfside Beach, you can eat barbecue and dance to the tropical sounds of a steel band. Fee of $40 per person includes all the food you can eat. Contact De Palm Tours (tel. 297/8–24545).

Take a 97-foot luxury cruiser to dine at the Marina Pirata. A four-hour round-trip jaunt on the *Maria Monica* will cost $38 per person, which includes dinner. Contact **Ronald de Cuba** (tel. 297/8–34424).

Explore the floor of the sea through a cruise on a glass-bottom boat for $15 per person, from either De Palm Tours (tel. 297/8–24545) or Pelican Watersports (tel. 297/8–24739).

Getting Around A dispatch office is located at Alhambra Bazaar and Boulevard
Taxis Center; you can also flag down taxis on the street. Since taxis do not have meters, rates are fixed and should be confirmed before you take your ride. All Aruba's taxi drivers have participated in the government's Tourism Awareness Programs and have received their Tourism Guide Certificate. An hour's tour of the island by taxi will run you between $20 and $22, for a maximum of five persons.

Rental Cars You'll need a valid U.S. or Canadian driver's license to rent a car, and you must be able to meet the age requirements of each rental service, instigated for insurance reasons. **Budget** (tel. 800/527–0700) requires drivers to be between 23 and 65, **Avis** (tel. 800/331–2112) requires drivers between 25 and 60, and **Hertz** (tel. 800/654–3131) requires drivers to be older than 21. Insurance is available starting at $6 per day, and all companies offer unlimited mileage. Budget and Avis generally have lower rates, but fees, which may range between $25 and $50 a day, are generally determined by the make of the vehicle.

Avis (Kolibristraat 14, tel. 297/8–28787, airport, tel. 297/8–25496), **Budget Rent-A-Car** (Kolibristraat 1, tel. 297/8–28600), **Hertz, De Palm Car Rental** (L. G. Smith Blvd. 142, Box 656, tel. 297/8–24545), **Dollar Rent-a-Car** (Grebedaweg 15, tel. 297/8–22783; airport tel. 297/8–25651, Manchebo tel. 297/8–26696), and **National** (Tank Leendert 170, tel. 297/8–21967, airport tel. 297/8–25451).

Motorcycle and Bike Rentals Rates vary according to the make of vehicle. For a Honda 450cc, ($35 per day), call **Donasine Cycle Car Rental** (Soledad 3, Tank Leendert, tel. 297/8–27041). For Suzuki scooters ($23 day, $100 week), contact **George Cycle Center** (Morgenster 27, Box 434, tel. 297/8–25975). For a fully automatic Moped ($22.50 per day), contact **Aruba Scooters and Mopeds Rentals** (1 Kolibristraat, tel. 297/8–28600).

Buses For inexpensive trips between the beach hotels and Oranjestad, buses run hourly. The fare is 90¢, and exact change is preferred. Contact the Aruba Tourist Bureau for a bus schedule or inquire at your front desk.

Telephones and Mail Local and international calls can be made via hotel operators or from the Government Long Distance Telephone Office, which is in the Post Office in Oranjestad. To dial direct to Aruba, dial 011–297–8, followed by the number in Aruba. When dialing locally in Aruba, simply dial the five-digit number.

Telegrams and telexes may be sent through the Government Telegraph and Radio Office at the Post Office Building in Oranjestad or via your hotel. There is also an ITT office located on Boecoetiweg 33 (tel. 297/8–21458).

You can send an airmail letter from Aruba to the United States for AFl 1.00, a postcard for AFl .60.

Opening and Closing Times Shops are generally open between 8 AM and 6:30 PM. Most stores open through the lunch hour of noon–2 PM, Monday through Saturday. Store hours vary at each hotel. Many stores open when cruise ships are in port on Sunday and holidays. Nighttime shopping at the Alahambra Bazaar runs 5 PM–midnight.

Beaches

Beaches in Aruba are legendary in the Caribbean: white sand, turquoise waters, and virtually no garbage, for everyone takes the "no littering" sign—"No Tira Sushi"—very seriously. The influx of tourists in the past decade, however, has crowded the major beaches, which back up to the hotels along the southwestern strip. These beaches are public, and you can make the one-hour hike from the Holiday Inn to the Bushiri Beach Hotel free of charge and without ever leaving sand. If strolling during the day, make sure you are well protected from the sun—it scorches fast. Luckily, there's at least one covered bar (and often an ice cream stand) at virtually every hotel you pass. If you take the stroll at night, you can literally hotel-hop for dinner, dancing, gambling, and late-night entertainment. On the northern side of the island, heavy tradewinds make the waters too choppy for swimming, but the vistas are great and the terrain is wonderfully suited to sunbathing and geological explorations. Among the finer beaches are these:

Fishermans' Hut. Next to the Holiday Inn, this beach is a windsurfer's haven. Take a picnic lunch (tables are available) and watch the elegant purple, aqua, and orange Windsurfer sails struggle in the wind.

Palm Beach. Called one of the 10 best beaches in the world by the *Miami Herald*, this is the stretch behind the Americana Aruba, Concorde, Aruba Palm Beach, and Holiday Inn hotels. It's the center of Aruban tourism, offering the best in swimming, sailing, snorkeling, fishing, and scuba diving. During high season, however, it's a sardine can.

Manchebo Beach. In front of the Manchebo Beach Resort, this impressively wide stretch of white powder is Aruba's "topless" beach. Most of the sunbathers, though, tend to remain horizontal, so feel free to stroll by.

Eagle Beach. Across the highway from La Quinta Resort, Eagle Beach is one of the last undiscovered stretches on the southern coast. In late 1988, very early in the morning, it was a nearly deserted isle, with only one or two joggers in sight.

Baby Beach. On the island's eastern tip, this tiny strip is as placid as a wading pool and only four to five feet deep—perfect for tots and terrible swimmers. Thatched shaded areas are good for cooling off.

B.A. Beach. On the north of San Nicolas, this gorgeous beach is perfect for windsurfing. The view from the highway is dramatic, with huge sloping dunes dotted with cacti and blue-green crashing waves.

Boca Grandi. Just west of B.A. Beach, on the northwest coast (near the Seagrape Grove and the Aruba Golf Club), Boca Grandi is excellent for wave jumping and windsurfing.

Boca Prince. Near the Fontaine Cave and Blue Lagoon, this beach is about as large as a Brazilian bikini, but with two rocky cliffs and tumultuously crashing waves, it's as romantic as you get in Aruba.

Exploring Aruba

Numbers in the margin correspond with points of interest on the Aruba map.

Oranjestad ❶ Aruba's charming Dutch capital is best explored on foot. Take a taxi or bus from your hotel to the corner of L.G. Smith Boulevard and Arnold Shuttestraat. Cruise ships dock very close to here, and if you arrive early enough, you may find a Venezuelan trade ship selling fruits, vegetables, and other goods right on the dock. At the corner of Shuttestraat is the **Bali Floating Restaurant,** where you can enjoy fine *rijstaffel* (a Indonesian rice dish) or a cool drink on the outdoor terrace *(see* Dining below).

To reach the main shopping district, turn left onto Shuttestraat, bear left to the plaza, and take the second right. You're now on **Nassaustraat,** the main shopping district of Aruba, offering a variety of clothes, curios, electronic equipment, perfume, and jewelry stores.

If you're interested in Dutch architecture, walk back to the corner of Olde School Straat and go three blocks south (toward the harbor) to **Wilheminastraat.** The oldest and most interesting buildings are located here, some dating back to 1790 when Oranjestad was founded. Walk west, and you'll pass old homes, the library, and the Protestant church.

When you reach Shuttestraat again, turn left and go one block south to Zoutmanstraat. The small **Archeology Museum** is located here, with two rooms of Indian artifacts, farm and domestic utensils, and even skeletons. *Zoutmanstraat 1, tel. 297/8–28979. Admission free. Open weekdays 8–noon, 1:30–4:30.*

One block to the east lies **Fort Zoutman,** the island's oldest building, constructed in 1796 and used as a major fortress in the skirmishes between British and Curaçao troops. The Willem III tower, named for the Dutch monarch of that time, was added in 1868. The fort's Historical Museum displays centuries' worth of Aruba relics and artifacts in an 18th-century lighthouse. *Willem III Toren, tel. 297/8–26099. Admission: 50¢. Open weekdays 9–4.*

Walk one block south and you'll chance upon **Wilhelmina Park,** a small grove of palm trees and flowers overlooking the sea. Head back to Nassaustraat and turn north to the corner of Hendrikstraat to see the **Saint Francis Roman Catholic Church.**

Just behind the church is the **Numismatic Museum,** displaying coins and paper money from more than 400 countries. *Iraussquinplein 2-A, tel. 297/8–28831. Admission free. Open weekdays 7:30–noon and 1–4:30.*

Time Out The motto at **Le Petit Café** (at Mainstreet, corner of Schlepstraat, tel. 297/8-26577) is "Romancing the Stone"—referring to tasty cuisine cooked on hot stones. The low ceiling and hanging plants makes an intimate lunch spot for shoppers. Jumbo shrimps, sandwiches, ice cream, and fresh fruit dishes are light delights.

The Countryside The "real Aruba"—what's left of a wild, untamed beauty—can be found only in the countryside. Before you rent a car and dash off, consider hiring a cab for $10 an hour. Although most of the main highways are well paved, some of the more interesting sights are difficult to find because there are few clear road signs. If you do decide to go it alone, rent a jeep. And get specific instructions. Traffic is sparse, but you'll need to keep a sharp eye out for cars that unexpectedly dart out of driveways. After a rainfall, the dirt roads turn to mush and are dangerous.

Few beaches outside the hotel strip have refreshment stands, so take your own food and drink. And one more caution: Note that there are *no* public bathrooms—anywhere—once you leave Oranjestad, except in the infrequent restaurant.

East to San Nicolas For a shimmering vista of blue-green sea, drive east on L. G. Smith Boulevard toward San Nicolas. Past the airport, you'll ❷ soon see the towering 54-foot peak of **Hooiberg** (Haystack Hill). If you have the energy, climb the 580 steps up to the top for an impressive view of the city.

Just past the drive-in theater (a popular hangout for Arubans), ❸ a road on your left will take you to **Frenchman's Pass:** a dark, luscious stretch of highway arbored by overhanging trees. Local legend claims the French and native Indians warred here during the 17th century for control of the island. Nearby are ❹ the cement ruins of the **Bushiribana Gold Mine** (take the dirt road veering to the right)—a lovely place to picnic, listen to the parakeets, and contemplate the towering cacti. A magnificent gnarled divi divi tree guards the entrance.

Returning to the main road, drive through the area called **⑤ Spanish Lagoon,** where pirates once hid to repair their ships.

⑥ Back on the main highway, pay a visit to **Savaneta,** Aruba's oldest village, also known as the Aruba Sunrise Side. During the heyday of the Exxon refineries, the town was a bustling port; now it's dedicated to tourism, with the main street promenade full of interesting kiosks. The **China Clipper Bar** on Main Street used to be a famous "whore" bar frequented by sailors docked in port. These days, the promenade features folkloric shows held at 6 PM on the first Thursday of every month.

Time Out Now an institution, **Charlie's Bar,** Zeppenfeldstraat 56, San Nicolas, tel. 297/8–45086, has been a San Nicolas hangout for artists, writers, and musicians for more than 50 years. During the oil-refinery days, it was a hopping bar for all kinds of rough-and-scrufs. Folks touring San Nicolas stop here for lunch and many leave mementoes behind—witness the bras, panties, shirts, shoes, and helmets hanging from the ceiling. The specialty is "shrimps—jumbo and dumbo." The bus to San Nicolas stops right at the door.

Anyone looking for geological exotica should head for the northern coast, driving northwest from San Nicolas. Stop at **⑦** the two old Indian caves **Guadirikiri** and **Fontein.** Both were used by the native Indians centuries ago, but you'll have to decide for yourself whether the "ancient Indian inscriptions" are genuine—rumor has it they were added by a European film company that made a movie here years ago. You may enter the caves, but there are no guides available, and bats are known to make appearances. Take your flashlights.

⑧ A few miles up the coast is the **Natural Bridge,** sculpted out of coral rock by centuries of raging wind and sea. Nearby is a café overlooking the water and a souvenir shop stuffed with trinkets, T-shirts, and postcards for reasonable prices.

West of Palm Beach Drive or take a taxi west from the hotel strip to Malmok, where Aruba's wealthiest families reside. Open to the public, **Malmok Beach** is considered one of the finest spots for shelling and snorkeling. Right off the coast here is the wreck of the German ship *Antilla,* which was scuttled in 1940—a favorite haunt for div-**⑨** ers. At the very end of the island stands the **California Lighthouse,** now closed, which is surrounded by huge boulders that look like extraterrestrial monsters; in this stark landscape, you'll feel as though you've just landed on the moon.

What to See and Do with Children

The **children's playground** on L. G. Smith Boulevard across the street from the Talk of the Town Hotel is open Tuesday–Saturday 3:30–6:30, Sundays 11–6:30. Admission: AFl 1 or about U.S. 60¢. For parties, call Mrs. Wekker (tel. 297/8–21059).

The Waterslide at Indian Rock Garden (Hoolberg 77, tel. 297/8–34030) is open on Saturday and Sunday 10–6 (phone during the week for special times). Fees are $1 per hour for pool use and $2 per hour for waterslide use.

Off the Beaten Track

Near the Fontaine and Guadirikiri Caves lies the **Tunnel of Love.** Marco Marlin, a local artist with a quirky sense of humor, will lead you on a 20-minute climb through the heart-shape tunnel past naturally sculpted rocks that look just like the Madonna, Abe Lincoln, and even a jaguar. Depending on your state of mind, the tour and Marco's jokes are either very scary or hysterically funny—and Marco just might call out his bats for you. Afterwards, calm your nerves with a beer at his bar without walls. Warning: The actual climb is difficult for anyone not in average physical condition, and it's definitely not recommended for elderly people or young children who lack coordination. The fee is $3 per person; no reservations are necessary.

Participant Sports

Deep-Sea Fishing With catches ranging from barracuda to kingfish, bonito, and black and yellow tuna, deep-sea fishing is great sport on Aruba, and many charter boats are available. Sail for a half day or a full day. **De Palm Tours** (L.G. Smith Blvd. 142, Box 656, Box 656, tel. 297/8–24400) can arrange parties for up to six people, in boats that range from 24 to 27 feet. Half-day tours, including all equipment, can be arranged for $125–$160 for two people, with special rates for up to six people. Private yachts, manned by independent sea captains, may also be arranged. Check with the Aruba Tourist Authority.

Golf The **Aruba Golf Club** (Golfweg 82, near San Nicolas, tel. 297/8–93485) features a nine-hole course with 20 sand traps, five water hazards, roaming goats, and lots of cacti. There are 11 oiled sand greens, enabling 18-hole tournaments. The clubhouse contains a bar, storage rooms, workshop, and separate men's and women's locker rooms. The course's official U.S. Golf Association rating is 67; greens fees are $4 and a caddy costs $5. Complete golf bags are available for $5.

Horseback Riding One-hour jaunts at **Rancho El Paso** (tel. 297/8–23310) will take you through countryside flanked by cactus, divi-divi trees, and aloe vera plants; two-hour trips also go to the beach. Remember to wear headgear and take lots of suntan lotion.

Snorkeling and With visibility up to 90 feet, Aruban waters are excellent for
Scuba Diving snorkeling in shallow waters, and scuba divers will discover exotic marine life and coral. The *Antilla* shipwreck—a German freighter sunk off the northwest coast of Aruba near Palm Beach—is a favorite spot with divers.

De Palm Tours (L.G. Smith Blvd. 142, Box 656, tel. 297/8–24545 or 297/8–24400; telex 5049 DPALM B+NA; Cable DPTOURS; fax 297/8–23012) has a near-monopoly on all water sports in Aruba; the company maintains a registration desk in the lobby of most of the large hotels, or you can make arrangements directly through its main office. Equipment for both snorkeling and scuba diving is available, as is certified instruction.

Pelican Watersports (Box 1193,, Oranjested, tel. 297/8–24739 or 297/8–23600, ext. 511 or ext. 329) also offers water-sports packages, including snorkeling, scuba diving, sailing, windsurfing, and deep-sea fishing.

Windsurfing **Pelican Watersports** (Box 1193, tel. 297/8–24739) rents equipment and offers instruction with a certified Mistral instructor. Stock boards and custom boards rent for $10 hour, $30 per day, $150 per week, with $100 deposit.

Roger's Windsurf Place (L.G. Smith Blvd. 472, tel. 297/8–21918) offers high-performance lessons with Kiepper and custom boards. Packages available include one complete sailboard plus hotel room for a week, double occupancy; cost is $295 per person during off season, $399 during high season.

Windsurfing is also available through **Windsurfing Aruba** (Boliviastraat 14, Box 256, tel. 297/8–21036), **Windward Leeward Watersports** (Beatrixstraat 29, tel. 297/8–22690), and **De Palm Tours** (L.G. Smith Blvd. 142, Box 656, tel. 297/8–24545).

Shopping

Nassaustraat—Aruba's chief shopping street—makes for a pleasant diversion from the beach and casino life. Duty-free is a magic word here. Major credit cards are welcome virtually everywhere, U.S. dollars are accepted almost as often as local currency, and traveler's checks may be cashed with proof of identity.

Aruba's souvenir and craft stores are full of Dutch porcelains and figurines, as befits the island's Netherlands heritage. Dutch cheese is a good buy (you are allowed to bring up to one pound of hard cheese through U.S. customs), as are hand-embroidered linens and any products made from the native plant aloe vera—sunburn cream, face masks, and skin refresheners. Since there is no sales tax, the price you see on the tag is the price you pay. But one word of warning: Don't pull any bargaining tricks. Arubans consider it rude to haggle.

Native Crafts **Artesania Arubiano** (L.G. Smith Blvd. 78, next to the Aruba Tourism Authority, tel. 297/8–25311). Charming home-crafted pottery and folklore objects d'art.

Good Buys **Artistic Boutique** (Nassaustraat 25, tel. 297/8–23142). Lively enough to have branches at the Aruba Concorde and the Holiday Inn, this chain features Aruba hand-embroidered linens, gold and silver jewelry, Persian carpets and dhurries, porcelain and pottery from Spain, and lots of antiques.

Aruba Trading Company (Nassaustraat 12, tel. 297/8–22600). A name synonymous with old-fashioned reliability, ATC offers internationally known brand names, at 30% discounts, but you have to hunt for them. Perfume and cosmetics are on the first floor, jewelry on the second. Both men's and women's clothes are sold. Low-priced liqueurs are a good buy.

Aquarius (Nassaustraat 9, tel. 297/8–24871). This store features the trendiest names in both apparel and decor; men, women, and children can stock up on Maud Frizon, Gianfranco Ferre, Valentino, Fiorucci, and Fendi merchandise. Chrome trim, track lighting, and ever-present rock music set a fast-track mood.

La Bonbonniere (Nassaustraat 75-AB, tel. 297/8–22375). This dollhouse-size gourmet shop is stocked with chocolates, rum cakes, caviar, and Cuban cigars.

El Globo Aruba (Nassaustraat 70, tel. 297/8–22900). Electronics, cameras, and souvenirs are sold here.

Gandelman's Jewelers (Nassaustraat 5-A, tel. 297/8–29143). A name of distinction in the Caribbean offers Gucci and Swatch watches at reasonable prices, gold bracelets, and pink and red coral. It carries a full line of Gucci accessories, from key chains to handbags.

Little Switzerland (Nassaustraat 14, tel. 2297/8–4360). The Curaçao-based giant in china, crystal, and fine tableware offers good buys on Omega and Rado watches, Swarovski silver, Baccarat crystal, and Lladro figurines. If you don't see what you want, ask and they ship it to you.

Palais Oriental (Nassaustraat 8, tel. 297/8–21510). One of the best stores for Lladro figurines, Delft hand-painted porcelain, jewel-beaded blouses made in India, Vuitton luggage, and Cristofle silver and assorted crystal.

J.L. Penha & Son's (Nassaustraat 11, tel. 297/8–24161). One of the most venerated names in Aruba merchandising, this clothes-and-cosmetics store features Pringle, Lanvin, Dior, and Castoni for women and Givenchy, Pierre Cardin, and Papillon for men.

Wulfsen's (Nassaustraat 51, tel. 297/8–24092). For 18 years one of the highest rated stores in the Netherlands Antilles, Wulfen's offers Italian, French, German, and Dutch fashions for both sexes. The Dutch-line Mexx is a favorite of hip teens Betty Buckley and Mondo are popular for women.

Shopping Malls **The Boulevard Shopping Center** (located on L. G. Smith Blvd., tel. 297/8–23754) is a wood-raftered covered mall that's a pleasure to stroll through, with more than 60 shops, including boutiques, restaurants, and perfumeries. The arcade is lined with tropical plants and caged birds. Shops are open from 9–6.

Dining

Aruba's restaurants serve a cosmopolitan variety of cuisines, although most menus are specifically designed to please American palates—you can get fresh surf and New York turf almost anywhere. Make the effort to try Aruban specialties—*pan bati* is a delicious beaten bread that resembles a pancake, and plantains are similar to cooked bananas.

Dress ranges from casual to elegant, but even the finest restaurants require at the most only a jacket for men, a sundress for women. The air-conditioning does get cold, so don't go bare-armed. And anytime you plan to eat in the open air, remember to douse yourself first with insect repellent—the mosquitos can get unruly.

On Sunday, it may be difficult to find a restaurant outside of the hotels that's open for lunch. One of the best bets is the extensive buffet at the Holiday Inn.

The most highly recommended restaurants are indicated by a star ★ .

Category	Cost*
Expensive	over $15

Moderate	$8-$15
Inexpensive	under $8

*per person, excluding drinks, service, and sales tax (15%)

★ **Chez Mathilde.** This elegant restaurant is in a renovated private home, one of the last surviving 19th-century dwellings in Aruba. The chef is Swiss, the owner is the honorary counsel of Germany, and the French-style menu is constantly being recreated. To the tune of Strauss waltzes, dine on frogs' legs or escargots Dijonaise, or try the *emincée à boeuf*—paper-thin slices of fillet beef spiked with horseradish. The wine list is one of the best on the island. *Havenstraat 23, Oranjestad, tel. 297/8-34968. Reservations required. AE, MC, V. Expensive.*

La Dolce Vita. At one of the most critically acclaimed restaurants in Aruba, start with antipasto (the antipasto bar is free with a coupon from the *Aruba Visitor's Guide*, available at your hotel), then progress to stuffed calamari, bartolucci (fried veal with cheeses and herbs), fettuccine, and zuppa de pesce. *Nassaustraat 164, Oranjested, tel. 297/8-25675. Reservations advised. AE, MC, V. Expensive.*

The Old Mill (Die Olde Molen). A gift from the Queen of Holland, this real Dutch mill was shipped brick by brick to Aruba and reassembled here. The present owner, Bill Waldron, is a native Virginian but has maintained the excellence of the international cuisine. For starters, try the seafood crepe Neptune, nestled in a delicate cheese bed. Also excellent is the shrimp with spinach and cream sauce, or the dutch fries—crunchy little nuggets of potato. Order the ice cream with chocolate liqueur and take the bottle home as a souvenir. A time-sharing condominium complex, including tennis courts, is now being added to the estate. *Palm Beach, tel. 297/8-22060. Reservations required. 2 dinner seatings: 6:30 and 9 PM. AE, MC, V. Expensive.*

★ **Papiamento.** Take Papiamento's winding staircase up 20 steps and enjoy French cuisine in the island's most elegant tropicalia, with massive brass chandeliers, an exquisite garden built into a wall of rock, and a beautiful mahogany floor. A private room with a circular glass window has an eight-seat table. The salad bar is luscious, and entrée specialties include rack of lamb and mixed seafood cooked on a stone. The prize, though, goes to the *poulet grand-mère*, which comes in a clay pot you break with a hammer and then take home. *Wilhelminisatraat 7, tel. 297/8-4544. Reservations required. AE, MC, V. Expensive.*

Talk of the Town Restaurant. Here you'll find candlelight dining and some of the best steaks in town—the owner comes from a family of Dutch butchers. Located in the Talk of the Town Hotel, between the airport and Palm Beach, this fine restaurant is now a member of the elite honorary restaurant society, Chaine de Rotisseurs. Saturday night is prime-rib-as-much-as-you-can-eat night, but seafood specialties are popular, too—such as the crabmeat crepes and the *escargots à la bourguignonne*. *L. G. Smith Blvd., Oranjestad, tel. 297/8-23380. AE, DC, MC, V. Expensive.*

Bali Floating Restaurant. Floating in its own Oriental houseboat and anchored in Oranjestad's harbor, the Bali is considered to have the best Indonesian food on the island. Bamboo rooftops and Indonesian antiques add charm. Sunday buffets are good for quantity and variety; full rijstaffel dinners (rice table with 21 different meat, chicken, shrimp, vegetable,

fruit, and relish dishes) run about $22 per person. Service is
terminally slow but well-meaning. Happy hour 6–8 PM. *L.G.
Smith Blvd., Oranjestad, tel. 297/8–22131. AE, MC, V. Moderate.*

Bon Appetit. With its yellow tablecloths, clay-potted plants,
and burnt-orange beams, this restaurant glows like a beautiful
tan—but it's the savory smells that hook you. Prepared by the
Curaçaoan chef Robert Volkerts, the international cuisine wins
acclaim—*Gourmet* magazine once requested the recipe for his
keshi yena, baked cheese stuffed with meat and condiments.
The roast rack of lamb is a winner. *Palm Beach 29, tel. 297/8–
25241. Reservations required. AE, DC, V. Moderate.*

★ **Boonoonoonoos.** The name—say it just like it looks!—means
extraordinary, and that's no hyperbole for this Austrian-owned
Caribbean bistroquet in the heart of town. Orchids and aloe
veras bloom on the tables and the waitresses wear folkloric ruf-
fled dresses. Roast chicken Barbados is sweet and tangy,
marinated in pineapple and cinnamon and simmered in fruit
juices. The Jamaican jerk ribs (a 300-year-old recipe) are tiny
but spicy, and the satin-smooth hot pumpkin soup drizzled with
cheese and served in a pumpkin shell might as well be dessert.
*Wilhelminastraat 18A, tel. 297/8–31888. Reservations ad-
vised. AE, V. Closed Sun. Moderate.*

Buccaneer Restaurant. Imagine you're in a sunken ship—fish
nets and turtle shells hang from the ceiling, and through the
portholes you see live sharks, barracudas, and groupers swimming by. That's the Buccaneer, snug in an old stone building
flanked by heavy black chains and boasting a fantastic 5,000-
gallon saltwater aquarium, plus 12 more porthole-size tanks.
The surf-and-turf cuisine is prepared by the chef-owners with
European élan, and the tables are always full. Order the fresh
catch of the day, or more exotic fare such as shrimps with pernod; smoked pork cutlets with sausage, sauerkraut, and
potatoes; or the turtle steak with a light cream sauce. Go early
(around 5:45 PM) to get a booth next to the aquariums. *Gasparito
11-C., Oranjestad, tel. 297/8–26172. Reservations not accepted. AE, MC, V. Closed Sun. Moderate.*

Cattle Baron. From the "Welcome pardner" sign on the front
door to the cattle horns, wagon wheels, and Jesse James
wanted posters, this Texas cowpokery feels very un-Aruban.
Situated next to La Quinta Resort Hotel, this is a cool dark
place to come into out of the sun. Prime rib, barbecued ribs,
sirloins, and Dutch steak are specialties; the porterhouse is immense. Other options include snapper Arubiano, panbroiled
with Creole sauce and served with fried plantains. *L.G. Smith
Blvd., 228 Eagle Beach, tel. 297/8–22977. AE, MC, V. Moderate.*

Old Cunucu House. Situated on a small estate in a residential
neighborhood three minutes from the high rises, this 70-year-
old Aruban home has been renovated into a restaurant of casual
élan. Dine on local recipes for red snapper, coconut-fried
shrimp, Cornish hen, and New York sirloins, or beef fondue à
deux. Private dining rooms hold groups up to 20. Happy hour
5–6 PM. *Palm Beach 150, tel. 297/8–31666. Reservations suggested. AE, DC, MC. Closed Mon. Moderate.*

★ **La Paloma.** "The Dove" has an air of low-key loveliness with no
gimmicks, and it's usually packed. The restaurant has its own
fishing boat, so the fish is always fresh. There's conch stew
with *pan bati* and fried bananas for exotic tastes. Minestrone

soup is a house specialty. *Noord 39, tel. 297/8–24611. AE, MC, V. Closed Tues. Moderate.*

Papagayo. This is a noisy restaurant crazy with the sound of cawing parrots and squeaking parakeets; it's even moist from the tropical plants that hang everywhere. Waitresses are dressed in tight mumus with flowers in their hair. The view of the harbor is superb and the northern Italian kitchen has a fine reputation for linguine with lobster, chicken Papagayo (stuffed breast), and prime cuts of meat. *Boulevard Shopping Center, Oranjestad, tel. 297/8–24140. Reservations required. AE, MC, V. Moderate.*

La Taurina. Spanish bullfighting fans will enjoy the paintings of toreadors as well as the antique gun and fans decorating the wall. Basic surf and turf is served; the shrimp with mushrooms is a big hit. *Nassaustraat 149, tel. 297/8–26780. AE, MC, V. Happy hour 5–7 PM. Moderate.*

Twinklebone's House of Roastbeef. Prime rib with Yorkshire pudding is the kitchen's pride, but there's a full international menu with dishes named after local friends and residents. The chef is known to leave the stove and sing Aruban tunes with the maitre d'. *Turibana Plaza, Noord 124, tel. 297/8–26806. Reservations advised. AE, MC, V. Closed Sun. Moderate.*

★ **Brisas del Mar.** A cozy, friendly 10-table place that is popular with tourists because you'll feel as if you're dining in an Aruban home overlooking the sea. The menu features mostly fried fish with spicy sauces of tomatoes and onions served with loads of *funchi* (cornmeal squares) and *pan bati*. To find it, drive east in Oranjestad on L. G. Smith Boulevard to the town of Savaneta, 10 miles away. *Savaneta 22A, tel. 297/8–47718. Reservations suggested. No credit cards. Closed Mon. Inexpensive.*

Lodging

All the hotels in Aruba are located west of Oranjestad along L. G. Smith Boulevard. They generally include a host of facilities—drugstores, boutiques, health spas, beauty parlors, casinos, restaurants, pool bars, and gourmet delis. Do not arrive in Aruba without a reservation; many hotels are booked seasons in advance. Their restaurants and clubs, however, are open to all guests on the island, so you can visit other properties no matter where you're staying. Look out for Charlie, the island's coconut expert, who makes constant rounds of the hotels demonstrating his special talent: devastating a coconut samurai style in three seconds.

The most highly recommended lodgings are indicated by a star ★.

Category	Cost*
Very Expensive	over $115
Expensive	$90–$115
Moderate	$60–$90
Inexpensive	under $60

All prices are for a standard double room for two, excluding 5% tax and a 10% service charge.

Casa del Mar Beach Resort. This beachfront low rise featuring completely furnished suites is one of Aruba's most expensive time-shares. The two-bedroom suites each have a dining table seating six; the full kitchen comes stocked with an eight-piece table service. Baby-sitters are on call, and a social hostess provides children's programs. *L. G. Smith Blvd. 53, Punta Brabo Beach, tel. 297/8–27000; in NY 212/563–6940. 32 2-bedroom suites, 75 2-bedroom suites. Facilities: restaurant (2 restaurants and pool bar at sister property), lobby bar, TVs with in-room movie satellite, fitness center, sauna and massage, pool, 2 Jacuzzis, 2 lighted tennis courts, children's playground, shops. AE, DC, MC, V. Very Expensive.*

Americana Aruba Hotel & Casino. This luxurious high rise located on Palm Beach, is a haven for Americans, with most of the social activity centered around the large pool area and casino. A shopping mall with seven boutiques makes trips into town nearly irrelevant. Guests at the spectacular Stellaris Gourmet Dinner Club enjoy nightly cabaret shows at 9:15 PM, with full-course dinners running about $25–$30. *L. G. Smith Blvd. 83, Palm Beach, tel. 297/8–24500 or 800/223–1588; in NY, 212/661 –4540. 406 rooms. Facilities: restaurants, coffee shop, ice cream parlor, swimming pool with pool bar, TV, tennis, ground tour/water-sports center, laundry/valet, car rentals, telex/xerox/typewriters, boutiques, beauty parlor/barber shop. AE, DC, MC, V. Expensive.*

Aruba Concorde Hotel & Casino. At 18 stories, the Concorde rates as Aruba's highest building. The terraced guest rooms are all air-conditioned; the marble-and-chrome lobby feels like a Four Seasons, only slightly downscaled. It's not a lobby to traipse through in your bikini, but during happy hour, the piano bar and surrounding couches make an elegant place to relax (and meet rich South Americans). The boutique row offers luxurious items, such as gold jewelry, designer clothes, fine perfumes, and leather bags. The Olympic-size pool and day-and-night tennis make fine alternatives to the omnipresent ocean sports. Dining possibilities befit the cosmopolitan ambience: from northern Italian (Adriana's) to the elegant Continental cuisine of Le Serre to intimate late-night suppering at Rendez-Vous Gourmet. Club Arubesque, off the main lobby, is a nightclub, complete with showgirls, and the casino competes with that of the Aruba Caribbean for biggest on the island. *L. G. Smith Blvd. 77, Palm Beach, tel. 297/8–24466 or 800/223–7944; in NY 212/757–8989. 500 rooms. Facilities: 6 restaurants, nightclub, casino, 3 cocktail lounges, pool, 2 lighted tennis courts, massage room, game room, car rental, ground tours and water sports, ballroom with meeting and banquet rooms, shops, beauty parlor, deli, children's corner. AE, DC, MC, V. Expensive.*

Aruba Palm Beach Hotel & Casino. Formerly a Sheraton and now government-owned, this pink-blue-and-white Moorish palazzo even has pink-swaddled palm trees dotting its drive. The lobby, with its impressive grand piano, is a haze of pink and purple, underlaid with cool marble. The large backyard sunning grounds are a well-manicured tropical garden, with a fleet of pesky parrots guarding the entrance. Guest rooms are air-conditioned, roomy, and cheerful, with tiny balconies, baths with separate dressing areas, and large walk-in closets. All overlook either the ocean, the pool, or the gardens. For entertainment, try the chrome-glitzed disco Galactica Lounge or the dinner-cum-floor-show (about $30 per person) at the elegant Rembrandt Room. *L. G. Smith Blvd. 79, Palm Beach, tel. 297/ 8–23900 or 800/344–1212; in NY 212/832–2277. 200 rooms. Fa-*

cilities: 2 restaurants, pool, coffee shop, disco, TV, shops, beauty shop. AE, DC, MC, V. Expensive.

★ **Divi Divi Beach Resort.** One of the more popular low rises, the Divi Divi's motto is "barefoot elegance," which means you can streak through the lobby in your bikini. The main section has 90 standard guest rooms, 20 lanai rooms, and 40 casitas (garden bungalows) that look out onto individual courtyards. A newer section, Divi Dos, contains 49 luxury rooms and 1 suite, all with ocean view and Jacuzzi bathtubs. All rooms are air-conditioned. Divi Divi has the reputation of being a honeymoon hotel —special packages that include champagne breakfast, "just married" signs, photo albums, and fruit baskets are available. The free-form pool includes a small island with a teahouse at the center, accessible by a bridge. A breakfast buffet is served on the Pelican Terrace, just steps away from the sea ($8.75 plus 15% service). Special theme nights include Tuesday's Carnaval and Saturday's Beach barbecue, with folkloric show and steel band. *L. G. Smith Blvd. 45, Punta Brabo Beach, tel. 297/8–23300 or 800/367–DIVI. 200 rooms. Facilities: 4 restaurants, TV, radio, ceiling fan, free-form pool, swimming pool, Jacuzzis, tennis courts, shuffleboard, shops, ground tours and water sports. AE, MC, V. Expensive.*

Tamarijn Beach Resort. A sprawling melange of two-story white stucco town houses opens onto one of the longest beachfronts (1 mile) in Aruba. The ambience is barefoot casual: the staff even discourages jackets. All rooms have a beachfront view and are air-conditioned. Guests can ride to the Alhambra Casino and the Divi Divi Beach Hotel in free carts, and exchange privileges have been arranged with the Divi Divi Beach resort, including nightly entertainment. The poolside bar stays open til 1 AM. *L. G. Smith Blvd. 64, Punta Brabo Beach, tel. 297/8–24150 or 800/367–DIVI. 236 rooms. Facilities: 1 restaurant, 2 bars, radio, pool, tennis courts, 2 Jacuzzis, shops, activities center. AE, MC, V. Expensive.*

Golden Tulip Aruba Caribbean Resort & Casino. Called La Grand Dame of the Caribbean, the Golden Tulip was the first high rise on the island and still lives up to its stylish standards, having been renovated in 1984–86. Liz Taylor used to stay here when she was married to Eddie Fisher, and the Queen of Holland still stays in the Royal Suite (available on request), so the staff is used to filling special needs. The turquoise-and-white tiled lobby gives the feeling of an Art Deco tropical palazzo, and even the hallways are lined with trees. The sunny air-conditioned rooms, all with some ocean view, are scattered among four buildings, with added balconies for private sunning. The fitness center on the top floor offers a Universal weight system, squash and raquetball courts, rowing machine, and aerobics classes. French and American wine tastings are held on Monday night; nightly shows are held in the blue-and-gold Fandango Nightclub. *L. G. Smith Blvd. 81, Palm Beach, tel. 297/8–33555. 400 rooms. Facilities: 4 restaurants, 4 bars, nightclub, meeting and banquet rooms, casino, pool, 4 lighted tennis courts, fitness center, ground tours and water sports, putting green, videogame room, laundry and dry cleaning, shops, beauty parlor, deli. AE, MC, V. Expensive.*

Playa Linda Beach Resort. Designed in a ziggurat of receding balconies, this time-share complex sits on a enticing stretch of white sandy beach sheathed in a facade of terra-cotta and cream. Accommodations are stylishly comfortable, outfitted with private kitchens, verandas, and air-conditioning. Units (all of which are suites) sleep four–six persons. Rates vary according to season. All three meals heartily served at the open-air Palapa Restaurant. Water sports and tennis can be arranged. *L. G. Smith Blvd. 87, Palm Beach, tel. 297/8–31000; in NJ 201/617–8877. 192 1-bedroom and 12 2-bedroom suites. Facilities: restaurant, bar, TV, radio, activity center, adults' and children's pools, tennis courts, minimarket/gift shop. AE, MC, V. Expensive.*

Aruba Beach Club. This attractive low-rise resort on Druif Beach also doubles as a time-share. The open-air lobby leads to a patio, gardens, and pool, with the beach only a few steps beyond. Action settles around the pool bar, with a clientele that's mostly American, mostly young-to-middle-aged marrieds. The rooms are air-conditioned and tastefully designed with balconies and kitchenettes. *L. G. Smith Blvd. 53, Punta Brabo Beach, tel. 297/8–23000. 133 suites. Facilities: 2 restaurants, cocktail lounge, pool bar, ice cream parlor, satellite TV, radio, pool (adult and children's), 2 lighted tennis courts, children's playground, baby-sitting service. AE, MC, V. Moderate.*

Atlantis Hotel & Villas. Set on the island side of Palm Beach, north of the high-rise hotels and near Malmok, this property offers fully furnished air-conditioned apartments that sleep five and have full kitchens. You'll have to cross the street to get to the beach, however. Weekly and monthly rates are available. *Salina Cerca 51, Nooord, Oranjestad, tel. 297/8–24343 or 800/223–6114; in NY 212/661–6565. 76 apartments. Facilities: restaurant, nightclub, satellite TV, pool, laundry service, game room, arrangements with water-sports and tour operators, baby-sitting. AE, MC, V. Moderate.*

★ **Best Western Talk of the Town Resort.** Originally a run-down chemical plant, Talk of the Town was transformed by two Floridians into a first-class resort. It gets its name from the excellent on-premises restaurant (*see* Dining, above). A huge pool is at the center of this two-story motel-like structure, with all the guest rooms overlooking the charming Spanish-style courtyard. Some accommodations have kitchens and all offer TV, air-conditioning, and minifridges. There's also a heated hydrotherapy whirlpool bath. The tropical cafe/cabaret Temptations on the beach is one of Aruba's jumpiest night spots, and add-on packages for dinner and entertainment elsewhere on the island can be bought at the hotel at a 20% discount. The beach is just 200 yards from your door and Oranjestad's shopping center is a 15-minute stroll away. *L. G. Smith Blvd. 2, tel. 297/8–23380; in NY 212/628–3319; or 800/233–1108. 63 rooms. Facilities: 3 restaurants, nightclub, cable TV, free scheduled transportation, facilities exchange with Manchebo Beach Hotel, gift shop, beach across the road. AE, MC, V. Moderate.*

Bushiri Beach Resort. This long, low attractive building is the first beach hotel you encounter driving out of Oranjestad. Associated with a hotel school, it's a real bargain and has an enthusiastic staff. All rooms are air-conditioned and have ocean views. The Flamboyan Restaurant makes for good dining. Due to its proximity to town, the Bushiri attracts businessmen. *L. G. Smith Blvd. 35, tel. 297/8–25216 or 800/622–7836. 150 rooms. Facilities: 2 restaurants, pool bar, cocktail lounge, piano bar, pool, satellite TV, tennis courts, night entertainment, beach, water sports center, drugstore. AE, DC, MC, V. Moderate.*

★ **La Quinta Beach Resort.** This new resort designed by a Venezuelan architect is in the middle of several phases of construction, but the work has been planned so as not to disturb guests. La Quinta is a low rise with the sophistication of a high rise; the one- and two-bedroom suites are spacious, with full cooking facilities, two TVs (including a VCR), and a shower/bath combo. The hotel is across the street from Eagle Beach and only a five-minute walk to the casino at Alhamrba (*see* Nightlife, below). *Eagle Beach, tel. 297/8–35010. Facilities: restaurant, bar, cocktail lounge, pool, cable TV, VCR with cassette rentals, fitness center, tennis courts, raquetball courts. AE, DC, MC, V. Moderate.*

Nightlife

Casinos The hottest casino action on the island can be found in the **Alhambra Casino** (L. G. Smith Blvd. 93, Oranjestad, tel. 297/8–25434), where a "Moorish slave" gives every gambler a hearty handshake upon entering. The Alhambra is decorated like a Morroccan bazaar, complete with numerous restaurants and more than 30 boutiques—including the New York Deli, which is open 24 hours. If you're staying at any of the three Divi Divi Hotels, you'll enjoy free transportation to and from your lobby.

There's also action along the Oranjestad "strip" in the casinos at the **Aruba Concorde Hotel** (L. G. Smith Blvd. 77, tel. 297/8–24466) and the **Golden Tulip Caribbean** (L. G. Smith Blvd. 81, tel. 297/8–33555). The **Holiday Inn's** casino (L. G. Smith Blvd., tel. 297/8–23600) is open 22 hours a day, with an adjacent New York–style deli open until 5 AM. The **Americana Hotel Casino** (L. G. Smith Blvd. 83, tel. 297/8–24500) opens daily at 1 PM for slots, 9 PM for all games. The **Aruba Palm Beach Hotel Casino** (L. G. Smith Blvd. 79, tel. 297/8–23900) opens at 9 PM.

Disco and Dancing **Alhambra's Roseland Night Club/Disco** (Alhambra Complex, L. G. Smith Blvd. 93, tel. 297/8–25434). Originally a bandstand, Roseland in the Alhambra complex looks dark and scary from the outside, but only lacks intimacy once you're inside. Mostly a disco for teens 16–18.
Le Visage (L. G. Smith Blvd. 93, tel. 297/8–35000). Almost like an adult amusement park, Le Visage is an in-spot disco for both Arubans and tourists. Arubans usually start partying late, and action doesn't start till around midnight, mostly on the weekends. Besides dancing, there are three slot machines, video games, two wide-screen TVs, two bars, five pool tables, ping pong, and pinball—and even condom machines in the bathroom. The Sirena Cocktail Lounge offers light snacks; the specialty is deep-fried chicken wings.
Contempo Disco (Talk of the Town Hotel, L. G. Smith Blvd. 2, Oranjestad, tel. 297/8–23380). This is a convenient place to dance after a festive meal at the Talk of the Town restaurant next door.
Club Scaramouche (Boulevard Shopping Center, Oranjestad, tel. 297/8–24954). In this trendy chrome-and-mirrored disco, you may brush shoulders with the local beauties who vie for the Mr. and Miss Aruba contests. Cushy banquettes surround a circular bar; there are also pool tables.
Temptations on the Beach (L. G. Smith Blvd. 2, across from, and owned by Talk of the Town hotel, tel. 297/8–23380). This beach-bum café-cum-cabaret is so casual that you mix your own drinks between 6 and 10:30 PM. Munch on tapas as you listen to jazz, disco, steel bands, and native merengues and tumbas.

Hotels with lounges that feature live bands include the **Aruba Concorde Hotel** (L. G. Smith Blvd. 77, Palm Beach, tel. 297/8–24466), the **Aruba Beach Club** (L. G. Smith Blvd. 53, Punta Brabu Beach, tel. 297/8–23000), the **Golden Tulip Aruba Caribbean Hotel** (L. G. Smith Blvd. 81, tel. 297/8–33555), the **Holiday Inn** (L. G. Smith Blvd. 230, tel. 297/8–23600), the **Best Western Manchebo Beach Resort Hotel** (L. G. Smith Blvd. 55, Punta Brabu Beach, tel. 297/8–23444), **Divi Divi Beach Resort** (L. G. Smith Blvd. 93, Punta Brabu Beach, tel. 297/8–23300), the **Bushiri Beach Resort** (L. G. Smith Blvd. 35, tel. 297/8–25216), the **Americana Hotel** (L. G. Smith Blvd. 83, tel. 297/8–24500), and the **Tamarijn Beach Resort** (L. G. Smith Blvd. 64, Punta Brabo Beach, tel. 297/8–24150).

Theater **Aruba Dance Theater** (L. G. Smith Blvd. 81, tel. 297/8–33555). Held at the Golden Tulip Hotel's Pelican Terrace, Saturday's Aruban night features native dancers in bright folkloric costumes in an open-air pavilion. Children will love the rooster dance and the maypole ribbons. Dine during the shows.

Aladdin Theater (L. G. Smith Blvd. 93, tel. 297/8–25434). This cabaret theater tucked into the Alhambra Bazaar features a variety of shows—the last one seen was unabashedly American, with film clips from *That's Entertainment* and skits out of *Gone with the Wind*. Go only if you're homesick. There's free popcorn.

5 Barbados

by Joan Iaconetti

A writer, photographer, and communications consultant based in New York, Joan Iaconetti is an avid scuba diver who spends winters on the island of Bequia. Her articles have appeared in Travel & Leisure, Travel-Holiday, Cosmopolitan, *and* Self.

Barbados seems to have a life of its own that goes on after the tourists have packed their sun-oils and returned home. Since the government is stable and unemployment relatively low, the difference between haves and have-nots is less marked—or at least less visible—than on other islands, and visitors are neither fawned upon nor resented for their assumed wealth. Genuinely proud of their country, the quarter million Bajans welcome visitors as privileged guests. Barbados is fine for people who want nothing more than to offer their bodies to the sun; yet the island, unlike many in the Caribbean, is also ideal for travelers who want to discover another life and culture.

Because the beaches of Barbados are open to the public, they lack the privacy that some visitors seek; but the beaches themselves are lovely, and many along the tranquil west coast—in the lee of the northwest trade winds—are backed by first-class resorts. Most of the hotels are situated along the beaches on the southern and southwestern coasts. The British and Canadians often favor the hotels of St. James Parish; Americans (couples more often than singles) tend to prefer the large south coast resorts.

To the northeast are rolling hills and valleys covered by acres of impenetrable sugarcane. The Atlantic surf pounds the gigantic boulders along the rugged east coast, where the Bajans themselves have their vacation homes. Elsewhere on the island, linked by almost 900 miles of good roads, are historic plantation houses, stalactite-studded caves, a wildlife preserve, and the Andromeda Gardens, one of the most attractive small tropical gardens in the world.

No one is sure whether the name *los Barbadoes* ("the bearded ones") refers to the beardlike root that hangs from the island's fig trees or to the bearded natives who greeted the Portuguese "discoverer" of the island in 1536. The name Los Barbados was still current almost a century later when the British landed—by accident—in what is now Holetown in St. James Parish. They colonized the island in 1627 and remained until it achieved independence in 1966.

Barbados retains a British accent. Afternoon tea is habitual at numerous hotels. Cricket is still the national sport, producing some of the world's top cricket players. Polo is played in winter. The British tradition of dressing for dinner is firmly entrenched; a few luxury hotels require tie and jacket at dinner, and in good restaurants most women will consider themselves inappropriately dressed in anything less formal than a sundress. (A daytime stroll in Bridgetown in a swimsuit is as inappropriate as it would be on New York's 5th Avenue.) Yet the island's atmosphere is hardly stuffy. When the boat you ordered for noon doesn't arrive until 12:30, you can expect a cheerful response, "He okay, mon, he just on Caribbean time." Translation: No one, including you, needs to be in a hurry here.

Before You Go

Tourist Information Contact the **Barbados Board of Tourism** (800 2nd Ave., New York, NY 10017, tel. 212/986-6516); additional offices are in Los Angeles and in Winter Park, Florida. Barbados is also represented by Peter Rotholtz Assoc., Inc. (380 Lexington Ave., New York, NY 10017, tel. 212/687-6565).

Arriving and Grantley Adams Airport in Barbados is a Caribbean hub.
Departing There are daily nonstop flights from New York on **American**
By Plane **Airlines** (tel. 800/433–7300), **Pan Am** (tel. 800/221–1111), and
BWIA (tel. 800/327–7401); from Washington, DC, on Pan Am;
from Miami on Pan Am and BWIA. From Canada, **Air Canada**
(tel. 800/422–6232) connects from Montreal through New York
or Miami and flies nonstop from Toronto. From London, **British
Airways** (tel. 800/247–9297) has nonstop service and BWIA connects through Trinidad.

Flights to St. Vincent, St. Lucia, Trinidad, and other islands
are scheduled on LIAT and BWIA; Air St. Vincent/Air
Mustique links Barbados with St. Vincent and the Grenadines.

From the Airport Airport taxis are not metered. A large sign at the airport an-
nounces the fixed rate to each hotel or area, stated in both
Barbados and U.S. dollars (about $20 to the west coast hotels,
$13 to the south coast). The new highway around Bridgetown
saves time and trouble in getting up the western coast.

By Boat A popular cruise port, Barbados has room for eight ships
(which is some indication of how crowded the Bridgetown shops
can be). Bridgetown Harbour is located on the northwest side
of Carlisle Bay, and most cruise ships organize transportation
to and from the new **Carlisle Bay Centre,** a "hotel without
rooms" for passengers on shore excursions. The CBC provides
changing facilities, a restaurant, gift shops, and water sports
facilities—including floats, snorkel equipment, Sunfish sailboats, waterskiing, Windsurfers—for a nominal fee.

Passports American and Canadian citizens need proof of citizenship plus a
and Visas return or ongoing ticket to enter the country. Acceptable proof
of citizenship is a valid passport or an original birth certificate
and a photo ID; a voter registration card is not acceptable. British citizens need a valid passport.

Customs Barbados is a noted free port where most duty-free items can
and Duties be bought over the counter when you show your passport or air/
sea ticket. Items that must be delivered to your point of departure are tobacco, wines, and video/stereo/computer equipment.

Language English is spoken everywhere, sometimes accented with the
phrases and lilt of a Bajan dialect.

Precautions Beach vendors of coral jewelry and beachwear will not hesitate
to offer you their wares, but they are mercifully less persistent
here than on other islands. One hotel's brochure gives sound
advice: "Please realize that encouraging the beach musicians
means you may find yourself listening to the same three tunes
over and over for the duration of your stay."

Water The water on the island, both in hotels and in restaurants, has
been treated and is safe to drink.

Insects Insects aren't much of a problem on Barbados, but if you plan to
hike or spend time on secluded beaches, it's wise to use insect
repellent.

Toxic Tree Little green apples that fall from the large branches of the
manchineel tree may look tempting, but they are poisonous to
eat and toxic to the touch. Even taking shelter under the tree
when it rains can give you blisters. Most manchineels are identified with signs; if you do come in contact with one, go to the
nearest hotel and have someone there phone for a physician.

Barbados

Cunard Paradise Beach Hotel, **46**
Discovery Bay Hotel, **36**
Divi St. James Beach Resort, **40**
Divi Southwinds Beach Hotel, **61**
Glitter Bay, **32**
Golden Palms, **35**
Grand Barbados Beach Resort, **47**
Heywoods Barbados, **27**
King's Beach Hotel, **28**
Marriott's Sam Lord's Castle, **66**
Ocean View, **55**
Sandy Beach Resort, **57**
Sandy Lane, **41**
Settlers' Beach, **31**
Sichris Hotel, **58**
Southern Palms, **62**

Crime	While there is little crime on Barbados, you don't want to invite trouble by leaving valuables unattended on the beach or in plain sight in your room.
Further Reading	*In the Castle of My Skin*, an autobiographical novel by George Lamming (who lives part of each year in the Atlantis Hotel), is a lyrical remembrance of growing up in the West Indies, told from a young boy's point of view.

Louis Lynch's *The Barbados Book* uses anecdotes to recount the social history of Barbados and to describe the island way of life, past and present.

Local News The daily newspapers include *The Barbados Advocate* and *The Nation* (which appears on Sunday as *The Sun*). They publish, respectively, *The Sun Seeker* and *The Visitor* to keep you informed of current entertainment and sightseeing. The Board of Tourism prepares the free "Official Guide to Barbados" and the "Things You Should Know" brochures; they are well worth reading before you begin a serious exploration of the island.

Staying in Barbados

Important Addresses **Tourist Information: The Barbados Board of Tourism** is on Harbour Road in Hastings (tel. 809/427–2623).

Emergencies **Emergency:** tel. 119.

Ambulance: tel. 61113.

Police: tel. 112.

Fire department: tel. 113.

Scuba diving accidents: Divers' Alert Network (DAN) (tel. 919/684–8762 or 919/684–2948). Barbados recompression chamber, Barbados Defense Force, St. Ann's Fort, Garrison, St. Michael Parish (tel. 809/427–8819).

Currency One Barbados dollar (BDS$1) equals about U.S.50¢. Because the value of the Barbados dollar is pegged to that of the U.S. dollar, the ratio remains constant. Both currencies and the Canadian dollar are accepted everywhere on the island, but changing your money to Barbados dollars will get you slightly better value. Prices quoted throughout this chapter are in U.S. dollars unless noted otherwise.

Taxes and Service Charges At the airport you must pay a departure tax of BDS$16 (about U.S.$8) in either currency before leaving Barbados.

A 10% service charge is added to your hotel bill and to most restaurant checks; any additional tip recognizes extraordinary service. When no service charge is added, tip maids $1 per room per day, waiters 10% to 15%, taxi drivers 10%. Airport porters and bellboys expect 25¢ to 50¢ per bag.

Guided Tours For an island of its size (14 miles by 21 miles), Barbados has a lot to see. A bus or taxi tour, which can be arranged by your hotel, is a good way to get your bearings. **L. E. Williams Tour Co.** (tel. 809/427–1043) offers an 80-mile island tour for about $40; a bus picks you up at 10 AM and takes you through Bridgetown, the St. James beach area, past the Animal Flower Cave, Farley Hill, Cherry Tree Hill, Morgan Lewis Mill, the east coast, St. John's Church, Sam Lord's Castle, Oistin's fishing village, and to St. Michael Parish, with drinks along the way and a West Indian lunch at the Atlantis Hotel in Bathsheba.

Custom Tours (tel. 809/425–0099 or 809/424–3516) arranges personalized tours for one to four persons. Staff members determine your particular interests (such as gardens, plantation houses, swimming at secluded beaches), pack a picnic lunch, and drive you in their own cars. They offer a familiarization tour for first-time visitors, and often they can take you to places that aren't normally open to the public.

Getting Around Taxis operate at a fixed rate (BDS$30 for the first hour, less af-
Taxis ter that); settle the rate before you start off, and be sure you agree on whether it's in U.S. or Barbados dollars. Most drivers will cheerfully narrate a tour, though the noise of the car may make it difficult for you to follow a rambling commentary colored with Bajan inflections.

Buses Public buses along Highway 1, St. James Road, are cheap (BDS$1, exact change appreciated), plentiful, reliable, and usually packed. The buses provide a great opportunity to experience local color, and your fellow passengers will be eager to share their knowledge.

Rental Cars It's a pleasure to explore Barbados by car, provided you take the time to study a good map and you don't mind asking directions frequently. The more remote roads are in good repair, yet few are well lighted at night, and night falls quickly at about 6 PM. Even in full daylight, the tall sugarcane fields lining a road can create near-zero visibility. Yet local residents are used to pointing travelers in the right direction, and some confused but intelligent drivers have been known to flag a passing taxi and pay to follow it back to a city area. Use caution: Pedestrians are everywhere. And remember, traffic keeps to the left throughout the island.

To rent a car you must have an international driver's license, obtainable at the airport and major car-rental firms for $5 if you have a valid driver's license. More than 40 offices rent minimokes for about $35 a day, usually with a three-day or four-day minimum; cars with automatic shift are $40–$50 a day. Gas costs just over BDS$1 a liter (about $2 a gallon) and is extra. The speed limit, in keeping with the pace of life, is 37 miles per hour (60 kilometers per hour) in the country, 21 miles per hour in town. To operate a motor bike also requires an international driver's license—and some skill and daring.

The principal car rental firms are National (tel. 809/426–0603), Courtesy Car Rentals (tel. 809/426–5871 or 809/428–6744), Dear's Garage on the south coast (tel. 809/429–9277 or 809/427–7853), Sunny Isle in Worthing (809/428–8009 or 809/428–2965), and Sunset Crest Rentals in St. James (tel. 809/432–1482).

Telephones The area code for Barbados (and the entire Caribbean) is 809.
and Mail Except for emergency numbers, all phone numbers have seven digits and begin with 42 or 43.

To send an airmail letter to the United States or Canada costs BDS65¢ per half ounce; an airmail postcard costs 45¢.

Opening and Stores are open weekdays 8–4, Saturday 8–noon. Some super-
Closing Times markets remain open daily 8–6. Banks are open Monday to Thursday 9–3, Friday 9–1 and 3–5.

Beaches

Barbados is blessed with some of the Caribbean's most beautiful beaches, all of them open to the public. (Access to hotel beaches may not always be public, but you can walk onto almost any beach from another one.)

West Coast Beaches The west coast has the stunning coves and white-sand beaches that are dear to postcard publishers—plus calm, clear water for snorkeling, scuba diving, and swimming. The afternoon clouds and sunsets may seem to be right out of a Turner painting; because there is nothing but ocean between Barbados and Africa, the sunsets are rendered even more spectacular by the fine red sand that sometimes blows in from the Sahara.

While beaches here are seldom crowded, the west coast is not the place to find isolation. Owners of private boats stroll by, offering waterskiing, parasailing, and snorkel cruises. There are no concession stands per se, but hotels welcome nonguests for terrace lunches (wear a cover-up). Picnic items and necessities can be bought at the Sunset Crest shopping center in Holetown.

Beaches begin in the north at **Heywoods** (about a mile of sand) and continue almost unbroken to Bridgetown at **Brighton Beach,** a popular spot with locals. There is public access through the Barbados Beach Club and the Barbados Pizza House (both good for casual lunches), south of the Discovery Bay Hotel.

Good spots for swimming include **Paradise Beach,** just off the Paradise Beach Hotel; **Brandon's Beach,** a 10-minute walk south; **Browne's Beach,** in Bridgetown; and **Greaves End Beach,** south of Bridgetown at Aquatic Gap, between the Holiday Inn and the Hilton in St. Michael Parish.

The west coast is the area for scuba diving, sailing, lunch-and-rum cruises on the red-sailed **Jolly Roger "pirate" party ship** (tel. 809/426–0767), and an undersea jaunt on the **Atlantis passenger submarine** (tel. 809/436–8929).

South Coast Beaches The heavily traveled south coast of Christ Church Parish is much more built up than the St. James Parish coast in the west; here are condos, high-rise hotels, many places to eat and shop, and the traffic (including public transportation) that serves them. These busier beaches generally draw a younger, more active crowd. The quality of the beach itself is consistently good, the reef-protected waters safe for swimming and snorkeling. Two of the best are in the St. Lawrence Gap area, near **Southern Palms** and **Casuarina Cove.** The **Barbados Windsurfing Club Hotel** in Maxwell caters specifically to windsurfing aficionados, and most hotels and resorts provide boards or rent them for a nominal fee.

Crane Beach has for years been a popular swimming beach. As you move toward the Atlantic side of the island, the waves roll in bigger and faster; the waves at the nearby Crane Hotel are a favorite with bodysurfers. (But remember that this is the ocean, not the Caribbean, and exercise caution.)

Nearby **Foul Bay** lives up to its name only for sailboats; for swimmers and alfresco lunches, it's lovely. **Needham's Point,** with its lighthouse, is one of Barbados's best beaches, crowded with locals on weekends and holidays.

North Coast Beaches Those who love wild natural beauty will want to head north up the east coast highway. With secluded beaches and crashing ocean waves on one side, rocky cliffs and verdant landscape on the other, the windward side of Barbados won't disappoint anyone who seeks dramatic views. But be cautioned: Swimming here is treacherous and *not* recommended. The waves are high, the bottom tends to be rocky, and the currents are unpredictable. Limit yourself to enjoying the view and watching the surfers—who have been at it since they were kids.

A worthwhile little-visited beach for the adventurous who don't mind trekking about a mile off the beaten track is **Morgan Lewis Beach**, on the coast east of Morgan Lewis Mill, the oldest intact windmill on the island. Turn east on the small road that goes to the town of Boscobelle (between Cherry Tree Hill and Morgan Lewis Mill), but instead of going to the town, take the even less traveled road (unmarked on most maps; you will have to ask for directions) that goes down the cliff to the beach. What awaits is more than 2 miles of unspoiled, uninhabited white sand and sweeping views of the Atlantic coastline. You might see a few Barbadians swimming or sunning or fishing, but for the most part you'll have privacy.

Return to your car, cross the island's north point on the secondary roads until you reach the west coast. About a mile west from the end of Highway 1B is **Maycock's Bay,** an isolated area in St. Lucy Parish about 2 miles north of Heywoods, the west coast's northernmost resort complex.

Exploring Barbados

Numbers in the margin correspond with points of interest on the Bridgetown map.

The island's most popular sights and attractions can be seen comfortably in four or five excursions, each lasting one day or less. The five tours described here begin with Bridgetown and then cover central Barbados, the eastern shore, north central Barbados, and the south shore. Before you set out in a car, minimoke, or taxi, ask at your hotel or the Board of Tourism for a free copy of the detailed Barbados Holiday Map and check performance or opening times.

Bridgetown ❶ **Bridgetown** is a bustling city complete with rush hours and traffic congestion; you'll avoid hassle by taking the bus or a taxi. Sightseeing will take only an hour or so, and the shopping areas are within walking distance.

❷ In the center of town, overlooking the picturesque harbor known as the Careenage, is **Trafalgar Square** with its impressive monument to Horatio, Lord Nelson. It predates the Nelson's Column in London's Trafalgar Square by about two decades (and for more than a century Bajans have petitioned to replace it with a statue of a Bajan). Here are also a war memorial and a three-dolphin fountain commemorating the advent of running water in Barbados in 1865.

❸ Bridgetown is a major Caribbean free port. The principal shopping area is **Broad Street,** which leads north from Trafalgar Square past the House of Assembly and Legislative Council

Bridgetown

Buildings. These Victorian Gothic structures, like so many
smaller buildings in Bridgetown, stand beside a growing number of modern office buildings and shops. Small colonial
buildings, their balconies trimmed with wrought iron, reward
the visitor who has patience and an appreciative eye.

4 The water that bounds Trafalgar Square is called the **Careenage,** a finger of sea that made early Bridgetown a natural harbor and a gathering place. Here working schooners were
careened (turned on their sides) to be scraped of barnacles and
repainted. Today the Careenage serves mainly as a berth for
fiberglass pleasure yachts.

While no one has proved it conclusively, George Washington, on
his only visit outside the United States, is said to have wor-
5 shiped at **St. Michael's Cathedral** south of Trafalgar Square.
The structure was nearly a century old when he visited in 1751,
and it has since been destroyed by hurricanes and rebuilt
twice, in 1780 and 1831.

The two bridges over the Careenage are the Chamberlain
Bridge and the Charles O'Neal Bridge, both of which lead to
6 Highway 7 and south to the **Fairchild Market.** On Saturdays the
7 activity there and at the **Cheapside Market** (on the north end of
Lower Broad Street, across from St. Mary's Church Square)
recall the lively days before the coming of the supermarket and
the mall, when the outdoor markets of Barbados were the daily
heart and soul of shopping and socializing.

About a mile south of Bridgetown on Highway 7, the unusually
8 interesting **Barbados Museum** has artifacts and mementos of

military history and everyday life in the 19th century. Here you'll see cane-harvesting implements, lace wedding dresses, ancient (and frightening) dentistry instruments, and slave sale accounts kept in a spidery copperplate handwriting. Wildlife and natural history exhibits, a well-stocked gift shop, and a good café are also here, in what used to be the military prison. *Hwy. 7, Garrison Savannah, tel. 809/435–6900. Admission: BDS$4. Open Mon.–Sat. 9–6.*

9 East of Bridgetown, **Queen's Park,** now being restored to its original splendor, is home to one of the largest trees in Barbados: an immense baobab more than 10 centuries old. The **10** historic **Queen's Park House,** former home of the commander of the British troops, has been converted into a theater—with an exhibition room on the lower floor—and a restaurant. Queen's Park is a long walk from Trafalgar Square or the museum; you may want to take a taxi. *Open daily 9–5.*

Central Barbados *Numbers in the margin correspond with points of interest on the Barbados map.*

The most interesting place for getting into the water is the **11** **Folkestone Underwater Park** (809/422–2814), north of Holetown. While Folkestone has a land museum of marine life, the real draw is the underwater snorkeling trail around Dottin's Reef, with glass-bottom boats available for use by nonswimmers. A dredge barge sunk in shallow water is the home to myriad fish, and it and the reef are popular with scuba divers. Huge sea fans, soft coral, and the occasional giant turtle are sights to see.

12 Highway 2 will take you to **Harrison's Caves.** These pale gold limestone caverns, complete with subterranean streams and waterfalls, are entirely organic and said to be unique in the Caribbean. Open since 1981, the caves are so extensive that tours are made by electric tram (hard hats are provided, but all that may fall on you is a little dripping water). *Admission: BDS$10. Open daily 9–4. Reservations are recommended.*

13 Continue along Highway 2 to reach the **Flower Forest,** 8 acres of fragrant flowering bushes, canna and ginger lilies, and puffball trees. Another hundred species of flora combine with the tranquil views of Mt. Hillaby to induce in visitors what may be a relaxing and very pleasant lightheadedness. *Admission: BDS$6. Open daily.*

14 The nearby **Welchman's Hall Gully,** a part of the National Trust in St. Thomas, affords another ideal opportunity to commune with nature. Here are acres of labeled flowers and trees, the occasional green monkey, and great peace and quiet.

15 Take either Highway 4 or the smaller roads to **Gun Hill** for a view so pretty it seems almost unreal: Shades of green and gold cover the fields all the way to the horizon, the picturesque gun tower is surrounded by brilliant flowers, and the white limestone lion behind the garrison is a famous landmark. Military invalids were once sent here to convalesce.

The Eastern Shore Take Highway 3 across the island to Bathsheba and the phenomenal view from the **Atlantis,** the oldest hotel in Barbados, where you may need help getting up from the table after sampling the lunch buffet. In the nearby **Andromeda Gardens,** a fascinating small garden set into the cliffs overlooking the sea, are unusual and beautiful plant specimens from around the world, collected by the horticulturist Iris Bannochie.

16
17 North of Bathsheba, **Barclay's Park** offers a similar view and picnic facilities in a wooded seafront area. At the **Chalky Mount Potteries,** less than 2 miles north on Highway 3, you'll find craftspersons making and selling their wares.

18 A drive north to the isolated Morgan Lewis Beach (*see* Beaches, above) or to Gay's Cove, which every Bajan calls Cove Bay, will put you in reach of the town of **Pie Corner.** Pie Corner is known not for baked goods but for artifacts left by the Caribe and Arawak tribes who once lived here.

19 The **Animal Flower Cave** at North Point, reached by Highway 1, displays small sea anemones, or seaworms, that resemble jewellike flowers as they open their tiny tentacles. For a small fee you can explore inside the cavern and see the waves breaking just outside it. *Admission: BDS$2. Open daily.*

North Central The attractions of north central Barbados might well be com-
Barbados bined with the tour of the eastern shore.

20 The **Barbados Wildlife Reserve** can be reached on Highway 1 from Speightstown on the west coast. Here are herons, land turtles, a kangaroo, screeching peacocks, innumerable green monkeys and their babies doing all manner of things, geese, brilliantly colored parrots, and a friendly otter. The fauna are not in cages, so step carefully and keep your hands to yourself. The preserve has been much improved in recent years with the addition of a giant walk-in aviary and natural history exhibits. Terrific photo opportunities are everywhere. *Admission: BDS$6. Open daily 10–5.*

21 Just to the south, **Farley Hill Mansion** is a national park in northern St. Peter Parish; the rugged landscape explains why they call this the Scotland area. Gardens, lawns, gigantic mahogany, whitewood, and casuarina trees, and an avenue of towering royal palms surround the imposing ruins of a once magnificent plantation great house. Partially rebuilt for the filming of *Island in the Sun*, the structure was later destroyed by fire. *Admission free. Open daily until dusk.*

22 **St. Nicholas Abbey** near Cherry Tree Hill, named for a former owner and the oldest (c. 1650) great house in Barbados, is well worth visiting for its stone and wood architecture in the Jacobean style. Fascinating home movies, made by the present owner's father, record scenes of Bajan town and plantation life in the 1920s and 1930s. There are no set showing times; you need only ask to see them. *Admission: $2.50. Open weekdays 10–3:30.*

The South Shore Driving east on Highways 4 and 4B, you'll note the many **chattel houses** along the route; the property of tenant farmers, these ever-expandable houses were built to be dismantled and moved when necessary. On the coast, the appropriately named
23 **Ragged Point Lighthouse** is where the sun first shines on Barbados and its dramatic Atlantic seascape. About 4 miles to the northwest, in the eastern corner of St. John Parish, the coralstone buildings and serenely beautiful grounds of
24 **Codrington Theological College,** founded in 1748, stand on a cliff overlooking Consett Bay.

Take the smaller roads southeast to reach **Sam Lord's Castle** (*see* Lodging, below), the Regency house built by the buccaneer. Most of the rooms are furnished with the fine antiques he is said to have acquired from passing ships (note the mahogany four-poster), but he had to hire Italian artisans to create the elaborate plaster ceilings. The tour is free to guests; others pay a small fee.

Participant Sports

Barbados offers a comprehensive variety of sports activity.

Golfing Golfers will find a championship 18-hole course at the **Sandy Lane Club** (tel. 809/422–1405), nine holes at the **Rockley Resort** (tel. 809/427–5890), and an 18-hole course at **Heywoods** (tel. 800/223–9815). All are open (for various fees) to nonguests.

Hiking Hilly but not mountainous, the interior of Barbados is ideal for hiking. The **Outdoor Club of Barbados** organizes escorted treks weekly. *Sturdee House, Bank Hall, St. Michael Parish, tel. 809/426–6739 or 809/426–0024. Cost: $15–$25.*

The **Barbados National Trust** (tel. 809/426–2421) sponsors free walks on Sunday, from 5 or 6 AM to about 9 AM, during the winter. Newspapers announce the time and meeting place (or you can call the Trust).

Horseback Riding **Sharon Hill Riding Stables** (tel. 809/425–0099) arranges horseback riding on the beach or through the hills, which can be an exhilarating experience.

Parasailing Parasailing, where you wear a parachute harness and take off from a raft as you're towed by a speedboat, is available, wind conditions permitting, on the beaches of St. James and Christ Church. Just ask at any hotel, then flag down a speedboat (though it may have found you first).

Sailing and Fishing Sailing and deep-sea fishing charters can be arranged through **Jolly Roger Watersports** (tel. 809/426–0767) and **Captain Patch Cruises** (tel. 809/427–2525). For day-long sails and party cruises, consult the **Barbados Cruising Club** (tel. 809/426–4434) or the **Barbados Yacht Club** (tel. 809/427–1125).

Scuba Diving Barbados is a rich and varied underwater destination, one of the few in the Caribbean that offers luxury and activity for both divers and nondivers. Many dive shops provide instruction (the three-hour beginner's "resort courses" and the week-long certification courses) followed by a shallow dive, usually on Dottin's Reef. Trained divers can explore reefs, wrecks, and the walls of "blue holes," the huge circular depressions in the ocean floor. Not to be missed by certified, guided divers is the *Stavronikita*, a 368-foot Greek freighter that was deliberately sunk at about 125 feet; hundreds of butterfly fish hang out around its mast, and the thin rays of sunlight that filter down through the water make exploring the huge ship a wonderfully eerie experience.

Dive Barbados (Jolly Roger Watersports, Sunset Crest Beach, near Holetown, St. James Parish, tel. 809/432–7090 or 703/893–4704) provides beginner's instruction (resort course) and reef and wreck dives with a friendly, knowledgeable staff.

The **Coral Reef Club** (St. James Beach, tel. 809/432–0833) has its own dive facility and school, available to nonguests. Les Wotton has retired; the school is now headed by Andrew Routley.

At **The Dive Shop, Ltd.** (on the beach, St. Michael Parish, tel. 809/426–9947), Paquia Diega leads experienced divers on deep dives to old wrecks to look for bottles and other artifacts (and you can usually keep what you find). Don't be put off by the grubby shop; the instructor knows his stuff.

Willie's Watersports (Cunard Paradise Beach Hotel, tel. 809/424–0888, ext. 7429, and Heywoods Hotel, tel. 809/422–4900, ext. 2831) offers instruction and a range of diving excursions.

Underwater Barbados (Southwinds Beach Hotel, St. Lawrence, Christ Church Parish, tel. 809/428–3504), the Peter Hughes diving facility, also does finders-keepers bottle dives.

Dive Boat Safari (Hilton Hotel, tel. 809/427–4350) offers full diving and instruction services.

Snorkeling Snorkeling gear can be rented for a small charge from nearly every hotel.

Squash Squash courts can be reserved at the **Rockley Resort** (tel. 809/427–5890) and the **Barbados Squash Club** (tel. 809/427–7193).

Submarining Submarines are enormously popular with families and those who enjoy watching fish without getting wet, and the 28-passenger *Atlantis* turns the Caribbean into a giant aquarium. The 45-minute trip takes you as much as 150 feet below the surface for a look at what even sport divers rarely see. The nighttime dives, using high-power searchlights, are spectacular. *Tel. 809/436–8929. Cost: about $45.*

Tennis The **Paragon Tennis Club** (tel. 809/427–2054) is one possibility, but most hotels have tennis courts that can be reserved day and night. Be sure to bring your whites; appropriate dress is expected on the court.

Waterskiing Waterskiing is widely available, often provided along St. James and Christ Church by the private speedboat owners. Inquire at your hotel, which can direct you to the nearest Sunfish sailing and Hobie Cat rentals as well.

Windsurfing Windsurfing boards and equipment are often guest amenities at the larger hotels and can be rented by nonguests. The best place to learn and to practice is on the south coast at the **Barbados Windsurfing Club Hotel** (Maxwell, Christ Church Parish, tel. 809/428–9095).

Spectator Sports

Cricket The island is mad for cricket, and you can sample a match at almost any time of year. While the season is June through late December, test matches are played all year long. The newspapers give the details of time and place.

Horse Racing Horse racing takes place on alternate Saturdays, from January to May and from July to November, at the **Garrison Savannah,** about 3 miles south of Bridgetown. Appropriate dress might be described as "casual elegance." *Tel. 809/426–3980. Admission: about $6.*

Polo Polo, the sport of kings, is played seriously in Barbados. Matches are held at the **Polo Club** in St. James on Wednesday and Saturday from September to March. *Admission: about $2.50.*

Rugby The rough-and-tumble game of rugby is played at the Garrison Savannah; schedules are available from the **Barbados Rugby Association** (tel. 809/435–6455).

Soccer The football, or soccer, season runs from January through June; game schedules are available from the **Barbados Football Association** (tel. 809/424–4413).

Shopping

While St. Thomas is the undisputed leader in designer consumerism in the Caribbean, Bridgetown has its own distinctive bargains and entertaining shopping. Most stores and boutiques are located on Broad Street; their hours are generally weekdays 8–4, Saturday 8–1. Many stores have an in-bound (duty-free) department where you must show your travel tickets or a passport to buy duty-free goods, and the reduced prices are worth taking the trouble to find.

Luxury Goods Bridgetown stores have values on fine bone china, crystal, cameras, stereo and video equipment, jewelry, perfumes, and clothing. **Cave Shepherd** and **Harrison's** department stores offer wide selections of goods at many locations and at the airport. **De Lima's** and **Da Costa's Ltd.** stock quality imports. Among the specialty stores are **Louis I. Bayley** (gold watches), **J. Baldini** (Brazilian jewelry and Danish silver), and **Correia's** (diamonds, pearls, semiprecious stones). The 20 small shops of **Mall 34** in Bridgetown's central district sell everything from luxury goods to crafts.

Handicrafts Island handicrafts are everywhere: woven mats and placemats, dresses, dolls, handbags, shell jewelry. The **Best of Barbados** shops, at the airport, the Sandpiper Inn, Mall 34 in Bridgetown (tel. 809/436–1416), and three other locations, offer the highest quality artwork and crafts, both "native style" and modern designs. A resident artist, Jill Walker, sells her watercolors and prints here and at **Walker's World** shops (tel. 809/428–1183) near the south shore hotels in St. Lawrence Gap.

At the **Pelican Village Handicrafts Center** (tel. 809/426–1966) on the Princess Alice Highway near the Cheapside Market in Bridgetown, in a cluster of conical shops, you can watch goods and crafts being made before you purchase them. Rugs and mats made from pandanus grass and khuskhus are good buys.

Antiques Antiques and fine memorabilia are the stock of **Greenwich House Antiques** (tel. 809/432–1169) in Greenwich Village, Trents Hill, St. James Parish, and at **Antiquaria** (tel. 809/426–0635) on St. Michael's Row next to the Anglican cathedral in Bridgetown.

Fabric Fine batik and colorful island-pattern fabrics are available at the **Caribatik Island Fabric** shop in the Crane Beach Hotel, where you'll find quality caftans, wall hangings, sundresses, neckties, and fabric by the yard.

Dining

The better hotels and restaurants of Barbados have employed chefs trained in New York and Europe to attract and keep their sophisticated clientele. Gourmet dining here usually means fresh seafood, beef, or veal with finely blended sauces.

The native West Indian cuisine offers an entirely different dining experience. The island's West African heritage brought rice, peas, beans, and okra to its table, the staples that make a perfect base for slowly cooked meat and fish dishes. Many side dishes are cooked in oil (the pumpkin fritters can be addictive). And be cautious at first with the West Indian seasonings; like the sun, they are hotter than you think.

Every menu features dolphin (the fish, not the mammal), kingfish, snapper, and flying fish prepared every way imaginable. Shellfish abound; so does steak. Everywhere for breakfast and dessert you'll find mangoes, soursop, papaya (called pawpaw), and, in season, mammyapples, a basketball-size, thick-skinned fruit with giant seeds.

Cou-cou is a mix of corn meal and okra with a spicy Creole sauce made from tomatoes, onions, and sweet peppers; steamed flying fish is often served over it. A version served by the Brown Sugar restaurant, called "red herring," is smoked herring and breadfruit in Creole sauce.

Pepperpot stew, a hearty mix of oxtail, beef chunks, and "any other meat you may have," simmered overnight, is flavored with *casareep*, an ancient preservative and seasoning that gives the stew its dark, rich color.

Christophenes and **eddoes** are tasty, potatolike vegetables that are often served with shrimp, chicken, or goat curries.

Buljol is a cold salad of codfish, tomatoes, onions, sweet pepper, and celery, marinated and served raw.

Callaloo is a soup made from okra, crabmeat, a spinachlike vegetable, and seasonings.

Among the liquid refreshments of Barbados, in addition to the omnipresent Banks Beer and Mount Gay rum, there are **falernum,** a liqueur concocted of rum, sugar, lime juice, and almond essence and **mauby,** a refreshing nonalcoholic beerlike drink made by boiling bitter bark and spices, straining the mixture, and sweetening it.

The most highly recommended restaurants are indicated by a star ★.

Category	Cost*
Expensive	over $25
Moderate	$15–$25
Inexpensive	under $15

Per person, excluding drinks and service charge. There is no sales tax on Barbados.

The following credit card abbreviations are used: AE, American Express; CB, Carte Blanche; DC, Diners Club; MC, MasterCard; and V, Visa.

Expensive   **Bagatelle Great House.** Occupying a converted plantation house in a hill area, Bagatelle Great House gives diners an impression of colonial life. The terrace allows intimate dining at tables for two, while inside the castlelike walls are much larger round tables. Here are candlelight dining, Continental and local cuisine, and an extensive wine list. *St. Thomas Parish, tel.*

809/425–0666. Reservations necessary. Jacket and tie required. AE, MC, V.

★ **Carambola.** The recently opened Carambola has been highly recommended by locals and tourists alike for its creative menu, superior service, and seaside setting. On a recent menu were grilled paillard of veal with cream, rum, and carambola (star fruit); poached flying fish with herbs. *St. James Parish, tel. 809/432–0832. Reservations necessary. AE, CB, DC, MC, V.*

La Cage aux Folles. Acclaimed as the island's true gourmet French restaurant, the intimate La Cage aux Folles seats only 22. The tropical French decor includes a cage of colorful parrots and macaws and lots of fresh flowers; soft music throughout the evening further sets the mood. The menu is simple, the lobster and beef are exceptional, the wine list is good. *Payne Bay, St. James Parish, tel. 809/432–1203. Reservations necessary. Jacket and tie required. AE, MC, V. Dinner only.*

Noelle's. Noelle's, a family-run restaurant, has an Old World inn atmosphere and a menu that is strong on local seafood and Continental fare. The service is excellent. *Holetown, St. James Parish, tel. 809/432–6159. Reservations necessary. AE, MC, V.*

Piperade. The elegant Piperade terrace restaurant in the Glitter Bay resort, decorated in shades of pink and green, offers entertainment nightly and an extensive wine list with selections from France, Italy, Spain, Germany, and Portugal. On the menu are distinctive shrimp dishes and a *filet de boeuf pecheur* (seasoned filet topped with mushrooms and curried shrimp). *Glitter Bay, St. James Parish, tel. 809/422–4111. Reservations necessary. Jacket and tie required. AE, MC, V. Dinner only.*

Moderate **Balmore House Restaurant.** New on the beach in St. James Par-
★ ish, the elegant Balmore House features English country-home furnishings in a colonial-style house with a paneled bar that opens onto a seaside terrace dining area. There are candles on the tables, and the service is attentive. Pepper steak and shrimp mousseline are featured. *Holetown, St. James Parish, tel. 809/432–1156. Reservations recommended. AE, MC, V. Closed Sun. and Mon.*

Brown Sugar. A special-occasion atmosphere prevails at Brown Sugar, located just behind the Island Inn outside Bridgetown. Dozens of ferns and hanging plants decorate the breezy multilevel restaurant with its indoor and outdoor rattan chairs and tile-top tables. The extensive and authentic West Indian lunch buffets, popular with local businessmen, include cou-cou, pepperpot stew, Creole orange chicken, and such homemade desserts as angelfood chocolate mousse cake and passionfruit and nutmeg ice cream. *Aquatic Gap, St. Michael Parish, tel. 809/426–7684. Reservations recommended. AE, MC, V. Closed Sun. No lunch Sat.*

Da Luciano Ristorante Italiano. The restored living room of an old Victorian home houses Da Luciano, where you'll find hearty servings of classic Italian fare. *Hastings, Christ Church Parish, tel. 809/427–5518. Reservations recommended. AE, MC, V.*

Flamboyant. Local residents who look forward to dining in a cozy old Barbadian home favor Flamboyant and its generous portions of West Indian and European dishes, some of them with a German influence. *Worthing, Christ Church Parish, tel. 809/427–5588. AE, MC, V. Dinner only.*

Koko's. For a dramatic beach setting, drive up Highway 1 to Koko's in Prospect, where the ocean view from the terrace is stunning. The "nu-Bajan" menu offers an imaginative West Indian twist on nouvelle cuisine. The *kohoblopot* soup recalls the all-in-one-pot the Arawak Indians are said to have kept going for a week, using casareep as a preservative; the shrimp Kristo is simmered in red gravy with christophenes. *Prospect, St. James Parish, tel. 809/424–4557. Reservations recommended. AE, MC, V. Dinner only.*

Ocean View Hotel. The gracious old dining room of the Ocean View Hotel overlooks the south coast sea. Airy and tropical, the setting is as pleasant as the service is attentive. Area residents have long favored the Ocean View for excellent Bajan dishes, among them "sea eggs" (sea urchins) in season. *Hastings, Christ Church Parish, tel. 809/427–7821. Reservations recommended. AE, MC, V.*

Plantation. Wednesday's Bajan buffet and Tuesday's entertainment are big attractions here. The Plantation is set in a renovated Barbadian residence surrounded by spacious grounds above the Southwinds Resort; its cuisine combines French and Barbadian influences, and you can eat indoors or on the terrace. *St. Lawrence, Christ Church Parish, tel. 809/428–5048. Reservations suggested. AE, MC, V. Dinner only.*

Rose and Crown. The casual Rose and Crown serves seafood and the ubiquitous flying fish prepared in a variety of ways. Indoors is a paneled bar, outdoors are tables on a wraparound porch. *Prospect, St. James Parish, tel. 809/425–1074. Reservations suggested. AE, MC, V.*

The Virginian. The locally popular Virginian offers intimate surroundings and some of the island's best dining values. The specialties are seafood, shrimp, and steaks. *Sea View Hotel, Hastings, Christ Church Parish, tel. 809/427–7963. Reservations suggested. AE, MC, V. Dinner only.*

Witch Doctor. The interior of the Witch Doctor is a cascade of tropical plants; the menu features traditional Barbadian dishes and local seafood. *St. Lawrence Gap, Christ Church Parish, tel. 809/428–7856. Reservations recommended. AE, MC, V. Dinner only.*

Inexpensive **Atlantis Hotel.** While the surroundings may be simple and the
★ rest room could use a coat of paint, the food and the magnificent ocean view at the Atlantis Hotel in Bathsheba on the east coast make it a real find. Enid Maxwell, who may be the best cook on the island, serves up an enormous Bajan buffet daily, where you're likely to find pickled souse (marinated pig parts and vegetables), pumpkin fritters, spinach balls, pickled breadfruit, fried "fline" (flying) fish, roast chicken, pepperpot stew, and West Indian–style okra and eggplant. Among the homemade pies are an apple and a dense coconut. *Bathsheba, St. Joseph Parish, tel. 809/423–1526. Reservations suggested. No credit cards.*

Lodging

The southern and western shores of Barbados are lined with hotels and resorts of every size and price, offering a variety of accommodations from private villas to modest but comfortable rooms in simple inns. At the same time, apartment and home rentals and time-share condominiums have become widely available and are growing increasingly popular among visitors to the island; information about these arrangements follows the hotel listings below.

Hotels are grouped here by parish, beginning with St. James in the west and St. Peter to the north, then St. Michael, Christ Church, St. Philip, and St. Joseph.

The most highly recommended lodgings are indicated by a star ★.

Category	Cost*
Very Expensive	over $200
Expensive	$150–$200
Moderate	$100–$150
Inexpensive	under $100

All prices are for a standard double room, excluding 10% service charge.

Hotels
St. James Parish

Coconut Creek Club. A luxury cottage colony, the Coconut Creek Club is set on handsomely landscaped grounds with a private beach and a bar pavilion for entertainment and dancing. MAP (breakfast and dinner) available. *Reservations: Box 249, Bridgetown; Hwy. 1, St. James Parish, tel. 809/432–0803. 53 rooms. Facilities: pool, dining room, pub. AE, DC, MC, V. Very Expensive.*

Colony Club. The seven-acre Colony Club a cottage colony on the beach, is a "residential club." All rooms have private patios. There is a dining room and cocktail terrace, and there are water sports on the beach. *Reservations: Box 429, Bridgetown; Hwy. 1, St. James Parish, tel. 809/422–2335. 76 rooms. Facilities: pool, dining room. AE, MC, V. Very Expensive.*

★ **Coral Reef Club.** The cottages of the Coral Reef Club are scattered over 12 flower-filled acres. Extensive water-sports activities include a scuba-diving school. Luncheon on a terrace, dining, dancing, and beach barbecues make you feel pampered. *Reservations: St. James Beach; Hwy. 1, St. James Parish, tel. 809/422–2372 or 800/223–1108. 70 rooms. Facilities: pool, entertainment. AE, MC, V. Very Expensive.*

★ **Discovery Bay Hotel.** The rooms of the quiet, white-columned recently renovated Discovery Bay Hotel open onto a central lawn and a pool. Some rooms have ocean views. Beach activities include windsurfing, Sunfish, Hobie Cats. *Hwy. 1, Holetown, St. James Parish, tel. 809/432–1301. 85 rooms. Facilities: pool, table tennis, terrace restaurant, boutique. AE, DC, MC, V. Very Expensive.*

Divi St. James Beach Resort. The Divi St. James, formerly the Club St. James, is the island's only all-inclusive property; week-long packages include accommodations, meals, beverages, and water sports. An exchange program allows the use of sports and recreation facilities of the Divi Southwinds, a sister property. Regular rates are available, too, as well as dive packages. *Holetown, St. James Parish, tel. 809/432–7840. 316 rooms. Facilities: golf, pool, Nautilus fitness center, sauna. No guests under age 16. AE, DC, MC, V. Very Expensive.*

Glitter Bay. Surrounded by tropical gardens at the edge of the sea, the large, airy units of the Glitter Bay resort comprise six three-bedroom penthouses, 12 two-bedroom suites, and three one-bedroom suites. All have fully equipped kitchens. The

Piperade restaurant offers gourmet dining, dancing, and entertainment. Water sports are available on the resort property. *Hwy. 1, Porters, St. James Parish, tel. 809/422–4111. 84 rooms. Facilities: pool, restaurant; golf nearby. AE, DC, MC, V. Very Expensive.*

★ **Sandy Lane.** A $4 million refurbishment has restored the original splendor of one of the Caribbean's most famous hotels, the beachfront Sandy Lane resort, a Trusthouse Forte Ltd. property. Ornate mirrors and crystal chandeliers set off coral-stone walls. Amenities include bathrobes, fine toiletries, and careful service. All water sports are available on the 1,000 feet of beach. *Hwy. 1, Sunset Crest, St. James Parish, tel. 809/432–1311 or 800/223–5672. 128 rooms. Facilities: pool, 5 tennis courts, golf course, 2 restaurants, 2 cocktail lounges, entertainment. AE, DC, MC, V. Very Expensive.*

Settlers' Beach. The accommodations at Settlers' Beach are two-story, two-bedroom homes with full kitchen and dining room (or one-story villas with atrium), arranged asymmetrically around a large courtyard filled with towering palms and a pool. The outdoor pool and bar area has just been renovated, and the new chef is from the Parker Meridien Hotel in Manhattan. Your neighbors may turn out to be British film stars. *Hwy. 1, St. James Parish, tel. 809/422–3052. 22 villas. Facilities: pool, restaurant. AE, MC, V. Very Expensive.*

Barbados Beach Village. Vacationers choose from twin-bedded rooms, studios, apartments, and duplexes at the Barbados Beach Village. The beach has a terrace bar, and the restaurant is seaside. *Hwy. 1, St. James Parish, tel. 809/425–1440. 88 rooms. Facilities: pool, restaurant, disco nightclub. AE, DC, MC, V. Moderate.*

Golden Palms. With one-, two-, and three-bedroom villas set around a shopping center with a supermarket, a deli, a beauty shop, a bank, and a department store, Sunset Crest resembles a small village. The resort is very popular with families (especially Canadians), who find here the ingredients of a reasonable self-catering holiday. The recreation area has a clubhouse, two pools, a pitch-and-putt golf course, and tennis courts. Across the road, the Beach Club has two pools, two restaurants, a bar and games room, and a fine stretch of beach. The calypso group Merrymen often entertains here. *Hwy. 1, St. James Parish, tel. 809/432–1290. 111 rooms. Facilities: 2 pools, tennis courts, shops, entertainment. AE, DC, MC, V. Moderate.*

St. Peter Parish **Cobblers Cove Hotel.** The comfortable, unpretentious Cobblers
★ Cove Hotel, about 11 miles up the coast from Bridgetown, offers luxury efficiency units with kitchenettes and balconies or patios. Water sports are available on the beach. *Hwy. 1, Road View, St. Peter Parish, tel. 809/422–2291. 38 rooms, 1 suite. Facilities: pool, dining terrace, bar. AE, MC, V. Very Expensive.*

Heywoods Barbados. Everything is on a grand scale here: The seven buildings of the Heywoods Barbados, each with its own theme and decor, house hundreds of luxury rooms. The mile-long beach has space for all water sports. Owned by the Barbados government, the property is worth a visit just for a look at the landscaping and the layout. *Hwy. 1, St. Peter Parish, tel. 809/422–4900. 306 rooms. Facilities: 3 pools, 5 lighted tennis courts, squash courts, 9-hole golf course, restaurants, bars, boutiques, entertainment. AE, DC, MC, V. Expensive.*

King's Beach Hotel. The newly opened King's Beach, a property of Tropical Resort Ltd., has a two-story, semicircular design and draws a European clientele. *Hwy. 1, Road View, St. Peter Parish, tel. 809/422–1690. 57 rooms. Facilities: pool, restaurant, bar, shops, library, games room. AE, MC, V. Expensive.*

St. Michael Parish **Grand Barbados Beach Resort.** Once a Holiday Inn, the Grand Barbados Beach Resort at Carlisle Bay is convenient to Bridgetown. Its renovated rooms have minibar and refrigerator, hair dryer, and satellite TV; 100 rooms have ocean views. "Executive floors" have a hospitality suite and secretarial services. *Box 639, Bridgetown; on Carlisle Bay, St. Michael Parish, tel. 809/426–0890 or 800/223–9815. 133 rooms. Facilities: restaurant, secretarial services. AE, DC, MC, V. Very Expensive.*

Barbados Hilton International. A large resort just five minutes from Bridgetown, the modern Hilton International is for those who like activity and having plenty of other people around. Its attractions include an atrium lobby, a man-made beach 1,000 feet wide with full water sports, and lots of shops. The cuisine is West Indian and international. All rooms and suites have balconies. *Needhams Point, St. Michael Parish, tel. 809/426–0200. 185 rooms. Facilities: pool, tennis courts, coffee shop, lounge. AE, CB, DC, MC, V. Expensive.*

Cunard Paradise Beach Hotel. A recently completed renovation added a conference center and upgraded the rooms and public areas of the Cunard Paradise Beach Hotel, formerly the Paradise Beach Resort, convenient to Bridgetown and popular with younger Canadians and Americans. The beach offers rental boats, water sports, and nocturnal goings-on for those who want constant activity. *Hwy. 1, St. Michael Parish, tel. 809/424–0888. 172 rooms. Facilities: dining rooms, bar, entertainment. AE, DC, MC, V. Expensive.*

Christ Church **Divi Southwinds Beach Hotel.** Situated on 20 lush acres, the
Parish Divi Southwinds offers rooms and luxury suites with private terrace or balcony, and the suites have fully equipped kitchens. The beach is fine white sand; complete scuba and water-sports activities are available. *St. Lawrence, Christ Church Parish, tel. 800/367–3484. 160 rooms. Facilities: 3 pools, 2 lighted tennis courts, putting green, shopping arcade, beauty salon. AE, DC, MC, V. Very Expensive.*

★ **Sandy Beach Resort.** All rooms face the sea at Sandy Beach, where there are drinks and entertainment poolside and the Green House Restaurant serves a weekly West Indian buffet. Water-sports activities include scuba-diving certification, deep-sea fishing, and harbor cruises. *Worthing, Christ Church Parish, tel. 809/435–8000. 139 rooms. Facilities: pool, restaurant, bar, entertainment. AE, CB, DC, MC, V. Expensive.*

Southern Palms. A luxurious plantation-style hotel on a fine 1,000-foot stretch of pink sand near the Dover Convention Center, Southern Palms is a convenient businessperson's hotel. You may choose from standard bedrooms, deluxe oceanfront suites with kitchenette, and a four-bedroom penthouse. Other attractions are a full water-sports center, Le Petit Flambe dining room, and the Unicorn I disco. *St. Lawrence, Christ Church Parish, tel. 809/428–7171. 95 rooms. Facilities: pool, tennis court, dining room, disco. AE, DC, MC, V. Expensive.*

Barbados Windsurfing Club Hotel. A small hotel that began as a gathering place for windsurfing enthusiasts, the Barbados Windsurfing Club is now a complete school and center for the sport. The spacious and comfortable yet unpretentious rooms overlook the fishing village of Oistins on the south coast. The bar and restaurant overlook the water and offer weekly jazz nights. All sports can be arranged, but windsurfing (learning, practicing, and perfecting it) is king. *Maxwell, Christ Church Parish, tel. 809/428–9095. 15 rooms. Facilities: restaurant, bar, entertainment. AE, MC, V. Moderate.*

Casuarina Beach Club. This luxury apartment hotel on 900 feet of pink sand takes its name from the towering casuarina pines that surround it, and the quiet setting provides a dramatic contrast to that of the platinum-coast resorts. The bar and restaurant are on the beach. Scuba diving, golf, and other activities can be arranged. The Casuarina Beach is popular with those who prefer self-catering holidays in a secluded setting, convenient to nightlife and shopping. *St. Lawrence Gap, Christ Church Parish, tel. 809/428–3600. 100 rooms. Facilities: pool, tennis courts, squash courts, restaurant, bar. AE, MC, V. Moderate.*

Sichris Hotel. The Sichris is a "discovery," more attractive inside than seen from the road, a comfortable and convenient self-contained resort that can be ideal for businesspeople who need a quiet place to work. Just minutes from the city, the air-conditioned one-bedroom suites all have kitchenettes and private balconies or patios. It's a walk of two or three minutes to the beach. *Worthing, Christ Church Parish, tel. 809/435–7930. 24 rooms. Facilities: pool, restaurant, bar. AE, MC, V. Moderate.*

Accra Beach Hotel. The Accra Beach offers neatly furnished housekeeping suites with dining room, cocktail lounge, beach bar, and water sports. *Rockley Beach, Christ Church Parish, tel. 809/427–7866 or 800/223–9815. 52 rooms. Facilities: dining room, lounge, beach bar, water-sports center. AE, MC, V. Inexpensive.*

Caribbee Hotel. The Caribbee has been popular for decades with those who want a simple, reasonable vacation hotel; its 36 one-bedroom apartments attract those seeking self-catering facilities. Shopping and dining are within walking distance. *Hastings, Christ Church Parish, tel. 800/223–6510. 54 rooms. AE, CB, DC, MC, V. Inexpensive.*

Ocean View. Antiques, a traditional atmosphere, and the hotel's proximity to Bridgetown make the Ocean View attractive to businesspeople. It's a homey place with an airy seaside restaurant, a popular dining spot known for seafood and traditional Bajan cuisine. *Hastings, Christ Church Parish, tel. 809/427–7821. 40 rooms. Facilities: restaurant. AE, MC, V. Inexpensive.*

St. Philip Parish **Crane Beach Hotel.** Although it has changed hands with alarming regularity, this remote hilltop property on a cliff overlooking the dramatic Atlantic coast remains one of the special places of Barbados. The Crane Beach has suites and one-bedroom apartments in the main building and additional bedrooms at the beach club next door. The restaurant has an extensive wine cellar. *Crane's Bay, St. Philip Parish, tel. 809/423–6220. 18 rooms. Facilities: 2 pools, restaurant, 2 bars. AE, DC, MC, V. Very Expensive.*

★ **Marriott's Sam Lord's Castle.** Set on the Atlantic coast about 14 miles east of Bridgetown, Sam Lord's Castle is not a castle with moat and towers but an impressive mansion surrounded by 71 acres of beautiful grounds, gardens, and beach. The seven rooms in the main house have canopied beds; downstairs, the public rooms have furniture by Sheraton, Hepplewhite, and

Chippendale. Spode china and paintings by Reynolds recall the days when only planters and pirates could afford this luxury. Additional guest rooms in surrounding cottages have more conventional hotel furnishings. The beach is a mile long, the Wanderer Restaurant offers Continental cuisine, and there are even a few slot machines, as befits a pirate's lair. *Long Bay, St. Philip Parish, tel. 809/423-7350. 256 rooms. Facilities: 2 pools, lighted tennis courts, restaurant, entertainment. AE, DC, MC, V. Very Expensive.*

St. Joseph Parish **Atlantis Hotel.** The Atlantis provides a warm, pleasant atmosphere in a pastoral location overlooking a majestically rocky Atlantic coast. The hotel is modest and in need of a bit of paint, yet the congeniality and the Bajan food more than make up for that. *Bathsheba, St. Joseph Parish, tel. 809/433-9445. 16 rooms. Facilities: dining room. No credit cards. Inexpensive.*

Rental Homes Private homes are available for rental south of Bridgetown in
and Apartments the Hastings–Worthing area, along the St. James Parish coast, and in St. Peter Parish. The **Barbados Board of Tourism** (tel. 809/427-2623) has a listing of rental properties and prices.

Beyond the Blue. Two one-bedroom villas and a three-bedroom (three baths) villa with maid service and access to the beach and facilities of the Cunard Paradise Beach Resort are available year-round. *Willie Hassell, Black Rock, St. Michael Parish, tel. 809/424-1808. No credit cards.*
Caribbean Home Rentals. Cook, maid, gardener, airport pickup, and the delivery of rental cars are available with the 125 properties listed here. Rates range from $150 a night in the off-season for a one-bedroom cottage to $2,600 a week for a six-bedroom villa in high season. *Box 710, Palm Beach, FL 33480, tel. 407/833-4454. No credit cards.*

Time-Share **Rockley Resort and Beach Club.** The Rockley Resort's air-
Condominiums conditioned one- and two-bedroom accommodations, with a balcony or a patio, are located about 5 miles from Bridgetown. On the grounds are a health club, six swimming pools, five tennis courts, a nine-hole golf course, squash courts, and volleyball and croquet facilities. A special playground for children, a free shuttle bus to the beach (five minutes), a dining room, and a cocktail lounge are further amenities. *Rockley Resort, Suite 512, Christ Church Parish, tel. 800/223-9815. 288 rooms. AE, CB, DC, MC, V.*

The Arts and Nightlife

The Arts **Barbados Art Council.** The gallery shows drawings, paintings, and other art, with a new show about every two weeks. *2 Pelican Village, Bridgetown, tel. 809/426-4385. Admission free. Open Mon.–Sat.*

Barbados Museum. Theater and a buffet dinner are the major attraction here twice a week in the courtyard. The professional Barbados Dance Theatre performs a show of history and folklore with terrific calypso, limbo, and stilt dancing. The costumes alone are worth a visit. The West Indian buffet is tasty, but don't arrive ravenous, for the line is long and slow (yet the desserts are worth waiting for). Stroll the museum exhibits before or after the performance. *Hwy. 7, Garrison Savannah, tel. 809/435-6900. Show and dinner, Sun. and Thurs., about $30. Reservations recommended.*

Plantation Restaurant and Garden Theatre. On Wednesday and Saturday the Tropical Spectacular Show bursts with high-energy dancing and nonstop steel band music; the eye-poppingly colorful costumes make up for some silly audience-participation material. On Monday and Friday the Calypso Cabaret Show features fire-eaters and steel bands playing non-stop reggae and calypso—and after enough rum punches, you may very well find yourself joining in the limbo contests. The show (outdoors, under tents), unlimited drinks, and the West Indian buffet are about $35; the show and drinks only, about $15. *St. Lawrence Road, Christ Church Parish, tel. 809/428–5048 or 809/428–2986. Dress: casual.*

Nightlife Nightlife in Barbados means music; the island's top reggae groups, steel bands, and calypso singers are followed with great interest and devotion. Most resort hotels have entertainment, dancing, and sometimes disco every evening: the **Flambeau Bar** at the Hilton, the **Hide-away** next door to the Bagatelle Great House, and the **Rendezvous** at the Rockley Resort are popular.

Alexandra's (Bishop Court, Bridgetown, tel. 809/422–1487), an elegant club set in a 170-year-old plantation house, features live music every night but Sunday.

Barbados Beach Club (Hwy. 1, St. James Parish, tel. 809/425–1440) has a wildly eclectic program of entertainment nightly: ragtime bands, jazz groups, Bajan shows with music and stand-up comics, steel bands, and dancing to live and recorded pop/disco/island music in a large outdoor facility. There are inexpensive cafeteria-style dinners of spaghetti and fish, drinks, and video games indoors. One of the two swimming pools is permanently populated by turtles and barracuda. A high cyclone fence keeps customers from strolling on the attractive stretch of sand.

Baxter's Road (Bridgetown) is the place to boogie with the Bajans, to hear some of the island's best calypso and steel bands, and to taste West Indian cooking at the stalls that line the street. The action begins around 11 PM.

Unicorn I (Southern Palms Hotel, St. Lawrence, Christ Church Parish, tel. 809/428–7171), a relatively new disco, is lively and popular with a young crowd.

Bars and Inns Barbados supports the rum industry in more than 1,600 "rum shops," simple bars where men congregate to discuss the world's ills, and in more sophisticated inns, where you'll find world-class rum drinks and the island's renowned Mount Gay and Cockspur rums. The following offer welcoming spirits: **The Ship Inn** (St. Lawrence Gap, Christ Church Parish, tel. 809/428–9605), **The Coach House** (Paynes Bay, St. James Parish, tel. 809/432–1163), **The Windsor Arms** (Hastings, Christ Church Parish, tel. 809/427–7831), **The Boat Yard** (Bay Street, Bridgetown, tel. 809/429–4806), **Barbados Windsurfing Club** (Maxwell, Christ Church Parish, tel. 809/428–9095), **The Abbeville Pub** (Rockley, Christ Church Parish, tel. 809/427–7524), **The Rosebank Inn** (Rockley, Christ Church Parish, tel. 809/427–7273), **Ye Olde English Pub** (St. Lawrence Gap, Christ Church Parish, tel. 809/428–5777), and **TGI Boomers** (St. Lawrence Gap, Christ Church Parish, tel. 809/428–8439).

6 Bonaire

by Pamela Bloom

Bonaire is a stark desert island, perfect for the rugged individualist who is turned off by the overcommercialized high life of the other Antillean islands. The island boasts a spectacular array of exotic wildlife—from fish to fowl to flowers—that will keep nature-watchers awestruck for days. It's the kind of place to rent a jeep and go dashing off madly in search of the wild flamingo, the wild iguana, or even the wild yellow-winged parrot named the Bonairian lora.

A mecca for divers, Bonaire offers one of the most unspoiled reef systems in the world. The water is so clear that you can lean over the dock and look the fish straight in the eye.

Kudos for the preservation of the 112-square-mile isle go to the people and government of Bonaire, who in 1970, with the help of the World Wildlife Fund, developed the Bonaire Marine Park—a model of ecological conservation. The underwater park includes, roughly, the entire coastline, from the high-water tidemark to a depth of 200 feet, all of which is protected by strict laws. Because the Bonairians desperately want to keep their paradise intact, any diver with a reckless streak is firmly requested to go elsewhere.

This is not the island for connoisseurs of fine cuisine, shopping maniacs, or those who prefer hobnobbing with society. The island itself may be lacking in splendor, but what lies off its shores keeps divers enthralled.

Before You Go

Tourist Information Contact the **Bonaire Government Tourist** Office (275 7th Ave., New York, NY 10001, tel. 212/242–7707) for advice and information on planning your trip.

Arriving and Departing
By Plane **American** (tel. 800/433–7300) and **ALM** (tel. 800/327–7230) will get you to Bonaire. ALM flies nonstop to Bonaire from New York once a week and from Miami twice a week. American offers daily flights from New York to Curaçao and Aruba, but you must connect to Bonaire through ALM—and the plane is small. ALM also has daily flights to Curaçao from Miami, with a connecting flight to Bonaire.

From the Airport Bonaire's airport is tiny, but you'll appreciate its welcoming ambience. The customs check is perfunctory if you are arriving from another Dutch isle; otherwise, you will have to show proof of citizenship, plus a return or ongoing ticket. Rental cars and taxis are available at the airport, but try to arrange the pickup through your hotel.

Passports and Visas U.S. and Canadian citizens need only offer proof of identity, so a passport, notarized birth certificate, or voter's registration card will suffice. British subjects may carry a British Visitor's Passport, available from any post office. All other visitors must carry an official passport. In addition, any visitor who steps onto the island must have a return or ongoing ticket and must confirm that reservation 48 hours before departure.

Customs and Duties U.S. residents returning to the United States may bring $400 worth of duty-free articles. Included may be one carton of cigarettes as well as one quart of liquor per person over 21. Articles in excess of $400 up to $1,000 are assessed at a flat rate of 10%.

Language The official language is Dutch, but few speak it, and even then only on official occasions. The street language is Papiamento, a mixture of Spanish, Portuguese, Dutch, English, African, and French—full of colorful Bonairian idioms that even Curaçaoans sometimes don't get. You'll light up your waiter's eyes, though, if you can remember to say *Masha danki* (thank you).

Precautions Because of violent trade winds pounding against the rocks, the windward (eastern) side of Bonaire is much too rough for diving. The *Guide to the Bonaire Marine Park* (available at dive shops around the island) specifies the level of diving skill required for 44 sites, and it knows what it's talking about. No matter how beautiful a beach may look, heed all warning signs regarding the rough undertow.

During the rainy season, the mosquitoes in Bonaire are nearly vampiric. Spray your hotel room before you go to bed. Smart, happy people douse themselves with repellent all day long, including their arms, legs, and face.

Get an orientation on what stings under water and what doesn't. As the island's joke goes, you won't appreciate Bonaire until you've stepped on a long-spiny urchin, but by then, you won't appreciate the joke.

Bonaire used to have a reputation for being the friendliest and safest island in the Caribbean, but this year, even residents are locking their car doors for safety. Don't leave your camera lying about, and tuck away money, credit cards, jewelry, and other valuables.

Further Reading Divers should buy the island's diving bible, *Guide to the Bonaire Marine Park*, by Tom van t'Hof, for in-depth descriptions of 44 dive sites. Available at the entrance to Washington/Slagbaai Park is the *Field Guide*, which details the park's geography, geology, history, and plant and animal life.

A must for any snorkeling or diving fanatic is the *Guide to the Coral and Fishes of Florida, the Bahamas and the Caribbean*, a waterproof, boatproof, childproof book that describes and illustrates over 260 species you're bound to encounter on your underwater expeditions. Kids will want to bring it to school for show-and-tell.

Staying in Bonaire

Important Addresses **Tourist Information:** The **Bonaire Tourist Board** (Kaya Grandi, tel. 599/7–8322/8649).

Emergencies **Police:** For assistance call 599/7–8000.

Hospitals: St. Francis Hospital, Kralendijk (tel. 599/7–8900).

Currency The great thing about Bonaire is that you don't need to convert your American dollars into the local currency, the NAf guilder. U.S. currency and traveler's checks are accepted everywhere, and the difference in exchange rates is negligible. Banks accept U.S. dollar banknotes at the official rate of NAf 1.77 to the U.S. dollar, checks at NAf 1.79. The rate of exchange at shops and hotels ranges from NAf 1.75 to NAf 1.80. The guilder is divided into 100 cents, and there are coins of 1 cent, 2½, 5, 10, 25, 50, 100, 250, and 500 guilders. Note: Prices quoted here are in U.S. dollars unless indicated otherwise.

Taxes and Service Charges Hotels and restaurants collect a 5% government tax. The departure tax is $10.

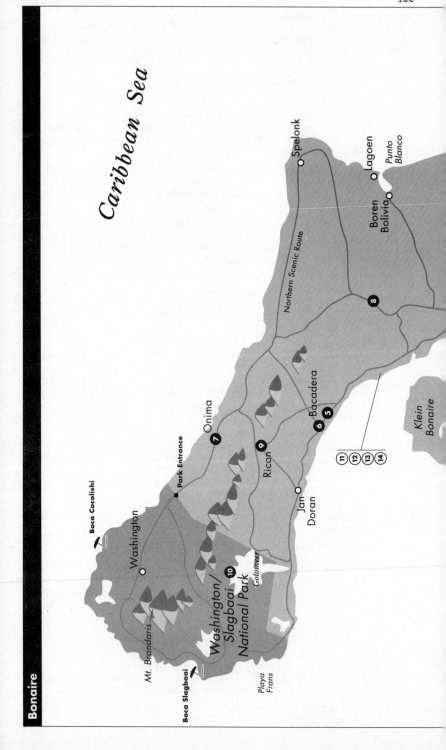

Bonaire

Caribbean Sea

Boca Cocolishi

Washington

Mt. Brandaris

Boca Slagbaai

Washington/
Slagbaai
National Park

⑩

Gotomeer

Playa
Frans

Park Entrance

Onima

⑦

Ricon

⑨

Jan
Doran

Bacadera

⑥ ⑤

⑪ ⑫ ⑬ ⑭

Klein
Bonaire

Northern Scenic Route

Spelonk

⑧

Boren
Bolivia

Lagoen

Punto
Blanco

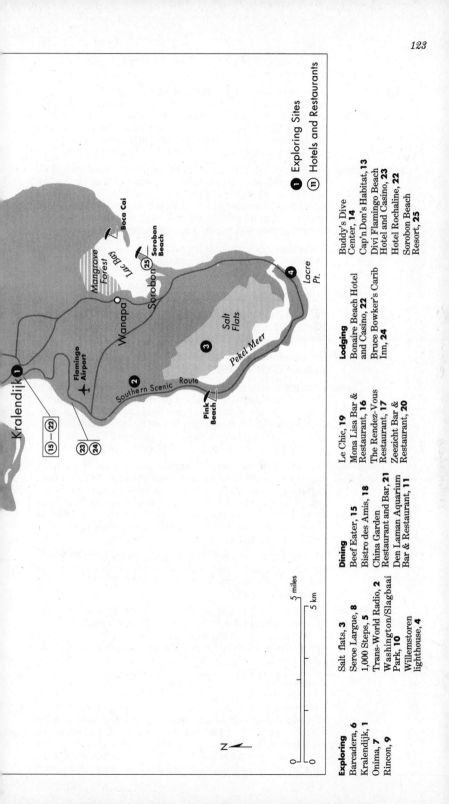

Hotels usually add a 10%–15% service charge to your bill; most restaurants add 15%.

Guided Tours If you don't like to drive, **Bonaire Sightseeing Tours** (tel. 599/7–8300, ext. 225) will chauffeur you around the island (about $10 per person) on two different two-hour tours, north and south. A complete three-hour expedition of the island goes for $15 per person, and parties of four may spend up to four hours exploring Washington National Park at a cost of $17 per person.

Getting Around You can zip about the island in a Suzuki jeep. Scooters and bicycles, which are also available, are less practical but can be fun, too. Just remember that there are at least 20 miles of unpaved road; the roller-coaster hills at the national park require strong stomachs; and during the rainy season, mud—called Bonairian snow—is unpleasant. All traffic stays to the right.

Rental Cars **Budget** has jeeps available from its three locations: Head Office (tel. 599/7–8300, ext. 25/242), at the airport (tel. 599/7–8315), and the Flamingo Beach Hotel & Casino (tel. 599/7–830, ext. 234). It's always a good idea to wire in advance: Cable BUDGET BONAIRE; telex 1280 BTC NA.

Scooters For scooters and two-seater 80-cc Yamahas, try **Happy Chappy Rentals** (tel. 599/7–8761) or the **Bonaire Trading Company** (tel. 599/7–8300, ext. 225). Rates are approximately $15 per day.

Bicycles The **Bonaire Beach Hotel** (tel. 599/7–8448) and the **Divi Flamingo Beach Hotel** (tel. 599/7–8285) rent bicycles by the half hour.

Taxis Taxis are unmetered; they have fixed rates. A trip from the airport to your hotel will cost about $4; from Hotel Bonaire to the Flamingo Beach Hotel, $5. Fares increase from 8 PM to midnight by 25% and from midnight to 6 AM by 50%. Taxi drivers are usually knowledgeable enough about the island to conduct half-day tours; they charge about $25–$30. Inquire at your hotel.

Telephones and Mail It's difficult for visitors to Bonaire to get involved in dramatic, heart-wrenching phone conversations or *any* phone discussions requiring a degree of privacy: There are no telephones in any hotel rooms on the island. All calls must be made from hotel front desks or from the central telephone company office in Kralendijk. To call Bonaire from the United States, dial 011–599–7 + the local four-digit number.

Airmail postage rates to the United States are NAf1.00 for letters and NAf.65 for postcards; to Canada, NAf1.10 for letters and NAf.70 for postcards; to Britain, NAf1.25 for letters and NAf.80 for postcards.

Opening and Closing Times Stores in the Kralendijk area are generally open Monday through Saturday 8–noon and 2–6 PM. On Sundays and holidays, when cruise ships arrive, most shops open for a few extra hours. Few restaurants besides those affiliated to hotels are open for lunch.

Beaches

In general, beaches in Bonaire are not runways for voyeurs—anybody with a roving eye is usually underwater looking at the fish. Consequently, figure-shy sunbathers will find Bonaire a pleasant, private place to relax. Don't come expecting Aruba-length stretches of glorious white sand. Bonaire's beaches are smaller, and though the water is indeed blue (several shades of it, in fact), the sand is not always white. You can have your pick of beach in Bonaire according to color: pink, black, or the more familiar white.

As the name suggests, the sand at **Pink Beach** boasts a pinkish tint that takes on a magical shimmer in the late afternoon sun. The water is suitable for swimming, snorkeling, and scuba diving. Take the South Scenic Route on the western side of the island, past the Trans-World Radio station, close to the slave huts. A favorite hang-10 site for Bonairians on the weekend, it is virtually deserted during the week.

Hermit crabs can be found along the shore at **Boca Cocolishi**, a black-sand beach in Washington/Slagbaai Park on the northeast coast. Tiny bits of dried coral and shells form the basin and beach, their dark hues giving the sand an unusual look. Virtually free of current, the spot is perfect for a nontaxing swim or an intimate picnic *à deux*. To get there, take the Northern Scenic Route to the park, then ask for directions at the gate.

Also inside Washington Park is **Boca Slagbaai,** a stretch of fine white powder that is totally free of coral at some points. The gentle surf makes it an ideal place for swimming, especially for children.

For uninhibited sun worshipers who'd rather enjoy the rays in the altogether, the private, "clothes-optional" beach at the **Sorobon Beach Resort** offers calm water and clean sand. Nonguests are welcome for a small fee.

If you enjoy water sports, find out which beaches are best for a specific sport: *See* Participant Sports, below.

Exploring Bonaire

Numbers in the margin correspond with points of interest on the Bonaire map.

Kralendijk Bonaire's capital city of Kralendijk (population: 2,500) is five
1 minutes from the airport and a short walk from the Carib Inn and the Flamingo Beach Hotel. There's really not much to explore here, but there are a few sights worth noting in this small, very tidy city.

Kralendijk has one main drag, J. A. Abraham Boulevard, which turns into **Breedestraat** (Broad Street) in the center of town. Along it are most of the island's major department stores, boutiques, restaurants, duty-free shops, and jewelry stores (*see* Shopping, below).

Crossing Breedestraat, opposite the Spritzer & Fuhrmann jewelry store, is **Kerkweg Street,** with several small supermarkets, the ALM office, a handful of snack shops, and some of the better restaurants, including Bistro des Amis and Rendez Vous (*see* Dining, below). Walk down the narrow waterfront avenue called C. F. B. Hellmundweg, which leads straight to the **North** and **South piers.** Along this route you will see **Fort Oranje,** with cannons pointing to the sea. Throughout the week, many seagoing vessels dock in the harbor, including the *Aquanaut Holiday,* a diver's cruise ship, and the *Freewinds,* owned by the Scientology Church. The elegant white structure that looks like a tiny Greek temple is the **Fish Market,** where local fishermen sell their early morning haul.

Time Out **Rendez Vous Restaurant** (3 Kaya L. D. Gerharts, tel. 599/7–8454) is a bistrolike café that serves soups, salads, and terrific vegetable entrées for lunch. The restaurant's terrace is an ideal locale for people watching.

Elsewhere on the Island   A complete tour around the 24-mile-long island is essential to really "do" Bonaire. Two tours, north and south, are possible; both will take from a few hours to a full day, depending upon whether you stop to snorkel, swim, dive, or lounge.

South Bonaire   The trail south from Kralendijk is chock-full of icons—both natural and man-made—that tell the minisaga of Bonaire. Rent a jeep (a heavy-treaded car will do, but during the rainy months this place becomes a virtual mudslide) and head south along the South Scenic Route.

2 The first icon you'll come to is the unexpected symbol of modernism—the towering 500-foot antennas of **Trans-World Radio,** one of the most powerful stations in Christian broadcasting. From here, evangelical programs and gospel music are transmitted daily in 20 languages to countries worldwide, including those of the Eastern bloc.

3 Keep on cruising about three more miles to the **salt flats,** voluptuous white drifts that look something like huge mounds of vanilla ice cream. Harvested twice a year, the "ponds" are owned by the Antilles International Salt Company, which has reactivated the 19th-century salt industry with great success. (One reason for that success is that the ocean on this part of the island is higher than the land—which makes irrigation a snap.) Keep a lookout for the three 30-foot obelisks—white, blue, and pink—which were used to guide the trade boats coming to pick up the salt. On this stark landscape, these obelisks look decidedly phallic; today, the blue one is used as a point of reference to direct traffic.

The gritty history of the salt industry is revealed down the road in **Rode Pan,** the site of two groups of tiny slave huts. During the 19th century, the salt workers, imported slaves from Africa, worked the fields by day, then crawled into these huts at night to sleep, returning to their homes in Rincon for the weekend. In recent years, the government has restored the huts to their original simplicity, complete with cane-thatch roofs.

4 Regain your bearings and head south to **Willemstoren,** Bonaire's first lighthouse, built in 1837 and still in use. Check out the shipwreck near the shore here—legend has it that the skipper just didn't take directions well.

Rounding the tip of the island, head north and notice how the waves, driven by the trade winds, play a crashing symphony against the rocks. Locals make a habit of stopping here to collect pieces of driftwood in spectacular shapes. To the north are two of the most picturesque beaches in Bonaire—**Sorobon Beach** and **Boca Cai** at Lac Bay. The road here winds through otherworldly desert terrain, full of organ-pipe cacti and spiny-trunk mangroves—huge stumps of saltwater trees that rise out of the marshes like witches. At Boca Cai, you'll be impressed by the huge piles of conch shells discarded by local fishermen. (Sift through them; they make great gifts—but pack them carefully.) On the weekends at Cai, live bands play daily from 10 to 4, and there's beer and food available at the local restaurant. When the mosquitoes arrive in late afternoon, it's time to hightail it home.

North Bonaire The northern tour takes you right into the heart of Bonaire's natural wonders—desert gardens of towering cacti, tiny coastal coves, dramatically shaped coral grottoes, and plenty of fantastic panoramas. A snappy excursion with the requisite photo stops will take about 2½ hours, but if you pack your swimsuit and a hefty picnic basket (forget finding a Burger King or any other restaurant outside Kralendijk), you could spend the entire day exploring this northern sector, including a few hours snorkeling in Washington Park.

Head out from Kralendijk on the Breedestraat until it turns into the Northern Scenic Route on the outskirts of town. Fifteen minutes north of the Bonaire Beach Hotel is a site called
⑤ **1,000 Steps,** a limestone staircase carved right out of the cliff on the left side of the road. Actually, there are only 67 steps, but if you take the trek down them, you'll discover a great place to snorkel and scuba dive.

Following the route northward, look closely for a turnoff marked Vista Al Mar Restaurant. A few yards ahead, you'll discover some stone steps that lead down into a cave full of stalactites and vegetation. Once used to trap goats, this cave,
⑥ called **Barcadera,** is one of the oldest in Bonaire; there's even a tunnel that looks intriguingly spooky.

Note that once you pass the antennas of the Radio Nederland, you cannot turn back to Kralendijk. The road becomes one way, and you will have to follow the cross-island road to Rincon and return via the main road through the center of the island.

If you continue toward the northern curve of the island, the green storage tanks of the **Bonaire Petroleum Corporation** become visible. The road to Rincon and Washington Park is clearly marked. The route to the left will carry you along the
⑦ east coast to **Onima.** Small signposts direct the way to a three-foot limestone ledge that juts out like a partially formed cave entrance. Inside you'll find red-stained designs and symbols inscribed on the limestone, said to have been the handiwork of the Arawak Indians when they inhabited the island centuries ago.

⑧ Follow that same fork and you'll come to **Seroe Largu,** the highest point on the southern part of the isle. During the day, a winding path leads to a magnificent view of Kralendijk's rooftops; at night, the twinkling city lights below make this a romantic stop. If you've got some time, sit on one of the stone benches and watch the friendly turquoise-footed lizards slithering about. They rely on tourists for their main source of crumbs, but if they should happen to ignore you, throw a pebble near them and they'll trot right over.

If you bear right at the fork south of the park you'll pass
⑨ through **Rincon**—a well-kept cluster of pastel cottages and century-old buildings that constitute Bonaire's oldest village. Watch your driving—herds of goats often sit right in the middle of the main drag.

Washington/ Once a plantation producing divi divi trees (whose pods were
Slagbaai Park used for tanning animal skins), aloe (used for medicinal lo-
⑩ tions), charcoal, and goats, **Washington/Slagbaai Park** is now a model of conservation, designed to maintain fauna, flora, and geological treasures in their natural state. Visitors may easily tour the 15,000-acre tropical desert terrain along the dirt roads. Although well marked, the roads sometimes rise and fall

like a roller-coaster, consequently four-wheel drive is a must. (Think twice about coming here if it rained the day before—the mud you may encounter will be more than inconvenient.) There are two different routes: The long one (21 miles) is marked by yellow arrows; the short one (15 miles) is marked by green arrows. Goats and donkeys may dart across the road, and if you keep your eyes peeled, you may catch sight of large, camouflaged iguanas in the shrubbery. Some folks even look out for shooting cacti.

Bird-watchers are really in their element here. Right inside the park's gate, flamingos roost on the salt pad known as **Salina Mathijs,** and exotic parakeets dot the foot of **Mt. Brandaris,** Bonaire's highest peak at 746 feet. Some 130 species of colorful birds fly in and out of the shrubbery in the park. Keep your eyes open and your binoculars at hand. (For choice beach sites in the park *see* Beaches, above.) *The park is open daily 8–5. Admission: $2 adults, children under 15 free. Swimming, snorkeling, and scuba diving are permitted, but visitors are requested not to frighten the animals or remove anything from the grounds. There is absolutely no hunting, fishing, or camping allowed. A useful guidebook to the park is available at the entrance to the park for about $4.*

Off the Beaten Track

Spiny-legged wild flamingos—affectionately called "pink clouds"—at first look like swizzlesticks. But they're magnificent birds to observe—and there are about 15,000 of them in Bonaire. The best time to catch them at home is March–May, when they tend to their blue-plumed young. One of their favorite hangouts is in **Gotomeer,** a saltwater lagoon on the north coast, easily reached by the Northern Scenic Route. At **Playa Frans,** on the northwest curve of the island, you're also sure to make a sighting, with a few turkeys, chickens, and ducks thrown in for good measure. Right inside the gate of **Washington/Slagbaai Park** is another flamingo haunt. And in the south, the birds camp out at the salt ponds, site of their largest breeding grounds.

Scuba Diving

Bonaire has the best reef diving this side of Australia's Great Barrier Reef. The island is unique primarily for its incredible dive sites; it takes only 5–25 minutes to reach your site, and many of the reefs have very sudden, steep drops. General visibility runs 60 to 100 feet, except during surges in November. An enormous range of coral can be seen, from knobby brain and giant brain coral to elkhorn, staghorn, mountainous star, and gorgonian, as well as the black coral that locals use to handcraft jewelry. You're also likely to encounter schools of parrotfish, surgeonfish, angelfish, eels, snappers, and groupers.

The well-policed Bonaire Marine Park, roughly the entire coastline around Bonaire and Klein Bonaire, remains an underwater wonder because visitors take the rules here seriously. Do not even think about (1) spearfishing, (2) dropping anchor, or (3) touching, stepping on, or collecting coral.

Bonaire Diving

Washington/
Slagbaai
National Park

Playa Funchi

Nukove

Gotomeer

Onima

Ricon

Karpata

Jan
Doran

Rappel

Bacadera

Cliff

La Machaca

Ebo's Special

Carl's Hill

Sampler
Klein
Bonaire

Something
Special

Southwest Corner

Calabas
Reef

Forest

Kralendijk

Caribbean Sea

Windsock Steep

Flamingo
Airport

Angel City

Wanapa

Alice in Wonderland

Southern Scenic Route

Salt Pier / Salt City

N

Pink Beach

Salt
Flats

0   5 miles
0   5 km

Pekel Meer

Lighthouse

Lacre Pt.

Dive Operations   All the hotels listed in this guide, with the exception of the Hotel Rochaline, have dive centers. The competition for quality
and variety is fierce. Before making a room reservation, inquire about specific dive/room packages that are available.
Many of the dive shops also have boutiques where you can purchase T-shirts, color slides showing underwater views, postcards, and tropical jewelry. Some of the larger centers include
Bonaire Scuba Center (Bonaire Beach Hotel; write Box 775,
Morgan, NJ 08879, or call tel. 201/566–8866 or 800/526–2370),
Buddy Dive Resort (tel. 599/7–8647/8065), **Habitat Dive Center**
(Cap'n Don Stewart's Habitat; write Box 237, Waitsfield, VT
05673, or call tel. 802/496–5067), and **Peter Hughes Dive Bonaire** (Flamingo Beach Hotel; contact Divi Hotels, tel. 800/367–
3484 or 607/277–3484).

Dive Sites The *Guide to the Bonaire Marine Park* lists 44 sites that have been identified and marked by moorings. In the past year, dive expert Don Stewart has added several sites through a conservation program called Sea Tether. Guides associated with the various dive centers can give you more complete directions. The following are a few popular sites to whet your appetite; these and selected other sites are pinpointed on our Bonaire Diving map.

Take the track down to the shore just behind Trans-World Radio station; dive in and swim south to **Angel City,** one of the most popular and shallowest sites in the reef complex called **Alice in Wonderland.** The boulders and green and tan coral are home to black margates, spanish hogfish, gray snappers, and the large purple sponge tube.

You'll need to catch a boat to reach **Forest,** a dive site off the coast of Klein Bonaire, so named for the abundant black-coral forest found there. Responsible for occasional currents, this site gets a lot of fish action, including what's been described as a "friendly" spotted eel who lives in a cave.

Calabas Reef, located off the Flamingo Beach Hotel, is the island's most frequently dived site. All divers using the hotel's facilities take their warm-up dive here where they can inspect the wreck sunk by Don Stewart for just this purpose. The site is replete with Christmas-tree sponges and fire coral adhering to the ship's hull. Fish life is frenzied, with the occasional octopus putting in an appearance.

Something Special, just south of the entrance of the marina, is famous for its garden eels that slither around the relatively shallow sand terrace.

Windsock Steep, situated in front of the small beach opposite the airport runway, is an excellent first-dive spot and a popular place for snorkeling close to town.

Rappel is one of the most spectacular dives, right near the Karpata Ecological Center. The shore is a sheer cliff and the lush coral growth is home to an unusual variety of marine life, including orange seahorses, squid, spiny lobsters, and a spotted trunkfish named Sir Timothy, who will befriend you for a banana or a piece of cheese.

Participant Sports

Horseback Riding Guided trips may be arranged at the **Tinis Stable** through the Bonaire Beach Hotel (*see* Lodging, below).

Snorkeling Don't consider snorkeling the cowardly diver's sport; in Bonaire the experience is anything but elementary. For only $4–$8 per day, you can rent a mask, fins, and snorkel at any hotel with a water-sports center (*see* Lodging, below). The better spots for snorkeling are on the leeward side of the island, where you have access to the reefs.

Swimming Beaches good for swimming can be found anywhere along the western coast of the island. Excellent sites are by the **Bonaire Beach Hotel** and the **Flamingo Beach Hotel,** where there is no undertow and the slope from the beach to deep water is gradual. Or hitch a ride on a diving expedition to **Klein Bonaire,** a tiny stretch of land where you can spend the day playing king of the dune. There is absolutely *nothing* on Klein Bonaire, except a few forgotten sneakers, so remember to take some food along. And don't miss the boat back home.

Tennis Guests play for free on the two courts at the **Bonaire Beach Hotel**; nonguests pay to play, $6 for 30 minutes of court time. A tennis pro can spruce up your technique, and racquets and balls may be borrowed without charge.

Shopping

You can get to know all the shops in Bonaire in a matter of a few hours, but sometimes there's no better way to enjoy some time out of the sun and sea than to go shopping, particularly if your companion is a dive fanatic and you're not. Almost all the shops are situated on the Kaya Grandi or in adjacent streets and tiny malls. There are several snazzy boutiques worth a browse. One word of caution: Buy as many flamingo T-shirts as you want, but don't take home anything made of goatskin or tortoiseshell; they are not allowed into the United States.

Good Buys The hippest boutique in Bonaire is **Birds of Paradise** (in the small courtyard off Kaya Grandi, tel. 599/7–8998), with merchandise ranging from flamingo earrings and other desert-chic jewelry to Esprit sportswear and stylish swimsuits.

Kibracha Souvenir and Gifts (33 Kaya Corsow, no phone) features wall hangings, exotic shells and driftwood, embroidered dresses, and Dutch curios.

Home Collection Shop (Kaya Grandi, tel. 599/7–8460) specializes in decorations for the home, including locally made *chibichibi* (sugar birds), tile paintings, Dutch souvenirs, and unusual stuffed fish and cloth parrots.

Spritzer & Fuhrmann (29 Kaya Grandi, tel. 599/7–8466) is the duty-free source for Baccarat, Lalique, Royal Doulton, Minton china, silver souvenir spoons, gold jewelry and watches.

Aries Boutique (33 Kaya Grandi, tel. 599/7–8901) is good for a browse in casual men's and women's fashions. It's also the place to pick up picnicking goods, such as Dutch cheeses, crackers, chocolates, and fine wines.

One shop that's sure to inspire a purchase is the **Ki Bo Ke Pakus**, or **What Do You Want?** (Flamingo Beach Hotel, tel. 599/7–8285), with an exquisite line of batiks, dashikis, and island-made jewelry. Swimsuits and beach cover-ups are very chi-chi, with prices to match.

A government-funded crafts center, **Fundashon Arte Industri Bonairiano** (J. A. Abraham Blvd., Kralendijk), offers locally made necklaces of coral in a variety of colors, hand-painted shirts and dresses, and the "fresh craft of the day."

Other locally made ceramics can be found at **MOR-ANG Ceramics** (J. A. Abraham Blvd., just north of Flamingo Beach).

Dining

Gourmets have not been sneaking off to Bonaire for five-star cuisine, but with a healthy variety of dining experiences, visitors should not go home hungry.

The most highly recommended restaurants are indicated by a star ★.

Category	Cost*
Expensive	over $25
Moderate	$15–$25
Inexpensive	under $15

per person, excluding drinks, service, and sales tax (5%)

Beef Eater. This is a Bonairian-run restaurant with old-English decor, but don't let the name mislead you into thinking it's a steak-'n'-aler. The amiable service and the likes of shrimp thermidor, pepper steaks, and fresh catch of the day make for adequate dining. A bar in the back sometimes features rowdy Bonairians—feel free to join in. *12 Kralendijk, Kaya Grandi, tel. 599/7–8081. Reservations required. AE, DC, MC, V. Expensive.*

★ **Bistro des Amis.** Expensive but worth every guilder. The Bistro's creative French menu and the sensual Folies Bergère ambience have all been designed by chef-owner Jan Van Tilburg; try to get this engaging Dutchman to talk about his specialties (though he's usually frantic in the kitchen), then savor his unforgettable red-pepper soup, duck with red-wine sauce, mousse of smoked eel, and red snapper steamed in fish stock. Or just have a drink around the mahogany bar. *1 Kaya L. D. Gerharts, tel. 599/7–8003. Reservations required. AE, MC, V. Closed Sun. Expensive.*

Den Laman Aquarium Bar & Restaurant. Don't let the low lights and open-air site fool you: This seafood restaurant is not exactly relaxing—you'll want to jump up every five minutes to see the barracudas, eels, mammoth turtles, and neon fish swimming by in the 9,000-foot aquarium. Fortunately, this fantastic "ocean-floor" show makes up for the infamously slow service. The conch Kralendijk is an awfully tough piece of meat overmarinated in vinegar, but the red snapper Creole is heavenly. Be sure to reserve a window seat. *77 Gouverneur Debrotweg, next to the Bonaire Beach Hotel, tel. 599/7–8955. Reservations required. AE, MC, V. Closed Mon. Expensive.*

Le Chic. A renovated 80-year-old home in town, Le Chic, with its French menu and pale-green decor, is leagues away from snorkels and wetsuits, so don't go grubby. A Dutch-schooled Aruban chef prepares specialties, such as *Le Pateau*, a meat-fish combo with two sauces, and interesting desserts. *Kaya C. E. B. Hellmund, tel. 599/7–8617. Reservations suggested. AE, DC, MC, V. Expensive.*

The Green Parrot. This restaurant, which is located on the dock of the Sand Dollar Condotel premises, features the biggest hamburgers and the best dacquiris on the island. The view of the setting sun from this casual eatery is spectacular. *Kay Grandi, tel. 599/7–8738. Reservations accepted. AE, MC, V. Moderate.*

★ **Mona Lisa Bar & Restaurant.** The restaurant offers local, Dutch, and Indonesian dishes at unbeatable prices. Its most famous plate is the pork tenderloin drizzled with a special peanut-butter sauce. Somehow, Mona Lisa has become renowned for fresh vegetables, though God knows where they come from, since nearly everything in Bonaire has to be imported. This is a late-night hangout for local shmoozing, and its bar can make light snacks until about 2 AM. *15 Kaya Grandi, tel. 599/7–8718. No reservations. AE, MC, V. Moderate.*

The Rendez Vous Restaurant. From the shaded terrace of this bistrolike café, watch the world of Bonaire go by as you fill up on warm bread, hearty soups, seafood, steaks, and vegetarian specialties. Or munch on light pastries accompanied by steamy espresso. Those in the know swear the Rendez Vous is the place to go to recover from disco-burnout. *3 Kaya L. D. Gerharts, tel. 599/7–8454. No reservations. AE. Closed Sun. morning and Tues. Moderate.*

Zeezicht Bar & Restaurant. Zeezicht (pronounced zay-zeekt and meaning sea view) is one of the better restaurants open for lunch in town. Dining is on the terrace overlooking the harbor or upstairs inside an air-conditioned enclave. Local fishermen are dedicated to this hangout, especially for the ceviche, conch sandwiches, local snails in hot sauce, and the Zeezicht special soup with conch, fish, shrimp, and oysters. *Kaya Corsow, across from the old fish market, tel. 599/7–8434. No reservations. AE, MC, V. Moderate.*

China Garden Restaurant and Bar. Despite its name, this place has an everything-you-could-ever-want menu, from American sandwiches to shark's fin soup, steaks, lobster, even omelets. The sweet-and-sour dishes are not bad. The cable TV at the large bar can be handy, but, in general, the decor is somewhat sleazy. *47 Kaya Grandi, tel. 599/7–8480. No reservations. No credit cards. Closed Tues. Inexpensive.*

Lodging

The most highly recommended lodgings are indicated by a star ★.

Category	Cost*
Expensive	$95–$150
Moderate	$55–$95
Inexpensive	under $55

* All prices are for a standard double room for two, excluding 5% tax and a 15% service charge.

Hotels **Bonaire Beach Hotel and Casino.** The island's largest hotel, the Bonaire Beach complex is undergoing extensive renovation, and at press time, its 1990 condition is not known. The property is spread across 12 acres and encompasses the 600-foot beach Playa Leche. For divers, the Bonaire Scuba Center offers a complete scuba and underwater photography center plus special packages that include diving and the free use of all water-sports equipment. Nondivers can rent Sunfish, Windsurfers, and snorkeling gear. *Gouverneur Debrotweg 75, Box 34, tel. 599/7–8448. U.S. rep.: ITR, tel. 800/223–9815. 145 rooms. Facilities: dining room, cocktail lounge, coffee shop, tennis courts, casino, beach bar, dive and water-sports center. AE, MC, V. Expensive.*

★ **Cap'n Don's Habitat.** With its recent expansion and massive renovation, the Habitat can no longer pass itself off as a mere guest house for divers, once a sort of extended home of Captain Don Stewart, the island's wildest sharp-shooting personality. New management has added a fabulous set of private apartments, which rank among the island's best: all with ocean-view verandas, full kitchens, and spacious, stylish arrangements. For entertainment, look up Captain Don, who lives on the premises, and whose uninhibited presence on Tex-Mex night can throw an entire room of diners into a roaring brawl. Visit his unusual rock garden and nursery on the grounds and ask him about his novels and the night he shot a mosquito with a shotgun. A full dive center, complete with PADI certification, rounds out the picture. *Kaya Gouverneur Debrotweg 103, Box 88, tel. 599/7–8290. U.S. reps: Scott Calder International, tel. 800/223–5581, and Habitat North American, tel. 800/327–6709. 9 cottages, 8 villas, 10 rooms. Facilities: bar, restaurant, gift shop, dive center, photo labs. AE, MC, V. Expensive.*

Divi Flamingo Beach Hotel and Casino. Flamingo is the closest thing you'll find to a small village on Bonaire—a plantation-style resort that will serve your every need. No matter which hotel you're staying at, reserve a table at the Chibi Restaurant, one of the most sought-after dining spots on the island, where you can see ocean waves pounding beneath the open floorboards. The dive facility, called Dive Bonaire, was founded by world-class expert Peter Hughes and features some of the best photo labs in the Caribbean. A special one-hour class in "Zen Diving" will help make divers more comfortable underwater and teach them how to preserve the reef. For those who need it, there's even the world's first barefoot casino. *J. A. Abraham Blvd., tel. 599/7–8285. U.S. rep.: Divi Hotels, tel. 800/367–3484. 110 rooms, 40 time-sharing units. Facilities: casino, 2 restaurants, 2 pools, dive shop, boutique. AE, MC, V. Expensive.*

Sorobon Beach Resort. Here's the perfect place to act out all your *Swept Away* fantasies. Avidly trying to outgrow its previous reputation as a sleazy nudist colony, the Sorobon is an intimate, family-style cluster of cottages on a private beach at Lac Bay, on the southeast shore. Today, about a quarter of the upscale, mostly European guests are not "naturalists," as the other guests prefer to be called—that is, no one will force you to disrobe and no one will force you to look. New Agers will like the natural look of the Scandinavian wood furniture. The heady windsurfing here, a result of the unbeatable combo of shallow bay and strong trade winds, draws raves. And who could hate massage and shiatsu right on the beach? Restaurant, bar, volleyball, nature-oriented book and video library are all for the asking, even a telescope to view the stunning night skies. But act blasé when the manager arrives wrapped in a towel. *Box 14, tel. 599/7–8738. 25 cottages. Facilities: kitchenettes, restaurant, bar, library, water-sports center. AE, MC, V. Expensive.*

★ **Bruce Bowker's Carib Inn.** Fifteen years ago, American diver Bruce Bowker started his small diving lodge out of a private home, continually adding on and refurbishing. Serious divers who like unpretentious digs get a kick out of the intimate college-dorm feel; Bowker knows everybody by name and loves to fill special requests. The two units with no kitchen have a refrigerator and electric kettle, but for more involved dining, you'll have to escape to town because there's no restaurant on the premises. Nervous virgin divers will enjoy Bowker's small scuba classes (one or two people); PADI certification is available. *Box 68, tel. 599/7–8819. 9 units. Facilities: pool, scuba classes, cable TV. AE, MC, V. Moderate.*

Buddy's Dive Center. Europeans who tend to eschew luxury and require only basic amenities with matching rates enjoy this growing complex situated on the beach. In keeping with its no-frills style, this hotel advertises "everyday only one clean towel per person." *Box 231, Marina area, tel. 599/7–8647/8065. 13 apartments. Facilities: pool with bar; restaurant under construction. AE, MC, V. Moderate.*

Hotel Rochaline. Stay in the Rochaline only as a last resort in Bonaire. It's gained a reputation for seediness, but check first: Renovations could have taken place. *Box 27, Kralendijk, tel. 599/7–8286. 35 rooms. Facilities: restaurant. AE, MC, V. Inexpensive.*

Home and Apartment Rentals **Carib Vacations LTD.** (tel. 800/666–8016) can help you locate suitable housing in Bonaire.

The Arts and Nightlife

The Arts Slide shows of underwater scenes keep both divers and nondivers fascinated in the evenings. The best is Dee Scarr, a dive guide, whose show "Touch the Sea" is presented Monday night at 8:45 PM at **Cap'n Don's Habitat** (tel. 599/7–8290). Check with the Habitat for other shows throughout the week. **Flamingo Beach Hotel** (tel. 599/7–8285) offers a free underwater video, "Discover the Caribbean," on Sunday night at 9:30 PM.

The best singer on the island is guitarist **Cai-Cai Cecelia,** who performs with his duo Thursday night at **Flamingo Beach Hotel** and Monday at **Habitat.** He sings his own compositions, as well as Harry Belafonte classics.

Nightlife Most divers are exhausted after they finish their third, fourth, or fifth dive of the day, which probably explains why there's only one disco in Bonaire. Nevertheless, **E Wowo** (Kralendijk, at the corner of Kaya Grandi and Kaya L. D. Gerharts) is usually packed in high season, so get there early. The name E Wowo means "eye" in Papiamento, illustrated with two flashing op-art eyes on the wall. Recorded music is loud, and the large circular bar seats a lot of action. The entrance fee varies according to the season.

For late-night conversations, **The Rendez Vous Restaurant** is open late, with light pastries and espresso, as is the **Mona Lisa** (*see* Dining, above).

The popular bar **Karel's** (no phone), on the waterfront across from the Zeezicht Restaurant, sits on stilts above the sea and is *the* place to flirt with diving pros. Closed Monday.

Bonaire has only two casinos: **Flamingo Beach Hotel Casino** opens at 4 PM, and the **Black Coral Casino at Bonaire Beach Hotel** opens at 9 PM.

7 The British Virgin Islands

by David L. Grambs

A freelance writer and editor from New York City, David L. Grambs is the author of two books—Dimboxes, Epopts, and Other Quidams: Words to Describe Life's Indescribable People and Words About Words—and a contributing editor to the Random House Dictionary of the English Language.

There's no gambling, no golf, no lavish nightly entertainment. Don Rickles has never cracked a joke here. Nassau hats and Hawaiian shirts look slightly gauche on Main Street, where there's little to buy, none of it duty free. On all the islands there are fewer beds than in the Caribe Hilton in San Juan. Hotels are by law no more than two stories high, and few have air-conditioning—just ceiling fans and a steady breeze brushed with the scent of frangipani blossoms, jasmine, and sage.

Three crucial facts you might want to know right off. One, you won't hear a great many Oxbridge accents; this is still the West Indies. Two, your American money is not only good here, it's the official currency. Three, many of the better resorts are rather expensive, even for the Caribbean.

On the map you'll find this destination 60 miles east of Puerto Rico, where you'll get your connecting flight if you don't choose as your stop-off the much closer island of St. Thomas. Tortola (not to be confused with various Tortugas) is the largest island, with a population of 9,200. Off Tortola's northern shores are the islands of Jost Van Dyke, Guana, and Great Camanoe, among others.

Tortola's sister in size and beauty is smaller, spindly Virgin Gorda to the east, which has a population of about 1,400 and geographically seems to leave a trail of jigsaw pieces parallel to (west to east) and south of Tortola: Norman, Peter, Salt, Cooper, and Ginger islands.

But the glory of this archipelago is less the islands themselves than the 5-mile-wide Sir Francis Drake Channel. It sparkles like a vast turquoise river in the sunlight as you careen along Tortola's curving Waterfront Drive (perhaps the only road in the BVI on which you'll hear cars whoosh by). It makes you want to visit one of the islands over there, or to just sail up and down its length; you're not sure which. Maybe to anchor over the wreck of the R.M.S. *Rhone*— off Salt Island, which, with Virgin Gorda's bouldered grotto called The Baths, is the prime tourist attraction in the BVI.

The British Virgin Islands are in fact a sailor's heaven. To "bareboat" here is not to go skinny-shipping but to be your own captain. From old yacht club members to young couples who hire a crew and captain, many BVI visitors sail happily from anchorage to anchorage, from Prickly Pear to Great Dog, from Sandy Cay to Scrub Island, from Pelican Island to Dead Chest —if not to mysterious Anegada, the unique coral island north of Virgin Gorda's North Sound. Hundreds of wrecks lie in these waters, and most of them lie around Anegada—its highest point is only 28 feet above sea level—and unlucky Horseshoe Reef.

Driving on the British Virgin Islands is never dull. On Tortola go as slowly as you can along the beautiful stretch from Long Bay to Cane Garden Bay or up the roller-coaster switchback from Road Town called Joe's Hill. On Virgin Gorda you can drive to the haunting and ruggedly beautiful place called Copper Mine Point or get to the highest point you can find overlooking Leverick Bay and North Sound for a view that will become a freeze-frame in your memory.

In the British Virgins, you won't find high-rise hotels, marble lobbies, shopping arcades, cruise-ship hordes, groaningly

ATLANTIC

Long
Pt.
Guana Island

*Great
Tobago*

Man
O'War
Bay

JOST VAN DYKE

West End
Pt.

*Great
Harbour*

Little
Harbour

Brewer's
Bay

Fahie
Hill

Long
Bay

White Bay

Pull &
Be Damn
Pt.

*Black
Pt.*

Cane Garden
Bay

Todman
Pk.

Fort
Shirley

Little Tobago

Carrot Bay

Road
Town

Road
Town
Harbour

*Great Thatch
Island*

West End

Mt.
Sage

West Pt.

Frenchman's
Cay

TORTOLA

*Great
Harbour*

Rock
Hole

*White
Bay*

Pelican Island

Privateer
Bay

ST. JOHN
UNITED STATES VIRGIN ISLANDS

Norman
Island

*Money
Bay*

ANEGADA
(15 miles north of Neckar Is.)

West End Pt.
Bones Bight
Loblolly Bay
Table Bay
Flamingo Pond
Red Pond
The Settlement
Lower Bay
Budrock Pond
Horse Shoe Reef
White Bay

O C E A N

Anegada Passage

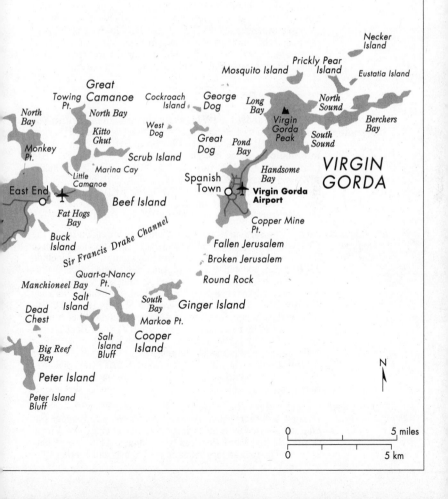

Necker Island
Prickly Pear Island
Eustatia Island
Mosquito Island
Great Camanoe
Towing Pt.
Cockroach Island
George Dog
Long Bay
North Sound
North Bay
North Bay
Kitto Ghut
West Dog
Virgin Gorda Peak
Berchers Bay
Monkey Pt.
Scrub Island
Great Dog
Pond Bay
South Sound
Marina Cay
Little Camanoe
VIRGIN GORDA
East End
Spanish Town
Handsome Bay
Beef Island
Fat Hogs Bay
Virgin Gorda Airport
Buck Island
Sir Francis Drake Channel
Copper Mine Pt.
Quart-a-Nancy Pt.
Fallen Jerusalem
Manchioneel Bay
Broken Jerusalem
Salt Island
Round Rock
Dead Chest
South Bay
Ginger Island
Markoe Pt.
Salt Island Bluff
Cooper Island
Big Reef Bay
Peter Island
Peter Island Bluff

N

| 0 | | | | | 5 miles |
| 0 | | | | | 5 km |

packed safari jams, traffic jams, or honeymoon-package hype. "Towns" are more like sleepy settlements. In fact you won't even find many room telephones or television sets. The BVI evidently will enter the 1990s contentedly uncommercialized — still the more virginal Virgins.

It must be the British influence, or reticence. The English, along with the Dutch and the French, began sniffing around these Indies cays in the 16th and 17th centuries when Spain didn't seem too serious about them. (They were sighted, in 1493, by Columbus.) English planters settled on Virgin Gorda in 1680, and eventually prospered on sugarcane and cotton, but when slavery ended in 1833 they fled elsewhere, leaving their lands in the hands of their former slaves. In 1893 there were only two whites on the islands, the deputy governor and the doctor. Until tourism began in the late 1960s, the BVI was a society of small farmers and fishermen.

Today most islanders own their own land and can afford to treat visitors as welcome guests. What will happen when hotel chains rattle at their doors is anyone's guess; but for now they're avoiding the plight of other West Indians, who are lucky to find jobs in high-rise hotels on land they and their families owned for generations. Hotels and shops are being established by white Americans and Europeans, but the BVI is home to them, and they have an equal stake in preserving the quality of island life. So far, the quality of life is more important than the pace, and nothing is still one of the nicest things to do.

Before You Go

Tourist Information Information about the BVI is available through the **British Virgin Islands Tourist Board** (370 Lexington Ave., Suite 511, New York, NY 10017, tel. 212/696–0400) or at **British Virgin Islands Information Offices** in San Francisco (1686 Union St., San Francisco, CA 94123, tel. 415/775–0344 or, in CA, 800/922–4873) and Ontario (801 York Mill Rd., Suite 201, Don Mills, Ontario, CAN MCB 1X7, tel. 416/443–1859). British travelers can write or visit the **BVI Information Office** (26 Hockerill St., Bishops Stortford, Herts., CM23 2DW, tel. 01/44279–54969).

Arriving and Departing
By Plane No nonstop service is available from the United States to the BVI; connections are usually made through San Juan, Puerto Rico, or St. Thomas, USVI. From San Juan, carriers include **Air BVI** (tel. 800/468–2485) and **American Eagle** (tel. 800/433–7300), which fly to both Beef Island/Tortola and Virgin Gorda. Airlines flying to those same two destinations from St. Thomas are Air BVI, **Virgin Islands Seaplane Shuttle** (tel. 800/524–2050) and (to Virgin Gorda only) American Eagle. More remote Anegada can be reached by flying Air BVI from Beef Island/Tortola. Service between the BVI and the islands of Anguilla, Antigua, St. Kitts, and St. Maarten is provided by either Air BVI or **Leeward Islands Air Transport (LIAT)** (tel. 809/462–0701). These and other islands can also be reached via **Gorda Aero Service** (Tortola, tel. 809/495–2271), a charter service.

By Boat Various water taxis connect St. Thomas, USVI, with Tortola. There is daily service via *Native Son, Oriole,* and *Voyager Eagle,* and service on Sundays between St. Thomas and Virgin Gorda. **Smiths Ferry Services** (tel. 809/494–4430 or 809/494–2355) carries passengers between St. Thomas and Tortola Mondays through Saturdays, and **Speedy's** (tel. 809/495–5240) connects those two islands Tuesdays, Thursdays, and Saturdays.

Between Tortola and Virgin Gorda service is offered by Smiths seven days a week and by Speedy's Mondays through Saturdays. Speedy's connects Tortola and Virgin Gorda with Anegada on Tuesdays and Sundays. Speedy's also goes from both Tortola and Virgin Gorda to St. John and back on Thursdays. **Varlack Ventures** (tel. 809/776–6412 or 809/776–6695) has daily ferries between St. Thomas, St. John, and Tortola, and **Inter-Island Boat Services'** *Sundance II* (tel. 809/776–6282) connects St. John and Tortola daily. Running daily between Virgin Gorda's North Sound (Bitter End Yacht Club) and Beef Island are **North Sound Express** boats (tel. 809/494–2746). There are also daily boats between Tortola's CSY Dock and Peter Island.

Passports and Visas U.S. and Canadian citizens must present proof of citizenship upon entering the BVI in the form of a passport, birth certificate, or voter's registration card.

Customs and Duties A $400 duty-free exemption on purchased goods is allowed by U.S. Customs as long as you have been out of the United States at least 48 hours. Such limits can be "pooled" by family members into a joint or collective duty-free allowance; thus a husband and wife are allowed $800 in duty-free exemption regardless of who bought what. For an article costing up to $1,000, the duty is 10% of the remainder or excess over the exempt amount; for example, for a $1,000 necklace, spouses traveling together will pay 10% duty on $200. Unlimited gifts may be mailed back home duty-free as long as the gift's value doesn't exceed $50 per day to any single address. The allowance on items classified as island crafts, art, or antiques is unlimited. The cigarette allowance is one carton duty-free (80¢ tax on additional cartons), and the liquor allowance one liter per person over 21. If you are traveling to St. Thomas, you may buy $400 worth of goods in the BVI and another $400 worth in St. Thomas.

Language British English, with a West Indian inflection, is the language of the BVI.

Precautions There are no perils from drinking the water in these islands. Insects, notably mosquitoes, are not usually a problem in these breeze-blessed isles, but it is always a good idea to bring some repellent along. Animals in the BVI are not dangerous but they can be road hazards, if shy ones. Give goats, sheep, horses, and cows the right of way.

Further Reading Robb White's *Our Virgin Island* is about Marina Cay a couple of decades ago (it became the Sidney Poitier and John Cassavetes movie *Virgin Island);* you still might be able to find a copy in a library.

Lito Valls's *What a Pistarckle!*, published in 1981 on St. John, USVI, is an entertaining paperback dictionary of Virgin Islands' English Creole. If you can't find a copy in Road Town, you will at the Sugar Mill hotel's little gift shop.

Margaret Truman's *Murder in the CIA* has a British Virgin Islands setting.

Once you've arrived in the BVI, the place to find numerous local books and pamphlets about these islands is **The Cockle Shop** (Main St., Road Town, near the post office, tel. 809/494–2525) or nearby **Past and Presents** (tel. 809/494–2747).

Staying in the British Virgin Islands

Important Addresses **Tourist Information:** On Tortola there is a **BVI Tourist Board Office** at the center of Road Town near the ferry dock, just south of Wickhams Cay I (Box 134, Road Town, Tortola, BVI, tel. 809/494–3134). For all kinds of useful information about these islands, including rates and phone numbers, get a free copy of *The Welcome Tourist Guide*, available at hotels and other places.

Emergencies **Police:** Dial 999.

Hospitals: Dial 998 for a medical emergency. On Tortola there is **Peebles Hospital** in Road Town (tel. 809/494–3497). Virgin Gorda has two clinics, one in Spanish Town or The Valley (tel. 809/495–5337) and one at North Sound (tel. 809/495–7310).

Pharmacies: Pharmacies in Road Town include **BVI Drug Center** (tel. 809/494–2702) and **Lagoon Plaza Drug Store** (tel. 809/494–2498). On Virgin Gorda, in Spanish Town, there is **J. R. O'Neal Marketing Associates** (tel. 809/495–5325).

Currency British though they are, the BVI have the U.S. dollar as the standard currency.

Taxes and Service Charges Hotels collect a 7% accommodations tax. For those leaving the BVI by air, the departure tax is $5; by sea it is $4. A tourist information card must also be filled out by visitors.

Guided Tours If you'd like to do some chauffeured sightseeing on Tortola, get in touch with **B.V.I. Taxi Association** ($10 per person, minimum three persons, tel. 809/494–2875, 809/494–2322, or 809/495–2378), **Style's Taxi Service** (tel. 809/494–2260 during the day or 809/494–3341 at night), or **Travel Plan Tours** (tel. 809/494–2872). An inclusive tour program is also offered by **Rancal Rent-a-Car** (tel. 809/494–4534, 809/494–4535, or 809/495–4330). **Scato's Bus Service** in Road Town (tel. 809/494–2365) provides public transportation, special tours with group rates, and beach outings.

Guided tours on Virgin Gorda can be arranged through **Andy's Taxi and Jeep Rental** (tel. 809/495–5252 or 809/495–5353).

Getting Around Whether you're behind the wheel yourself or not, motoring about on Tortola or Virgin Gorda is pleasurable, scenic, and sometimes exciting. Roads tend to have simple names rather than highway numbers. If there is a traffic light anywhere in the BVI, only a secret society knows where it is. Ascents and descents can be thrilling, particularly when the views to the side are so astoundingly lovely as to be distracting. If chugging up Joe's Hill from Road Town doesn't have you holding your breath a bit, the roll down to the northern coast—or the view of Cane Garden Bay—on the other side of the ridge, will. The same holds for the main road on Virgin Gorda from Spanish Town to Gun Creek and North Sound.

Driving is *à l'Anglais*, on the left side of the road. You can get used to this by driving slowly. This is easily done since the speed limit is 30 m.p.h., 10 to 15 m.p.h. in residential areas.

Taxis Your hotel will be happy to summon you a taxi when you want one. There is a taxi stand in Road Town near the ferry dock (tel. 809/494–2322) and one on Beef Island, where the airport is (tel. 809/495–2378). You can also usually find a taxi at Sopers Hole, West End, where water taxis or ferries come in from St. Thomas.

Buses For information about rates and schedules, call **Scato's Bus Service** (tel. 809/494–2365).

Mopeds Scooters can be rented on Tortola from **Hero's Bicycle Rental** (tel. 809/494–3536 or 809/494–3746).

Rental Cars You must have a valid driver's license and you must pay $10 for a temporary BVI driver's license, valid for three months. You can pick up the license at a police station or purchase it as part of the paperwork when you are renting a car.

Car-rental agents on Tortola are **Alphonso Car Rentals** (tel. 809/494–3137 or 809/494–4886), **Anytime Car Rental** (tel. 809/494–2875 or 809/494–3107), **Avis** (tel. 809/494–3322 or 809/494–2193), **Budget** (tel. 809/494–2639), **Caribbean** (tel. 809/494–2595), **Inner Harbour Marina Car Rentals** (tel. 809/494–4502/3/4/5), **International** (tel. 809/494–2516 or 809/494–2517), **Island Suzuki** (tel. 809/494–3666), **National** (tel. 809/494–3197), and **Rancal** (tel. 809/494–4534, 809/494–4545, or 809/495–4330).

On Virgin Gorda you can lease a vehicle from **Speedy's** (tel. 809/495–5235 or 809/495–5240). **Mahogany Rentals** (tel. 809/495–5542 or 809/494–5322) does not accept credit cards but has lower rates and *especially* courteous and helpful service.

Telephones and Mail The area code for the BVI is 809, which, of course, needn't be dialed for a local call. Furthermore, only the last five digits of a number have to be dialed here: instead of dialing 494–1234, just dial 4–1234. A local call from a public pay phone costs 25¢. For long-distance calls, the best place to hook up with public phones on Tortola is **Cable & Wireless,** in Road Town; on Virgin Gorda, at the Yacht Harbour.

There are post offices in Road Town on Tortola and in Spanish Town on Virgin Gorda. Postage for a first-class letter to the United States is 40¢ and for a postcard 30¢. (It might be noted that postal efficiency is not first-class in the BVI.)

Opening and Closing Times Stores are generally open from 9 to 5 Monday through Saturday. Bank hours are Monday through Thursday 9–2:30 and Friday 9–2:30 and 4:30–6.

Beaches

Beaches here are less developed than, say, on St. Thomas or St. Croix. You'll also find fewer people. Try to get out on a boat at least one day during your stay in these islands, whether a dive-snorkeling boat or a day-trip sailing vessel. It's sometimes the best way to get to the most virgin Virgin beaches (some have no road access). The beaches mentioned below can be reached by car or jeep, possibly with a little walking involved, too. Rent a jeep if you're a seeker of remote beaches and want to be able to handle the worst kind of terrain to get there. If you explore numerous beaches in a single drive, know that most of the best ones on both Tortola and Virgin Gorda are on the northern coasts.

Are you welcome at a beach that seems to belong to a particular resort? Technically, yes, and technically, no: you're welcome on the beach, but not always welcome on the private property you have to cross in order to get to it. While welcoming your use of their beach, most resorts also hope to safeguard the prerogatives and privacy of their own guests. (Little Dix Bay Resort on Virgin Gorda is particularly concerned with privacy.) In short, it's a gray area. Feel free to hit the sand anywhere but don't leave your manners at home.

Tortola **Cane Garden Bay** rivals St. Thomas's Magens Bay in majesty but is besieged by visiting hordes. It's a grand beach for jogging if you can resist veering into that translucent water. You can rent sailboards and such, and for noshing or sipping there is Stanley's Welcome Bar, Rhymer's, and Quito's Gazebo. From Road Town you'll drive a steep uphill and a steep downhill to get here, and you'll feel like you've landed in Paradise.

At **Smuggler's Cove** (Lower Belmont Bay) you'll really feel like you've found a hidden place and will hardly notice the has-seen-better-days hotel back in the overgrowth. There is a fine view of the island of Jost Van Dyke. The snorkeling is good.

Long Bay on Beef Island is gorgeous and visited only by a knowledgeable few. The view of Little Camanoe and Great Camanoe islands is appealing, and if you walk around the bend to the right, you can see little Marina Cay and Scrub Island. Take the Queen Elizabeth Bridge to Beef Island and watch for a small dirt turnoff before the airport. Drive across that dried-up marsh flat—there really is a beach (with interesting seashells) on the other side.

If you want to surf, **Apple Bay** (Cappoons Bay) is the spot. Sebastians, the very casual hotel here, caters especially to those in search of the perfect wave. Good waves are never a sure thing, but January and February are usually high times here.

About the only thing you'll find moving at **Trunk Bay** is the surf. It's directly north of Road Town, midway between Cane Garden Bay and Beef Island, and you'll have to hike down a *ghut* (defile) from the high Ridge Road.

The water at **Brewers Bay** is good for either snorkeling (calm) or surfing (swells). There's a campground here, but in the summer you'll find almost nobody around. The beach and its old sugar mill and rum distillery ruins are just north of Cane Garden Bay on the road near Luck Hill.

Virgin Gorda **Savannah Bay** is a lovely place, and though it may not be deserted it seems wonderfully private for a beach just north of Spanish Town (on the north side of where the island narrows, at Black Rock). From town it's only 15 minutes or so on foot.

It's worth going out to **Long Bay** (near Virgin Gorda's northern tip, past the Diamond Beach Club) for the snorkeling (Little Dix Bay resort has outings here). Going north from Spanish Town, go left at the fork near Pond Bay. Part of the route there is dirt road.

Leverick Bay is a small, busy beach-cum-marina that fronts a resort restaurant and pool. Don't come here to be alone or to jog. But if you want a lively little place and a break from the island's noble quiet, take the road north and turn left before

Gun Creek. The view of Prickly Pear Island is an added plus, and there's a dive facility right here to motor you out to beautiful Eustatia Reef just across North Sound.

Anybody going to Virgin Gorda must experience swimming or snorkeling among its unique boulder formations. But why go to The Baths, usually crowded, when you can get your rocks next door—just north—at **The Crawl?** And right next to it is **Guavaberry's Spring Bay** beach, which is a gem.

Other Islands Beaches on other islands, reachable only by boat, include Jost Van Dyke's **Little Harbour** and **White Bay; Marina Cay;** Peter Island's **Big Reef Bay, White Bay,** and **Dead Man's Bay;** Mosquito Island's **Limetree Beach, Long Beach,** and **Honeymoon Beach;** Cooper Island's **Manchioneel Bay;** and farther-off, reef-laced **Anegada.**

Exploring Tortola

Numbers in the margins correspond with points of interest on the Tortola map.

❶ This outing begins at the populous indentation in the middle of Tortola called **Road Town.** The route will acquaint you with this mountainous island's western half, where its more popular beaches and views are to be found. You will drive along both the southern and northern coasts with chances to stop at lovely bays, and there will be some heady mountain roads, a misty rain forest, and one of the best panoramic views in all the Caribbean. Be sure to bring your swimsuit!

We'll start at **Wickhams Cay.** This is the center of the action in Road Town and a place to enjoy a broad view of the wide harbor, home to countless sailing vessels and yachts and a base for the well-known yacht-chartering enterprise called The Moorings. You'll find a **BVI Tourist Board** office to serve you right here as well as banks, a post office, and most of Tortola's stores and boutiques. If you walk about to do a little shopping, don't miss **The Pusser's Co. Store and Pub.** This handsome emporium has a nautical theme, and its sporty knickknacks, Pusser's rum mugs, and all-cotton clothes make attractive purchases. Outside the store, along the main harbor-front sidewalk, you'll also find some good clothing buys from street vendors. Check out some of the unusual BVI T-shirts (seconds), some of which cost only a couple of dollars.

Hitting the road, head west on the one and only main street, which hugs the island's southern coast. The turret-like building perched on that little hill to your right is **Fort Burt,** once an old Dutch fort and now a nice little hotel with an esteemed restaurant. Just ahead on the left is the comfortable **Prospect Reef** resort, catering especially to vacationers who don't like to keep their feet dry. You might want to park for a moment to get a look at the property's lagoons, canals, pools, and amazing seafront pool. They're all man-made, but the sun-gilded **Sir Francis Drake Channel** out there—some 20 miles long and 5 miles wide—was definitely made by higher powers.

Continue west on the ever-curving shore road. You're about to enjoy 5 miles or so of the nicest driving in all the British Virgin Islands: a well-paved road, no hills, little traffic, lots of curves to keep things interesting, and the lovely, island-studded chan-

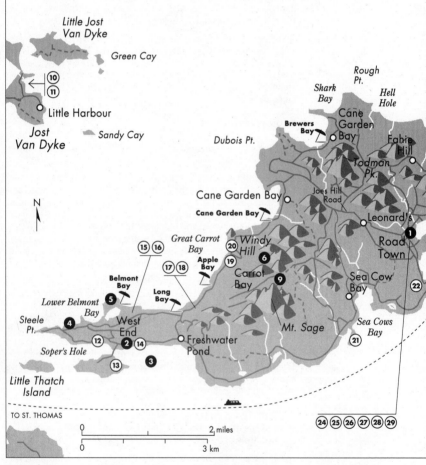

ATLANTIC OCEAN

Little Jost Van Dyke

Green Cay

Little Harbour

Jost Van Dyke

Sandy Cay

Dubois Pt.

Rough Pt.

Shark Bay

Hell Hole

Brewers Bay

Cane Garden Bay

Fahie Hill

Todman Pk.

Joes Hill Road

Cane Garden Bay

Leonard's

Road Town

Great Carrot Bay

Windy Hill

Apple Bay

Carrot Bay

Belmont Bay

Lower Belmont Bay

Long Bay

Sea Cow Bay

Steele Pt.

West End

Freshwater Pond

Mt. Sage

Sea Cows Bay

Soper's Hole

Little Thatch Island

TO ST. THOMAS

N

0   2 miles
0   3 km

Exploring	**Dining**	**Lodging**	Frenchman's Cay Resort Hotel, **13**
Beef Island, **7**	The Cloud Room, **24**	Anegada Reef Hotel (Anegada Island), **36**	Guana Island Club (Guana Island), **34**
Belmont Pond/Belmont Point, **5**	Elena's, **25**	Cane Garden Bay Beach Hotel, **35**	Hotel Castle Maria, **12**
Callwood Distillery, **6**	Fort Burt Restaurant, **31**	Fort Burt, **18**	Jolly Roger Inn, **29**
Frenchman's Cay, **3**	Jule's Place, **19**	Fort Recovery, **14**	Long Bay Beach Resort, **16**
Marina Cay, **8**	Long Bay Beach Resort, **15**		Maria's by the Sea, **28**
Road Town, **1**	The Pusser's Deli, **27**		Marina Cay Hotel (Marina Cay), **35**
Sage Mountain National Park, **9**	Spaghetti Junction, **26**		
Smuggler's Cove, **4**	Sugar Mill, **17**		
West End, **2**			

TO ANEGADA
36

Wash
Ballock
Pt.

Long
Pt.

*Muskmellon
Bay*

*North
Bay*

Great
Camano

*Guana
Island*   **34**

*White
Bay*

*Lee
Bay*

Kitto Ghut

*Scrub
Island*

Monkey Pt.

*Little
Camanoe*

*Rogue's
Pt.*

**Trunk
Bay**

*Long
Bay*

*Marina
Cay*

8 **35**

**Long
Bay**

*Trellis
Bay*

Bufa Mt.

Long
Look

**East
End**

Parham
Town

Long Swamp

Queen
Elizabeth
Bridge

7

30

Mt. Belle-Vue

*Bluff
Bay*

*Beef
Island*

Ft. Shirley

*Fat Hogs
Bay*

*Road
Town
Harbour*

31 **32** **33**

*Paraquita
Bay*

*Buck
Island*

TO VIRGIN
GORDA

TO PETER
ISLAND

23

Sir Francis Drake Channel

1 Exploring Sites

10 Hotels and Restaurants

nel on your left. At Sea Cow Bay the road bends inland just a bit to pass through a small residential area, but it soon rejoins the water's edge. Jutting out into the channel is **Nanny Cay**. You might want to swing left here to see the marina and Peg Leg Landing, a lively restaurant on stilts worth coming back to for a sunset drink or a moonlit dinner. The hotel here has recently come under Ramada management.

After Nanny Cay this pleasant, wide-open coastal road passes **Fort Recovery**. There are now vacation villas here but the ruins of the 17th-century Dutch fort are still to be seen. The road ❷ straightens out and brings you to **West End** and **Sopers Hole,** where—if you didn't fly in to Beef Island Airport—you probably arrived by boat. The boat terminal and customs and immigration offices are here. Turn left over the bridge to ❸ **Frenchman's Cay** and bear right on the other side of the bridge. There's a marina and a lovely view across the peaceful waters of Sopers Hole and west toward Little Thatch Island.

Leaving Frenchman's Cay, turn right and follow the coast road back toward Road Town. Take the left turn just down the road at Zion Hill—and shift into low gear. There's a steep hill ahead with a sharp-angled turn. This is Tortola's narrowest north–south point and leads quickly to the island's cherished skein of pristine north-shore beaches. On the other side of the hill, at Long Bay, detour left up a rather twisty dirt road. Suspend your doubts and drive slowly ahead until you come to the small ❹ dead-end clearing at **Smuggler's Cove**. You may well have this hideaway beach to yourself (and a friendly resident dog, who loves sprinting after coconuts in the surf). This cove (actually Lower Belmont Bay) always seems a secret or forgotten place. There is a hotel of sorts back in the brush here, but you'd scarcely know it.

The rocky road back will give you a brief but stunning prospect ❺ of **Belmont Pond** and pyramidal **Belmont Point** to your left. Ahead—returning, thankfully, to a paved road—you'll pass Long Bay and, again, at a curve on the hill just past this resort, there is a car-halting view of Long Bay's brilliant white beach extending down to the seemingly carved green hump of Belmont Point (somehow a little reminiscent of Rio de Janeiro's Sugar Loaf Mountain). The road levels out now as you pass Little Apple Bay, Apple Bay, Little Carrot Bay, and Great Carrot Bay, all presenting equally enticing vistas to the northwest of **Jost Van Dyke** and smaller **Sandy Cay**. These waters draw many avid surfers to Tortola. Just past Sebastians on the Beach, a casual hostelry for the hang-five set, you'll notice a curiously decorated—or graffitoed—ramshackle beach hut on the left, **Bomba Shack**. It may look like a giant semi-collapsed wooden wind chime, but it's actually a bar of sorts run by an unconventional local gentleman. Just ahead is Sugar Mill, one of Tortola's nicest places to eat if you're game for some truly intimate, candlelit ambience.

So many of Tortola's best sights seem to be preceded by a hill or two, and **Cane Garden Bay** is no exception. After zigzagging up and down Windy Hill you glide down to this long and curved beach justly celebrated as one of the most beautiful in all the Caribbean. Its sparkling calm waters attract many boats seeking an idyllic place to drop anchor. You'll want to walk at least part of its length, maybe even rent a Windsurfer and do a little stand-up sailing.

Time Out Have a snack and cooling soda or beer at **Stanley's Welcome Bar** (Cane Garden Bay, tel. 809/495–4520) right on Cane Garden's beach, which will give you a place out of the sun.

6 Before leaving the area, stop at the **Callwood Distillery** nearby, sort of a Tortolan version of a backwoods still, but a legal one. If you're interested, venturesome, and not a brand-name-only type, you can purchase a bottle of Callwood's potent moonshine rum for very little.

You'll roll over a little bridge as you proceed east from Cane Garden Bay. Don't relax. You have a long thrill of a hill to drive up here—not even Tortolans seem to be sure of its official name, but some call it Soldiers Hill. Drive along the high central ridge of the island and down Joe's Hill back to Road Town. If you want to continue exploring, don't return to Road Town but continue along the central ridge east past the communities of Wesley Will and Long Swamp, to the modestly slender
7 **Queen Elizabeth Bridge.** Over the bridge is quite flat **Beef Island** and its airport. If you like interesting seashells, **Long Bay**
8 is a find. Also worth a visit is **Marina Cay,** a tiny reef-fringed island resort and marina that can be reached by boat (a short ride) from a dock near the airport.

You have another option at this point before returning to Road Town. The area at the top of the Cane Garden Bay hill (called Meyers) is where four different roads more or less converge. If you bear to the right at the top of the hill and go straight (don't turn off toward the radio tower on your right), you'll come to
9 the parking lot for **Sage Mountain National Park.** Sage Mountain, at 1,716 feet, is the highest peak in the Virgin Islands.

Your best unobstructed views up here are actually from the parking area. From here a trail will lead you around in a loop not only to the peak itself but also to the island's rain forest, sometimes shrouded in mist. Most of the island's forest was cut down over the centuries to clear land for sugarcane, cotton, other crops, pastureland, and timber. But in 1964 this park was established to preserve the remaining rain forest, which not only has exotic trees and plants but also serves an important function in preserving water for Tortola's aquifer. Up here you can see mahogany trees, white cedars, mountain guavas, elephant-ear vines, mamey trees, and giant bulletwoods, to say nothing of such birds as mountain doves and thrushes. As you walk the trail to the main gate, you'll also have good views on your right of the Sir Francis Drake Channel.

If you're not feeling like a naturalist or hiker, from Meyers you can bear left instead of right at the top of the Cane Garden Bay incline and shoot up that steep, driveway-like hill to Skyworld restaurant. The panoramic vista from here is a marvel. There are telescopes on the highest terrace, but even your naked eye will appreciate that this is one of the best views in the Leeward seas—particularly at sunset. Islands, islands everywhere. From here it's a short, gravity-assisted drive back down to Road Town.

Exploring Virgin Gorda

Numbers in the margin correspond with points of interest on the Virgin Gorda map.

Virgin Gorda, with its mountainous central portion connected by skinny necks to southern and northern appendages—on a map they look like they might break away—is quite different from Tortola. Paved roads are few, alternate routes are limited, and there are few places where you can actually drive right along the coast. Yet it has a simple and primitive beauty and is small enough that you can easily get a good fix on most areas of the island in a single day.

❶ From **Spanish Town,** or **The Valley,** as it's sometimes called, drive south past Fischer's Cove Hotel, which is on your right. Continue south until you see a road to the left. Take the left and then the next right. Notice how distinctively dry and desert-like the terrain and plant life are at this end of Virgin Gorda, as evidenced by cactus growth. The road bends east toward the coast. There's an abrupt hill, some badly paved spots, and then no paving at all. But in minutes the rocky dirt road brings you

❷ to spectacular **Copper Mine Point.** A tall, chimney-like stone tower stands amid broken walls and rubble at this windswept promontory, those being the ruins of a 400-year-old Spanish copper mine. You are at the southeastern tip of Virgin Gorda, a rugged, seemingly unvisited place that has something haunting about it. There is a special vividness about the greenish blues of the sea here and the jagged coast it washes against. This is also one of the few places in the British Virgin Islands where you won't see islands dotting the horizon.

Follow the road back north but turn left at the first intersection and then left again. Driving south, you will pass the **Guavaberry Spring Bay** resort, where guests stay in elevated-deck cottages nestled up against huge boulders—the singular feature of Virgin Gorda's southern end. At the end of the road

❸ you'll reach the island's most famous attraction, **The Baths,** where clusters of behemoth prehistoric rocks form cool grottoes. Walk—squeeze—into this cave-like formation to see the shallow pools and the play of sunlight slanting in through crevices. Outside you can enjoy some unusual boulder snorkeling, though you may bump into more people than boulders. The Baths tend to be a little crowded, and many of its visitors come from all those boats you see anchored just offshore. The less besieged beaches just north of here also have majestic boulders.

Drive north from The Baths to **Spanish Town.** At the **Virgin Gorda Yacht Harbour** you can enjoy a stroll along the dock front or do a little browsing in the shops there, such as the Virgin Gorda Craft Shop, Pelican's Pouch Boutique, Island Woman, or The Wine Cellar.

Time Out Settle down by the fountain on the cool patio of the **Bath and Turtle** (Virgin Gorda Yacht Harbour, tel. 809/495–5239), an English-style pub off the marina mall courtyard, and have a burger or fish sandwich with a mug of Courage or your favorite rum drink.

Having seen a bit of the island's arid and relatively flat southern leg, we can look forward to some very different scenery north of Spanish Town. On the way out of town you'll pass the extensive, beautifully cared-for property of **Little Dix Bay,** the Rockresort retreat that is the grandmother of all British Virgin Islands resorts. Much of its sloping 400 acres of verdant grounds looks like a golf course invaded by beautiful tropical trees.

Past Little Dix the road takes you quickly out of town and downhill to the island's thin neck at Savannah Bay. The view—the Sir Francis Drake Channel to the north and the mainstream Caribbean to the south—might make you want to pull over to **4** be sure it's real. It is, and this scenic elbow is called **Black Rock.** The road forks as it goes uphill. The left prong winds past the Mango Beach and Diamond Beach Club resorts (and not much else) to Long Bay and not quite to Mountain Point. To continue exploring, take the road on the right, which winds uphill and looks down on beautiful South Sound. You'll notice that you see nary a dwelling or sign of mundane civilization up here, only a green mountain slope on your left and a spectacular view down to South Sound on the right. From here, too, you can also look back and get a wonderful, living sense of Virgin Gorda's stringy, crooked shape: Back there, looking flat and almost like a separate island, is Spanish Town, which you've just left. Because of this shape, Virgin Gorda is one of those places where you can get a bird's-eye (or map's-eye) view of things from right inside your car.

5 You'll see a small sign on the left for the trail up to **Virgin Gorda Peak,** the island's summit at 1,359 feet. It's about a 15-minute hike up to a small clearing, where you can climb a ladder to the platform of a wood observation tower. If you're keen for some woodsy exercise or just stretching your legs, go for it. But the view at the top is somewhat tree-obstructed and may not be as good as the one you have right here at roadside.

No trip to Virgin Gorda would be complete without seeing **6** some of its **North Sound** area. This is a yachtsman's paradise, but you can appreciate its isolated beauty from a car as well. The route ahead will lead you merely to a view—but what a view!

This corniche comes to a hilly little settlement—there's a clinic, church, and school—just above Gun Creek. Go left, or north, and you'll come out at **Leverick Bay.** There is a resort here, with a cozy beach and marina area and some luxurious hillside villas to rent, all a little like a tucked-away tropical suburb. Low-gear your way up one of the narrow hillside roads (you're not on a driveway, it only seems that way) to one of those topmost Leverick dwellings, where you can park for a moment. (Three of the highest, if you can find them, are called Seaview, Tamarind, and Double Sunrise.)

Out to the left, across Blunder Bay, you'll see **Mosquito Island;** the hunk of land straight ahead is **Prickly Pear,** which has just been named a National Park to protect it from development. At the neck of land to your right, across from Gun Creek, is **Biras Creek,** and around the bend to the north of that you'll see the Danish-roof buildings of the **Bitter End Yacht Club,** these being two of the British Virgin Islands' finest resorts. Between the Bitter End and Prickly Pear you should be able to make out **7** **Saba Rock,** home of one of the Caribbean's best-known diving entrepreneurs, Bert Kilbride—a man who knows where all the wrecks are buried and is recognized and commissioned by the Queen of England.

That magical color change in the sea near Prickly Pear reveals **8** **Eustatia Sound** and its valued reef. Beyond that are Horseshoe

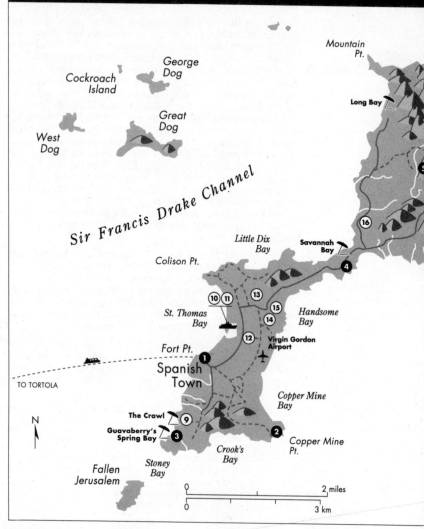

Virgin Gorda

Mountain Pt.

Long Bay

Cockroach Island

George Dog

Great Dog

West Dog

Sir Francis Drake Channel

Little Dix Bay

Colison Pt.

Savannah Bay

St. Thomas Bay

Handsome Bay

Virgin Gordon Airport

Fort Pt.

Spanish Town

TO TORTOLA

Copper Mine Bay

N

The Crawl

Guavaberry's Spring Bay

Copper Mine Pt.

Crook's Bay

Fallen Jerusalem

Stoney Bay

0   2 miles

0   3 km

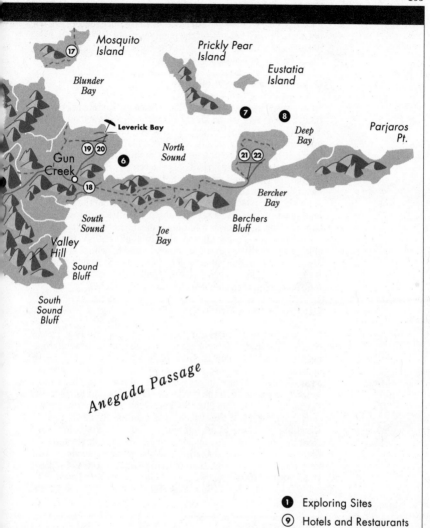

Mosquito Island

Prickly Pear Island

Eustatia Island

Blunder Bay

17

7

8

Deep Bay

Parjaros Pt.

Leverick Bay

19 20

6

North Sound

21 22

Gun Creek

18

Bercher Bay

South Sound

Joe Bay

Berchers Bluff

Valley Hill

Sound Bluff

South Sound Bluff

Anegada Passage

● Exploring Sites

⑨ Hotels and Restaurants

Reef and the flat coral island of Anegada. Out there is where most of those wrecks *are* buried and where bareboaters are not permitted to sail because of the perilous reefs. But you can easily take a boat to Biras Creek or the Bitter End. In fact, that's the only way you can get there.

Other British Virgin Islands

Just across the channel from Road Town on Tortola is **Peter Island,** a 1,000-acre island known for its hotel and yacht club. **Jost Van Dyke,** the sizable island north of Tortola's western tip, is a good choice for travelers in search of isolation and good hiking trails; it has three hostelries and a campground, but only one small town and no cars, roads, or electricity. Hikers also enjoy the nature trails and wildlife sanctuary on **Guana Island,** a private island just above the eastern tip of Tortola. **Marina Cay** is a snug six-acre islet near Great Camanoe, just north of Beef Island, east of Tortola. **Anegada,** about 20 miles north of Virgin Gorda's North Sound, is a flat mass of coral 11 miles long and 3 miles wide with a population of only about 250. Visitors are chiefly scuba divers and fishermen, some of whom are interested in the bonefishing here. The island can be reached by Air BVI as well as by boat (Speedy's, tel. 809/495–5240). (For more information on these islands, *see* Lodging, below.)

Off the Beaten Track

Get yourself some snorkeling gear and hop a dive boat to the wreck of the **R.M.S. *Rhone,*** off Salt Island (just across the channel from Road Town on Tortola). This is your chance to float on crystal-clear water over or near one of the world's best wrecks: a royal mail steamer 310 feet long that sank here in a hurricane in 1867. It was used in the movie *The Deep.* Its four parts are at various depths of from 20 to 80 feet. Even if you can't see down to the main part of the wreck, you'll definitely be fascinated watching the moves and bubbles of scuba divers below you. Nearby Rhone Reef is only 20 to 50 feet down. Simple and safe flotation devices are available, and the scuba supervisors will keep an eye on you. Call **Baskin in the Sun** (tel. 809/494–2858), **Underwater Safaris** (tel. 809/494–3235), **Blue Water Divers** (tel. 809/494–2847), **Island Diver, Ltd.** (tel. 809/494–3878), or **Caribbean Images** (tel. 809/495–2563).

Participant Sports

Horseback Riding   On Tortola, equestrians should get in touch with **Tamarind Country Club Hotel** (East End, tel. 809/495–2477) or **Mr. Ellis Thomas** (Sea Cows Bay, tel. 809/494–4442). On Virgin Gorda call **Little Dix Bay** (The Valley, tel. 809/495–5555).

Sailboarding   **Boardsailing B.V.I.** (Long Look, Tortola, tel. 809/495–2447) has private lessons for $45 per hour and cheaper group rates. **The Nick Trotter Sailing School** (Bitter End Yacht Club, North Sound, Virgin Gorda, tel. 800/872–2392) has both beginner's and advanced courses.

Sailing/Boating   The BVI has been a charter boat paradise for the past 20 years, and the flagship of charter operators has all along been **The Moorings,** at The Moorings-Mariner Inn in Road Town's harbor, Tortola (tel. 809/494–2331 or 800/535–7289; AE, MC, V). About 25 other sailing enterprises offer crewed or bareboat charters or both, and some also have arrangements for cruise trips or day sails.

Tortola **B.V.I. Bareboats** (Road Town, tel. 809/494–4289) offers both bareboat and skippered charters. **Go Vacations** (East End, tel. 809/495–2374) has cat boats, sloops, ketches, and trawlers for bareboat or crewed hire. **Patsy Lady/Foxy Lady** (Road Town, tel. 809/494–3540) will rent you a 24' or 43' twin-engine motorcruiser.

Virgin Gorda **The Bitter End Yacht Club** (North Sound, tel. 809/494–2746 or 800/872–2392, AE, DC, MC, V) is island headquarters for most sailing activity and offers Cal; 27 charters **Malcolm & Niki** (Yacht Harbor, tel. 809/495–5555) rents the *Beruthiel*, a 35' ocean-going catamaran.

Scuba Diving and Snorkeling The famed wreck of the R.M.S. *Rhone*, off Salt Island, is reason enough to do some diving before your BVI stay is over. Except for wall diving, there is a great variety of dive sites along the channel and north of Tortola, including an underwater pinnacle called Blonde Rock. **Baskin in the Sun** (Prospect Reef Hotel; Road Town, tel. 800/233–7938, 809/494–2858, or 809/494–2859, AE, MC, V), the successor to Aquatic Centres, offers resort courses and packages as well as day and night dives and works with six hotels on the island. **Caribbean Images** (Road Town, tel. 809/495–2563 or 809/494–3311) specializes in snorkeling tours and also has glass-bottom boats and photo and video services. **Dive B.V.I.** (tel. 809/495–5513; AE, MC, V), with shops at both the Yacht Harbour and Leverick Bay in Virgin Gorda, has both three-day and five-day packages

Sportfishing A number of companies can transport and outfit you for a few hours of reel fun; try **Charter Fishing Virgin Islands** (Prospect Reef, Tortola, tel. 809/494–3311), **Harrigan's Rent-A-Boat** (Yacht Harbour, Virgin Gorda, tel. 809/495–5542), or **Kingfisher** (Yacht Harbour, Virgin Gorda, tel. 809/495–5230 or 809/495–5336).

Tennis Resorts on Tortola that have tennis courts are **Frenchman's Cay, The Moorings-Mariner Inn, Long Bay Hotel, Prospect Reef,** and **Treasure Isle Hotel.** You may reserve court time at **Prospect Reef** without being a guest there (Road Town, tel. 809/494–3311). There is also the **Tortola Tennis Club,** in Road Town (tel. 809/494–3733). On Virgin Gorda **Biras Creek** at North Sound (tel. 809/494–3555) and **Little Dix Bay** in The Valley (tel. 809/495–5555) have courts.

Shopping

Unlike the U.S. Virgin Islands, the British Virgins are not known as a shopping haven. There isn't a lot to choose from on these tranquil isles, but what is there is select and sophisticated.

Shopping Districts Most of the shops and boutiques on Tortola are clustered on and off Road Town's Main Street. The Wickhams Cay shopping area adjacent to the Marina has a number of new shops that have an upscale feel, and upscale prices. On Tortola's resort-crested sister isles most boutiques are located within the individual hotel complexes. One of the best is the one in the Little Dix Bay Rockresort on Virgin Gorda. Other properties on the same island—Biras Creek, the Bitter End, and Leverick Bay—have small but equally select boutiques, and there's a more than respectable and diverse scattering of shops in the minimall adjacent to the bustling yacht harbor in Spanish Town.

Drake's Anchorage on Mosquito Island has one of the best resort shops; American owner Jamy Faust stocks both maillots and basic bikinis, T-shirts, shell jewelry, pareos, and straw hats, as well as sun lotions and other sundries. Other resorts with on-site shops include the Peter Island Hotel and Yacht Club on Peter Island, the Marina Cay and the Anegada Reef on Anegada, and the Sandcastle on Jost Van Dyke.

Specialty Stores

Art **Collector's Corner** (Columbus Centre, Wickhams Cay, Tortola, tel. 809/494–3550) has serious Caribbean art at serious prices. They also carry antique maps and a collection of eelskin wallets, bags, and belts.

The Courtyard Gallery (Main St., Road Town, Tortola) shows its exclusive Carinia Collection, delicate crushed-coral sculptures depicting darting hummingbirds, angelfish, nesting pelicans, and flowers.

Naucraft Galleries (Wickhams Cay II, Road Town, Tortola, tel. 809/494–4790) has a wide range of Caribbean art (and prices); its offerings include original watercolors, oils, and acrylics, as well as signed prints, limited-edition serigraphs, and turn-of-the-century sepia photographs.

Sunny Caribbee Skyworld Boutique and Art Gallery (Skyworld Restaurant, Ridge Rd., Tortola, tel. 809/494–3567) has one of the largest displays of paintings throughout the Caribbean; the collection is hung in the restaurant's dining room and is heavy on Haitian primitive. They also sell their own line of spices, soaps, and sun-protection creams.

Clothing **Island Woman** (The Valley, Virgin Gorda, tel. 809/495–5237) offers an array of cotton Java Wraps and belts, beads, bracelets, and other accessories from Indonesia.

Sally Bell's (Main St., Road Town, Tortola, tel. 809/494–4670) has a sophisticated selection of British and French fashions (some trendy, some classic) for men and women.

Sea Urchin (Columbus Centre, Road Town, Tortola, tel. 809/494–3129) has a good selection of island-living designs: print shirts and shorts, slinky swimsuits, sandals, and, of course, T-shirts.

Turtle Dove Boutique (Flemming St., Road Town, Tortola, tel. 809/494–3611) is among the best of the best in the BVI for French perfume, international swimwear, and premium cotton batiks from Thailand.

Food and Drink **The Ample Hamper** (Village Cay Marina, Wickhams Cay, Tortola, tel. 809/494–2494), the leader in gourmet foods in Tortola, offers serious take-home packages that can serve as the foundation for an elegant picnic.

The Pusser's Company Store & Pub (Main St. and Waterfront Rd., Road Town, Tortola, tel. 809/494–2467) is a find for both rum lovers and teetotalers. Those who drink appreciate the free rum tastings and the assortment of handsome bottles of this renowned brew (available here for about half of what they cost elsewhere). Those who don't shop for nautical memorabilia, ship models, marine paintings, and an entire line of clothes and gift items bearing the Pusser's logo.

The Sunny Caribbee Herb & Spice Company (Main St., Road Town, Tortola, tel. 809/494–2178), located in a brightly painted West Indian house, packages its own herbs, teas, coffees, herb vinegars, hot sauces, and natural soaps and skin lotions.

Gifts **Carousel Gift Shop** (Tropic Aisle, Wickhams Cay, Tortola, tel. 809/494–2442) carries fine crystal and china, embroidered table and bed covers, and French perfume.

Past and Presents (Main St., Road Town, Tortola, tel. 809/494–2747 or 809/494–2163), now in its 20th year of operation, has quality books from the British Isles, United States, and Canada, as well as a good selection of paperbacks for the beach. They also have a very good (if small) selection of antique silver and china.

Jewelry **Flaxcraft Jewellers** (Main St., Road Town, Tortola, tel. 809/494–2892) carries fine gold and silver jewelry; many of the pieces are one-of-a-kind creations incorporating shells and fragments of coral.

Little Denmark (Main St., Road Town, Tortola, tel. 809/494–2455) stocks handsome, streamlined designs from Scandinavia as well as brand-name china.

Local Crafts **The Basket Case** (Cell 5 Complex, The Rufus L. deCastro Centre, Tortola, tel. 809/494–4608) has the best selection of hand-woven baskets from islands throughout the Caribbean as well as a sampling of other local crafts.

Delightfully Yours (opposite the Post Office in Road Town, Tortola) is a yellow-and-cream century-old shop that houses a choice selection of ceramics, wood carvings, woven fabrics, and pewter and sandstone pieces made by BVI craftsmen.

The Shipwreck Shop (Main St., Road Town, Tortola, tel. 809/494–2567) is one of a chain of Shipwreck Shops scattered throughout the Caribbean, all of which offer distinctive items at very reasonable prices: woven baskets, hammocks, shell and coral jewelry, hand-blocked pareos, painted T-shirts (long and short), and wood plates and bowls. If you enjoy a challenge, consider the Arawak Indian game of *warri;* the sets here come with a carved wood board and beans that are used as markers.

Textiles **Bonker's Gallery** (Main St., Road Town, Tortola, tel. 809/494–2535) features designs created by the owner along with the muted-color sarongs from Java Wraps. There's also a swimwear and T-shirt corner as well as a selection of miscellaneous gifts and trendy ties for the hair or waist.

Zenaida (Cutlass House, Wickhams Cay, Road Town, Tortola, tel. 809/494–2113) displays the fabric finds of Argentinian Vivian Helm, who travels through South America, Africa, and India in search of batiks, hand-painted and hand-blocked fabrics, and interesting weaves that can be made into pareos or wall hangings. The shop also offers a selection of unusual bags, belts, and beads.

Dining

The most popular choices in BVI restaurants are seafood dishes. Almost everything else has to be imported and thus tends to be more expensive. Most restaurants offer varied fare, including seafood and an array of Continental dishes.

The most highly recommended restaurants are indicated by a star ★.

Category	Cost*
Very Expensive	over $35

Expensive	$25–$35
Moderate	$15–$25
Inexpensive	under $15

*per person, excluding drinks and service; there is no sales tax in the BVI

Tortola   **Sugar Mill.** Low candles, low breezes, and low music comple-
★ ment an ever-creative menu and ample wine list. The
tenderloin cooked in red-wine sauce is excellent, and a typical
potage is curried banana soup. Owners/chefs Jeff and Jinx Morgan somehow also find time to write for *Bon Appetit* magazine.
*West End (North Shore), Apple Bay, tel. 809/494–4355. Reser-
vations advised. AE, MC, V. Very Expensive.*

The Cloud Room. Not only do you have a mountain-top view,
but the roof moves to make things alfresco. The proprietors
pick up guests from local hotels, then return them after dinner.
The menu is varied. *Ridge Rd., above Road Harbour, tel. 809/
494–2821. Reservations required. AE, MC, V. Dinner only.
Expensive.*

Fort Burt Restaurant. This respected restaurant is situated on
the site of a 17th-century Dutch fort on a roadside hill overlooking the harbor. Its entrees range from pan-fried dolphin and
lobster Thermidor to tournedos of beef, mixed grill, and
beefsteak-oyster-ale pie. *Fort Burt, Road Town, tel. 809/494–
2587. Reservations advised. AE, MC, V. Expensive.*

★ **Long Bay Beach Resort.** Recent renovation here has involved
only the building, not the menu, which needs none. From a
chicken-and-melon salad or pâté appetizer you can go on to
West Indian curry with rice and peas or pork, duck, or filet mignon. *West End (North Shore), Long Bay, tel. 809/495–4252.
Reservations advised. AE, MC, V. Expensive.*

Elena's. You can sit outdoors or in the handsome Tea Room. The
chef serves an eclectic mix of dishes, among them Oriental stirfry, chicken pineapple, Mandarin shrimp crepes, and chili.
*Road Town at Fonseca Corner, tel. 809/494–2790. AE, MC, V.
Moderate.*

Jules' Place. If you really want to go island in food and atmosphere, this open-air hut—once a festival booth—on the sea will
fill the bill of fare. Local dishes include conch fritters, West Indian pâtés, fish soup with coconut milk, and barbecued meat
and fish dishes. *Carrot Bay, tel. 809/495–4822. No credit cards.
Happy hour 6–7 PM. Moderate.*

★ **Spaghetti Junction.** At this merry, airy little upstairs box of a
restaurant, unbeatable selections are stuffed mushrooms, Caesar salad with sun-dried tomatoes, artichoke linguini, and the
tortellini. The salads are as fresh as you'll ever have. *Road
Town, across from Wickhams Cay I, tel. 809/494–4880. Reservations advised. Moderate.*

The Pusser's Deli. This pub-like eatery is a good place to know,
whether your budget is limited or strained. You'll find English
shepherd's pie and chicken-and-asparagus pie, roast beef and
other deli sandwiches, and even some Mexican dishes. You can
also get a Key lime pie or a milk shake. *Main St., Road Town,
tel. 809/494–2467. Inexpensive.*

Virgin Gorda   **Biras Creek.** You come by boat (provided free) to this serene
★ restaurant on a turret-like terrace with the sea on one side and
a beautiful North Sound marina on the other. The excellent
dishes are never heavy, and the wine list is considerable. There

is a prix fixe dinner of five courses. *North Sound, tel. 809/494–3555 or 809/495–4356. Reservations advised. AE, MC, V. Expensive.*

Chez Michelle. The restaurant is simply decorated and the building is nondescript—cuisine is the thing. Entrees include broiled lobster, seafood fettucine Alfredo, rack of lamb, and Chicken Cordon Chic (slices of banana and Black Forest ham encased in chicken breast, roasted and served with curry sauce). A favorite here is the Caesar salad with garlic walnuts. *The Valley, near the Yacht Harbour, tel. 809/495–5510. Reservations requested. MC, V. Dinner only, 6:30–9:30. Expensive.*

★ **Olde Yard Inn.** The high thatch ceiling, background classical music, and sofas and chess set near the bar are thoroughly enticing—and the dishes equally so. The pasta and breads are all homemade. Entrees include Caribbean lobster and sirloin steak; the breast of chicken is prepared with rum, cream, and nuts. *The Valley, tel. 809/495–5544. Reservations requested. MC, V. Moderate.*

Salty Whale Pub & Eatery. Out North Sound way, this outdoor terrace faces a small, cove-like marina and offers chicken, ribs, or local fish dishes at modest prices, as well as Continental entrees and fiery chicken wings. *Leverick Bay, tel. 809/495–5421 or 809/495–5433. AE, MC, V. Moderate.*

Lodging

The number of rooms available in the BVI is small as compared to other destinations in the Caribbean; what is available is also often in great demand, and the prices are not low. The top-of-the-line resorts here are among the most expensive in the Caribbean and are sometimes difficult to book even off-season. Even the more moderately priced hotels command top dollar during the season; off-season, however, they are legitimate bargains at about half the price. There are some inexpensive hotels, but their accommodations are often Spartan; their locations, however, sometimes more than make up for that.

The most highly recommended lodgings are indicated by a star ★.

Category	Cost*
Very Expensive	over $200
Expensive	$125–$200
Moderate	$65–$125
Inexpensive	under $65

All prices are for a standard double room, excluding 7% accommodation tax.

Tortola **Nanny Cay Resort and Marina.** This new Ramada marina resort has its own nub of land, just off Tortola's south coast road between Road Town and West End. All rooms have kitchenettes, cable TV, telephone, air-conditioning and ceiling fans, and a patio or balcony. Peg Leg Landing restaurant, on stilts, is perfect for viewing sunsets. *Box 281, Road Town, tel. 809/494–4895. 41 rooms. Facilities: beach, 2 pools (1 saltwater), restaurant, bar, marina. AE, MC, V. Very Expensive.*

Fort Recovery. The simple, air-conditioned beachfront villas have garden patios, full kitchens, and an ideal view of the Sir Francis Drake Channel. On the grounds stands part of a Dutch fort built in 1600. A small commissary sells home-cooked entrees for quick reheating. The resort is located close to Frenchman's Cay and West End. *Box 239, Road Town, tel. 809/ 495–4354, 212/929–7929, or 518/377–7216. 7 1-bedroom villas, 1 2-bedroom villa, and 1 4-bedroom luxury house. Facilities: beach, snorkeling, commissary. AE. Expensive.*

Frenchman's Cay Resort Hotel. The breezes blow strong at this finely situated 12-acre resort connected to Tortola's coastal road by a small bridge. The one- and two-bedroom villas have full kitchens and shaded terraces. *Box 1054, West End, tel. 809/ 494–4844 or 800/223–9832. 23 rooms. Facilities: beach, restaurant, bar, tennis courts, pool, water sports. AE, MC, V. Expensive.*

★ **Long Bay Beach Resort.** Set along one of the longest sweeps of white-sand beach on Tortola, the Long Bay offers hillside units, beachfront cabanas, and deluxe new beachfront rooms that share a large porch. Most rooms have kitchenettes. The excellent restaurant has been totally renovated, and a new Modified American Plan (MAP) allows you to have breakfast late into the afternoon. *Box 433, Road Town, tel. 809/495–4396 or 800/537– 6247. 52 rooms. Facilities: beach, 2 restaurants, 2 bars, pool, 9-hole pitch-and-putt golf course, tennis court, commissary. AE, MC, V. Expensive.*

★ **Prospect Reef.** This large resort is a paradise for water-sports enthusiasts. It has its own harbor inlet, bridges, lagoon, and craggy, rock-terraced sea pool. Every room overlooks the water. Garden rooms have air-conditioning, and superior and deluxe studios have kitchens. The panoramic channel view of islands to the south is never less than irresistible. *Box 104, Road Town, tel. 809/494–3311 or 800/356–8937. 131 rooms. Facilities: man-made beach area, 3 pools (2 freshwater: 1 Olympic-size and 1 for diving), children's splash pool, 6 tennis courts, pitch-and-putt golf course, water sports, restaurant and bars, shopping arcade. AE, MC, V. Expensive.*

★ **Sugar Mill.** Dine at night here, where candles flicker within old walls hung with Haitian paintings and voices are never too loud against the roll of the Apple Bay surf, and you'll know the magic of Tortola. Owners Jeff and Jinx Morgan are also writers and gourmet cooks and know all the ingredients of inn-like peacefulness and romance; with manager Patrick Conway they are ever personable and helpful hosts. Buildings are on a snug hillside property, and deluxe accommodations have kitchenettes and balconies. *Box 425, Road Town, tel. 809/495–4355. 20 rooms. Facilities: beach, restaurant, 2 bars, pool. AE, DC, MC, V. Expensive.*

Fort Burt. This well-run small hotel is perched neatly by itself on a small hill—site of a 1666 Dutch fort—overlooking Road Harbour. All rooms face the water. The restaurant is one of Tortola's best, and the cool, well-like bar area is an interesting place to quaff. A boat takes guests to a private beach. *Box 187, Road Town, tel. 809/494–2587. 7 rooms. Facilities: bar, restaurant, pool. AE, MC, V. Moderate.*

★ **Sebastians on the Beach.** This casual north-shore outpost, at Little Apple Bay, is a favorite of surfers and Europeans. (Surfboards can be rented.) All rooms have refrigerators, and most have a queen-size and a twin bed. The restaurant fare is simple, mainly grilled fish or meat. A homey atmosphere prevails. *Box 441, Road Town, tel. 809/495–4212. 26 rooms. Facilities: beach,* *restaurant, bar, water sports, and commissary. AE. Moderate.*

Treasure Isle Hotel. Renovation is ongoing at this lively hillside hotel recently purchased by The Moorings, a yacht-charter company. All rooms have telephones, are air-conditioned, and some even have rattan double swings. Daily transportation is provided to two beaches, and you can be brought by boat to the hotel's own beach club on Cooper Island. *Box 68, Road Town, tel. 809/494–2501 or 800/526–4789. 40 rooms. Facilities: restaurant, bar, pool, 2 tennis courts, squash court, water sports, marina. AE, MC, V. Moderate.*

Cane Garden Bay Beach Hotel. Beautiful Cane Garden Bay and the stunning white beach cradled by steep mountain greenery are the main attractions here. The simple hotel rooms have beach-view balconies, ceiling fans, and screened windows. Snorkeling equipment, Windsurfers, Sunfish, and other paraphernalia for water activities can be rented on the beach. The hotel is only a 15-minute drive from Road Town. *Box 570 CGB, tel. 809/495–4639 or 809/495–4215. 27 rooms. Facilities: beach, restaurant, bar, water sports. AE, MC, V. Inexpensive.*

Hotel Castle Maria. This clean hotel gets lovely breezes through its balconies, which have wide, cushioned chairs. The many island-scene paintings give the place a friendly West Indian atmosphere. Some rooms have air-conditioning and cable TV and all have small refrigerators. *Box 206, Road Town, tel. 809/494–2553. 30 rooms. Facilities: restaurant, bar, pool. AE, MC, V. Inexpensive.*

Jolly Roger Inn. A money-saver just west of the ferry dock at the sunset end of Tortola, this very unfancy place has just a few rooms with shared bath and a few with private bath: stay six nights and the seventh is free. The turnoff to north-shore beaches is conveniently just down the road. *West End, Sopers Hole, tel. 809/495–4559. 6 rooms. Facilities: restaurant, bar, harborside bar, dinghy dock. No credit cards. Inexpensive.*

Maria's by the Sea. The sea here is Road Harbour, as this simple two-story building is situated on a flat patch of land at Wickhams Cay I. There are balconies on the air-conditioned rooms, which have kitchenettes and rattan furniture. Local food is served at the restaurant. Don't look for shade here on this sandy spit of waterfront. *Box 206, Wickhams Cay I, Road Town, tel. 809/494–2595. 14 rooms. Facilities: restaurant, pool. AE, MC, V. Inexpensive.*

Campgrounds **Brewers Bay Campground.** This campground, which opened in 1976 as the BVI's first, is at a beautiful location. Bare sites are in a grove 150 feet from the beach. Tent sites come with floor, beds and linens, propane-gas stove and lantern, ice chest, cooking and eating utensils, and picnic table and bench. Toilets and showers are in a separate building. *Box 185, Road Town, tel. 809/494–3463. 15 beds. Facilities: beach, beach bar, commissary. Baby-sitters available. No credit cards or personal checks.*

Virgin Gorda **Biras Creek.** A turret-like stone building (clubhouse and dining
★ room) quietly watches over this magically private resort, which is neatly fit into a North Sound isthmus and can be reached only by boat. From your two-unit modern cottage—with bedroom, living room, and elegant open-air walled shower—you can bicycle (provided free) down a desert-garden path to the ocean-view pool, tennis courts, a salt-pond bird sanctuary, or the Deep Bay swimming beach, which has an honor bar, raft, and

water-sports equipment. A few super-deluxe suites are also available. There are no roads, only miles of hiking trails (and one Iguana Crossing). The restaurant and wine list are first-rate. British hosts Brian and Judith Connelly might allow you to guess which one of them is the former Yorkshire mayor and which the sometime singer and impersonator. There is not a dram of pretention in them. *Box 54, tel. 809/494–3555 or 809/494–3556. 32 rooms. Facilities: beach, restaurant, bar, tennis courts, marina, pool, water sports, hiking trails. AE, MC, V. Very Expensive.*

Bitter End Yacht Club. When the Caribbean yachting set want to get their feet dry or whistles wet, this sporty village-length North Sound resort is a favorite anchorage. Guests stay in hillside or beachfront villas or chalets—or on a live-aboard yacht. Pick your boat, your restaurant, your bar, your sailing-instruction course, or your dive package. You will be taxied around on People Mover carts, a Hillevator, or pontoon shuttle boats. For maximum peace and quiet, the topmost hillside chalets or endmost beachfronts are your best bet. *Box 46, North Sound, tel. 809/494–2746. 100 rooms. Facilities: beach, 3 restaurants, bar, marina, pool. AE, DC, MC, V. Very Expensive.*

★ **Little Dix Bay.** Set on 400 verdant acres along the Sir Francis Drake Channel, this quiet Rockresort property is possibly the most famous resort in the BVI. The curving beach is magnificent, and a broad, sheltering reef completes its circle. Cone-roof guest cottages, some on stilts, are furnished with elegant understatement in a Caribbean way, and all have a terrace or balcony. *Box 70, tel. 809/495–5555. 102 rooms. Facilities: beach, restaurant, bar, water sports, marina, 7 tennis courts. AE, DC, MC, V. Very Expensive.*

Fischer's Cove Beach Hotel. A short walk from the Virgin Gorda Marina, this casual beachfront hotel with unmanicured grounds is West Indian in atmosphere and gets good breezes. The 11 buildings each have two guest units; there are also two two-bedroom cottages with kitchens. The rooms are oddly shaped but spacious and cool. *Box 60, The Valley, tel. 809/495–5252 or 809/495–5253. 22 rooms. Facilities: beach, restaurant, bar, water sports, discotheque. AE, MC, V. Expensive.*

★ **Olde Yard Inn.** You'll find beach chairs under physic nut trees, hammocks, and a few Virgin Gordan boulders on these peaceful grounds. There are private patios, and upstairs rooms look out to sea. But most special about this homey oasis is its octagonal library pavilion, with handsome books, a chess set, and a George Steck spinet kept in perfect tune. (It could be a gentleman's club room in 19th-century Kenya.) It's all enough to make you forget about the beach, which is a 20-minute walk away. *Box 26, Spanish Town, tel. 809/495–5544. 14 rooms. Facilities: restaurant and bar, library, horseback riding. AE, MC, V. Expensive.*

Leverick Bay Resort and Marina. Nestled on a picturesque, steep bend of Gorda Sound, this resort is centered on a clustered beach area, marina dock, and pool. Its luxury villas at various levels of the hillside are rentable by the week and have one, two, or three bedrooms. Only the studio apartments have air-conditioning. Prickly Pear Island and some excellent reefs are part of the resort's view. *North Sound Yacht Charter, Ltd., Box 1077, tel. 809/495–7421 or 809/495–5433. 41 rooms. Facilities: 2 beaches, beach restaurant and bar, marina, pool, water sports. AE, MC, V. Moderate–Expensive.*

Mango Beach Resort. The Italians have landed at Mahoe Bay and built this array of modern white duplex villas, tucked privately downhill from the north-coast road winding out of Spanish Town. Everything is very new, spacious, and airy, including the terraces. Each villa is divided into separate one- and two-bedroom units with full kitchens. The lagoonlike waters are tranquil, and there is a small dock. *Box 1062, tel. 809/ 495–5672 or 809/495–5673. 21 rooms. Facilities: beach, dock, snorkeling. No credit cards. Moderate–Expensive.*

Guavaberry Spring Bay Vacation Homes. From the exquisite tamarind-shaded beach you can swim to the mammoth boulders and shaded basins of the famed Baths, which adjoin this property. The one- and two-bedroom cottages, all with kitchen facilities, have curved decks and are a bit like tree houses. You'll hear twittering birds and branches swaying in the breeze. Guests emphatically do not miss telephones. *Box 20, tel. 809/495–5227. 16 rooms. Facilities: beach, commissary. No credit cards. Moderate.*

Ocean View Hotel. You can save money here, but management also saves with 25-watt lightbulbs, loud ceiling fans, and velvet wall art. On the other hand, it's cheap and right across the road from the marina shops of Spanish Town. *Box 66, tel. 809/495– 5230. 12 rooms. Facilities: restaurant and bar. AE, MC, V. Inexpensive.*

Peter Island **Peter Island Hotel and Yacht Club.** This resort is close to the last word in luxury in all the Caribbean. There are 52 rooms and five villas and every imaginable living, dining, or recreational amenity, including a gourmet restaurant, saltwater pool, tennis, and horseback riding. *Box 211, Road Town, Tortola, BVI, tel. 809/494–2561 or 800/346–4451. AE, MC, V. Very Expensive.*

Anegada **Anegada Reef Hotel.** The only hotel on Anegada, this resort has 12 rooms, a beach, beach bar, restaurant, dive shop, gift shop, anchorage with moorings, and taxi service. *Lowell Wheatley, Anegada Reef Hotel, Anegada, BVI, tel. 809/494–3111 (marine operator) or, in St. Thomas, 809/776–8282. No credit cards. Expensive.*

Jost Van Dyke **Sandcastle,** at White Bay, has four beach cottages and a restaurant and bar. *Box 540, Pawley's Island, SC 29585, tel. 803/237– 8999. No credit cards. Expensive.*

Rudy's Mariner Inn, at Great Harbour, has three rooms with kitchenettes and dining areas. There is a restaurant and beach bar. *Great Harbour, Jost Van Dyke, BVI, tel. 809/775–3558 (USVI). No credit cards. Expensive.*

Tula's N & N Campground offers bare sites and 8 × 10 or 9 × 12 tents. *Reservations: Box 8364, St. Thomas, USVI 00801, tel. 809/775–3073 or 809/774–0774.*

Guana Island **Guana Island Club.** This luxurious hideaway has 15 rooms, terrace dining, tennis, nature trails, and water sports for its guests. *Box 32, Road Town, Tortola, BVI, tel. 809/494–2354 or 800/54GUANA. No credit cards. Very Expensive.*

Mosquito Island **Drake's Anchorage.** The bungalows at this secluded getaway are West Indian in style. Besides the 12 ocean-front rooms (two of them suites), there are two fully equipped villas. There is a restaurant, hiking trails, and water-sports facilities. *Box 2510, North Sound, Virgin Gorda, BVI, tel. 809/494–2254 or 800/624 –6651. AE, MC, V. Very Expensive.*

Marina Cay **Marina Cay Hotel.** A favorite spot for sailing visitors, this resort has 12 colorful rooms, two restaurants and bars, and water-sports facilities. *Box 76, Road Town, Tortola, BVI, tel. 809/494–2174. AE, MC, V. Very Expensive.*

Nightlife

If going out on the town is to be a big part of your Caribbean vacation, well, you won't find much in the way even of towns in the British Virgin Islands. Most BVI guests are content to find their nightlife at the resort (or boat) where they're staying.

Tortola But on the evening when you just have to drive somewhere to hear some music, clinking glasses, and conversational din, one spot on Tortola that might fit the bill is **The Pub** (Fort Burt Marina, tel. 809/494–2608), which has a buzzing bar and live bands (rock, reggae, or calypso) on Friday and Saturday nights. Another playroom, built on stilts at a marina, is **Peg Leg Landing** (Nanny Cay, tel. 809/494–2512). Down at Sopers Hole, West End, are **Pusser's Landing** (tel. 809/495–4554 or 809/495–4553), which has a steel band Thursday nights and, with a slightly more raw and hard-drinking ambience, **The Jolly Roger** (tel. 809/495–4559). For West Indian entertainment try **Skylight** (Fat Hog's Bay, tel. 809/495–2584).

Virgin Gorda The biggest noise, literally, on Virgin Gorda is in The Valley at **Andy's Chateau de Pirate** (tel. 809/595–5253), a disco that pumps at full volume at Fischer's Cove Hotel, where the crowd is mostly young local residents. But for setting, conviviality, and a sporty atmosphere, you can't do much better than to join the yachting crowd—who will not be in formal dress—and guests from the States at the **Bitter End Yacht Club** on beautiful North Sound (tel. 809/494–2746).

8 Cayman Islands

by John English

A native of Athens, Georgia, John English teaches journalism in the university in that city.

The venerable old *Saturday Evening Post* dubbed them "the islands that time forgot." The paper did not survive long enough to see the Cayman Islands, a British Crown colony comprising Grand Cayman, Cayman Brac, and Little Cayman, become one of the Caribbean's hottest tourist destinations.

Why do metropolis-weary visitors continue to trek to these islands 480 miles south of Miami? Why do they fill the hotels and condominiums that line Grand Cayman's famed Seven Mile Beach, even during the traditionally slow summer season? Their dollars certainly go farther in other Caribbean destinations, for in Cayman—which positively reeks of prosperity, bulging as it does with some 500 offshore banks located in George Town, the capital, on Grand Cayman—the U.S. dollar is worth 80 Cayman cents, and the cost of living is 20% higher than in the United States.

Certainly it is not because of overwhelming advertising in the United States. The Department of Tourism's ad budget is miniscule compared with the budgets of tourist rivals like the Bahamas and Jamaica.

The secret is word-of-mouth testimonials. The Cayman Islanders—the population is 18,000, almost all of it residents of Grand Cayman—are renowned for the courteous and civil manners befitting their British heritage. If they sometimes appear to be slightly aloof, truth is the attitude is born of innate shyness. Visitors will find no hasslers or panhandlers, and no need to look apprehensively over their shoulder on dark evenings, for the colony is virtually crime-free. Add to that permanent political and economic stability, and you have a fairly rosy picture.

The Caymans are a paradise for divers: Transluscent waters and a colorful variety of marine life are protected by the government, which has designated various marine parks.

Columbus is said to have sighted the islands in 1503, but he didn't stop off to explore. He did note that the surrounding sea was alive with turtles, so the islands were named Las Tortugas. The name was changed later to Cayman.

The islands stayed largely uninhabited until the latter part of the 1600s, when Britain took over the Cayman Islands and Jamaica from Spain under the Treaty of Madrid. Cayman attracted a mixed bag of settlers, pirates, refugees from the Spanish Inquisition, shipwrecked sailors, and deserters from Oliver Cromwell's army in Jamaica. Today's Caymanians are the descendants of those nationalities.

The islands were a happy hunting ground for pirates of the ilk of Blackbeard and Sir Henry Morgan, who plundered Spanish galleons that were hauling riches from the New World of South America to Spain. Many a ship also fell afoul of the reefs surrounding the islands, often with the help of the Caymanians, who lured the vessels to shore with beacon fires. Some of the old pioneer homes on the islands were made from the remains of those galleons.

The legend of the Wreck of the Ten Sails was to have a lasting effect on the Caymanians. In 1788, a convoy of 10 Jamaican ships bound for England foundered on the reefs, but the islanders managed to rescue everyone. Royalty was purportedly aboard, and a grateful George III decreed that Caymanians should forever be exempt from conscription and never have to pay taxes.

The islands were a dependency of Jamaica until the 1961 formation of the West Indies Federation. Jamaica opted for independence from Britain, but Cayman chose to remain a colony, and it has since remained loyal to the Crown.

Queen Elizabeth II is represented in the Cayman islands by a Governor—at present, H.E. (for His Excellency) Alan Scott—who appoints three official members to the Legislative Assembly. Twelve other members are elected every four years. The governor has to accept the advice of the Executive Council in all matters except foreign affairs, defense, internal security, and civil service appointments.

Before You Go

Tourist Information For the latest information on activities and lodging, write or call any of the following offices of the **Cayman Islands Department of Tourism:** 250 Catalonia Ave., Suite 604, Coral Gables, FL 33134, tel. 305/444–6551; 2 Memorial City Plaza, 820 Gessner, Suite 170, Houston, TX 77024, tel. 713/461–1317; 420 Lexington Ave., Suite 2312, New York, NY 10017, tel. 212/682–5582; 1 Magnificent Mile, 980 N. Michigan Ave., Suite 1260, Chicago, IL 60611, tel. 312/944–5602; 3440 Wilshire Blvd., Suite 1202, Los Angeles, CA 90010, tel. 213/738–1969; 234 Eglinton Ave. E., Suite 306, Toronto, Ont. M4P 1K5, tel. 416/485–1550; Knightsbridge House, 197 Knightsbridge, London SW7 1RB, tel. 01/581–4463.

Arriving and Departing
By Plane Grand Cayman is serviced by **Northwest Orient** (tel. 800/447–4747), **Cayman Airways** (tel. 800/422–9626), and **Air Jamaica** (tel. 800/523–5585). Cayman Airways also operates daily flights to Cayman Brac and service every day except Tuesday to Little Cayman. Flights land at Owen Roberts Airport, Gerrard Smith Airport, or Edward Bodden Airport.

Upon arrival, some hotels offer free pickup at the airport. Taxi service and car rentals are also available.

Passports and Visas Passports are not required for American and Canadian citizens, but they must show some proof of citizenship, such as a birth certificate or voter registration card, plus a return ticket. British and Commonwealth subjects do not need a visa but must carry a passport. Visitors to the islands cannot be employed without a work permit.

Customs and Duties You may bring into the United States $400 worth of merchandise duty-free if you've been out of the country more than 48 hours, provided that you've not used any part of it during the preceding 30 days. In addition, you may send $50 worth of gifts to friends daily and take back one liter of liquor and five cartons of cigarettes duty free. U.S. taxes beyond the limit are 10% on the first $1,000 above the $400 quota.

Turtle products are banned in the United States and will be seized upon importation.

Canadian citizens are permitted items worth $300 duty-free once a year, or $100 quarterly, or $25 any time. Forty ounces of liquor and two cartons of cigarettes may also be imported duty-free.

British subjects are entitled to £28 worth of merchandise duty-free, plus 200 cigarettes and one liter of alcoholic spirits.

Grand Cayman

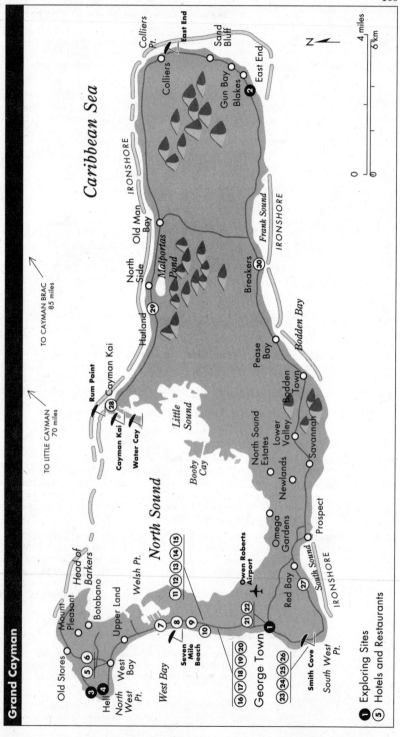

Caribbean Sea

Colliers Pt.

East End

Sand Bluff

Colliers

Gun Bay

Blakes

East End

IRONSHORE

Old Man Bay

North Side

Malportas Pond

Hutland

Breakers

Frank Sound

IRONSHORE

TO CAYMAN BRAC
85 miles

TO LITTLE CAYMAN
70 miles

Rum Point

Cayman Kai

Water Cay

North Sound

Little Sound

Booby Cay

Pease Bay

Bodden Bay

North Sound Estates

Lower Valley

Bodden Town

Savannah

Newlands

Prospect

South Sound

IRONSHORE

Omega Gardens

Red Bay

Owen Roberts Airport

George Town

Smith Cove

South West Pt.

Mount Pleasant

Botabano

Old Stores

Hell

Upper Land

West Bay

North West Pt.

Head of Barkers

Welsh Pt.

Seven Mile Beach

● Exploring Sites

⑤ Hotels and Restaurants

N

0   4 miles

0   6 km

Cayman Brac and Little Cayman

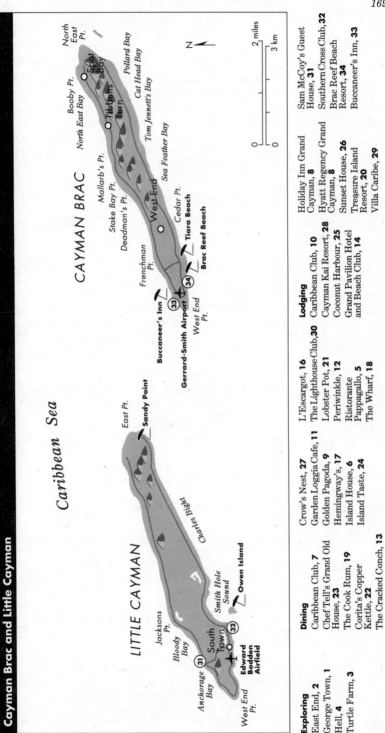

Caribbean Sea

LITTLE CAYMAN

West End Pt.
Anchorage Bay
Bloody Bay
Jacksons Pt.
South Town
Edward Bodden Airfield
Smith Hole Sound
Owen Island
Charles Bight
East Pt.
Sandy Point

CAYMAN BRAC

North East Pt.
Scot Bay
Booby Pt.
North East Bay
Pollard Bay
Cat Head Bay
Tibbetts Turn
Mallarb's Pt.
Stake Bay Pt.
Deadman's Pt.
Tom Jennett's Bay
Sea Feather Bay
West End
Cedar Pt.
Frenchman Pt.
Tiara Beach
Buccaneer's Inn
Gerrard-Smith Airport
Brac Reef Beach
West End Pt.

N

0   2 miles
0   3 km

Exploring
East End, **2**
George Town, **1**
Hell, **4**
Turtle Farm, **3**

Dining
Caribbean Club, **7**
Chef Tell's Grand Old House, **23**
The Cook Rum, **19**
Corita's Copper Kettle, **22**
The Cracked Conch, **13**

Crow's Nest, **27**
Garden Loggia Cafe, **11**
Golden Pagoda, **9**
Hemingway's, **17**
Island House, **6**
Island Taste, **24**

L'Escargot, **16**
The Lighthouse Club, **30**
Lobster Pot, **21**
Periwinkle, **12**
Ristorante Pappagallo, **5**
The Wharf, **18**

Lodging
Caribbean Club, **10**
Cayman Kai Resort, **28**
Coconut Harbour, **25**
Grand Pavilion Hotel and Beach Club, **14**

Holiday Inn Grand Cayman, **8**
Hyatt Regency Grand Cayman, **8**
Sunset House, **26**
Treasure Island Resort, **20**
Villa Caribe, **29**

Sam McCoy's Guest House, **31**
Southern Cross Club, **32**
Brac Reef Beach Resort, **34**
Buccaneer's Inn, **33**

Language English is spoken here with a slight Caribbean accent. The local daily newspaper, the *Caymanian Compass*, is also in English.

Precautions Remember that traffic is on the left in the Cayman Islands.

Locals make a constant effort to conserve fresh water, so don't waste a precious commodity.

Penalties for drug importation and possession of controlled substances include large fines and prison terms.

Though theft is uncommon in the Caymans, it is only prudent to watch your valuables when outdoors. Marauding blackbirds called "ching chings" have been known to carry off jewelry if it is left out in the open.

Staying in the Cayman Islands

Important **Tourist Information:** The main office of the **Department of Tour-**
Addresses **ism** is located in the Tower Building (N. Church St., tel. 809/949–7999). There is also an information booth in the George Town Craft Market, on Cardinal Avenue, which is open when cruise ships are in port (tel. 809/949–8342).

Emergencies **Police:** The emergency number is 999.

Hospitals: For emergencies, call 555.

Pharmacies: The most central pharmacy is **Cayman Drug**, in downtown George Town on Panton Street (tel. 809/949–2597).

Airport Information: For flight information, call 809/949–7733.

Divers' Decompression Chamber: Call 809/949–4234.

Currency Although the American dollar is accepted everywhere, you'll save money if you go to the bank and exchange U.S. dollars for Cayman Island (C.I.) dollars, which are worth about $1.25 each. The Cayman dollar is divided into a hundred cents with coins of 1¢, 5¢, 10¢, and 25¢, and notes of $1, $5, $10, $25, $50, and $100. There is no $20 bill.

Prices are often quoted in Cayman dollars, so it's best to ask. All prices quoted here are in U.S. dollars, unless otherwise noted.

Taxes and Service Hotels collect a 6% government tax. The departure tax is
Charges $7.50.

Hotels add a 10% service charge to your bill. Many restaurants add a 10%–15% service charge.

Guided Tours The most impressive sights are underwater. Snorkeling, diving, glass-bottom-boat and submarine rides can be arranged at any of the major aquatic shops: **Bob Soto's Diving Ltd.** (tel. 809/947–4631), **Nick's Aqua Sports** and **Don Foster's Dive Grand Cayman** (tel. 809/949–5679 for both), **Aqua Delights** (tel. 809/947–4786), the **Watersports Center** (tel. 809/947–0762), and **Atlantis Submarine** (tel. 809/949–7700).

To see the island, rent a car or take a tour with a taxi driver or with a local tour service. **Evco Tours** (tel. 809/949–2118) offers six-hour, round-island tours, from the Tortuga Club at the East End to the Turtle Farm and village of Hell in West Bay. **Majestic Tours** (tel. 809/949–7773) guide Buddy Wood takes vanloads of passengers to visit island high points on regular morning tours. All-day tours also can be arranged with **Tropicana Tours** (tel. 809/949–4599), **Rudy's** (tel. 809/949–2308), **Reids** (tel. 809/949–6531), and **GreyLine** (tel. 809/949–2791).

Getting Around If your accommodations are along Seven Mile Beach, you can walk to the shopping centers, restaurants, and entertainment spots along West Bay Road. Public buses run frequently into the downtown area—stops are marked with small white signs.

Taxis Taxis offer islandwide service. Fares are determined by an elaborate rate structure set by the government and, although it may seem pricey for a short ride (fare from Seven Mile Beach to the airport ranges from $7 to $11), cabbies rarely try to rip off tourists. Ask to see the chart if you want to double-check the quoted fare.

Rental Cars To rent a car bring your current driver's license and the car-rental firm will issue you a temporary permit ($3). Most firms have a range of models available, from compacts to Jeeps to minibuses. The major agencies have offices in a building next to the airport terminal, where you can pick up and drop off vehicles.

Car-rental companies are **Ace Hertz** (tel. 809/949–2280), **Budget** (tel. 809/949–5695), **CICO-Avis** (tel. 809/949–2468), **Coconut** (tel. 809/949–4037), **Dollar** (tel. 809/949–2981), **Holiday Payless** (tel. 809/949–7074), and **National** (tel. 809/949–4790).

For mopeds, motorbikes, and bicycles: **Caribbean Motors** (tel. 809/949–4051 or 809/947–4466), **Cayman Cycle** (tel. 809/947–4020), **Honda** (tel. 809/947–4466), and **Soto Scooters** (tel. 809/947–4652).

Telephones and Mail For international dialing to Cayman, the area code is 809. To call outside, dial 0+1+ area code and number. You can call anywhere, anytime through the Cable and Wireless system and local operators. To dial locally, simply dial the last five digits of the number, excluding the country code and exchange.

Beautiful stamps and first-day covers are available at the main post office in downtown George Town, weekdays from 8:30 to 4. Sending a postcard to the United States, Canada, the Caribbean, or Central America costs C.I. 10¢. An airmail letter is C.I. 25¢ per half ounce. To Europe and South America, the rates are C.I. 15¢ for a postcard and C.I. 50¢ per half ounce for airmail letters.

Opening and Closing Times Banking hours are generally Monday–Thursday 9–2:30 and Friday 9–1 and 2:30–4:30. Shops are open Monday–Saturday 9–5 and are usually closed on Sunday.

Beaches

Grand Cayman You may read or hear about the "dozens of beaches" of these islands, but that's more exaggeration than reality. Grand Cayman's west coast, the most developed area of the entire colony, is where you'll find its famous **Seven Mile Beach** (actually 5½ miles long) and its expanses of powdery white sand. The beach is litter free and sans peddlers, so you can relax in an unspoiled, hassle-free atmosphere. This is also Grand Cayman's busiest vacation center, and most of the island's accommodations, restaurants, and shopping centers are located on this strip.

The seaside bar and pool at the Holiday Inn are "party central" to repeat visitors on the island; the bar features on-tap frozen piña coladas. Aqua Delights, the water-sport company operating out of the Holiday Inn, has one-of-a-kind rentals such as Aqua trikes, Paddle Cats, and Banana Rides. You'll find headquarters for the island's aquatic activities scattered along the strip (*see* Participant Sports, below).

Grand Cayman has several smaller beaches that might better be called coves, including **Smith's Cove,** off South Church Street, south of the Grand Old House—a popular bathing spot on weekends with residents.

The best snorkeling locations are off **the ironshore** (coral ledge area) south of George Town on Grand Cayman's west coast, and in the reef-protected shallows of the island's north and south coasts, where coral and fish life are much more varied and abundant.

Other good beaches include **East End,** at Colliers, by the Tortuga Club, which can be lovely if it's kept clean of seaweed tossed ashore by trade winds. Seldom discovered by visitors unless they're staying out there are the beautiful beach areas of **Cayman Kai, Rum Point,** and, even more isolated and unspoiled, **Water Cay.** These are favored hideaways for residents and popular Sunday picnic spots.

Cayman Brac Both **Tiara Beach** and **Brac Reef Beach** resorts have fine small beaches, better for sunning than snorkeling. Excellent snorkeling can be found immediately offshore of the **Buccaneer's Inn** on the north coast.

Little Cayman **Sandy Point,** on the eastern tip, and **Owen Island,** off the south coast, beaches are exquisite isolated patches of powder great for sunbathing and worth every effort to reach by boat.

Exploring the Cayman Islands

Numbers in the margin correspond with points of interest on the Grand Cayman and Cayman Brac and Little Cayman maps.

George Town Start to explore George Town at the **Cayman Maritime and**
❶ **Treasure Museum,** located on the waterfront on North Church Street, about 150 yards from the downtown area. This little museum is a real find. Dioramas show how Caymanians became seafarers, boat builders, and turtle breeders. An animated figure of Blackbeard the Pirate spins salty tales about the pirates and buccaneers who "worked" the Caribbean. Since the museum is owned by a professional treasure-salvaging firm, it's not surprising that there are a lot of artifacts from shipwrecks. There is even a gold bar that visitors can lift to appreciate its weight. *Harbour Dr., tel. 809/949–7470. Admission: C.I.$5. Open Mon.–Sat. 9–4:30.*

In the Soto Building is **McKee's Treasure Museum,** which features the booty recovered from the deep by diver and salvager Art McKee. His collection of relics comes from the remains of sunken Spanish galleons, shipwrecked in the early 17th century. Artifacts are arranged by type—warfare, navigation, religious, everyday life, coins, and jewelry. *No phone. Guided tours are available. Admission: C.I.$5. Open Mon.–Sat. 9–4:30.*

Along the waterfront, heading along North Church Street toward town, notice part of the original wall of the old Fort George, which is being restored. Across the street is the Wholesome Bakery, which adds the homey smell of baking bread to the sea breezes off George Town Harbour. Try one of their delicious meat patties.

Turn left onto **Fort Street,** a main shopping street where you'll find the People's Boutique and a whole row of jewelry shops featuring black coral products—Bernard Passman, Island Treasures, Finiterre, Smith's, and the Jewellery Factory.

At the end of the block is the heart of downtown George Town. At the corner of Fort Street and **Edward Street,** notice the small clock tower dedicated to Britain's King George V and the huge fig tree, manicured into an umbrella shape. The Cayman Islands **Legislative Assembly Building** is next door to the 1919 **Peace Memorial Building,** which is the old town hall. You can have a look inside the Legislative building during office hours (weekdays 8:30–5) or arrange a guided tour.

Turning right on Edward Street, the charming **Library,** built in 1939, has English novels, current newspapers from the United States, and a small reference section. It's worth a visit just for the Old World atmosphere. Across the street is the new **Court House.** Down the next block, a stroller enters the "financial district," where banks from all over the world have offices.

Straight ahead is the **General Post Office,** also built in 1939, with its strands of decorative colored lights and some 2,000 private mailboxes on the outside. (Mail is not delivered on the island.) Behind the post office is **Elizabethan Square,** a new shopping and office complex on **Shedden Road** that houses various food, clothing, and souvenir establishments. The courtyard has a pleasant garden and fountain as well as outdoor tables at La Fontaine, a French restaurant. In the evenings, a live band converts this spot into an outdoor nightclub.

If you walk out the side entrance of Elizabethan Square, you'll be in a parking lot from which you can see the main government office building, called the **Glass House.** At four stories, it was until recently the tallest structure and featured the only elevator on the island. Both claims to fame were stolen when the Hyatt opened its five-story luxury resort hotel in 1987.

Exiting Elizabethan Square onto Shedden Road and walking past Anderson Square and Caymania Freeport, turn right back onto Edward Street, then left at the Royal Bank of Canada onto **Cardinal Avenue.**

This street is the main shopping area. On the right is the chic Kirk Freeport Plaza, which is known for its emeralds and fancy watches. On the left is the George Town Craft Market, a tourist information office, and the Native Taste café with outdoor tables.

Turn left on **Harbour Drive** and make your way back to Shedden Road, passing the English Shoppe, a souvenir outlet that looks more like it belongs on Shaftesbury Avenue in London than in the West Indies, and the Cayside Galleries, with its maritime antiques and cameras.

Walking back into town on Harbour Drive, one can have a leisurely stroll along a waterfront sidewalk. A new public park with a circular wood structure is where visitors from the cruise ships disembark, but the park offers no shade from the sun.

Across the street is a pleasant church, the **Elmslie Memorial United.** Its vaulted ceiling with wood arches and a sedate nave should remind visitors of the quietly religious nature of island residents.

The Outer Districts Venturing away from the Seven Mile Beach strip, travelers will encounter the more down-home character of the islands. Heading out on South Church Street, you can see some of the old houses, which feature elaborate Victorian gingerbread on modest frame homes. Heading east in a district called **Pantonville,** after the Pantons who live there, there are three pretty cottages with lacy woodwork. Then at **South Sound** you see larger residences, some with fine detail and gracious verandas.

In the Savannah district, **Pedro's Castle,** built in 1780, lays claim to being the oldest structure on the island. Pedro's is now a restaurant with a great view from the bar. At **Bodden Town,** you'll find an old cemetery on the shore side of the road. Graves with A-frame structures are said to contain the remains of pirates, but, in fact, they may be those of early settlers. A curio shop serves as entrance to what's called the **Pirate's Caves,** where you'll pass by a minizoo en route to these partially underground caves. The natural formations are interesting, but the place is more hokey than spooky.

Time Out The large and airy **Lighthouse Club** (Breakers, tel. 809/947–2047) has booth seating around spectacular waterfront windows. Island dishes and German fare are served daily. The Key lime pie is memorable.

2 The village of **East End** is the first recorded settlement on the island. Its major claim to fame these days is that it's where a renowned local musician called the "Violin Man," aka Radley and His Happy Boys, lives and occasionally performs his distinctive form of music (more akin to Louisiana's backwater zydeco than reggae). It's also the site of a number of shipwrecks and the **Tortuga Club,** whose guests are mostly avid divers.

3 At the other end of the island is the **West Bay** community, whose main attraction is the **Turtle Farm.** The farm, which was started about 20 years ago, is the most popular attraction on the island today, with some 70,000 visitors a year. There are turtles of all ages, from day-old hatchlings to huge 600-pounders that can live to be 100 years old. The Turtle Farm was set up both as a conservation and a commercial enterprise; it releases about 5% of its stock back out to sea every year, harvests turtles for local restaurants, and exports the by-products. (Note: U.S. citizens cannot take home any turtle products due to a U.S. Customs regulation banning their import.) In the adjoining café, one can sample turtle soup or turtle sandwiches while looking over an exhibit about turtles. *West Bay Rd., tel. 809/ 949–3893. Admission: $5 adults, $2.50 children 6–12. Open daily 9–5.*

The other area of West Bay that is of brief interest is the tiny **4** village of **Hell,** which is little more than a patch of incredibly jagged rock formations called ironshore. The big attraction here is a small post office and card shop, which does a box-office business selling stamps and postmarking cards from Hell. Souvenir shops called Devil's Den and Hades Hideaway also exploit the concept. Almost unbelievably, a nearby nightclub, called the Club Inferno, is run by the McDoom family.

Cayman Brac

Brac, the Gaelic word for bluff, aptly identifies this island's most distinctive feature, a rugged limestone cliff that runs down the center of the island's 12-mile length. At the eastern end, the bluff soars to 140 feet—rather dramatic for the Caribbean. Cayman Brac lies 89 miles east of Grand Cayman and can be a pleasant day trip via a Cayman Airways package, which includes a morning flight, sightseeing tour, and lunch at a hotel with the afternoon free to swim, snorkel, and sun. Only 1,700 people live on this island, in rural communities with such names as Watering Place, Cotton Tree, Halfway Ground, and Spot Bay. The variety of flora includes unusual orchids and tropical fruits such as mangoes and papaya, and the Caymanian parrot lives among the Brac's bird population. Parts of the island are unpopulated, so visitors can explore truly isolated areas both inland and along the shore.

Two hotels catering to divers, the Tiara Beach and the Brac Reef Beach Resort, are located on sandy beaches in a lagoon on the south side.

Little Cayman

Only 2 miles away from Cayman Brac is Little Cayman Island, which boasts a population of only two dozen on its 12 square miles. This tiny place really is paradise for those intent on getting away from crowds—it has no shops, no restaurants, no movies, no gas stations or central electricity supply, and only three private phones and one pay phone on the entire island. It does have ample accommodations for visitors, however, in three small lodges—the Southern Cross Club, Sam McCoy's Diving and Fishing Lodge, and Pirate's Point. In addition to privacy, the real attractions of Little Cayman are diving, which is most spectacular off the north coast, and fishing, which includes angling for tarpon and bonefish.

And if ever Little Cayman gets too busy, there is one final retreat—**Owen Island,** which is just 200 yards offshore. Accessible by rowboat, it has a blue lagoon and a sandy beach. Take your own picnic if you plan to spend the day.

What to See and Do with Children

Don't miss the one-hour **Atlantis Submarine** (tel. 809/949–7700) ride, which takes 28 passengers, a driver, and a guide down along the Cayman Wall to depths of 150 feet. This $2.8 million submarine, which recorded its 100,000th guest in 1988, has all sorts of safety features, including a constantly circling surface monitor boat, and is air-conditioned. Through its large windows, one can see huge barrel sponges, corals of extraterrestrial-like configurations, strange eels, and schools of beautiful and beastly fish. Night dives are quite dramatic because the artificial lights of the ship make the colors more vivid than in daytime excursions.

Turtle Farm (*see* Exploring, above).

Older children can also enjoy many of the water sports and beach games available. Hotels politely say that they do not organize activities for children, so be prepared to do so on your own.

Off the Beaten Track

Two architectural curiosities are worth a look if you are driving around. One is the little pink and white house on West Bay Road just past the cemetery. This 100-year-old cottage is made of mahogany and ironwood. Another odd residence is the conch house, near the power plant. This house was covered with conch shells years ago, but a recent renovation has added modern skylights and a garish satellite dish in the front yard.

Carey Cayman Coral (no phone) is a workshop out in South Sound run by Carey Hurlstone. Carey, a gentle bear of a man with tattoos covering his skin, professes he was a biker with the Hell's Angels before coming home to Cayman to work as a craftsman. He also carves glass. Carey's workmanship is superb and his prices are quite reasonable for the quality.

Participant Sports

Diving To say that the Cayman Islands are a scuba diver's paradise would not be overstating the case. Everything a diver could want is here: pristine water (often exceeding 100-foot visibility), breathtaking coral formations, plentiful and exotic marine life, and a host of top-notch dive operations offering a variety of services, instruction, and equipment.

Divers are required to be certified and possess a "C" card or take a short resort or full certification course. A certification course, including classroom, pool, and boat sessions as well as checkout dives, takes about six days and costs up to $300. A resort course usually lasts a day and costs about $75. It introduces the novice to the sport and teaches the rudimentary skills needed to make a shallow, instructor-monitored dive.

All dive operations on Cayman are more than competent; among them are **Bob Soto's** (tel. 809/949–2022), **Don Foster's** (tel. 809/949–7025), **Aqua Delights** (tel. 809/947–4786), and **Nick's Aqua Sports** (tel. 809/949–8745). Literature on all operators can be obtained through the Department of Tourism.

On Cayman Brac, **Peter Hughes' Dive Tiara** (tel. 809/948–7553) offers scuba and snorkeling.

Most operations can rent all diving gear, including equipment for underwater photography; they also have facilities for film processing. Courses of instruction can be arranged at most shops.

Deep-Sea Fishing If you enjoy action fishing, Cayman waters have plenty to offer—blue and white marlin, yellowfin tuna, sailfish, dolphin, and wahoo. Bonefish and tarpon are also plentiful off Little Cayman. Some 25 boats are available for charter. Since 1984 a Million Dollar Month fishing tournament has been held in June, and registered anglers can win cash prizes by landing record-breaking catches. Each of the five tournaments has its own rules, records, and entrance fees. For information and applications, write Million Dollar Month Committee (Box 878, Grand Cayman, Cayman Islands, B.W.I.).

Other Water Sports Water-skiing, windsurfing, Hobie Cats, and jet skis are available at many of the aquatic shops along Seven Mile Beach (*see* Diving, above).

Tennis Most hotels and condo complexes have tennis courts for guests.

Golf The **Grand Cayman–Britannia** golf course, which is located next to the Hyatt Regency, was designed by Jack Nicklaus. The course is really three in one—a nine-hole championship course, an 18-hole executive course, and a Cayman course, which is played with a Cayman ball that goes about half the distance of a regulation ball. Greens fees range from $25 to $50.

Fitness A **Nautilus Fitness Center,** with machines, weights, sauna, and whirlpool, is in operation on Crewe Road, just across from the airport. Daily membership is $10; weekly, $25.

Shopping

If your motto is "Born to Shop," then Grand Cayman has two money-saving attributes—duty-free merchandise and the absence of sales tax. Prices on imported merchandise—English china, Swiss watches, French perfumes, and Japanese cameras and electronic goods—are relatively cheaper than elsewhere. Expensive jewelry is another good buy, and the selection is vast. If you've been postponing buying such luxury goods, you might consider this opportunity.

Good Buys
Black Coral Black coral products are popular and exquisite choices. There are a number of local craftsmen who create original designs and finish their own work. Among those who have retail outlets in downtown George Town are **Coral Art Collections by Mitzi** (tel. 809/949–7805), in the Old Fort building on North Church Street; **Bernard Passman** (tel. 809/949–4948), whose creations won the approval of the English royal family, on Fort Street; and **Black Coral Jewelry and Other Fine Gems** (tel. 809/949–7156), whose creators Richard and Rafaela Barile have attracted lots of celebrities to their shop on Harbour Drive (*see also* Off the Beaten Track, above).

Arts and Crafts Debbie van der Bol runs an arts and crafts shop called **Pure Art** (tel. 809/949–7716) in a home on Church Street. She features the work of such local artists as Janet Walker, who does watercolors; woodworker Ralph Terry; and lacemaker Karin Baur. Ms. van der Bol is also an artist, and her sketches and card series are among the best buys in the place.

The **Grand Cayman Craft Market** (tel. 809/949–2195) downtown on Cardinal Avenue, has an assortment of local crafts, as does the **Heritage Crafts Shop** (no phone), upstairs on Shedden Road.

T-shirt shops abound all over town, especially along Harbour Drive, supporting the notion that they are the most popular souvenir.

Dining

Grand Cayman's restaurants should satisfy every palate and pocketbook. Gourmet Continental cuisine is available to the high rollers. Ethnic food can be had at moderate prices. West Indian fare in dining spots serving locals offers the best in meals and value. Fast-food franchises are there for those who must.

Seafood, not surprisingly, appears on most restaurant menus. Fish, including grouper, snapper, dolphin, tuna, wahoo, and marlin, is served either simply or Cayman style, with peppers, onions, and tomatoes. Conch, the meat of a large pink mollusk, is ubiquitous in stews and chowders, as fritters or pan-fried ("cracked"). Caribbean lobster is available, but often quite expensive, and other shellfish are in short supply in local waters. The only traditional culinary treat of the islands is turtle soup, stew, or steak, but only a few restaurants carry it these days.

Dining out on Grand Cayman can be expensive, so replenish your billfold because some places do not accept plastic. Prices are usually quoted in Cayman dollars.

All of the restaurants reviewed below are located on Grand Cayman. The most highly recommended restaurants are indicated by a star ★.

Category	Cost*
Expensive	over $20
Moderate	$15–$20
Inexpensive	under $15

per person, excluding drinks and service

★ **Caribbean Club.** The Continental menu of this quiet and well-appointed restaurant is one of the best in the Caymans. Among its seafood dishes, the lobster sausage is highly recommended, served as an appetizer or entrée. The service is meticulous and unhurried. The upstairs bar is worth a stop for the vista. *West Bay Rd., tel. 809/947–4099. Reservations are a must. Jacket and tie required. AE, MC, V. Expensive.*

★ **Chef Tell's Grand Old House.** TV celebrity chef Tell Erhardt has been running this popular establishment since 1986. His menu features Continental entrées and a few local specialties. Among the spicier appetizer choices is grouper Beignete, marinated and deep-fried grouper served with curry sauce and minted yogurt. On the bland side is Lobster Chef Fred's Way, dipped in egg batter and sautéed with shallots, mushrooms, and white wine. The back porch dining room with its Victorian trim and ceiling fans is the liveliest and best spot to dine. The excellent service adds to this gracious dining experience. *S. Church St., tel. 809/949–2020. Reservations necessary for dinner, suggested for lunch. AE, MC, V. Closed for lunch weekends. Expensive.*

L'Escargot. Fine china, crystal, and silverware; waiters in tuxedoes; and live piano music make this one of the island's most romantic dining spots. The view of the garden and pool competes with the elegant decor of the salon. The French and Continental menu features escargot in many forms. Sunday luncheon buffet is served from noon to 2:30. *Treasure Island Resort, tel. 809/949-7255. Reservations mandatory for dinner. Jacket and tie required for dinner. AE, MC, V. Expensive.*

Garden Loggia Cafe. The Hyatt's indoor-outdoor café opens onto the most beautifully landscaped garden courtyard on the island. The Caribbean decor includes pastel colors, ceiling fans, and marble-top tables. The menu combines European and Caribbean tastes. The Friday night seafood buffet and sumptuous Sunday champagne brunch feature everything from roast suckling pig, king crab, and lobster to waffles and custom-made omelets. Live music is featured at breakfast and dinner except Sunday. *Hyatt Regency Grand Cayman, West Bay Rd., tel. 809/949-1234. Reservations a must. AE, MC, V. Expensive.*

Lobster Pot. The second-floor terrace of this cozy restaurant overlooks the bay downtown, so the sunsets are an extra attraction. Its menu features both Continental dishes and such Caribbean specialties as conch chowder, turtle soup, steak, seafood curry, and, of course, lobster. This place is popular, so the constant turnover makes the atmosphere feel rushed. If you can't make dinner, drop by the pub and have a frozen banana daiquiri. *N. Church St., tel. 809/949-2736. Reservations recommended. MC, V. Expensive.*

Periwinkle. This Italian restaurant, decorated in soothing pink and gray, is quiet and romantic. The menu features such Italian fare as seafood lasagne and chicken cacciatore, grouper Caymanian style. During summer months, a grill is set up on the patio to charcoal dishes like fresh swordfish. *West Bay Rd., tel. 809/949-2927. Reservations accepted. AE, MC, V. Expensive.*

Ristorante Pappagallo. On a remote point near Spanish Cove, this thatch-roof restaurant's highlight is exotic decor that includes macaws in cages. Curiously, its menu is northern Italian cuisine, with predictable antipasti, pasta, and veal dishes. The biggest drawbacks: its inconvenient location and inconsistancy. *West Bay at Villas Pappagallo, tel. 809/949-3479. Reservations required. AE, MC, V. Expensive.*

The Cracked Conch. This popular seafood restaurant has the ambience of a crowded fish house. Specialties include conch fritters, conch chowder, spicy Cayman-style snapper, and three types of turtle steak. The Key lime pie is divine. Take-out service is available. The bar has live entertainment and is a local hangout. *Selkirk's Plaza, West Bay Rd., tel. 809/949-5717. Reservations suggested in winter. AE, MC, V. Moderate.*

Crow's Nest. With the ocean right in its backyard, this secluded small restaurant is a great spot to snorkel as well as to lunch. One drawback: Insect repellent is required for patio dining in the evening. Specialties here include shrimp, conch, and conch fritters. The dessert of raisins and rum cake is scrumptious. *South Sound, tel. 809/949-6216. Reservations accepted. MC, V. Closed Sun. Moderate.*

Golden Pagoda. The oldest Chinese restaurant in the Caymans features Hakka-style cooking. Among their specialties are Mahlah chicken, butterfly shrimp, and chicken in black bean sauce. Takeout is available. *West Bay Rd., tel. 809/949-5475. Reservations accepted. Dress: no shorts at dinner. AE, MC, V. Moderate.*

Hemingway's. Located right on Seven Mile Beach, this classy restaurant features open-air dining with a sea view and breezes. Zesty seafood dishes include Pirate's Stew Pot, conch and turtle steak prepared in coconut milk and green bananas, or beer-batter coconut shrimp. For a tropical drink, try the Seven Mile Meltdown, with dark rum, peach schnapps, pineapple juice, and fresh coconut. There is superb service and Caribbean decor. Buffet dinner is served on the *Spirit of Ppalu*, a glass-bottom catamaran. *Hyatt/Brittania Beach Club, tel. 809/949–1234. Reservations accepted. AE, MC, V. Moderate.*

The Lighthouse Club. This airy converted lighthouse offers oceanfront dining on the island's southeast coast. Seating is in comfy booths or at tables next to big screened windows overlooking the ocean. The menu includes such island specialties as mango shrimp, sea whelks, and conch, and such German fare as sauerbraten, schnitzel, and venison. The drive from town takes at least 15 minutes, but it's worth it. *Breakers, tel. 809/947–2047. Reservations accepted. AE, MC, V. Moderate.*

The Wharf. This restaurant, which opened in 1989, is stylishly decorated in blue and white and looks onto a veranda and the nearby sea. On the menu are such Caribbean specialties as turtle steak, conch chowder, and sea scallops Provençale. Daily specials include seafood paella and soft-shell and stone crabs. Live music entertains diners. The Ports of Call bar is a perfect spot to watch the sun set. *N. Church St., tel: 809/949–2231. MC, V. Moderate.*

★ **The Cook Rum.** This restaurant with a tin roof and a frontporch view of the bay features West Indian fare, including turtle stew, salt beef and beans, and pepper pot stew. Dessert specials are yam cake and coconut cream pie. *N. Church St., tel. 809/949–8670. No credit cards. Inexpensive.*

★ **Corita's Copper Kettle.** Here is a tidy downtown diner featuring Jamaican breakfasts and such native specials as conch and lobster burgers. The fare is tasty and plain. *Edward St., tel. 809/949–2696. No reservations. No credit cards. Inexpensive.*

Island House. The café atmosphere of this renovated 100-year-old Caymanian house is the main attraction. Standards have slipped in recent years, service is slow, and the food is unpredictable. Its best dishes are turtle steak and filet of grouper. *Church St., West Bay, tel. 809/949–3017. No credit cards. Inexpensive.*

Island Taste. Caribbean decor (a hodgepodge of stone, bamboo, and rope) and island music set the laid-back pace here. A Caribbean luncheon buffet is served daily on a table made from the timbers of an old ship. Skip the bland seafood soup. *S. Church St., tel. 809/949–4945. AE, MC, V. Inexpensive.*

Lodging

The success of the Cayman Islands as a resort destination has an attendant problem—a scarcity of accommodations during the winter season. Visitors have to book ahead for holidays, especially at Christmastime. During the summer season, it is possible to find suitable lodging even on short notice. If you choose to stay in a condominium, you can book on a daily basis and stay any length of time. While about a third of the visitors come for the diving, a growing number are young honeymooners. There are few accommodations in the economy range, so guests must be prepared for resort prices.

Category	Cost*
Very Expensive	over $100
Expensive	$100–$160
Moderate	$85–$100
Inexpensive	under $85

*All prices are for a standard double room for two, excluding 6% tax and a 10% service charge.

Hotels
Grand Cayman

★ **Caribbean Club.** Eighteen one- and two-bedroom villas (six located on the beach) comprise a quiet island getaway. All units are individually decorated and contain full kitchens, living and dining rooms, patios, and a bathroom for every bedroom. Secluded and luxurious. *Box 504, Grand Cayman, tel. 809/947-4099 or 800/327-8777. 18 villas. Facilities: tennis courts, water-sports center, restaurant, bar. AE, MC, V. Very Expensive.*

Grand Pavilion Hotel and Beach Club. This five-star hotel is where the English royal family stays when they are in the Cayman Islands. Rooms are exquisitely furnished with Louis XV–style furniture and canopy beds. The Pavilion is a favorite with international business travelers who return for the hotel's impeccable style and service. Guests have access to beach-club facilities across the road. *Box 69, Grand Cayman, tel. 809/947-4666 or for reservations in U.S., 800/421-9999. 79 rooms and 3 suites. Facilities: 2 restaurants, 2 bars, meeting rooms, beach club, pool and pool bar. AE, MC, V. Very Expensive.*

★ **Hyatt Regency Grand Cayman.** One of the things that makes this hotel special is that it's adjacent to the only golf course on Grand Cayman. The rooms are exquisite, each with a marble entrance, oversize bathtub, bar, French doors, and a veranda. The Hyatt's beach club offers every water sport imaginable. Regency Club accommodations include complimentary Continental breakfast, early evening hors d'ouevres and 24-hour concierge service. *Box 1698, Grand Cayman, tel. 809/949-1234 or 800/553-1300. 236 rooms, 43 rooms in Regency Club, 1-, 2-, and 3-bedroom Britannia villas. Facilities: pool, golf course, tennis courts, private marina, full-service water-sports center, 3 restaurants, conference rooms. AE, MC, V. Very Expensive.*

Treasure Island Resort. Owned by a consortium of country music stars (Randy Travis and Larry Gatlin among other notables), the five-story resort aptly promotes itself as a place where the "fun never sets." All rooms are decorated in tropical colors and have views of either the beach or the pool. *Box 1817, Grand Cayman, tel. 809/949-7777 or for reservations in U.S., 800/ 874-0027. 290 rooms. Facilities: 2 restaurants, 3 bars, nightclub, 2 pools, Jacuzzi, water-sports center. AE, CB, DC, MC, V. Very Expensive.*

★ **Coconut Harbour.** There's only one drawback to this diver's retreat: It's located near a field of oil storage tanks. This delightful resort has a dive shop, waterfront thatch-roof bar, and an informal restaurant. There's excellent diving offshore at Waldo's Reef, which is known for its population of tame marine life. *Box 2086, Grand Cayman, tel. 809/949-7486, or for U.S.*

reservations, 800/552–6281. 33 rooms, all with kitchens. Facilities: bar/grill, dive shop. AE, MC, V. Expensive.

Holiday Inn Grand Cayman. This hotel was the pioneer resort establishment on the beach and it's still loose and fun. Don't miss the "Barefoot Man," who performs nightly outside on the patio. *Box 904, Grand Cayman, tel. 809/947–4444 or for reservations, 800/421–9999. 137 double and 78 king-size rooms. Facilities: restaurant, 3 bars, tennis, water-sports center. AE, MC, V. Expensive.*

Cayman Kai Resort. Nestled next to a coconut grove, each sea lodge features a full kitchen, dining and living areas, and two screened-in porches overlooking the ocean. *Box 1112, North Side, tel. 809/947–9556 or for reservations, 800/223–5427. 46 rooms, 26 lodges. Facilities: restaurant, 2 bars, tennis court, diving, fishing and water-sports shop. AE, MC, V. Moderate.*

★ **Sunset House.** Low-key and laid-back describes this motel on the ironshore south of George Town. A well-run dive operation, congenial staff, and popular bar make this resort a favorite with divers. The relaxed atmosphere on the deck in the evening makes it a great place to meet people. *Box 479, S. Church St., tel. 809/949–5966. 42 rooms, 2 suites. Facilities: restaurant, bar, dive shop, fishing and sailing charters. AE, MC, V. Moderate.*

Villa Caribe. On the north coast, the Caribe offers Cayman-style and fine traditional cuisine. *Box 1410, North Side, tel. 809/947–9636 or for reservations, 800/367–0041. 14 rooms. Facilities: restaurant. Inexpensive.*

Cayman Brac **Brac Reef Beach Resort.** Designed, built, and owned by Bracker Linton Tibbets, the resort lures divers and vacationers who come to savor the special ambience of this tiny island. Quality accommodations, a pool, a beach, snorkeling, and the restaurant are additional reasons to stay here. *Box 235, Cayman Brac, tel. 809/948–7323. 42 rooms. Facilities: restaurant, 2 bars, pool, Jacuzzi, beach, dive shop. AE, MC, V. Moderate.*

Tiara Beach Hotel. This resort is dedicated to divers, with an excellent diving facility complimented by the DIVI chain's standards: tile floors, rattan furniture, louvered windows, balconies, and ocean views. *Box 238, Cayman Brac, tel. 809/948–7553 or for reservations, 800/FOR–DIVI. 58 rooms. Facilities: restaurant, bar, pool, Jacuzzi, tennis, dive operation, water-sports center, fishing. AE, MC, V. Moderate.*

Buccaneer's Inn. This 36-room property is simple but very friendly. It's located opposite Brac Reef, but on the West End's north shore, with the airport runway separating the two at this tip of the island point. All rooms are air-conditioned, with a private bath and patio. A bar on the beach features entertainment at the edge of the sea. The restaurant is one of the inn's delights, as is its location on the north coast, with excellent diving and snorkeling right offshore. *Box 68, Cayman Brac, tel. 809/948–7257. 36 rooms. Facilities: restaurant, bar, pool, and water-sports center. AE, MC, V. Moderate.*

Little Cayman **Sam McCoy's Guest House.** This small, cozy diving and fishing resort opened in 1985 on Little Cayman's north coast. Very reasonable rates and the owner's infectious good nature are the hallmarks of this locally run resort. Superb diving and snorkeling right offshore. Meals are included in rates. *Little Cayman, tel. 809/948–8326 or 809/948–3251. 8 rooms. Moderate.*

Southern Cross Club. Three family-style meals a day are included with your room. A bus for tours, excellent bird-watching, and diving make a stay at the club all-inclusive and relaxing. *Little Cayman, tel. 809/948-3255 or 317/636-9501 in U.S. 10 rooms. Facilities: diving, fishing, bird-watching in sanctuary. Moderate.*

Condominiums   The **Cayman Islands Department of Tourism** provides a complete list of condominiums and small rental apartments in the Moderate to Inexpensive range. Rates are higher during winter season, so check before you book. **Cayman Rent a Villa** (Box 681, Grand Cayman, tel. 809/947-4144) can help locate a rental house or cottage. **Reef House Ltd. Property Management** (Box 1540, Grand Cayman, tel. 809/949-7093) also rents villas, houses, and apartments on all three islands.

Nightlife

Each of the island hot spots attract a different clientele. The rowdy crowd gathers at the **Wreck of the Ten Sails** at the Holiday Inn where the "Barefoot Man" entertains. The dance floor is always crowded, and it's also a great spot to people-watch. Admission is $5; hotel guests pay no admission charge.

Silver's Nightclub (tel. 809/949-7777) at the Treasure Island Resort is a spacious, tiered club that is usually filled to capacity. A lively house band plays Monday–Saturday nights.

Monkey Business (upstairs at the Falls Shopping Center, tel. 809/947-4024) is a disco with an ersatz jungle decor, complete with dummy monkeys. The flashing lights and pulsating beat keep the dance floor hopping.

For current entertainment, look at the freebie newspaper, *Cayman After Dark*, which gives listings of music, movies, theater, and other entertainment possibilities.

9 Curaçao

by Pamela Bloom Forty miles north of Venezuela and 42 miles east of Aruba is Curaçao, the largest of the islands in the Netherlands Antilles. The sun smiles down on Curaçao, but it never gets stiflingly hot: the gentle trade winds refresh. Water sports attract enthusiasts from all over the world, and some of the best reef diving is here, though Curaçao's 38 beaches and coves hardly compare in size with those of its nearby sister islands of Aruba and Bonaire.

As seen from the Otrabanda of Willemstad by the first-time visitor, Curaçao's "face" will be a surprise—spiffy rows of pastel-colored town houses that look transplanted from Holland. Although the gabled roofs and red tiles show a Dutch influence, the absurdly gay colors of the facades, as novelist Christopher Isherwood once described them, are peculiar to Curaçao. It is said that the first governor of Curaçao developed a terrible allergy to the color white (it gave him migraines), so all the houses were painted in colors. The dollhouse look of the architecture makes a cheerful contrast to the stark cacti and the dramatic shrubbery dotting the countryside.

The history books still cannot agree on who discovered Curaçao—one school of thought believes it was Alonzo de Ojeda, another says it was Amerigo Vespucci, but they seem to agree that it was around 1499. The first Spanish settlers arrived in 1527. In 1634, the Dutch came via the Netherlands West India Company. They promptly shipped off the Spaniards and the few remaining Indians—survivors of the battles for ownership of the island, famine, and disease—to Venezuela. Eight years later, Peter Stuyvesant ruled as governor until he left for New York around 1645. Twelve Jewish families arrived from Amsterdam in 1651 and built a synagogue; today, it is the oldest synagogue still in use in the Western Hemisphere. Over the years, the city built massive fortresses to defend itself against French and British invasions—many of those ramparts now house unusual restaurants and hotels. The Dutch claim to Curaçao was finally recognized in 1815 by the Treaty of Paris. In 1954, Curaçao became an autonomous part of the Kingdom of the Netherlands, with an elected Parliament and island council, and is ruled by a governor appointed by the queen.

Today Curaçao's population is derived from more than 50 nationalities blending together in an exuberant mix of Latin and African roots. The island is known for its religious tolerance, and tourists are warmly welcomed. In the past few years, millions of dollars have been poured into restoring the old colonial landmarks and upgrading and modernizing hotels. The International Trade Center, a major convention hall that opened in 1989, is expected to attract enormous business to the island. Within the complex, construction on two new hotels—a Ramada and a Sonesta—should be finished sometime in 1990.

Before You Go

Tourist Information Contact the **Curaçao Tourist Office** (400 Madison Ave., New York, NY 10017, tel. 212/751–8266 or 800/332–8266) for information.

Arriving and
Departing
By Plane

If you're flying from New York, **American** (tel. 800/433–7300) and **ALM** (tel. 800/327–7230) will take you direct to Curaçao; only ALM flies nonstop to Curaçao from Miami and San Juan. From Curaçao, ALM flies to the other Antilles islands, including Aruba, Bonaire, and St. Martin. **BWIA** (tel. 800/327–7401) flies to Antigua with a **LIAT** (tel. 809/462–0700) connection to Curaçao.

Passports
and Visas

U.S. and Canadian citizens traveling in Curaçao need only proof of citizenship. A voter's registration card or a notarized birth certificate (not a photocopy) will suffice—a driver's license will *not*. All British citizens must produce a passport. Visitors must show an ongoing or return ticket.

Customs
and Duties

U.S. residents returning to the United States may bring in $400 worth of duty-free articles. Included may be 200 cigarettes, one quart of liquor, locally made souvenirs and handicrafts, film, art, books, antiques, caviar, truffles, and jewelry made in the Netherlands Antilles (be sure to get a certificate from the place of purchase that your jewelry was made on the island). Articles in excess of $400 up to $1,000 are assessed at a flat rate of 10%.

Language

Dutch is the official language, but the vernacular is Papiamento—a tough one to master. Like Chinese, it's a tonal language, which means that the slightest shift in pitch changes the meaning of the word. Developed during the 18th century by Africans, Papiamento evolved in Curaçao as the mode of communication between landowners and their slaves. These days, however, English, as well as Spanish, and, of course, Dutch, are studied by schoolchildren. Anyone involved with tourism—shopkeepers, restaurateurs, and museum guides—speaks English.

Precautions

Mosquitoes in Curaçao do not seem as vicious and bloodthirsty as they do on Aruba and Bonaire, but that doesn't mean they don't exist. To be safe, you should douse yourself with insect repellent before dining alfresco and spray your hotel room at night—especially if you've opened a window.

If you plan to go into the water, beware of Portuguese man-of-war, moon jellyfish, red fire sponges, and long-spined sea urchins, which can cause pain and discomfort if you come in contact with them.

Do not eat any of the little green apple-like fruits of the manchineel tree: They're poisonous. In fact, steer clear of the trees altogether; raindrops or dewdrops dripping off the leaves can blister your skin. If contact does occur, rinse the affected area with water and, in extreme cases, get medical attention. Usually, the burning sensation won't last longer than two hours.

Further Reading

Before venturing into the Caribbean waters, pick up a copy of the *Guide to Corals and Fishes of Florida, the Bahamas and the Caribbean*, a waterproof paperback available through the publisher (Seahawk Press, 6840 S.W. 92nd St., Miami FL 33156) and in bookstores and dive shops around Curaçao. Both children and adults will enjoy the easily understood text and the colorful drawings of more than 260 aquatic species. Tom van t' Hof's *Guide to the Curaçao Underwater Park* is an invaluable introduction to diving on the isle. *Curaçao: Scenes and Behind the Scenes* by Jos de Roo discusses the island's history and architecture.

Staying in Curaçao

Important **Tourist Information:** The **Curaçao Tourist Board** has three of-
Addresses fices on the island, where multilingual guides are ready to
answer questions. You can also pick up maps, brochures, and a
copy of *Curaçao Holiday*. The main office is located at Waterfront Plaza, next to the Curaçao Plaza Hotel (tel. 599/961–
3397); other offices are in Schouwburgweg (tel. 599/977–1222)
and at the airport (tel. 599/98–6789).

Emergencies **Police** may be reached at tel. 599/94–4444.

Hospitals: For medical emergencies, call **St. Elisabeth's Hospital** (tel. 599/962–4900) or an ambulance (tel. 599/962–5822).

Pharmacies: Botica Popular (Madurostraat 15, tel. 599/61–
1269).

Currency U.S. dollars—in cash or traveler's checks—are accepted nearly everywhere, so there's no need to worry about exchanging
money. However, you may need small change for pay phones,
cigarettes, or soda machines. The currency in the Netherlands
Antilles is the guilder, or florin, as it is also called, indicated by
an fl. or NAf. on price tags. The U.S. dollar is considered very
stable; the official rate of exchange at press time was NAf 1.77
to U.S. $1. Note: Prices quoted here are in U.S. dollars unless
indicated otherwise.

Taxes and Hotels collect a 5% government tax.
Service Charges The departure tax is $5.75.

Hotels add a 10% service charge to the bill; restaurants add
10%–15%.

Guided Tours You don't really need a guide to show you downtown Willemstad—it's an easy taxi or bus ride from most major hotels and
small enough for a self-conducted walking tour. To see the rest
of the island, however, a guided tour can save you time and energy. Most hotels have tour desks where arrangements can be
made with reputable tour operators. For very personal, amiable service, try **Casper Tours** (tel. 599/95–3010). For $25 per
person, you'll be escorted around the island in an air-
conditioned van, with stops at the Juliana Bridge, the salt
lakes, Knip Bay for a swim, the grotto at Boca Tabla, and lunch
at Janchi Christiaan's, which is famous for its native cuisine. A
sunset cruise includes beer, wine, and cheese and runs $22.50
per head. **Taber Tours** (tel. 599/97–7637) offers a 3½-hour city
and country tour ($10), which includes visits to the Curaçao Li-
queur Factory, the Botanical Garden, the Breivennat Church,
and the old fort.

Taber Tours (tel. 599/97–7637) offers a two-hour sunset cruise,
costing $25 for adults and $15 for children, that includes a feast
of French bread, cheese, and wine. For a daytime excursion,
try the Coral sailing tour around Santa Marta Bay. The package includes transportation to and from your hotel, lunch at the
Coral Cliff Hotel, and beer and soft drinks during the trip. The
cost is $35 for adults, $25 for children.

Getting Around Taxi drivers have an official tariff chart, with fares from the
Taxis airport vicinity running about $11 to Willemstad to $9 to

Curaçao

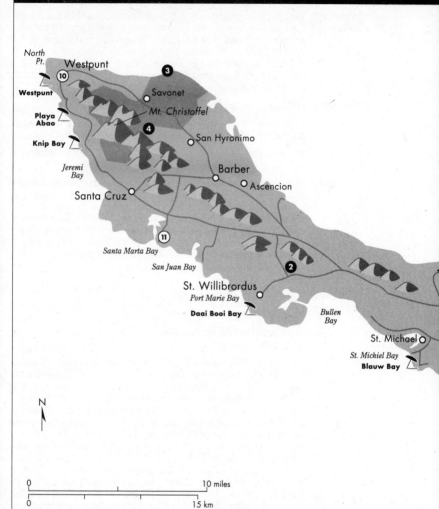

North Pt.

Westpunt

Westpunt **10**

Playa Abao

Knip Bay

Jeremi Bay

3

Savonet

Mt. Christoffel

4

San Hyronimo

Barber

Ascencion

Santa Cruz

Santa Marta Bay

11

San Juan Bay

St. Willibrordus

Port Marie Bay

Daai Booi Bay

2

Bullen Bay

St. Michael

St. Michiel Bay

Blauw Bay

N

0 ——————— 10 miles

0 ——————— 15 km

Caribbean Sea

Curaçao International Airport

Brievengat

Santa Caterina

St. Joris Bay

Great St. Joris

Little St. Joris

Santa Rosa

Mt. Tafelberg

Ostpunt

Julianadorp

St. Anna Bay

Bottelier

Brakkaput

Spanish Water

Willemstad

Piscadera Bay

Jan Thiel Bay

Caracas Bay

Santa Barbara Beach

Nieuwpoort

Curaçao Underwater Park

1 Exploring Sites

10 Hotels and Restaurants

Lodging

Avila Beach Hotel, **24**

Coral Cliff Resort and Beach Club, **11**

Curaçao Caribbean Hotel and Casino, **23**

Curaçao Plaza Hotel and Casino, **25**

Golden Tulip Las Palmas and Vacation Village, **12**

Holiday Beach Hotel and Casino, **26**

Princess Beach Hotel and Casino, **28**

Trupial Inn, **27**

Picadera Bay. Taxis at other times are moderately priced, but confirm the fare with the driver before departure. There is an additional 25% surcharge after 11 PM. Taxis are readily available at hotels; in other cases, call Central Dispatch at 599/968–4574.

Rental Cars You can rent a car from **Budget** (tel. 599/98–3198), **Avis** (tel. 599/961–1255), and **National Car Rental** (tel. 599/98–3489) at the airport or have it delivered free to your hotel. A typical rate is about $28 a day for a Volkswagen Beetle to about $50 for a four-door sedan. If you're planning to do country driving or rough it through Christoffel Park, a Jeep is best. All you'll need is a valid U.S. or Canadian driver's license.

Telephones and Mail Phone service in Curaçao eventually does connect, but you can spend up to a half hour waiting to reach your party—and some of the connections will require yelling. Hotel operators will put the call through for you, but if you make a collect call, do check immediately afterward that the hotel does not charge you as well. To call Curaçao direct, dial 011–599–9 plus the number in Curaçao. To airmail a letter to the United States costs NAf 1; a postcard costs NAf .60.

To place a call from Curaçao to the United States, dial 1, area code, and local number. To place a local call on the island, dial the six- or seven-digit local number.

Opening and Closing Times Most shops are open Monday–Saturday 8–noon and 2–6. Banks are open on weekdays 8:30–noon and 1:30–4:30.

Beaches

Curaçao has some 38 beaches, and the best way to find "your" beach is to rent a Jeep, cycle, or heavy-treaded car. Ask your hotel to pack a picnic basket for you and go exploring. Getting lost and ending up in some undiscovered cove is half the fun. Curaçao doesn't have Aruba's long, powdery stretches of sand; instead, you'll discover the joy of inlets: tiny bay openings to the sea marked by craggy cliffs, exotic trees, and scads of interesting pebbles. Imagine a beach that's just big enough for your party of four—or a party of just two. Keep an eye out for flying fish. They propel their tails through the water until they reach a speed of 44 mph, then spread their fins and soar.

Hotels with the best beach properties include **The Avila Beach Hotel** (impressively long), the **Princess Beach** (impressively sensuous) and the **Coral Cliff Resort** (impressively deserted). No matter which hotel you're staying at, beach hopping to other hotels can be fun.

Westpunt, on the northwest tip of the island, is rocky but shady in the morning. It doesn't have much sand, but you can sit on a shaded ledge. On Sunday, watch the divers jump from the high cliff. The bay view is worth the trip. For lunch, stop at Janchie Christiaan's nearby (*see* Dining, below).

Knip Bay has two parts: Big (Grote) Knip and Little (Kleine) Knip. Both are shaded with huge trees—these are manchineels, so steer clear of them. Both have alluring white sand, but neither one has a place to change. Take the road to the Knip Landhouse, then turn right. Signs will direct you. In between the big and the little bay is a superb scenic route. The protected cove, backed by sheer cliffs, is usually a blast on weekends when there is live music.

Starting from the church of St. Willibrordus, signs will direct you to **Daai Booi Bay**, a sandy shore dotted with thatched shelters. The road to this public beach is a small paved highway flanked on either side by thick lush trees and huge organpipe cacti. The beach is curved, with shrubbery rooted into the side of the rocky cliffs: a great place to swim.

Santa Barbara on the eastern tip has changing facilities and a snack bar but charges a small fee, usually around $3.35 per car.

One of the largest, more spectacular beaches on Curaçao is **Blauw Bay** (Blue Bay). There's plenty of white sand and lots of shady places, showers, and changing facilities, but since it's a private beach, you'll pay an entrance fee of about NAf.4 per car. Take the road that leads past the Holiday Beach Hotel and the Curaçao Caribbean north toward Julianadrop. At the end of the stretch of straight road, a sign will instruct you to bear left for Blauwbaai and the fishing village of San Michiel. The latter is a good place to dive.

Playa Abao boasts crystal-clear turquoise water; amenities include a snack center and public toilets. It is located at the northern tip of the island, near West Pointe Bay.

Exploring Curaçao

Numbers in the margin correspond with points of interest on the Curaçao map.

Willemstad **The capital city, Willemstad,** is a favorite cruise stop for two
❶ reasons: The shopping is considered the best in the Caribbean, and a quick tour of most of the downtown sights can be managed within a six-block radius. Santa Anna Bay slices the city down the middle: On one side is the Punda, and on the other is the Otrabanda (literally, the "other side"). Think of the Punda as the side for tourists, crammed with shops, restaurants, monuments, and markets. Otrabanda is for the natives—narrow winding streets full of private homes notable for their picturesque gables and Dutch-influenced designs.

There are three ways to make the crossing from one side to the other: (1) Drive or take a taxi over the Juliana Bridge, (2) traverse the Queen Emma Pontoon Bridge on foot, or (3) ride the free ferry when it's running. If you're staying in a hotel on the Otrabanda side, a free shuttle bus that stops by the lobby will leave you near the Rif Fort; you'll need only to take a short walk north to reach the foot of the Pontoon Bridge.

Our walking tour of Willemstad starts at the **Queen Emma Bridge,** affectionately called "the Lady" by the natives. During the hurricane season in 1988, the 700-foot floating bridge practically floated right out to sea; it was later taken down for major reconstruction. If you're standing on the Otrabanda side, take a few moments to scan Curaçao's multicolored "face" on the other side of Santa Anna Bay. If you wait long enough, the bridge will swing open (at least 30 times a day) to let the seagoing ships pass through. The original bridge, built in 1888, was the brainchild of the American consul Leonard Burlington Smith, who made a mint off the tolls he charged for the bridge. Initially, the charge was 2¢ per person if he was wearing shoes, free if he was barefoot. Today it's free.

Take a breather at the peak of the bridge and look north to the 1,625-foot-long **Queen Juliana Bridge,** completed in 1974 and standing 200 feet above water. That's the bridge you drive over to cross to the other side of the city, and although the route is time consuming (and more expensive if you're going by taxi), the view from this bridge is worth it. At every hour of the day, the sun casts a different tint over the city, creating an ever-changing panorama; the nighttime view, rivaling Rio's, is breathtaking.

When you cross the bridge and arrive on the Punda side, turn left and walk down the waterfront, along **Handelskade.** You'll soon pass the ferry landing. Now take a close look at the buildings you've seen only from afar; the original red tiles of the roofs came from Europe and arrived on trade ships as ballast.

Walk down to the corner and turn right at the customs building onto Sha Caprileskade. This is the bustling **floating market,** where each morning dozens of Venezuelan schooners arrive laden with tropical fruits and vegetables. Fresh mangoes, papayas, and exotic vegetables vie for space with freshly caught fish and unusual fabrics. It's probably too much to ask a tourist to arrive by 6:30 AM when the buying is best, but there's plenty of action to see throughout the afternoon. Any produce bought here, however, should be thoroughly washed before eating.

When the sun is beating down, the **Reading Corner** in the Maduro and Curiel's Bank building (right in front of the floating market) will feel like an oasis. It's an open-air reading room, where you can sit and catch up on the latest newspapers from the United States, Venezuela, and Holland. You might even be able to find a recent *Time* magazine or a *Business Week*.

Keep walking down Sha Caprileskade. Head toward the Wilhelmina Drawbridge, which connects Punda with the once-flourishing district of **Scharloo,** where the early Jewish merchants first built stately homes. Scharloo is now a red-light district.

At the bridge, turn left and walk up Columbusstraat to the **Mikveh Israel-Emanuel Synagogue,** founded in 1651 and the oldest temple still in use in the Western Hemisphere. One of the most important sights in Curaçao, it draws 20,000 visitors a year. Enter through the gates around the corner on Hanchi Snoa and ask the front office to direct you to the guide on duty. A unique feature is the brilliant white sand covering the synagogue floor, a remembrance of Moses leading his people through the desert; the Hebrew letters on the four pillars signify the names of the Four Daughters of Israel: Eve, Sarah, Rachel, and Esther. A quaint museum in the back displays Jewish antiques (including a set of circumcision instruments) and artifacts from Jewish families collected from all over the world. The gift shop near the gate has excellent postcards and commemorative medallions. *29 Kerkstraat, tel. 599/961–1067). Open weekdays 9–11:45 and 2:30–5. Services conducted by an American rabbi are held Fri. at 6:30 PM and on Sat. at 10 AM. Jacket and tie required.*

Continue down Columbusstraat till you reach the courthouse, with its stately balustrade, and the impressive Georgian facade of the Bank of Boston. The statue keeping watch over the park is of Queen Wilhelmina, a popular monarch of the Netherlands, who gave up her throne to her daughter Juliana after her Golden Jubilee in 1948. At Breedestraat, turn left and browse at two of the best jewelry shops in the Caribbean: **Spritzer & Furhman** and **Gandleman's Jewelers.** Take Breedestraat down to the Pontoon Bridge, then turn left at the waterfront. At the foot of the bridge are the mustard-colored walls of **Fort Amsterdam.** Take a few steps through the archway and enter another century. The entire structure dates back to the 1700s, when it was actually the center of the city and the most important fort on the island. Now it houses the governor's residence, the Fort Church, the ministry, and several other government offices. Next door is the **Plaza Piar,** dedicated to Manuel Piar, a native Curaçaoan who fought for the independence of Venezuela under the liberator Simon Bolívar. On the other side of the plaza is the **Waterfort,** a bastion dating back to 1634. The original cannons are still positioned in the battlements. The foundation, however, now forms the walls of the Curaçao Plaza Hotel. Following the sidewalk around the plaza, you'll discover the most delightful shopping area on the island, newly built under the **Waterfort arches** (*see* Shopping, below, for details).

Western Side The road through the village of Soto that leads to the northwest tip of the island winds through landscape that Georgia O'Keefe might have painted—towering cacti, flamboyant dried shrubbery, and thatch-roof houses. Throughout this *cunucu*, or countryside, you'll see native fishermen hauling in their nets, women pounding cornmeal, and donkeys blocking traffic. Landhouses, large estate houses from centuries past, dot the countryside, though most are closed to the public. Their facades, though, can often be glimpsed from the highway. For a splendid view, food, drinks, and music, try to stop at **Landhuis Jan Kock** (tel. 599/964–8087), built in the mid-17th century, which is reputed to be haunted. Hours are irregular, so do call in advance.

Next, head toward Christoffel Park on the highway. Make a stop at **Boca Tabla,** where the sea has carved a magnificent grotto. Safely tucked in the back, you can watch and listen to the waves crashing ferociously against the rocks. About an hour from Willemstad, off the Westpunt highway, is **Christoffel Park,** a fantastic 4,450-acre garden and wildlife preserve with the towering Mt. Christoffel at its center. Open to the public since 1978, the park consists of three former plantations with individual trails that take about one to 1½ hours each to traverse. You may drive your own car (heavy-treaded wheels) or rent a Jeep with or without an accompanying guide. Start out early (by 10 AM the park starts to feel like a sauna), and if you're going solo, first study the *Excursion Guide to Christoffel Park* (sold at the front desk), which outlines the various routes and identifies the flora and fauna found here. No matter what route you take, you'll be treated to interesting views of hilly fields full of prickly pear cacti, divi divi trees, bushy-haired palms, and exotic flowers that bloom unpredictably after April showers. There are also caves with ancient Indian inscriptions. For the strong of heart: Walk through the bat caves on the Savonet route (marked in blue); you'll hear bat wings rustling in the corners and see a few scary, but nonpoisonous, scorpion spiders scuttling over the walls. Make sure you're wearing the proper shoes; the ground is covered with *guano* (bird and bat droppings) that almost seems alive because of the millions of harmless mites. It's not all a shop of horrors, though—if you make it to the last chamber, you'll discover a magnificent white-faced barn owl.

As you drive through the park, keep a lookout for tiny deer, goats, and other small wildlife that might suddenly dart in front of your car. The snakes you could encounter—the whip-snake and the minute silver snake—are not poisonous. White-tail hawks may be seen on the green route, white orchids and crownlike passion flowers on the yellow route.

Climbing up the 1,230-foot Mt. Christoffel on foot is an exhilarating experience and a definite challenge to anyone who hasn't grown up scaling the Alps. The guidebook claims the round-trip will take you one hour, and Curaçaoan adolescent boys do make a sport of racing up and down, but it took this writer 2½ sweaty hours to make it back to camp. And the last few feet are deadly. The view from the peak, however, *is* thrilling—a panorama of the island, including Santa Marta Bay and the tabletop mountain of St. Hironimus. On a clear day, you can even see the mountain ranges of Venezuela, Bonaire, and Aruba. *Tel. 599/964–0363. Admission: $1.25 adults, 75¢ children 6–15, free after 2 PM. Open daily 8–3.*

Eastern Side To explore the eastern side of the island, take the coastal road out from Willemstad past the zoo and botanical gardens (neither is exceptional) about 2 miles to Jan Thiel Bay. There you'll find the Seaquarium and the Underwater Park.

The **Curaçao Seaquarium** is *the* place to see the island's underwater treasures without getting your feet wet. In fact, it's the world's only public aquarium where sea creatures are raised and cultivated totally by natural methods. You can spend several hours here, mesmerized by the 75 freshwater tanks full of over 400 varieties of exotic fish and vegetation, including sharks, lobsters, turtles, corals, and sponges. Look out for their eight-foot mascot, Herbie the cewfish, a lugubrious fish who, with luck, has been moved to a bigger tank by the time you get there. Water slides designed for both adults and children are big pleasers. There's also an excellent Indonesian restaurant, steakhouse, and snack bar. A 495-yard, man-made beach of white sand is well suited to novice swimmers and children, and bathroom and shower facilities are available. A souvenir shop sells some of the best postcards and coral jewelry on the island. *Tel. 599/961–6666. Admission: $5 adults, $2.50 children. Open daily 9 AM–10 PM.*

Curaçao Underwater Park consists of about 12½ miles of untouched coral reef that have been granted the status of national park. Mooring buoys have been placed at the most interesting dive sites on the reef to provide safe anchoring and to prevent damage to the reef. The park stretches along the south shore from the Princess Beach Hotel in Willemstad to the eastern tip of the island. Admission is free.

Landhuis Brievengat (tel. 599/97–8344) is a 10-minute drive northeast of Willemstad, near the Centro Deportivo sports stadium. On the last Sunday of the month, it holds an open house with crafts demonstrations and folkloric shows. You can see the original kitchen still intact, the 18-inch-thick walls, fine antiques, and the watchtowers, once used for lovers' trysts. The restaurant serves a fine rijstaffel.

❽ Nearby is the **Arawak Clay Products** (tel. 599/97–7658) with a factory showroom of native-made crafts. You can purchase a variety of tiles, plates, pots, and tiny replicas of landhouses. Tour operators can arrange trips.

Wind southward past Spanish Bay, where you'll pass several private yacht clubs that attract sports anglers from all over the world for international tournaments. And make a stop at **Santa Barbara Beach,** especially on Sundays, when the atmosphere approaches party time (*see* Beaches, above). **Caracas Bay,** off the coast, is a popular diving site, with a sunken ship so close to the surface that even snorkelers can balance their flippers on the helm.

Curaçao for Free

Located on the side of Willemstad in Cholobo, the **Senior Liqueur Factory** distills and distributes the original Curaçao liqueur. Don't expect to find a massive factory—it's just a small showroom in the open-air foyer of a beautiful 17th-century landhouse. There are no guides, but you can read the story of the distillation process on posters, and you'll be graciously offered samples in various flavors. If you're interested in buying—the chocolate liqueur is fantastic over ice cream—you can choose from a complete selection, which is bottled in a variety of fascinating shapes, including Dutch ceramic houses.

What to See and Do with Children

The **Curaçao Caribbean** and **Las Palmas** hotels work hard to provide a variety of activities for children—crafts, volleyball, water sports, and other group games. If you are staying elsewhere, talk to the activities director or hostess of your hotel for suggestions; they're usually very creative and might even plan a party for your child's birthday if other children are available.

Sports programs for youngsters can be found at **Chirino** (12 Orionweg, tel. 599/961–3346), a sport and recreation center. It also offers classes called *arte infantil*, where children sing, dance, act, and play. Also available is a fully equipped gym for adults, complete with aerobics classes, fitness training, jazz dancing, massage, and sauna.

Off the Beaten Track

Beth Haim, the oldest Caucasian burial ground still in use in the Western Hemisphere, is a wonderful off-beat stop. Consecrated before 1659, the Jewish cemetery has more than 2,500 graves on 3 acres, and grand history can be read from the inscriptions on the magnificently carved tombstones.

Participant Sports

Horseback Riding No one in Curaçao offers romps down the beach, but you can ride the trail inside **Rancho Alegre** (tel. 599/97–9160) by the hour or longer by reservation. Or call **Joe Pineda** (tel. 599/98–1616) for a $10-an-hour ride at his ranch.

Jogging The **Rif Recreation Area** stretches from the water plant at Mundo Nobo to the Curaçao Caribbean Hotel, along the sea. It comprises more than 1.2 miles of palm-lined beachfront, a wading pond, and a jogging track with an artificial surface, as well as a big playground. There is good security and street lighting along the entire length of the beachfront.

Tennis Most hotels (including Curaçao Caribbean, Las Palmas, Princess Beach, Holiday Beach, and the Trupial Inn) offer well-paved courts, illuminated for day and night games.

Water Sports Curaçao has facilities for all kinds of water sports, thanks to the government-founded **Curaçao Underwater Park**, which includes almost a third of the island's southern diving waters. Scuba divers and snorkelers can enjoy over 12½ miles of protected reefs and shores, with normal visibility from 60 to 80 feet (up to 150 feet on good days). With water temperatures ranging from 70 to 80° F, wet suits are generally unnecessary. No coral collecting, spearfishing, or littering is allowed. An underwater nature trail, which is especially handy for snorkelers, has been chartered along the shallows between the Seaquarium and Jan Thiel Beach, but it's accessible only by boat. An exciting wreck to explore is the SS *Oranje Nassau*, which ran aground about 80 years ago and now hosts hundreds of exotic fish and unusually shaped coral.

Most hotels either offer their own program of water sports or will be happy to make arrangements for you. An introductory scuba lesson (or one-time dive) usually runs around $25–$30.

Peter Hughes Underwater Curaçao (tel. 599/961–6666) is a world-renowned diving operation connected with the Divi Hotels and offers complete vacation/dive packages in conjunction with the Holiday Beach Hotel, Las Palmas, Princess Beach Hotel, and Trupial Inn. Its fully stocked dive shop, located next to the Curaçao Seaquarium, offers equipment for both sale and rental. Personal instruction and group lessons are conducted on state-of-the art dive boats personally designed by Peter Hughes. One dive will run you $25; packages are available. Glass-bottom-boat tours are also a fun way to go down under without getting your ears wet.

Piscadera Watersports (tel. 599/962–5000, ext. 177), at the Curaçao Caribbean Hotel, specializes in snorkeling and scuba-diving trips to reefs and underwater wrecks in every type of water vehicle—from pedal boats and water scooters to waterskis and windsurf boards. A five-dive package costs $110. Snorkeling gear costs about $2 an hour to rent. Die-hard fishermen with companions who prefer to suntan will enjoy the day trip to Little Curaçao, the "clothes optional" island between Curaçao and Bonaire, where the fish are reputed to be lively: Plan on $40 per person. Deep-sea fishing for a maximum of six people can also be arranged; it costs $225 for a half day, $450 for a full day.

Seaquarium Dive Shop, at the Seaquarium, includes a spacious patio overlooking the marina and is equipped with personal storage bins and wash tanks. Take a dive/snorkeling trip on the *Coral Sea*, a 40-foot twin diesel yacht-style dive boat, or the *Coral View*, a monohull flat-top glass-bottom boat that makes regular 30-minute excursions. A full range of equipment may be rented.

Dive Curaçao & Watersports (tel. 599/961–4944, ext. 20) at the Princess Beach Hotel both rents equipment and conducts diving and snorkeling trips. Scuba lessons run $30, including equipment. Take a 1½-hour snorkeling tour around the underwater park for $10. Also available is a cabin cruiser for half-day or full-day deep-sea fishing excursions, for $150.

Other dive shops include **Masterdive** (13 Fokkerweg, tel. 599/95–4312) and **Sun Dive** at the Holiday Beach Hotel (tel. 599/962–4888).

For windsurfing, check out the **Curaçao High Wind School** (Princess Beach Hotel, tel. 599/961–4944).

Spectator Sports

The graceful Windsurfers, bobbing sailboats, and commercial ships passing through the harbor make an ongoing sport spectacle in Curaçao. Soccer matches, from March through October, are held in the modern and comfortable **Centro Deportivo** stadium, located about 10 minutes from town. For more information, contact the Curaçao Tourist Board Office (400 Madison Ave., New York, NY 10017, tel. 212/751–8266 or 800/332–8266).

Shopping

Curaçao has long enjoyed the reputation of having some of the best shops in the Caribbean, but don't expect posh Madison Avenue boutiques. With a few exceptions (such as Benetton's, which recently moved into the Caribbean with a vengeance), the quality of women's fashions here lies along the lines of sales racks.

If you're looking for bargains on Swiss watches, cameras, crystal, or electronic equipment, do some comparison shopping back home and come armed with a list of prices.

Shopping Areas Most of the shops are concentrated in one place—**Punda**—in downtown Willemstad, within about a six-block area. The main shopping streets are **Heerenstraat, Breedestraat,** and **Madurostraat. Heerenstraat** and **Gomezplein** are both pedestrian malls, closed to traffic, and their roadbeds have been raised to sidewalk level and covered with pink inlaid tiles.

The hippest shopping area lies under the **Waterfort arches,** along with a variety of restaurants and bars. Our three favorite shops under the arches are **Bamali** (tel. 599/961–2258), which sells Indonesian batik clothing, leather bags and briefcases, and charming handicrafts; **The African Queen** (no phone), an exotic bazaar of fine African jewelry, antiques, and artifacts; and **Gino's European Boutique** (tel. 599/961–5583), full of snazzy hats with plumes and trendy accessories that look wonderfully out of place on a Caribbean isle.

Good Buys The leading jewelers in the Netherlands Antilles, **Spritzer & Fuhrman** (Heerenstraat 2, tel. 599/961–1511) carries Danish silver, delftware, Limoges, diamonds, emeralds, china, and Lladro figurines. The service is elegant.

Julius L. Penha & Sons (Heerenstraat 1, tel. 599/961–2266), in front of the Pontoon Bridge, sells French perfumes, Hummel figurines, linen from Madeira, delftware, and handbags from Argentina, Italy, and Spain. The store also has an extensive cosmetics counter.

Boolchand's (Heerenstraat 4B, tel. 599/961–2798) handles an interesting variety of merchandise behind a facade of red-and-white checked tiles. Stock up here on French perfumes, British cashmere sweaters, Italian silk ties, Dutch dolls, Swiss watches, and Japanese cameras.

Benetton's (Madurostraat 4, tel. 599/961–4919) has winter stock in July and summer stock in December; both stocks are 20% off the retail price.

Crazy Look (Madurostraat 6, no phone) has French, Italian, and Dutch fashions with a hip Eurotrash look, as well as trendy sweat shirts and baggy pants.

Toko Zuikertuintje (tel. 599/97–0188), a supermarket built on the original 17th-century Zuikertuintje Landhuis, is where most of the local elite shop. Enjoy the free tea and coffee while you stock up on all sorts of European and Dutch delicacies.

Local Crafts Native crafts and curios are on hand at **Fundason Obra di Man** (Bargestraat 57, tel. 599/961–2413). Particularly impressive are the posters of Curaçao's architecture.

Black Koral (Princess Beach Hotel, tel. 599/961–4944) is owned by Dutch-born artisan Bert Knubben, one of Curaçao's true characters. For the past 30 years, he's been designing and sculpting the most exciting black-coral jewelery in the Caribbean—and even dives for it himself, with special permission from the government. Dolphin pendants and twiglike earrings finished in 14-karat gold are excellent buys. Call before you drop by.

Dining

Restaurateurs in Curaçao believe in whetting appetites with a variety of cuisines and intriguing ambience: Dine under the boughs of magnificent old trees, in the romantic gloom of wine cellars in renovated landhouses, or on the ramparts of 18th-century forts. Curaçaoans partake of some of the best Indonesian food in the Caribbean, and they also find it hard to resist the French, Swiss, Dutch, and Swedish delights. Dress in restaurants is almost always casual, but if you feel like putting on your finery, there will always be a place for you. Do take a wrap or a light sweater with you—for some reason, most restaurants have their air-conditioners going full blast.

The most highly recommended restaurants are indicated by a star ★.

Category	Cost*
Expensive	$15–$25
Moderate	$5–$15
Inexpensive	under $5

per person, excluding drinks and service

★ **Bistro Le Clochard.** The charming Dutch couple who own this harborside restaurant still laugh about the 1988 hurricane that blew out the big picture windows and sent ocean trout swimming through the dining area. A romantic gem, the bistro is built into the 18th-century Rif Fort and is suffused with the cool, dark atmosphere of ages past. The use of fresh ingredients in the consistently well-prepared French and Swiss dishes make dining here a dream. Try the fresh-fish platters or the tender veal in mushroom sauce. Savor the fondue and let yourself get carried away by the unusual setting; just save room for the chocolate mousse. *On the Otrabanda Rif Fort, tel. 599/962–5666. Reservations required. Closed Sat. for lunch and Sun. off-season. AE, DC, MC, V. Expensive.*

★ **De Taveerne.** From the intricate detail of its centuries-old antiques to its impressive Continental menu, this restaurant rates as one of the most elegant, romantic spots on the island. Dining is in the whitewashed wine cellar of this magnificent renovated country estate, built in the 1800s by an exiled Venezuelan revolutionary. The best appetizer is the slices of tangy, smoked dolphin. The young Dutch chef Hennie also excels in grilled lobster and works wonders with veal. For dessert, there's better-than-average cheesecake, and the absolutely unforgettable broiled pears, topped with vanilla ice cream and drenched with Curaçao chocolate liqueur. *LandhuisGroot Davelaar, on Fridsanusweg, near the Promenade Shopping Center, tel. 599/97–0669. Reservations required. AE, DC, MC, V. Closed Sun. Expensive.*

La Bistroelle. The rustic Victorian splendor of the chandeliers, dark wood beams, and plush velvet chairs here will make you think that you've wandered into a French country inn. A favorite of residents who can afford it, the marvelous French cuisine includes octopus, steak in champagne, mussels in whiskey sauce, and hearty bouillabaisse. The crêpes Suzettes and *poires flambée* are not to be missed. The owners cater private parties in one of their plantation houses upon request. *Astroidenweg/Schottegatweg in the Promenade Shopping Center, tel. 599/97–6929. Reservations required. AE, DC, MC, V. Expensive.*

Fort Nassau Restaurant. This is *the* place to witness the twinkling magic of Curaçao at night. High on a hilltop overlooking Willemstad, the restaurant is built into an 18th-century fort and gives a 360-degree panoramic view of the city's rooftops. Go for a drink in the breezy, trendy Battery Terrace bar or dine in air-conditioned civility in front of the huge bay windows. The view might surpass the food, but best bets include the onion soup, the *keshi yena* (stuffed Edam cheese), and the red snapper. Afterward, check out the action in the Infinity Club downstairs, one of the sexiest, plushest discos we've ever seen. *Near Point Juliana, tel. 599/961–3086. Reservations required. AE, DC, MC, V. Expensive.*

Belle Terrace. Tucked into the quaint Avila Beach Hotel, this seaside restaurant sits right underneath the boughs of an ancient tree. Each night it features a different specialty, from Curaçao dishes like *keshi yena* to *sopito* (fish and coconut soup) to salted boiled breast of duck and filet mignon. In between stops at the creative salad bar, watch the fish jumping out of the sea—they fly up to 20 feet. *Penstraat 13–134, tel. 599/961–4377. Reservations required. AE, DC, MC, V. Moderate.*

Bellevue Restaurant. A mom, pop, and son operation that's acquired the reputation of serving some of Curaçao's best native-cuisine—the queen of Holland and the president of Venezuela have even stopped by. Forty-three years ago, it started out as an American naval base—Charles Lindbergh landed his seaplane here. Choose from a lineup of soups, including oyster, iguana, turtle, okra, and papaya, as well as sauerkraut and goat-meat stews. The seafood-combination platter is so big you won't know where to start. And the caramel pudding is wicked. *Baai Macolaweg, Parera, tel. 599/95–4291. AE, DC, MC, V. Moderate.*

★ **Janchi Christiaan's Restaurant.** Tour buses stop regularly at this open-air restaurant for lunch and for weird-sounding, but mouth-watering, native dishes. For starters, try the okra soup, the cactus soup, or the goat-meat stew; the main-course specialty is a hefty platter of fresh-caught fish, potatoes, and vegetables. Curaçaoans joke that Janchi's "iguana soup is so strong it could resurrect the dead"—truth is, it tastes just like chicken soup, only better. But Janchi, Jr., says if you want iguana, you order iguana in advance "because we have to go out and catch them." He's not kidding. *Westpunt 14, tel. 599/964–0354. No reservations required. No credit cards. Moderate.*

Golden Star Restaurant. This place looks and feels more like a friendly roadside diner than a full-fledged restaurant, but the native food here is among the best in town. Owner Marie Burke turns out Antillean specialties like *bestia chiki* (goat stew), shrimp Creole, and delicately seasoned grilled conch, all served with generous heaps of rice, fried plantains, and avocado. Steaks and chops can be had for the asking. *Socratestraat 2, tel. 599/965–4795. No reservation required. AE, DC, MC, V. Moderate.*

★ **Rijstaffel Indonesia Restaurant.** No steaks or chops here, just one dish after another of exotic delicacies that make up the traditional Indonesian banquet called *rijstaffel.* Try some sweet-and-sour barbecue ribs at the mahogany bar first, then choose from 16–36 traditional dishes that are set buffet style around you. Wash it all down with Bintang, a tangy Indonesian beer. Lesser appetites will enjoy the lighter meals, such as the fried noodles, fresh jumbo shrimps in garlic, or combination meat and fish platters. Desserts are nearly mystical; a "ladies only" ice cream comes with a red rose. The coconut ice cream comes packed in a coconut shell you can take home. The walls are stocked with beautiful Indonesian puppets ($25–$40) that will make stunning gifts. Curaçaoans love this restaurant. *Mercurriusstraat 13–15, Salinja, tel. 599/961–2999. Reservations required. Happy hour daily 5–7. AE, DC, MC, V. Moderate.*

Cozzoli's Pizza. Fast, cheap, hearty New York–style pizzas oven-baked, just like they make them in Brooklyn, are offered here. Pig out on calzones, sausage rolls, and lasagna. It is right in the middle of downtown Willemstad. *Breedestraat 2, tel. 599/961–7184. No credit cards. Inexpensive.*

Gipsy. This is a spic-and-span fast-food counter in the middle of the shopping district—drop by if all you want is a diet Coke or a roast-beef sub. Amstel beer, capuccinos, and espresso are quick pick-me-ups. *On Madurostraat, near the floating market. No phone. No credit cards. Inexpensive.*

Lodging

Hotels in Curaçao all have their pluses and minuses. If you're a business traveler, you'll appreciate the Curaçao Plaza, with easy access to the city center, but you'll have a long trek to the beach. Guests at the Curaçao Caribbean, Las Palmas, and Holiday Beach hotels enjoy their own beaches, but they're some distance from town. The Avila Beach Hotel has a beautiful beach, but the rooms are small and ascetic. Most hotels offer free shuttle bus services to downtown.

The most highly recommended lodgings are indicated by a star ★.

Category	Cost*
Expensive	over $75
Moderate	$55–$75
Inexpensive	under $55

All prices are for a standard double room for two, excluding 5% tax and a 10% service charge.

Hotels

★ **Curaçao Caribbean Hotel and Casino.** Formerly a Hilton, this government-owned hotel has a beach the size of a sandbox, but the lounging yard behind it is sprawling and perfect for sunbathing. It's five minutes by car from the center of town. The high-rise complex is self-contained, with one of the best organized activities program on the island, including crab races, Papiamento lessons, crafts, walking tours, ping-pong and jousting tournaments, and special theme nights for dinner and dancing. Adults can safely leave their kids in the hands of friendly and energetic hostesses who will entertain them. Water sports include everything imaginable. And the row of boutiques means you never have to leave the premises to shop. Across the street is the new International Trade Center. *Box 2133, Piscadera Bay, tel. 599/962–5000 or 800/444–1010. 200 rooms. Facilities: 2 restaurants, 2 bars, pool, casino, beauty salon, barber shop, lighted tennis courts, boutiques, drugstore, secretarial services, telex, meeting and convention rooms. AE, DC, MC, V. Expensive.*

Golden Tulip Las Palmas and Vacation Village. The drive from the main highway to the main building takes you through a luxurious tropical garden. Las Palmas has the feel of a laid-back hacienda, with the three-story main building and compact casitas spread out on the hilly gardens. However, you must be an energetic walker to navigate the grounds; the private beach is 800 yards from the main lobby, with a steep incline to negotiate, and the pool and casino are also a hike. A courtyard full of vines, a lily pond, and bamboo arches make for a relaxing dining experience. The air-conditioned rooms are comfortable, but the acoustics—let's just say your room had better not be next to a honeymoon couple's. The casino is tiny, but nightly entertainment is usually big and noisy, with steel bands, fire-eating limbo dancers, folklore shows, and exotic buffets. *Box 2179, Piscadera Bay, Willemstad, tel. 599/962–5200. 98 rooms; 94 2-bedroom villas. Facilities: restaurant, coffee shop, pool, casino, private beach with snack bar, minimarket, lighted tennis courts, drugstore. AE, DC, MC, V. Expensive.*

★ **Avila Beach Hotel.** The royal family of Holland and its ministers stay at this 200-year-old mansion for three good reasons: the privacy, the personalized service, and the austere elegance. Americans used to luxurious resorts might find the rooms stark, but the hotel's true elegance lies in the spectacular beach, the largest in Curaçao, as well as in the fabulous tree-shaded, outdoor dining area. The Danish chefs who specialize in a Viking pot, local dishes, and weekly smorgesbord also smoke their own fish and bake their own bread. Classical concerts, often performed by the owner, a budding tenor, take place on Sunday mornings. Recent renovations, include a new coffee shop with an open-air sea view and a conference room. *Box 791, Penstraat 130134, Willemstad, tel. 599/961–4377. 87 rooms; 20 apartments with ocean view, some with kitchenettes. Facilities: restaurant, coffee shop, bar, elevator, conference room, shuttle bus to city center. AE, DC, MC, V. Moderate.*

Coral Cliff Resort and Beach Club. Seclusion and rustic simplicity are everything here. A half hour from the center of Willemstad, the grounds boast a beach so enticing that it even attracts native islanders who are desperate for a weekend retreat. The caged iguanas near the restaurant are the only ones you will see in captivity on the island, and you're apt to find low-flying trupials, parrots, and parakeets alighting on your dinner table. All rooms are air-conditioned and overlook the sea. Cottages are equipped with kitchenettes. *Box 3782, Santa Marta Bay, tel. 599/964–1820 or 800/223–9815. 35 rooms. Facilities: casino, pool, 2 restaurants, bar, car-rental agent, marina, watersports center, and PADI 4-star dive shop. AE, DC, MC, V. Moderate.*

Curaçao Plaza Hotel and Casino. "Please don't touch the passing ships" is the slogan of the Curaçao Plaza, the only hotel in the world with marine-collision insurance. The ships do come close to the island's first high-rise hotel, which is built right into the massive walls of a 17th-century fort at the entrance of Willemstad's harbor. At the Plaza, you give up beachfront (you have beach privileges at major hotels, however) for walking access to the city's center—consequently, it's a business traveler's oasis, complete with executive floors and secretaries who will fax, telex, type, translate, and read out stock prices for you. The Queens and Kings Room is where the executives gather to network, read international papers, enjoy breakfast on the house, and indulge in the honor bar. The ramparts rising from the sea offer a fantastic evening view of the twinkling lights of the city. Most rooms are lacking in the decor department, but many have windows that provide a view of the Venezuelan coast. The new boutiques built under the adjacent arches are the best in Curaçao. *Box 229, Plaza Piar, Willemstad, tel. 599/961–2500. 254 rooms, 135 of which are in the tower, many with a sea view and some with balconies. All with bath, shower, color cable TV, air-conditioning, and 24-hr room service. Beach privileges with other hotels a taxi drive away. Facilities: 2 restaurants, nightclub, bar, casino, outdoor saltwater pool, discotheque, poolside barbecue and elaborate Sun. buffet, newsstand, drugstore, gift shop, and flower shop. Babysitter and house physician on call. AE, DC, MC, V. Moderate.*

Holiday Beach Hotel and Casino. This low-rise building was put up in 1966 and has undergone major reconstruction with an eye toward making beach life even more accessible. The lobby has been totally redesigned, and a beach bar and restaurant have been built close to the water. Despite the major renovations, however, the individual rooms remain uninspiring, not the kind you'd want to do more than sleep in. Clientele include business travelers and honeymooners, with a large cultural mix in the low season, including South Americans. *Box 2178, Otrabanda, Pater Euwensweg, Willemstad, tel. 599/962–5400. 197 rooms; 2* suites. *Facilities: playground, beauty shop, boutique, drug-store, gift shop, car-rental agent, casino. AE, MC, V. Moderate.*

★ **Princess Beach Hotel and Casino.** The beach, lined with lime trees, is one of the most beautiful in Curaçao, and is located right in front of the underwater park and next door to the Seaquarium. The rooms are huge, most with breathtaking ocean or garden views. (The garden-view rooms are the more spacious of the two.) The pathway to guest rooms is through lush, tropical grounds full of chirping birds. The new freshwater pool has the added bonus of a staff to offer drinks to guests as they paddle about on floats. Dinner in the Ballroom is black tie. The casino is the most exciting in Curaçao. Time-sharing apartments with terraces are now available. The **Curaçao High Wind School** is on the premises. *M. L. King Blvd. 8, tel. 599/961-4944 or 800/223-9815. 203 rooms. Facilities: restaurant, special theme nights, pool with bar, boutiques, drugstore, dive shop, spa, refrigerators on request. AE, DC, MC, V. Moderate.*

Trupial Inn. The price and its central location are the best things going for this informal inn. *Groot Davelaarweg 5, Willemstad, tel. 599/97-8200, telex 1410 TRUIN NA. 74 air-conditioned rooms (with 8 suites), some with kitchenettes. Facilities: restaurant, cocktail lounge, tennis court, pool, sauna, men's boutique, drugstore, free shuttle to town. AE, DC, MC, V. Inexpensive.*

Home and Apartment Rentals There are very few rentals available on the island. Your best bet is to contact the **Curaçao Tourist Board** or write to the **Caribbean Home Rentals** (Box 710, Palm Beach, FL 33480).

The Arts and Nightlife

The Arts **The Curaçao Museum,** housed in a century-old former plantation house, is filled with artifacts, paintings, and antique furnishings that trace the island's history. *Across from the Holiday Beach Hotel, off Pater Euwensweg, tel. 599/962-3777. Admission: $1.50. Open Tues.–Sun. 8–noon and 2–5. Closed last Sun. of the month.*

Gallery 86 (no phone), in the Bloksteeg (Punda) opposite the Bank of the Netherland Antilles, features the work of local artists and occasionally those of South Americans and Africans.

Nightlife The once-a-month open house at Landhuis Brievengat (*see* Exploring, Eastern Side, above) is a great way to meet interesting locals—it usually offers a folkloric show, snacks, and local handicrafts. The Curaçao Plaza, Holiday Beach, Las Palmas, and the Princess Beach hotels all have casinos that are open 2 PM–4 AM, with the exception of San Marco and the Curaçao Caribbean, which are open 9 AM–4 AM.

Blue Note Jazz Cafe (Schout bij N. Doormanweg, tel. 599/937-0685) is a singles bar-cum-Dutch pub that fills up fast. There's likely to be more TV-watching than dancing. There is live jazz on Wednesday 9:30 PM–2 AM and Sunday noon–5 PM.

La Fontaine (78 Cas Coraweg, tel. 599/97-8596), about a 10-minute drive from town, is a psychedelic-lit disco that's popular with locals. Occasional live shows feature hard-rock acts that attract a teenage crowd.

Infinity (tel. 599/61-34-50), a tiny club underneath the Fort Nassau Restaurant, is so dark that you might not notice the couple making out on the couch next to you. Everything—from the plushy couches to the waterfall wall—has been designed to induce intimate contact.

Considered the most colorful disco in town, **Naick's Place** (Lindbergweg 32, Salina, tel. 599/96–14640) is about as hip as Curaçao gets. It's dark and cool, with huge bamboo chairs for lounging. The men cruise and the women are dressed to kill. There are two disco floors with flashing lights and an intense aural assault. It's packed on Thursday, Friday, and Saturday nights.

The new nightclub and disco **Sabine's** (Plaza Hotel, tel. 599/961–2500), is open daily 10 PM–3 AM. There's no cover charge for the live entertainment that's featured on Friday and Saturday nights.

10 Dominica

by Honey Naylor

The national motto emblazoned on the coat of arms of the Commonwealth of Dominica reads "*Après Bondi, c'est la ter.*" It is a French-Creole phrase meaning "After God, it is the land." On this unspoiled isle, the land is indeed the main attraction. The Smithsonian Institution has called Dominica a giant plant laboratory, unchanged for 10,000 years.

Do not travel to Dominica seeking sleek casinos, glitzy discos, duty-free shops, and posh resorts. There aren't any. The grandeur of Dominica (pronounced dom-in-*ee*-ka) is not man-made. This untamed, ruggedly beautiful land, located in the eastern Caribbean between Guadeloupe to the north and Martinique to the south, is a 290-square-mile nature retreat; 29 miles long and 15 miles wide, the island is dominated by some of the highest elevations in the Caribbean and has 365 rivers running through it. Much of the interior is covered by a luxuriant rain forest, a wild place where you almost expect Tarzan to swing howling by on a vine. This exotic spot is home to such unusual critters as the Sisserou (or Imperial) parrot and the red-necked (or Jacquot) parrot, neither of which can be found elsewhere in the world.

Dominica is home, too, to the last remnants of the Carib Indians, whose ancestors came paddling up from South America more than a thousand years ago. The fierce, cannibalistic Caribs kept Christopher Columbus at bay when he came to call during his second voyage to the New World. Columbus turned up at the island on Sunday, November 3, 1493. In between Carib arrows he hastily christened it Dominica (Sunday Island), and then beat a retreat.

For almost two centuries the British and French tried unsuccessfully to subdue the Caribs, and in 1749 they agreed to let the Caribs keep the island. However, French and English planters, unable to resist the lure of the fertile land, began to fight one another for squatter's rights. Their frequent and ferocious fights caused even the Caribs to call the island *waitukubuli* (land of many battles). In 1795, the English paid a "ransom" of 12,000 pounds to the French, and Dominica became a British possession. In 1967, the British colony became self-governing, and on November 3, 1978 Dominica became a fully independent republic. Despite (or maybe because of) its ferocious past, Dominica today is a quiet, peaceful place. There are about 87,000 people who live on the island, and they are some of the friendliest people in all of the Caribbean.

Before You Go

Tourist Information
The **Caribbean Tourism Association** (20 E. 46th St., New York, NY 10017, tel. 212/682–0435) has little information on hand, so you will do better to contact the **Dominica Tourist Board** (Box 73, Roseau, Dominica, W.I. tel. 809/448–2186 or 809/448–2351. Telex 8649 TOURIST DO). However, if you write to the island allow at least two to three weeks for your letter to arrive as the mail is notoriously slow, and if you call you may not get a very good connection.

Arriving and Departing
By Plane
No major airlines fly into Dominica, but **LIAT** (tel. 809/462–0700) connects with flights from the United States on Antigua, Barbados, Guadeloupe, Martinique, and San Juan, Puerto

Rico. **Air Caribe** (tel. 809/449–1117) flies direct from San Juan, **Air Martinique** (tel. 809/449–1060) from Fort de France, and **Air Guadeloupe** (tel. 809/449–1060) from Pointe-à-Pitre.

From the Airport **Canefield Airport** (about 3 miles north of the capital city of Roseau) at present can take only small aircraft, but a project to lengthen the runway and add lights for night landings is under way. Dominica's older and larger **Melville Hall Airport,** on the northeast (Atlantic) coast, can manage larger commercial aircraft and night landings; however, it is a rather harrowing 90-minute drive from there to Roseau, and the taxi cost is $13 per person, as opposed to the $6-per-car fare from Canefield to Roseau. The moral of the story: Opt for Canefield, if at all possible.

Passports and Visas The only entry requirements for U.S. or Canadian citizens are proof of citizenship, such as a birth certificate or voter registration card, and an ongoing or return airline ticket. British citizens are required to have passports but visas are not necessary.

Customs and Duties In addition to items for personal use, you may bring in 200 cigarettes or 50 cigars and 8 ounces of tobacco, a quart of alcohol, and 6 ounces of perfume.

Language The official language is English, but most Dominicans also speak a French-Creole patois.

Precautions Be sure to bring insect repellent. If you are prone to carsickness, you will also want to bring along some pills. The roads twist and turn dramatically, and the (expert) local drivers barrel across them at a dizzying pace.

Staying in Dominica

Important Addresses **Tourist Information:** The main office of the **Dominica Tourist Board** (Bath Estate, Roseau, tel. 809/448–2186 or 809/448–2351) and the tourist desks at the **Old Market Plaza** (Roseau, tel. 809/448–2186), **Canefield Airport** (tel. 809/449–1242), and **Melville Hall Airport** (tel. 809/445–7051) are open weekdays 8–1 and 2–4.

Emergencies **Police, Fire, and Ambulance:** Call 999.

Hospitals: Princess Margaret Hospital (Federation Dr., Goodwill, tel. 809/448–2231 or 809/448–2233).

Pharmacies: Jolly's Pharmacy (33 Great George St., Roseau, tel. 809/448–3388).

Currency The official currency is the Eastern Caribbean dollar (E.C.), but U.S. dollars are accepted everywhere. At press time the rate was E.C.$2.67 to U.S.$1. Local prices, especially in shops frequented by tourists, are often quoted in both currencies, so be sure to ask. Prices quoted here are in U.S. dollars unless noted otherwise.

Taxes and Service Charges Hotels collect a 10% government tax; restaurants a 3% tax. The departure tax is $6.

Most hotels and restaurants add a 10% service charge to your bill. Taxi drivers expect a 10% tip.

Guided Tours A wide variety of hiking and photo safari tours are conducted by **Dominica Tours** (tel. 809/448–2638) in sturdy four-wheel-

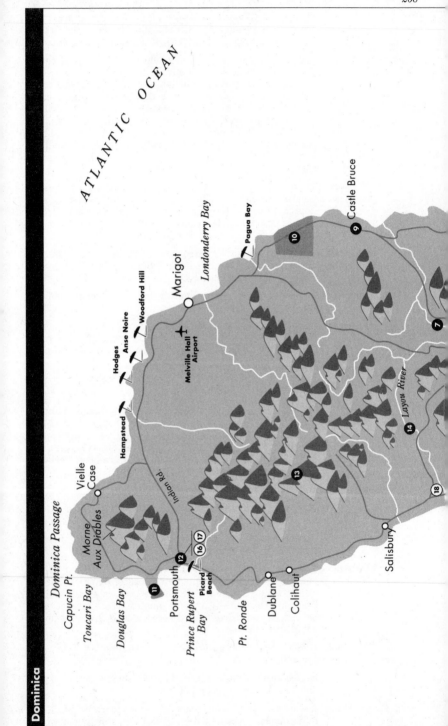

drive vehicles. Prices range from $5 to $40 per person, depending upon the length of the trip and whether picnics and rum punches are included. There are also boat tours that include snorkeling and swimming.

Rainbow Rover Tours (tel. 809/448–8650) are conducted in an air-conditioned Land Rover. Tours take in the island for a half or full day at a per-person cost of $30–$50, which includes food and drink.

The taxi driver who picks you up at the airport will almost certainly ask, "Is this your first visit to Dominica?" If your answer is "Yes," he will offer his services as a guide at the cost of $15 an hour, with tip extra. It's a good idea to get a recommendation from the Dominica Tourist Board (*see* Tourist Information, above) before selecting a guide and driver.

Getting Around If it doesn't bother you to drive on the left on potholed moun-
Rental Cars tainous roads with hairpin curves, rent a car and strike out on you own. Daily car-rental rates begin at $30 (weekly $160), and you'll have to put down a deposit and purchase a visitor's driving permit for E.C.$20. You can rent a car from **Wide Range Car Rentals** (81 Bath Rd., Roseau, tel. 809/448–2198), **Valley Rent-A-Car** (Goodwill Rd., Roseau, tel. 809/448–3233), **Shillingford Car Rental** (10 Winston La., Goodwill, tel. 809/448–3151), **S.T.L. Rent-A-Car** (Goodwill Rd., Roseau, tel. 809/448–2340 or 809/448–3376), or **CNC Rent-A-Car** (37 Kennedy Ave., Roseau, tel. 809/448–2207 or 809/449–6375).

Remember: Driving is on the left.

Telephones To call Dominica from the United States, dial area code 809 and
and Mail the local access code, 44. On the island, you need to dial only the five-digit number. Direct telephone, telegraph, telefax, teletype, and telex services are via **Cable & Wireless** (West Indies) Ltd.

First-class (airmail) letters to the United States and Canada cost E.C.60¢; postcards cost E.C.35¢.

Opening and Business hours are 8–4 weekdays and 8–1 Saturdays. Banks
Closing Times are open Monday–Thursday 8–noon, Friday 8–noon and 3–5.

Beaches

Don't come to Dominica in search of powdery white-sand beaches. If you do, you'll be disappointed. Which is not to say that there are no beaches. Most of them are of dark sand, evidence of the island's volcanic origins. The best beaches are found at the mouths of rivers and in protected bays. Scuba diving, snorkeling, and windsurfing are all excellent here. Check with Derek Perryman (**Dive Dominica**, tel. 809/448–2188) about scuba-diving expeditions and with **Dominica Tours** (tel. 809/448–2638) about swimming and snorkeling excursions.

Picard Beach, on the northwest coast, is the island's best beach. Great for windsurfing and snorkeling, it's a 2-mile stretch of gray sand fringed with coconut trees. The Castaways and Coconut Beach hotels are both on this beach.

The scuba diving is excellent at **Soufrière Bay,** a sandy beach south of Roseau.

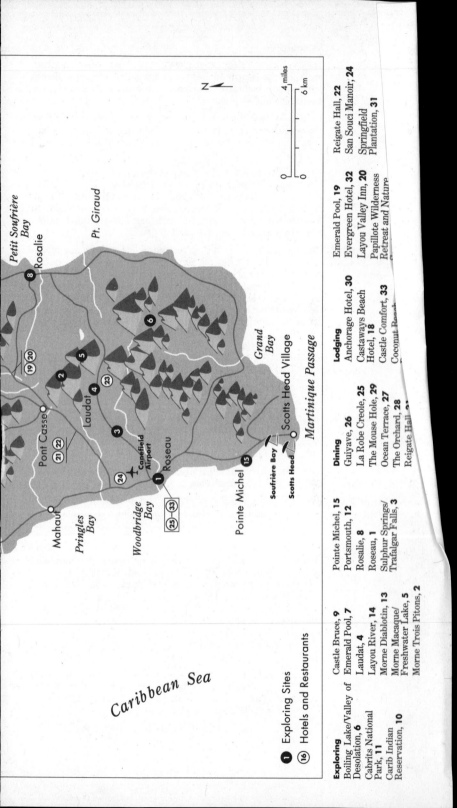

Caribbean Sea

Petit Soufrière Bay

Rosalie

Pt. Giraud

8

Pont Casse

19 20
21 22

2

5

24

23

Laudat

4

3

Mahaut

Pringles Bay

Woodbridge Bay

25 33

1

Roseau

Canefield Airport

Pointe Michel

6

Grand Bay

Soufrière Bay

Scotts Head

Scotts Head Village

Martinique Passage

N

0 ───── 4 miles
0 ───── 6 km

● Exploring Sites
⑯ Hotels and Restaurants

Exploring
Boiling Lake/Valley of Desolation, **6**
Cabrits National Park, **11**
Carib Indian Reservation, **10**
Castle Bruce, **9**
Emerald Pool, **7**
Laudat, **4**
Layou River, **14**
Morne Diablotin, **13**
Morne Macaque/Freshwater Lake, **5**
Morne Trois Pitons, **2**
Pointe Michel, **15**
Portsmouth, **12**
Rosalie, **8**
Roseau, **1**
Sulphur Springs/Trafalgar Falls, **3**

Dining
Guiyave, **26**
La Robe Creole, **25**
The Mouse Hole, **29**
Ocean Terrace, **27**
The Orchard, **28**
Reigate Hall, **2**

Lodging
Anchorage Hotel, **30**
Castaways Beach Hotel, **18**
Castle Comfort, **33**
Coconut Beach
Emerald Pool, **19**
Evergreen Hotel, **32**
Layou Valley Inn, **20**
Papillote Wilderness Retreat and Nature

Reigate Hall, **22**
San Souci Manoir, **24**
Springfield Plantation, **31**

Pagua Bay is on the Atlantic coast, a quiet, secluded beach of dark sand.

Layou River has the best swimming on the island, and its banks are great for sunbathing.

The beaches from Roseau to **Scotts Head** at the southernmost tip of the island are good for scuba diving and snorkeling.

Woodford Hill, Hampstead, Anse Noir, and **Hodges,** all on the northeast coast, are excellent beaches for snorkeling and scuba diving.

Exploring Dominica

Numbers in the margin correspond with points of interest on the Dominica map.

Given the small size of this almond-shape island, virtually any destination is within reach on any easy day trip. The amount of time you spend hiking, mountain climbing, birdwatching, or just enjoying the scenery will determine how much you can see during one round-the-island trip. The highways ringing the island's perimeter have been upgraded in recent years, making many sights and towns easier to reach in self-drive cars. However, it is advisable when heading toward some of the more remote destinations to hire a driver with a car, or to take an escorted tour *(see* Guided Tours, above).

Roseau

① All the hotels and virtually all the island's population are on the leeward, or Caribbean, side of the island. Twenty thousand or so inhabitants reside in **Roseau,** a town on the flat delta of the Roseau River. Stop first in the Tourist Office in the **Old Market Plaza.** Then stroll through the center of town, where craft shops and tiny cafes are tucked into old buildings of wood, stone, and concrete. On Victoria Street is the **Fort Young Hotel,** which was originally built as a fort in the 18th century. Directly across the street is the **Government House;** the **Public Library** and the **old Court House** are both nearby.

Across from the Court House is the **National Park Service,** which has a wealth of information about this exotic island. *Open Mon. 8–1 and 2–5, Tues.–Fri. 8–1 and 2–4.*

Now, backtrack along Victoria Street and walk along the harbor, where you can watch bananas, citrus, and spices being loaded onto ships.

Time Out | Stop in the **Cartwheel Cafe** (corner of Bay St. and John La., tel. 809/448–5353) for sandwiches, pastries, or snacks.

Elsewhere on the Island

② **Morne Trois Pitons** is a blue-green hill of three peaks, the highest of which is 4,403 feet. The mountain is usually covered with swirling mists and clouds, and the 16,000-acre national park over which it looms is awash with cool mountain lakes, waterfalls, and rushing rivers. Ferns grow 30 feet tall and wild orchids sprout from trees. Sunlight leaks through green canopies, and a gentle mist rises over the jungle floor.

The road from the capital to the Morne Trois Pitons National Park runs through the **Roseau River Valley.** About 5 miles out of

③ Roseau, a side road juts off to the splendid **Sulphur Springs** (visible evidence of the island's volcanic origins) and the spectacular triple **Trafalgar Falls,** with a drop of 200 feet into a pool strewn with rocks.

❹ The village of **Laudat** (about 7 miles from Roseau) is a good starting point for a venture into the park. Two miles northeast ❺ of Laudat, at the base of **Morne Macaque** (3,500 feet), you'll find **Freshwater Lake,** with a fringe of greenery and purple hyacinths floating on the water.

From Freshwater Lake there are several sights to be seen, but ❻ the hiking trails are not for the faint of heart. **Boiling Lake** and the **Valley of Desolation** are reached by a rugged 6-mile ramble, and you should go only with an experienced guide *(see* Participant Sports, below).

Boiling Lake, the world's second largest boiling lake, is like a caldron of gurgling gray-blue water. It is 70 yards wide, and the water temperature ranges from 180 to 197 degrees Fahrenheit. Its depth is unknown. It is believed that the lake is not a volcanic crater, but a flooded fumarole—a crack through which gases escape from the molten lava below.

The Valley of Desolation lies below Boiling Lake, and it lives up to its name. Harsh sulfuric fumes have destroyed virtually all the vegetation in what was once a lush forested area. Hikers in the Valley of Desolation are advised to stay on the trail in order to avoid breaking through the crust that covers the hot lava below.

❼ **Emerald Pool** is 3½ miles northeast of Pont Casse, which is on the road that leads to Castle Bruce. Lookout points along the trail provide sweeping views of the windward coast and the forested interior. Emerald Pool is a swirling, fern-bedecked basin into which splashes a 50-foot waterfall.

A good map and steady nerves are necessary for driving along the rugged, ragged windward (Atlantic) coast. A few miles east of Pont Casse there is a fork in the road where a right turn will take you to the southeast coast and a left to the northeast coast.

❽ The south coast road goes to **Rosalie,** where there is a river for swimming, a black-sand beach, an old aqueduct, and a waterwheel. There is also a waterfall that dashes down a cliff into the ocean. A hike leads to **Petite Soufrière,** where another dramatic waterfall cascades to the sea below.

❾ The northerly road leads to the little fishing village of **Castle Bruce.** On the beach here you can watch dugout canoes being made from the trunks of rubber trees. About 6 miles north of ❿ Rosalie lies the **Carib Indian Reservation,** which was established in 1903 and covers 3,700 acres. Don't expect a lot in the way of ancient culture and costume. The folks who gave the Caribbean its name live pretty much like other West Indians, as fishermen and farmers. However, they have maintained their traditional skills at woodcarving, basket weaving, and canoe building. Their wares are displayed and sold in little thatch-top huts. The reservation's Roman Catholic church at Salibia has an altar that was once a canoe. Another point of interest on the reservation is **L'Escalier Tête Chien** ("trail of the snake staircase" in Creole patois)—a hardened lava flow that juts down to the ocean.

Continuing north from the reservation you'll go past lovely **Pagua Bay**, with its beach of dark sand. A bit farther along, near Melville Hall Airport, is **Marigot**, the largest (population: 5,000) settlement on the east coast. On the northeast coast, steep cliffs rise out of the Atlantic, which flings its frothy waters over dramatic reefs, and rivers crash through forests of mangroves and fields of coconut. The beaches are excellent for snorkeling, and scuba diving at **Woodford Hill, Hampstead, Anse Noir,** and **Hodges.** From this vantage point you can see the French island of Marie Galante in the distance.

The road continues through banana plantations to Portsmouth, but a side road leads up to the village of **Vieille Case** and **Capuchin Point,** at the northernmost tip of the island. **Morne Au Diable** soars 2,826 feet over this area, and slopes down to **Toucari Bay** and **Douglas Bay** on the west coast, where there are spectacular white-sand beaches.

⑪ Just 2 miles south of Douglas Bay, the 250-acre **Cabrits National Park** is surrounded on three sides by the Caribbean Sea. Lush vegetation covers the remains of **Fort Shirley,** a military complex built between 1770 and 1815. In 1982, local historian Lennox Honychurch began developing Fort Shirley as an interpretive center. Some of the buildings have been restored, and there is a small museum in the park. The park is connected to the mainland by a freshwater swamp, verdant with ferns, grasses, and trees, where you can see a variety of migrant birds.

Time Out The bar in the **Purple Turtle Guest House** (Portsmouth, tel. 809/445–5296) is a fine place for a rum punch before or after a tour through the town of Portsmouth.

⑫ **Portsmouth,** 2 miles south of Cabrits, is a peaceful little town with a population of about 5,000. **Prince Rupert Bay,** site of a naval battle in 1782 between the French and the English, is far and away the island's most beautiful harbor. There are more than 2 miles of sandy beaches fringed with coconut trees and the island's only beachfront hotels. The **Indian River** flows to the sea from here, and a canoe ride takes you through an exotic rain forest.

⑬ Just south of Indian River is **Pointe Ronde,** the starting point for an expedition to **Morne Diablotin,** the island's highest summit at 4,747 feet. This is not an expedition you should attempt alone; the uninhabited interior is an almost impenetrable primeval forest. You'll need a good guide (*see* Participant Sports, below), sturdy shoes, a warm sweater, and firm resolve.

⑭ The west coast road dips down through the little villages of **Dublanc, Colihaut,** and **Salisbury** before reaching the mouth of the **Layou River.** The Layou River Valley is rich with bananas and cacao, citrus fruits, and tobacco. The river is the island's longest and largest, with deep gorges, quiet pools and beaches, waterfalls and rapids–a great place for a full day's outing of swimming and shooting the rapids, or just sunning and picnicking.

⑮ Just south of Roseau the road forks, with a treacherous road leading east to **Grand Bay** where there is a lovely beach. If you continue due south from Roseau you'll go through **Pointe Michel,** settled decades ago by Martiniquais who fled the catastrophic eruption of Mont Pelée. The stretch all the way from Roseau to Scotts Head at the southernmost tip of the island has excellent beaches for scuba diving and snorkeling.

Participant Sports

Boating Motorboat and sailing trips can be arranged through **Dominica Tours** (tel. 809/448–2638).

Hiking Trails range from the easygoing to the arduous. For the former, all you'll need are sturdy, rubber-sole shoes and an adventurous spirit.

For the hike to Boiling Lake or the climb up Morne Diablotin you will need hiking boots and a guide. Guides will charge about $15–$25 per day and can be contacted through the Tourist Office or the Forestry Division (tel. 809/533–1866).

Scuba Diving **Dive Dominica** (Castle Comfort, tel. 809/448–2188) offers instruction for beginners, as well as challenging day-long dive excursions.

Snorkeling Two major island operators rent equipment: **Anchorage Limited** (tel. 809/448–2188) and **Castaways Hotel** (tel. 809/449–6244 or 809/449–6245).

Swimming River swimming is extremely popular on Dominica, and the best river to jump into is the Layou River (*see* Exploring, above). Also *see* Beaches, above, for our pick of best beaches to swim, snorkel, or surf in.

Windsurfing Contact either **Anchorage Limited** or **Castaways Hotel** (*see* Snorkeling, above).

Shopping

Gift Ideas The handicrafts of the Carib Indians include colorful baskets made of dyed reeds and waterproofed with tightly woven banana leaves. Their crafts are sold on the reservation, as well as in Roseau's shops. Dominica is also noted for its spices, hot peppers, and coconut-oil soap; its vetiver-grass mats are sold all over the world.

Shops Stop in **Caribana Handcrafts** (31 Cork St., Roseau, tel. 809/-448–2761), where you'll find soaps, spices, stacks of handmade hats and baskets.

At **Tropicrafts Ltd** (Turkey La. and Queen Mary St., Roseau, tel. 809/448–2747) you can not only buy a vetiver-grass rug or mat but also watch it being made. The shop also has handmade baskets, hats, and dolls.

Dining

The fertile Dominican soil produces a cornucopia of fresh vegetables, and chefs here utilize them to great advantage, most often with a Creole flair. There are sweet green bananas, kush-kush yams, breadfruit, and dasheen (known as taro elsewhere, a tuber similar to the potato). You'll find fresh fish on virtually every menu, as well as "mountain chicken," a euphemism for a large frog called *crapaud*.

The most highly recommended restaurants are indicated by a star ★.

Category	Cost*
Expensive	$35–$45
Moderate	$25–$35
Inexpensive	under $25

*per person, excluding drinks, service, and sales taxes (3%)

★ **La Robe Creole.** A cozy place with wood rafters, ladderback chairs, and colorful Madras cloths, this restaurant has an eclectic à la carte listing. A specialty is callaloo and crab soup, made with dasheen and coconut. You can also have steak au poivre, crêpes of lobster and conch, charcoal-grilled fish and meats, pizza, barbecued chicken, and salads. *3 Victoria St., Roseau, tel. 809/448–2896. Reservations advised. AE. Closed Sun. Expensive.*

★ **Reigate Hall.** In this stylish French restaurant an old-fashioned waterwheel turns while you dine. Among the specialties are breast of duck in port-wine sauce, mountain chicken in champagne sauce, and coq au vin. Dessert selections include crème caramel and poire Belle Hélène. *Reigate Hall Hotel, Roseau, tel. 809/445–4031. Reservations advised. AE, DC, MC, V. Expensive.*

Guiyave. Have a drink at the second-floor bar and then repair to the table-filled balcony for dining. Spareribs, lobster, rabbit, and mountain chicken are offered, as is a variety of light snacks and sandwiches. This restaurant is noted for its fresh tropical fruit juices, and its homemade pies, tarts, and cakes. *15 Cork St., Roseau, tel. 809/448–2930. No credit cards. Moderate.*

Ocean Terrace. As the name suggests, this eatery in the Anchorage Hotel is on a terrace overlooking the ocean. Grilled lamb chops with mint jelly, Creole-style fish courtbouillon, and chilled lobster in a chives-vinaigrette marinade are among the à la carte specialties. There is live Caribbean entertainment three nights a week. *Anchorage Hotel, Roseau, tel. 809/448–2638. Reservations advised. AE, DC, MC, V. Moderate.*

★ **The Orchard.** You can dine indoors in a spacious, unadorned dining room or in a pleasant covered courtyard surrounded by latticework. Chef Joan Cools-Lartique offers Creole-style coconut shrimp, lobster, black pudding, mountain chicken, and callaloo soup with crabmeat, among other delicacies. Sandwiches are also on the menu. *31 King George V St., Roseau, tel. 809/448–3051. MC, V. Moderate.*

The Mouse Hole. This is the place to pack for your picnic in the park. There are sandwiches, salads, and snacks, all for takeout only. It's downstairs from, and affiliated with, La Robe Creole (*see* above). *3 Victoria St., tel. 809/448–2396. No credit cards. Inexpensive.*

Lodging

Hotels on Dominica range from Spartan to chic, but even in the swankiest places informality is the rule. There are only 430 rooms on the entire island, but an additional 80 or so are planned for the near future. The only beachfront hotels are in the Portsmouth area. Roseau's seaside facilities have a splendid view of the Caribbean but are beachless. There are also a few exceptional nature retreats perched in the rain forest. A variety of meal plans is available. It's a good idea to check current credit-card policy.

The most highly recommended lodgings are indicated by a star ★.

Category	Cost*
Expensive	$70–$100
Moderate	$50–$70
Inexpensive	under $50

All prices are for a standard double room for two, excluding 10% tax and a 10%–15% service charge.

Hotels **Anchorage Hotel.** A three-story, galleried section of this hotel ★ has spacious rooms, each with a double and a twin bed, and a private balcony overlooking the sea. Smaller, somewhat dark rooms are located by the swimming pool. The hotel is headquarters for Dominica Tours *(see* Guided Tours, above). *Box 34, Roseau, tel. 809/448–2638. 36 rooms with bath. Facilities: restaurant, bar, pool, squash court, yacht mooring. AE, DC, MC, V. Expensive.*

Castaways Beach Hotel. This hotel is popular with young people, mostly because of its young and energetic manager, Linda Harris. The island's first resort hotel, it's located in Mero, 11 miles north of Roseau on a mile-long, black-sand beach. Rooms have double beds, balconies overlooking tropical gardens, and come with or without air-conditioning. The restaurant serves French-Creole cuisine, and island music plays nightly in the beach bar. *Box 5, Roseau, tel. 809/449–6245 or 800/223–9815 in USA. 27 rooms with shower or bath. Facilities: beach, restaurant, 2 bars, tennis court, water-sports center. AE, MC, V. Expensive.*

★ **Papillote Wilderness Retreat and Nature Sanctuary.** You have to be in pretty good shape to navigate up the steep hill that leads to this inn, which is smack in the rain forest. The setting is spectacular, and Florida-born owner Anne Jean-Baptiste, who has lived on Dominica for more than 25 years, can provide all sorts of helpful tips about nature walks, tours, and such. Her inn is small and Spartan and has a loyal following of nature lovers. A hot tub bubbles right next to the open-air restaurant. *Box 67, Roseau, tel. 809/448–2287. 7 rooms, all share 4 baths. Facilities: restaurant, bar, boutique, nature tours. AE, MC, V. Expensive.*

★ **Reigate Hall.** Perched high on a steep cliff, this is a stunning stone-and-wood facility. The suite has a magnificent carved-wood four-poster bed, bar, and Jacuzzi. All rooms have air-conditioning, private balconies, embroidered bedspreads on double or twin beds, bidets, and handsome hardwood floors. *Box 200, Roseau, tel. 809/448–4031, 800/223–9815 in USA, 800/468–0023 in Canada. 16 rooms with bath. Facilities: restaurant, 2 bars, pool, lighted tennis court, sauna, exercise room, clock radios. AE, DC, MC, V. Expensive.*

Springfield Plantation. This former plantation home, complete with sweeping veranda, has been enlarged, and is furnished in a tropical-cum-antique style. The compound includes hotel rooms as well as apartments with kitchens. The Anthurium River is right there for freshwater swimming. *Box 41, Roseau,* tel. 809/449–1401. 7 rooms with bath. Facilities: restaurant, 2 bars. AE. Expensive.

Emerald Pool. If you really want to get away from it all and commune with nature, this may be the place for you. There isn't even a telephone here—you have to telex for reservations. The setting is idyllic—it's just a mile from Emerald Pool—but there is very little in the way of amenities. There are accommodations in A-frame cabins and in a two-room bungalow. This hotel is a favorite of European travelers. *Box 483, Roseau, telex 8631 TONGE. 10 rooms with bath. Facilities: restaurant, bar, pools, and rivers on property. No credit cards. Inexpensive–Expensive.*

Coconut Beach Resort. The hotel's 25 acres include 1,000 feet of beach. Apartments and beachfront bungalows have double rooms that are cooled by air-conditioning or fans. *Box 50, Roseau, tel. 809/445–5393 or 809/445–5415. 11 rooms with bath. Facilities: beach, restaurant, bar, water sports. AE, MC, V. Moderate.*

★ **Evergreen Hotel.** A small gem perched on the Caribbean Sea, Mena Winston's hotel has air-conditioned rooms, simple traditional furnishings, and small vases of fresh flowers in each room; some rooms have private terraces. Winston and her family turn out exceptionally fine fare, and the spacious dining room is a popular spot where locals gather to watch cable TV. *Box 309, Roseau, tel. 809/448–3288. 10 rooms with bath. Facilities: restaurant, lounge. AE, DC, MC, V. Moderate.*

Portsmouth Beach Hotel. Many of the hotel's rooms are used by students from the nearby medical school, so things can sometimes get a bit noisy here, but it *is* right on the beach. This hotel is a companion to the Anchorage Hotel in Roseau, and it's possible to arrange north–south stays. *Box 34, Roseau, tel. 809/445–5142. 76 rooms with bath. Facilities: beach, restaurant, 2 bars. AE, V. Inexpensive.*

Guest Houses **Layou Valley Inn.** This small inn is located in the foothills of Morne Trois Pitons, not far from Emerald Pool and the Carib Indian Reservation. It's an ideal setting for hikers and nature lovers. *Box 196, Roseau, tel. 809/449–6203. 5 rooms with bath. Facilities: restaurant and bar. AE, MC, V. Expensive.*

★ **Castle Comfort.** If this guest house is especially homey, it's because it is the home of the genial Mrs. Dorothy Perryman, whose sister owns the Evergreen Hotel next door. The rooms are all air-conditioned and have twin beds and baths with showers. This is home to *Dive Dominica*, and the dive packages offered include room, meal plan, and diving excursions. Perryman has recently expanded the facility with the addition of five rooms. *Box 63, Roseau, tel. 809/448–2188. 6 rooms with bath. Facilities: restaurant, dive shop. AE, MC, V. Moderate.*

Sans Souci Manor. Two miles from Roseau, Sans Souci offers three luxury apartments complete with kitchens. Meal service is available at an extra charge. In the mornings, a chauffeur drives guests into Roseau. *Box 373, Roseau, tel. 809/448–2306. 3 apartments. Facilities: TV, pool. AE, MC, V. Moderate.*

Nightlife

Discos If you're not too exhausted from mountain climbing, swimming, and such, you can join the locals on weekends at **The**

Warehouse (tel. 809/449–1303) and **Aqua Cade** (tel. 809/449–1489), both in Roseau.

Nightclubs Apart from the discos, the only other nightlife is centered in hotels such as **Reigate Hall** and the **Anchorage** (see Lodging, above) which offer local entertainment on a weekly basis.

11 Dominican Republic

by Honey Naylor

Sprawling over two-thirds of the island of Hispaniola, the Dominican Republic is the spot where European settlement of the Western hemisphere really began. Santo Domingo, its capital, is the oldest continuously inhabited city in this half of the globe, and history buffs who visit have difficulty tearing themselves away from the many sites that boast of antiquity in the city's 16th-century Colonial Zone. Sun-seekers head for the luxury beach resorts of Puerto Plata, Samaná, and La Romana; at Punta Cana, beachcombers tan on the Caribbean's longest stretch of white-sand beach. The highest peak in the West Indies is here: Pico Duarte lures hikers to the central mountain range, and ancient sunken galleons and coral reefs divert divers and snorkelers.

Columbus happened upon this island on December 5, 1492, and on Christmas Eve his ship, the *Santa Maria,* was wrecked on the Atlantic shore. He named it *La Isla Española* ("the Spanish island"), established a small colony, and sailed back to Spain on the *Pinta* to report his discovery. A year later, he returned, only to find that the Spanish colony had been destroyed by the Taino Indians, the island's original inhabitants. But Columbus established another colony nearby, leaving his brother Bartholomew in charge. Santo Domingo, which is located on the south coast where the Rio Ozama spills into the Caribbean Sea, was founded in 1496 by Bartholomew Columbus and Nicolas de Ovando, and during the first half of the 16th century became the bustling hub of Spanish commerce and culture in the New World.

Hispaniola (a derivation of "La Isla Española") has had an unusually chaotic history, replete with bloody revolutions, military coups, yellow-fever epidemics, invasions, and bankruptcy. In the 17th century, the western third of the island was ceded to France; a slave revolt in 1804 resulted in the establishment there of the first black republic, Haiti. Dominicans and Haitians battled for control of the island on and off throughout the 19th century. After two abortive attempts, in 1821 and 1844, the Dominicans finally declared themselves an independent republic in 1865, but the country was in bankruptcy by the turn of the century. The United States helped to administer the island's finances, and eventually U.S. Marines occupied the country from 1916 to 1924, until a new Dominican constitution was signed. Rafael Trujillo ruled the Dominican Republic with a dictator's iron fist from 1930 until his assassination in 1961; it was not until the early 1970s that the Dominican Republic became politically stable.

In recent years, tourism has played a more important role in the government's scheme of things. Like Puerto Rico, its cousin to the east across the Mona Channel, the Dominican Republic is gearing up for a grand and glorious 500th celebration of its discovery by Christopher Columbus.

Before You Go

Tourist Information Contact the **Dominican Tourist Information Center** at any of the following addresses: 485 Madison Ave., New York, NY 10022, tel. 212/826–0750; 2355 Sanzedo St., Coral Gables, FL 33134, tel. 305/444–4592; 29 Bellair St., Toronto, Ontario, Canada M5R 2C8, tel. 416/928–9188; 1464 Crescent St., Montreal, Quebec, Canada H3G 2B6, tel. 514/289–9398.

Arriving and Departing By Plane The Dominican Republic has two major international airports: Las Américas International Airport, about 20 miles outside Santo Domingo, and La Unión International Airport, about 25 miles east of Puerta Plata on the north coast. Two international airports share the runway. **American Airlines** (tel. 800/433–7300), **Pan Am** (tel. 800/221–1111), and **Dominicana** (tel. 718/459–5720 or 800/635–3560) fly nonstop from New York to Santo Domingo; American and Dominicana fly from New York to Puerto Plata; Pan Am and Dominicana fly from Miami to Santo Domingo; Pan Am and Dominicana fly from Miami to Puerto Plata; American and Dominicana fly from San Juan to Santo Domingo, and Dominicana provides nonstop service from San Juan to Puerto Plata. Dominicana flies nonstop from San Juan to Samaná.

The opening of a new airport in Barahona in January 1990 should greatly alleviate the year-round long lines and confusion at Las Américas. Overworked customs and immigration officials are often less than courteous, and luggage theft is rife. Try to travel with carry-on luggage, and keep a sharp eye on it.

From the Airport Taxis are available at the airport, and the 25-minute ride into Santo Domingo averages R.D. $65 (about U.S. $10).

Passports and Visas U.S. and Canadian citizens must have either a valid passport or proof of citizenship, such as an original (not photocopied) birth certificate, and a Tourist Card. Legal residents of the United States must have an Alien Registration Card (green card), a valid passport, and a Tourist Card. British citizens need only a valid passport; no entry visa is required. The requisite Tourist Card costs $10, and you should be sure to purchase it at the airline counter when you check in, and then fill it out on the plane. You can purchase the card on arrival at the airport, but you'll encounter long lines and a hassle. Keep the bottom half of the card in a safe place because you'll need to present it to immigration authorities when you leave.

Customs and Duties No customs duty is levied on personal belongings or gifts valued at $100 or less. Tortoiseshell is a big seller in the Dominican Republic, but the hawksbill turtle, which has a better grade of tortoiseshell, is on the U.S. list of endangered species: Anything manufactured from it that you bring home will probably be impounded by U.S. Customs.

Language Before you travel to the Dominican Republic, you should know at least a smattering of Spanish. Guides at major tourist attractions and front-desk personnel in the major hotels speak a fascinating form of English, though they often have trouble understanding tourists. The people who serve you in the hotel coffee shop are usually speechless when English is spoken to them, as are people you meet in the streets of Santo Domingo. Traffic signs and restaurant menus are in Spanish. Using smiles and gestures will help, but a nodding acquaintance with the language or a phrase book is more useful.

Precautions Beware of the *buscones* at the airports. They offer to assist you, and do so by relieving you of your luggage and disappearing with it. Avoid also the black marketers, who will offer you a tempting rate of exchange for your U.S. dollars. If the police catch you changing money on the street, they'll haul you off to jail (the *calabozo*). Also, buy amber only from reputable shops. The attractively priced piece offered by the street vendor is more than likely plastic. Guard your wallet or pocketbook in

Dominican Republic

Cofresi Beach
Luperón Beach
36 — 47
Montecristi
35
Playa Dorada
Cabarete Beach
Puerto Plata
31
33 48
Sosúa
32
Guayubin
49
Dajabón
La Unión International Airport
Santiago de los Caballeros
Moca
San Francisco de Macóris

HAITI

30

Bánica

DOMINICAN

H I S P A N I O

San Juan

Lago Enriquillo

Neiba

Azua

Duvergé

Bani

Pedernales

Barahona

Bahía de Ocoa

Oviedo

Isla Beato   Cabo Beato

0   50 miles

0   75 km

N

Cabo
Francés Viejo

Playa Grande

ATLANTIC OCEAN

Bahia
Escocesá

Nagua

Capo Samaná

Samaná

34 71

Bahia de Samaná

REPUBLIC

Miches

L A

Monte Plata   Hato Mayor

El Seibo

El Macao

Mona Channel

Cabo Engaño

50 — 70

Higüey

San
Cristóbal   27

Las Américas
International
Airport

72 — 74

*Rio
Charón*

76   **Punta Cana
Beach**
75

**Boca
Chica**

28

San Pedro
de Macorís

**Juan
Dolio**

29   La Romana

Minitas
Bayahibe

*Bahia
de Yuma*

Pta. Palenque

Santo Domingo

1 — 26

Isla Saona

*Mona
Passage*

Caribbean Sea

1   Exploring Sites

35   Hotels and Restaurants

Lodging

Bahía Beach Resort, **71**
Bavaro Beach
Resort, **75**
Casa de Campo, **72**
Club Medeterranée, **76**
Cofresi Beach
Resort, **35**
Dorado Naco, **36**
Eurotel Playa
Dorado, **37**

Gran Hotel Lina
and Casino, **67**
Heavens, **38**
Hostal Nicolás
de Ovando, **69**
Hotel El Embajador
and Casino, **68**
Hotel Montemar, **43**

Hotel Santo
Domingo, **64**
Jack Tar Village, **39**
Jaragua Resort Hotel,
Casino, and European
Spa, **65**
Playa Chiquita, **48**
Playa Dorado Beach
Resort, **40**
Puerto Plata Beach
Resort & Casino, **41**

Punto Galeta Beach
Resort, **49**
Radisson Puerto
Plata, **42**
San Gerónimo and
Casino, **70**
Santo Domingo
Sheraton Hotel and
Casino, **66**

Santo Domingo, especially around the Malecón, which seems to teem with pickpockets.

Staying in the Dominican Republic

Important Addresses

Tourist Information: There is a **Tourist Information Center** in Santo Domingo (George Washington Ave., tel. 809/682–8181) and in Puerto Plata (Playa Long Beach, tel. 809/586–3676). Hours are weekdays 9–2:30.

Emergencies

Police: In Santo Domingo, call 809/682–3000; in Puerto Plata, call 809/586–2331.

Hospitals: Santo Domingo emergency rooms that are open 24 hours are **Centro Médico Universidad Central del Este** (UCE) (Av. Máximo Gómez 66, tel. 809/682–0171), **Clínica Abreu** (Calle Beller 42, tel. 809/688–4411), and **Clínica Gómez Patino** (Av. Independencia 701, tel. 809/685–9131 or 685–9141). In Puerto Plata, you can go to **Clínica Dr. Brugal** (Calle José del Carmen Ariza 15, tel. 809/586–2519).

Pharmacies: The following pharmacies are open 24 hours a day: in Santo Domingo, **San Judas Tadeo** (Av. Independencia 57, tel. 809/689–2851 or 809/685–8165); in Puerto Plata, **Farmacia Deleyte** (Av. John F. Kennedy 89, tel. 809/586–2583).

Currency

The coin of the realm is the Dominican peso, which is divided into 100 centavos. It is written R.D.$, and fluctuates relative to the U.S. dollar. At press time, U.S.$1 was equivalent to R.D.$6.33. *Note:* prices quoted here are in U.S. dollars unless otherwise indicated.

Taxes and Service Charges

Hotels add a 21% government tax (which includes a 10% service charge) to your bill; restaurants add a 6% tax. The departure tax is $10.

Although hotels add a 10% service charge, it is customary to leave a dollar per day for the hotel maid. Restaurants and nightclubs add a 10% service charge to your bill. However, you may want to leave an additional 5%–10% tip for a job well done. Taxi drivers expect a 10% tip. Skycaps and hotel porters expect 25¢ per bag.

Guided Tours

Prieto Tours (tel. 809/682–8426) operates Gray Line of the Dominican Republic. It offers half-day bus tours of Santo Domingo, nightclub tours, beach tours, tours to Cibao Valley and the Amber Coast, and a variety of other tours.

Turinter (Bahía Beach Hotel, Samaná, tel. 809/685–4020) tours include dinner and a show or casino, a full-day tour of Samaná, as well as specialty tours (museum, shopping, fishing).

Apolo Tours (tel. 809/586–2751) offers a full-day tour of Playa Grande and tours to Santiago (including a casino tour) and Sosúa.

Getting Around

Taxis

Taxis, which are government regulated, line up outside hotels and restaurants. The taxis are unmetered, and the minimum fare within Santo Domingo is R.D.$20 (about U.S.$3). You can also negotiate a fare with the driver, assuming there is no language barrier. Just be certain both clearly understand in advance which currency is to be used in the agreed-upon fare. Taxis can also drive you to destinations outside the city. Rates are posted in hotels and at the airport. **Taxi la Baloma** (tel. 809/562–3460) or **Taxi Raffi** (tel. 809/689–5468) will transport you.

In a separate category are radio taxis, which are convenient if you'd like to schedule a pickup and academic if you don't speak Spanish. The fare is negotiated over the phone when you make the appointment.

Buses *Públicos* are small blue-and-white or blue-and-red cars that run regular routes, stopping to let passengers on and off. The fare is less than a peso. Competing with the públicos are the *conchos*, or *colectivos* (privately owned buses) whose drivers tool around the major thoroughfares, leaning out the window or jumping out to try to persuade passengers to climb aboard. It's a colorful, if cramped, way to get around town. The fare is about 50 centavos. Privately owned air-conditioned buses make regular runs to Santiago, Puerto Plata, and other destinations. You should reserve by calling **Metro Buses** (Av. Winston Churchill tel. 809/566–6596), **La Experiencia Bus Line** (Calle M. Aybar Av., tel. 809/594–0356), or **Dominican Express** (11 Independencia tel. 809/682–6610). One-way bus fare from Santo Domingo to Puerto Plata is R.D.$7.50.

Rental Cars You'll need a valid U.S. driver's license and a major credit card and/or cash deposit. Cars can be rented at the airport and at many hotels. Among the known names are **Avis** (tel. 809/533–3530), **Budget** (tel. 809/562–6812), **Hertz** (tel. 809/688–2277), and **National** (tel. 809/566–2747). Rates vary from $20 to $60 per day, depending upon the make and size of the car. Driving is on the right. Bear in mind that many Dominicans drive recklessly, often taking their half of the road out of the middle, and tend to screech suddenly to a halt for a cup of *café con leche*.

If, for some unavoidable reason, you must drive on the narrow, unlighted mountain roads at night, use extreme caution. The 80-kph (50-mph) speed limit is strictly enforced. Finally, keep in mind that gas stations are few and far between in some of the remote regions.

Telephones and Mail To call the Dominican Republic from the United States, dial area code 809 and the local number. Connections are clear and easy to make. Trying to place calls from the Dominican Republic, however, is another matter. The system is, to put it kindly, archaic.

Airmail postage to the United States for a letter or a postcard is about 50¢.

Opening and Closing Times Regular office hours are weekdays 8 AM–noon and 2–5 and Saturday 8–noon. Government offices are open weekdays 7:30–2:30. Banking hours are weekdays 8:30–4:30.

Beaches

The Dominican Republic has more than 1,000 miles of beaches, including the Caribbean's longest strip of white-sand beach, Punta Cana.

Boca Chica is the nearest beach to Santo Domingo (2 miles east of Las Américas Airport, 21 miles from the capital) and crowded with city folks on weekends. Five years ago, this beach was virtually a four-lane highway of fine white sand. "Progress" has since cluttered it with plastic beach tables, chaise longues, pizza stands, and beach cottages for rent. But the sand is still fine, and you can walk far out into clear blue water, which is protected by natural coral reefs that help keep the big fish at bay.

About 20 minutes east of Boca Chica is another beach of fine white sand, **Juan Dolio.** The Villas del Mar Hotel and Punta Garza Beach Club are on this beach.

Moving counterclockwise around the island, you'll come to **La Romana** area, with its miniature **Minitas** beach and lagoon, and the long white-sand, palm-lined crescent of **Bayahibe** beach, which is accessible only by boat. La Romana is the home of the 7,000-acre Casa de Campo resort (*see* Lodging, below), so you're not likely to find any private place in the sun here.

The gem of the Caribbean, **Punta Cana** is a 20-mile strand of pearl-white sand shaded by trees and coconut palms. Located on the easternmost coast, it is the home of Club Med and the Bavaro Beach Resort (*see* Lodging, below).

Playa Grande, on the north coast, is a long stretch of powdery sand that is slated for development. At present, it's undisturbed, but you'd better hurry if you want to enjoy it in solitude.

The beach at **Sosúa,** on the north coast, is lovely. Calm waters gently lap at long stretches of soft white sand. An unfortunate backdrop is a string of tents, and hawkers pushing cheap souvenirs. However, you can also get snacks and rent water-sports equipment from the vendors.

On the north Amber Coast, **Puerto Plata** is situated in a developed and still-developing area that is about to outdo San Juan's famed Condado strip. The beaches are of soft ecru or white sand, with lots of reefs for snorkeling. The Atlantic waters are great for windsurfing, waterskiing, and fishing expeditions.

About an hour west of Puerto Plata lies **Luperón Beach,** a wide white-sand beach fit for snorkeling, windsurfing, and scuba diving. The Luperón Beach Resort is handy for rentals and refreshments.

Exploring the Dominican Republic

Numbers in the margin correspond with points of interest on the Santo Domingo map.

Santo Domingo
❶
We'll begin our tour where Western civilization began, in the 12-block area of Santo Domingo called the **Colonial Zone.** This historical area is now a bustling, noisy district with narrow cobbled streets, shops, restaurants, residents, and traffic jams. Ironically, all the noise and congestion make it somehow easier to imagine this old city as it was when it was yet a colony—when the likes of Columbus, Cortés, Ponce de León, and pirates sailed in and out, and colonists were settling themselves in the New World. Tourist brochures boast that "history comes alive here"—a surprisingly truthful statement.

A quick taxi tour of the old section takes about an hour, but if you're interested in history, you'll want to spend a day or two exploring the many old "firsts," and you'll want to do it in the most comfortable shoes you own. (Note: Hours and admission charges are erratic, and you should check with the Tourist Office to get up-to-date information.)

Santo Domingo

Alcázar de Colón, **10**

Calle Las Damas, **13**

Capilla de los
Remedios, **15**

Casa de Bastidas, **18**

Casa de Tostado, **20**

Casa del Cordón, **9**

Catedral Menor de
Santa Maria, **6**

Concepción Fortress, **4**

Hospital de San Nicolás
de Bari, **7**

Hostal Nicolás de
Ovando, **16**

Iglesia y Convento
Dominico, **21**

Jardin Botanico
Nacional Dr. Rafael M.
Moscoso, **26**

La Atarazana, **11**

La Iglesia de Regina
Angelorum, **22**

Malecón, **24**

Montesina, **2**

Museo de las Casas
Reales, **14**

National Pantheon, **17**

Parque Colón, **5**

Parque Indepen-
dencia, **3**

Plaza de la Cultura, **25**

Puerta de la
Misericordia, **23**

San Francisco
Monastery, **8**

Santa Bárbara
Church, **12**

Santo Domingo, **1**

Torre del
Homenaje, **19**

One of the first things you'll see as you approach the Colonial Zone is a statue, only slightly smaller than the Colossus of Rhodes, staring out over the Caribbean Sea. It is **Montesina,** the Spanish priest who came to the Dominican Republic in the 16th century to appeal for human rights for Indians.

Parque Independencia, on the far western border of the Colonial Zone, is a big city park dominated by the marble and concrete **Altar de la Pátria.** The impressive mausoleum was built in 1976 to honor the fathers of the country (Duarte, Sánchez, and Mella).

To your left as you leave the square, the **Concepción Fortress,** within the old city walls, was the northwest defense post of the colony. *Calle Palo Hincado at Calle Isidro Duarte, no phone. Admission free. Open Tues.–Sun. 9–6.*

From Independence Square, walk eight blocks east on Calle El Conde and you'll come to **Parque Colón.** The huge statue of Columbus dates from 1897 and is the work of French sculptor Gilbert. On the west side of the square is the **old Town Hall** and on the east, the **Palacio de Borgella,** residence of the governor during the Haitian occupation of 1822–44.

Towering over the south side of the square is the coral limestone facade of the **Catedral Primada de América,** the first cathedral in America. Spanish workmen began building the **Catedral Menor de Santa María** in 1514 but left off construction to follow the trail of gold to Mexico. The church was finally finished in 1540. Inside, the high altar is of beaten silver, and in the nave, four baroque columns, carved to resemble royal palms, guard the magnificent bronze and marble sarcophagus within which lies (so say Dominican historians) the remains of Christopher Columbus. (Cuba and Spain also lay claims to the famed remains.) Columbus died in Spain in 1506. His last wish was that he be buried in Santo Domingo, and upon completion of the cathedral, his remains were deposited there. In the late 18th century, both Cuba and Spain got hold of exhumed corpses that they claimed were the remains of somebody named Columbus. Cuban and Spanish historians say it was Christopher; Dominican authorities say that the relocated remains are those of Christopher's grandson Luis, and that Christopher still rests in Santo Domingo. In any case, be sure to see the gold and silver displays in the cathedral's Treasury. *Calle Arzobispo Merino, tel. 809/689–1920. Admission free. Open Mon.–Sat. 9–6; Sun. masses begin at 6 AM.*

When you leave the cathedral, turn right, walk past Columbus Square and turn left on Calle El Conde. Walk one more block and turn right on Calle Hostos and continue for two more blocks. You'll see the ruins of the **Hospital de San Nicolás de Bari,** the first hospital in the New World, which was built in 1503 by Nicolás de Ovando. *Calle Hostos, between Calle Mercedes and Calle Luperón, no phone. Admission free. Open Tues.–Sun. 9–6.*

Continue along Calle Hostos, crossing Calle Emiliano Tejera, and about mid-block on your left are the majestic ruins of the **San Francisco Monastery.** Constructed between 1512 and 1544, the building contained the church, chapel, and convent of the Franciscan order. Sir Francis Drake's demolition squad significantly damaged the monastery in 1586, and in 1673 an earthquake nearly finished the job, but when it's floodlit at night the old monastery is indeed a dramatic sight.

Walk west for two blocks along Calle Emiliano Tejera. Opposite
⑧ the post office on Calle Isabel la Católica, the **Casa del Cordón** is recognizable by the sash of the Franciscan order carved in stone over the arched entrance. This house, built in 1503, is the Western Hemisphere's oldest surviving stone house. Columbus's son Diego Colón, viceroy of the colony, and his wife lived here until the Alcazar was finished. It was in this house, too, that Sir Francis Drake was paid a ransom to prevent him from totally destroying the city. The house is now home to the Banco Popular. *Corner of Calle Emiliano Tejera and Calle Isabel la Católica, no phone. Admission free. Open Tues.–Sun. 9–6.*

⑨ To reach the **Alcázar de Colón,** walk one block east along Calle Emiliano Tejera. You'll come across the imposing castle, with its balustrade and double row of arches. The castle of Don Diego Colón, built in 1514, was painstakingly reconstructed and restored in 1957. Forty-inch-thick coral limestone walls were patched and shored with blocks from the original quarry. There are 22 rooms, furnished in a style to which the viceroy of the island would have been accustomed—right down to the dishes and the viceregal shaving mug. Many of the period paintings, statues, tapestries, and furnishings were donated by the University of Madrid. *Just off Calle Emiliano Tejera at the foot of Calle Las Damas, tel. 809/689–5946. Admission: 50¢. Open daily 9–6.*

⑩ Across from the Alcázar, **La Atarazana** was the colonial commercial district, where naval supplies were once stored. There are eight restored buildings, the oldest of which dates from 1507. It now houses crafts shops, restaurants, and art galleries.

Time Out Stop for a pizza and a bloody Mary at **Bloody Mary's Pub** (Calle La Atarazana, no phone). It's right across the street from the main post office.

⑪ To reach the **Santa Bárbara Church,** go back to Calle Isabela la Católica, turn right, and walk four blocks. This combination church and fortress, the only one of its kind in Santo Domingo, was completed in 1562. *Calle Mella, between Calle Isabel la Católica and Calle Arzobispo Merino, no phone. Admission free. Open Mon.–Sat. 9–6. Sun. masses begin at 6 AM.*

Retrace your steps to Calle Isabel la Católica, turn left on Calle
⑫ Emiliano Tejera, and walk one block to **Calle Las Damas,** where you'll make a right turn to the New World's oldest street. The "Street of the Ladies" was named after the elegant ladies of the court who, in the Spanish tradition, promenaded in the evening.

On your left you'll see a sundial dating from 1753, and across
⑬ the street from it is the **Museo de las Casas Reales** (Museum of the Royal Houses). The collections in the museum are displayed in two early 16th-century palaces that have been altered many times over the years. Exhibits cover everything from antique coins to replicas of the *Niña,* the *Pinta,* and the *Santa María.* There are statue and cartography galleries, coats of armor and coats of arms, coaches and a royal court room, gilded furnish-

ings, and Indian artifacts. The first room of the former Governor's Residence has a wall-size map marking the routes sailed by Columbus's ships on expeditions beginning in 1492. If you like museums, you may have a hard time taking leave of this one. *Calle Las Damas, corner Calle Mercedes, tel. 809/682-4202. Admission: 50¢ adults, 25¢ children. Open Tues.–Sun. 9–6.*

⑮ Across the street is the **Capilla de los Remedios** (Chapel of Our Lady of Remedies), which was originally built as a private chapel for the family of Francisco de Dávila. Early colonists worshiped here as well before the completion of the cathedral. Its architectural details, particularly its lateral arches, are evocative of the Castilian-Romanesque style. *Calle Las Damas, at the foot of Calle Mercedes, no phone. Admission free. Open Mon.–Sat. 9–6; Sun. masses begin at 6 AM.*

⑯ Just south of the chapel on Calle Las Damas, the **Hostal Nicolás de Ovando** (*see* Lodging, below), now a highly praised hotel, was once the residence of Nicolás de Ovando, one of the principal organizers of the colonial city.

⑰ Across the street from the hotel looms the massive **National Pantheon.** The building, which dates from 1714, was once a Jesuit monastery and later a theater. Trujillo had it restored in 1955 with an eye toward being buried there. Instead, it contains the remains of the martyrs who assassinated him. A commemorative mural of the assassination is painted on the ceiling above the altar, where an eternal flame burns. The impressive chandelier was a gift from Spain's Generalissimo Franco. *Calle Las Damas, near the corner of Calle Mercedes, no phone. Admission: 50¢. Open Mon.–Sat. 9–6.*

Continue south on Calle Las Damas and cross Calle El Conde. **⑱** Look on your left for the **Casa de Bastidas,** where there is a lovely inner courtyard with tropical plants. *Calle Las Damas, just off Calle El Conde, no phone. Admission free. Open Tues.–Sun. 9–6.*

⑲ You won't have any trouble spotting the **Torre del Homenaje** (Tower of Homage) in the Fort Ozama. The fort sprawls two blocks south of the Casa de Bastidas, with a brooding crenelated tower that still guards the Ozama River. The fort and its tower were built in 1503 to protect the eastern border of the city. The sinister tower was the last home of many a condemned prisoner. *On Paseo Presidente Bellini, overlooking Río Ozama, no phone. Admission free. Open Tues.–Sun. 9–6.*

When you leave the fortress, turn left off Calle Las Damas onto **⑳** Calle Padre Bellini. A two-block walk will bring you to **Casa de Tostado.** The house was built in the first decade of the 16th century and was the residence of writer Don Francisco Tostado. Its twin Gothic windows are the only ones still in existence in the New World. It now houses the **Museo de la Familia Dominicana** (Museum of the Dominican Family), which features exhibits on the well-heeled Dominican family in the 19th century. *Calle Padre Bellini, near Calle Arzobispo Merino, tel. 809/689–5057. Admission: 50¢ adults, 25¢ children. Open daily 9–6.*

Walk two blocks west on Calle Padre Bellini to the corner of Calle Duarte. The graceful building with the rose window is **㉑** the **Iglesia y Covento Dominico** (Dominican Church and Convent), founded in 1510. In 1538, Pope Paul III visited here and was so impressed with the lectures on theology that he granted it the title of university, making it the oldest institution of higher learning in the New World. *Calle Padre Bellini and Av. Duarte, tel. 809/682–3780). Admission free. Open Tues.–Sun. 9–6.*

㉒ Continue west on Calle Padre Bellini for two blocks, and at the corner of Calle José Reyes, you'll see another lovely church, **La Iglesia de Regina Angelorum** (Church of Regina Angelorum), which dates from 1537. The church was damaged during the Haitian regime, from 1822 to 1844, but you can still appreciate its Baroque dome, and its Gothic arches and traceries. *Corner of Calle Padre Bellini and Calle José Reyes, tel. 809/682–2783. Admission free. Open Mon.–Sat. 9–6.*

㉓ Walk four blocks east on Calle Padre Bellini, turn left on Calle Palo Hincado, and keep going straight till you reach the **Puerta de la Misericordia** (Gate of Mercy), part of the old wall of Santo Domingo. It was here on the plaza, on February 27, 1844, that Ramón Mata Mella, one of the country's founding fathers, fired the shot that began the struggle for independence from Haiti.

Parque Independencia separates the old city from the new. Avenidas 30 de Marzo, Bolivar, and Independencia traverse the park and mingle with avenues named George Washington, John F. Kennedy, and Abraham Lincoln. Modern Santo Domingo is a sprawling, noisy city with a population of close to 2 million.

㉔ Avenida George Washington, which features tall palms and extravagant tourist hotels, breezes along the Caribbean Sea. The Parque Litoral del Sur, better known as the **Malecón**, borders the avenue from the colonial city to the Hotel Santo Domingo, a distance of about 3 miles. The seaside park, with its cafés and places to relax, is a popular spot, but beware of pickpockets.

㉕ Avenida Máximo Gómez comes down from the north. Take a right turn on it, cross Avenida Bolivar, and you'll come to the landscaped lawns, modern sculptures, and sleek buildings of the **Plaza de la Cultura.** Among the buildings are the **National Theater** (tel. 809/687–3191), which stages performances in Spanish; the **National Library,** in which the written word is Spanish; and museums and art galleries, whose notations are in Spanish. The following museums on the plaza are open Tuesday–Saturday from 9 to 5, and admission to each is 50¢: The **Museum of Dominican Man** (tel. 809/687–3622) traces the migrations of Indians from South America through the Caribbean islands. The **Museum of Natural History** (tel. 809/689–0106) examines the flora and fauna of the island. In the **Gallery of Modern Art** (tel. 809/682–8260), the works of 20th-century Dominican and foreign artists are displayed.

㉖ North of town in the Arroyo Hondo district is the **Jardin Botanico Nacional Dr. Rafael M. Moscoso** (Dr. Rafael M. Moscoso National Botanical Gardens), the largest garden in the Caribbean. Its 445 acres include a Japanese Garden, a Great Ravine, a gorgeous display of orchids, and an enormous floral clock. You can tour the gardens by train, by boat, or by horse-drawn carriage. *Arroyo Hondo, no phone. Admission: 50¢ adults, 25¢ children. Open daily 10–6.*

In the 320-acre **Parque Zoologico Nacional** (National Zoological Park), not far from the Botanical Gardens, animals roam free in natural habitats. There is an African plain, a children's zoo, and what the zoo claims is the world's largest bird cage. *Av. Máximo Gómez at Av. de los Proceres, no phone. Admission: 50¢ adults, 25¢ children. Open daily 10–6.*

La Romana *Numbers in the margin correspond with points of interest on the Dominican Republic map.*

Head east on Las Américas Highway toward La Romana, about a two-hour drive along the southeast coast. About 1½ miles out-side the capital, you'll come to the **Parque de los Tres Ojos** (Park of the Three Eyes). The "eyes" are cool blue pools peering out of deep limestone caves, and it's actually a four-eyed park. If you've a mind to, you can look into the eyes more closely by climbing down into the caves.

About 20 minutes outside the city is **Boca Chica Beach,** popular because of its proximity to the capital. Another 45 minutes or so away is the city of **San Pedro de Macorís,** where the na-tional sport and the national drink are both well represented. Some of the country's best *béisbol* games are played in **Tetelo Vargas Stadium,** which you can see off the highway to your left. The **Macorís Rum distillery** is on the eastern edge of the city.

The two big businesses around La Romana used to be cattle and sugarcane. That was before Gulf + Western created (and sub-sequently sold) the **Casa de Campo** resort, which is a very big business indeed, and **Altos de Chavón,** a re-creation of a 16th-century village and art colony.

Casa de Campo means "house in the country," and, yes, you could call it that. This particular "house" is a resort that sprawls over 7,000 acres and offers two golf courses (one of them, a teeth-clencher called Teeth of the Dog, has seven holes that skirt the sea), 16 tennis courts, horseback riding, polo, archery, trap shooting, and every imaginable water sport. Os-car de la Renta designed much of the resort and has a boutique in Altos de Chavón. He also owns a villa at Casa de Campo.

Altos de Chavón sits on a bluff overlooking the Rio Chavón, about 3 miles east of Casa de Campo. You can drive there easily enough, or you can take one of the free shuttle buses from the resort. In this re-creation of a medieval Spanish village, there are cobblestone streets lined with lanterns, wrought-iron bal-conies, and courtyards swathed with bougainvillea. More than a museum piece, this village is a place where artists live, work, and play. There is an art school, affiliated with New York's Par-sons School of Design, a disco, an archaeological museum, five restaurants, and a 5,000-seat outdoor amphitheater where Frank Sinatra and Julio Iglesias have entertained. The focal point of the village is **Iglesia St. Stanislaus,** which is named af-ter the patron saint of Poland in tribute to the Polish Pope John Paul II, who visited the Dominican Republic in 1979 and left some of the ashes of St. Stanislaus behind.

The Amber Coast The Autopista cuts northwest across the country from Santo Domingo to the north, or Amber Coast, so-called because of the large deposits of amber in the region. The drive to the city of Puerto Plata on the north coast, a distance of about 150 miles, will take about four hours. **Pico Duarte** (10,477 feet), the high-est peak in the West Indies, is to the west, and the mountainous road you'll be traveling on is lined with lush banana plantations, rice fields, fields of tobacco, and Royal Poinciana trees. Coconut palms are stuck in the hills like candles on a birthday cake. All along the road there are stands where, for just a few centavos, you can buy ripe pineapples, mangoes, avocados, chicharrones (fried pork rinds), and fresh fruit drinks.

About 90 miles north of the capital you'll come to the industrial city of **Santiago de los Caballeros,** where huge monuments guard the entrance to the city. Santiago, the capital of the province of Cibao, is the Dominican Republic's second largest city but holds little of interest to tourists. Squeeze through the city's narrow teeming streets and continue northward to **③** **Puerto Plata.**

The coastal area around Puerto Plata is a region of splashy resorts. The north coast boasts more than 70 miles of beaches, with condominiums and villas going up fast.

In the city of Puerto Plata, the **Museum of Dominican Amber,** housed in a lovely galleried mansion, is one of several tenants in the Tourist Bazaar. The museum displays and sells the Dominican Republic's national stone. Semiprecious, translucent amber is actually fossilized pine resin that dates back about 50 million years, give or take a few millennia. The north coast of the Dominican Republic has the largest deposits of amber in the world (the only other deposits are found in Germany and the U.S.S.R.), and jewelry crafted from the stone is the best-selling item on the island. *Calle Duarte 61, tel. 809/586–2848. Admission: $1. Open Mon.–Sat. 9–5.*

To the west of Puerto Plata, you can take a cable car to the top **③②** of **Mt. Isabel de Torres,** which soars 2,600 feet above sea level. On the mountain is a botanical garden, a huge statue of Christ, and a spectacular view. *The cable car operates Tues., Thurs., Fri., Sat., and Sun. 8–6. Round-trip is 75¢.*

Take the Autopista east from Puerta Plata about 15 miles to **③③** **Sosúa,** a small community settled during World War II by Austrian and German Jews. After the war, many of the Jews returned to Europe or went to the United States, and most of those who remained married Dominicans. Only a few Jewish families reside in the community today, and there is only one small, one-room synagogue. The flavor of the town is decidedly Spanish. There are numerous hotels, condominiums, and apartments in Sosúa. (The roads, off the Autopista, incidentally, are terrible and horribly punctured with potholes.)

Sosúa is actually two communities, **El Batey** and **Los Charámicos,** which are separated by a cove and one of the island's prettiest beaches (*see* Beaches, above). The sand is soft and white and the water gin-clear and calm. The walkway above the beach is packed with tents full of souvenirs, pizzas, and even clothing for sale, a jarring note in this idyllic setting.

Time Out **P. J. International Bar** (Calle Pedro Clisante, El Batey, Sosúa, tel. 809/571–2325), in the center of Sosúa, is a hot spot for tacos, hamburgers, and a rum punch or two.

Continue east on the Autopista past **Playa Grande.** At press time, this powdery white beach was undisturbed and unspoiled. But the area is slated for development, and by the time you read these pages, business may be booming.

The Autopista rolls along eastward and rides out onto a **③④** "thumb" of the island, where you'll find **Samaná.** Back in 1824, a sailing vessel called the *Turtle Dove*, carrying several hundred escaped American slaves from the Freeman Sisters' underground railway, was blown ashore in Samaná. The escapees settled and prospered, and today their descendants number several thousand. The churches here are Protestant, the worshipers live in villages called Bethesda, Northeast, and Philadelphia, and the language spoken is English.

About 3,000 humpback whales winter off the coast of Samaná from December to March. Plans are under way for organizing major whale-watching expeditions, such as those out of Massachusetts, that will boost the region's economy without scaring away the world's largest mammals.

In the meantime, sport fishing at Samaná is considered to be some of the best in the world. A beautiful bay and beach round out Samaná's attractions.

Dominican Republic for Free

Concerts. The quadrangle of Santo Domingo's Plaza de la Cultura is the site for occasional classical music concerts that you can hear for a song. There are also open-air concerts along the Malecón. Check with local newspapers, your hotel, or the Tourist Office for dates and programs.

Colonial Zone. Many of the ancient buildings have no admission charge, notably the Catedral Menor de Santa María, the Tower of Homage, the San Francisco Monastery, and the Casa del Cordón (*see* Exploring, above).

Parque de los Tres Ojos. The Park of the Three Eyes, 10 minutes east of Santo Domingo, is free to the public (*see* Exploring, above).

What to See and Do with Children

Dr. Rafael Moscoso National Botanical Gardens (*see* Exploring, above).

National Zoological Park (*see* Exploring, above).

Parque de los Tre Ojos (*see* Exploring, above).

Parque Quisqueya. Santo Domingo's amusement park has a merry-go-round, swings, see-saws, and other playground attractions. *Av. Bolívar and Av. Tiradentes, tel. 809/682–9191. Admission: R.D.$1. Open Thurs.–Sun. 10–10.*

Off the Beaten Track

Laguna Gri-Gri is a swampland smack out of the bayou country in south Louisiana, with the added attraction of a cool blue grotto that almost outdoes the Blue Grotto of Capri. About 90 minutes west of Puerta Plata, in Río San Juan, you can board a boat for a peaceful trip through the swamps and into the grotto. Contact the Tourist Board for arrangements.

Participant Sports

Although there is hardly a shortage of outdoor activities here, the resorts have virtually cornered the market on sports, including every conceivable water sport. In some cases, facilities may be available only to guests. You can check with the Tourist Board for more details. Listed below is a mere smattering of the island's athletic options:

Archery Robin Hood never had it so good. Bows and arrows can be had at **Club Med** (Punta Cana, tel. 809/567–5228) and **Bavara Beach Resort** (Punta Cana, tel. 809/682-2162).

Bicycling Pedaling is easy on pancake-flat beaches, but there are also steep hills in these parts. Bikes are available at **Villa Doradas** (Playa Dorada, Puerto Plata, tel. 809/586–3000), **Dorado Naco** (Dorado Beach, tel. 809/586–2019), **Jack Tar Village** (Puerto Plata, tel. 809/586–3800), and **Cofresi Beach Hotel** (Puerto Plata, tel. 809/586–2898).

Boating Hobie Cats and pedal boats are available at **Heavens** (Puerto Plata, tel. 809/586–5250). Check also at **Casa de Campo** (La Romana, tel. 809/682–2111) and **Club Med** (Punta Cana, tel. 809/567–5228).

Deep-Sea Fishing Marlin and wahoo are among the fish that folks angle for here. Arrangements can be made through **El Mirador** (Puerto Plata) and **Casa de Campo** (La Romana).

Golf **Casa de Campo** resort (La Romana) has two 18-hole Pete Dye courses, one of which is a seaside challenger called Teeth of the Dog. Guests in Santo Domingo hotels are usually allowed to use the 18-hole course at the **Santo Domingo Country Club,** but membership does have its privileges, that is, members tee off before visitors.

Horseback Riding **Casa de Campo** (La Romana) has a dude ranch on its premises, saddled with 2,000 horses.

Polo You can arrange for lessons at **Casa de Campo** (La Romana).

Sailing Sailboats are available at **Club Med** (Punta Cana) and **Casa de Campo** (La Romana).

Scuba Diving and Snorkeling Ancient sunken galleons, undersea gardens, and offshore reefs are the lures here. For equipment and trips contact **Mundo Submarino** (Santo Domingo, tel. 809/566–0344).

Tennis There must be a million nets laced around the island, and most of them can be found at the large resorts (*see* Lodging, below).

Spectator Sports

Greyhound Races The dogs make tracks every day except Tuesday at **Canodromo El Coco**. *Av. Monumental, La Yuca—about 15 min north of the capital, tel. 809/565–8333. Admission: R.D.$1–R.D.$4. Races Mon.–Sat. 7:30 PM, Sun. and holidays 4 PM.*

Horse Racing There are races year-round at the **Hipódromo Perla Antillana.** *Av. San Cristobal, Santo Domingo. Admission free. Post time: Mon., Thurs., Sat. 1:45 PM.*

Polo The ponies pound down the field at **Sierra Prieta** (Santo Domingo) and at **Casa de Campo** (La Romana). The season runs from October through May. For information about polo games, call 809/565–6880.

Shopping

The hot ticket in the Dominican Republic is amber jewelry. This island has the world's largest deposits of amber, and the prices here for the translucent, semiprecious stone are unmatched anywhere. The stones, which range in color from pale lemon to dark brown, are actually petrified resin from coniferous trees that disappeared from Earth about 50 million years ago. The most valuable stones are those in which tiny insects or small leaves are embedded. (Don't knock it till you've seen it.)

The Dominican Republic is the homeland of designer Oscar de la Renta, and you might want to stop in some of the chic shops that carry his creations. In the crafts department, hand-carved wood rocking chairs are big sellers, and they are sold unassembled and boxed for easy transport. Look also for the delicate ceramic Lime figurines that symbolize the Dominican culture.

Bargaining is both a game and a social activity in the Dominican Republic, especially with street vendors and at the stalls in El Mercado Modelo. Vendors are disappointed and perplexed if you don't haggle. They also tend to be tenacious, so unless you really have an eye on buying don't even stop to look—you may get stuck buying a souvenir to get rid of an annoying vendor.

Shopping Districts In Santo Domingo is **El Mercado Modelo,** a covered market in the Colonial Zone bordering Calle Mella. The restored buildings of **La Atarazana** (across from the Alcázar in the Colonial Zone) are filled with shops, art galleries, restaurants, and bars. The main shopping streets in the Colonial Zone are **Calle El Conde** and **Calle Duarte.** (Some of the best shops on Calle Duarte are north of the Colonial Zone, between Calle Mella and Av. Las Américas). **Plaza Criolla** (corner of Av. 27 de Febrero and Av. Anacaona) is filled with shops that sell everything from scents to nonsense. Duty-free shops selling liquors, cameras, and such are at the **Centro de los Héroes** (Av. George Washington), the **Embajador Hotel, Santo Domingo Sheraton,** and at **Las Américas Airport.**

In Puerto Plata, the seven showrooms of the **Tourist Bazaar** (Calle Duarte 61) are in a wonderful old galleried mansion with a patio bar. Another cluster of shops is at the **Plaza Shopping Center** (Calle Duarte at Av. 30 de Marzo).

In **Altos de Chavón,** art galleries and shops are grouped around the main square.

Good Buys **Ambar Tres** (La Atarazana 3, Colonial Zone, Santo Domingo,
Amber/Jewelry tel. 809/688–0474) carries a wide selection of the Dominican product.

Dominican Art Galleries in Santo Domingo are **Arawak Gallery** (Av. Pasteur 104, Santo Domingo, tel. 809/685–1661) and **Galería de Arte Nader** (La Atarazana 9, Colonial Zone, Santo Domingo, tel. 809/688–0969).

Macaluso's (Calle Duarte 32, Puerto Plata, tel. 809/586–3433) and **The Collector's Corner Gallery and Gift Shop** (Plaza Shopping Center, Calle Duarte at Av. 30 de Marzo, Puerto Plata, no phone) are the better-known galleries in Puerto Plata.

Wood Crafts Visit the stalls of **El Mercado Modelo** in the Colonial Zone, Santo Domingo, and **El Conde Gift Shop** (Calle El Conde 153, Santo Domingo, tel. 809/682–5909).

In Puerto Plata, browse and shop at **Macaluso's** (Calle Duarte 32, Puerto Plata, tel. 809/586–3433), **The Collector's Corner Gallery and Gift Shop** (Plaza Shopping Center, Puerto Plata, no phone), and **Artesania Lime** (Autopista Duarte, Km 21–2, Santiago, tel. 809/582–3754).

Dining

Dining out is a favorite form of entertainment for Dominicans, and (probably influenced by Dominican designer Oscar de la Renta) they tend to dress up for the occasion. Most restaurants begin serving dinner around 6 PM, but the locals don't generally turn up until 9 or 10. There are French, Italian, and Chinese restaurants, as well as those serving traditional Dominican fare. Some favorite local dishes you should sample are paella, *sancocho* (a thick stew), *arroz con pollo* (rice with chicken), and *tortilla de jamón* (spicy ham omelet). Country snacks include *chicharrones* (fried pork rinds) and *calletas* (flat biscuit crackers). Many a meal is topped off with *majarete*, a tasty corn-meal custard. Presidente and Bohemia are the local beers; Bermúdez and Brugal the local rums. Wine is on the expensive side because it has to be imported.

The most highly recommended restaurants are indicated by a star ★.

Category	Cost*
Expensive	$30–$45
Moderate	$20–$30
Inexpensive	under $20

per person, excluding drinks, service, and sales tax (6%)

Santo Domingo
Continental
★

Alcazar. Oscar de la Renta designed this elegant Moorish setting. Start with lobster bisque, followed by sea bass with crabmeat au gratin or filet Mignon with béarnaise sauce. A lunch buffet is served each day, with Mexican food on Tuesday, Chinese on Wednesday, Italian on Thursday, and so forth. *Hotel Santo Domingo, tel. 809/532–1511. Jackets and reservations required. AE, DC, MC, V. Expensive.*

Antoine's. In this *très intime* eatery, hotel guests rub shoulders with well-heeled Dominicans, with whom the restaurant is popular. Starters include black-bean soup, and among the main dishes on the extensive menu are lobster thermidor and imperial stew, made with lobster, shrimp, and scallops. There are no fewer than 20 dessert offerings. *Hotel Sheraton, Av. George Washington, tel. 809/686–6666. Jacket and reservations required. AE, DC, MC, V. Expensive.*

★ **Lina.** Lina was the personal chef of Trujillo, and she taught her secret recipes to the chefs of this stylish contemporary restaurant. Paella is the best-known specialty, but other offerings include steak au poivre and a casserole of mixed seafood flavored with Pernod. *Hotel Lina, Av. Máximo Gómez, tel. 809/689–5185. Jackets and reservations required. AE, DC, MC, V. Expensive.*

Mesón de la Cava. The capital's most unusual restaurant is more than 50 feet below ground in a natural cave complete with stalagmites and stalactites. Specialties include prime fillet with Dijon flambé, tournedos Roquefort, and excellent seafood dishes. Live music and dancing nightly until 1 AM. *Av. Mirador del Sur, tel. 809/533–2818. Jacket and reservations required. AE, DC, MC, V. Expensive.*

De Armando. Lobster, seafood, and steaks are the specialties in this restaurant, which has a sister restaurant in Puerta Plata. For dessert, the majarete is particularly good. A guitar trio entertains every night. *Av. Santiago 205, tel. 809/689–3534. Jackets and reservations required. AE, MC, V. Moderate.*

Fonda de la Atarazana. This patio restaurant in the Colonial Zone is especially romantic at night when music and dancing are added. Try the kingfish, shrimp, or *chicharrones de pollo* (bits of fried Dominican chicken). *La Atarazana 5, tel. 809/689–2900. No reservations. AE, MC, V. Moderate.*

Lucky Seven. Baseball is the big deal here. Owner Evelio Oliva has two satellite dishes, and telecasts of six major-league games go on at once. Incidentally, there's also steak, chicken, and seafood to satisfy pre- or postgame appetites. *Casimiro de Moya and Av. Pasteur, tel. 809/682–7588. No reservations. No credit cards. Moderate.*

Dominican **La Bahía.** An unpretentious spot where the catch of the day is
★ tops. Conch appears in a variety of dishes. For starters, try the *sopa palúdica*, a thick soup made with fish, shrimp, and lobster, served with tangy garlic bread. Then move on to kingfish in coconut sauce, or *espaguettis a la canona* (spaghetti heaped with seafood). *Av. George Washington 1, tel. 809/682–4022. No reservations. MC, V. Inexpensive.*

El Castillo del Mar. Another seafood restaurant on the Malecón, this one has an open-air setting by the sea. Start with fish soup, then feast on lobster thermidor or sea bass smothered in onions, tomatoes, peas, and basil. *Av. George Washington 2, tel. 809/688–4047. No reservations. MC, V. Inexpensive.*

French **Cafe St. Michel.** The cream of pumpkin soup and steak tartare
★ should clue you into why this popular restaurant has won many gastronomical awards. Desserts include a prize-winning chocolate torte and spectacular soufflés. *Av. Lope de Vega 24, tel. 809/562–4141. Jacket and reservations suggested. AE, MC, V. Moderate.*

Italian **Il Buco.** Informal and friendly, this restaurant has a full menu that lists dishes from all over Italy. Sample the antipasti, then move on to the green lasagna alla garisenda, which garnered one of the awards for this prize-winning restaurant. *Calle Arzobispo Merino 152-A, tel. 809/685–0884. Reservations required. AE, DC, MC, V. Expensive.*

★ **Vesuvio.** Capital-city denizens flock to this superb Italian restaurant, where everything on the lengthy menu is either freshly caught, homemade, or homegrown. Start with antipasti, then try the seafood platter, *calamares al vino blanco* (squid in white wine sauce) or *scaloppina al tarragon* (veal with tarragon). (**Vesuvio II** is at Av. Tiradentes 17, tel. 809/562–6090.) *Av. George Washington 521, tel. 809/682–2766. Jacket required. No reservations. DC, MC, V. Expensive.*

Spanish **El Caserio.** An extensive menu lists specialties such as paella Valenciana, seafood zarzuela, bluefish with anchovies, and leg of lamb Segovia. For dessert, swallow your diet and order chocolate cake Caserio. *Av. George Washington 459, tel. 809/685–3392. Jackets and reservations required. AE, DC, MC, V. Expensive.*

La Romana **La Casa del Río.** In a dining room perched high on a cliff above
★ the Río Chavón, you can feast on Continental specialties such as

duck soup, ragout of lobster, and veal medallions. *Altos de Chavón, tel. 809/682–9656, ext. 2345. Jacket and reservations required. AE, DC, MC, V. Expensive.*

Tropicana. An elegant pavilion swept with cooling breezes, this eatery specializes in beef and fresh-caught seafoods. Shrimp and lobster are always offered, and sea bass is prepared in a variety of ways. *Casa de Campo, tel. 809/596–8885. Jackets and reservations required. AE, DC, MC, V. Expensive.*

Café del Sol. This is an outdoor café in a 16th-century village setting. You can sample pizza and assorted light dishes while enjoying the view of the distant mountain range. *Altos de Chavón, tel. 809/682–9656, ext. 2346. No reservations. AE, DC, MC, V. Moderate.*

Puerto Plata **De Armando.** Here on the north coast, a restaurant in a pretty blue-and-white house dishes up steak, seafood, and Continental dishes, all served to the tune of a guitar trio. *Calle Separación, corner Calle Antera Mota, tel. 809/586–3418. Reservations required. MC, V. Expensive.*

Flamingo's. You can dine either indoors in a stately room or outside on the balcony overlooking the pool. In any case, you can feast on fettuccine al pesto, lobster fricassee in sherry sauce, and medallions of beef with béarnaise sauce. *Dorado Naco Hotel, tel. 809/586–2019. Reservations suggested. AE, DC, MC, V. Expensive.*

★ **Jimmy's.** Within this old Victorian house, you'll be served chateaubriand, filet Mignon, and a variety of creatures from the sea. Be sure to top it all off with something flambéed. *Calle Beller 72, tel. 809/586–4325. Jackets and reservations required. AE, MC, V. Moderate.*

Roma II. This is just an open-sided stand with a metal roof, but the pizzas, which are cooked in a wood-burning oven, are some of the best you'll ever eat. The pizza dough and pasta are made fresh daily. Other specialties include *spaghetti con pulpo* (octopus), *filete chito* (steak with garlic), and a host of other pastas and special sauces. *Corner Calle E. Prudhomme and Calle Beller, tel. 809/586–3904. No reservations. No credit cards. Inexpensive.*

Lodging

Your options here vary from the New World's first hotel to some of the world's newest and poshest resorts. An ambitious development plan continues, especially at Puerto Plata on the north coast, where there are already so many adjoining resorts that when you go out for a stroll you have to flag landmarks to find your way back to the one where your luggage is. Be sure to inquire about special packages when you call to reserve. Our prices, in U.S. dollars, are based on a double room during the high season.

The most highly recommended lodgings are indicated by a star ★.

Category	Cost*
Very Expensive	over $150
Expensive	$100–$150
Moderate	$75–$100

Inexpensive	under $75

*All prices are for a standard double room for two, excluding 21% tax and a 10%–15% service charge.

Santo Domingo　**Hotel Santo Domingo.** Oscar de la Renta designed the interiors of this very *haut* hotel. There are acres of marble and tile, bold colors, ceiling fans, and hand-crafted Dominican furniture throughout. The air-conditioned hotel, on 14 beautifully landscaped acres, overlooks the Caribbean. The rooms have balconies, and most have two double beds. The Alcazar is the elegant Continental restaurant; Las Palmas is the place for dancing. VIPs (and there are many who stay here) check into the Premier Club for extra perks. *Box 2112, Santo Domingo, tel. 809/532–1511 or 800/223–6620. 220 rooms. Facilities: 3 restaurants, 2 bars, pool, sun deck, sauna, 3 tennis courts (2 lighted). AE, DC, MC, V. Expensive.*

Jaragua Resort Hotel, Casino and European Spa. This palatial pink complex is set in 14 acres of gardens, waterfalls, and fountains. Top-name entertainers are booked into the 800-seat nightclub, master chefs from four countries tend to the cuisine, and a staff doctor supervises the diet program in the spa. Air-conditioned accommodations are in Garden or Tower rooms, and all have 3 phones, 21-channel satellite TV, minibar, and hair dryer. Twelve cabanas surround the Olympic-size freeform pool, and the casino covers 20,000 square feet. *Av. George Washington 367, Santo Domingo, tel. 809/685–4151; 800/223–9815; or in Canada, 800/468–0023. 355 rooms, including 18 suites. Facilities: casino, pool, 5 restaurants, 5 bars, 4 tennis courts (1 lighted), golf (at the Santo Domingo Country Club), and European spa with exercise/diet programs, saunas, Jacuzzis, whirlpool. AE, MC, V. Expensive.*

★　**Santo Domingo Sheraton Hotel and Casino.** This 11-story, ultramodern, air-conditioned hotel is on Avenida George Washington, and many of the rooms have balconies overlooking the sea. Most of the rooms have a minibar, and all have color TV with English-language movies. *Box 1493, Santo Domingo, tel. 809/685–5151 or 800/325–3535. 260 rooms. Facilities: casino, pool, Antoine's restaurant, bar, disco, 2 lighted tennis courts, beauty salon, saunas, health club, facilities for the handicapped. AE, DC, MC, V. Expensive.*

★　**Gran Hotel Lina and Casino.** This ultramodern balconied hotel, on Avenida Máximo Gómez near the Plaza de la Cultura, has a contemporary, stylish decor. Rooms are air-conditioned, spacious, and carpeted, with double beds, minifridges, huge marble baths, and cable TV. The staff is friendly and helpful. *Box 1915, Santo Domingo, tel. 809/686–5000. 220 rooms and suites. Facilities: casino, restaurant, piano bar, nightclub, coffee shop, health club, 2 tennis courts, pool facilities for the handicapped. AE, DC, MC, V. Moderate.*

Hotel El Embajador and Casino. The rooms in this air-conditioned hotel are spacious, with carpeting, twin or king-size bed, radio, cable TV, and balconies with either a mountain or ocean view (choose the latter). *Av. Sarasota 65, Santo Domingo, tel. 809/533–2131 or 800/457–0067. 316 rooms, including 12 suites. Facilities: casino, pool, free transport to beach, 4 tennis courts, 2 restaurants, 2 bars, shopping arcade, facilities for the handicapped. AE, DC, MC, V. Inexpensive.*

★　**Hostal Nicolás de Ovando.** The oldest hotel in the New World, and the only hotel in the Colonial Zone, was home to the first governor in the early 1500s. The decor is Spanish, with carved mahogany doors, beamed ceilings, tapestries, arched colonnades, and a courtyard with splashing fountain. Dominican specialties are served in the restaurant. *Calle Las Damas, Santo Domingo, tel. 809/687–3101. 60 rooms. Facilities: restaurant, bar, pool. No credit cards. Inexpensive.*

San Gerónimo and Casino. On Avenida Independencia, this small hotel offers air-conditioned rooms with bath, cable TV, and phone. Some of the rooms have kitchenettes. *Box 15, Santo Domingo, tel. 809/533–8181. 72 rooms. Facilities: casino, restaurant, bar, pool, nightclub. AE, DC, MC, V. Inexpensive.*

The Amber Coast
★

Dorado Naco. This is a sprawling complex of air-conditioned villas with spacious carpeted one- and two-bedroom apartments. The living/dining area has a sofa bed, cable TV, two phones, dining table that seats four, and a counter bar. Each apartment has a large patio or terrace surrounded by tropical flowers and plants. The Dorado features an aggressive activities program that arranges beach barbecues, bonfires, and such. *Box 162, Playa Dorada, tel. 809/586–2019 or 800/322–2388. 202 rooms. Facilities: pool, restaurant, 4 bars, coffee shop, game room, minimarket, bicycle rental, horseback riding, tennis, golf, and water-sports center. AE, DC, MC, V. Expensive.*

Eurotel Playa Dorada. A cascading pool washes down to the two-mile beach upon which sit clusters of small low-rise buildings. This large resort, completed in 1986, is done in bold, imaginative designs. Standard rooms have one double or two twin beds; one-bedroom apartments have a pull-out couch in the living room, and some have kitchens. There's always a lot going on at the beach club. *Box 337, Playa Dorada, tel. 809/586–3663 or 800/826–3447. 402 rooms, including 186 suites. Facilities: 3 restaurants, 3 bars, 5 lighted tennis courts, golf, horseback riding, water-sports clinic, bicycles, scooters. AE, DC, MC, V. Expensive.*

Heavens. No, you don't enter through a pearly gate, but you can work out in the Heavenly Bodies Gym. The emphasis here is on earthly pleasures, especially water sports—windsurfing, sailing, scuba diving, waterskiing, fishing excursions, sea sleds, snorkeling, and water-sports clinics. After you dry off, you can play in the Andromeda Disco Cabaret. Standard bedrooms or one-bedroom apartments are located in three low-rise buildings, each with 50 air-conditioned rooms. (The suites have kitchenettes.) Minimum stay during holiday periods is seven days. *Playa Dorado, tel. 809/586–5250; or 800/223–9815; in Canada, 800/468–0023. 146 rooms. Facilities: restaurant, bar, disco, bicycling, Hobie Cats, parasailing, water-sports center. AE, MC, V. Expensive.*

Jack Tar Village. At this link in the all-inclusive chain of JTVs, everything, including drinks and golf greens fees, is included in the cost of your accommodation. There is a very active activities program, plus nightly entertainment and all manner of enjoyable pursuits. Accommodations are in Spanish-style villas near the beach. There is free transportation to town, but the all-inclusive deal will probably keep you on the premises. *Box 368, Playa Dorada, tel. 809/586–3800 or 800/527–9299. 240 rooms. Facilities: 3 restaurants, 3 bars, golf, horseback riding, day and night tennis, water-sports center. AE, MC, V. Expensive.*

Playa Dorada Beach Resort. This beach resort is known for its lively nightlife. It's set on a mile-long white-sand beach, and there are a variety of social and sports programs. The grounds are beautifully landscaped, and the pool, with swim-up bar, is just a few steps from the beach. Air-conditioned rooms come with cable TV and either two doubles or a king-size bed. *Box 272, Playa Dorada, tel. 809/586–3988 or 800/423–6902. 253 rooms, including 1 suite. Facilities: pool, 4 restaurants, 4 bars, ice-cream parlor, golf, tennis courts, horseback riding, bikes, jogging trail, water-sports center. AE, DC, MC, V. Expensive.*

★ **Puerto Plata Beach Resort and Casino.** This is a 7-acre village with cobblestone pathways, colorful gardens, the Amber Coast's only casino, and suites in 23 two- and three-story buildings. An activities center sets up water-sports clinics, rents bicycles, and so forth. This resort also caters to the little ones, with children's games and enclosures for them at the shallow end of the pool. La Lechuza is the resort's glitzy disco. *Box 600, Av. Malecón, Puerta Plata, tel. 809/586–4243 or 800/223–9815. 216 suites. Facilities: pool, 4 restaurants, bar, outdoor Jacuzzi, horseback riding, 3 lighted tennis courts, water-sports center. AE, MC, V. Expensive.*

★ **Radisson Puerto Plato.** New in 1988, this is a luxurious resort with accommodations in 44 two-story pastel-colored villas. Rooms are air-conditioned, with remote-control cable TV, minibar. The free-form pool has a swim-up terrace, and there's free shuttle service to the beach. Nightly entertainment and dancing in the patio lounge and lobby bar. *Playa Dorada, tel. 809/586–5350 or 800/777–7800. 336 rooms and junior suites. Facilities: 2 restaurants, 3 bars/lounges, pool, 7 lighted tennis courts, health club, gym, spa, Jacuzzi, golf, room service. AE, MC, V. Expensive.*

Cofresi Beach Resort. The rooms here are simply furnished (twin beds, bath with tub and shower), but the setting is breathtaking. The all-inclusive resort is built on the reefs along the Atlantic, which spritzes its waters into the peaceful man-made lagoon and pools along the beach. There are jogging and exercise trails, paddleboats for the lagoon, scuba-diving clinics, and evening entertainment, including a disco. Everything, including unlimited drinks, is included. *Box 327, Costamar, tel. 809/586–2898 or 800/828–8895; in NY, 212/840–6636; in Canada, 800/468–0023. 150 rooms. Facilities: 2 restaurants, 3 bars, disco, nightclub, 2 pools, (1 saltwater), bicycling, horseback riding, paddleboats, tennis, water-sports center. AE, MC, V. Moderate.*

★ **Playa Chiquita.** In this new Sosúa resort, you register in a broad breezeway that leads past the free-form pool right to the small private beach. The all-suites, air-conditioned complex has contemporary tropical decor, with terra-cotta floors, cable TV, double or a king-size beds, wet bar, kitchenettes, and patios or balconies. A sun deck overlooks the ocean. The pool has a swim-up bar for adult guests and a shallow section for the little ones. *Sosúa, tel. 809/689–6191. 90 rooms. Facilities: restaurant, coffee shop, pool, gift shop, horseback riding, water sports. MC, V. Moderate.*

Punta Goleta Beach Resort. The resort is set in 100 tropical acres across the road from the Cabarete beach, where windsurfing is the big deal. All the hotel's rooms are air-conditioned and most have terraces or patios with gingerbread trim. There is a lot of activity here, such as volleyball in the pool or on the beach, frog and crab racing, board games, merengue lessons, disco, and boating on the lagoon. *Box 318,*

Cabarete, tel. 809/531–3036 or 800/874–4637. 128 rooms plus 2 3-bedroom villas. Facilities: 2 restaurants, 4 bars, disco, jogging track, pool, lagoon, horseback riding, golf, tennis, watersports center. AE, DC, MC, V. Moderate.

Hotel Montemar. Located on the Malecón, between Puerto Plata and Playa Dorada, this is a good choice for a cost-conscious holiday. All rooms have an ocean view. Superior rooms are air-conditioned, but small standard rooms are not. There is a daily schedule of activities, and transportation to the beaches at Playa Dorada. This hotel doubles as a school for young Dominicans interested in hospitality-industry careers. *Box 382, Puerta Plata, tel. 809/586–2800. 101 rooms. Facilities: restaurant, coffee shop, bar, 2 tennis courts, beach club, golf, horseback riding. AE, MC, V. Inexpensive.*

La Romana **Casa de Campo.** This luxury resort is—in a word—awesome. It
★ occupies 7,000 landscaped acres along the edge of the Caribbean. Much of the resort was designed by Oscar de la Renta, who owns a villa here and also has a boutique in Altos de Chavón, the re-created village and art colony on the property (*see* Exploring, above). There are 350 casitas, casita suites, and one-, two-, and three-bedroom golf and tennis villas, plus 150 condominium apartments. There is a ranch with 2,000 horses, three polo fields, and two 18-hole Pete Dye golf courses. Minibuses provide free transportation around the resort, but you can also rent electric carts, scooters, and bicycles. *Box 140, La Romana, tel. 809/682–2111 or 800/223–6620. 740 rooms. Facilities: 9 restaurants, 8 bars, 13 pools, 13 tennis courts (6 lighted), fitness center, Jacuzzi, sauna, polo fields, ranch, 2 18-hole golf courses, boutiques, marina, airstrip. AE, DC, MC, V. Very Expensive.*

Punta Cana **Bavaro Beach Resort.** More than 20 miles of the Caribbean's
★ best beach are to be found in front of this four-star luxury resort. Rooms are in five low-rise buildings by the beach or overlooking the gardens. Each room is air-conditioned and has a private balcony or terrace and refrigerator. A social director coordinates a wide variety of daily activities. *Higüey, tel. 809/682–2162. 1,001 rooms. Facilities: 3 restaurants, 3 bars, 2 pools, cable TV, archery, bicycles, horseback riding, tennis, disco, water sports. AE, MC, V. Expensive.*

Club Méditerranée. Everything but hard liquor is included in the price you pay for a stay in this 70-acre facility on the Punta Cana beach. Its air-conditioned, double-occupancy rooms are in three-story beach and coconut-grove lodgings, with twin beds and showers. There's a disco on the beach, plus the whole spectrum of Club Med activities, from archery to yoga. *Punta Cana, tel. 809/567–5228 or 800–CLUBMED; In NY 212/750–1670. 332 rooms. Facilities: 2 restaurants, bar, disco, pool, 14 tennis courts (6 lighted), golf driving range and putting green, archery, bocce ball, volleyball, boat rides, soccer, ping-pong, aerobics classes, water-sports center. AE, MC, V. Moderate.*

Samaná **Bahía Beach Resort.** On a cliff above the beach in one of the best game-fishing areas of the Caribbean, the Bahía offers air-conditioned rooms with ocean view on the mainland, plus fan-cooled cottages on an island 5 miles offshore. A favorite of young Dominicans, this is another all-inclusive resort. *Samaná Bay, tel. 809/685–6060 or 800/327–7737. 85 rooms in the main hotel, 29 on the island. Facilities: restaurant, bar, pool, 2 tennis courts, disco, water sports. AE, MC, V. Moderate.*

The Arts and Nightlife

Check with your hotel and get a copy of the magazine *Vacation Guide* and the newspaper *Touring*, both of which are available free at the Tourist Office, to find out what's happening around the island. Look also in the *Santo Domingo News* for listings of events.

Casinos The greatest concentration of casinos is in the major hotels of Santo Domingo, but there are others here and there, and all offer blackjack, craps, and roulette. Casinos are open daily 3 PM–4 AM. You must be 18 to enter, and jackets are required. In Santo Domingo, the most popular casinos are in the **Dominican Concorde** (Calle Anacaona, tel. 809/562–8222), the **Jaragua** (Av. Independencia, tel. 809/685–4151), the **El Embajador** (Av. Sarasota, tel. 809/533–2131), the **Hotel Lina** (Av. Máximo Gómez, tel. 809/689–5185), the **Naco Hotel** (Av. Tirandentes 22, tel. 809/562–3100), the **San Géronimo** (Av. Independencia 1067, tel. 809/533–8181).

12 Grenada

Grenada, a tiny island only 21 miles long and 12 miles wide, is bordered by dozens of beaches and secluded coves; crisscrossed by nature trails; and filled with spice plantations, tropical forests and cozy hotels clinging to hillsides overlooking the sea.

Known as the Isle of Spice, Grenada is a major producer of nutmeg, cinnamon, mace, cocoa, and many other common household spices. The pungent aroma of spices fills the air, at the outdoor markets, where they're sold from large burlap bags; in the restaurants, where chefs believe in using them liberally; and in the pubs, where cinnamon and nutmeg are sprinkled on the rum punches. If the Irish hadn't beaten them to it, Grenada might have been called the Emerald Isle, for the lush pine forests and the thick brush on the hillsides give it a great, green beauty that few Caribbean islands duplicate.

Located in the Eastern Caribbean 90 miles north of Trinidad, Grenada is the most southerly of the Windward Islands. It is a nation composed of three inhabited islands and a few uninhabited islets: Grenada island is the largest, with 120 square miles and a population of 110,000; Carriacou, 16 miles north of Grenada, is 13 square miles and has a population of 7,000; and Petit Martinique, 5 miles northeast of Carriacou, has 486 acres and a population of 600. Although Carriacou and Petit Martinique are popular for day trips and fishing and snorkeling excursions, most of the tourist action is on Grenada. Here, too, you will find the nation's capital, St. George's, and its largest harbor, St. George's Harbour.

Until 1983 when the United States/Eastern Caribbean invasion of Grenada catapulted this tiny nation into the forefront of international news, it was a relatively obscure island providing a quiet hideaway for those who love fishing, snorkeling, or simply lazing in the sun.

Today Grenada is back to normal, a safe and secure vacation spot with enough good shopping, restaurants, and pubs to make it a regular port of call for major cruise lines, and plenty of beaches and coves for those who want to scuba dive, snorkel, or just sit and stare at the waves.

Although Grenada's tourism industry is undergoing an expansion, it is a controlled expansion, counterbalanced by the island's West Indian flavor. No building can stand taller than a coconut palm, and new construction on the beaches must be at least 165 feet from the high-water mark. The hotels, resorts, and restaurants remain small and are mostly family-owned by people who get to know their guests and pride themselves on giving personalized service. They're typical of the islanders as a whole—friendly and hospitable.

Grenada was sighted by Columbus in 1498. Although he never stepped foot on the island, he nevertheless named it Concepción. Throughout the 17th century it was the scene of bloody battles between the indigenous Carib Indians and the French. The French finally captured the island in 1650, and lost it in 1762 to the British. This was the beginning of the seesaw of power between the two nations that became a familiar tale on many of the Windward Islands.

In 1967 Grenada became part of the British Commonwealth; seven years later it was granted total independence. The New Jewel Movement (NJM) seized power in 1979, formed the People's Revolutionary Government, and named Maurice Bishop prime minister. He established ties with Cuba, the Soviet Union, and other communist governments. His prime ministry lasted until 1983, when a coup d'état led to his execution, along with many of his supporters. Bernard Coard, NJM deputy prime minister, and Army Commander Hudson Austin took over the government. At that point the United States was encouraged to intervene. U.S. troops invaded the island on October 25, 1983, and evacuated the American students who were attending St. George's University Medical School. Coard and Austin were arrested and resistance to the invasion was quickly put down.

If the U.S. invasion—which Grenadians refer to as "the rescue"—was deemed controversial elsewhere, it was greeted with almost unanimous support throughout the Caribbean. American visitors to Grenada will find themselves treated as if they had personally liberated the country.

Herbert A. Blaize was elected prime minister in December 1984. With $57.2 million in U.S. aid, his government began reorganizing Grenada's economy, focusing on agriculture, light manufacturing, and tourism. The country started to rebuild roads, and a new telephone system, with direct-dial from the United States, replaced the outdated, inefficient system. Point Salines International Airport opened in 1984, enabling jets to land on the island and also allowing night landings, both firsts for Grenada.

In 1988 construction was completed on the first phase of Camerhogne Park, a recreation and conference center at Grand Anse Bay, where many of the hotels and resorts are located. The park, designed primarily for the use of visiting cruise-ship passengers, has picnic tables, locker and shower facilities, food concessions, and a jetty for water taxis.

Before You Go

Tourist Information Contact the **Grenada Tourist Office:** in the United States (Suite 701, 141 E. 44th St., New York, NY 10017, tel. 800/638–9852, or 212/687–9554); in Canada (Suite 820, 439 University Ave., Toronto, Ontario M5G 1Y8, tel. 416/595–1339); or in Britain (1 Collingham Gardens, London SW5, tel. 1/370–516).

Arriving and Departing
By Plane **BWIA** (tel. 212/581–3200) flies from New York, Miami, Toronto, and London to Grenada, via Trinidad. **American Airlines** (tel. 800/334–7400), **Pan Am** (tel. 800/421–5330), and **Air Canada** (tel. 800/422–6232) fly to Barbados, where **LIAT** (Leeward Islands Air Transport; tel. 809/462–0700) connects with flights to Grenada. LIAT has scheduled service between Grenada and Carriacou and also serves Trinidad and Venezuela.

From the Airport Taxis and minivans are available at the airport to take you to your hotel. Rates to St. George's and the hotels of Grand Anse and L'Anse aux Epines are about $12.

Passports and Visas Passports are not required of United States, Canadian, and British citizens, provided they have two proofs of citizenship (one with photo) and a return air ticket. A passport, even an expired one, is the best proof of citizenship; a driver's license with photo *and* an original birth certificate or voter's registration card will also suffice.

Exploring

Annandale Falls
Visitors' Centre, **8**
Bacolet Bay, **5**
Concord Falls, **2**
Dougaldston Estate, **3**
Grand Etang Lake and
Visitors' Centre, **7**
Grenville, **6**
St. George's, **1**
St. George's University
Medical School, **9**
Westerhall, **4**

Dining

Betty Mascoll's Great
House, **10**
The Bird's Nest, **24**
The Boatyard, **33**
The Calabash, **31**
Coconut's Beach, **25**
Delicious Landing, **11**
Le Balisier, **12**
Mama's, **13**
The Nutmeg, **14**
Ristorante Italia, **15**
Rudolf's, **16**
The St. James Hotel, **17**
Secret Harbour
Hotel, **32**
Spice Island Inn, **23**
Tropicana, **18**

Lodging

Blue Horizons Cottage
Hotel, **28**
The Calabash, **34**
Cassiday Bay Resort
(Carricou), **38**
Coral Cove, **20**
Coyaba, **29**
Gem Apartments, **30**
Horse Shoe Beach
Hotel, **19**
La Sagesse Centre, **37**
No Problem Apartment
Hotel, **21**
Prospect Lodge
(Carricou), **39**
Ramada Renaissance
Hotel, **27**
The St. James Hotel, **22**
Secret Harbour
Hotel, **35**
Spice Island, **26**
Twelve Degrees
North, **36**

Grenada

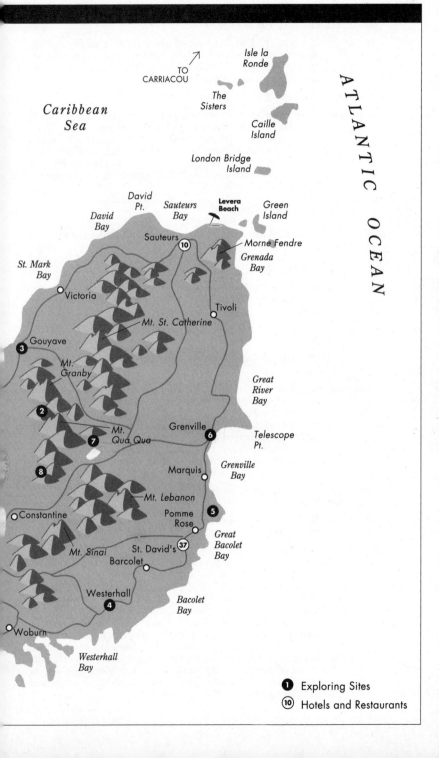

To Carriacou

Isle la Ronde

The Sisters

Caille Island

Caribbean Sea

ATLANTIC OCEAN

London Bridge Island

David Pt.

David Bay

Sauteurs Bay

Levera Beach

Green Island

Sauteurs ⑩

Morne Fendre

Grenada Bay

St. Mark Bay

Victoria

Tivoli

Mt. St. Catherine

❸ Gouyave

Mt. Granby

Great River Bay

❷

Grenville ❻

Telescope Pt.

❼ Mt. Qua Qua

Marquis

Grenville Bay

❽

Mt. Lebanon

Pomme Rose

❺

○ Constantine

Mt. Sinai

St. David's �337

Great Bacolet Bay

Barcolet

Westerhall

❹

Bacolet Bay

○ Woburn

Westerhall Bay

❶ Exploring Sites

⑩ Hotels and Restaurants

Customs and Duties You are allowed to bring into Grenada 200 cigarettes, 20 cigars, and 40 ounces of spirits.

If you're bringing in foreign-made articles, such as cameras, binoculars, and expensive timepieces, it's wise to keep the receipts with your travel documents. Otherwise, you may be charged duty when returning home.

Language English is the official language of Grenada.

Precautions Reasonable security with your personal property is a good idea. The only problem with walking late at night in the Grand Anse/L'Anse aux Epines (pronounced lance-au-peen) hotel districts is the lack of street lights. Unless there's a full moon, it's so dark that it's easy to bump into things, maybe even into one of the cows that graze silently by the roadside. St. George's is equally safe.

Staying in Grenada

Important Addresses **Tourist Information:** The **Grenada Tourist Office** is located in St. George's (the Carenage, tel. 809/440–2001). It has maps, brochures, and information on accommodations, tours, and other services.

Emergencies **Police, Fire,** and **Ambulance:** In St. George's, Grand Anse, and L'Anse aux Epines, call 911. For other areas, check with your hotel.

Hospitals: St. George's Hospital (tel. 809/440–2051; 809/440–2052; 809/440–2053).

Pharmacies: Gittens (Halifax St., St. George's, tel. 809/440–2165).

Currency Grenada uses the Eastern Caribbean (E.C.) dollar. At press time, the exchange rate was E.C.$2.64 to U.S.$1. Be sure to ask which currency is referred to when you make purchases and business transactions; prices are often quoted in E.C. Money can be exchanged at any bank or hotel. U.S. currency and traveler's checks are widely accepted. Most hotels and major restaurants accept credit cards. *Note:* Prices quoted here are in U.S. dollars unless indicated otherwise.

Taxes and Service Charges Hotels add an 8% government tax; restaurants add a 10% tax. The departure tax is E.C. $25.

Hotels and most restaurants add a 10% service charge to your bill. A 10%–15% gratuity should be added for a job well done.

Guided Tours **Grenada Tours and Travel** (Young St., St. George's, tel. 809/440–3316) offers a wide selection of tours. "Around the Island" is a 6½-hour trip up the west coast to a spice plantation at Gouyave, then to the Mascoll plantation house, Morne Fendue, for lunch. The return route is through the east-coast town of Grenville and across scenic St. David's Parish. The tour costs about $28 per person. The "Day Sail" tour includes a stop for swimming, snorkeling, and beachcombing in a deserted cove, plus lunch and rum punches, for $25. Deep-sea game-fishing expeditions cost about $20 per person, per hour, for a minimum of three hours. A day tour of the neighboring island of Carriacou includes air transportation, a barbecue lunch, and snorkeling for about $118 per person.

A number of car-rental agencies and tour operators in St. George's offers standard tours such as the "Royal Drive," which includes the town of St. George's; scenic Westerhall Point, across the island on the Atlantic; a small fishing village; a sugar-processing factory; and Grand Anse Beach. Those offering such tours include **Otways Tours** (the Carenage, tel. 809/440–2558) and **McIntyre Brothers** (Lagoon Rd., tel. 809/440–2044 or 809/440–2901). In Grand Anse, try **Carin's,** just south of the shopping center (tel. 809/444–4363 or 809/444–4364). **Henry's Tours** offers hiking trips for about $20 per person. Included are a trek to Fedon's Camp and an excursion to the Seven Sisters Falls (tel. 809/443–5313).

Getting Around Minivans ply the winding road between St. George's and Grand
Taxis Anse Beach, where many of the hotels are located. Hail one anywhere along the way, pay E.C.$1 and settle in for one of the most hair-raising rides of your life. Taxis are plentiful and rates are posted at the hotels and at the pier on the Carenage in St. George's. The trip from downtown to Grand Anse is about $6; from the airport to Grand Anse, about $12. Cabs are plentiful at all hotels, at the pier, and next to the Tourist Office on the Carenage.

Rental Cars To rent a car, you will need a valid driver's license. Driving is on the left. Rental cars cost about $40 a day or $220 a week with unlimited mileage. Gas costs about $2.50 per gallon. Your hotel can arrange a rental for you. Car-rental agencies in St. George's include **David's** (Church St., tel. 809/440–2351), **Huggins** (Young St., tel. 809/440–3316), **MCR Car Rental** (Paddocks, 809/444–2832; after hours, 809/444–4486; 809/440–5448 or 809/440–5513), and **MacIntyre Brothers** (Young St., tel. 809/440–3316; 809/440–2514; after hours, 809/440–3428). In Grand Anse, try **Royston's** (tel. 809/444–4316).

Telephones Telephone service on the island has much improved in the last
and Mail few years. Grenada can be dialed directly from the United States and Canada. Long-distance calls from Grenada must still be placed through hotel operators, but this is expected to change very soon.

Airmail rates for letters to the United States and Canada are E.C. $.90 for a half-ounce letter and E.C. $.60 for a postcard.

Opening and Store hours are generally from 8–noon and 1–4 weekdays; 8–
Closing Times noon, Saturday; they are closed Sunday. Banks are open weekdays 9–noon.

Beaches

Grenada has some 80 miles of coastline, 65 bays, and 45 white-sand beaches, many with secluded little coves. All the beaches are public and within an easy cab ride of St. George's. Most are located on the Caribbean, south of St. George's in the Grand Anse and L'Anse aux Epines areas, where most of the hotels are clustered. Virtually every hotel, apartment complex, and residential area has its own beach or tiny cove.

The loveliest and most popular beach is **Grand Anse,** about a 10-minute taxi ride from St. George's. It's a gleaming, 2-mile curve of sand and clear, gentle surf. At its southern end is a palm-covered point; to the north you can see the narrow mouth of St. George's Harbour and the pastel houses on the hillsides above it. The sunset is particularly beautiful at Grand Anse—

enjoy it over cocktails at Spice Island Inn, where tables line the beach.

Levera Beach is at the northern tip of the island where the Caribbean meets the Atlantic. The first of the Grenadines is visible in the distance. The surf is rougher here than on the Caribbean beaches, but it is great for body surfing or watching the waves roll in.

Morne Rouge Beach is on the Caribbean side, about 1 mile south of Grand Anse Bay and 3 miles south of St. George's Harbour. The beach forms a ½-mile-long crescent and has a gentle surf excellent for swimming. A small café serves light meals during the day. In the evening, there's the Sur la Mer Restaurant (*see* Dining, below), and a disco, Fantazia 2001 (*see* Nightlife, below).

Exploring Grenada

Numbers in the margin correspond with points of interest on the Grenada map.

St. George's Grenada's capital city and major port is one of the most
❶ picturesque and truly West Indian towns in the Caribbean. Pastel warehouses cling to the curving shore along the horseshoe-shape Carenage, the harborside thoroughfare; rainbow-colored houses rise above it and disappear into the green hills. A walking tour of St. George's can be made in about two hours.

Start on the **Carenage,** a walkway along St. George's Harbour and the town's main thoroughfare. Ocean liners dock at the pier at the eastern end, and the **Delicious Landing** restaurant (tel. 809/440–3948), with outdoor tables, is at the western end. In between are the **post office,** the **public library,** a number of small **shops,** the **Grenada Tourist Office,** and two more good restaurants, **Rudolf's** and the **Nutmeg** (*see* Dining, below), boasting a huge open window providing a great view of the harbor.

You can reach the **Grenada National Museum** by walking along the west end of the Carenage and taking Young Street west to Monckton Street. The museum has a small, interesting collection of ancient and colonial artifacts and recent political memorabilia. *Young and Monckton Sts., no phone. Admission: 50¢ adults, 10¢ children. Open weekdays 9–3.*

Across the street are **York House** (now the Supreme Court building) and the **Registry,** both built around 1800. Since both are used as public buildings, visits are unstructured. *Church and Young Sts., no phone. Admission free. Open weekdays 9–3:45.*

Walk west along Young Street, turn left on Cross Street, and you'll reach the **Esplanade,** the thoroughfare that runs along the ocean side of town. In the middle of the Esplanade you'll find **Grencraft,** the National Handicrafts Center (tel. 809/440–2655), where local goods are sold. Also on the Esplanade, where Cross Street intersects, is the **Yellow Poui Art Gallery** (tel. 809/440–3001), which exhibits and sells Caribbean art, antique engravings, and other fine arts. Directly across the street, on Cross Street, is a row of tiny shops selling similar goods, as well as treats such as guava jelly (a soft candy) and coconut fudge. *Shopping hours: weekdays 8–noon and 1–4, Sat. 8–noon; closed Sun.*

Take the Esplanade north to Granby Street and turn right. Granby Street will take you to **Market Square,** which comes alive every Saturday morning from 8–noon with vendors selling baskets and fresh produce, including tropical fruit you can eat on the spot.

Walk back on Granby Street to Halifax Street and turn left. At the intersection of Halifax and Church streets is **St. Andrew's Presbyterian Church,** built in 1830. Follow Church Street east to Gore Street, to **St. George's Anglican Church,** built in 1828. It's lined with plaques representing Grenada in the 18th and 19th centuries. **St. George's Methodist Church,** built in 1820, is on a hill a few blocks north, on Green Street near Tyrrel Street.

Take Tyrrel Street west to the corner of Park Lane to see the **Marryshow House.** Built in 1917, it combines Victorian and West Indian architecture. The Marryshow also houses the **Marryshow Folk Theatre,** Grenada's first cultural center. Plays, West Indian dance and music, and poetry readings are presented here on occasion. *Tyrrel St., near Bain Alley, tel. 809/440–2451. Admission free. Open weekdays 10–4.*

Head west on Tyrrel Street and turn left onto Church Street. **Fort George** is at the southern tip of Church Street. The fort, rising above the point that separates the harbor from the ocean, was built by the French in 1708. The inner courtyard now houses the police headquarters. *Church St., no phone. Outer courtyard open to the public. Admission free. Open daily during daylight hours.*

The fastest way from the Carenage to the Esplanade is through the **Sendall Tunnel,** slightly north of Fort George. Take it if you're too tired to walk up the steep hill.

The West Coast The coast road north from St. George's winds past soaring mountains and valleys covered with banana and breadfruit trees, palms, bamboo, and tropical flowers. You can drive to ② **Concord Falls,** about 8 miles north of St. George's, and then hike for 2 miles up into the hills to a second waterfall. About 15 minutes farther north is the town of **Gouyave,** center of the nutmeg industry.

③ **Dougaldston Estate,** near the entrance to the town, has a spice factory where you can see cocoa, nutmeg, mace, cloves, cinnamon, and other spices in their natural state, laid out on giant trays to dry in the sun. Old women walk barefoot through the spices, shuffling them so they dry evenly. *Gouyave, no phone. Admission free. Open weekdays 9–4.*

Time Out For lunch, head south for the short drive to Betty Mascoll's old plantation house, **Morne Fendue** (St. Patrick's Parish, tel. 809/440–9330). The large, two-story house was built by Mrs. Mascoll's father in 1912 of hand-chiseled, colored stones mortared with lime and molasses. Outside, poinsettias grow in profusion; inside, amid Victorian antiques and dainty lace curtains, Mrs. Mascoll serves superb West Indian cuisine and one of the best rum punches on the island.

The East Coast

④ Start your tour at **Westerhall,** a residential area about 5 miles southeast of St. George's, known for its beautiful villas, gardens, and panoramic views. From here, take a dirt road north
⑤ to **Bacolet Bay,** a jagged peninsula on the Atlantic, where the surf pounds against deserted beaches. About 15 or 20 miles
⑥ north is **Grenville,** the island's second largest city. From here you can watch schooners set sail for the outer islands. As in St. George's, Saturday is market day, and the town fills with local people doing their shopping for the week. Cooking enthusiasts may want to see the town's spice-processing factory, which is open to the public.

If you take the interior route back to St. George's, you'll fully appreciate the lush, mountainous nature of the island. There is only one paved road that cuts across the island. Leaving Grenville and heading for St. George's, you'll wind upward through the rain forest until you're surrounded by mist, then you'll descend onto the sunny hillsides. In the middle of the island is
⑦ **Grand Etang Lake and Visitors' Centre.** The lake, in the crater of an extinct volcano, is a 13-acre glass-like expanse of cobalt-blue water. The area is a bird sanctuary and forest reserve, where you can go fishing, hiking, and swimming. *Main interior rd., halfway between Grenville and St. George's, tel. 809/440–7425. Open Mon.–Sat. 8–4.*

⑧ Another place to stop is **Annandale Falls and Visitors' Centre,** where a mountain stream cascades 50 feet into a pool surrounded by such exotic tropical flora as liana vines and elephant ears. This, too, is a good swimming and picnic spot. *Main interior rd., 15 min east of St. George's, tel. 809/440–2542. Open Mon.–Sat. 8–4.*

Grand Anse and Most of the island's hotels and its nightlife are in Grand Anse or
the South End the adjacent community of L'Anse aux Epines, which means
⑨ Cove of Pines. Here you will find one of the two campuses of **St. George's University Medical School.** American students were evacuated from the university during the U.S. invasion in 1983.

The second campus is in **True Blue,** a residential area near L'Ansè aux Epines. To reach it, take Grand Anse Road south toward the airport and turn left just before you reach the airport. Although the road is unnamed, it is the only road off Grand Anse Road.

The **Grand Anse Shopping Centre** has a supermarket/liquor store, a clothing store, shoe store, and a gift shop with quality souvenirs and such luxury items as English china and Swedish crystal *(see* Shopping, below). Prices are competitive with duty-free shops elsewhere in the Caribbean.

Grenada's **Carriacou, Petit Martinique,** and a handful of uninhabited
Grenadines specks that comprise the nation of Grenada are north of Grenada island and part of the Grenadines, a chain of 32 tiny islands and cays.

Carriacou's colonial history parallels Grenada's; its tiny size has restricted its political role to a minor part in the area's history. It, too, is verdant and mountainous. A chain of hills cuts a wide swath through its center, from Gun Point in the north to Tyrrel Bay in the south. LIAT has daily flights to and from Grenada island, and schooners leave from St. George's Harbour twice a week. Hillsborough is the main town. In August, the Carriacou Regatta attracts yachts and sailing vessels from throughout the Caribbean.

Five miles northeast of Carriacou is Petit Martinique, the smallest of Grenada's inhabited islands. Like Carriacou and Grenada, Petit Martinique was settled by the French.

Grenada for Free

A good way to spend an afternoon without spending money is to watch fishing boats of all sizes and descriptions pull in and out of St. George's Harbour. On Tuesday afternoons you can watch the boats being loaded with crates and bags of fruit and vegetables bound for Trinidad. It's also fun to roam through the Saturday markets in St. George's and Grenville, which are ablaze with color and humming with activity. Farm women sitting under umbrellas sell bananas, papayas, oranges, yams, plantains, exotic roots and vegetables, and fresh spices; ask the women for their permission before grabbing a photo opportunity. At the nearby fish market, just a short stroll down the Esplanade, you can see the day's catch on display.

Participant Sports

Fishing Deep-sea fishing around Grenada is excellent, with marlin, tuna, yellowfin, and dolphin topping the list of good catches. The annual **Game Fishing Tournament** is held in mid-January. Half-day and full-day excursions are available, plus tours to Sandy Island, Carriacou, and the Grenadines. Contact **Capt. Terry Lampert** (tel. 809/444–4657 or 809/440–2508) to set sail on one of his two fishing boats, the 30-foot *Royal Chappy* and the 41-foot *Free Spirit*.

Golf The Grenada Golf and Country Club in Grand Anse (tel. 809/444–4244) has a nine-hole golf course that charges very low rates; your hotel will make arrangements for you.

Sailing, Diving, and Snorkeling You can rent 30- to 40-foot yachts, with or without crew, from **Go Vacations** at the Spice Island Marina in L'Anse aux Epines (tel. 809/440–3670; from the United States, 800/387–3998). Diving is excellent in this area, with visibility as much as 200 feet. Hundreds of varieties of fish and more than 40 species of coral await underwater explorers. Snorkeling can cost as little as $5 per person, per day, including equipment. A superb spot for scuba diving is at the site of the largest shipwreck in the Caribbean, the *Bianca C*, a cruise ship that caught fire and sank in 1961. It settled in waters more than 100 feet deep and is now home to giant turtles, spotted eagle rays with 15-foot wing spans, and a 350-pound grouper that lives in the ship's smokestack.

The **HMC Diving Centre** at Grand Anse Beach (at Spice Island Inn, tel. 809/444–4258; Ramada Renaissance, tel. 809/444–4372; and Coyaba, tel. 809/444–4129), and **Virgo Watersports** at Prickly Bay (Horseshoe Beach Hotel, tel. 809/444–4410) to the south, both offer a variety of scuba courses, as well as certification for novices. HMC Diving Centre also takes expert divers to the reefs and shipwrecks.

Swimming	Take your pick from Grenada's 45 beaches and secluded coves, but don't miss Grand Anse Beach. **Commodore Peter,** on Grand Anse Beach in front of Spice Island Inn (tel. 809/444–4258), will take you in his boat to a deserted island where he and his wife will prepare a delicious barbecue lunch while you swim, snorkel, or sunbathe.
Other Water Sports	The major hotels on Grand Anse Beach have water-sports centers where you can rent small sailboats, Windsurfers, and Sunfish equipment. The centers are located in front of the hotels. Your hotel can make arrangements for you, or you can call one of the major hotels for information.
Tennis	Several hotels have tennis courts that are free to their guests, including **Calabash** (tel. 809/444–4234), **Secret Harbour** (tel. 809/444–4548), **Coyaba** (tel. 809/444–4129), **Spice Island Inn** (tel. 809/444–4258), **Ramada Renaissance** (tel. 809/444–4371), and **Twelve Degrees North** (tel. 809/444–4580). If there are no courts where you're staying, you can play at some private clubs on the island. Two that accept guests are **Richmond Hill Tennis Club** (tel. 809/440–2537) in Richmond Hill, a suburb of St. George's, and **Tanteen Tennis Club** (tel. 809/440–3010) in St. George's. Your hotel desk clerk can contact them for you.

Shopping

The best souvenirs to pick up in Grenada are little spice baskets filled with cinnamon, nutmeg, mace, bay leaf, vanilla, and ginger. You can find them in practically every shop. Vendors who stroll the beach in Grand Anse also sell spice baskets as well as fabric dolls; T-shirts; hats, fans, and visors woven from green palm; and black-coral jewelry. Shops are open weekdays 8–4. Many are closed noon–1. Saturday hours are 8–noon. Shops are closed Sunday.

Good Buys *St. George's*	In St. George's, **Grencraft,** the **National Handicrafts Centre** (Melville St. at the Esplanade, tel. 809/440–2655), sells locally made furniture, black- and white-coral jewelry, and jewelry made from tortoise shells; crafts of wood, wicker, straw, and fabrics; and T-shirts, postcards, local juices, preserves, candy, and sauces. **Spice Island Perfumes** on the Carenage (tel. 809/440 –2006) is a treasure trove of local perfumes, body oils, natural extracts of spices and herbs, shampoos, suntan oils and lotions, teas, spices, and some nice batiks, and hand-screened T-shirts. **Sea Change,** also on the Carenage (tel. 809/440–2056), carries books, magazines, postcards, stamps, film, paintings, prints, and gift items.
Grand Anse	In Grand Anse, the **Grand Anse Shopping Centre** houses **The Gift Shop,** an outlet for luxury goods such as watches, leather goods, fine jewelry, imported crystal and china, and framed prints, all at competitive prices. The center also has a clothing boutique for children and adults, with sportswear, novelty T-shirts, bathing suits, and some English wool sweaters; a record shop; and a shoe store.

Dining

Unlike most Caribbean islands that have a scarcity of fresh produce, Grenada has everything from cabbage and tomatoes, to bananas, mangoes, papaya (called paw paw), plantains, melon, callaloo (similar to spinach), breadfruit, oranges, tangerines, limes, christophine (similar to squash), avocado—the list is endless. In addition, fresh seafood of all kinds, including lobster and oyster, is also plentiful. Conch, known here as lambi, is very popular and appears on most menus in some form. Be sure to try one of the exotic ice creams made from avocado or nutmeg. Almost all the Grenadian restaurants serve local dishes, which are varied enough to be continually interesting.

Rum punches are served everywhere, but no two places make them exactly alike. The local beer, Carib, is also very popular.

The most highly recommended restaurants are indicated by a star ★.

Category	Cost*
Expensive	$20–$40
Moderate	$10–$20
Inexpensive	under $10

per person, excluding drinks, service, and sales tax (10%)

The Calabash. The open-air restaurant here is small and pretty, surrounded by palms and tropical flowers. Try the callaloo soup. There is a fixed-price dinner and menu each evening. *L'Anse aux Epines, tel. 809/444–4234. Reservations suggested. AE, MC, V. Expensive.*

Secret Harbour Hotel. This open-air restaurant is at the most elegant hotel on the island. Decorated in Spanish tile and red brick, it is cooled by the breezes of Mt. Hartman Bay. Allow time for cocktails or a nightcap in the cozy lounge. There is usually a fixed menu for dinner. *L'Anse aux Epines, tel. 809/444–4439 or 809/444–4548. Reservations suggested. AE, MC, V. Expensive.*

★ **Spice Island Inn.** The dining room, open on three sides, is just a few steps from the beach. The Friday-night buffet is exceptional and a great way to sample the various types of local seafood and salads. *Grand Anse, tel. 809/444–4258. Reservations required late Dec.–mid-Apr. AE, MC, V. Expensive.*

★ **Betty Mascoll's Great House.** Although it's a one-hour drive from St. George's, this restaurant is definitely worth the trip *(see* Exploring, above*).* The owner, Mrs. Mascoll, serves only lunch—and what a lunch! The buffet usually includes her legendary pepperpot, a stew of pork, oxtail, and other meats. The rum punches are among the best on the island. *St. Patrick's Parish, near Sauteurs, tel. 809/440–9330. Reservations required. No credit cards. Moderate.*

The Bird's Nest. This is a Chinese restaurant serving excellent food in a very relaxed setting. *Next to the Grand Anse Shopping Centre, tel. 809/444–4264. AE, MC, V. Moderate.*

The Boatyard. Smack in the middle of a marina, this restaurant is a lively place, filled with embassy personnel and expatriates. Lunches include burgers, fish and chips, and deep-fried shrimp. Dinner features club steaks, lobster, and different types of meat and seafood brochettes. In season (late Dec.–mid-Apr.) there's a steel band on Saturday night, jazz on Sunday, and disco music on Friday night. *L'Anse aux Epines, tel. 809/444–4662. MC, V. Moderate.*

Coconut's Beach. Better known as "The French Restaurant," this cozy spot is set in a pretty Creole-style house on the beach, with tables of varying shapes and sizes set on the sand. Local cuisine is served with flair and with a French touch. In season, you can enjoy barbecues and listen to steel bands. It's also open for breakfast. *Grand Anse, tel. 809/444-4644. Reservations suggested. No credit cards. Moderate.*

Delicious Landing. This very informal place sits at the end of the Carenage overlooking the water. The menu includes seafood fritters, salads, lobster served a half-dozen different ways, barbecued chicken, sukiyaki, and some vegetarian specialties. *The Carenage, St. George's, tel. 809/440-3948. MC, V. Moderate.*

Le Balisier. You can dine poolside here on a large terrace that offers a sweeping view of St. George's. Dinner focuses on local specialties, such as shrimp Creole; curried or stewed lobster; lambi (conch); and fresh fish, which may be ordered broiled, poached, steamed, or fried, and with curry, white wine, or calypso sauces. *Richmond Hill, St. George's, tel. 809/440-2346. Reservations suggested. MC, V. Moderate.*

★ **Mama's.** This restaurant is more like a diner, West Indian style and very charming. There are no menus, and one of Mama's daughters will set before you whatever specialties Mama has cooked—probably some roast turtle, fried chicken, lobster salad, christophine salad, cabbage salad, or fried plantain. You will not leave hungry. Don't miss it. *Lagoon Rd., St. George's, tel. 809/440-1459. Reservations required. No credit cards. Moderate.*

The Nutmeg. Fresh seafood is the specialty of this second-floor restaurant that has a great view of the harbor. Try the grilled turtle steaks. *The Carenage, St. George's, tel. 809/440-2539. Informal. AE, MC, V.*

Ristorante Italia. True to its name, this restaurant features delicious pizza, pasta, and other Italian dishes. Located above Spice Island Perfumes shop, the restaurant has broad windows overlooking scenic St. George's Harbour. *The Carenage, St. George's, tel. 809/440-3986. No credit cards. Moderate.*

Rudolf's. This informal, pub-like place offers both West Indian cuisine (crab back and lobster salad are specialties) and some Asian dishes such as Tung Po (breaded pork chops with honey, peaches, and rice). Try the cold tomato-and-orange soup. *The Carenage, St. George's. Closed Sun. No credit cards. Moderate.*

The St. James Hotel. This genteel old hotel was a private home 100 years ago. Its restaurant serves satisfying Grenadian cuisine on white linen tablecloths set with antique Sheffield silver. The chutney alone makes this restaurant worth a visit. *Lagoon Rd., St. George's, tel. 809/440-2041 or 809/440-2042. Reservations recommended. No credit cards. Moderate.*

Tropicana. You can dine on the terrace or in a small dining room here and enjoy an extensive list of both Chinese and West Indian specialties. Open for both lunch and dinner, it serves massive portions. The Tropicana also provides take-out service. *Lagoon Rd., St. George's, tel. 809/440-1586. AE, MC, V. Moderate.*

Lodging

Grenada's accommodations range from simply furnished kitchenette suites to suites representing Caribbean-style elegance. There are no pretentious hotels—Grenada is a simple place and its hotels have been furnished accordingly. Most of the hotels are owned and operated by Grenadians; those that aren't are usually run by British or American expatriates who thrive on the simplicity of Grenadian life. The hotels tend to be small (10 to 20 rooms in most cases), but they exude a sense of intimacy, with friendly managers or owners.

For confirmation on reservations at any of the 24 members of the **Grenada Hotel Association,** call, in the United States, 800/CALL–GND; in New York State, 212/840–6636; and in Canada, 800/468–0023.

During the winter season, some hotels offer MAP (Modified American Plan, two meals daily). Prices for the summer are discounted by 20% to 40%.

The most highly recommended lodgings are indicated by a star ★.

Category	Cost*
Very Expensive	over $150
Expensive	$100–$150
Moderate	$75–$150
Inexpensive	under $75

All prices are for a standard double room for two, excluding 8% tax and a 10% service charge.

Hotels
Grenada
★

The Calabash. This all-suite hotel is set on a wide green lawn overlooking a curved beach, a yacht harbor, and charter-boat anchorage in Prickly Bay, L'Anse aux Epines. The deluxe suites have their own private swimming pool. *Box 382, St. George's, tel. 809/444–4234. 22 suites. Facilities: restaurant, beach bar, pool, water-sports center, tennis. In season, MAP only. AE, MC, V. Very Expensive.*

Secret Harbour Hotel. The island's most exclusive resort is now an all-inclusive property for couples only. It has spacious, Mediterranean-style villas set on a ridge overlooking Mt. Hartman Bay. Each villa has two antique four-poster beds, a balcony with a sweeping view of the bay, and a giant bathroom with a window overlooking the sea. *Box 11, L'Anse aux Epines, St. George's, tel. 809/444–4548. 20 villas. Facilities: restaurant, lounge, tennis, beach with bar, pool, water-sports center, nightly entertainment. AE, MC, V. Very Expensive.*

★ **Spice Island Inn.** This is a charming hotel with completely refurbished beachside bungalows, many with private pools. *Box 6, Grand Anse, St. George's, tel. 809/444–4258 or 809/444–4423. 42 bungalows. Facilities: pool, water-sports center, restaurant, lounge. AE, MC, V. Very Expensive.*

Horse Shoe Beach Hotel. Really a cluster of six Spanish-style villas, this hotel clings to a hillside overlooking a small beach and a pool. Each suite is furnished with antiques and giant, mahogany four-poster beds, fit for royalty. All the villas have private patios and a kitchen in an outdoor courtyard where a maid prepares breakfast each morning. The hotel has a new water-sports center and diving school and offers dive packages. *Box 174, St. George's, tel. 809/444–4410 or 809/444–4244. 12 suites. Facilities: pool, restaurant, lounge. AE, MC, V. Expensive.*

Ramada Renaissance Hotel. Since Ramada took over this resort, formerly the Grenada Beach Hotel, it has spent $15 million on renovation. It is the island's largest hotel and is noted for its efficient, friendly service. All rooms have king-size or extra-large beds and satellite TV. *Box 441, Grand Anse, St. George's, tel. 809/444–4371. 186 rooms, including 2 luxury suites. Facilities: 2 restaurants, lounge, pool. AE, DC, MC, V. Expensive.*

Twelve Degrees North. Six apartments, with one and two bedrooms, sit atop a hill that slopes to a swimming pool and, beyond that, a small beach that's good for snorkeling. Each apartment is stocked with food staples, which are billed to you at cost; a staff member is on hand to drive you to the supermarket if you want to buy more food. There's no restaurant on the premises but a maid prepares breakfast and lunch for you in your apartment. The complex is within walking distance or a short cab ride to the restaurants of Grand Anse and L'Anse aux Epines. Children under 12 are not allowed. A minimum stay of one week is required during high season. *Box 241, L'Anse aux Epines, St. George's, tel. 809/444–4580. 6 apartments. Facilities: pool, tennis, sailing dinghy for rent. No credit cards. Expensive.*

Blue Horizons Cottage Hotel. This comfortable hotel is set among the palms around a large, sunny lawn and swimming pool on 6½ acres. Grand Anse Beach is a six-minute walk down the hill. Royston's Rental Cars is based here. *Box 41, Grand Anse, St. George's, tel. 809/444–4316. 22 suites with terraces. Facilities: restaurant, lounge, pool. AE, MC, V. Moderate.*

Coral Cove. Secluded and serene, this hotel has cottages with one and two bedrooms, all with views of the sea, offshore islands, and the mountains. The nearby beach is excellent for snorkeling. *Box 187, St. George's, tel. 809/444–4217. 18 cottages. Facilities: pool, tennis courts. MC, V. Moderate.*

★ **Coyaba.** *Coyaba* means "heaven" in the Arawak Indian language. Guests will agree that the name is an apt one for this beachfront hotel. All the rooms have patios, satellite TV, radio, telephone, and a hair dryer. *Box 336, Grand Anse, St. George's, tel. 809/444–4129. 30 rooms. Facilities: pool with swim-up bar, tennis courts, water-sports center, restaurant, bar, lounge. AE, DC, MC, V. Moderate.*

Gem Apartments. Furnishings here are basic, but the one- and two-bedroom apartments on Morne Rouge Beach are spacious and comfortable, and all are air-conditioned. On the premises is the popular Fantazia 2001 disco, Sur La Mer restaurant, and Aquarius beach bar. *Gems BBC Ltd., Morne Rouge, St. George's, tel. 809/444–4224; 809/443–5536. 4 2-bedroom, 12 1-bedroom apartments. Facilities: disco, restaurant, beach bar. AE, DC, MC, V. Inexpensive.*

La Sagesse Nature Centre. Set on a bay 10 miles from Point Salines Airport, the center has a guest house with basic, but spacious, rooms. There's an old sugar mill and rum distillery at the entrance. Mangroves, a salt-pond bird sanctuary, and hiking trails provide a peaceful, unspoiled setting. *Box 44, St. David's, tel. 809/444–6458. 5 rooms. Facilities: restaurant, bar, art gallery. MC, V. Inexpensive.*

No Problem Apartment Hotel. "No problem" might refer to the convenient location of this small apartment complex just 1 mile from the airport, 2 miles from Grand Anse, and within walking distance of several deserted Point Salines beaches. Each apartment has twin beds, a sofa bed, well-equipped kitchen, TV, and telephone. Laundry service is provided. *Box 280, St. George's,* *tel. 809/444–4336. 20 suites. Facilities: pool, terrace restaurant, honor bar, barbecue, open kitchen, 14 bicycles. AE, DC, MC, V. Inexpensive.*

★ **The St. James Hotel.** This 100-year-old former private home has been a hotel since 1950. It's on the west end of St. George's, on a hill between the Carenage and the Esplanade, and is a gracious retreat amidst the bustle of town. There's shuttle-bus service to Grand Anse Beach. *Grand Etang Rd., St. George's, tel. 809/ 440–2041. 16 rooms, most with private bath; some share bath with adjoining room. Facilities: restaurant. MC, V. Inexpensive.*

Carriacou   **Cassaday Bay Resort.** Set in a peaceful atmosphere, this resort has a panaromic view of the ocean. Privacy is the byword here. *Carriacou, tel. 809/443–7494. 18 suites with veranda. Facilities: restaurant, bar, water-sports center. AE, DC, MC, V. Inexpensive.*

Prospect Lodge. Located on the leeward coast of Carriacou, the lodge overlooks the Caribbean and provides a quiet setting for those who want to enjoy the beach and the sun. *Prospect, Carriacou, tel. 809/443–7380. 10 apartments. Facilities: restaurant, water-sports center. AE, DC, MC, V. Inexpensive.*

Villa and Private-Home Rentals   Two local agencies handle rentals of villas and private homes: **Bain and Bertrand Realtors** (Lagoon Rd., St. George's, tel. 809/ 440–2848) **and Grenada Property Management** (Melville St., St. George's, 809/440–1896). In-season rates range from about $600 a week for a two-bedroom home with a pool, to about $3,500 for a six-bedroom home on the beach.

Nightlife

Grenada's nightlife centers on the hotel lounges and bars. During winter, many of the hotel lounges have steel, reggae, and pop bands in the evenings. **Spice Island Inn, The Calabash, Coyaba,** and the **Ramada Renaissance** hotels are among the most lively (*see* Lodging, above). Check with your hotel or the Tourist Information Office to find out where various bands are performing on a given night.

Fantazia 2001 is a popular disco on Morne Rouge Beach. *Gem Apartments premises, Morne Beach, tel. 809/444–4224. No cover or minimum.*

13 Guadeloupe

by Honey Naylor   It's a steamy hot Saturday in mid-August. There may be a tropical depression brewing somewhere to the west. It's that time of year. But the mood in Pointe-à-Pitre, Guadeloupe's commercial center, is anything but depressing. Amid music and laughter, women adorned with gold jewelry and the traditional madras and foulard parade through the streets. Balanced on their heads are huge baskets decorated with miniature kitchen utensils and filled with mangoes, papaya, breadfruit, christophine, and other island edibles. The procession wends its way to the Cathédrale de St. Pierre et St. Paul where a high mass is celebrated. A five-hour feast with music, song, and dance will follow.

The *Fête des Cuisiniéres* (Cooks' Festival) takes place annually in honor of St. Laurent, patron saint of cooks. The parading *cuisinieres* are the island's women chefs, an honored group. This festival gives you a tempting glimpse of one of Guadeloupe's stellar attractions—its cuisine. The island's more than 100 restaurants serve some of the best food in all of the Caribbean.

But there is more here than meets the palate. Night owls and nature enthusiasts, hikers and bikers, scuba divers, sailors, mountain climbers, beachcombers, and hammock potatoes all can indulge themselves in Guadeloupe.

Actually, Guadeloupe doesn't appeal to every pleasure seeker. Guadeloupe does not market its hospitality. Sugar, not tourism, has been its mainstay, though tourism rates as the island's third most important industry. French is the official language here. But even if your tongue twirls easily around a few French phrases, you will sometimes receive a cool response. As in any foreign place, you'll find some less-than-friendly people here. Hang loose and you'll enjoy the island's many treasures.

Guadeloupe looks like a giant butterfly resting on the sea between Antigua and Dominica. Its two wings—Basse-Terre and Grande-Terre—are the two largest islands in the 659-square-mile Guadeloupe archipelago, which includes the little offshore islands of Marie-Galante, La Désirade, and Les Saintes, as well as French St. Martin and St. Barthélemy to the north. Mountainous 312-square-mile Basse-Terre (lowland) lies on the leeward side, where the winds are "lower." Smaller, flatter Grande-Terre (218 square miles) gets the "bigger" winds on its windward side. The Rivière Salée, a four-mile sea-water channel flowing between the Caribbean and the Atlantic, forms the "spine" of the butterfly. A drawbridge over the channel connects the two islands.

If you're seeking resort hotels, casinos, and white sandy beaches, your target is Grande-Terre. Basse-Terre's Natural Park, laced with mountain trails and washed by waterfalls and rivers, is a 74,100-acre haven for hikers, nature lovers, and anyone yearning to peer into the steaming crater of an active volcano. If you want to get away from it all, head for the offshore islands of Les Saintes, Désirade, and Marie-Galante.

Not surprisingly, Christopher Columbus "discovered" Guadeloupe. On November 4, 1493, he landed at Ste. Marie on the southern shore of Basse-Terre and named the island Santa Marie de Guadelupe de Estremadura. The Carib inhabitants, who had already polished off the peaceful Arawaks, had no intention of relinquishing the land they called *Karukera* (Island of Beau-

Guadeloupe

La Luisiane, **77**
La Mandingo, **59**
La Mouette, **83**
La Plantation, **53**
Le Balata, **57**
Le Barbaroc, **50**
Le Bistrot, **68**
Le Foyal, **42**
Le Flibustier, **69**
Le Galion, **58**
Le Houlimont, **38**
Le Karacoli, **35**
Le Paille En Queue, **60**
Le Zagaya, **78**
Les Gommiers, **78**
Les Oiseaux, **40**
Relais de Iles, **43**
Relais du Moulin, **71**
Rosini, **55**

Lodging
Auberge de la
Distillerie, **48**
Auberge de la Vielle
Tour PLM-Azur, **63**
Auberge des
Anacardies, **45**
Auberge du Grand
Large, **75**
Bois Joli, **46**
Callinago-PLM
Azur, **67**
Cap Sud Caraibes, **66**
Club Med
Caravelle, **72**
Fler d'Epée
Novotel, **65**
Grand Anse Hotel, **41**
Hamak, **80**
Hotel Les Trois
Mats, **82**
La Creole Beach, **64**
La Toubana, **73**
Los Santo-PLM
Azur, **47**
Meridien, **81**
Relais du Moulin, **74**
Village Creole, **44**

tiful Waters). The Spaniards gave up on the island in 1604. In 1635, the French laid claim to it. They ran the Caribs off, brought in African slaves to work their sugar plantations, and in 1674 Guadeloupe was annexed by France. The British also had designs on the island, and they gained control of it from 1759 until 1763 when they relinquished it in exchange for all French rights to Canada. During the French Revolution battles broke out between royalists and revolutionaries on the island. In 1794, Britain responded to the call from Guadeloupe royalists to come to their aid, and that same year France dispatched Victor Hugues to sort things out. (In virtually every town and village you'll run across a "Victor Hugues" street, boulevard, or park.) After his troops banished the British, Hugues issued a decree abolishing slavery and guillotined recalcitrant planters. The ones who managed to keep their heads fled to Louisiana or hid in the hills of Grande-Terre, where their descendants now live. Hugues was soon relieved of his command, slavery was reestablished by Napoleon, and the French and English continued to battle over the island. The 1815 Treaty of Paris restored Guadeloupe to France, and in 1848, due largely to the efforts of Alsatian Victor Schoelcher, slavery was permanently abolished. The island has been a full-fledged *departement* of France since 1946, and in 1974 it was elevated to a *region*, administered by a prefect appointed from Paris by the Minister of the Interior.

Before You Go

Tourist Information Call or write to the **French West Indies Tourist Office** (610 5th Ave., New York, NY 10020, tel. 212/757–1125). You may also obtain information from the **French Government Office** at any of the following addresses: 628 5th Ave., New York, NY 10020, tel. 212/757–1125; 9454 Wilshire Blvd., Beverly Hills, CA 90212, tel. 213/272–2661; 645 N. Michigan Ave., Chicago, IL 60611, tel. 312/337–6301; 103 World Trade Center, Dallas, TX 75258, tel. 214/742–7011; 1 Hallidie Plaza, Suite 250, San Francisco, CA 94102, tel. 415/986–4161; 1981 Ave. McGill College (490), Montreal, Que., Canada H3A 2W9, tel. 514/288–4264; 1 Dundas St. W, Suite 2405, Toronto, Ont., Canada M5G 1Z3, tel. 416/593–4717; 178 Piccadilly, London, United Kingdom W1V 0AL, tel. 01/499–6911.

Arriving and Departing
By Plane **American Airlines** (tel. 800/433–7300) flies from more than 100 U.S. cities direct to San Juan with connections to Guadeloupe. **Air Canada** (tel. 800/422–6232) flies direct from Montreal and Toronto. **Air France** (tel. 800/237–2747) flies nonstop from Paris and Fort-de-France, and has direct service from Miami, San Juan, and Port-au-Prince. **Air Guadeloupe** (tel. 599/5–44212) flies daily from St. Martin and St. Maarten, St. Barts, Marie-Galante, La Désirade, and Les Saintes. **LIAT** (tel. 212/269–6925) flies from St. Croix in the north and Trinidad in the south.

From the Airport You'll land at La Raizet International Airport, 2½ miles from Pointe-à-Pitre. Cabs are lined up outside the airport.

By Boat Major cruise lines call regularly, docking at berths in downtown Pointe-à-Pitre about a block from the shopping district. **Trans Antilles Express** (tel. 590/83–12–45) provides ferry service to and from Marie-Galante, Les Saintes, and Désirade. The *Jetcat* and *Madras* ferries depart daily from the pier at Pointe-à-Pitre for Marie Galante; the *Princess Caroline* leaves Trois

Rivières for the 30-minute trip to Les Saintes (allow 1½ hours to get from Pointe-à-Pitre to Trois Rivières); and *Socimade* runs between Désirade and St. François.

Passports and Visas U.S. and Canadian citizens need only proof of citizenship. A passport is best (even one that's expired not longer than five years ago). Other acceptable documents are a notarized birth certificate with a raised seal (not a photocopy) or a voter's registration card. With either you'll need a government-authorized photo ID. A free temporary visa, good only for your stay in Guadeloupe, will be issued to you upon your arrival at the airport. British citizens need a valid passport, but no visa. In addition, all visitors must hold an ongoing or return ticket.

Customs and Duties Items for personal use, such as tobacco, cameras, and film are admitted without tax or formalities, provided they are not in "excessive quantity."

Language The official language is French. Everyone also speaks a Creole patois, which you won't be able to understand even if you're fluent in French. In the major tourist hotels at least one person at the front desk speaks English. Waiters and waitresses often do not speak English, and neither do people in the countryside. Some taxi drivers speak a little English. Arm yourself with a phrase book, a dictionary, patience, and a sense of humor.

Precautions Put your valuables in the hotel safe. Don't leave them unattended in your room or on the beach. Keep an eye out for motorcyclists riding double. They sometimes play the notorious game of veering close to the sidewalk and snatching shoulder bags. It isn't a good idea to walk around Pointe-à-Pitre at night because it's almost deserted after dark. If you rent a car, always lock it with luggage and valuables stashed out of sight.

The rough Atlantic waters off the northeast coast of Grande-Terre are dangerous for swimming.

Ask permission before taking a picture of an islander, and don't be surprised if the answer is a firm, "No." Guadeloupeans are also deeply religious and traditional. Don't offend them by wearing short shorts or swimwear off the beach.

Staying in Guadeloupe

Important Addresses Tourist Information: The **Office Departmental du Tourism** has offices in Pointe-à-Pitre (23 rue Delgrès, corner rue Schoelcher, tel. 590/82–09–30), in Basse-Terre (Maison du Port, tel. 590/81–24–83), and in Saint-François (Ave. de l'Europe, tel. 590/88–48–74). All offices are open weekdays 8–5, Saturday 8–noon.

Emergencies **Police:** In Pointe-à-Pitre (tel. 590/17 or 590/82–00–17), in Basse-Terre (tel. 590/81–11–55).

Fire: In Pointe-à-Pitre (tel. 590/18 or 590/82–00–28), in Basse-Terre (tel. 590/81–19–22).

SOS Ambulance: Tel. 590/82–89–33.

Hospitals: There is a 24-hour emergency room at **Pointe-à-Pitre Central Hospital** (Abymes, tel. 590/82–98–80 or 590/82–88–88.) There are several clinics located around the island. The Tourist Office or your hotel can assist you in locating an English-speaking doctor.

Pharmacies: Pharmacies alternate in staying open around the clock. The Tourist Office or your hotel can help you locate the one that's on duty.

Currency Legal tender is the French franc, which is comprised of 100 centimes. At press time, U.S.$1 bought 5.96F, but the franc fluctuates relative to the dollar. Check the current rate of exchange. Some places accept U.S. dollars, but it's best to change your money into the local currency. Credit cards are accepted in most major hotels, restaurants, and shops, less so in smaller places and in the countryside. Prices are quoted here in U.S. dollars unless otherwise noted.

Taxes and A *taxe de séjour* varies from hotel to hotel but never exceeds $1
Service Charges per person, per day.

Most hotel prices include a 10%–15% service charge; if not it will be added to your bill.

Restaurants are legally required to include 15% in the menu price. No additional gratuity is necessary. Tip skycaps and porters about 5F. Many cab drivers own their own cabs and don't expect a tip. You won't have any trouble ascertaining if a 10% tip is expected.

Guided Tours There are set fares for taxi tours to various points on the island. The Tourist Office or your hotel can arrange for an English-speaking taxi driver and even organize a small group for you to share the cost of the tour.

George-Marie Gabrielle (Pointe-à-Pitre, tel. 590/82–05–38) and **Petrelluzzi Travel** (Pointe-à-Pitre, tel. 590/82–82–30) both offer half- and full-day excursions around the island. A modern bus with English-speaking guide will pick you up at your hotel.

At Raizet Airport, helicopter tours can be arranged through **Caraibe Air Tourisme** (tel. 590/91–61–24) and **Safari Tours** (tel. 590/84–06–74).

Organization des Guides de Montagne de la Caraibe, O.G.M.C., (Maison Forestière, Matouba, tel. 590/80–05–79) provides guides for hiking tours in the mountains.

Getting Around Fares are regulated by the government and posted at the air-
Taxis port, at taxi stands, and at major hotels. During the day you'll pay about 29F from the airport to Pointe-à-Pitre, about 58F to Gosier, and about 167F to St. François. Between 9 PM and 7 AM fares are hiked 40%. If your French is in working order, you can contact radio cabs at 590/82–15–09, 590/83–64–27, and 590/84–37–65.

Buses Modern public buses run from 5:30 AM to 7:30 PM. They stop along the road at bus stops and shelters marked *arrêtbus*, but you can also flag one down along the route.

Vespas or Bikes If you opt to tour the island by bike, you won't be alone. Biking is a major sport here (*see* Participant Sports, below, for rental information).

Vespas can be rented at **Vespa Sun** (Pointe-à-Pitre, tel. 590/82–17–80), **Location de Motos** (Meridien Hotel, St. François, tel. 590/88–51–00), and **Dingo Location Scooter** (Gosier, tel. 590/90–97–01).

Rental Cars Your valid driver's license will suffice for up to 20 days, after which you'll need an international driver's permit. Guadeloupe has 1,225 miles of excellent roads (marked as in Europe), and driving around Grande-Terre is relatively easy. However, you may be more comfortable with a Guadeloupean behind the wheel in the mountains of Basse-Terre. Guadeloupeans are skillful drivers, but they do like to drive fast. Cars can be rented at **Avis** (tel. 590/82–33–47 or 800/331–1212), **Budget** (tel. 590/82–95–58 or 800/527–0700), **Hertz** (tel. 590/82–00–14 or 800/654–3131), and **National-Europcar** (tel. 590/82–50–51 or 800/468–0008).

Telephones and Mail To call from the United States, dial 011 + 590 + the local six-digit number. (To call person-to-person, dial 01–590.) It is not possible to place collect or credit card calls to the United States from Guadeloupe, and there are no coin pay telephones. If you need to make calls outside of your hotel, purchase a *Telecarte* at the post office or other outlets marked *Telecarte en Vente Ici*. Telecartes look like credit cards, and are used in special booths marked "Telecom." Local and long-distance calls made with the cards are cheaper than operator-assisted calls.

To call the United States from Guadeloupe, dial 19 + 1 + the area code and phone number. To dial locally in Guadeloupe, simply dial the six-digit phone number.

Postcards to the United States need 2.80F; letters up to 20 grams, 4.40F. For Canada, postcards are 2F; letters, 2.70F. Stamps can be purchased at the post office, *café-tabacs*, hotel newsstands, or souvenir shops.

Opening and Closing Times Banks are open weekdays 8–noon and 2–4. Credit Agricole, Banque Populaire, and Société Générale de Banque aux Antilles have branches that are open Saturday. During the summer most banks are open 8–3. Banks close at noon the day before a legal holiday that falls during the week. As a rule, shops are open weekdays 8 or 8:30–noon and 2:30–6, but hours are flexible when cruise ships are in town.

Beaches

As a rule, Guadeloupe's beaches, all free and open to the public, have no facilities. For a small fee, hotels allow nonguests to use changing facilities, towels, and beach chairs. You'll find long stretches of white sand on Grande-Terre. On the south coast of Basse-Terre the beaches are gray volcanic sand, and on the northwest coast the color is golden-tan. There are several nudist beaches (noted below), and topless bathing is prevalent at the resort hotels. Note that the Atlantic waters on the northeast coast of Grande-Terre are too rough for swimming.

Ilet du Gosier is a little speck off the shore of Gosier where you can bathe in the buff. Make arrangements for water-sport rentals and boat trips to the island through the Creole Beach Hotel in Gosier (tel. 590/84–26–26). Take along a picnic for an all-day outing. *Beach closed weekends.*

Some of the island's best beaches of soft white sand lie on the south coast of Grande-Terre from Ste. Anne to Pointe des Châteaux.

One of the longest and prettiest stretches is just outside the town of Ste. Anne at **Caravelle Beach.** Protected by reefs, it makes a fine place for snorkeling. At the hotel La Toubana (tel. 590/88–25–78) in the hills above you can rent fins and masks, as well as canoes and Windsurfers. Club Med, with its staggering array of activities, occupies one end of this beach.

Just outside of St-François is **Raisin-Clairs,** home of the Meridien Hotel (tel. 590/88–51–00), which rents Windsurfers, water skis, and sailboats.

Tarare is a secluded nudist strip at the tip of Pointe des Châteaux. There are no facilities, but it, too, is near St-François's rentals and rum punches.

Located just outside of Deshaies on the northwest coast of Basse-Terre, La Grande Anse is a secluded beach of soft beige sand sheltered by palms. There's a large parking area but no facilities other than the Karacoli restaurant, which sits with its "feet in the water," ready to serve you rum punch and Creole dishes.

From **Malendure** beach, on the west coast of Basse-Terre, Pigeon Island lies just offshore. Jacques Cousteau called it one of the 10 best diving places in the world. The Nautilus Club at Malendure is one of the island's top scuba operations (tel. 590/ 98–85–89).

Souffleur, on the west coast of Grande-Terre, just outside of Port Louis, has brilliant flamboyant trees that bloom in the summer. There are no facilities on the beach, so take along a picnic. Stick around long enough for a super sunset.

Place Crawen, Les Saintes' quiet, secluded beach for skinny dipping, is a half mile of white sand on Terre-de-Haut. Facilities are within a five-minute walk at Bois Joli hotel (tel. 590/99– 50–38).

Petit Anse, on Marie-Galante, is a long gold-sand beach crowded with locals on weekends. During the week it's quiet, and there are no facilities other than the little seafood restaurant, La Touloulou.

Exploring Guadeloupe

Numbers in the margin correspond with points of interest on the Guadeloupe map.

Pointe-à-Pitre
❶

Pointe-à-Pitre is a city of some 100,000 people in the extreme southwest of Grande-Terre. It lies almost on the "backbone" of the butterfly, near the bridge that crosses the Salee River. In this bustling, noisy city, with its narrow streets, honking horns, and traffic jams, there is little of the relaxed, joyful mood one finds on many other Caribbean islands.

Life has not been easy for Pointe-à-Pitre. The city has suffered severe damage over the years as a result of earthquakes, fires, and hurricanes. The most recent damage was done in 1979 and 1980 by Hurricanes Frederick and David. Standing on boulevarde Frébault you can see on one side the remaining French colonial structures and on the other the modern city.

Stop at the Office of Tourism, a block off the quays where the cruise ships dock, to pick up maps and brochures. *Bonjour, Guadeloupe,* the free visitors' guide, is very useful.

When you leave the office, turn left, walk one block along rue Schoelcher, and turn right on rue Achille René-Boisneuf. Two more blocks will bring you to the **Musée St-John Perse.** The restored colonial house is dedicated to the Guadeloupean poet who won the 1960 Nobel Prize in Literature. (Nearby, at No. 54, rue René-Boisneuf, a plaque marks his birthplace.) The museum contains a complete collection of his poetry, as well as some of his personal effects. There are also works written about him, and various mementoes, documents, and photographs. *Corner rues Noizières and Achille René-Boisneuf, no phone. Admission: 10F. Open Mon.–Sat. 9–12:30 and 2–6.*

Rues Noizières, Frébault, and Schoelcher are Pointe-à-Pitre's main shopping streets. In sharp contrast to the duty-free shops is the bustling **Marketplace,** which you'll find by backtracking one block from the museum and turning right on rue Frébault. Located between rues St.-John Perse, Frébault, Schoelcher, and Peynier, the market is a cacophonous and colorful place where housewives bargain for papayas, breadfruit, christophine, tomatoes, and a vivid assortment of other produce.

Take a left at the corner of rues Schoelcher and Peynier. The **Musée Schoelcher** honors the memory of Victor Schoelcher, the 19th-century Alsatian abolitionist who fought slavery in the French West Indies. The museum contains many of his personal effects and the exhibits trace his life and work. *24 rue Peynier, tel. 590/82–08–04. Admission: 5F. Open weekdays 9–noon and 2:30–5:30.*

Walk back along rue Peynier past the market for three blocks. You'll come to **Place de la Victoire,** surrounded by wood buildings with balconies and shutters. The square was named in honor of Victor Hugues's 1794 victory over the British. The sandbox trees in the park are said to have been planted by Hugues the day after the victory. During the French Revolution, Hugues's guillotine in this square lopped off the heads of many a white aristocrat. Today the large palm-shaded park is a popular gathering place.

Rue Duplessis runs between the southern edge of the park and La Darse, where fishing boats dock and fast motorboats depart for the choppy ride to Marie-Galante and Les Saintes.

Rue Bebian is the western border of the square. Walk north along it (away from the harbor) and turn left on rue Alexandre Isaac. You'll see the imposing **Cathedral of St. Peter and St. Paul,** which dates from 1847. Mother Nature's rampages have wreaked havoc on the church, and it is now reinforced with iron ribs. Note the lovely stained glass windows.

Grande-Terre This round-trip tour of **Grande-Terre** will cover about 85 miles. Drive south out of Pointe-à-Pitre on Route N4 (named the "Riviera Road" in honor of the manmade beaches and resort hotels of Bas-du-Fort). The road goes past the marina, which is always crowded with yachts and sailboats.

② The road turns east and heads along the coast. In 2 miles you'll sight **Fort Fleur d'Epée,** an 18th-century fortress that hunkers on a hillside behind a deep moat. This was the scene of hard-fought battles between the French and English. You can explore the well-preserved dungeons and battlements, and on a clear day take in a sweeping view of Iles des Saintes and Marie-Galante.

③ The **Guadeloupe Aquarium** is just past the fort off the main highway. This aquarium, the Caribbean's largest and most modern, also ranks third in all of France. *Rte. N4, tel. 590/90–*

92–38. Admission: 15F adults, 10F children. Open weekdays 8:30–12:30 and 2:30–5:30, Sat. 8:30–5:30.

4 **Gosier,** a major tourist center 2 miles farther east, is a busy place indeed, with big hotels and tiny inns, cafés, discos, shops, and a long stretch of sand. The Creole Beach, the Auberge de la Vielle Tour–PLM Azur, and its cousin the Callinago–PLM Azur are among the hotels here.

Breeze along the coast through the little hamlet of St. Felix and on to **Ste. Anne,** about 8 miles east of Gosier. Only ruined sugar **5** mills remain from the days in the early 18th century when this village was a major sugar-exporting center. Sand has replaced sugar as the town's most valuable asset. The soft white-sand beaches here are among the best in Guadeloupe. The Club Med Caravelle occupies a secluded spot on the Caravelle Beach to the west of town, and there are several small Relais Creoles with their "feet in the sand." The hotel La Toubana sits on a bluff with its bungalows tumbling down to the beach, and the Relais du Moulin occupies one of the old sugar mills. On a more sober note, you'll pass St. Anne's lovely cemetery with stark-white above-ground tombs.

Don't fret about leaving the beaches of Ste. Anne behind you as you head eastward. The entire south coast of Grande-Terre is scalloped with white-sand beaches. Eight miles along, just be-**6** fore coming to the blue-roof houses of **St-François,** you'll come to the Raisins Clairs beach, another beauty.

St-François was once a simple little village primarily involved with fishing and tomatoes. The fish and tomatoes are still here, but so are some of the island's ritziest hotels. This is the home of the Hamak and the Meridien. Avenue de l'Europe runs between the well-groomed 18-hole Robert Trent Jones municipal golf course and the man-made marina. On the marina side, a string of shops and restaurants cater to tourists.

7 To reach **Pointe des Châteaux,** take the narrow road east from St. François and drive 8 miles out onto the rugged promontory that is the easternmost point on the island. The Atlantic and the Caribbean waters join here and crash against huge rocks, carving them into castle-like shapes. The jagged, majestic cliffs are reminiscent of the headlands of Brittany. The only human contribution to this dramatic scene is a white cross high on a hill above the tumultuous waters. From this point there are spectacular views of the south and east coasts of Guadeloupe and the distant cliffs of Désirade.

Time Out **Paillote** (no phone) is a tiny roadside stand right on the *pointe* where you can get libations and light bites.

About 3 miles from the farthest point, a rugged dirt road crunches off to the north and leads to the nudist beach, Pointe Tarare.

Take Route N5 north from St. François for a drive through fragrant silvery-green seas of sugarcane. About four miles beyond **8** St. François you'll see **Zévalos,** a handsome colonial mansion that was once the manor house of the island's largest sugar plantation.

9 Four miles northwest you'll come to **Le Moule,** a port city of about 17,000 people. This busy city was once the capital of

Guadeloupe. It was bombarded by the British in 1794 and 1809, and by a hurricane in 1928. Canopies of flamboyants hang over narrow streets where colorful vegetable and fish markets do a brisk business. Small buildings are of weathered wood with shutters, balconies, and bright awnings. The town hall, with graceful balustrades, and a small 19th-century neoclassical church are on the main square. Le Moule also has a beautiful crescent-shape beach.

⑩ North of Le Moule archaeologists have uncovered the remains of Arawak and Carib settlements. The **Edgar-Clerc Archaeological Museum** contains Amerindian artifacts from the personal collection of this well-known archaeologist and historian. There are several rooms with displays pertaining to the Carib and Arawak civilizations. *La Rosette, tel. 590/23-57-43. Admission free. Open Mon., Wed.–Fri., and Sun. 9:30–12:30 and 2:30–5:30; Sat. 9:30–5:30.*

From Le Moule you can turn west on Route D101 to return to Pointe-à-Pitre or continue northwest to see the rugged north coast.

⑪ To reach the coast, drive 8 miles northwest along Route D120 to Campêche, going through Gros Cap. At 1½ miles beyond Campêche, turn north on Route D122. **Porte d'Enfer** (Gate of Hell) marks a dramatic point on the coast where two jagged cliffs are stormed by the wild Atlantic waters. One legend has it that a Madame Coco strolled out across the waves carrying a parasol and vanished without a trace.

⑫ Four miles from Porte d'Enfer, **La Pointe de la Grande Vigie** is the northernmost tip of the island. Park your car and walk along the paths that lead right out to the edge. There is a splendid view from here of the Porte d'Enfer, and on a clear day you can see Antigua 35 miles away.

⑬ **Anse-Bertrand,** the northernmost village in Guadeloupe, lies 4 miles south of Pointe de la Grande Vigie along a gravel road. Drive carefully. En route to Anse Bertrand you'll pass another good beach, Anse Laborde. The area around Anse Bertrand was the last refuge of the Caribs. Most of the excitement these days takes place in the St. Jacques Hippodrome, where horse races and cockfights take place.

⑭ Route N6 will take you 5 miles south to **Port-Louis,** a fishing village of about 7,000. As you come in from the north, look for the turnoff to the Souffleur beach, one of the island's prettiest. The sand is fringed by flamboyant trees whose brilliant orange-red flowers bloom during the summer and early fall. The beach is crowded on weekends, but during the week it's blissfully quiet. The sunsets here are something to write home about.

Time Out **Poisson d'Or** is a rustic seaside restaurant that features spicy Creole dishes. *Rue Sadi Carnot, Port Louis, tel. 590/84-90-22. No credit cards.*

⑮ From Port Louis the road leads 5 miles south through mangrove swamps to Petit Canal where it turns inland. Three miles east of Petit Canal turn right on the main road. Head 6 miles south to **Morne-à-l'Eau,** an agricultural city of about 16,000 people. Morne-à-l'Eau's unusual amphitheater-shape cemetery is the scene of a moving (and photogenic) candlelight service on

All Saint's Day. Take Route N5 out of town along gently undulating hills past fields of sugarcane and dairy farms.

Just south of Morne-à-l'Eau are the villages of **Jabrun du Sud** and **Jabrun du Nord,** which are inhabited by the descendants of the "Blancs Matignon," the whites who hid in the hills and valleys of the Grands Fonds after the abolition of slavery in 1848.

Continue on Route N5 to Pointe-à-Pitre.

Basse-Terre: There is high adventure on the butterfly's west wing, which **The Southern Half** swirls with mountain trails and lakes, waterfalls, and hot springs. Basse-Terre is the home of the Old Lady, as the Soufrière volcano is called locally, as well as of the capital, also called Basse-Terre.

Guadeloupe's de rigueur tour takes you through the 74,100-acre Natural Park, a sizable chunk of Basse-Terre. Before going, pick up a *Guide to the Natural Park* from the Tourist Office, which rates the hiking trails according to difficulty.

The Route de la Traversée (La Traversée) is a good paved road that runs east–west, cutting a 16-mile-long swath through the park to the west coast village of Mahaut. La Traversée divides Basse-Terre into two almost equal sections. The majority of mountain trails falls into the southern half. Allow a full day for this excursion. Wear rubber-sole shoes, and take along both swimsuit and sweater, and perhaps food for a picnic.

Begin your tour by heading west from Pointe-à-Pitre on Route N1, crossing the Rivière Salée on the Pont de la Gabare drawbridge. At the Destrelan traffic circle turn left and drive 6 miles south through sweet-scented fields of sugarcane to the Route de la Traversée (aka D23), where you'll turn west.

As soon as you cross the bridge you'll begin to see the riches produced by Basse-Terre's fertile volcanic soil and heavier rainfall. La Traversée is lined with masses of thick tree-ferns, shrubs, flowers, tall trees, and green plantains that stand like soldiers in a row.

Five miles from where you turned off Route N1 you'll come to a junction. Turn left and go a little over a mile south to **Vernou.** Traipsing along a path that leads beyond the village through
⑯ the lush forest you'll come to the pretty waterfall at **Saut de la Lezard,** the first of many you'll see.

Back on La Traversée, 3 miles farther, you'll come to the next
⑰ one, **Cascade aux Ecrevisse.** Park your car and walk along the marked trail that leads to a splendid waterfall dashing down into the Corossol River (a fit place for a dip). Walk carefully— the rocks along the trail can be slippery.

⑱ Two miles farther along La Traversée you'll come to the **Parc Tropical de Bras-David,** where you can park and explore various nature trails. The **Maison de la Forêt** (admission free, open daily 9–5) has a variety of displays that describe (for those who can read French) the flora, fauna, and topography of the Natural Park. There are picnic tables where you can enjoy your lunch in tropical splendor.

Two and a half miles more will bring you to the two mountains
⑲ known as **Les Mamelles**—Mamelle de Petit-Bourg at 2,350 feet, and the Mamelle de Pigeon at 2,500 feet. (*Mamelle* means breast, and when you see the mountains you'll understand why

they are so named.) There is a spectacular view from the pass that runs between the Mamelles to the south and a lesser mountain to the north. From this point, trails ranging from easy to arduous lace up into the surrounding mountains. There's a glorious view from the lookout point 1,969 feet up the Mamelle de Pigeon. If you're a climber, you'll want to spend several hours exploring this area.

20 You don't have to be much of a hiker to climb the stone steps leading from the road to the **Zoological Park and Botanical Gardens.** Titi the Raccoon is the mascot of the Natural Park. There are also cockatoos, iguanas, and turtles. *La Traversée, no phone. Admission: 20F adults, 10F children. Open daily 9–5.*

On the winding 4-mile descent from the mountains to **Mahaut** you'll see patches of the blue Caribbean through the green trees. In the village of Mahaut turn left on Route N2 for the drive south along the coast. In less than a mile you'll come to **Malendure.** The big attraction here is offshore on **Pigeon Island** (*see* Beaches, above). Club Nautilus and Chez Guy, both on the Malendure Beach, conduct dive trips, and the glass-bottom *Aquarium* and *Nautilus* make daily snorkeling trips to the spectacular site.

Time Out At **La Touna,** (Malendure Beach, tel. 590/98–70–10) right by the sea, you can sit on the veranda with a rum punch, feast on the catch of the day, and also arrange for fishing excursions at the Fishing Club Antilles.

21 From Malendure continue through neighboring **Bouillante,** where hot springs burst up through the earth, and
22 **Vieux-Habitants,** one of the oldest settlements on the island. Pause to see the restored church, which dates from 1650, before driving 8 miles south to the capital city.

Basse-Terre **Basse-Terre,** the capital and administrative center, is an active
23 city of about 15,000 people. Founded in 1640, it has had even more difficulties than Pointe-à-Pitre. The capital has endured not only foreign attacks and hurricanes but sputtering threats from La Soufrière as well. More than once it has been evacuated when the volcano began to hiss and fume. The last major eruption was in the 16th century. But the volcano seemed active enough to warrant the evacuation of more than 70,000 people in 1975.

The centers of activity are the port and the market, both of which you'll pass along Boulevard Général de Gaulle. The 17th-century **Fort St. Charles** at the extreme south end of town, and the **Cathedral of Our Lady of Guadeloupe** to the north, across the Rivière aux Herbes, are worth a short visit. Drive along Boulevard Felix Eboue to see the colonial buildings that house government offices. Follow the boulevard to the **Jardin Pichon** to see its beautiful gardens. Stop off at **Champ d'Arbaud,** an Old World square surrounded by colonial buildings. Continue along the boulevard to the **Botanical Gardens,** another pleasant place to stop and smell the flowers. A steep, narrow road leads 4
24 miles up to the suburb of **St-Claude,** on the slopes of La Soufrière. In St-Claude there are picnic tables and good views of the volcano. You can also get a closer look at the volcano by driving up to the Savane à Mulets. From there leave your car and hike the strenuous two-hour climb (with an experienced guide) to the summit at 4,813 feet, the highest point in the

Lesser Antilles. Water boils out of the eastern slope of the volcano and spills into the Carbet Falls.

㉕ Drive 2 miles farther north from St-Claude to visit **Matouba, a** village settled by East Indians whose descendants still practice ancient rites including animal sacrifice. If you've an idle 10 hours or so, take off from Matouba for a 19-mile hike on a marked trail through the Monts Caraibes to the east coast.

Descend and continue east on Route N1 for 4 miles to
㉖ **Gourbeyre.** Visit **Etang As de Pique.** Reaching this lake, located 2,454 feet above the town, is another challenge for hikers, but you can also reach it in an hour by car via paved Palmetto Road. The 5-acre lake, formed by a lava flow, is shaped like an *as de pique* (ace of spades).

From Gourbeyre you have the option of continuing east along Route N1 or taking the roller-coaster Route D6 along the coast. Either route will take you through lush greenery to **Trois Rivières** on the southeast coast.

㉗ Not far from the ferry landing for Les Saintes, the **Parc Archéologique des Roches Gravées** contains a collection of rock engravings dating from the Arawak and Carib periods. Pick up an information sheet at the park's entrance. Displays interpret the figures of folk and fauna depicted on the petroglyphs. The park is set in a lovely botanical garden. *Trois Rivières, no phone. Admission free. Open daily 9–5.*

Continue through banana fields and the village of Bananier for
㉘ 5 miles to reach the village of **St. Sauveur,** gateway to the magnificent **Chutes du Cabaret** (Cabaret Falls). Three of the *chutes,* which drop from 65 feet, 360 feet, and 410 feet, can be reached by following the narrow, steep, and spiraling Habituée Road for 5 miles up past the **Grand Etang** (Great Pond). At the end of the road you'll have to proceed on foot. Well-marked but slippery trails lead to viewing points of the *chutes.*

Time Out   You can have a hearty lunch of Creole chicken, goat curry, or crayfish at **Chez Dollin-Le Crepuscule** (Habituée Village, tel. 590/86–34–56) before or after viewing the falls. There's also a four-course menu.

Continue along Route N1 for 3 miles to **Capesterre-Belle-Eau.**
㉙ You'll cross the Carbet River and come to **Dumanoir Alley,** lined with century-old royal palms.

Three miles farther along, through fields of pineapple, banan-
㉚ as, and sugarcane, you'll arrive at **Ste. Marie,** where Columbus landed in 1493. In the town there is a monument to the Great Discoverer.

Seventeen miles farther north you'll return to Pointe-à-Pitre.

Iles des Saintes   This eight-island archipelago, usually referred to as Les
㉛ Saintes, dots the waters off the south coast of Guadeloupe. The islands are Terre-de-Haut, Terre-de-Bas, Ilet à Cabrit, Grand Ilet, La Redonde, La Coche, Le Pâté, and Les Augustins. Columbus discovered the islands on November 4, 1493, and christened them Los Santos in honor of All Saints' Day.

Of the islands, only Terre-de-Haute and Terre-de-Bas are inhabited, with a combined population of 3,260. Les Saintois, as the islanders are called, are fair-haired, blue-eyed descendants of Breton and Norman sailors. Fishing is the main source of income for Les Saintois, and the shores are lined with their fishing boats and *filets bleus* (blue nets dotted with burnt-orange buoys). The fishermen wear hats called *salakos*, which look like inverted saucers or coolie hats. They are patterned after a hat said to have been brought here by a seafarer from China or Indonesia. Almost no English is spoken on the islands.

With 5 square miles and a population of about 1,500, Terre-de-Haut is the largest island and the most developed for tourism. Its big city is Bourg, which boasts one street and a few bistros, cafés, and shops. Clutching the hillside are trim white houses with bright red or blue doors, balconies, and gingerbread frills.

Arrival on Terre-de-Haut is an exhilarating affair, whether by land or by sea. Air Guadeloupe has regularly scheduled flights, and your whole life may flash before your eyes as you soar down to the tiny airstrip. However, the flight is mercifully brief and you may prefer it to the choppy ferry crossings from Trois Rivières.

Terre-de-Haut's ragged coastline is scalloped with lovely coves and beaches, including the nudist beach at Anse Crawen. The beautiful bay, complete with sugarloaf, has been called a "mini Rio." This is a quiet, peaceful getaway, but it may not remain unspoiled. At present, tourism accounts for 20%–30% of the economy. Although government plans call for a total of only 250 hotel rooms, the tourist-related industries are making a major pitch for tourists.

There are three paved roads on the island, but don't even think about driving here. The roads are ghastly, and backing up is a minor art form choreographed on those frequent occasions when two vehicles meet on one of the steep, narrow roads. There are four minibuses that transport passengers from the airstrip and the wharf and double as tour buses. However, the island is so small you can get around by walking. It's a mere five-minute stroll from the airstrip to downtown Bourg.

32 **Fort Napoleon** is a relic from the period when the French fortified these islands against the Caribs and the English, but nobody has ever fired a shot at it or from it. The nearby museum contains a collection of 250 modern paintings. You can also visit the well-preserved barracks, prison cells, and museum, and admire the surrounding botanical gardens. From the fort you can see Fort Josephine across the channel on the Ilet à Cabrit. *Bourg, no tel. Admission: 10F. Open daily 9–noon.*

For so tiny a place, Terre-de-Haut offers a variety of hotels and restaurants. For details, *see* Dining and Lodging, below.

Marie-Galante
33 If you take the ferry to this flat island, you'll put in to Grand Bourg, its major city with a population of about 8,000. A plane will land you 2 miles from Grand Bourg. If your French or your phrase book are good enough, you can negotiate with the taxi drivers for a price for touring the island.

With about 60 square miles, this is the largest of Guadeloupe's offshore islands. It is dotted with ruined 19th-century sugar mills, and sugar is still one of its major products (the others are cotton and rum). One of the last refuges of the Caribs when they were driven from the mainland by the French, the island is a favorite retreat of Guadeloupeans who come on weekends to enjoy the beach at Petite Anse.

Columbus discovered the island on November 3, 1493, the day before he landed at Ste. Marie on Basse-Terre. He named it for his flagship, the *Maria Galanda*, and sailed on.

There are several places near the ferry landing where you can get an inexpensive meal of seafood and Creole sauce. If you want to stay over, you can choose from the La Salut, in St.-Louis (15 rooms, tel. 590/97–02–67); Auberge de l'Arbre à Pain (7 rooms, tel. 590/97–73–69) or Soledad (20 rooms, tel. 590/97–75–45) in Grand Bourg. An entertainment complex in Grand Bourg El Rancho has a 400-seat movie theater, restaurant, terrace grill, snack bar, disco, and a few double rooms.

La Désirade According to legend, this island is the "desired land" of
34 Columbus's second voyage. He spotted it on November 3, 1493. The 8-square-mile island, 5 miles east of St. François, was for many years a leper colony. The main settlement is Grande Anse, where there is a pretty church and a hotel called La Guitoune. Nothing fancy, but the restaurant serves excellent seafood. Most of the 1,600 inhabitants are fishermen.

There are good beaches here, notably Souffleur and Baie Mahault, and there's little to do but loll around on them. The island is virtually unspoiled by tourism and likely to remain so, at least for the foreseeable future.

Three or four minibuses meet the flights and ferries, and you can negotiate with one of them to give you a tour.

Participant Sports

Bicycling The relatively flat terrain of Grande-Terre makes for easy wheeling. See Christian Rolle at **Veló-Vert** (Pointe-à-Pitre, tel. 590/83–15–74) to rent bikes and maps that cover a 270-mile tour. **Le Relais du Moulin** (near Ste. Anne, tel. 590/88–23–96) offers bike tours. You can also rent bikes at **Cyclo-Tours** (Gosier, tel. 590/84–11–34), **Le Flamboyant** (St. François, tel. 590/84–45–51), and **Rent-a-Bike** (Meridien Hotel, St. François, tel. 590/84–51–00). For information about cycling tours from the United States to Guadeloupe, contact **Country Cycling Tours** (140 W. 83rd St., New York, NY 10024, tel. 212/874–5151).

Boating If you plan to sail these waters, you should be aware that the winds and currents of Guadeloupe tend to be strong. There are excellent, well-equipped marinas in Pointe-à-Pitre, Bas-du-Fort, Deshaies, St. François, and Gourbeyre. Bare-boat or crewed yachts can be rented in Bas-du-Fort at **Locaraibes** (tel. 590/90–82–80), **Vacances Yachting Antilles** (tel. 590/90–82–95), and **Soleil et Voile** (tel. 590/90–81–81). All beachfront hotels rent Hobie Cats, Sunfish, pedal boats, motorboats, and water skis.

Deep-Sea Fishing Half- and full-day trips in search of bonito, dolphin, captainfish, barracuda, kingfish, and tuna can be arranged through **Fishing Club Antilles** (Bouillante, tel. 590/84–15–00), **Nautilus Club** (Bouillante, tel. 590/98–85–69), and **Papyrus** (Marina Bas-du-Fort, tel. 590/90–92–98).

Fitness The **PLM Azur Marissol** (Bas-du-Fort, tel. 590/90–84–44) offers gym facilities for calisthenics, stretching, water exercises in pool or sea, yoga, and beauty care.

Golf   Golf Municipal Saint-François (St-François, tel. 590/88–41–87) has an 18-hole Robert Trent Jones course, an English-speaking pro, a clubhouse, a pro shop, and electric carts for rental.

Hiking   Basse-Terre's Natural Park is laced with fascinating trails, many of which should be attempted only with an experienced guide. Trips for up to 12 people are arranged by **Organisation des Guides de Montagne de la Caraibe (O.G.M.C.)** (Maison Forestière, Matouba, tel. 590/80–05–79).

Horseback Riding   Beach rides, picnics, and lessons are available through **Le Criolo** (St. Felix, tel. 590/84–38–90) and **Le Relais du Moulin** (Châteaubrun, between Ste. Anne and St. François, tel. 590/88–23–96).

Scuba Diving   Guides and instructors here are certified under the French CMAS rather than PADI or NAUI. To explore the wrecks and reefs, contact **Nautilus Club** (Bouillante, tel. 590/98–85–69) or **Chez Guy** (Bouillante, tel. 590/98–81–72).

Sea Excursions and Snorkeling   Most hotels rent snorkeling gear and post information about excursions. The *Papyrus* (Marina Bas-du-Fort, tel. 590/90–92–98) is a glass-bottom catamaran that offers full-day outings replete with rum, dances, and games, as well as moonlight sails. Glass-bottom boats also make snorkeling excursions to Pigeon Island (*see* Scuba Diving, above). The sailing school **Evasion Marine** (locations in St. François and Bas-du-Fort, tel. 590/84–46–67) offers excursions on board the *Ginn Fizz*, the *Ketch*, or the *Sloop*.

Tennis   Courts are located at the following hotels: **Arawak** (2 courts), **Auberge de la Vielle Tour** (1 court), **Caravelle/Club Med** (6 courts), **La Creole Beach** (2 courts), **Golf Marine Club** (2 courts), **Hamak** (1 court), **Les Marines de St. François** (2 courts), **Meridien** (5 courts), **Novotel Fleur d'Epée** (2 courts), **PLM Azur Marissol** (2 courts), **Relais du Moulin** (1 court), **Residence Karukera** (1 court), **Salako** (2 courts), and **Toubana** (1 court). Games can also be arranged through the **St. François Tennis Club** (tel. 590/88–41–87).

Windsurfing   Immensely popular here, windsurfing rentals and lessons are available at all beachfront hotels.

Shopping

If shopping is your goal and you're headed for a French island, head for Martinique—service is friendlier and the language less of a barrier. But if you insist on shopping in Guadeloupe, visit Pointe-à-Pitre. Get an early start as it gets very hot and sticky around midday.

Many stores offer a 20% discount on luxury items purchased with traveler's checks or, in some cases, major credit cards. You can find good buys on anything French—perfumes, crystal, china, cosmetics, fashions, scarves. As for local handcrafted items, you'll see a lot of junk, but you can also find island dolls dressed in madras, finely woven straw baskets and hats, salako hats made of split bamboo, madras table linens, and wood carvings. And, of course, the favorite Guadeloupean souvenir—rum.

Shopping Areas   In Pointe-à-Pitre the main shopping streets are **Rue Schoelcher, Rue Nozières,** and **Rue Frébault.** Bas-du-Fort's two shopping districts are the **Mammouth Shopping Center** and the

Marina, where there are 20 or so boutiques and several restaurants. In **St-François** there are also several shops surrounding the marina. Many of the resorts have fashion boutiques. There are also a number of duty-free shops at Raizet Airport.

Good Buys
China, Crystal, and Silver For Baccarat, Lalique, Porcelaine de Paris, Limoges, and other upscale tableware, check **Selection** (rue Schoelcher, Pointe-à-Pitre, no phone), **A la Pensée** (44 rue Frébault, Pointe-à-Pitre, tel. 590/82–10–47), and **Rosebleu** (5 rue Frébault, Pointe-à-Pitre, tel. 590/82–93–44).

Cosmetics Guadeloupe's exclusive purveyor of Orlane, Stendhal, and Germaine Monteil is **Vendome** (8–10 rue Frébault, Pointe-à-Pitre, tel. 590/83–42–84).

Native Crafts **Tim Tim** (16 rue Henri IV, tel. 590/83–48–71) is an upscale nostalgia shop with elegant (and expensive) antiques ranging from Creole furniture to maps. For doudou dolls, straw hats, baskets, and madras table linens, try **Au Caraibe** (4 rue Frébault, Pointe-à-Pitre). Anthuriums and other plants that pass muster at U.S. customs are packaged at **Casafleurs** (42 rue René-Boisneuf, tel. 590/82–31–23, and Raizet Airport, tel. 590/82–33–34) and **Floral Antilles** (80 rue Schoelcher, tel. 590/82–18–63, and Raizet Airport, tel. 590/82–97–65).

Perfumes Sweet buys can be found at **Phoenicia** (3 locations in Pointe-à-Pitre: 93 rue de Nozières, tel. 590/82–17–66; 8 rue Frébault, tel. 590/83–50–36; and 121 rue Frébault, tel. 590/82–22–22), **Au Bonheur des Dames** (49 rue Frébault, Pointe-à-Pitre, tel. 590/82–00–30), and **L'Artisan Parfumeur** (rue Schoelcher, Pointe-à-Pitre, no phone).

Rum and Tobacco **Delice Shop** (45 rue Achille René-Boisneuf, Pointe-à-Pitre, tel. 590/82–98–24), **Ets Azincourt** (13 rue Henry IV, Pointe-à-Pitre, tel. 590/82–21–02), and **Comptoir sous Douane** (Raizet Airport, tel. 590/82–22–76) have good choices of island rum as well as tobacco.

Dining

The food here is superb. Many of Guadeloupe's restaurants feature seafood (shellfish is a great favorite), often flavored with rich herbs and spices à la Creole. Favorite appetizers are *accras* (codfish fritters), *boudin* (highly seasoned pork sausage), and *crabes farcis* (stuffed land crabs). Christophine is a vegetable pear (as plantain is considered a vegetable banana—served as a side dish) that appears in a variety of costumes. *Blaff* is a spicy fish stew. Lobster, turtle steak, and *lambi* (conch) are often among the main dishes, and homemade coconut ice cream is a typical dessert. The island boasts 100 restaurants, including those serving classic French, Italian, African, Indian, Vietnamese, and South American fare. The local libation of choice is the *'ti punch* (little "poonch," as it is pronounced)—a heady concoction of rum, lime juice, and sugarcane syrup. The innocent-sounding little punch packs a powerful wallop.

The most highly recommended restaurants are indicated by a star ★.

Category	Cost*
Expensive	over $35
Moderate	$25–$35
Inexpensive	under $25

*per person, excluding drinks

Grande-Terre **Auberge de St-François.** Claude Simon's country home is set in
★ an orchard and his tables are set with Royal Doulton china and
fine crystal. Dining is indoors or on one of the flower-filled patios, with a superb view of Marie Galante and Pointe des
Châteaux. The house specialty is crayfish served several different ways. Also try brochette of smoked shark with a pepper
sauce or conch. *St-François, tel. 590/88-51-71. Reservations
essential. Jacket required. Closed Sun. No credit cards. Expensive.*

★ **Auberge de la Vielle Tour.** A Guadeloupean favorite where chef
Gilles Ballereau's superb cuisine is artistically presented in a
stylish, air-conditioned room with intimate lighting. The large
windows afford a splendid view of Ilet du Gosier. A la carte offerings include fresh duck foie gras, sliced pork fillet in saffron
sauce, and salmon and dorado with banana butter. Finish with
French cheeses and a cup of potent coffee. There is an extensive
(and expensive) wine list. *Gosier, tel. 590/84-23-23. Reservations required. Jackets required. No lunch. AE, DC, MC, V.
Expensive.*

Le Balata. Pierre and Marie Cecillon present classic Lyonnaise
cuisine with Creole touches. Begin with chicken liver in aspic,
then contemplate the catch of the day with parslied butter. A
special businessman's lunch is available at 90F, including wine.
Reserve early for one of the eight tables on the terrace with a
view of Fort Fleur d'Epée. *Route de Labrousse, Gosier, tel. 590/
90-88-25. Closed Sun. for dinner. AE, DC, V. Expensive.*

Le Bistrot. A path from the main road leads down to this eatery,
from which there is a splendid view of the coast. Openers include a spicy fish soup. Among the main dishes are stingray
with black-butter sauce, shark steak with fresh pasta, crayfish
mousse, and rib steaks. For dessert, don't miss the walnut pie
and praline ice cream with chocolate-rum-raisin sauce. *Petit
Havre, between Gosier and Ste. Anne, tel. 590/88-91-82. Reservations suggested for dinner. Closed Sun., Mon., and July.
AE, V. Expensive.*

★ **La Canne à Sucre.** Some of the best food in the Caribbean comes
out of the kitchen of this restored colonial house in the center of
the city. The original and unusual recipes of Gerard Virginius
include chicken breast stuffed with conch and sea urchins sautéed with lime and spices. Partner Bruno Deligne created
grilled lobster "Bruno-style." Among the lavish desserts is
coupe Canne à Sucre, with rum, coconut sherbet, banana, caramel, whipped cream, and a dash of cinnamon. *17 rue Henri IV,
Pointe-à-Pitre, tel. 590/82-10-19 or 590/83-58-48. Reservations essential. Jackets required. No lunch Sat.; closed Sun.
AE, V. Expensive.*

Château de Feuilles. Take a dip in the pool or stroll around the
2-acre farm of this country home while waiting for your lunch.
The changing menu may include goose *rillettes*, breaded conch,
tuna carpaccio, swordfish with sorrel, or sardines grilled with
lime and green pepper. Follow the green and white arrows that
begin outside Le Moule or Anse Bertrand. *Campèche, tel. 590/*

22–19–10. Reservations required. V. No dinner. Expensive.

Le Flibustier. This rustic hilltop farmhouse is a favorite with staffers from neighboring Club Med. A complete dinner of mixed salad, grilled lobster, coconut ice cream, petit punch, and half a pitcher of wine is $26. A lively, fun place. *La Colline, Fonds Thézan (between Ste. Anne and St. Felix, tel. 590/88–23–36. Closed Mon., no lunch Sun. No credit cards. Moderate–Expensive.*

★ **Le Galion.** The Ecotel Hotel's dining room is a training ground for student cooks, waiters, and waitresses. The menu changes with the visiting French master chefs and apprentices, but usually includes red snapper and lobster prepared in various ways. Gourmet galas are prepared twice a month by visiting chefs for about $36 per person. *Ecotel, Montauban, Gosier, tel. 590/84–15–66. Reservations suggested. Jackets required. No lunch. AE, DC, MC, V. Moderate–Expensive.*

Les Oiseaux. Claudette and Arthur Rolle's menu includes filet en croute with red wine sauce, as well as some unusual dishes such as *Marmite de Robinson,* a fish fondue with dorado, kingfish, tuna, shrimp, and local vegetables. Shellfish aficionados should try *cigale de mer,* which is sea cricket, a member of the shrimp family. *Anse des Rochers, tel. 590/88–56–92. Reservations essential. Closed Thurs., Sun. dinner. V. Moderate–Expensive.*

★ **Relais du Moulin.** The restaurant of this inn overlooks a restored windmill. Inside, nouvelle cuisine includes the house specialty: grouper and lobster in puff pastry with saffron flowers. Crème caramel in coconut sauce is among the sumptuous desserts. By day sunlight floods through large windows; by night, candles flicker on crisp white cloths. *Châteaubrun (between Ste. Anne and St-François), tel. 590/88–13–78. AE, DC, MC, V. Moderate–Expensive.*

★ **La Grande Pizzeria.** Open late and very popular, this seaside spot serves pizza, pasta, salads, and some Milanese, Bolognese, and other Italian seafood specialties. *Bas-du-Fort, tel. 590/92–82–64. No reservations. Moderate.*

La Mandingo. In a gardenside dining room, chef Gilles Dontevieux turns out smoked kingfish salad, spicy palourdes Gouverneur, giant Guyanese grilled shrimp, and chicken with crayfish. At lunch, grilled meat and fish are served on an outdoor terrace. It's a popular disco by night. *Gosier Beach, tel. 590/84–35–59. MC, V. Moderate.*

★ **La Mouette.** Tables in a gazebo and in the front yard for barefoot and bathing-suit lunching. Grilled lobster, curried goat, ragouts, accras, and stuffed or roasted trunkfish are on the menu. *Pointe des Châteaux, tel. 590/88–62–52. Closed Tues. and Sun. dinner. No credit cards. Moderate.*

Le Paille En Queue. For a change of pace you might try the Vietnamese, Chinese, and Reunionnaise offerings in this large, informal terrace setting. If your taste buds can't take tearproducing spices, stay away from the Reunionnaise dishes. There are à la carte listings as well as $16 menus that change every other day. *La Rocade, Gosier, tel. 590/84–16–20. V. Moderate.*

Le Zagaya. Dine with a background of classical music on crabes farcis or accras for openers, and lobster, fish, and meat cooked on an outdoor grill in this small, romantic seaside terrace restaurant. The desserts are homemade. *Rue de la République, St-François, tel. 590/88–40–94. No credit cards. Closed Mon. Moderate.*

★ **Chez Violetta-La Creole.** Head of Guadeloupe's association of cuisinières (lady chefs), award-winning Violetta Chaville presents an à la carte menu of traditional Creole dishes. You'll be served by waitresses in madras and foulard garb. The restaurant is popular with American visitors. *Eastern outskirts of Gosier Village, tel. 590/84–10–34. No credit cards. Moderate-Inexpensive.*

★ **L'Amour en Fleurs.** Close to Club Med (and very popular with its guests), this is an unpretentious little roadhouse where the award-winning Madame Tresor Amanthe prepares spicy blaffs, boudin, a tasty blend of conch, octopus, rice and beans, and court bouillon. Don't miss the homemade coconut ice cream. *Ste. Anne, tel. 590/88–23–72. No credit cards. Inexpensive.*

★ **Le Barbaroc.** People come from all over the island to the rustic 12-table restaurant to feast on Félicité Doloir's imaginative Creole creations. Among the three dozen dishes listed are pureed breadfruit, *poulet du pays cuit fume* (smoked chicken), breadfruit and other vegetable soufflés, and sweet potato noodles. She also brews beer and concocts *moabie*, a nonalcoholic drink made from tree bark, and "punch de maison," a secret mixture of local fruits and rum. The energetic Madame Doloir also conducts culinary/historic tours of the area. *Petit Canal, tel. 590/22–62–71. Reservations advised. No credit cards. Dinner only, closed Wed. Inexpensive.*

Folie Plage. North of Anse Bertrand, this lively spot is especially popular with families on weekends. In addition to the reliable Creole food of Prudence Marcelin, there is a children's wading pool, a boutique, and a disco on weekends. Superb courtbouillon and imaginative curried dishes. *Anse Laborde, tel. 590/22–11–17. Reservations suggested. No credit cards. Inexpensive.*

Basse-Terre ★ **Chez Clara.** This restaurant is popular and crowded even in the off-season. Clara Laseur and her mother turn out Creole dishes with daily specials listed on the blackboard. Clara (whose English is excellent) gave up a jazz-dancing career in Paris to run her family's seaside restaurant. Clara takes the orders, and the place is often so crowded with her friends and fans that you may have to wait for her to get around to you. The food is worth the wait. *Ste. Rose, tel. 590/28–72–99. Reservations advised. Closed Wed., Sun. dinner, Oct. CB, MC, V. Moderate-Inexpensive.*

★ **Le Karacoli.** Lucienne Salcede's rustic seaside restaurant is well-established and well-regarded. The restaurant has its feet firmly planted in the sands of Grande Anse, a great place for a swim. Creole boudin is a hot item here, as are accras. Other offerings include coquilles Karacoli, courtboullion, fried chicken, and turtle ragout. For dessert, try the banana flambé. *Grande Anse, north of Deshaies, tel. 590/28–41–17. No dinner Sat.-Thurs., closed Fri. CB, MC, V. Moderate-Inexpensive.*

★ **Chez Jacky.** Jacqueline Cabrion serves Creole and African dishes in her cheerful seaside restaurant. Creole boudin is featured, as are lobster (grilled, vinaigrette, or fricassee), fried crayfish, and ragout of lamb. There's also a wide selection of omelets, sandwiches, and salads. For dessert, try peach melba or banana flambé. *Anse Guyonneau, Pte. Noire, tel. 590/98–06–98. Closed Sun. dinner. AE, MC, V. Inexpensive.*

Les Gommiers. Lovely peacock chairs grace the bar of this stylish restaurant. The changing menu may list beef tongue in mango sauce, lobster in sauce piquante, filet of beef Roquefort, escallopes of veal, and grilled entrecote. Banana split and profiterolles are on the dessert list. Light lunches include salade Nicoise. *Rue Baudot, Pte. Noire, tel. 590/98–01–79. Closed Mon., Wed. dinner. CB, MC, V. Inexpensive.*

Iles des Saintes, Terre-de-Haute
★ **Le Foyal.** This delightful seaside terrace restaurant serves a sophisticated mélange of Creole and Continental dishes. Begin with a warm crepe filled with lobster, conch, octopus, and fish; crabe farci; or a rillette of smoked fish. A house specialty is an assiette of smoked fish served cold; another is stuffed fish fillet served in a white wine sauce. A special plate for children under 10 is also offered. *Anse Mirre, tel. 590/99–50–92. No credit cards. Moderate–Inexpensive.*

★ **Relais des Iles.** Select your lobster from the *vivier* and enjoy the splendid view from this hilltop eatery while your meal is expertly prepared by Bernard Mathieu. Imaginative things are done with local vegetables. For dessert try the melt-in-your-mouth chocolate mousse. Choose your spirits from an excellent wine list. *Rte. de Pompierre, tel. 590/99–53–04. Reservations suggested in high season. No credit cards. Moderate–Inexpensive.*

Lodging

Gosier is the main venue for resort hotels, but the areas around St. François and St. Anne also have their fair share of resorts. You can choose between a splashy hotel with a full complement of resort activities or head for a small inn called a Relais Creole. All the inns have met certain guidelines for their beauty or location by the Guadeloupe tourist office and all have a decidedly Gallic accent. But if French is not your forte, you'll fare better in the large hotels. Most hotels include Continental breakfast in their rates (a few include full American breakfast).

The most highly recommended lodgings are indicated by a star ★.

Category	Cost*
Very Expensive	over $280
Expensive	$150–$280
Moderate	$110–$150
Inexpensive	under $110

All prices are for a standard double room for two, excluding a taxe de séjour that varies from hotel to hotel, and a 10%–15% service charge.

★ **Hamak.** Five landscaped acres, a private white-sand beach, and even a small fleet of twin-engine planes for transporting guests make this a superb place for getting away from it all in high style. One-bedroom suites are in bungalows. Each unit has a living room, small bedroom, kitchenette, a private rear patio with outdoor freshwater shower and a front terrace with hammock. All are air-conditioned, with large bath, twin beds, hair dryer, and international direct-dial phone. TV and videos are available. *St-François 97118, tel. 590/88–59–99 or 800/366–1510). 56 units. Facilities: restaurant, 2 bars, lighted tennis court, water-sport center. AE, DC, MC, V. Very Expensive.*

★ **Auberge de la Vielle Tour PLM-Azur.** This fine hotel with the ambience of a country inn is only three blocks from the Gosier center. The main building occupies a hilltop on a 7-acre estate, with green hills rolling down to the rooms and small private beach. Some of the rooms are rather small and simply furnished, though outfitted with minibars, TV, air-conditioners, and spacious baths. Eight rooms have upscale amenities, such as terry-cloth robes. At press time, rooms were being upgraded. In high season, breakfast, lunch, and barbecues are served at the terrace restaurant at the pool level. Robert Zarkis's orchestra plays nightly in the formal dining room. Water-sport equipment is available for guests Callinago PLM-Azur. *Montauban Gosier 97190, tel. 590/84–23–23 or 800/223–9862. 80 rooms. Facilities: 2 restaurants, bar, boutiques, 2 lighted tennis courts, pool. AE, DC, MC, V. Expensive.*

La Creole Beach. Set in 10 acres of tropical greenery, this Leader Hotel boasts two beaches and spacious rooms. All rooms have individually controlled air-conditioners, TV, VCR, radio, international direct-dial phones, and sliding glass doors onto a balcony. Water activities include boat excursions to Ilet du Gosier. *Box 19, Gosier 97190, tel. 590/84–26–26 or 800/366–1510. 156 rooms. Facilities: restaurant, bar, pool, 2 lighted tennis courts, car-rental desk, boat excursions, water-sport center. Expensive.*

Fleur d'Epée Novotel. This upscale beachfront property offers rooms with a queen-size and a single bed, blue onyx baths, satellite TV, radio, phones, and balconies (some with a sea view). An activities director organizes steel band shows and other entertainment. *Bas du Fort, Gosier 97190, tel. 590/90–81–49 or 800/221–4542. 186 rooms. Facilities: 2 restaurants, 1 snack bar, pool, 2 tennis courts, water-sports center. AE, DC, MC, V. Expensive.*

Club Med Caravelle. Occupying 50 secluded acres at the western end of a magnificent white-sand beach, this version of the well-known villages has air-conditioned twin-bed rooms, some with balconies. Activities include a French-English language lab, yoga, volleyball, calisthenics, and water sports. *Ste. Anne 97180, tel. 590/88–21–00 or 800/258–2633. 275 rooms. Facilities: restaurant, pub, boutiques, 6 lighted tennis courts (with pro), pool, water-sports center. AE. Moderate–Expensive.*

★ **Meridien.** This hotel is recommended for those who want to pack as much activity as possible into a vacation. This 150-acre resort puts out its own *A to Z Leisure Guide*, and broadcasts from Radio Meridien to let you know about resort activities. The activities director organizes everything from bocci to book lending. The hotel's beach hut is a busy place even off-season. The spacious, breezy lobby is filled with Haitian artwork and fresh flowers. Standard rooms are rather modest, but all are air-conditioned with king-size or twin beds, radio, direct-dial phones, and balconies, about half of which face the sea. *St-François 97118, tel. 590/88–51–00 or 800/543–4300. 265 rooms, 10 suites. Facilities: 4 restaurants, 2 bars, disco, boutiques, pool, 5 tennis courts, (3 lighted), bike rental, car-rental desk, water-sports center. AE, DC, MC, V. Moderate–Expensive.*

★ **La Toubana.** Red-roof bungalows are sprinkled on a hilltop overlooking the Caravelle Peninsula, arguably the best beach on the island. The bungalows are air-conditioned, and all rooms have private bath, phone, and an ocean view. Seven suites have kitchenettes and private terraced gardens. The pool is rather small. There's evening entertainment at the French-Creole restaurant, including a piano bar. Pets are welcome. *Box 63, Ste. Anne 97180, tel. 590/88–25–78 or 800/223–9815. 57 rooms and suites. Facilities: restaurant, bar, pool, tennis court, water-sports center. AE, DC, V. Moderate–Expensive.*

Cap Sud Caraibes. This is a tiny Relais Creole on a country road between Gosier and Ste. Anne, just a five-minute walk from a quiet beach. Guests are presented with a welcome cocktail, and although English is not the first language here, every attempt is made to make you feel at home. Individually decorated rooms are air-conditioned, and each has a balcony and an enormous bath. There's a big kitchen that guests are welcome to share. *Gosier 97190, tel. 590/88–96–02, or 800/223–9815, 800/468–0023. 12 rooms. Facilities: transfer from airport to hotel, bar, drycleaning and laundry facilities, snorkeling equipment. Moderate.*

★ **Relais du Moulin.** A restored windmill serves as the reception room for this Relais Creole tucked in Châteaubrun, near Ste. Anne. A spiral staircase leads up to a TV/reading room from which there is a splendid view. Accommodations are in air-conditioned bungalows; rooms are immaculate and tiny, with twin beds, small terraces, and kitchenettes. Horseback riding can be arranged, and bikes are available. The fine restaurant serves West Indian nouvelle cuisine. *Châteaubrun, Ste. Anne 97180, tel. 590/88–23–96, 800/223–9815, or 800/468–0023. 40 rooms. Facilities: restaurant, bar, pool, tennis court, archery. AE, MC, V. Moderate.*

★ **Callinago-PLM Azur.** In this hilltop complex above the beach you've a choice between the Callinago Hotel and the Callinago Village. The former offers air-conditioned rooms with full bath, phone, and private balcony with a view of the sea or the gardens. The village offers studios and duplex apartments with kitchenettes. You'll be offered a welcome drink. There's dancing in the bar, and frequent entertainment by folkloric groups and steel bands. *Box 1, Gosier 97110, tel. 590/84–25–25 or 800/223–9862. 154 units. Facilities: 2 restaurants, 1 bar, car-rental desk, dive shop, pool, water-sports center. AE, DC, MC, V. Inexpensive–Moderate.*

★ **Auberge de la Distillerie.** This is an excellent choice for those who want to be close to the Natural Park and its hiking trails. The small country inn has air-conditioned studios with phone (you'll have to share a bath) and a TV lounge. There's also a rustic wood chalet that sleeps two–four people. Boat trips are arranged on the Lezarde River, in which you can also swim. Pets are welcome. *Vernou 97170, Petit-Bourg, tel. 590/94–25–91, 800/223–9815, or 800/468–0023. 7 studios, 1 chalet. Facilities: restaurant, bar, piano bar. AE, V. Inexpensive.*

Auberge du Grand Large. This casual family-style inn on the grand Ste. Anne beach has bungalows on the beach or tucked in a garden. All are air-conditioned with private bath. The restaurant serves Creole specialties. Pets are welcome. *Ste. Anne 97180, tel. 590/88–20–06, 800/223–9815, or 800/468–0023. 10 rooms. Facilities: restaurant, bar. AE, MC. Inexpensive.*

Grand Anse Hotel. Located near the ferry landing from which you leave for Les Saintes, this Relais Creole offers air-conditioned bungalows with shower baths, phones, and little balconies. The view of the mountains is spectacular. It's less than a mile from a black-sand beach, and water sports can be arranged. A good choice for nature lovers. *Trois Rivières*

97114, tel. 590/92–92–21 or 800/468–0023. 20 bungalows. Facilities: restaurant, bar. V. Inexpensive.

Les Saintes **Village Creole.** Baths by Courreges, dishwashers, freezers,
★ satellite TV/videos, and international direct-dial phones are
among the amenities in this apartment hotel. Ghyslain Laps,
the English-speaking owner, will help you whip up meals in
the kitchen. If you'd prefer not to cook, he can provide you
with a cook and housekeeper for an extra charge. A sailboat
is available for excursions to Marie-Galante and Dominica.
*Pte. Coquelet 97137, Terre-de-Haut, tel. 590/99–53–83 (telex
919671). 22 duplexes. Facilities: airport shuttle service, daily
maid service, safe deposit, business center, scooter and boat
rentals, water-sport center. MC, V. Moderate–Inexpensive.*

★ **Auberge des Anacardies.** Trimmed with trellisses, topped by
dormers, and owned by the mayor, this inn offers air-
conditioned, twin-bed rooms with phone and bath. Casement
windows open to a splendid view of the gardens, the hills, and
the bay. This hostelry possesses the island's only swimming
pool. Steak au poivre, grilled lobster, and steaks are among the
restaurant's offerings. *La Savane 97137, Terre-de-Haut, Les
Saintes, tel. 590/99–50–99. 10 rooms. Facilities: restaurant,
bar, pool. AE, MC, V. Inexpensive.*

Bois Joli. You'll need to reserve three months in advance for a
room here in high season. Facing the "Sugarloaf" on the island's beautiful bay, the hotel consists of modern rooms in
bungalows, 14 of which are air-conditioned. You have to be
pretty flexible about baths here. There are no private baths.
Water sports can be arranged, and the Anse Crawen nudist
beach is a five-minute walk away. Pets are allowed. *Terre-de-
Haut 97137, tel. 590/99–52–53 or 800/223–9815. 21 rooms.
Facilities: restaurant, 2 bars, airport transfers. MC, V.
Inexpensive.*

★ **Los Santos-PLM Azur.** These red-top balconied bungalows are
all air-conditioned, with phone and private bath; 10 have kitchenettes. Dives and boat and cycling trips can be arranged.
*Terre-de-Haut 97137, tel. 590/99–50–40 or 800/223–9862. 54
rooms. Facilities: restaurant, bar, boutique, TV lounge, video
club, nursery, water-sport center. AE, DC, MC, V. Inexpensive.*

Home and For information about villas, apartments, and private rooms in
Apartment Rental modest houses contact **Gites de France** (tel. 590/82–09–30). For
additional information about apartment-style accommoda-
tions, contact the **ANTRE Association** (tel. 590/88–53–09).

The Arts and Nightlife

Cole Porter notwithstanding, Guadeloupeans maintain the beguine began here (the Martiniquais make the same claim for
their island). Discos come, discos go, and the current music
craze is "zouk," but the beat of the beguine remains steady.
Many of the resort hotels feature dinner dancing, as well as entertainment by steel bands and folkloric groups.

Casinos There are two casinos on the island. Neither has one-armed
bandits, but both have American-style roulette, blackjack, and
chemin de fer. The legal age is 21. Admission is $10, and you'll
need a photo ID. Tie and jacket are not required, but "proper
attire" means no shorts. The **Casino de Gosier les Bains** (Gosier,
tel. 590/84–18–33) has a bar, restaurant, and nightclub, and is

open Monday–Saturday 9 PM–dawn. The **Casino de St-François** (Marina, St-François, tel. 590/84–41–40) has a snack bar and nightclub and is open Tuesday–Sunday 9 PM–3 AM.

Discos A mixed crowd of locals and tourists frequent the discos. Night owls should note that carousing is not cheap. Most discos charge an admission of at least $8, which includes one drink. Drinks cost about $5 each. Some of the enduring hot spots are **Le Foufou** (Marissol PLM-Azur, Bas-du-Fort, tel. 590/90–84–44), **Ti Raccoon** (Creole Beach Hotel, Pointe de la Verdure, tel. 590/84–26–26), **Le Mandingo** (Gosier Beach, tel. 590/84–35–39), **Le Caraibe** (Salako, Gosier, tel. 590/84–22–22), the **Bet-a-Feu** (Meridien Hotel, St-François, tel. 590/88–51–00), and the very Parisian **Elysée Matignon** (Rte. des Hôtels, Bas-du-Fort, tel. 590/90–89–00).

Bars and Nightclubs If discos are not your dish, tune in to the **Auberge de la Vielle Tour** (Gosier, tel. 590/84–23–23), where Robert Zarkis's orchestra plays for touch-dancing, which is never passé here. There's also a popular piano bar. **La Toubana** (Ste. Anne, tel. 590/88–25–78) offers a piano bar; there's nightly entertainment at the **Lele Bar** (Meridien, St-François, tel. 590/88–51–00); and an orchestra plays dance music at the **Marissol PLM-Azur** (Bas-du-Fort, tel. 590/90–84–44).

14 Jamaica

by John DeMers

John DeMers, who makes his home in New Orleans, served for several years as food editor of United Press International. He is the author of the cookbook Caribbean Cooking.

Jamaica was in the news briefly in September 1988 in the aftermath of Hurricane Gilbert, the island's most unwelcome visitor in 50 years. While the inland residential areas saw the full force of the storm and suffered damage that was expected to take months and even years to repair completely, the popular tourist areas were more lightly affected, with many establishments in operation again within days or weeks and nearly all of them fully recovered by the beginning of 1989. For the casual visitor to Jamaica, the hurricane's legacy has been freshly repainted and redecorated hotels and restaurants and a renewed appreciation of the importance of the tourist to the Jamaican economy.

The third largest island in the Caribbean (after Cuba and Puerto Rico), the English-speaking nation of Jamaica enjoys a considerable self-sufficiency based on tourism, agriculture, and mining. Its physical attractions include jungled mountaintops, clear waterfalls, and unforgettable beaches, yet the country's greatest resource may be the Jamaicans themselves. Although 95% of the population trace their bloodlines to Africa, their national origins lie in Great Britain, the Middle East, India, China, Germany, Portugal, South America, and many of the other islands in the Caribbean. Their cultural life is a wealthy one; the music, art, and cuisine of Jamaica are vibrant with a spirit easy to sense but as hard to describe as the rhythms of reggae or a flourish of the streetwise patois.

Jamaica is unusual in that, in addition to such pleasure capitals of the north coast as Montego Bay and Ocho Rios, it has a real capital in Kingston. For all its congestion, and for all the disparity between city life and the bikinis and parasails to the north, Kingston is the true heart and head of the island. This is the place where politics, literature, music, and art wrestle for acceptance in the largest English-speaking city south of Miami, its actual population of nearly 1 million bolstered by the emotional membership of virtually all Jamaicans.

The first people known to have reached Jamaica were the Arawaks, Indians who paddled their canoes from the Orinoco region of South America about a thousand years after the death of Christ. (It is possible that a more primitive group, the Ciboneys, had already spent time here on their trek from Florida to other Caribbean islands.) The Arawaks, who left their imprint on Jamaica, were basically a gentle folk who liked to hunt, fish, farm when the weather was good, and enjoy a rich collection of games and festivals. Then, in 1494, Christopher Columbus stepped ashore at what is now called Discovery Bay. Having spent four centuries on the island, the Arawaks had little notion that his feet on their sand would mean their extinction within 50 years.

What is now St. Ann's Bay was established as New Seville in 1509 and served as the Spanish capital until local government crossed the island to Santiago de la Vega (now Spanish Town). The Spaniards were never impressed with Jamaica; their searches found no precious metals, and they let the island fester in poverty for 161 years. When 5,000 British soldiers and sailors appeared in Kingston harbor in 1655, the Spaniards did not put up a fight.

The arrival of the English, and the three centuries of rule that followed, provided Jamaica with the surprisingly genteel underpinnings of its present life—and the rousing pirate tradition fueled by rum that enlivened a long period of Caribbean history. The British buccaneer Henry Morgan counted Jamaica's governor as one of his closest friends and enjoyed the protection of His Majesty's government no matter what he chose to plunder. Port Royal, once said to be the "wickedest city of Christendom," grew up on a spit of land across from present-day Kingston precisely because it served so many interests. Morgan and his brigands were delighted to have such a haven, and the people of Jamaica profited in being able to buy pirate booty at Port Royal at terrific bargains. In a sense, Port Royal may have been the world's first outlet store.

Morgan enjoyed a prosperous life; he was knighted and made lieutenant governor of Jamaica before the age of 30, and like every good bureaucrat, he died in bed and was given a state funeral. Port Royal fared less well. On June 7, 1692, an earthquake tilted two-thirds of the city into the sea, the tidal wave that followed the last tremors washed away millions in pirate treasure, and Port Royal simply disappeared. In recent years divers have turned up some of the treasure, but most of it still lies in the depths, adding an exotic quality to the water sports pursued along Kingston's reefs.

The very British 18th century was a time of prosperity in Jamaica. This was the age of the sugar baron, who ruled his plantation great house and made the island the largest sugar-producing colony in the world. Because sugar fortunes were built on slave labor, however, production became less profitable when the Jamaican slave trade was abolished in 1807 and slavery in 1838.

As was often the case in colonies, a national identity came to supplant the British allegiance in the hearts and minds of Jamaicans. This new identity was given official recognition on August 6, 1962, when Jamaica became an independent nation with loose ties to the Commonwealth. The island today has a democratic form of government led by a prime minister and by a cabinet of fellow ministers. The 60 members of the House of Representatives are chosen in general elections every five years; the 21 members of the Senate are nominated by the government and the opposition party, then appointed by the governor general.

The elections of February 1989 gave the People's National Party more than two-thirds of the seats in the House and made Michael N. Manley prime minister. Manley replaced Edward P. G. Seaga, leader of the Jamaica Labor Party, who was credited with the recovery of the national economy by instituting unpopular austerity measures. Under Seaga, tourism became Jamaica's major industry, with thousands of talented young Jamaicans choosing it as their career. The mining of bauxite is expected to expand in the near future, and agriculture has been given a fresh look with a new crop of winter vegetables intended to compete with those of Florida and Mexico. While Hurricane Gilbert may have set back efforts to revitalize the economy in 1988, the "Product of Jamaica" label is one the world should soon be seeing on fruit and vegetables again.

Jamaica

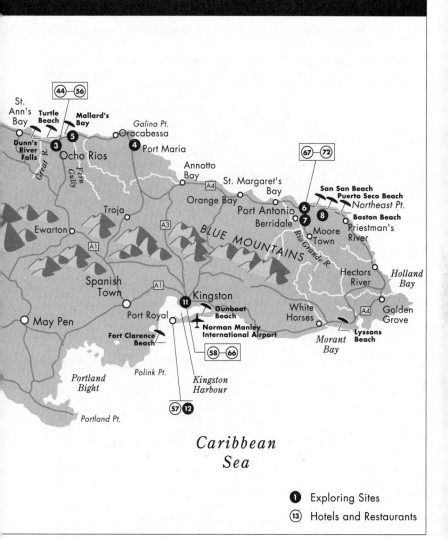

- Exploring Sites
- ⑬ Hotels and Restaurants

Before You Go

Tourist Information	Contact the **Jamaica Tourist Board** (866 2nd Ave., New York, NY 10017, tel. 212/688–7650).
Arriving and Departing *By Plane*	**Donald Sangster International Airport** in Montego Bay (tel. 809/952–5530) is the most efficient point of entry for visitors destined for Montego Bay, Round Hill-Tryall, Ocho Rios, Runaway Bay, and Negril. **Norman Manley Airport** in Kingston (tel. 809/924–8452) is better for visitors to the capital or Port Antonio. Trans Jamaica Airlines (tel.809/929–5624) provides shuttle services on the island.

Air Jamaica (tel. 718/830–0303 or 800/523–5585) and **American Airlines** (tel. 212/619–6991 or 800/433–7300) fly nonstop from New York, while Air Jamaica comes in from Miami, **BWIA** (tel. 800/327–7401) from San Juan, and **Aeroflot** (tel. 809/929–2251) from Havana. Air Jamaica provides the most frequent service from U.S. cities, flying to the island from Newark, Philadelphia, Atlanta, Chicago, Tampa, Los Angeles, New York, and Miami. The national carrier also flies from Toronto. **Air Canada** (tel. 800/422–6232) offers service from Toronto and Montreal, and both **British Airways** (tel. 800/247–9297) and Air Jamaica connect the island with London.

Passports and Visas	Passports are not required of visitors from the United States or Canada, but every visitor must have proof of citizenship such as a birth certificate or a voter registration card (a driver's license is *not* enough). British visitors need passports but not visas. Each visitor must possess a return or ongoing ticket and sufficient funds to maintain himself on the island. Declaration forms are distributed in flight in order to keep customs formalities to a minimum.
Customs and Duties	Luggage is searched upon arrival in Jamaica. The importation of illegal drugs, fresh fruit, flowers, and meat is restricted. Jamaican law prohibits bringing arms or ammunition onto the island; firearms must be surrendered to authorities at the point of entry, to be returned at the time of departure. The laws forbidding the use of "ganja" (marijuana) in Jamaica are strict. Financial penalties, jail terms, and deportation await anyone who scoffs at the laws. Enforcement includes Coast Guard patrols and ganja-sniffing police dogs.
Language	The official language of Jamaica is English. Islanders sometimes speak a patois among themselves, and they may use it when they don't want you to understand something.
Precautions	Do not let the beauty of Jamaica cause you to relax the caution and good sense you would use in your own hometown. Never leave money or other valuables in your hotel room; use the safe deposit boxes that most establishments make available. Carry your funds in traveler's checks, not cash, and keep a record of the check numbers in a secure place. Never leave a rental car unlocked, and never leave valuables even in a locked car. Finally, resist the call of the wild when it presents itself as a scruffy-looking native offering to show you the "real" Jamaica. Jamaica *on* the beaten path is wonderful enough; don't take chances by wandering far from it. And ignore his efforts, however persistent, to sell you a ganja joint.

Staying in Jamaica

Important Addresses	**Tourist Information:** The main office of the **Jamaica Tourist Board** is in Kingston (Tourism Central Bldg., New Kingston Box 360, Kingston Sides, tel. 809/929–9200). There are also JTB desks at both Montego Bay and Kingston airports, and JTB offices in all resort areas.
Emergencies	**Police, Fire, Ambulance:** Police and Air-Rescue is 119. Fire department and ambulance is 110.
	Hospitals: University Hospital at Mona in Kingston (tel. 809/927–6621), **Cornwall Regional Hospital** (Mt. Salem, in Montego Bay, tel. 809/952–5100), and **Port Antonio General Hospital** (Naylor's Hill in Port Antonio, tel. 809/993–2646).
	Pharmacies: Pegasus Hotel in Kingston (tel. 809/926–8174), **McKenzie's Drug Store** (16 Strand St. in Montego Bay, tel. 809/952–2467), and **Great House Pharmacy** (Brown's Plaza in Ocho Rios, tel. 809/974–2352).
Currency	By law, anything purchased in Jamaica must be paid for with Jamaican dollars. The Jamaican dollar is worth about U.S. 20 cents. Currency can be exchanged at airport bank counters, exchange bureaus, or a commercial bank. Be sure to keep all your exchange transaction receipts; you'll need them when you're ready to change your leftover Jamaican currency on leaving the country. Jamaican currency may not be taken out of the country. Prices quoted below are in U.S. dollars, unless otherwise noted.
Taxes and Service Charges	Hotels collect a 6% government tax on room charges. The departure tax is $8.

Many hotels and restaurants add a 10% service charge to your bill. Otherwise, tips may average 10%–15%. |
Guided Tours	Half-day tours are offered by a variety of operators in the important areas of Jamaica. The best Great Houses tours include Rose Hall, Greenwood, and Devon House. Plantations to tour are Prospect and Brimmer's Hall. The Governor's Coach Tour uses a diesel rail car to visit villages, plantations, and a rum distillery. The increasingly popular waterside folklore feasts are offered on the Dunn's, Great, and White rivers. The significant city tours are those in Kingston, Montego Bay, and Ocho Rios. Quality tour operators include **Martin's Tours** (tel. 809/327–5767), **Tropical Tours** (tel. 809/952–1110), **Greenlight Tours** (tel. 809/926–2014), and **Estate Tours Services** (tel. 809/947–2058). A ride in a hot-air balloon is the highlight of the **Hilton High Day Tour** (tel. 809/952–3343), which has been dubbed "Up, Up, and Buffet."
Getting Around *Taxis*	Some but not all of Jamaica's taxis are metered. If you accept a driver's offer of his services as tour guide, be sure to agree on a price *before* the vehicle is put into gear. All licensed taxis display red Public Passenger Vehicle (PPV) as well as regular license plates. Cabs can be summoned by telephone or flagged down on the street. Taxi rates are per car, not per passenger, and 25% is added to the metered rate between midnight and 5 AM. Licensed minivans are also available and bear the red PPV plates.
Rental Cars	Jamaica has dozens of rental car companies throughout the island. Because rentals can be difficult to arrange once you've

arrived, you should make a reservation before you start on your trip. Best bets are the same names you would think of at home: **Avis** (tel. 800/331–2112), **Dollar** (tel. 800/421–6868), **Hertz** (tel. 800/654–3001), **National** (tel. CAR–EUROPE). In Jamaica, try the branch offices in your resort area or **United Car Rentals** (tel. 809/952–3077 or 809/952–1781). You must be at least 21 years old to rent a car, and you must have a valid driver's license (from any country). You may be required to post a security of several hundred dollars before taking possession of your car; ask about this when you make the reservation.

Traffic keeps to the left in Jamaica, and those who are unfamiliar with driving on the left will find that it takes some getting used to. Be cautious until you are comfortable with it.

Trains The diesel train between Kingston and Montego Bay reveals virtually every type of scenery Jamaica has to offer in a trip of nearly five hours.

Buses Buses are the mode of transportation Jamaicans use most, and consequently some buses are very crowded and slow. Yet the service is quite good between Kingston and Montego Bay and between other significant destinations. Schedule or route information is available at bus stops, or from the bus driver.

Cycles The front desks of most major hotels can arrange the rental of bicycles, mopeds, and motorcycles. Daily rates run from about $16 for a moped to $125 for a Honda 125. Deposits of $80 or more are required.

Telephones and Mail The area code for all Jamaica is 809. Direct telephone, telegraph, telefax, and telex services are available.

Airmail postage from Jamaica to the United States or Canada at press time was JM$.45 for letters, JM$.35 for postcards.

Opening and Closing Times Normal business hours for stores are weekdays 8–4, Saturdays 8–1. Banking hours are generally Monday–Thursday 9–2, Friday 9–noon and 2:30–5.

Beaches

Jamaica has some 200 miles of beaches, some of them still uncrowded. The beaches listed below are public places, and they are among the best Jamaica has to offer. In addition, nearly every resort has its own private beach complete with towels and water sports. Some of the larger resorts sell day passes to nonguests.

Doctor's Cave Beach at Montego Bay shows a tendency toward population explosion, attracting Jamaicans and tourists alike; at times it may resemble Fort Lauderdale at spring break. The 5-mile stretch of sugary sand has been spotlighted in so many travel articles and brochures over the years that it's no secret to anyone. On the bright side, Doctor's Cave is well fitted out for all its admirers with changing rooms, colorful if overly insistent vendors, and a large selection of snacks.

Two other popular beaches in the Montego Bay area are **Cornwall Beach,** farther up the coast, which is smaller, also lively, with lots of food and drink available, and **Walter Fletcher Beach,** on the bay near the center of town. Fletcher offers protection from the surf on a windy day and therefore unusually fine swimming; the calm waters make it a good bet for children, too.

Ocho Rios appears to be just about as busy as Mo Bay these days, and the busiest beach is usually **Mallard's.** The Mallard's Beach and the Club Americana hotels are both here, spilling out their large convention groups at all hours of the day. To the south, it is **Turtle Beach** that the islanders consider the place to go swimming in Ocho Rios.

Not too long ago, the 7 miles of white sand at **Negril Beach** offered a beachcomber's vision of Eden. Today much of it is fenced off and littered with the debris of construction. The nude beach areas are sectioned off, and some new resorts are building accommodations overlooking their nude beaches, thereby adding a new dimension to the traditional notion of "ocean view."

Elsewhere in Negril, the action-oriented **Hedonism II** is a favorite of the young singles crowd, with facilities for a range of activities from jet-skiing to weightlifting and an array of social hoopla. Its reputation for the risqué may make it unappealing or unsuitable for some people. Hedonism's beach is a private hotel beach; nonguests must pay fee to use the facilities.

In Port Antonio, head for **San San** or **Boston Bay.** Any of the shacks spewing scented smoke along the beach at Boston Bay will sell you the famous peppery delicacy jerk pork. On your return along the coast toward Montego Bay, **Puerto Seco Beach** at Discovery Bay can provide a sunny and sandy break from driving.

Kingston may seem an unlikely place for beach lovers, yet Kingstonians enjoy the water, too. **Gunboat Beach** is the most popular choice, and there are other options. **Fort Clarence,** a black-sand beach in the Hellshire Hills area southwest of the city, has changing facilities and entertainment. Sometimes Kingstonians are willing to drive 32 miles east to the lovely **Lyssons Beach** in Morant Bay or, for a small negotiable fee, to hire a boat at the Morgan's Harbor Marina at Port Royal to ferry them to **Lime Cay.** This island, just beyond Kingston Harbor, is perfect for picnicking, sunning, and swimming.

Those who seek beaches off the main tourist routes will want to explore Jamaica's unexploited south coast. Nearest to "civilization" is **Bluefields Beach** near Savanna-la-Mar, south of Negril along the coast. **Crane Beach** at Black River is another great discovery. And the best of the south shore has to be **Treasure Beach,** 20 miles farther along the coast beyond Crane.

Exploring Jamaica

Numbers in the margin correspond with points of interest on the Jamaica map.

Montego Bay
❶
The number and variety of its attractions make Montego Bay on the island's northwest corner the logical place to begin an exploration of Jamaica. Confronting the string of high-rise developments that crowd the water's edge, you may find it hard to believe that little of what is now Montego Bay (the locals call it Mo Bay) existed before the turn of the century. Today many explorations of Montego Bay are conducted from a reclining chair on Doctor's Cave Beach, a table nearby to hold frothy drinks.

Rose Hall Great House, perhaps the greatest in the West Indies in the 1700s, enjoys its popularity less for its architecture than for the legend surrounding its second mistress. Annie Palmer was credited with murdering three husbands and a plantation overseer who was her lover; the story is told in two novels sold everywhere in Jamaica, *The White Witch of Rose Hall* and *Jamaica White*. The great house is east of Montego Bay, just across the highway from the Rose Hall resorts. *Tel. 809/953-2323. Open daily 9–6:30.*

Time Out For a lunch break between great houses, stop in at **Wyndham Rose Hall** (tel. 809/953–2650). On entering the hotel lobby, buy a ticket for the lively buffet at the Cat Cay Brasserie and Terrace, where the main attractions are the chili and the Jamaican rice and peas.

Greenwood Great House, 15 miles east of Montego Bay, has no spooky legend to titillate visitors, but it's much better than Rose Hall at evoking the atmosphere of life on a sugar plantation. The Barrett family, from which the English poet Elizabeth Barrett Browning was descended, once owned all the land from Rose Hall to Falmouth, and the family built several great houses on it. The poet's father, Edward Moulton Barrett ("the Tyrant of Wimpole Street"), was born at Cinnamon Hill, currently the private estate of the country singer Johnny Cash. Highlights of Greenwood include oil paintings of the Barretts, china made especially for the family by Wedgwood, a library filled with rare books printed as early as 1697, fine antique furniture, and a collection of exotic musical instruments. *Open daily 10–6.*

One of the most popular excursions in Jamaica is rafting on the **➋ Martha Brae River.** The gentle waterway takes its name from that of an Arawak Indian who killed herself because she refused to reveal the whereabouts of a local gold mine to the Spanish. According to legend, she finally agreed to take them there and, on reaching the river, used magic to change its course and drowned herself along with the greedy Spaniards. Her *duppy* (ghost) is said to guard the mine's entrance to this day. Bookings are made through hotel tour desks. The trip is $26 per person, including transportation, about 28 miles from most hotels in Montego Bay.

The **Governor's Coach Tour** takes you through the lush hills and countryside around Montego Bay in a diesel rail car. You'll get a look at Jamaican villages, plantations growing banana and coconut, coffee groves, and the facility that turns out Appleton Rum. The full-day excursion includes a riverside lunch and a rum punch. *Tel. 809/952-2887. Cost: $35 per person. The tour departs Tues.–Fri. at 9:30 AM from Montego Bay Railway Station, returning at 5:30.*

An Evening on the Great River is a must for tour groups, yet fun nonetheless. The adventure includes a boat ride up the torchlit river, a full Jamaican dinner, a native folklore show, and dancing to a reggae band. *Tel. 809/952–5047 or 809/952–5097. $36 per person, $33 when you drive your own car. Sun., Tues., and Thurs.*

Ocho Rios Perhaps more than anywhere else in Jamaica, Ocho Rios—67 **➌** miles east of Montego Bay—presents a striking contrast of natural beauty and recreational development. The Jamaicans can fill the place by themselves, especially on a busy market day, when cars and buses from the countryside clog the heavily traveled coastal road that links Port Antonio with Montego Bay. Add a tour bus or three and the entire passenger list from a cruise ship, and you may find yourself mired in a considerable traffic jam.

Yet a visit to Ocho Rios is worthwhile, if only to enjoy its two chief attractions, Dunn's River Falls and Prospect Plantation. Both are considered so central to the Jamaican Experience that in the wake of Hurricane Gilbert the cruise lines insisted they be cleaned up before their ships would dock. A few steps away from the main road in Ocho Rios await some of the most charming inns and oceanfront restaurants in the Caribbean. Lying on the sand of what will seem to be your private cove, or swinging gently in a rope chair with a tropical drink in your hand, you'll soon forget the traffic a brief stroll away.

No, Ocho Rios is not from the Spanish for "eight rivers"; the name is a corruption of *chorreras*, which describes a seemingly endless series of cascades that sparkle from the limestone rocks along this stretch of coast. For as long as anyone can remember, Jamaicans have favored Ocho Rios for their own escape from the heat and the crowds of Kingston.

Dunn's River Falls is an eye-catching sight: 600 feet of cold, clear mountain water splashing over a series of stone steps to the warm Caribbean. The best way to enjoy the falls is to climb the slippery steps. Don a swimsuit, take the hand of the person ahead of you, and trust that the chain of hands and bodies leads to an experienced guide. Those who lead the climbs are personable fellows who reel off bits of local lore while telling you where to stop. *Dunn's River Feast*, a nocturnal variation on this popular entertainment on Thursdays at 7:30 PM, includes a Jamaican buffet followed by a nighttime climb, a folklore performance, a fashion show, and dancing to reggae.

Prospect Plantation Tour (tel. 809/974-2058)is the best of several offerings that delve into the island's former agricultural lifestyle. It's not just for specialists; virtually everyone enjoys the beautiful views over the White River Gorge and the tour by jitney (a canopied open-air cart pulled by a tractor) through a plantation with exotic fruits and tropical trees planted over the years by such celebrities as Winston Churchill and Charlie Chaplin. Horseback riding over 1,000 acres is available.

The third "must" in Ocho Rios—and the newest—is **Carinosa,** a pet project of the former prime minister Edward Seaga. This amazing 20-acre garden perched on a hillside above the town offers some of the loveliest orchids anywhere, a dramatic weave of streams and waterfalls, and a tropical aviary. *Eden Bower Rd., tel. 809/974-5346. Tours daily from 9 AM.*

Time Out | Try to plan your Carinosa visit around lunch or dinner, for the **Garden Restaurant** (tel. 809/974-5346) offers a delightful terrace and New Jamaican cuisine. Best bets are the smoked marlin and the Seville chicken julienne.

The only major historic site in Ocho Rios is **The Old Fort,** built in 1777 as a defense against invaders from the sea. The original "defenders" spent much of their time sacking and plundering as far afield as St. Augustine, Florida, and sharing their bounty with the local plantation owners who financed their missions.

❹ Two area residences are of more than passing interest. **Firefly,** about 20 miles east of Ocho Rios in Port Maria, was once Sir Noël Coward's vacation residence and is now preserved in all its hilltop wonder by the National Trust of Jamaica. Coward used to entertain jet-setters and royalty in the surprisingly spartan digs in an Eden-like setting. The Jamaicans who sometimes give impromptu tours of Firefly used to work for Sir Noël, and they show a moving reverence for his simple grave on the grounds.

❺ **Golden Eye,** just east of Ocho Rios on the main coast road, was used in wintertime by Ian Fleming, the creator of James Bond, from 1946 until his death in 1964. Since then Golden Eye has served as home to the reggae legend Bob Marley and to the founder of Island Records, Chris Blackwell. Today it can be seen only by those who can afford to rent it from the record company. It's an airy complex of deep blue buildings, walls and bookcases bursting with Bond memorabilia, and a private cove reached by stone steps that would have delighted 007 (provided the Dom Perignon would not be badly shaken during the descent).

Port Antonio Every visitor's presence in Port Antonio pays homage to the
❻ beginnings of Jamaican tourism. Early in the century the first tourists arrived here on the island's northeast tip, 133 miles east of Montego Bay, drawn by the exoticism of the island's banana trade and seeking a respite from the New York winters. The original posters of the shipping lines make Port Antonio appear as foreign as the moon, yet in time it became the tropical darling of a fast-moving crowd and counted Clara Bow, Bette Davis, Ginger Rogers, Rudyard Kipling, J. P. Morgan, and William Randolph Hearst among its admirers. Its most passionate devotee was the actor Errol Flynn, whose spirit still seems to haunt the docks, devouring raw dolphin and swigging gin at 10 AM. Flynn's widow runs a boutique in Port Antonio at the posh Trident Villas and Hotel.

Although the action has moved elsewhere, the area can still weave a spell. Robin Moore wrote *The French Connection* here, and Broadway's tall and talented Tommy Tune found inspiration for the musical *Nine* while being pampered at Trident.

With the help of recent renovations, a stroll through the town suggests a step into the past. A couple of miles north of Port Antonio's main street, **Queen Street** in the residential Titchfield area offers fine Georgian architecture. **DeMontevin Lodge** (21 Fort George, tel. 809/993–2604), owned by the Mrs. Mullings who long served as Errol Flynn's cook, and the nearby **Musgrave** are in the traditional sea-captain style that one finds along coasts as far away as New England.

The town's best-known landmark is **Folly,** on the way to Trident, a Roman-style villa in ruins on the eastern edge of East Harbor. The creation of a Connecticut millionaire in 1905, the manse was made almost entirely of concrete. Unfortunately, the cement was mixed with sea water, and it began to crumble as it dried. According to local lore, the millionaire's bride took one look at her shattered dream, burst into tears, and fled forever. Little more than the marble floor remains today.

Time Out **The Blue Hole** (San San Beach, tel. 809/993–2495), known as The Blue Lagoon after the Brooke Shields movie, is a popular spot near San San Beach. Take a table alongside the water, peel and eat "pepper shrimp" from a piece of newspaper, and down a cold Red Stripe.

7 Rafting on the **Rio Grande River** (yes, Jamaica has a Rio Grande, too) is a must. This is the granddaddy of the river-rafting attractions, an 8-mile-long, swift green waterway from Berrydale to Rafter's Rest. Here the river flows into the Caribbean at St. Margaret's Bay. The trip of about three hours is made on bamboo rafts pushed along by a raftsman who is likely to be a character. You can pack a picnic lunch and eat it on the raft or along the river bank; wherever you lunch, a vendor of Red Stripe beer will appear at your elbow. A restaurant, bar, and souvenir shop are at Rafter's Rest (tel. 809/993–2778). About $25 per two-person raft.

8 Another interesting excursion takes you to **Somerset Falls,** where you can climb the 400 feet with some assistance from a concrete staircase. A brief raft ride takes you part of the way. Tickets are sold just west of Rafter's Rest (tel. 809/993–2778). Another part of the complex is **Athenry Gardens,** a 16-acre tropical wonderland, and **Nonsuch Cave,** whose underground beauty has been made accessible by concrete walkways, railed stairways, and careful lighting.

A short drive east from Port Antonio deposits you at **Boston Beach,** which is popular with swimmers and enshrined by lovers of jerk pork. The spicy barbecue was originated by the Arawaks and perfected by runaway slaves called the Maroons. Eating almost nothing but wild hog preserved over smoking coals enabled the Maroons to survive years of fierce guerilla warfare with the English.

For as long as anyone can remember, Port Antonio has been a center for some of the finest deep-sea fishing in the Caribbean. Dolphins (the delectable fish, not the lovable mammal) are the likely catch here, along with tuna, kingfish, and wahoo. In September the week-long *Blue Marlin Tournament* attracts anglers from around the world. By the time enough beer has been consumed, it's a bit like the running of the bulls at Pamplona, except that fish stories carry the day.

Negril Negril, situated 52 miles southwest of Montego Bay on the
9 winding coast road, is no longer Jamaica's best-kept secret. In fact, it has begun to shed some of its bohemian, ramshackle atmosphere for the attractions and activities traditionally associated with Montego Bay. Applauding the sunset from Rick's Cafe may still be the highlight of a day in Negril, yet increasingly the hours before and after have come to be filled with conventional recreation.

One thing that has not changed around this west coast center (whose only true claim to fame is a 7-mile beach) is the casual approach to life. As you wander from lunch in the sun to shopping in the sun to sports in the sun, you'll find that swimsuits are common attire. Want to dress for a special meal? Slip a caftan over your bathing suit.

Even though you may be staying at one of the charming smaller inns in Negril, you might enjoy spending a day at **Hedonism II,** a kind of love poem to health, Mother Nature, and good (mostly clean) fun. The owners love to publicize the occasional nude volleyball game in the pool at 3 AM, but most of the pampered campers are in clothes and in bed well before that hour. And what if Hedonism II is not the den of iniquity it likes to appear to be? What it is, and what your day pass ($55) gets you, is a taste of the spirit as well as the food—and participation in snorkeling, parasailing, and jet skiing.

After sunset, activity centers on **West End Road,** Negril's main (and only) thoroughfare, which comes to life in the evening with bustling bistros and ear-splitting discos. West End Road may still be unpaved, yet it leads to the town's only building of historical significance, the **Lighthouse.** All anyone can tell you about it, however, is that it's been there for a while. Even historians find it hard to keep track of the days in Negril.

Negril today stretches along the coast north from the horseshoe-shaped **Bloody Bay** (named during the period when it was a whale-processing center), along the calm waters of **Long Bay** to the Lighthouse section and the landmark **Rick's Cafe** (tel. 809/957–4335). Sunset at Rick's is a tradition, one not unlike the event observed at Mallory Square in Key West. Here there are jugglers and fire-eaters; 50-foot cliffs and divers who go spiraling downward into the deep green depths.

In the 18th century Negril was where the English ships assembled in convoys for the dangerous ocean crossing. Not only were there pirates in the neighborhood, the infamous Calico Jack and his crew were captured right here, while they guzzled the local rum. All but two of them were hanged on the spot; Mary Read and Anne Bonney were pregnant at the time, and their execution was delayed.

Mandeville
❿
More than a quarter of a century after Jamaica achieved its independence from Great Britain, Mandeville seems like a hilly tribute to all that is genteel and admirable in the British character. At 2,000 feet above sea level, 70 miles southeast of Montego Bay, Mandeville is considerably cooler than the coastal area 25 miles to the south. Its vegetation is more lush, thanks to the mists that drift through the mountains. The people of Mandeville live their lives around a village green, a Georgian courthouse, tidy cottages and gardens, even a parish church. The entire scene could be set down in Devonshire, were it not for the occasional poinciana blossom or citrus grove.

Mandeville is omitted from most tourist itineraries even though its residents are increasingly interested in showing visitors around. It is still much less expensive than any of the coastal resorts, and its diversions include horseback riding, cycling, croquet, hiking, tennis, and golf.

The town itself is characterized by its orderliness. You might stay here several days, or a glimpse of the lifestyle may satisfy you and you'll scurry back to the steamy coast. **Manchester Club** features tennis, nine holes of golf, and well-manicured greens; **Mrs. Stevenson's Gardens** are lovely with orchids and fruit trees; the natural **Bird Sanctuary** shows off 25 species indigenous to Jamaica; and **Marshall's Pen Great House** offers an array of walking tours. The cool, crisp air will make you feel up to any stroll in Mandeville. Further information on Mandeville is available from the area coordinator, Elizabeth Ross (tel. 809/962–3265).

Kingston The reaction of most visitors to the capital city, situated on the
⑪ southeast coast of Jamaica, is anything but love at first sight. In
fact, only a small percentage of visitors to Jamaica see it at all.
Kingston, for the tourist, may seem as remote from the resorts
of Montego Bay as the loneliest peak in the Blue Mountains. Yet
the islanders themselves can't seem to let it go. Everybody
talks about Kingston, about their homes or relatives there,
about their childhood memories. More than the sunny havens
of the north coast, Kingston is a distillation of the true Jamaica. Parts of it may be dirty, crowded, often raucous, yet
it is the ethnic cauldron that produces the cultural mix that
is the nation's greatest natural resource. As one Jamaican
has put it, "You don't really know Jamaica until you know
Kingston."

The best way to approach this city is from within, staying in
one of the quiet residential sections and dining with the local
inhabitants in restaurants that seem to have no names (people
refer to them by their addresses, such as 73 or 64, and everyone
knows where to meet). The first-time business or pleasure
traveler may prefer to begin with New Kingston, a former
racetrack property that now glistens with hotels, office towers,
apartments, and boutiques. Newcomers may feel more comfortable settling in here and venturing forth from comfort they
know will await their return.

Kingston's colonial past is very much alive away from the high
rises of the new city. **Devon House** (tel. 809/929–6602), our first
stop, is reached through the iron gates at 26 Hope Road. Built
in 1881 and bought and restored by the government in the
1960s, the mansion has period furnishings. Shoppers will appreciate Devon House, for the firm Things Jamaican has
converted portions of the space into some of the best crafts
shops on the island. On the grounds you'll find one of the few
mahogany trees to survive Kingston's ambitious but not always
careful development.

Time Out The **Coffee Terrace** and the **Gourmet Restaurant** at Devon
House (26 Hope Rd., tel. 809/929–6602) have ackee and
saltfish, curry goat, and other island specialties created by
Enid Donaldson, known as the Julia Child of Jamaica for her appearances on television.

Among nearby residences, **Kings House,** farther along Hope
Road, is the home of Jamaica's governor general, and **Vale Royal** on Montrose Road is home to the prime minister. The latter
structure, originally built as a plantation house in the 1700s, is
one of the few still standing in the capital that has a lookout tower for keeping an eye on ships in the harbor. *Tel. 809/927–6424.
Open weekdays, 10–5.*

Once you have accepted the fact that Kingston doesn't look like
a travel poster—too much life goes on here for that—you might
see your trip here for precisely what it is, the single best introduction to the people of Jamaica. Near the waterfront, the
Institute of Jamaica (tel. 809/922–0620) is a museum and library
that traces the island's history from the Arawaks to current
events. The charts and almanacs here make fascinating browsing; one example, famed as the Shark Papers, is made up of
damaging evidence tossed overboard by a guilty sea captain
and later recovered from the belly of a shark.

From the Institute, push onward to the **University of the West Indies** (tel. 809/927–1660) in the city's Mona section. A cooperative venture begun after World War II by several West Indian governments, the campus is set in an eye-catching cradle of often misty mountains. In addition to a bar and a disco where you can meet the students (they pay dues, while tourists enter free), the place seems a monument to the conviction that education and commitment lead to a better life for the entire Caribbean.

Jamaica's rich cultural life is evoked at the **National Gallery** (12 Ocean Blvd., tel. 809/922–1561), which was once part of Devon House and can now be found at Kingston Mall near the reborn waterfront section. The artists represented here may not be household words in other nations, yet the paintings of such intuitive masters as John Dunkley, David Miller, Sr., and David Miller, Jr., reveal a sensitivity to the life around them that transcends academic training. Among other highlights from the 1920s through the 1980s are works by Edna Manley and Mallica Reynolds, better known as Kapo.

Reggae fans touring the National Gallery will want to look for Christopher Conzalez's controversial statue of Bob Marley, and they will feel transfixed by **Tuff Gong International** (56 Hope Rd.). Painted in Rastafarian red, yellow, and green, this recording studio was built by Marley at the height of his career. The house has since become the **Bob Marley Museum** (tel. 809/927–9152), with impromptu tours given by just about anyone who may be around. Certainly there is much here to help the outsider understand Marley, reggae, and Jamaica itself. The Ethiopian flag is a reminder that Rastas consider the late Ethiopian emperor Haile Selassie to be the Messiah, a descendant of King Solomon and the Queen of Sheba. A striking mural by Ever Brown, *The Journey of Superstar Bob Marley*, depicts the hero's life from its beginnings in a womb shaped like a coconut to enshrinement in the heart of the Jamaican people.

A distinct change of pace is offered by the **Royal Botanical Gardens at Hope** (tel. 809/927–1085), a cooling sanctuary donated to Jamaica by the Hope family following the abolition of slavery. Some 200 acres explode with tropical trees, plants, and flowers, each clearly labeled and lovingly discussed by qualified guides. Free concerts are given here on the first Sunday of each month.

12 Unless your visit must be very brief, you shouldn't leave Kingston without a glimpse of "the wickedest city in the world." **Port Royal** has hardly been that since an earthquake tumbled it into the sea in 1692, yet the spirits of Henry Morgan and other buccaneers add a great deal of energy to what remains. The proudest possession of **St. Peter's Church,** rebuilt in 1725 to replace Christ's Church, is a silver communion plate donated by Morgan himself.

You can no longer down rum in Port Royal's legendary 40 taverns, but you can take in a draft of the past at the **Archaeological and Historical Museum** (tel. 809/924–8706), located within the Police Training School building. In the same building are a small **Maritime Museum** and a tipsy, angled structure known as **Giddy House.** Nearby is a graveyard in which rests a man who died twice. According to the tombstone, Lewis Goldy was swallowed up in the great earthquake of 1692, spewed into the sea, rescued, and lived another four decades in "Great Reputation." Port Royal attractions are open daily 9–5.

Jamaica for Free

Fifteen years ago Jamaica introduced the *Meet the People* concept that has become so popular in the Caribbean. One of the best free attractions anywhere, it allows visitors to get together with islanders who have compatible interests and expertise. The nearly 600 Jamaican families who participate in Meet the People on a voluntary basis offer their guests a spectrum of activities from time at a business or home to musical or theatrical performances. The program's theme is Forget Me Not, the name of a tiny blue flower that grows on Jamaican hillsides. Once you've met these people, you're likely not to forget them. It's important to arrange your occasion in advance of your trip through the Jamaica Tourist Board.

Off the Beaten Track

The Cockpit Country, 15 miles inland from Montego Bay and one of the most primitive areas in the West Indies, is a terrain of pitfalls and potholes carved by nature in limestone. For nearly a century from 1655 it was known as the Land of Look Behind because British soldiers rode their horses back to back in pairs, looking out for the savage freedom fighters known as Maroons. Fugitive slaves who refused to surrender to the invading English, the Maroons eventually won a treaty of independence and continue to live apart from the rest of Jamaica in the Cockpit Country. The government leaves them alone, untaxed and ungoverned by outside authorities. The Jamaica Tourist Board has information on minibus tours from Montego Bay to Maroon headquarters at Accompong.

Admirers of Jamaica's wonderful coffee may wish to tour the **Blue Mountains.** The best way to do this is in your own rental car, driving into the mountains from Kingston along Highway A3. Before departing, you should obtain directions either to **Pine Grove** or to the Jablum coffee plant at **Mavis Bank,** then follow the handlettered signs after you leave A3. It's an exciting excursion and a virtual pilgrimage for many coffee lovers. Pine Grove, a working coffee farm that doubles as an inn, has a restaurant that serves the owner Marcia Thwaites' Jamaican cuisine. Mavis Bank is delightfully primitive—considering the retail price of the beans it processes. There is no official tour; ask someone to show you around.

Spanish Town, 12 miles west of Kingston on the A1, was the island's capital under Spanish rule. British until 1872, the town boasts the noblest Georgian square (Government Square) and the oldest cathedral (St. James) in the Western Hemisphere. Spanish Town's original name was Santiago de la Vega, which the English corrupted to St. Jago de la Vega, both meaning St. James of the Plains.

Participant Sports

The Tourist Board licenses all operators of recreational activities, which should ensure you of fair business practices as long as you deal with companies that display the decals.

Fishing Deep-sea fishing can be great around the island. Port Antonio gets the headlines with its annual blue marlin tournament, and Montego Bay and Ocho Rios have devotees who talk of the sailfish, yellowfin tuna, wahoo, dolphin, and bonita. Licenses are not required. Boat charters can be arranged at your hotel.

Golf The best courses may be found at **Caymanas** and **Constant Spring** in Kingston; **Eden, Half Moon, Rose Hall, Tryall,** and **Ironshore** in Montego Bay; and **Runaway Bay** and **Upton** in Ocho Rios. A nine-hole course in the hills of Mandeville is called **Manchester Club** (tel. 809/962–2403).

Horseback Riding This is not only terrific recreation, it's also an ideal way to tour certain areas. The island is fortunate to have the best equestrian facility in the English-speaking Caribbean, Chukka Cove (write Box 160, Ocho Rios, St. Ann, tel. 809/972–2506) near Ocho Rios. The resort, complete with stylishly outfitted villas, offers packages with full instruction in riding, polo, and jumping.

Tennis Many hotels have tennis facilities that are free to their guests, but some will allow you to play for a fee. The sport is a highlight at **Tryall** in Sandy Bay, **San Souci** in Ocho Rios, and **Half Moon** in Montego (*see* Lodging, below).

Water Sports The major areas for swimming, windsurfing, snorkeling, and scuba diving are Negril in the west and Port Antonio in the east. All the large resorts rent equipment for a deposit and/or a fee. Diving is perhaps the only option that requires training, for you need to show a C-card to participate. However, some dive operators on the island are qualified to certify you. **Blue Whale Divers** (Negril Tree House, tel. 809/957–4438), **Sun Divers** (Club Caribbean, Runaway Bay, tel. 809/973–2340), and **Caribbean Amusement** (Trelawny Beach Hotel, Falmouth, tel. 809/954–2123) offer certification courses and dive trips. Some tour operators offer day trips that include an off-shore trip, snorkel equipment, lunch, and cocktails. For the best swimming spots, *see* Beaches, above.

Shopping

by Sandra Hart Shopping in Jamaica goes two ways: things Jamaican and things imported. The former are made with style and skill; the latter are duty-free luxury finds. Jamaican crafts take the form of resortwear, hand-loomed fabrics, silk screening, wood carvings, paintings, and other fine arts.

Jamaican rum is a great take-home gift. So is Tia Maria, Jamaica's world-famous coffee liqueur.

Some bargains, if you shop around, include Swiss watches, Irish crystal, jewelry, cameras, and china. The top-selling French perfumes also are available alongside Jamaica's own fragrances—Royal Lyme, Royall Spyce, and Royall Bay aftershave for men, and Khus Khus toilet water for women.

Shopping Areas A shopping tour of the Kingston area should begin at **Constant**
Kingston **Spring Road** or **King Street.** No matter where you begin, keep in mind that the trend these days is shopping malls, and Jamaica has caught on with a fever and an ever growing roster: **Twin Gates Plaza, May Pen Shopping Plaza, New Lane Plaza, Tree Plaza.**

A day at **Devon House** (26 Hope Rd., Kingston, tel. 809/929–6602) should be high on your shopping list. This is the place to find old and new Jamaica. The Great House is now a museum with antiques and furniture reproductions, and the new Lady Nugent's Coffee Terrace outside. There are 10 boutiques in what were once the house's stables: A branch of Things Jamaican; Tanning and Turning for leather finds; first-rate furnishings and antique reproductions at Jacaranda; silver and pewter recreations (many from centuries-old patterns) at The Olde Port Royal; and some of the best tropical-fruit ice cream (mango, guava, pineapple, and passion fruit) at I-Scream.

Montego Bay and Ocho Rios A must to avoid are the "craft" stalls in MoBay and Ocho Rios that are literally filled with peddlers desperate to sell touristy straw hats, T-shirts, and cheap jewelry. You may find yourself purchasing an unwanted straw something in order to get out alive. If you're looking to spend money, head for Overton Plaza or Westgate Plaza in Montego Bay; the Coconut Grove Plaza in Ocho Rios. It's also a good idea to chat with salespeople, who can enlighten you about the newer boutiques and their whereabouts.

Special Buys The **Gallery of West Indian Art** (1 Orange La., MoBay, tel. 809/
Arts and Crafts 952–4547) is the place to find Jamaican and Haitian paintings. A corner of the gallery is devoted to hand-turned pottery (some painted) and beautifully carved birds and jungle animals.

Cheap sandals are good buys in shopping centers throughout Jamaica. While workmanship and leathers don't rival the craftsmanship of those found in Italy or Spain, neither do the prices (about $20 a pair). In Kingston there are two booteries that share the same address, the **Shoe Scene** and **Taurus** (27 Half Way Tree Rd., tel. 809/926–6476; 809/926–4168, respectively). There's also **Lee's** (New Kingston Shopping Center) and **Bata** (217 Spanish Town Rd., Kingston, tel. 809/923–6020). In Ocho Rios, the **Pretty Free Shoe Shop** (Ocean Village Shopping Centre, tel. 809/974–5040) is a good bet. In Montego Bay, try **Overton Plaza** or **Westgate Plaza.**

Things Jamaican (Devon House, Hope Rd., Kingston, tel. 809/929–6602; 68 Spanish Town Rd., Kingston, tel. 809/923–8928; Fort St., MoBay, tel. 809/952–5650) has three outlets and two airport stalls, which display and sell some of the best native crafts made in Jamaica. The Devon House branch offers items that range from carved wood bowls and trays, to reproductions of silver and brass period pieces.

Books and Records Books about Jamaica and the Caribbean, many not available in the United States, can be found at the three branches of **Sangster's Bookstores** (97 Harbour St., Kingston, tel. 809/922–3640; Constant Spring Rd. Mall, Kingston, tel. 809/926–2271; Westgate Shopping Centre, MoBay, tel. 809/952–0319). Jonathan Routh's *Jamaica Holiday: The Secret Life of Queen Victoria* makes a great gift and/or souvenir. For terrific beach reading dive into *The Book of Jamaica*, by Russell Banks, or anything by novelist Jean Rhys.

Reggae tapes by world famous Jamaican artists, such as Bob Marley, Ziggy Marley, Peter Tosh, and Third World, can be found easily in U.S. or European record stores, but a pilgrimage to **Randy's Record Mart** (17 N. Parade, Kingston, tel. 809/922–4859) should be high on the reggae lover's list. Also worth checking is the **Record Plaza** (Tropical Plaza, Kingston, tel.

809/926–7645) and **Record City** (Westgate Plaza, MoBay, tel. 809/993–2836). While Kingston is the undisputed place to purchase, the determined somehow (usually with the help of a local) will find **Jimmy Cliff's Records** (Oneness Sq., MoBay, no phone), owned by reggae star Cliff.

Gift Ideas Fine "acanudo" cigars, with monogrammed cigar bands, in beautiful wood humidors (also monogrammed), make sensational gifts. An order will take about one week to fill, so place an order with **Gore Brothers** (27 Upper Waterloo Rd., Kingston, tel. 809/925–0030) upon your arrival. (Cost is around $50 for the humidors alone.) The hard-to-find Blue Mountain coffee can sometimes be found at **John R. Wong's Supermarket** (1 Tobago Ave., Kingston, tel. 809/926–4811). If they're out of stock you'll have to settle for High Mountain coffee, the natives' second preferred brand. If you're set on Blue Mountain you might try **Magic Kitchen Ltd.** (Village Plaza, Kingston, tel. 809/929–6602).

Jamaican-brewed rums and Tia Maria can be bought at either the Kingston or MoBay airports before your departure. While the airport prices are not any cheaper, there's no toting of heavy, breakable bottles from the hotel to the airport.

Specialty Shops Belts, bangles, and beads are the name of the game at the factory of **Ital-Craft** (Twin Gates Plaza Shopping Centre, Kingston, tel. 809/926–8291). Belts are the focus of this savvy operation, but they also produce some intriguing jewelry and purses (many made from reptile skins). While Ital-Craft's hand-made treasures are sold in boutiques throughout Jamaica, we recommend a visit to the factory for the largest selection of these belts, made of spectacular shells, combines with leather, feathers, or fur. (The most ornate belts sell for about $50.)

Silk batiks, by the yard or made into chic designs, are at **Caribatick** (tel. 809/954–2314), the studio of Muriel Chandler, two miles east of Falmouth. Drawing on patterns in nature, Chandler has translated the birds, seascapes, flora, and fauna into works of art.

Teeny-weeny bikinis, which more than rival Rio's, are designed by **Sonia Vaz** and sold at her manufacturing outlet (77 East St., Kingston, tel. 809/952–5650) and at the Sandal's and Super Clubs resorts *(see* Lodging, below).

Sprigs and Things (St. James Pl., Gloucester Ave., MoBay, tel. 809/952–4735) is where artist Janie Soren sells T-shirts featuring her hand-painted designs of birds and animals. She also paints canvas bags and tennis dresses.

Annabella Proudlock sells her unique wood Annabella Boxes, the covers depicting reproductions of Jamaican paintings at a restored great house, Harmony Hall (an eight-minute drive from Ocho Rios, east on A-1; tel. 809/974–4222). Reproductions of paintings, lithographs, and signed prints of Jamaican scenes are also for sale along with shell work and hand-carved wood combs. Stay for high tea and enjoy the locally grown teas, jams, and jellies on the Great House's veranda.

Dining

Sampling the island's cuisine introduces you to virtually everything the Caribbean represents. Every ethnic group that has made significant contributions on another island has made them on Jamaica, too, adding to a Jamaican stockpot that is as rich as its melting pot. So many Americans have discovered the Caribbean through restaurants owned by Jamaicans that the very names of the island's dishes have come to represent the region as a whole.

Jamaican food represents a true cuisine, organized, interesting, and ultimately rewarding. It would be a terrible shame for anyone to travel to the heart of this complex culture without tasting several typically Jamaican dishes. Here are a few:

Rice and Peas. A traditional dish, known also as Coat of Arms and similar to the *moros y christianos* of Spanish-speaking islands: white rice cooked with red beans, coconut milk, scallions, and seasoning.

Pepperpot. The island's most famous soup—a peppery combination of salt pork, salt beef, okra, and the island green known as callalloo—is green, but at its best it tastes as though it ought to be red.

Curry Goat. Young goat is cooked with spices and is more tender and has a gentler flavor than the lamb for which it was a substitute for immigrants from India.

Ackee and Saltfish. Salted fish was once the best islanders could do between catches, so they invented this incredibly popular dish that joins saltfish (in Portuguese, *bacalao*) with ackee, a vegetable (introduced to the island by Captain Bligh of *Bounty* fame) that reminds most people of scrambled eggs.

Jerk Pork. Created by the Arawaks and perfected by the Maroons, jerk pork is the ultimate island barbecue. The pork (the purist cooks the whole pig) is covered with a paste of hot peppers, berries, and other herbs and cooked slowly over a coal fire.

Patties are spicy meat pies that elevate street food to new heights. While, in fact, they originated in Haiti, Jamaica can give patty lessons to anybody.

Where restaurants are concerned, Kingston has the widest selection; its ethnic restaurants offer Cantonese, German, Thai, Indian, Korean, and Continental fare. There are fine restaurants as well in all the resort areas, and the list includes many located in large hotels.

The most highly recommended restaurants are indicated by a star ★.

Category	Cost*
Expensive	over $25
Moderate	$15–$25
Inexpensive	under $15

per person, excluding drinks and service charge (or tip)

Kingston ★ **Blue Mountain Inn.** The elegant Blue Mountain Inn is a 30-minute taxi ride from downtown and worth every penny of the fare. (The inn operates a special limo, costing less than $5, from the Pegasus, Oceana, Courtleigh, and Terra Nova hotels.) A former coffee plantation great house built in 1754, the inn complements its atmosphere with Continental cuisines. All the classics of the beef and seafood repertoires are here, including steak Diane and lobster Thermidor. *Gordon Town, tel. 809/ 927-7400. Reservations required. Dress: dressy. AE, CB, DC, MC, V. Expensive.*

Ristorante d'Amore. Located on the 17th floor of the Wyndham New Kingston, this Northern Italian restaurant offers a spectacular view of the city along with homemade pasta dishes, many of them prepared tableside. Veal may be served in sauces from a simple lemon butter to dark stock reductions with wine. Flaming desserts are another specialty. *Wyndham New Kingston, tel. 809/926-5430. Reservations recommended. Dress: dressy. AE, CB, DC, MC, V. Expensive.*

Talk of the Town. Another room with a view, the Talk of the Town is situated at the top of a 23-story New Kingston hotel. The Continental dishes are supplemented by intriguing renditions of Caribbean, such as snapper wrapped in callaloo and served with a veloute sauce. *Jamaica Pegasus Hotel, tel. 809/ 926-3690. Reservations required. Dress: dressy. AE, CB, DC, MC, V. Expensive.*

Hotel Four Seasons. The Four Seasons has been pleasing local residents for more than 25 years with its cuisine from the German and Swiss schools and local seafood. The setting tries to emulate Old World Europe without losing its casual island character. *18 Ruthven Rd., tel. 809/926-8805. Reservations recommended. AE, CB, DC, MC, V. Moderate.*

Restaurant Korea. You'll meet more of Jamaica than you might think in this popular Korean dining room, for the islanders love ethnic food. Bugoki is the specialty, a kind of marinated barbecue than can be made with beef, pork, or chicken. Chinese and Japanese dishes are also available. *73 Kuntsford Blvd., tel. 809/ 926-1428. Reservations optional. AE, CB, DC, MC, V. Moderate.*

The Hot Pot. Jamaicans love the Hot Pot for breakfast, lunch, and dinner. Frying chicken is the specialty. It's not far from the New Kingston hotel district, but it can be difficult to find, so you might ask a taxi driver to take you (he probably will have just come from the place). *2 Altamont Terr., tel. 809/926-3906. Reservations unnecessary. No credit cards. Inexpensive.*

Montego Bay   **Georgian House.** A landmark restaurant in the heart of town, the Georgian House occupies two restored 18th-century buildings set in a shady garden courtyard. An extensive wine cellar complements the Continental and Jamaican cuisine, the best of which are the steaks and the dishes made with the local spiny lobster. Free pickup from Montego Bay hotels. *Union and Orange Sts., tel. 809/952-0632. Reservations required. Dress: dressy. AE, CB, DC, MC, V. Expensive.*

Julia's. Even if Julia's didn't run a free minibus to hotels all over Montego Bay, visitors would have discovered it. The kitchen turns out an "Italian gourmet" fixed price dinner for $30 per person, lining up carefully prepared pastas (Alfredo, primavera, etc.) and quality veal. The hillside location above the town and harbor, enhanced by an abundance of windows on three sides, allows the area's single most spectacular view. *Bogue Hill, tel. 809/952-1772. Reservations recommended. Dress: chic. AE, CB, DC, MC, V. Expensive.*

Pier 1. Despite its sharing a name with the American "import" store, Pier 1 writes the book daily on waterfront dining. After tropical drinks at the deck bar, you'll be ready to dig into the international variations on fresh seafood, the best of which are the grilled lobster and any preparation of island snapper. *Just off Howard Cooke Blvd., tel. 809/952-2452. Reservations recommended. AE, CB, DC, MC, V. Expensive.*

★ **Sugar Mill.** One of the finest restaurants in Jamaica, the Sugar Mill (formerly the Club House) is where seafood is served with flair—on a terrace. Steak and lobster are usually offered in a pungent sauce that blends Dijon mustard with Jamaica's own Pickapeppa. Other wise choices are the daily specials and anything flamed tableside—and the taste will rival the theater. *At Half Moon Golf Course, tel. 809/953-2560. Reservations required for dinner, recommended for lunch. AE, CB, DC, MC, V. Expensive.*

Calabash. The specialty of the Calabash, a casual eating place with seating for 80, is a kind of Caribbean casserole featuring lobster, shrimp, crabmeat, and whatever else strikes the chef as freshest, all baked in a cheese and brandy sauce. *Queen's Dr., tel. 809/952-3891. Reservations recommended. AE, CB, DC, MC, V. Dinner only. Moderate.*

Town House. Most of the rich and famous who have visited Jamaica over the decades have eaten at the Town House. You won't find innovative cuisine here, just good versions of standard ideas (red snapper papillot is the specialty, with lobster, cheese, and wine sauce) in a colonial setting of shuttered windows, high ceilings, and hard-to-get old brick. *16 Church St., tel. 809/952-2660. Reservations recommended. Dress: smart. AE, CB, DC, MC, V. Moderate.*

★ **Pork Pit.** This open-air hangout three minutes from the airport must introduce more travelers to Jamaica's fiery jerk pork than any other place on the island. The Pork Pit is a local phenomenon down to the Red Stripe beer, yet it's accessible in both location and style. Plan to arrive around noon, when the jerk begins to be lifted from its bed of coals and pimento wood. *Adjacent to Casa Montego Hotel, no phone. No reservations. No credit cards. Inexpensive.*

Ocho Rios **Casanova.** Deta Plunkett, the chef at Casanova, is a little Jamaican lady who for 25 years had been turning out some of the best food on the island. The Sans Souci Hotel is imaginative enough to serve her homemade pastas in a comfortable open-air setting. All the Italian items are fine, and so are the smoked marlin, the spiny lobster, and the "catch of the day." At lunch you must try chicken à la Deta, a spicy island version of barbecue; if it's not on the menu, ask for it. *Sans Souci Hotel, tel. 809/974-2353. Reservations recommended. Dress: dressy at dinner. AE, CB, DC, MC, V. Expensive.*

The Ruins. A 40-foot waterfall dominates the open-air Ruins restaurant, and in a sense it dominates the food as well. Surrender to local preference and order the Lotus Lily Lobster, a stirfry of the freshest local shellfish, then settle back and enjoy the tree-shaded deck and the graceful footbridges that connect the dining patios. *DaCosta Dr., tel. 809/974-2442. Reservations recommended. Dress: smart. AE, CB, DC, MC, V. Expensive.*

★ **Almond Tree.** One of the most popular restaurants in Ocho Rios, the Almond Tree offers Jamaican dishes enlivened by a European culinary tradition. The swinging rope chairs of the terrace bar and the tables perched above a lovely Caribbean cove are great fun. The pumpkin and pepperpot soups, the dramatic tableside preparations, and, among the entrees, the

Dining

Calabash, **32**
Georgian House, **34**
Julia's, **37**
Pier 1, **36**
Pork Pit, **31**
Sugar Mill, **23**
Town House, **35**

Lodging

Carlyle on the Bay, **29**
Half Moon Club, **24**
Holiday Inn
Rose Hall, **25**
Richmond Hill Inn, **33**
Round Hill, **38**
Sandals, **27**
Sandals Club
Fantasy, **30**
Sandals Royal
Caribbean, **26**
Sea Garden Beach
Resort, **28**
Wyndham Rose Hall
Beach and Country
Club, **22**

Montego Bay Dining and Lodging

family mementos. *21 Fort George St., tel. 809/993–2604. Reservations required. AE, CB, DC, MC, V. Moderate.*

Negril   **Cafe au Lait.** The proprietors of Cafe au Lait are French and Jamaican, and so is the cuisine. Local seafood and produce are prepared with delicate touches and presented in a setting overlooking the sea. *Charela Inn on Lighthouse Rd., tel. 809/957–4277. Reservations recommended. AE, CB, DC, MC, V. Moderate.*

★   **Rick's Cafe.** Here it is, the local landmark complete with cliffs, cliff divers, and powerful sunsets, all perfectly choreographed. It's a great place for a sunny brunch of omelets, eggs Benedict, or toast and plantains. In the sunset ritual, the crowd toasts Mother Nature with fresh fruit daiquiris. *Lighthouse Rd., tel. 809/957–4335. Reservations recommended. AE, CB, DC, MC, V. Moderate.*

Lodging

The island has a variety of destinations to choose from, each of which offers its own unique expression of the Jamaican experience. **Montego Bay** has miles of hotels, villas, apartments, and duty-free shops set around Doctor's Cave Beach. Although it's lacking much cultural stimuli, MoBay presents a comfortable island backdrop for the many conventions and conferences it hosts.

Ocho Rios, on the northwest coast halfway between Port Antonio and Montego Bay, long enjoyed the reputation of being Jamaica's most favored out-of-the-way resort, but the late-blooming Negril has since stolen much of that distinction. Ocho Rios' hotels and villas are all situated within walking distance of shops and one of Jamaica's most scenic attractions, Dunn's River Falls.

Port Antonio, described by poet Ella Wheeler Wilcox as "the most exquisite port on earth," is a seaside town nestled at the foot of verdant hills toward the east end of the north coast. The two best experiences to be had here are rafting the Rio Grande and a stop at the Trident, arguably the island's classiest watering hole.

Negril, some 50 miles west of Montego Bay, has become a byword for hedonism (its best-known resort, Hedonism II, sums that up). Negril itself is only a small village, so there isn't much of historical significance to seek out. Then again, that's not what brings the sybaritic singles and couples here.

Mandeville, 2,000 feet above the sea, is noted for its cool climate and proximity to secluded south coast beaches.

The smallest of the resort areas, **Runaway Bay** has a handful of modern hotels and fine 18-hole golf courses.

Kingston is the most culturally active place on Jamaica. Some of the island's finest hotels are located here and those high towers are filled with rooftop restaurants, English pubs, and jazz clubs.

Jamaica was the birthplace of the Caribbean all-inclusive, the vacation concept that took the Club Med idea and gave it a lusty, excess-in-the-tropics spin. From Negril to Ocho Rios, resorts make their strongest statement by including everything, even drinks and cigarettes, in a single price of $150–$200 per night. At times they may feel a bit like Pleasure Island, where Pinocchio picks up long ears and a tail for doing everything bad he ever wanted to do. Yet their financial structure and their wealth of "free" recreation have a definite appeal. The all-inclusives are now branching out, some of them courting families, others going after an upper crust that would not even have picked up a brochure two or three years ago.

In the survey of accommodations that follows, the all-inclusives are listed first in each area, followed by other lodgings from the Very Expensive to the Inexpensive.

The most highly recommended lodgings are indicated by a star ★.

Category	Cost*
Very Expensive	over $200
Expensive	$150–$200
Moderate	$90–$150
Inexpensive	under $90

All prices are for a standard double room for two, MAP (breakfast and dinner), excluding 6% tax and any service charge.

Falmouth **Trelawny Beach Hotel.** The dependable Trelawny Beach resort offers seven stories of rooms overlooking 4 miles of beach. In recent years it has become an all-inclusive with an emphasis on families. Children under 14 get free room and board during the off-season when they share accommodations with their parents. *Box 54, Falmouth, tel. 809/954–2450. 350 rooms. Facilities: 2 dining rooms, tennis courts, pool, complimentary use of water sports equipment. AE, CB, DC, MC, V. Moderate.*

Kingston **Jamaica Pegasus.** The Jamaica Pegasus is one of two fine business hotels in the New Kingston area. The 17-story complex near downtown is virtually a convention center, with some good restaurants and at least a little pampering. *Box 333, Kingston, tel. 809/926–3690. 350 rooms. Facilities: meeting rooms for 1,000, audiovisual services, restaurants, cocktail lounges, shops, pool, jogging track, health club, tennis courts. Meals not included. AE, CB, DC, MC, V. Expensive.*

★ **Wyndham New Kingston.** The main competition to Jamaica Pegasus on the Kingston business beat, the high-rise Wyndham New Kingston also has 17 stories but adds seven cabana buildings. *Box 83, Kingston, tel. 809/926–5430. 400 rooms. Facilities: Olympic-size pool, gardens, conference space for 800, meeting rooms, tennis courts, health club, 3 restaurants, 2 bars, disco. Meals not included. AE, CB, DC, MC, V. Expensive.*

Hotel Oceana. The high-rise Hotel Oceana property affords convenient access to the National Gallery, government offices, and the ferry to Port Royal. *Box 986, Kingston, tel. 809/922–0920. 150 rooms. Facilities: meeting space for 1,200, cocktail lounge, shopping arcade, pool. Meals not included. AE, CB, DC, MC, V. Moderate.*

Mandeville **Hotel Astra.** A hotel with guest-house charm, the Hotel Astra
★ is situated 2,000 feet up in the hills, providing an ideal getaway

for nature lovers and outdoors enthusiasts. *Ward Ave., Box 60, Mandeville, tel. 809/962–3265. 22 rooms. Facilities: sauna, fitness program, restaurant; golf, tennis, riding, bird-watching nearby. AE, CB, DC, MC, V. Inexpensive.*

Mandeville Hotel. The Victorian Mandeville Hotel, set in tropical gardens, bills itself as a "highland rendezvous." *Box 78, Mandeville, tel. 809/962–2420. 60 rooms. Facilities: restaurant, cocktail lounge, golf privileges at nearby Manchester Club. Meals not included. AE, CB, DC, MC, V. Inexpensive.*

Mahoe Bay **Sandals Royal Caribbean.** An all-inclusive for couples only, the Royal Caribbean is enlivened by Jamaican-style architecture arranged in a semicircle around attractive gardens. It's a sister in both theme and quality to other Sandals resorts. *Box 167, Montego Bay, tel. 809/953–2231. 165 rooms. Facilities: pool, private beach, tennis, putting green, dining room. AE, CB, DC, MC, V. All-inclusive.*

Montego Bay **Carlyle on the Bay.** Now a part of the Sandals group, the Carlyle operates as an all-inclusive for singles, couples, and families; its rooms have balconies facing the sea. It is convenient to shopping in Montego Bay. *Box 412, Montego Bay, tel. 809/952–4140. 52 rooms. Facilities: beach privileges, pool, restaurant, pub. AE, CB, DC, MC, V. All-inclusive.*

Sandals Club Fantasy. The all-inclusive Club Fantasy, formerly the Casa Montego, sports high-rise design and a Mediterranean flair. All nine stories have terraces. *Opposite Cornwall Beach, Box 16, Montego Bay, tel. 809/952–4150. 129 rooms. Facilities: open-air bar, dining room, saltwater pool, disco, shopping arcade. AE, CB, DC, MC, V. All-inclusive.*

★ **Sandals.** The largest private beach in Montego Bay is the spark that lights Sandals, one of the most popular couples resorts in the Caribbean. The all-inclusive, seven-day format includes airport transfers, government taxes, sports equipment, aerobics classes, meals, theme parties, and other entertainment. It's a bit like a cruise ship that remains in port, with air-conditioned rooms overlooking the bay. *Box 100, Montego Bay, tel. 809/952–5510. 173 rooms. Facilities: pool, water-sports center, dining room, nightclub. AE, CB, DC, MC, V. All-inclusive.*

SeaGarden Beach Resort. The 50-year-old SeaGarden Beach Resort, once known as Club Paradise, is working hard to change its image. Behind the white gingerbread it has adopted an all-inclusive stance, following the trend and the business along Jamaica's north coast. *Box 300, Montego Bay, tel. 809/ 952–4780 or 800/526–2422. 100 rooms. Facilities: exercise equipment, pool, sailing, snorkeling, tennis, volleyball, shopping. AE, CB, DC, MC, V. All-inclusive.*

★ **Half Moon Club.** For more than three decades the 400-acre Half Moon Club resort has been a destination unto itself with a reputation for doing the little things right. The apartments on the beach can give you the feeling that Jamaica is your own private island. *East of Montego Bay (7 mi), tel. 809/953–2211. 197 rooms. Facilities: golf course, squash courts, health spa, water sports center, pool, restaurants. AE, CB, DC, MC, V. Very Expensive.*

Round Hill. You can spot the peninsula on which Round Hill stands for miles as you drive along the coast. At the resort you can choose between a hotel suite and a villa on the hill with a private pool, all surrounded by the tropical gardens of a 98-acre playground. *Box 64, Montego Bay, tel. 809/952–5150. 101 un-*

its. Facilities: tennis, horseback riding, water-sports center, restaurant. AE, CB, DC, MC, V. Very Expensive.

★ **Wyndham Rose Hall Beach and Country Club.** The veteran Wyndham Rose Hall, a self-contained resort, goes all out to attract a business clientele, mixing recreation with a top-flight conference setup. *Box 999, Montego Bay, tel. 809/953–2650. 500 rooms. Facilities: pool, water sports, 6 tennis courts, golf course, restaurant, coffee shop, nightclub, disco, audiovisual and teleconferencing equipment. AE, CB, DC, MC, V. Expensive.*

Holiday Inn Rose Hall. Here the great equalizer of hotel chains has done much to raise a run-down campground to the level of a full-service property with activities day and night and many tour facilities. *Box 480, Montego Bay, tel. 809/953–2485. 520 rooms. Facilities: pool, water-sports center, restaurant, shops. AE, CB, DC, MC, V. Moderate.*

★ **Richmond Hill Inn.** The hilltop Richmond Hill Inn attracts repeat visitors by providing spectacular views of the Caribbean and a great deal of peace, compared with Mo Bay's hustle. *Union St., Box 362, Montego Bay, tel. 809/952–3859. 22 rooms. Facilities: pool, terrace dining room. AE, CB, DC, MC, V. Inexpensive.*

Negril ★ **Grand Lido.** The opening of the Super Club's all-inclusive Grand Lido in 1989 broke new ground by extending a popular concept to upper income and taste levels. Would the "everything in one bag" vacation concept be accepted by travelers accustomed to treating each purchase as a corporate decision? The resort itself is striking, sitting in splendor next door to the original Super Club, Hedonism II. *Box 88, Negril, tel. 809/957–4317. 200 suites. Facilities: 3 restaurants, satellite TV, 24-hour room service, valet, concierge, water-sports center, pools, clothed and nude beaches, use of squash courts at Hedonism II. AE, CB, DC, MC, V. All-inclusive.*

★ **Hedonism II.** Here is the resort that introduced the Club Med-style all-inclusive to Jamaica a little over a decade ago. Still wildly successful, Hedonism appeals most to vacationers who like a robust mix of physical activities, all listed daily on a chalkboard. *Box 25, Negril, tel. 809/957–4200. 280 rooms. Facilities: water-sports center, fitness center, open-air buffet dining room, disco and bar, horseback riding, lighted tennis courts, shuffleboard, volleyball, squash. AE, MC, V. All-inclusive.*

Negril Inn. One of the prettiest palm-speckled sandy beaches in Jamaica is the center of almost everything the all-inclusive Negril Inn does for its guests. *Negril, tel. 809/957–4209 or 800/634–7456. 46 rooms. Facilities: restaurant, dancing, entertainment, satellite TV, water-sports center. AE, CB, DC, MC, V. All-inclusive.*

Sandals Negril. The opening in 1989 of Sandals, built from the best parts of the old Sundowner and Coconut Cove resorts made this 7-mile beach available to a new category of popular traveler. *Negril, tel. 809/957–4216; Unique Vacations, 7610 SW 61st St., Miami, FL 33143, tel. 800/327–1991. 186 rooms. Facilities: 2 freshwater pools, swim-up bar, private island, water-sports center, Jacuzzis, saunas, fitness center, movies, satellite TV, disco, piano bar. AE, CB, DC, MC, V. All-inclusive.*

Negril Gardens. A study in colonial pink and white, the new Negril Gardens bills itself as the "friendly alternative" to

Negril's all-inclusive scene. It is attractive and refined, and it offers a nice beach with water sports. *Negril, Westmoreland, tel. 809/957–4408. 54 rooms. Facilities: terrace restaurant, disco. AE, CB, DC, MC, V. Very Expensive.*

Charela Inn. Intimacy is special at the Charela Inn, each of the quiet rooms offering a balcony or a covered patio. The owners' French-Jamaican roots find daily expression in the kitchen, and there's an excellent selection of wines. *Box 33, Negril, Westmoreland, tel. 809/957–4277. 26 air-conditioned rooms. Facilities: beach. AE, CB, DC, MC, V. Moderate.*

Ocho Rios

★ **Boscobel Beach.** Boscobel Beach is a parent's dream for a Jamaican vacation, an all-inclusive that makes families feel welcome. Everybody is kept busy all week for a single package price, and everyone leaves happy. *Box 63, Ocho Rios, tel. 809/ 974–3291 or 800/858–8009. 208 rooms, half of them suites. Facilities: Nautilus gym, Jacuzzi, windsurfing, sailing, snorkeling, tennis, volleyball, golf. AE, CB, DC, MC, V. All-inclusive.*

Couples. No singles, no children, no TV: The emphasis at Couples is on romantic adventure and discovery, and the all-inclusive concept eliminates the decision-making that can intrude on social pleasure. Couples has the highest occupancy rate of any resort on the island—and perhaps the most suggestive logo as well. There may be a correlation. *Tower Isle, St. Mary, tel. 809/974–4271. 152 rooms, 8 villas. Facilities: pool, island for nude swimming, tennis courts, Nautilus gym, golf at Runaway Bay. AE, CB, DC, MC, V. All-inclusive.*

Eden II. Once upon a time this was the Jamaica Hilton; now it's a successful couples-only all-inclusive, located on a fine stretch of beach. The rooms have private balconies. *Mammee Bay, Box 51, Ocho Rios, tel. 809/972–2300. 265 rooms. Facilities: 5 tennis courts, water-sports center, sightseeing tours, horseback riding. AE, CB, DC, MC, V. All-inclusive.*

Sandals Ocho Rios. The newest of several couples-only all-inclusives, the nine-acre Sandals Ocho Rios resort, opened in late 1988, follows the formula perfectly. The mix of white and sand colors contrasts nicely with the vegetation and the sea. Accommodations are available in four grades, from deluxe ocean view to standard. *Ocho Rios, tel. 800/327–1991. 237 units. Facilities: restaurant, fitness center, water-sports center. AE, CB, DC, MC, V. All-inclusive.*

Chukka Cove. The battle cry at Chukka Cove is "Saddle Up." Chukka Cove earns its bread and butter by maintaining some of the best equestrian facilities in the Western Hemisphere. In addition to polo, experienced riders will want to investigate Chukka Cove's Jamaican Riding Holiday, an exploration of the north coast by horseback. *Box 160, Ocho Rios, tel. 809/972– 2506. 6 two-bedroom suites. Facilities: stables, equestrian instruction (all levels), cooks to prepare meals in villas, swimming from rocks. AE, CB, DC, MC, V. Very Expensive.*

★ **Jamaica Inn.** This vintage property is a special favorite of the privileged from both the United States and Europe, a clientele fascinated by the combination of class and quiet. There are weeks in season when every single guest is on at least his or her second visit. Each room has its own veranda on the beach. *Box 1, Ocho Rios, tel. 800/243–9420 or 203/438–3793. 50 rooms. Facilities: Continental and Jamaican dining, golf; tennis and horseback riding nearby. AE, CB, DC, MC, V. Very Expensive.*

Plantation Inn. This plantation actually looks like one—the

Deep South variety à la *Gone with the Wind*. The whole place serves up a veranda-soft existence. The rooms have dramatic views down to the sea. *Box 2, Ocho Rios, tel. 809/974–2501. 79 rooms. Facilities: dining and dancing by candlelight, shops, tennis courts. No children under 12. AE, CB, DC, MC, V. Very Expensive.*

Sans Souci Hotel, Club, and Spa. This pastel-pink cliffside fantasyland looks and feels like a lovely dream, if indeed the dreamer had absolute taste and no need to fret over the bill. Cuisine at the five-star Casanova Restaurant not only delights resort guests but attracts diners from other properties for breakfast, lunch, and dinner. It's all here—comfort, exoticism, celebrities getting away from the crush. *Ocho Rios, tel. 809/ 974–2353 or 800/237–3237. 80 rooms and suites. Facilities: health and fitness center, 2 freshwater pools, tennis courts, scuba diving, water-sports center. AE, CB, DC, MC, V. Very Expensive.*

Mallards Beach Resort. The largest hotel in Ocho Rios and formerly the Sheraton, this property draws most of its clientele from conferences and incentive travel. *Box 245, Ocho Rios, tel. 809/974–2201. 370 rooms. Facilities: Vivaldi's restaurant, water-sports center. AE, CB, DC, MC, V. Moderate.*

Shaw Park Beach Hotel. Another popular property with groups from Great Britain, Shaw Park offers a pleasant alternative to downtown high rises. The grounds are especially colorful and well-tended, while the Silks disco is a favorite for late-night carousing. *Cutlass Bay, Box 17, Ocho Rios, tel. 809/ 974–2552 or 800/243–9420. 118 rooms. Facilities: restaurant, water-sports center. AE, CB, DC, MC, V. Moderate.*

Port Antonio **Trident Villas and Hotel.** Both Hurricane Allen in 1980 and
★ Hurricane Gilbert in 1988 took their toll on this elegant hotel, yet both times the owner brought it back even posher than before. In fact, if a single hotel had to be voted the most likely for coverage by "Lifestyles of the Rich and Famous," this would have to be it. The pool, buried in a rocky bit of land jutting out into crashing surf, is a memory unto itself. The oh-so-formal restaurant is also a classic. *Box 119, Port Antonio, tel 809/962– 3265. 12 villas, 16 suites. Facilities: water-sports center. AE, CB, DC, MC, V. Very Expensive.*

★ **Goblin Hill.** For a while this was known as the Jamaica Hill resort, but it is once again going by its original, evocative name. It's a lush 13-acre estate atop a hill overlooking San San cove. Each villa comes with its own dramatic view, plus a maid and butler to handle the housekeeping, cooking, and general caretaking. *Box 26, Port Antonio, tel. 809/993–3286. 28 villas. Facilities: pool, beach, 2 tennis courts. AE, CB, DC, MC, V. Expensive.*

Admiralty Club at Navy Island. This 64-acre private island was once the home of Errol Flynn, Port Antonio's most beloved "character." Casual elegance is the theme here, with a general sense of knowing the world's pleasures. Service is quite attentive. *Box 188, Port Antonio, tel. 809/993–2667 or 800/225–3614. 7 studio cottages, 6 villas. Facilities: beach, cove for nude swimming, dining. AE, CB, DC, MC, V. Moderate.*

Bonnie View Hotel. Though the main appeal of this property is to the budget, it does have a few nice rooms with private verandas overlooking spectacular scenery. Its restaurant atop a 600-foot hill offers the finest view of all. *Box 82, Port Antonio, tel.*

809/993–2752. 30 rooms. Facilities: pool, sun deck. AE, CB, DC, MC, V. Inexpensive.

Port Royal **Morgan's Harbour Hotel, Beach Club, and Yacht Marina.** A favorite of the sail-into-Jamaica set, the small Morgan's Harbour Hotel boasts 22 acres of beachfront at the very entrance to the old pirate town. Every room has air-conditioning and ceiling fans. *Port Royal, tel. 809/924–8464. 24 rooms. Facilities: full-service marina, pier bar, restaurant, access to Lime Cay. AE, CB, DC, MC, V. Moderate.*

Runaway Bay **Jamaica, Jamaica.** One of the best Super Clubs, this all-
★ inclusive was a pioneer in emphasizing the sheer Jamaican-ness of the island, rather than generic sensuality. The cooking is particularly first-rate. It used to be the Runaway Bay Hotel and Golf Club. *Box 58, Runaway Bay, tel. 809/973–2436. 152 rooms. Facilities: water sports center, tennis, horseback riding, sightseeing tours, disco. Guests must be over 16. Minimum 1-wk stay. AE, CB, DC, MC, V. All-inclusive.*

H.E.A.R.T. Country Club. It's a shame more visitors don't know about this place, perched above Runaway Bay and brimming with Jamaica's true character. While providing training for young islanders interested in the tourism industry, it also provides a remarkably quiet and pleasant stay for guests. The employees make an effort to please. *Box 98, St. Ann, tel. 809/973–2671. 20 rooms. Facilities: satellite TV, golf, beach shuttle, restaurant. AE, CB, DC, MC, V. Inexpensive.*

Sandy Bay **Tryall Golf, Tennis, and Beach Club.** Part of a posh residential development 12 miles west of Montego Bay, Tryall clings to a hilltop overlooking the golf course and the Caribbean. Here you choose between accommodations in the former guest house of a 3,000-acre island plantation and one of the private villas dotted about the landscape. *Sandy Bay, Hanover, tel. 809/952–5110. 52 rooms, 40 villas. Facilities: golf course, tennis courts, pool with swim-up bar (bouillon served), terrace restaurant. AE, CB, DC, MC, V. Very Expensive.*

The Arts and Nightlife

Jamaica—especially in the city of Kingston—supports a lively community of musicians. For starters there is reggae, popularized by the late Bob Marley and the Wailers and performed internationally by Jimmy Cliff and many others. If your experience of Caribbean music has been limited to steel drums and Harry Belafonte, then the political, racial, and religious messages of reggae may set you on your ear; listen closely and you just might hear the heartbeat of the people. Those who already love reggae may want to plan a visit in mid-August for the Reggae Sunsplash. The four-night concert at the Bob Marley Performing Center in Montego Bay showcases local talent and attracts such performers as Rick James, Skeeter Davis, Gladys Knight and the Pips, the Beach Boys, and Aretha Franklin.

Nightlife and Bars For the most part, the liveliest late-night happenings throughout Jamaica are in the major resort hotels. Some of the best music will be found at the **Disco** at Hedonism II (tel. 809/957–4200), the **Negril Tree House,** and **Club Kokua** in Negril (no phone). The most popular spots in Kingston today are **Mingles** at the Courtleigh (tel. 809/974–5524), **Illusions** in the New Lane Plaza (tel. 809/929–2125), and **Jonkanoo** in the Wyndham New Kingston (no phone).

The principal clubs in Ocho Rios are **Silks** in the Shaw Park Beach Hotel (tel. 809/974–2552), and the **Little Pub on Main Street** (tel. 809/974–5825). The hottest places in Montego Bay are the **Cave** disco at the Seawinds Beach Resort (tel. 809/952–4070), **Sir Winston's Reggae Club** on Gloucester Street (tel. 809/952–2084), and the **Rose Hall Beach Holiday Inn** (tel. 809/953–2485). Some of the all-inclusives offer a dinner and disco pass for about $30. Like the daytime activity passes, these tickets let you sample one style of living without having to commit an entire vacation to it.

15 Martinique

by Honey Naylor

Not for naught did the Arawaks name Martinique *Mandinina*, which means "Island of Flowers." This is one of the most beautiful islands in the Caribbean, lush with exotic wild orchids, frangipani, anthurium, jade vines, flamingo flowers, and hundreds of vivid varieties of hibiscus. Trees bend under the weight of such tropical treats as mangoes, papayas, bright red West Indian cherries, lemons, limes, and bananas. Acres of banana plantations, pineapple fields, and waving green seas of sugarcane show the bounty of the island's fertile soil.

The towering mountains and verdant rain forest in the north lure hikers, while underwater sights and sunken treasures attract snorkelers and scuba divers. Martinique appeals as well to those whose idea of exercise is turning over every 10 or 15 minutes to get an even tan or whose adventuresome spirit is satisfied by finding booty in a duty-free shop. Francophiles in particular will find the island enchanting.

This 425-square-mile island, the largest of the Windward Islands, is 4,261 miles from Paris, but its spirit (and language) is French with more than a mere soupçon of West Indian spice. Tangible, edible evidence of that fact is the island's cuisine, which is a tempting blend of classic French and Creole dishes.

Columbus sailed near Martinique in 1493, but it was not until his fourth voyage in 1502 that he came ashore at Le Carbet. He paused long enough to remark, "My eyes would never tire of contemplating such vegetation," and to put ashore a number of goats to provide fresh meat for future visits. His eyes very quickly tired of the snakes he saw slithering about in his newfound Eden, so he weighed anchor and put water between him and them, never to return.

By the time Columbus made his way to Martinique, the cannibalistic Caribs had long since arrived on the island and eaten the Island of Flowers's Arawaks. Carib arrows kept outsiders at bay until 1635, when Pierre Belain d'Esnambuc, a Norman nobleman and adventurer, landed with a group of 100 settlers at the mouth of the Roxelane River. The French promised the Caribs the western half of the island, but instead polished them off and imported African slaves to work their sugarcane plantations.

By the mid-17th century, Martinique was an important sugar-producing island. Britain wanted to pluck the pearl away from the French, and the two nations fought over the island until the mid-19th century. In 1815, the island was ceded by treaty to France, and French it has remained ever since.

Martinique became an overseas department of France in 1946 and a *région* in 1974, a status not unlike that of an American state vis-à-vis the federal government. The Martiniquais vote in French national elections and have all the benefits of France's social and economic systems. The island is governed by a prefect who is appointed by the French minister of the interior. Martinique has one of the highest standards of living in the Caribbean.

Before You Go

Tourist Information Contact the **French West Indies Tourist Office** (610 5th Ave., New York, NY 10020, tel. 212/757–1125.) You may also obtain

information from the **French Government Offices** (628 5th Ave.,
New York, NY 10020, tel. 212/757–1125; 9454 Wilshire Blvd.,
Beverly Hills, CA 90212, tel. 213/272–2661; 645 N. Michigan
Ave., Chicago, IL 60611, tel. 312/337–6301; 103 World Trade
Center, Dallas, TX 75258, tel. 214/720–4010; 1 Hallidie Plaza,
Suite 250, San Francisco, CA 94102, tel. 415/986–4161; 1981
Ave. McGill College (490), Montreal, Quebec, Canada H3A
2W9, tel. 514/288–4264; 1 Dundas St. W, Suite 2405, To-
ronto, Ont., Canada M5G 1Z3, tel. 416/593–4717; and 178
Piccadilly, London, United Kingdom W1V 0AL, tel. 01/499–
6911).

Arriving and **American** (tel. 800/433–7300) has daily service from more than
Departing 100 U.S. cities to San Juan, from which the airline's American
By Plane Eagle wing flies on to Martinique. **Air France** (tel. 800/237–
2747) flies direct from Miami and San Juan; **Air Canada** (tel.
800/422–6232) has service from Montreal and Toronto; **LIAT**
(tel. 809/462–0700) flies in from neighboring islands; and **Air
Martinique** (tel. 596/51–09–90) has service to and from St. Martin, Dominica, Barbados, St. Lucia, St. Vincent, Mustique, Union Island, and Trinidad.

From the Airport You'll arrive at Lamentin International Airport, which is about
a 15-minute taxi ride from Fort-de-France and about 40 min-
utes from the Trois-Ilets peninsula where most of the hotels are
located.

Passports U.S. and Canadian citizens must have a passport (an expired
and Visas passport may be used as long as the expiration date is no more
than five years ago) or proof of citizenship, such as an original
(not photocopied) birth certificate or a voter's registration card
accompanied by a government-authorized photo identification.
British citizens are required to have a passport and a visa. In
addition, all visitors must have a return or ongoing ticket.

Customs Items for personal use, including tobacco, cameras, and film,
and Duties are admitted free.

Language The official language is French, and you will have difficulty unless you have either a nodding acquaintance with the language
or a good phrase book. While it is true that front-desk personnel in the tourist hotels speak some English, they often have
difficulty understanding it. Most menus are in French, and
even in the major tourist areas, waiters and waitresses often do
not speak English. And rare is the Martiniquais in the countryside who speaks English. Outside the major tourist areas,
you'll certainly have to resort to charades if you lack a smattering of French.

Precautions Exercise the same safety precautions as you would in any other
big city: Leave valuables in the hotel safe-deposit vault
and lock your car, with luggage and valuables stashed out of
sight. Also, don't leave jewelry or money unattended on the
beach.

Beware of the *mancenillie* (manchineel) trees! These pretty
trees with little green fruits that look like apples are poisonous. Sap and even raindrops falling from the trees onto your
skin can cause painful, scarring blisters. The trees have red
warning signs posted by the Forestry Commission.

If you plan to ramble through the rain forest, be careful where
you step. Poisonous snakes, cousins of the rattlesnake, slither
through the lush tropical Eden.

Martinique

Martinique Passage ㉔㉕㉖

Grand-Rivière
Macouba ⑫
Basse-Pointe ⑪

Anse-Ceron

Mont Pelée

Ajoupa-Bouillon ⑩

N1

Le Lorrain

Marigot ㉗

Le Prêcheur ⑦

Morne Jakob

N3

Le Morne Rouge ⑧
㉘㉙

N2

Rade de St-Pierre

⑥
⑤
St-Pierre

④
Le Carbet

N3

⑨
St-Joseph
Pitons du Carbet

N2

Bellefontaine ③

Case-Pilote ㉝

㊲—㊽

Fort-de-France

Schoelcher ②①
Baie des Flamands

Pointe du Bout

㊾
㊿
51
52
53

Baie de Fort-de-France

Anse-Mitan

Anse-à-l'Ane ⑰

54
55
56
57
58

La Villa Creole
Les Trois-Ilets ⑯
Mt. Bigot
D7

59
60

Le Diamant

Anse-d'Arlets
Grande Anse du Diamant
D37

⑱

Caribbean Sea

N

Diamond Rock

61 62 63

0 _____ 10 miles
0 _____ 15 km

1 Exploring Sites

24 Hotels and Restaurants

Bambou, **50**
Club Med/Buccaneer's Creek, **65**
Diamont Les Bains, **63**
Diamont-Novotel, **62**
Imperatrice, **48**
La Bakoua, **47**
La Batelière Hotel and Casino, **32**
The Last Resort, **64**
Le Méridien Trois-Ilets, **58**
Leyritz Plantation, **26**
Madras, **30**
Manoir de Beauregard, **68**
Martinique Cottages, **35**
PLM Azur-Carayou, **49**
PLM Azur La Pagerie, **51**
Rivage Hotel, **53**
Saint Aubin, **32**

Except for the area around Cap Chevalier, the Atlantic waters are rough and should be avoided by all but expert swimmers.

Staying in Martinique

Important Addresses

Tourist Information: The **Martinique Tourist Office** (Blvd. Alfassa, tel. 596/63–79–60) is open Monday–Thursday 7:30–12:30 PM and 2:30–5:30, Friday 7:30–12:30 and 2:30–5, Saturday 8–noon.

Emergencies

Police: Call 596/17.

Fire: Call 596/18.

Ambulance: Call 596/70–36–48 or 596/71–59–48.

Hospitals: There is a 24-hour emergency room at **Hôpital La Meynard** (Châteauboeuf, just outside Fort-de-France, tel. 596/50–15–15)

Pharmacies: Pharmacies in Fort-de-France include **Pharmacie de la Paix** (corner rue Victor Schoelcher and rue Perrinon, tel. 596/71–94–83) and **Pharmacie Cypria** (Blvd. de Gaulle, tel. 596/63–22–25).

Consulate: The **United States Consulate** (14 rue Blenac, Fort-de-France, tel. 596/63–13–03).

Currency

The coin of the realm is the French franc, which consists of 100 *centimes* (for example, the cost of an airmail stamp is 4.40F: 4 francs, 40 centimes). At press time, the rate was 5.96F to U.S. $1, but check the current exchange rate before you leave home. U.S. dollars are accepted in some of the tourist hotels, but for convenience, it's better to convert your money into francs. Banks give a more favorable rate than do hotels. A currency-exchange service, **Change Caraibes,** is open daily at the Arrivals Building at Lamentin Airport, at the Galerie des Flibustiers in Fort-de-France, and at the entrance to Club Med in Ste-Anne (tel. 596/51–51–51, ext. 11–41, or 596/60–28–40). *Note:* Prices quoted here are in U.S. dollars unless indicated otherwise.

Major credit cards are accepted in hotels and restaurants in Fort-de-France and the Pointe du Bout areas; few establishments in the countryside accept them. There is a 20% discount on luxury items paid for with traveler's checks or with certain credit cards.

Taxes and Service Charges

A resort tax varies from hotel to hotel; the maximum is $1 per person per day.

The departure tax is $1.

Rates quoted by hotels usually include a 10% service charge; some hotels add 10% to your bill. All restaurants include a 15% service charge in their menu prices.

Guided Tours

For a personalized tour of the island, ask the Tourist Office to arrange for a tour with an English-speaking taxi driver. There are set rates for tours to various points on the island, and if you share the ride with two or three other sightseers, the price will be whittled down.

Madinina Tours (tel. 596/73–35–35) offers half- and full-day jaunts, with lunch included in the all-day outings. Boat tours are also available, as well as air excursions to the Grenadines and to St. Lucia. Madinina has tour desks in most of the major hotels.

Hélicaraïbes (tel. 596/73–30–03) provides charter tours by helicopter for a mere $700 or so per hour.

Parc Naturel Regional de la Martinique (Regional Nature Reserve, tel. 596/73–19–30) organizes inexpensive guided hiking tours year-round. Descriptive folders are available at the Tourist Office.

Getting Around

Taxis Taxi stands are located at Lamentin Airport, in downtown Fort-de-France, and at major hotels. Rates are regulated by the government. The minimum charge during the day is 9.50F (about $1.50). The cost from the airport to Fort-de-France is about 53F ($8 or $9); from the airport to Pointe du Bout, about 136F ($20 or $22). A 40% surcharge is in effect between 8 PM and 6 AM.

Buses Public buses and eight-passenger minivans (license plates bear the letters TC) are an inexpensive means of getting from point to point around the island. Buses are always crowded and are not recommended for the timid traveler. In Fort-de-France, the main terminal for the minivans is at Pointe Simon on the waterfront. There are frequent departures from early morning until 8 PM; fares range from $1 to $5.

Ferries Weather permitting, *vedettes* (ferries) operate daily between Fort-de-France and the Marina Meridien in Pointe du Bout and between Fort-de-France and Anse-Mitan and Anse-à-l'Ane. The Quai d'Esnambuc is the arrival and departure point in Fort-de-France. At press time, the one way fare was 10F; round-trip 15F. Ferry schedules are listed in the visitors' guide, *Choubouloute*, available at the Office of Tourism.

Bicycles or Motorbikes Bikes and motorbikes can be rented from **Vespa** (tel. 596/71–60–03), **Funny** (tel. 596/63–33–05), or **T. S. Autos** (tel. 596/63–42–82), all of which are located in Fort-de-France.

Rental Cars Martinique has about 175 miles of well-paved and well-marked roads (albeit the markings are *en français*). Streets in Fort-de-France are narrow and clogged with traffic, country roads are mountainous with hairpin curves, and the Martiniquais drive with abandon. If you drive in the country, be sure to take along a good phrase book and a copy of the detailed map, *Carte Routière et Touristique*, available in bookstores.

A valid driver's license is needed to rent a car for up to 20 days. After that, you'll need an International Driver's Permit. Major credit cards are accepted by most car-rental agents. Rates are about $35–$40 per day. Among the many agencies are **Avis** (tel. 596/70–11–60 or 800/331–1212), **Budget** (tel. 596/63–69–00 or 800/527–0700), **Hertz** (tel. 596/60–64–64 or 800/654–3131), and **Europcar/National Car Rental** (tel. 596/73–33–13 or 800/328–4567).

Telephones and Mail To call Martinique station-to-station from the United States, dial 011 plus 596 plus the local six-digit number. For person-to-person calls, dial 01 plus 596 plus the local number. It is not possible to make collect or credit calls from Martinique to the United States. There are no coin telephone booths on the island. If you need to make calls outside your hotel, go to the post office and purchase a *Telecarte*, which looks like a credit card and is used in special booths marked *Telecom*. Long-distance calls made with *Telecartes* are less costly than are operator-assisted calls.

To place an intraisland call, dial the local six-digit number. To call the United States from Martinique, dial 19–596–1, area code, and the number you are trying to reach.

Airmail letters to the United States are 4.40F for up to 20 grams; postcards, 2.80F.

Opening and Closing Times Stores that cater to tourists are generally open weekdays 8:30–6; Saturday 8:30–1. Banking hours are weekdays 7:30–noon and 2:30–4.

Beaches

All Martinique's beaches are open to the public, but hotels charge a fee for nonguests to use changing rooms and facilities. There are no official nudist beaches, but topless bathing is prevalent at the large resort hotels. Unless you're an expert swimmer, steer clear of the Atlantic waters, except in the area of Cap Chevalier and the Caravelle Peninsula. The soft, white-sand beaches are along the southern coast; to the north the beaches are of gray volcanic sand.

Les Salines is a 1½-mile cove of soft white sand lined with coconut palms. A short drive south of Ste-Anne, it's awash with families and children during holidays and on weekends, but quiet and uncrowded during the week even at the height of the winter season. Take along some picnic food and towels because there are no facilities.

The soft white beaches of **Pointe du Bout** are man-made, superb, and lined with luxury resorts, among them the Meridien and the Bakoua.

Anse-Mitan was created by Mother Nature, who placed it just to the south of Pointe du Bout and sprinkled it with white sand. The waters around this beach offer superb snorkeling opportunities. Hotels on the beach are the Auberge de l'Anse-Mitan and the Bambou.

On the beach at **Anse-à-l'Ane,** you can spread your lunch on a picnic table, browse through the nearby shell museum, and cool off in the bar of the Calalou Hotel.

Diamant, the island's longest beach (2½ miles), has a splendid view of Diamond Rock, but the waters are rough and the currents are strong. This area is home to the Diamant-Novotel and Diamant les Bains hotels.

Near Les Salines, **Pointe Marin** stretches north from Ste-Anne. A good windsurfing and waterskiing spot, it also has campsites, sanitary facilities, and a 5F admission charge. Club Med occupies the northern edge, and the Manoir de Beauregard is in the nearby town of Ste-Anne.

Anse-Trabaud is on the Atlantic side, across the southern tip of the island from Ste-Anne. There is nothing here but white sand and the sea.

Exploring Martinique

Numbers in the margin correspond with points of interest on the Martinique map.

The starting point of the tour is the capital city of Fort-de-France, where almost a third of the island's 320,000 people live. From here, we'll tour St-Pierre, Mont Pelée, and other points north, go along the Atlantic coast, and finish with a look at the sights in the south.

Fort-de-France   **Fort-de-France** lies on the beautiful Baie des Flamands on the
❶   island's Caribbean (west) coast. With its narrow streets and pastel buildings with ornate wrought-iron balconies, the capital city is reminiscent of the French Quarter in New Orleans. However, where New Orleans is flat, Fort-de-France is hilly. Public and commercial buildings and residences cling to its hillsides.

Stop first at the **Office of Tourism,** which shares a building with Air France on the boulevard Alfassa, right on the bay near the ferry landing. English-speaking staffers provide excellent, free material, including detailed maps; a visitors' guide called *Choubouloute,* which lists events; and *Bienvenue en Martinique (Welcome to Martinique),* which has further information.

Thus armed, walk across the street to **La Savane.** The 12½-acre landscaped park is filled with gardens, tropical trees, fountains, and benches. It's a popular gathering place and the scene of promenades, parades, and impromptu soccer matches. A statue of Pierre Belain d'Esnambuc, leader of the island's first settlers, is upstaged by Vital Dubray's flattering white Carrara marble statue of the Empress Josephine, Napoleon's first wife. Sculpted in a high-waisted Empire gown, Josephine gazes toward Trois-Ilets across the bay, where in 1763 she was born Marie-Joseph Tascher de la Pagerie. Near the harbor is a **marketplace** where beads, baskets, pottery, straw hats, and the like are for sale. On the edge of the Savane, you can catch the **ferry** for the beaches at Anse-Mitan and Anse-à-l'Ane and for the 20-minute run across the bay to the resort hotels of Pointe du Bout.

Rue de la Liberté runs along the west side of La Savane. Look for the main Post Office (rue de la Liberté, between rue Blenac and rue Antoine Siger). Just across rue Blenac from the Post Office is the **Musée Departementale de Martinique,** which contains exhibits pertaining to the pre-Columbian Arawak and Carib periods. On display are pottery, beads, and part of a skeleton that turned up during excavations in 1972. One exhibit examines the history of slavery; costumes, documents, furniture, and handicrafts from the island's colonial period are on display. *9 rue de la Liberté, tel. 596/71–57–05. Admission: 5F. Open weekdays 8–noon and 3–5, Sat. 8–noon.*

Leave the museum and walk west (away from La Savane) on rue Blenac to rue Victor Schoelcher. There you'll see the Romanesque **St-Louis Cathedral,** whose steeple rises high above the surrounding buildings. The cathedral has lovely stained-glass windows. A number of Martinique's former governors are interred beneath the choir loft.

Rue Schoelcher runs through the center of the capital's primary shopping district, which consists of a six-block area bounded by rue de la République, rue de la Liberté, rue de Victor Severe, and rue Victor Hugo. Stores feature Paris fashions and French perfume, china, crystal, and liqueurs, as well as local handicrafts.

Time Out **Drugstore de la Galerie** (46 rue Ernest Duproge, tel. 596/73–90–85) is a combination restaurant, cafeteria, and tearoom, where you can rest your feet and get a light repast every day from 7 AM to midnight.

Three blocks north of the cathedral, make a right turn on rue Perrinon and go one block. At the corner of rue de la Liberté is the **Bibliothèque Schoelcher,** the wildly elaborate Byzantine-Egyptian-Romanesque–style public library. It's named after Victor Schoelcher, who led the fight to free the slaves in the French West Indies in the 19th century. The eye-popping structure was built for the 1889 Paris Exposition, after which it was dismantled, shipped to Martinique, and reassembled piece by ornate piece on its present location.

Follow rue Victor Severe five blocks west, just beyond the Hotel de Ville, and you'll come to Place Jose-Marti. The **Parc Floral et Culturel** will acquaint you with the variety of the exotic flora on this island. There's also an aquarium showing fish that can be found in these waters. *Place Jose-Marti, Sermac, tel. 596/71–66–25. Admission free. Open Mon.–Sat. 9–noon and 3–6.*

The Levassor River meanders through the park and joins the bay at **Pointe Simon,** where yachts can be chartered. The river divides the downtown area from the ritzy residential district of Didier in the hills.

The North The tour of the north is divided into two sections: a day trip and an overnight excursion. Martinique's "must do" is the drive north along the coast from Fort-de-France to St-Pierre. The 40-mile round-trip to St-Pierre can be made in an afternoon, although there is enough to see to fill an entire day. The drive to the north coast will appeal primarily to nature lovers, hikers, and mountain climbers. If you are interested in climbing Mont Pelée or hiking, plan to spend at least a night on the road *(see* Participant Sports, below, for guided hikes). Bear in mind that a 20-mile mountain drive takes longer than driving 20 miles on the prairie.

Tour 1 Head west out of Fort-de-France on Route N2. You'll pass
② through the suburb of **Schoelcher,** home of the University of the French West Indies and Guyana. La Batelière Hotel, noted for its sports facilities, is also located here.

Just north of Schoelcher is Fond-Lahaye, where the road begins to climb sharply. About 4½ miles farther along, you'll come to the fishing village of **Case-Pilote,** named after a Carib chief to whom the French took kindly and called Pilote.

Time Out **La Glou-Glou** (Rte. N2 at the turnoff to Case-Pilote) is a little sidewalk café that is good for sandwiches, burgers, ice cream, and other snacks.

Continuing along the coastal road, you'll see red-roof houses
③ clinging to the green mountainside on the way to **Bellefontaine,**

4 miles north. This is another fishing village, with pastel houses on the hillsides and colorful boats bobbing in the water. One of the houses here is built in the shape of a boat.

4 Continue north along the coast until you get to **Le Carbet.** Columbus is believed to have landed here on June 15, 1502. In 1635, Pierre Belain d'Esnambuc arrived here with the first French settlers.

Le Carbet is home to the **Amazona Zoological Gardens,** which has crocodiles from the Amazon, armadillos, lions, and ocelots. *Le Coin, Le Carbet, tel. 596/78-00-64. Admission: adults 8F, children 5F. Open daily 9-6.*

5 Just north of Carbet is **Anse-Turin,** where Paul Gauguin lived for a short time in 1887. The **Musée Gauguin** traces the history of the artist's Martinique connection through documents, letters, and reproductions of some of the paintings he did while on the island. There is also a display of Creole costumes. *Anse-Turin, tel. 596/77-22-66. Admission: 5F. Open daily 10-5.*

6 Two miles farther brings you to **St-Pierre,** the island's oldest city, which now has a population of about 6,000. At the turn of this century, St-Pierre was a flourishing city of 30,000 and was called the Paris of the West Indies. In spring 1902, Mont Pelée began to rumble and spit out ash and steam. By the first week in May, all wildlife had wisely vacated the area. City officials, however, ignored the warnings. At 8 AM on May 8, 1902, the volcano erupted, belching forth a cloud of burning ash with temperatures over 3,600°F. In the space of three minutes, Mt. Pelée transformed the Paris of the West Indies into Martinique's Pompeii. The entire town was destroyed and its inhabitants were instantly calcified. There was only one survivor, a prisoner named Siparis, who was saved by the thick walls of his underground cell. (He was later pardoned and for some years afterward was a sideshow attraction at the Barnum & Bailey Circus.) You can wander through the site to see the ruins of the island's first church, built in 1640; the theater; the toppled statues; and Siparis's cell. *For a guided tour of the area, contact Syndicat d'initiative, La Guinguette Restaurant, tel. 596/77-15-02. Tours: 15F adults, 10F children. Open weekdays 9-noon.*

The **Musée Vulcanologique** was established in 1932 by American volcanologist Franck Perret. His collection includes photographs of the old town, documents, and a number of relics excavated from the ruins, including molten glass, melted iron, and contorted clocks stopped at 8 AM, the time of the disaster. *St-Pierre, tel. 596/77-15-16. Admission: 5F adults, 1F children. Open Mon.-Sat. 9-noon and 3-5, Sun. 9-noon.*

Time Out **Le Factorerie** (Quartier Fort, tel. 596/77-12-53) rose from the ruins of a Benedictine monastery. The hillside alfresco eatery belongs to an agricultural training school and offers two daily three-course lunch menus featuring seafood and Creole dishes.

In St-Pierre, Route N2 turns inland toward Morne Rouge, but before going there, you may want to follow the coastal road 8 **7** miles north to **Le Prêcheur.** En route, you'll pass what is called the Tomb of the Carib Indians. The site is actually a formation of limestone hills from which the last of the Caribs are said to have flung themselves to avoid capture by the French. The village of Le Prêcheur was the childhood home of Françoise d'Aubigné, later to become the Marquise de Maintenon and the second wife of Louis XIV.

Return to St-Pierre and drive 4 miles east on Route 2 to reach **⑧ Le Morne Rouge.** Lying on the southern slopes of Mont Pelée, the town of Morne Rouge, too, was destroyed by the volcano. It is now a popular resort spot with spectacular mountain scenery. This is the starting point for a climb up the 4,600-foot mountain, but you must have a guide *(see* Participant Sports, below).

At this point, you have the option of returning to Fort-de-France or continuing on for a tour of the north and Atlantic coasts.

If you choose to return to the capital, take the Route de la Trace (Rte. N3) south from Le Morne Rouge. The winding, two-lane paved road is one of the island's great drives, snaking through dense tropical rain forests.

⑨ La Trace leads to **Balata,** where you can see the **Balata Church,** an exact replica of Sacré-Coeur Basilica in Paris, and the **Jardin de Balata** (Balata Gardens). Paths in the gardens lead past thousands of varieties of tropical flowers and plants. There are shaded benches where you can relax and take in the panoramic views of the mountains. *Rte. de Balata, tel. 596/64–48–73. Admission: 30F adults, 10F children. Open daily 9–5.*

From Balata, Route N3 continues 8 miles south to the capital city.

If you've opted to continue exploring the north and Atlantic coasts, take Route N3 north from Morne Rouge. You'll pass through Petite Savane and wind northeast to the flower-filled **⑩** village of **Ajoupa-Bouillon,** a 17th-century settlement in the midst of pineapple fields.

A mile and a half east of Ajoupa-Bouillon, Route N3 deadends at Route 1, which runs north–south. Turn left and drive 3 miles through sugarcane, pineapple, and banana fields to **Basse-Pointe,** which lies at sea level on the Atlantic coast. Just before reaching Basse-Pointe you'll pass a Hindu temple, one of the relics of the East Indians who settled in this area in the 19th century. The view of the eastern slope of Mont Pelée is lovely from here. Route D21 leads inland to the estimable **Leyritz Plantation,** a fine place to stay, to play, and to eat.

⑪ The **Musée de Poupées Végétales** contains a collection of exotic and unusual dolls. The dolls, depicting famous women of French history, are made entirely of plants and leaves. They are the work of local artisan Will Fenton. *Leyritz Plantation, tel. 596/75–53–08. Admission: 10F. Open daily 8–6.*

⑫ Three miles along, you'll come to **Macouba** on the coast. From here, the island's most spectacular drive leads 6 miles to **Grand-Rivière,** on the northernmost point. Perched on high cliffs, this village affords magnificent views of the sea, the mountains, and, on clear days, the neighboring island of Dominica. From Grand-Rivière, you can trek 11 miles on a well-marked path that leads through lush tropical vegetation to the beach at Anse-Ceron on the northwest coast. The beach is lovely and the diving is excellent, but the currents are very strong and swimming is not advised.

From Grand-Rivière, you can backtrack 13 miles to the junction of Routes N1 and N3 and continue down the Atlantic coast.

Time Out Stop in at **Chez Vava** (Rte. 1 on the eastern edge of Grand-Rivière, tel. 596/75–52–81) for a rum punch and a lunch of seafood and Creole dishes.

From the junction of Routes N1 and N3, continue 10 miles on Route 1 along the Atlantic coast, driving through the villages ⑬ of Le Lorrain and Marigot to **Ste-Marie,** a town of about 20,000 Martiniquais and the commercial capital of the island's north. There is a lovely mid-19th-century church in the town and, on a more earthy note, a rum distillery.

The **Musée du Rhum,** operated by the St. James Rum Distillery, is housed in a graceful galleried Creole house. Guided tours of the museum take in displays of the tools of the trade and include a visit to the distillery. And, yes, you may sample the product. *Ste-Marie, tel. 596/69–30–02. Admission free. Open weekdays 9–noon and 2–4:30, weekends 9–noon.*

⑭ **La Trinité,** a subprefecture in the north, is 6 miles to the south in a sheltered bay. From La Trinité, the **Caravelle Peninsula** thrusts 8 miles into the Atlantic Ocean. Much of the peninsula is under the auspices of the Regional Nature Reserve and offers places for trekking, swimming, and sailing. This is the home of the **Morne Pavilion,** an open-air sports and leisure center operated by the nature reserve *(see* Participant Sports, below). To reach it, turn right at Tartane on the Spoutourne Morne Pavilion road.

At the eastern tip of the peninsula, you can root through the ⑮ ruins of the **Dubuc Castle.** This was the home of the Dubuc de Rivery family, which owned the peninsula in the 18th century. According to legend, young Aimée Dubuc de Rivery was captured by Barbary pirates, sold to the Ottoman Empire, became a favorite of the sultan, and gave birth to Mahmoud II.

Tour 2 Return to La Trinité and take Route N4, which winds 20 miles through lush tropical scenery back to Fort-de-France.

The loop through the south is a round-trip of about 100 miles. This excursion will include the birthplace of the Empress Josephine, Pointe du Bout and its resort hotels, a few small museums, and many large beaches. You can spend an afternoon, a day, or a couple of weeks exploring this region, depending on the time at your disposal and your frame of mind.

From Fort-de-France, take Route N5, which leads south through Lamentin, where the airport is located. A 20-mile drive will bring you to Rivière-Salée, where you'll make a right ⑯ turn on Route D7 and drive 4½ miles to the village of **Les Trois-Ilets.**

Trois-Ilets, named after the three rocky islands nearby, is a lovely little village with a population of about 3,000. It's known for its pottery, straw, and wood works and as the birthplace of Napoleon's Empress Josephine. On the village square, you can visit the simple church were she was baptized Marie-Joseph Tascher de la Pagerie. To reach the museum and the old sugar plantation on which she was born, drive a mile west on Route D7 and turn left on Route D38.

A stone building that held the kitchen of the estate is now home to the **Musée de la Pagerie**. It contains an assortment of memorabilia pertaining to Josephine's life and loves (she was married first to Alexandre de Beauharnais). There are family portraits; documents, including a marriage certificate; a love letter written to her in 1796 by Napoleon; and various antique furnishings, including the bed she slept in as a child. *Trois-Ilets, tel. 596/68–34–55. Admission: 10F. Open Tues.–Sun. 8:30–5.*

The **Maison de la Canne** will teach you everything you ever wanted to know about sugarcane. Exhibits take you through three centuries of sugarcane production, with displays of tools, scale models, engravings, and photographs. *Trois-Ilets, tel. 596/68–32–04. Admission: 15F. Open Tues.–Sun. 9:30–5:30.*

⑰ You can reach **Pointe du Bout** and the beach at **Anse-Mitan** by turning right on Route D38 west of Trois-Ilets. This area is filled with resort hotels, among them the Bakoua and the Meridien. The Pointe du Bout marina is a colorful spot where a whole slew of boats are tied up. The ferry to Fort-de-France leaves from this marina.

Time Out **Food-Amour** (Marina, Pte. du Bout, tel. 596/66–02–00) is a friendly spot by the marina where you can get pizza, burgers, ice cream, beer, and wine to enjoy on the patio.

When you return to Route D7, turn right and head west. You'll pass by the **Empress Josephine Golf Course** on the way to **Anse-à-l'Ane**, where there is a pretty white-sand beach complete with picnic tables.

South from Anse-à-l'Ane, Route D7 turns into a 10-mile roller coaster en route to **Anse-d-'Arlets,** another popular beach. You'll see fishermen's nets strung up on the beach to dry and pleasure boats on the water.

From the center of town, take Route D37 along the coast down to Morne Larcher and on to **Le Diamant.** Several hotels sit on the 2½-mile beach (the island's longest, though not the best
⑱ beach), and from here, there is a splendid view of **Diamond Rock** a couple of miles offshore.

In 1804, during the squabbles over possession of the island between the French and the English, the latter commandeered the rock, armed it with cannons, christened it HMS *Diamond Rock*, and proceeded to use it as a warship. For almost a year and a half, the British held the rock, bombarding any French ships that came along. The French got wind of the fact that the British were getting cabin fever on their isolated ship-island and arranged a supply of barrels of rum for those on the rock. The French easily overpowered the inebriated sailors, ending one of the most curious engagements in naval history.

The hotels Diamant Les Bains and Diamant-Novotel are both in this area. At Le Diamant, Route D37 joins up with Route D7, which strikes out in a northeasterly direction at Taupinière. A mile's drive will bring you to a fork in the road; one branch heads north to Fort-de-France and the other continues south along the coast. Take the southerly route.

Three miles down the coastline lies **Ste-Luce,** another fishing village with a pretty white beach. From Ste-Luce, you can take

⑲ Route D17 north 1 mile to the **Forêt de Montravail,** where arrows point the way to Carib rock drawings.

Time Out **La Vague du Sud** (Rue Schoelcher, Ste-Luce, tel. 596/62–44–96) is an unpretentious little eatery serving seafood.

You'll say good-bye to Route D7 in Ste-Luce and hook up with Route D18, which will take you northeast 4 miles to **Rivière Pilote,** a town of about 12,000 people. From there, Route D18A trickles down south to **Pointe Figuier,** where the scuba diving is excellent. Stay with Route D18A and curve around the beautiful Cul de Sac inlet through **Le Marin.** Just east of Le Marin, turn right on Route D9 and drive all the way down to the sea. En route you'll pass the turnoff to Buccaneer's Creek/Club Med ⑳ and the pretty village of **Ste-Anne,** where a Roman Catholic church sits on the square facing a lovely white beach. Not far away, at the southernmost tip, is the island's best beach, the **Grande Anse des Salines.** It's 1½ miles of soft white sand, calm waters, and relative seclusion (except on weekends).

In sharp contrast to the north, this section of the island is arid and dry. If you walk from Les Salines to Anse-Trabaud, you'll ㉑ go through the **petrified forest,** which would look eerie and otherworldly any place, but especially on the Island of Flowers.

Backtrack 9 miles to Le Marin. From there, Route N6 goes ㉒ north 7 miles to **Le Vauclin,** skirting the highest point in the south, **Mt. Vauclin** (1,654 feet). Le Vauclin is an important fishing port on the Atlantic coast, and the return of the fishermen shortly before noon each day is a big event.

㉓ Continue north 9 miles on Route N6 to **Le François,** a sizable city of some 16,000 Martiniquais. This is a great place for snorkeling. Offshore are a number of shallow basins with white-sand bottoms between the reefs.

There is a lovely bay 6 miles farther along at **Le Robert.** You'll also come to the junction of Route N1, which will take you west to Fort-de-France, 12½ miles away.

Participant Sports

Bicycling The *Parc Naturel Regional de la Martinique* (tel. 596/64–42–59) has designed biking itineraries off the beaten track. Bikes can be rented from **Funny** (tel. 596/63–33–05), **Vespa** (tel. 596/71–60–03), and **T. S. Autos** (tel. 596/63–42–82), all located in Fort-de-France.

Boating For boat rentals and yacht charters, check with **Ship Shop** (6 rue Joseph-Compère, Fort-de-France, tel. 596/71–43–40), **Carib Charter** (Habitation Croix du Sud, Pointe Jaham, Schoelcher, tel. 596/71–58–96), **Soleil et Voile** (Marina Pointe du Bout, tel. 596/66–07–74), **Alize Plus** (Marina Pointe du Bout, tel. 596/66–04–81), or **Star Voyages Antilles** (Marina Pointe du Bout, tel. 596/66–00–72).

Deep-Sea Fishing Fish cruising these waters include tuna, barracuda, dolphin, kingfish, and bonito. For a day's outing on the 37-foot *Egg Harbor,* with gear and breakfast included, contact **Bathy's Club** (Méridien Hotel, tel. 596/66–00–00). Charters of up to five days can be arranged on Captain Réné Alaric's 37-foot **_Rayon Vert_** (Auberge du Vare, Case-Pilote, north of Fort-de-France, tel. 596/78–80–56).

Golf At **Golf de l'Imperatrice Joséphine** (tel. 596/68–32–81), there is an 18-hole Robert Trent Jones course with an English-speaking pro, fully equipped pro shop, a bar, and restaurant. Located at Trois-Ilets, a mile from the Pointe du Bout resort area and 18 miles from Fort-de-France, the club offers special greens fees for hotel guests and cruise-ship passengers.

Hiking Inexpensive guided excursions in which tourists can participate are organized year-round by the *Parc Naturel Regional de la Martinique* (Regional Nature Reserve, Caserne Bouille, Fort-de-France, tel. 596/73–19–30).

Horseback Riding Excursions and lessons are available at **Ranch Jack** (near Anse-d'Arlets, tel. 596/68–63–97), the **Black Horse Ranch** (near La Pagerie in Trois-Ilets, tel. 596/66–00–04), and **La Cavale** (near Diamant on the road to the Novotel hotel, tel. 596/76–22–94).

Sailing Hobie Cats, Sunfish, and Sailfish can be rented by the hour from hotel beach shacks. If you're a member of a yacht club, show your club membership card and enjoy the facilities of **Club de la Voile de Fort-de-France** (Pointe Simon, tel. 596/70–26–63) and **Yacht Club de la Martinique** (Blvd. Chevalier, Ste-Marthe, tel. 596/70–26–63).

Scuba Diving To explore the old shipwrecks, coral gardens, and other undersea sites, you must have a medical certificate and insurance papers. Among the island's dive operators are **Bathys Club** (Hotel Meridien, tel. 596/66–00–00), **Carib Scuba Club** (Hotel Latitude, north of Fort-de-France, tel. 596/78–08–08), and the **Caraibe Coltri Club** (Diamant-Novotel, tel. 596/76–42–42).

Sea Excursions and Snorkeling The *Aquarium* (Fort-de-France, tel. 596/61–49–49) is a glass-bottom boat that does excursions. For information on other sailing, swimming, snorkeling, and beach picnic trips, contact **Affaires Maritimes** (tel. 596/71–90–05).

Sports Center The **Morne Pavilion** (tel. 596/73–19–30), on the Caravelle Peninsula, is an open-air sports and leisure center offering sailing, tennis, and other activities.

Tennis In addition to its links, the **Golf de l'Imperatrice Joséphine** (Trois-Ilets, tel. 596/68–32–82) has three lighted tennis courts. There are also two courts at the **Bakoua Beach Hotel** (tel. 596/66–02–02); six courts at **La Batelière Hotel** (tel. 596/61–49–49); seven courts at **Buccaneer's Creek/Club Med** (tel. 596/76–74–52); two courts at **Diamant-Novotel** (tel. 596/76–42–42); one court at the **Leyritz Plantation** (tel. 596/75–53–92); and two courts at the **Meridien Hotel** (tel. 596/66–00–00). For additional information about tennis on the island, contact **La Ligue de Tennis** (Petit Manoir, Lamentin, tel. 596/51–08–00).

Shopping

French fragrances and designer scarves, fine china and crystal, leather goods, and liquors and liqueurs are all good buys in Fort-de-France. Purchases are further sweetened by the 20% discount on luxury items when paid for by traveler's checks and major credit cards. Among local items, look for Creole gold jewelry, such as loop earrings, heavy bead necklaces, and slave bracelets; white and dark rum; and handcrafted straw goods, pottery, and tapestries. In addition, U.S. Customs allows you to bring some of the local flora into the country.

Shopping Areas The area around the cathedral in Fort-de-France has a number of small shops carrying luxury items. Of particular note are the shops on **rue Victor Hugo, rue Moreau de Jones, rue Antoine Siger,** and **rue Lamartine.** There is also a duty-free shop at the airport. On the outskirts of Fort-de-France, shopping malls include **Centre Commercial de Cluny, Centre Commercial de Dillon,** and **Centre Commercial de Bellevue.**

Good Buys *China and Crystal* Look for Lalique, Limoges, and Baccarat at **Cadet Daniel** (72 rue Antoine Siger, Fort-de-France, tel. 596/71–41–48) and **Roger Albert** (7 rue Victor Hugo, Fort-de-France, tel. 596/71–71–71).

Flowers Anthuriums, torch lilies, and lobster claws are packaged for shipment at **MacIntosh** (31 rue Victor Hugo, Fort-de-France, tel. 596/70–09–50, and at the airport, tel. 596/51–51–51) and **Les Petites Floralies** (75 rue Blenac, Fort-de-France, tel. 596/71–66–16).

Local Handicrafts A wide variety of dolls, straw goods, tapestries, pottery, and other items are available at the **Caribbean Art Center** (Centre de Metiers Arts, opposite the Tourist Office, Blvd. Alfassa, Fort-de-France (tel. 596/70–32–16).

Perfumes Dior, Chanel, and Guerlain are among the popular scents at **Roger Albert** (7 rue Victor Hugo, Fort-de-France, tel. 596/71–71–71).

Rum Rum can be purchased at the various distilleries, including **Duquesnes** (Fort-de-France, tel. 596/71–91–68), **St. James** (Ste-Marie, tel. 596/69–30–02), and **Trois Rivières** (Ste-Luce, tel. 596/62–51–78).

Dining

Martinique has, arguably, the best food in all the Caribbean, with restaurants serving classic French cuisine and Creole dishes and wine cellars filled with fine French wines. Some of the best restaurants are tucked away in the countryside, and therein lies a problem. The farther you venture from tourist hotels, the less likely you are to find English-speaking folk. If you don't speak French and want to savor the countryside cuisine, take along a sophisticated phrase book. The local Creole specialties are *colombo* (curry), *accras* (cod or vegetable fritters), *crabbes farcies* (stuffed land crab), *écrevisses* (freshwater crawfish), *boudin* (Creole blood sausage), *lambi* (conch), *langouste* (clawless Caribbean lobster), *soudons* (sweet clams), and *oursin* (sea urchin). The local favorite libation is *le 'ti punch,* a "little punch," concocted of white rum, sugar, syrup, lime, and ice.

The most highly recommended restaurants are indicated by a star ★.

Category	Cost*
Expensive	over $40
Moderate	$25–$40
Inexpensive	under $25

per person, excluding drinks and service

Fort-de-France **La Biguine.** Downstairs is a cozy, casual café with red-and-white check cloths and upstairs, a more formal candlelit dining room. Local fish poached in Creole sauce, shark cooked in tomato sauce, and duck fillet with pineapple or orange sauce are among the à la carte offerings, with homemade tarts for dessert. *11 Rte. de la Folie, tel. 596/71–40–07. Jackets required for dinner. Reservations required for dinner. AE. Closed Sun. Expensive.*

★ **La Belle Epoque.** The nine tables on the terrace of this turn-of-the-century house are much in demand. You can feast on duck fillet in mango sauce, hot spinach mousse, and veal kidneys. Yves Coyac is the talented Martiniquais chef. *Km 2.5, Rte. de Didier, tel. 596/64–01–09. Jackets and reservations required for dinner. DC, MC, V. Closed Sun. and Mon. Expensive.*

Le Bristol. Selecting from a long list of rum drinks is the first order of business in this handsome terrace restaurant. The menu changes monthly, but you may find gazpacho or escargots in garlic butter for starters and main dishes, such as lobster fricassee and magret de canard as well as a variety of beef and fish dishes. Hot apple tarts and feathery coconut soufflés are usually on the dessert list. *0.2 km., rue Martin Luther King, tel. 596/63–66–76. Jackets and reservations required for dinner. AE. Expensive.*

★ **La Fontane.** In a pastoral setting, this lovely gingerbread house with a wrap-around veranda is shaded by mango trees. Inside you'll find Oriental rugs, fresh flowers, and a display of antiques that includes a handsome gramophone and a grandmother's clock. *Le Bambou de la Fontane* is a mixed salad with fish, tomato, corn, melon, and crawfish. Other dishes served here are cream soup with crabs, crayfish bisque, red snapper with lemon/lime sauce, magret de canard, and steak au poivre. *Km 4 Rte. de Balata, tel. 596/64–28–70 or 596/71–38–28. Jackets and tie required. Reservations essential. AE, CB. Closed Sun. Expensive.*

La Grand 'Voile. Crisp white cloths, fine china and crystal, and lots of windows overlooking the harbor contribute to a lovely dining room. Starters include chilled chicken liver mousse and fresh steamed mussels. Main dishes include lobster in Creole sauce and fillet of beef Rossini (with artichoke hearts, foie gras, truffles, and Madeira sauce). The *Menu Degustation* (a variety of sample-size portions) is a practical way to savor the restaurant's specialties. Service here is sometimes on the slow side. *Pte. Simon, tel. 596/70–29–29. Jacket and reservations suggested. AE, MC, V. Open daily for lunch and dinner. Expensive.*

Le Tiffany. Claude Pradine presides over the kitchen and the magic shows put on every Friday night. Dining is on candlelit terraces or in a cozy room filled with Pradine's collection of antiques. The menu consists of French cuisine as well as Creole dishes, which include terrine of red snapper, fish soup, crabbe farcie or boudin, grilled fish, Creole courtbouillon, and curried lamb. Linger late over coffee, which is served with homemade chocolate truffles and cognac. *Ancienne Rte. de Schoelcher, near Croix de Bellevue, tel. 596/71–33–82. Reservations required for dinner. MC, V. No lunch Sat.; closed Sun. Expensive.*

★ **Le Coq Hardi.** At press time, plans were under way to knock out a wall and expand the restaurant to take care of the crowds that flock here for the best steaks in town. You can pick out your own steak and feel confident that it will be cooked to perfection.

Steak tartare is the house specialty, but there are tournedos Rossini (with artichoke hearts, foie gras, truffles, and Madeira sauce), entrecote Bordelaise, prime ribs, and T-bone steaks, among the wide selection of beef offerings. For dessert, there's a selection of sorbets, profiteroles, and pear Belle Hélène. *0.6 km., rue Martin Luther King, tel. 596/71–59–64. Reservations suggested. AE, DC, MC, V. Closed all day Wed. and Sat. at noon. Moderate.*

Diamant Creole. Claudine Victoire's popular seven-table restaurant is on the second floor of a little red-and-white house. The old-fashioned Creole dishes served include tiny local clams in white wine or with chives and shallots; fish or conch brochette; Creole paella; and soups and local vegetables not offered on most island menus. *7 Blvd. de Verdun, tel. 596/73–18–25. Reservations suggested. AE, MC, V. Closed Sun. Moderate.*

Chez Gaston. Its cozy upstairs dining room, very popular with local residents, features a Creole menu. The brochettes are especially recommended. The kitchen stays open late, and there's a small dance floor. The downstairs section serves snacks all day. A French phrase book will be very helpful. *10 rue Felix Eboue, tel. 596/71–45–48. Reservations accepted. No credit cards. Inexpensive.*

Le Crew. Meals are served family style in rustic dining rooms, where the bill of fare features a few Creole dishes and lots of typical French bistro dishes: fish soup and stuffed mussels, snails, country pâté, frogs' legs, tripe, grilled chicken, and steak. The portions are ample, and there's a daily 60F three-course tourist menu that simplifies ordering. *42 rue Ernst Deproge, tel. 596/73–04–14. Reservations accepted. No credit cards. Closed Sat. evening and Sun. Inexpensive.*

Les Trois-Ilets **L'Amphore.** Dining is either on the front terrace, where there's a nice view of the bay, or in a gas-lit garden. Lobster is the menu's highlight, but there are Creole specialties and classic French dishes as well. During dinner, a guitarist strums and sings in several languages. *Anse-Mitan, tel. 596/66–03–09. Reservations accepted. No credit cards. Closed Mon.; no dinner Sat. Moderate.*

Matador. Fresh flowers adorn each table in this simply furnished terrace restaurant. Creole boudin, quiche, or sea urchins are good for openers. Main dishes include turtle steak, Creole bouillaibaise, lobster Thermidor, and fillet of beef with port wine and mushrooms. *Anse-Mitan, tel. 596/68–05–36. Reservations suggested in high season. AE, DC, MC, V. Closed Wed. Moderate.*

★ **La Villa Creole.** The steak béarnaise, curried dishes, conch, courtbouillon, and other dishes are all superb. However, the real draw here is owner Guy Dawson, a popular singer and guitarist who entertains during dinner, either solo or en duo with Roland Manere or Guy Vadeleux. The setting is romantic, with oil lamps flickering in the lush back garden of this very popular place. *Anse-Mitan, tel. 596/66–05–53. Reservations essential. AE, DC, V. Closed Sun. Moderate.*

Bambou Restaurant. This casual place, right on the beach, serves omelets and salads, as well as lamb cutlets, curried chicken, steak au poivre, codfish pie, and sole meunière. For dessert, there's coconut flan or banana or pineapple flambé. *Anse-Mitan, tel. 596/66–01–39. Reservations accepted. AE, DC, MC, V. Inexpensive.*

Anse-d'Arlets **Tamarin Plage Restaurant.** The lobster *vivier* in the middle of the room gives you a clue to the specialty here, but there are other recommendable offerings as well. Fish soup or Creole boudin are good starters, then consider courtbouillon, chicken fricassee, and curried mutton. The beachfront bar is a popular local hangout. *Anse-d'Arlets, tel. 596/68–67–88. Reservations accepted. No credit cards. Moderate.*

★ **Ti Sable.** This restaurant has a dramatic setting right on a beautiful beach and is shaded by a huge sea-grape tree. Seating is either on a broad seaside veranda or in an open pavilion with a billowing parachute ceiling. Specialties include grilled crawfish, poached sea urchins, and curried mutton. *Anse-d'Arlets, tel. 596/68–62–44. Reservations suggested. AE, V. Closed Sun. and Mon. Moderate.*

Ste-Anne **Aux Filets Bleus.** This breezy open-air eatery is right on the
★ beach, and you can go for a swim before or after dining. Turtle or fish soup, stuffed crab, and avocado vinaigrette are all good opening bids. In addition to an assortment of lobster entrées, there is grilled or steamed fish and octopus with red beans and rice. *Pointe Marin, tel. 596/76–73–42. Reservations essential. No credit cards. Closed Mon. Moderate.*

La Dunette. Bright blue awnings shade the terrace, which is filled with wrought-iron chairs and tables, and there is an abundance of hanging plants. Your choices for lunch or dinner include fish soup, grilled fish or lobster, poached sea urchins, pork en brochette with pineapple, and several curried dishes. *Ste-Anne, tel. 596/76–73–90. Reservations suggested in high season. V. Closed Wed. Inexpensive.*

François **Club Nautique.** While this little place is not going to turn up in
★ *Architectural Digest*, the food that comes fresh daily out of the sea is exquisitely prepared. Have a couple of rum punches, then dig into turtle steak or charcoal-broiled lobster. The restaurant is right on the beach, and boat trips leave here for snorkeling in the nearby coral reefs. *Le François, tel. 596/54–31–00. Reservations accepted. AE, DC, MC, V. Open for lunch only. Inexpensive.*

Diamant **Diamant Plage.** This split-level terrace faces the post office in the village of Diamant. Octavia Gabrielle turns out, among other things, Creole turtle, shark stew, stuffed shrimp or conch, and superb grilled fish. *Le Diamant, tel. 596/76–40–48. Reservations accepted. V. Inexpensive.*

Lamentin **Le Verger.** An orchard is the setting for this lovely country
★ house, not far from the airport. Pheasant and duck, as well as game, are on the extensive menu, which also includes classic French and Creole dishes. Follow the signs for La Trinité; the entrance to the restaurant is on the right immediately after the Esso and Shell stations. *Place d'Armes, tel. 596/51–43–02. Reservations suggested. AE, DC, MC, V. Closed Sat. afternoon and Sun. night. Moderate–Expensive.*

Morne-des-Esses **Le Colibri.** In the northwestern reaches of the island, this is the
★ domain of Clotilde Palladino, who presides over the kitchen while her children serve. Choice seating is at one of the seven tables on the back terrace. For starters, try *buisson d'écrevisses*, six giant freshwater crayfish accompanied by a tangy tomato sauce flavored with thyme, scallions, and tiny bits of crayfish. Stuffed pigeon, lobster omelets, suckling pig, and coconut chicken are among the main dishes. *Morne-des-*

Esses, *tel. 596/69–91–95. Reservations essential. AE, DC, MC, V. Closed Mon. Moderate–Expensive.*

Basse-Pointe **Leyritz Plantation.** The pride of Martinique is *the* place all the
★ cruise passengers head as soon as they disembark. The restored 18th-century plantation has the ambience of a country inn and a dramatic view of Mont Pelée. The menu is mostly Creole, featuring boudin, chicken with coconut, and several curried dishes. *Basse-Pointe, tel. 596/75–53–92. Reservations essential. DC, MC. Moderate–Expensive.*

Restaurant Mally. Unpretentious and popular, Mally Edjam's home has a few tables inside and only four on the side porch under an awning. The lady is a legend on the island, and although it's a long drive up, you'll be rewarded with the likes of papaya soufflé, spicy Creole concoctions such as curried pork and stuffed land crabs, and fresh local vegetables. Her exotic *confitures* of guava, pineapple, and cornichon top off the feast, along with a yogurt or light coconut cake. *Rte. de la Côte Atlantique, tel. 596/75–51–18. Reservations required. No credit cards. Inexpensive.*

Le Morne Rouge **Auberge de la Montagne Pelée.** The restaurant is open for dinner by reservation only, but the real treat is lunch on a clear day, when you can see Mont Pelée's summit from the terrace. Creole and French dishes are featured, including a Caribbean style pot-au-feu, with whitefish, scallops, salmon, crayfish, and tiny vegetables. *Rte. de l'Aileron, tel. 596/52–32–09. Reservations essential. MC, V. Moderate.*

La Trinité **L'Ami Fritz.** Local gourmets flock to Fritz's for his Muenster
★ cheese, game, sauerkraut, and fine wines. The lovely country mansion nestles in rolling hills, surrounded by flowers and greenery. *Brin d'Amour, tel. 596/58–20–18. Jacket and tie required. Reservations suggested. V. Closed Mon. Expensive.*

Lodging

Martinique's range of accommodations runs from tiny French inns called *Relais Creoles* to splashy tourist resorts, with an 18th-century plantation to round things out. The majority of the hotels are clustered in Pointe du Bout and Anse-Mitan on the Trois-Ilets peninsula across the bay from Fort-de-France, but there are other notable lodgings scattered around the island. Attractive packages are offered by many of the hotels during the year, and it's a good idea to ask what's available when you call to reserve. Remember that in the small country inns, you'll need a French phrase book.

The most highly recommended lodgings are indicated by a star ★.

Category	Cost*
Very Expensive	over $200
Expensive	$130–$200
Moderate	$75–$130
Inexpensive	under $75

All prices are for a standard double room for two, excluding $1 per person per night tax and a 10% service charge.

Hotels

★ Le Bakoua. Named after the pointed straw hats worn by the local fishermen, the Bakoua is locally owned and operated. Located in Pointe du Bout, the hotel has accommodations in three hillside buildings and a fourth on its man-made white-sand beach. The decor is cushy-cum-rustic, with wooden furnishings and tile floors. All rooms have a balcony or patio, TV, radio, king-size bed, direct-dial phone, and air-conditioning. Most accommodations are spacious but some are small and less desirable; these are known in hotel parlance as mother-in-law rooms. Entertainment consists of live music and shows nightly, including dinner dancing, limbo, and Friday-night performances of Les Grands Ballets de la Martinique. Most of the staff speak commendable English. Be sure to inquire about special package deals. *Box 589, Fort-de-France, tel. 596/66–02–02; in NY, 212/696–1323; in U.K., 01/730–7144. 140 rooms, including 2 1-bedroom suites. Facilities: 2 restaurants, bar, pool, 2 lighted tennis courts, boutique, beauty salon, water-sports center. AE, DC, MC, V. Very Expensive.*

★ Le Méridien Trois-Ilets. There is a great deal of activity here, even in the low season, much of it revolving around the pool and the long strip of white-sand beach. All rooms are air-conditioned, with wall-to-wall carpeting, built-in hair dryers, and boat-size tubs; some have balconies with a splendid view of the bay and of Fort-de-France. English is spoken well here, and there's live entertainment nightly. *Trois-Ilets 97229, tel. 596/66–00–00 or 800/543–4300; in NY, 212/245–2920. 303 rooms including 10 suites. Facilities: 2 restaurants, bar, casino, disco, pool, 2 lighted tennis courts, duty-free shops, marina, car-rental desk, tour desk, water-sports center. AE, DC, MC, V. Very Expensive.*

La Batelière Hotel and Casino. This beachfront property boasts the island's largest rooms, and arguably the best tennis courts. The hotel overlooks the sea, and all rooms are air-conditioned, with direct-access phone, cable TV, radio, and private balcony or patio. Ask about the scuba and honeymoon packages. *Schoelcher; 97233, tel. 596/61–49–49. 207 rooms and suites. Facilities: 2 restaurants, 3 bars, casino, pool, 6 lighted tennis courts, sauna, shops, water-sports center. AE, DC, MC, V. Expensive–Very Expensive.*

★ Diamant-Novotel. This self-contained resort occupies half an island in an ideal windsurfing location. Just beyond the registration area, a footbridge spans a large pool on the way to the guest rooms. Rooms are air-conditioned with wall-to-wall carpeting, twin beds, and large terraces. There are four beaches on the 5-acre property, and scuba packages offered by dive masters Claude and Dominique Cavazale attract both French and U.S. visitors. A shuttle bus offers complimentary rides daily into Fort-de-France, and little pink monoplanes are available for soaring over the beach. The staff speaks English. *Le Diamant 97223, tel. 596/76–42–42 or 800/221–4242; in NY, 212/354–3722. 180 rooms. Facilities: 3 restaurants, 4 bars, 2 tennis courts, pool, dive shop, car-rental desk, water-sports center. AE, DC, MC, V. Expensive–Very Expensive.*

Club Med/Buccaneer's Creek. Occupying 48 landscaped acres, Martinique's Club Med is an all-inclusive village with plazas, cafés, restaurants, boutiques, and a small marina. Air-conditioned pastel cottages contain twin beds and private shower/bath. The only money you need spend here is for bar drinks and personal purchases. There's a white-sand beach, a plethora of water sports, and plenty of nightlife. *Point Marin 97180, tel. 596/76–72–72 or 800/CLUBMED; in NY, 212/750–1670. 300 rooms. Facilities: 2 restaurants and bars, 6 tennis courts (4 lighted), pool, fitness and water-sports center. AE, V. Moderate–Expensive.*

★ **Leyritz Plantation.** The pride of Martinique is an 18th-century restored plantation that occupies 16 acres on a lush tropical mountain. You can stay either in one of the antique-filled rooms in the manor house or opt for a rustic cabin, the carriage house, or one of the other restored buildings. But don't let the look of opulence fool you: The ambience here is of a cozy country inn. The management has done a superb job of retaining the old while keeping a foot firmly planted in the health-conscious late 20th century. The plantation maintains a well-equipped spa center with Jacuzzi, solarium, personalized nutrition and beauty programs, figure-improvement classes, facials, and massages. There's free transportation to the beach, which is about 30 minutes away. *Basse-Pointe 97218, tel. 596/78–53–08. 53 rooms. Facilities: restaurant, bar, spa, health-and-fitness center, horseback riding, tennis courts, pool. DC, MC. Moderate–Expensive.*

PLM Azur-Carayou. The style here is definitely tropical. The reception area has rattan furniture and, overhead, quaint wood rafters. The rooms, built around the large swimming pool in the garden, are air-conditioned, equipped with TV, direct-dial phones, and well-stocked minibars. There are lots of sporting options for daytime activity, and a popular disco for evening. The hotel is well run, and the staff is helpful and friendly. *Pointe du Bout 97229, tel. 596/66–04–04. 200 double rooms. Facilities: 3 restaurants, 2 bars, 2 tennis courts, pool, archery, golf practice, scuba diving, fishing, waterskiing, sailing. AE, DC, MC, V. Moderate–Expensive.*

Bambou. The young and the hardy will enjoy this complex of rustic A-frame "chalets" with shingled roofs. The rooms are paneled in pink; they are tiny and Spartan, albeit with modern conveniences, such as air-conditioning, phones, and shower baths. The hotel is open year-round, and during high season, entertainment is featured five nights a week. *Anse-Mitan 97229, tel. 596/66–01–39; in NY, 212/757–1175. 118 rooms. Facilities: restaurant and bar, pool, water-sports center. AE, DC, MC, V. Moderate.*

★ **Diamant Les Bains.** Although manager Hubert Andrieu and his family go all out to make their guests comfortable, you won't feel quite at home unless you speak at least a little French. A few of the rooms are in the main house, where the restaurant is located, but most are in bungalows. All rooms are air-conditioned, with private bath, TV, and phone; eight have kitchenettes. Fishing excursions and other sports activities can be arranged. *Le Diamant 97223, tel. 596/76–40–14; in the United States, 800/112–9815; in Canada, 800/468–0023; in NY, 212/840–6636. 24 rooms. Facilities: restaurant, bar, car rental, pool, water-sports center. DC, MC. Moderate.*

Imperatrice. Overlooking La Savane park in the center of the city, the Imperatrice's air-conditioned rooms are in a 1950s five-story building (with an elevator). The rooms in the front are either the best or the worst, depending upon your sensibilities: They are noisy, but they overlook the city's center of activity. All rooms have TV and a private bath; 20 have balconies. Children under 8 stay free in the room with their parents, children 8–15 stay at 50% of the room rate. The hotel also has a popular sidewalk café. *Fort-de-France 97200, tel. 596/63–06–82; in the United States, 800/223–9815; in Canada, 800/468–0023; in NY, 212/840–6636. 24 rooms. Facilities: restaurant, café, bar. AE, DC, MC, V. Moderate.*

★ **Manoir de Beauregard.** If you're looking for glitz, look elsewhere. This is for the romantic. Madame St. Cyr's hotel is an 18th-century manor house whose original walls and black-and-white tile floors date back to 1720. There are carved mahogany four-poster beds, some of which are a century old, and handsome old armoires. "Old" is the operative word, since the inn definitely shows its years. Still, its modern conveniences include air-conditioning, phones, and private baths. *Ste-Anne 97227, tel. 596/76–73–40; in the United States, 800/223–6510. 27 rooms. Facilities: restaurant, bar, pool. AE, DC, MC, V. Moderate.*

★ **PLM Azur La Pagerie.** With its galleries, colonettes, and lush courtyard, La Pagerie looks as if it had been plucked out of south Louisiana and planted near the marina in Pointe du Bout. Fully air-conditioned, the hotel has small rooms and studios, some with kitchenettes, all with private bath. It's within a short stroll of the resort hotels, restaurants, and activity. Continental breakfast is available. *Pointe du Bout 97229, tel. 596/66–05–30; in the United States, 800/223–9862; in NY, 212/757–6500. 98 rooms. Facilities: pool, water-sports center. AE, MC, V. Moderate.*

★ **Saint Aubin.** This restored colonial house is in the countryside above the Atlantic coast. The rooms are modern, with air-conditioning, TV, phone, and private bath. This is a peaceful retreat, and only 3 miles from La Trinité, 2 miles from the Spoutourne sports center and the beaches on the Caravelle Peninsula. The inn's restaurant is reserved for hotel guests and is closed during June and October. *Box 52, La Trinité, 97220, tel. 596/69–34–77; in the United States, 800/223–9815; in Canada, 800/468–0023; in NY, 212/840–6636. 15 double rooms. Facilities: restaurant, bar, pool. AE, DC, MC, V. Moderate.*

Auberge de l'Anse-Mitan. This beachfront hotel, established in 1930, is the island's oldest family-run inn. The rooms are Spartan, but all are air-conditioned and have a shower/bath. Views are either of the bay or the tropical garden, and some rooms have balconies. Informal meals are served on the terrace for guests. Things are peaceful and quiet here—even more so if you don't speak French. *Anse-Mitan 97229, tel. 596/66–01–12; in the United States, 800/223–9815; in Canada, 800/468–0023; in NY, 212/840–6636. 20 rooms. Facilities: restaurant, bar. AE, DC. Inexpensive.*

Auberge de la Montagne Pelée. There are three rooms and six studios with kitchenettes in this hillside inn that faces the famed volcano. Accommodations are simple; the view from the restaurant terrace is spectacular. *Le Morne Rouge 97260, tel. 596/53–32–09. 9 rooms. Facilities: restaurant. No credit cards. Inexpensive.*

The Last Resort. John and Véronique Deschamps's bed-and-breakfast on rue Osman Duquesnay is in the former gendarmerie annex. Language will be no problem here, since the Deschampses once lived in Sausalito, but you'll have to be flexible enough to share a bathroom with the other guests on your floor. A small communal kitchen is available, and an excellent family-style dinner is served nightly. *Le Marin 97290, tel. 596/74–83–88. 7 rooms. Facilities: restaurant. No credit cards. Inexpensive.*

Madras. If you're a sports-minded, French-speaking person traveling on a tight budget, this may be just the place for you. These simple, clean seaside rooms are at the entrance to the Presqu'ile de la Caravelle Nature Preserve, about a 30-minute drive from Fort-de-France. Hiking, biking, tennis, and water sports are available at the nearby Anse Spoutourne sports center, and excursions with fishermen are easy to arrange (assuming you speak French). *Tartane 97220, tel. 596/58–21–44. 16 rooms. Facilities: restaurant, bar. No credit cards. Inexpensive.*

Martinique Cottages. These garden bungalows in the countryside have kitchenettes, cable TV, and phones. Operating the cottages is a family affair: The Arnauds built the bungalows, and son Jean-Marc and his sister Peggy speak English and Spanish as well as French. The restaurant here, La Plantation, is a gathering spot for gourmets. The beaches are about a 15-minute drive away. The cottages are difficult to find, and you should take advantage of the property's airport transfers. *Lamentin 97232, tel. 596/50–16–08. 16 rooms. Facilities: restaurant, bar, pool, Jacuzzi. AE, MC, V. Inexpensive.*

Rivage Hotel. Maryelle and Jean Claude Riveti's garden studios have kitchenettes, air-conditioning, TV, phones, and private baths. It's located right across the road from the beach. Breakfast and light meals are served in the friendly, informal snack bar. You get good value for your money, and you should have no difficulty communicating: English, Spanish, and French are spoken. *Anse-Mitan 97229, tel. 596/66–00–53. 17 rooms. Facilities: snack bar, pool, poolside barbecue pit. No credit cards. Inexpensive.*

Home and Villa Rentals The **Villa Rental Service** of the Martinique Tourist Office (tel. 596/63–79–60) can assist with rentals of homes, villas, and apartments. Most are in the south of the island near good beaches and can be rented on a weekly or monthly basis.

The Arts and Nightlife

The island is dotted with lively discos and nightclubs, but entertainment on Martinique is not confined to partying.

Be sure to catch a performance of **Les Grands Ballets de Martinique** (tel. 596/63–43–88). The troupe of young, exuberant dancers, singers, and musicians is one of the best folkloric groups in the Caribbean. They perform on alternate nights at the Bakoua, Méridien, La Batelièré, and Carayou-PLM Azur.

Discos As in most places, this season's hot spot may be history next season. Your hotel or the Tourist Office can put you in touch with the current "in" places. It's also wise to check on opening and closing times and admission charges. For the most part, the discos draw a mixed crowd of locals and tourists, the young and the not so young. Some of the currently popular places are **Le New Hippo** (24 blvd. Allegre, Fort-de-France, tel. 596/71–74–60), **Le Sweety** (rue Capitaine Pierre Rose, Fort-de-France, no phone), **Le Must** (20 blvd. Allegre, Fort-de-France, tel. 596/60–36–06), **Le Vesou** (Carayou-PLM Azur, tel. 596/66–04–04), **VonVon** (Hotel Méridien, tel. 596/66–00–00), **La Cabane de Pêcheur** (Diamant-Novotel, tel. 596/76–42–42), **L'Oeil** (Petit Cocotte, Ducos, tel. 596/56–11–11), **Palladium Club** (La Batalière, tel. 596/61–49–49), and **Zipp's Dupe Club** (Dumaine, Le François, tel. 596/54–47–06).

Casinos The island's two casinos are open from 9 PM to 3 AM. You have to be at least 21 (with a picture ID); jacket and tie are not required. The **Casino Trois-Ilets** (Méridien Hotel, tel. 596/66-00-00) has American and French roulette, blackjack, and an admission charge of 58F. **La Batelière** (Schoelcher, tel. 596/61-49-49) also has American and French roulette, blackjack, and craps. Admission is 55F.

16 Montserrat

by Honey Naylor

Montserrat lies a distant 3,000 miles from Ireland, but St. Patrick's Day is celebrated on the 40-square-mile island with much the same fanfare and festivity one would expect to encounter on that occasion in, say, Dublin. Such Irish names as O'Donoghue, O'Brien, O'Garra, and Ryan abound on the island; its Government House is adorned with a shamrock, and its immigration officials validate visitors' passports with a shamrock stamp. Montserrat flies the Union Jack on ceremonial occasions—it's a British Crown Colony—but its official badge shows the Irish Lady and the Harp.

The Caribbean's own Emerald Isle was colonized by settlers who arrived from St. Kitts, an event recalled by a stone memorial donated by the Montserrat National Trust that reads: "Site of 1st Colony, AD 1632." Some historians believe those first settlers were Irish, attempting to escape religious persecution on British-held St. Kitts. Other Irish immigrants began to arrive, from Ireland, from Barbados, and even from Virginia. By 1648, there were more than 1,000 Irish families living on Montserrat. Many were poor, but among the prosperous landowners were the Blakes of Galway. In the late 18th century, the Blakes built an estate whose ruins can still be seen in the southeastern part of the island.

Columbus spotted this little green link in the Leeward Islands chain during his second voyage in 1493. It's said that he named it after the similarly shaped sawtooth mountain in Barcelona Province upon whose cliffs clings one of Spain's greatest religious shrines, the Benedictine monastery of Santa María de Montserrat. During the 18th century, the island of Montserrat was turned into a battlefield by the French and the British, who fought to possess it. The 1783 Treaty of Paris gave the island to the British, who have held it ever since.

Little is known of the island's development during the 19th century, apart from its having sugarcane plantations. African slaves were imported to till the soil, but they eventually rebelled. When slavery was abolished in 1834, the labor force disappeared and the sugar industry went sour. Limes replaced sugarcane, and by the mid-19th century, Montserrat was the prime supplier of lime juice to England. A transplanted Gloucestershire Quaker, Joseph Sturge, is credited with developing the crop on the island.

Everything grows in rich profusion on the pear-shaped volcanic island. The central mountains are covered with forests and green vegetation. The tiny island, only 7 miles long and 11 miles across at its widest point, has three mountain ranges: the Silver Hills at its northernmost point, the Centre Hills, and, to the south, Chance's Peak, at 3,002 feet, the highest.

The island's population includes medical students at the American University of the Caribbean, who may chuckle at the promotion of the island as a quiet and peaceful retreat. For the most part, it *is* relaxing, with little to do but a bit of mountain climbing, golfing, sea-related things, and poking through a few historical sites.

It's a different story for musicians, for this is the home of Air Studios, one of the world's most sophisticated recording studios, founded in 1979 by former Beatles producer George Martin. Sting, Boy George, Jimmy Buffet, and Paul McCartney have all recorded at the studio. Mighty Arrow, local hero and international calypso star, cut "Hot, Hot, Hot" at Air Studios. Although there are attractive lodgings here, the great majority of the island's visitors are day-trippers. Montserrat is not set up for mass tourism. As the tourist brochures say, this is the Caribbean the way it used to be.

Before You Go

Tourist Information You can get information about Montserrat through **Tromson Monroe Public Relations** (40 E. 49th St., New York, NY 10017, tel. 212/752–8660).

Arriving and Departing By Plane Antigua is not only the gateway, it's the best way to reach Montserrat. **American Airlines** (tel. 800/334–7200), **BWIA** (tel. 212/581–3200), and **Pan Am** (tel. 800/421–5330) fly here from New York; **BWIA** and Pan Am fly from Miami; **Air Canada** (tel. 800/422–6232) and BWIA, from Toronto, and **British Airways** (tel. 01/897–4000 in Britain, 800/247–9297 in the United States) from London.

From Antigua's **V. C. Bird International Airport**, you can make your connections with **LIAT** (tel. 809/491–2200) and **Montserrat Air** (tel. 809/491–2362) for the 15-minute flight to Montserrat.

Your knuckles and hair may turn white in the process, but you will land on the 3,400-foot runway at **Blackburne Airport,** on the Atlantic coast, about 11 miles from Plymouth.

From the Airport Taxis meet every flight, and the government-regulated fare from the airport to Plymouth is E.C. \$21 (U.S.\$10).

Passports and Visas U.S. and Canadian citizens only need proof of citizenship, such as a passport, a notarized birth certificate, or voter's registration card. A driver's license is *not* sufficient. British citizens must have a passport; visas are not required. All visitors must hold an ongoing or return ticket.

Customs and Duties You may bring into the country duty-free 200 cigarettes or 50 cigars or eight ounces of tobacco, and one quart of liquor, plus any personal items.

Language It's English with a brogue, a result of the Irish legacy. You'll also hear a patois that's heard on most of the islands.

Precautions Ask for permission before taking pictures. Some residents may be reluctant photographic subjects, and they will appreciate your courtesy.

Most Montserrattians frown at the sight of skimpily dressed tourists; do not risk offending them by strolling around in shorts and swimsuits.

Staying in Montserrat

Important Addresses **Tourist Information:** The **Montserrat Tourist Board** (Church Rd., Plymouth, tel. 809/491–2230) is open weekdays 8–noon and 1:30–4 PM.

Emergencies **Police** (tel. 809/491–2552).

Hospitals: There is a 24-hour emergency room at **Glendon Hospital** (Plymouth, tel. 809/491–2552).

Pharmacies: **Lee's Pharmacy** (Marine Dr., Plymouth, tel. 809/491–3274) and **Daniel's Pharmacy** (George St., Plymouth, tel. 809/491–2908).

Montserrat

Currency The official currency is the Eastern Caribbean dollar (E.C.$) often called beewee. At press time (winter 1989), the exchange rate is E.C.$2.70 to U.S.$1. U.S. dollars are readily accepted, but you'll often receive change in beewees. Note: Prices quoted here are in U.S. dollars unless noted otherwise.

Taxes and Service Charges Hotels collect a 7% government tax. The departure tax is $8. Hotels add a 10% service charge. Most restaurants add a 10%–15% service charge. If restaurants do not add the service charge, it's customary to leave a 10% or 15% tip. Taxi drivers should be given a 10% tip.

Guided Tours There are no bus tours of the island. If this is your first visit, ask the Tourist Board to make arrangements for a taxi tour of the island. It will cost $8 per hour.

The Rotary Club conducts garden tours during February and March. Details can be obtained from the Tourist Board.

Getting Around
Taxis The Tourist Board issues a list of taxi fares to the popular destinations. Taxis are always available at the airport and at the hotels. You can also call the **Taxi Stand** in Plymouth (tel. 809/491–2261).

Car Rentals The island has more than 150 miles of good roads. Unless you're uncomfortable about driving on the left, you won't have any trouble exploring. You'll need a valid driver's license, plus a Montserrat license, which is available at the airport or the police station. The fee is E.C.$7.50. Rental cars cost about $25–$30 a day. The local Avis outlet is **Pauline Car Rentals** (Plymouth, tel. 809/491–2345 or 800/331–1084). Other agencies are **Neville Bradshaw** (Olverton, tel. 809/491–5270) and **Jefferson's Car Rental** (Dagenham, tel. 809/491–2126).

Telephones and Mail To call Montserrat from the United States, dial area code 809 and access code 491 plus the local four-digit number. International direct-dial is available on the island; both local and long-distance calls come through clearly. To call locally on the island, you need to dial only the local four-digit number.

Airmail letters and postcards to the United States and Canada cost E.C.$1.15 each. Montserrat is one of several Caribbean islands whose stamps are of interest to collectors. You can buy them at the main post office in Plymouth (open Mon. and Tues., Thurs. and Fri. 8:15–3:55; Wed. and Sat. 8:15–11:25 AM).

Beaches

The sand on the beaches on Montserrat's south coast is of volcanic origin; usually referred to as black, it's actually light to dark gray. On the northwest coast, the sand is beige or white. The three most popular destinations for swimming and sunning are **Rendezvous Bay, Little Bay,** and **Carr's Bay,** all on the northwest coast; they are best reached via the sailing and snorkeling excursions arranged by the **Vue Pointe Hotel** (tel. 809/491–5210).

Sugar Bay, to the south of Plymouth, is a beach of fine gray volcanic sand. The Yacht Club overlooks this beach.

Fox's Bay has a lovely strip of gray sand on the bay just north of the Bird Sanctuary.

Road Bay and Isles Bay are on the coast north of Fox's Bay (4 miles north of Plymouth) and have stretches of gray-sand beaches.

Exploring Montserrat

Numbers in the margin correspond with points of interest on the Montserrat map.

Plymouth About a third of the island's population of 12,500 live in
❶ **Plymouth,** the capital city that faces the Caribbean on the southwest coast. The town is neat and clean, its narrow streets lined with trim Georgian structures built mostly of stones that came from Dorset as ballast on old sailing vessels. Most of the town's sights are set right along the water. On the south side, a bridge over the Fort Ghaut ("gut," or ravine) leads to Wapping, where most of the restaurants are located.

We'll begin at **Government House** on the south side of town just above Sugar Bay. The frilly Victorian house, decorated with a shamrock, dates from the 18th century. Beautifully landscaped gardens surround the building; period furnishings are inside it. *Peebles St. Contact the Tourist Office for information. Admission free. Grounds open Mon., Tues., Thurs., and Fri. 10:30–noon. House open Wed. 10:30–noon.*

Follow Peebles Street north and cross the bridge. Just over the bridge at the junction of Harney, Strand, and Parliament streets you'll see the **Market,** where islanders bring their produce every Saturday, a very colorful scene.

From the market, walk along Strand Street for one block to the tall white **War Memorial,** with a bell turret. The memorial is a tribute to the soldiers of both world wars. Next to the monument is the **Post Office and Treasury,** a galleried West Indian-style building by the water, where you can buy stamps that make handsome souvenirs.

Walk away from the water on George Street, which runs alongside the War Memorial. The town's main thoroughfare, Parliament Street, cuts diagonally north–south through the town. A left turn onto Parliament Street, at the corner of George Street, will take you to the Methodist Church and the Court House. If you continue straight on George Street, you'll come to the Roman Catholic Church. North of the church is the **American University of the Caribbean,** a medical school with many American students.

Elsewhere on From here on, you'll need wheels. Take Highway 2, the main
the Island road north out of Plymouth. On the outskirts of town there's a stone marker that commemorates the first colony in 1632.

Tour 1 **St. Anthony's Church,** which is just north of town, was
❷ consecrated some time between 1623 and 1666. It was rebuilt in 1730 following one of the many clashes between the French and the English in the area. Two silver chalices displayed in the church were donated by freed slaves after emancipation in 1834. An ancient tamarind tree stands near the church.

Richmond Hill rises northeast of town. Here you will find the
❸ **Montserrat Museum** in a restored sugar mill. The museum contains maps, historical records, artifacts, and all sorts of memorabilia pertaining to the island's growth and development. *Richmond Hill, tel. 809/491–5443. Admission free. Open Sun. and Wed. 2:30–5.*

Take the first left turn past the museum to Grove Road; it will
❹ take you to the **Fox's Bay Bird Sanctuary,** a 15-acre bog area.
Marked trails lead into the interior, which is aflutter with
egrets, herons, coots, and cuckoo birds.

The **Bransby Point Fortification** is also in this area and contains
a collection of restored cannons.

Backtrack on Grove Road to Highway 2, drive north and turn
❺ right on Highway 4 to **St. George's Fort.** It's overgrown and of
little historical interest, but the view from the hilltop is well
worth the trip.

Highway 2 continues north past the **Belham Valley Golf Course**
to **Vue Pointe Hotel,** on the coast at Lime Kiln Bay. Head west
to the green slopes of Centre Hills, almost in the center of the
❻ island, for **Air Studios,** a recording studio founded in 1979 by
former Beatles producer George Martin. Sting, Boy George,
and Paul McCartney have all cut records at the studio. *Centre
Hills, tel. 809/491–5678. Admission free. Tours by appointment only.*

About 1½ miles farther north, a scenic drive takes you along
❼ **Runaway Ghaut.** Two centuries ago, this peaceful green valley
was the scene of bloody battles between the French and the English. **Little Bay, Carr's Bay,** and **Rendezvous Bay,** the island's
three most popular beaches, are along the northwest coast.
(Since driving in these parts can be treacherous, it's a good idea
to sign up for one of the day sails through the Vue Pointe Hotel.)

Tour 2 The next tour of the island will be considerably more arduous,
taking in the mountains, rain forests, and *soufrières* (volcanic
craters with sulfuric springs) to the south and east of Plymouth. You will need a guide to go mountain climbing; the
Tourist Board or your hotel can arrange one for you. The
guide's fee will be about $6. Wear rubber-soled shoes.

A 15-minute drive south of Plymouth on Old Fort Road will
bring you to the village of **St. Patrick's.** From there, a scenic
drive takes you to the starting point of the hour's hike through
❽ thick rain forests to **Great Alps Waterfall.** The falls cascade 70
feet down the side of a rock and splash into a shallow pool,
where you can see a rainbow in the mist.

❾ A rugged road leads eastward to **Galways Soufrière,** where another hike is involved, this one lasting about 20 minutes. Once
there, you'll see volcanic rock, boiling water, and small vents of
gurgling, molten sulfur. City people are fond of complaining in
the summertime of streets so hot you could fry an egg on them.
Here, your guide will almost certainly fry an egg to demon-
strate the intense heat of the rocks.

❿ The island's highest point, **Chance's Peak,** pokes up 3,000 feet
through the rain forests. The climb to the top is arduous—and
you shouldn't attempt it without a guide—but if you do make it
to the top, what little breath you may have left will be taken
away by the view.

Also in this area is the old **Galways Estate,** a plantation built in
the late 17th century by prosperous Irishmen John and Henry
Blake, who came to Montserrat from Galway. All that remains
now of the fine estate is the ruins of the house and factory and

some rusted machinery. This is also the site of archaeological digs.

Off the Beaten Track

The place is **The Village Place,** and it is run by Andy Lawrence, who describes himself as owner, waiter, bartender, and cook. Sting drops by this roadside tavern whenever he's on the island; so does Eric Clapton. Regular customers include medical students from the American University of the Caribbean in Plymouth, plus a lot of locals. There are a few crude wood picnic tables outside and a bar and a billiard table inside. The menu includes fried chicken, West Indian dishes, beer, and rum punch. Plain and simple it may be, but the Village Place is *the* place to be on Friday night. *Salem, tel. 809/491–5202. Closed Tues. No credit cards.*

Participant Sports

Boating
: Boats are available through **Cruise Villa Charters** (tel. 809/491–5665), **Captain Martin** (tel. 809/491–4738), or **Vue Pointe Hotel** (tel. 809/491–5210).

Sailing and Snorkeling
: Snorkeling equipment is provided on the day cruises to the white-sand coves on the west coast; lunch is included. Arrangements can be made through **Vue Pointe Hotel** (tel. 809/491–5210) or **Captain Martin** (tel. 809/491–5738).

Windsurfing
: Contact the **Vue Pointe Hotel** (tel. 809/491–5210) to rent boards.

Golf
: There is an 11-hole course at the **Belham Valley Golf Course** (tel. 809/491–5220). The fairways run from the beach up the mountainside and are so well kept and challenging that most golfers go around twice.

Horseback Riding
: Trail rides, lessons, and vacation packages are offered by **Sanford Farms** (contact Barbara Tipsen, tel. 809/491–3301). Your hotel can arrange for riding on the beach or in the mountains.

Tennis
: There are lighted tennis courts at the **Vue Point Hotel** (tel. 809/491–5210) and the **Montserrat Springs Hotel** (tel. 809/491–2481).

Spectator Sports

Cricket is the national passion. Cricket and soccer matches are held from February through June in **Sturge Park. Shamrock Car Park** is the venue for volleyball and basketball games. Contact the Tourist Board (tel. 809/491–2230) for schedules.

Shopping

Sea-island cotton clothing and handicrafts, such as ceramics, straw goods, and leather jewelry, make ideal presents and souvenirs.

Shops are scattered around Plymouth, and a few are to the north in Olde Towne.

Good Buys *Clothes*
: Top-rated is the **Montserrat Sea Island Cotton Co.** (corner of George and Strand Sts., Plymouth, tel. 809/491–2557). **Carol's**

Corner (Vue Pointe Hotel, Olde Towne, tel. 809/491–5210) also
has sea-island cotton dresses.

Crafts   Upstairs at the **John Bull Shop** (Wapping, tel. 809/491–2520),
the *Tapestries of Montserrat* are a must-see. There are hand-
tufted wall hangings, tote bags, and other hand-woven items.
Dutchers Studio (Olde Towne, tel. 809/491–5253) has hand-cut,
hand-painted decorative pieces made from old bottles. **Carol's
Corner** (Vue Pointe Hotel, tel. 809/491–5210) sells leather jewelry, as well as souvenir Montserrat stamps. **Montserrat Sea
Island Cotton Co.** (George and Strand Sts., tel. 809/491–2557)
also has leather and ceramic gift items.

Dining

The national dish is goatwater, a thick stew made with goat
meat and vegetables, similar to Irish stew. Goat meat is reminiscent of mutton. Mountain chicken (actually enormous frogs)
is also a great favorite. Yam, breadfruit, christophene (a green
vegetable), lime, mango, papaya, and a variety of seafood are
served in most restaurants.

The most highly recommended restaurants are indicated by a
star ★ .

Category	Cost*
Expensive	over $20
Moderate	$10–$20
Inexpensive	under $10

**per person, excluding drinks and service. If the service charge
is not added to the bill, leave a 10% to 15% tip*

Montserrat Springs Hotel. The split-level dining room at the
Montserrat Springs Hotel, enclosed on three sides, faces a
large pool and a sun deck. Openers include chilled melon;
among the main courses is a variety of chicken and seafood
dishes. *Richmond Hill, Plymouth, tel. 809/491–2481. Reservations suggested in season. AE, MC, V. Expensive.*

★   **Vue Pointe.** Candlelit dining in the hotel's restaurant overlooking the sea makes this a very romantic place. The menu may
include West Indian curried chicken; beef Wellington; red snapper with Creole sauce; and, for dessert, a luscious lime pie or
cheesecake. The Wednesday-night barbecue, accompanied by
music from a steel band, is a popular island event. *Olde Towne,
tel. 809/491–5210. Reservations suggested for dinner. AE, MC,
V. Expensive.*

★   **Belham Valley.** Under new ownership since late 1988, this restaurant is now open for lunch as well as dinner. In a tropical
setting, the erstwhile private home has wood floors, a tiny terrace, and a large menu. Appetizers include conch fritters and
liver pâté. Main dishes include Seafood Delight (sautéed lobster, red snapper, and sea scallops in a vermouth sauce) and
broiled baby lobster tails. Scrumptious desserts are mango or
lime mousse, lemon cake, and coconut cream cheesecake. At
lunchtime, the offerings are lighter: There are omelets, salads,
and sandwiches. *Olde Towne, tel. 809/491–5553. Reservations
required for dinner. No lunch weekends; closed Mon. AE, V.
Moderate–Expensive.*

The Attic. By the time you climb the long flight of stairs to the Attic, you'll feel both hungry and thirsty. Tables are set on a terrace, and house specialties are chicken, breaded shrimp, lobster tail, and calf's liver smothered with onions. The Attic is a popular local hangout, and the crowd here is friendly. *Marine Dr. Plymouth, tel. 809/491–2008. Reservations suggested in season. No credit cards. Moderate.*

Danny's. The lure here is patio dining and West Indian dishes, such as curried mutton, conch, or chicken. *Wapping, tel. 809/ 491–2920. Closed Sun. No credit cards. Moderate.*

★ **Emerald Café.** Dining is relaxed at four tables inside and on the terrace, where there are white tables shaded by blue umbrellas. Burgers, sandwiches, goatwater stew, and plate lunches are served at lunchtime. For dinner, starters include Avocado Royale or Emerald Café pâté. Chicken Parmigiana, mountain chicken, and lobster are among the entrée listings. The homemade pastries, such as Island Coconut Pie, are superb. There's also an ample list of liqueurs and wines. *Wapping, tel. 809/491–3821. Dinner reservations suggested in season. Closed Sun. No credit cards. Moderate.*

The Gallery. Pizza is the specialty here, but you can also get escargot, fish and chips, lasagna, and burgers. On Friday night, the Masquerade band plays calypso, rhythm and blues, rock, and blues. *Wapping, tel. 809/491–2579. Reservations suggested in season. No credit cards. Closed Mon. and Tues. Moderate.*

Iguana. This is an American-owned eatery set in a 200-year-old stone building that was a cotton mill. Pumpkin soup, lobster mousse, and homemade ice cream are among the offerings. *Wapping, tel. 809/491–3637. Closed Mon. and Tues. No credit cards. Moderate.*

Oasis. A 200-year-old stone building houses this restaurant, where you can dine indoors or on the patio. Entrées include mountain chicken, jumbo shrimp Provençal, and red snapper with lime butter. *Wapping, tel. 809/491–2328. Reservations suggested in season. No credit cards. Moderate.*

Chez Nous Chinese Saloon. The cuisine here ranges from French to Chinese to Tex-Mex. You can get steak and eggs for breakfast in this upstairs country kitchen, but the emphasis is Asian—sweet-and-sour pork, ginger chicken, and bamboo shoots. BLTs and burgers are also served. *Lower Dagenham, tel. 809/491–2752. Closed Wed. No credit cards. Inexpensive.*

Golden Apple. In this large, galleried stone building, you'll be served goatwater, spareribs, and mountain chicken, among other selections. *Cork Hill, tel. 809/491–2187. No credit cards. Inexpensive.*

Yacht Club. This simple, popular eatery and local hangout overlooks the water. Lunchtime offerings include curried chicken, sandwiches, and burgers. Mountain chicken, lasagna, and shrimp Creole are featured on the dinner menu. Friday-night entertainment consists of calypso, rhythm and blues, blues, and soul music played by a band. *Wapping, tel. 809/491–2237. Reservations required for dinner in season. No credit cards. Inexpensive.*

Lodging

Most of Montserrat's hotels operate on the modified American plan (MAP: Breakfast and dinner are included in the rate).

The most highly recommended lodgings are indicated by a star
★.

Category	Cost*
Very Expensive	over $150
Expensive	$120–$150
Moderate	$80–$120
Inexpensive	under $80

All prices are for a standard double room for two, excluding 7% tax and a 10% service charge.

Hotels

★ **Villas of Montserrat.** If you've ever wanted to do an island in style, this is the way to do it. You'll be flown in on a private plane, chauffeured to your villa, and treated to a lobster dinner at Belham Valley the night of your arrival. Each three-bedroom villa is decorated island-style, and each has a color TV, microwave oven, dishwasher, three bathrooms, and a Jacuzzi. The cluster of villas overlooks Isle Bay and the Caribbean. *Plymouth, tel. 809/491-5165 or in the U.S. 212/752-8660. 3 villas. Facilities: pool. No credit cards. Very Expensive.*

Vue Pointe. This 5-acre property is the island's largest hotel, as well as its showplace. Accommodations are in the main building and in the popular octagonal cottages that spill down to the gray-sand beach on Lime Kiln Bay. Each cottage has a large bedroom, great view, and privacy. There's a lounge in the main building where you can watch cable TV or chat with the other guests and the Osbornes, who own the hotel and who host Monday-night cocktail parties. The Vue Pointe is the center for water-sports activity on the island, and the Belham Valley Golf Course is nearby. The Wednesday-night barbecue, with steel bands and other entertainment, is an island event for locals as well as tourists. There is a 125-seat conference center that also serves as a theater and a disco. *Box 65, Plymouth, tel. 809/491-5210. 12 rooms, 28 cottages. Facilities: restaurant, bar, gift shop, putting green, pool, 2 lighted tennis courts, water-sports center. AE, MC, V. Very Expensive.*

★ **Montserrat Springs Hotel and Villas.** This air-conditioned facility has a variety of accommodations. There are Garden Rooms (two double beds, shower, and dressing area) and one- and two-bedroom suites (sitting room, two double beds, tub and shower, washing machine, and kitchen). The rooms, which are located in a wing of the main building and in the cottages along the steep hillside that slopes to the beach, are spacious (tubs are the size of rowboats). All have private balconies, phone, and TV. The split-level restaurant overlooks the 70-foot pool. On Friday night, there is a barbecue with live island entertainment. *Box 259, Plymouth, tel. 809/491-2482 or 800/223-9815; in Canada, 800/468-0023; in NY 212/840-6636. 29 rooms, including 6 suites. Facilities: restaurant, 2 bars, pool, hot/cold mineral-water Jacuzzi, 2 lighted tennis courts, 24-hr switchboard. AE, MC, V. Moderate-Expensive.*

★ **Coconut Hill.** Built in the 1800s as a plantation house, this building has been a hotel since 1908. There are hardwood floors, galleries, beamed ceilings, and a marvelous Victorian parlor. Some rooms (No. 5 is one) have carved mahogany four-poster beds and open onto the upstairs gallery. All rooms have phones; you've a choice of twin or double beds. The restaurant serves West Indian–style cuisine. The hotel is a half mile outside Plymouth, 6 miles from the airport. *Box 337, Plymouth, tel. 809/491–2144. 9 rooms with bath. Facilities: restaurant, bar. AE, MC, V. Moderate.*

Belham Valley Hotel. On a hillside overlooking Belham Valley and the Belham Valley River, this hotel has four self-catering units. There is a cottage, often let on a long-term basis, and three apartments (a studio, a one-bedroom, and a two-bedroom). *Box 409, Plymouth, tel. 809/491–5553. 4 units. Facilities: restaurant, maid service. AE, MC. Inexpensive.*

Flora Fountain Hotel. This rambling hotel in the heart of Plymouth is built around a courtyard with an enormous fountain that's lighted at night. The rooms, all with tile bath, are air-conditioned and have wall-to-wall carpeting and phones. The restaurant serves the catch of the day, barbecue pork chops, Creole chicken, and steaks. *Box 373, Church Rd., Plymouth, tel. 809/491–3444. 18 rooms. Facilities: restaurant, bar. MC, V. Inexpensive.*

Condominiums   **Shamrock Villas.** On a hillside overlooking the sea, the villas offer 45 one- and two-bedroom apartments and town-house condominiums. One-bedrooms in season are $350 per week; $1,350 by the month. *Contact Doug Kennedy, Montserrat Condominiums, Ltd., Box 180, Plymouth, Montserrat, WI.*

Home and Apartment Rentals   Villas here tend to be luxurious, with sweeping views of the sea, private pools, and terraces. The services of a domestic helper and gardener are usually included in the rate. For information, contact **Neville Bradshaw Agencies Ltd.** (Box 270, Plymouth, tel. 809/491–5270), **D.R.V. Edwards** (Box 58, Plymouth, tel. 809/491–2974), **Lime Court Apartments** (Box 250, Plymouth, tel. 809/491–3656), or the **Montserrat Tourist Board** (Box 7, Plymouth, tel. 809/491–2230).

Nightlife

The hotels offer regularly scheduled barbecues and steel bands, and the small restaurants feature live entertainment in the form of calypso, reggae, rock, rhythm and blues, and soul.

The **Yacht Club** (Wapping, tel. 809/491–2237) has live island music on Friday, as do the **Gallery** (Wapping, tel. 809/491–2479) and the **Village Place** (Salem Village, tel. 809/491–5202).

The **Plantation Club** (Wapping, upstairs over the Oasis, tel. 809/491–2892) is a lively late-night place with taped rhythm and blues, soul, and soca (Caribbean music).

La Cave (Evergreen Dr., Plymouth, no phone) and **747 Disco** (Harney St., Plymouth, no phone), both West Indian–style discos with Caribbean and international music, are popular among the young locals.

17 Nevis

by Honey Naylor In 1493, when the gentleman from Genoa spied a cloud-crowned volcanic isle during his second voyage to the New World, he named it *Nieves*, the Spanish word for "snows." It reminded him of the snowcapped peaks of the Pyrenees. Nevis (pronounced Neevis) rises out of the water in an almost perfect cone, the tip of its 3,232-foot central mountain smothered in clouds. It's lusher and less developed than its sister island of St. Kitts.

Tour groups are not attracted to an island that has no nonstop flights from the United States; that has virtually no glittering nightlife or shopping, and no high-rise hotels. Visitors tend to be self-sufficient types who know how to amuse themselves and who appreciate the warmth and character of country inns.

In 1607, Captain John Smith and his crew, on their way to establish the colony in Jamestown, Virginia, stopped off in Nevis to hang some mutineers; he noted: "Here we found a great poole, wherein bathing ourselves we found much ease." The mineral springs of the "great poole" didn't do much for the mutineers, but by 1778 the waters had become so famous that the luxurious Bath Hotel was built adjacent to them. This tiny, 36-square-mile island became known as the Spa of the Caribbean, attracting fashionable Europeans.

John Smith is not the only famous name associated with Nevis and with American history. Alexander Hamilton, who was to become treasury secretary under President George Washington, was born in Charlestown, Nevis, in 1755. His home in Charlestown has been restored and is now a museum.

Admiral Lord Nelson, who was headquartered in Antigua for a time, found Nevis a convenient stop for fresh water; it was where he met the comely Frances Nisbet. They were married at Montpelier Estate (as attested to in the records of St. John's Church in Fig Tree Parish). The Duke of Clarence, who later became King William IV of England, stood up for the admiral.

This island is known both for its natural beauty—long beaches with white and black sand, lush greenery—for a half-dozen mineral spa baths, and for the restored sugar plantations that now house some of the Caribbean's most elegant hostelries. In 1628, settlers from St. Kitts sailed across the 2-mile channel that separates the two islands. At first they grew tobacco, cotton, ginger, and indigo, but with the introduction of sugarcane in 1640, Nevis became the island equivalent of a boom town. As the mineral baths were drawing crowds, the island was producing an abundance of sugar. Slaves were brought from Africa to work on the magnificent estates, many of them nestled high in the mountains amid lavish tropical gardens.

The restored plantation homes that now operate as inns are the island's most sybaritic lures for the leisurely life. There is plenty of activity for the energetic—mountain climbing, swimming, tennis, horseback riding, snorkeling. But the going is easy here, with hammocks for snoozing, lobster bakes on palm-lined beaches, and candlelit dinners in stately dining rooms and on romantic verandas.

Nevis is linked politically with St. Kitts. The two islands, together with Anguilla, achieved self-government as an Associated State of Great Britain in 1967. In 1983, St. Kitts-Nevis became fully independent nations. Nevis papers sometimes

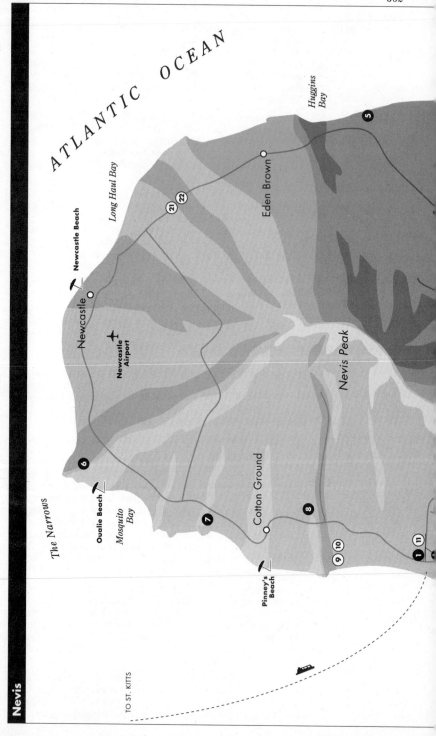

Nevis

ATLANTIC OCEAN

The Narrows

TO ST. KITTS

Mosquito Bay

Oualie Beach

Long Haul Bay

Newcastle Beach

Newcastle

Newcastle Airport

Huggins Bay

Eden Brown

Nevis Peak

Cotton Ground

Pinney's Beach

363

● Exploring Sites
⑨ Hotels and Restaurants

● 1 Exploring Sites
⑨ 9 Hotels and Restaurants

Exploring
Bath Springs, **2**
Charlestown, **1**
Eden Brown Estate, **5**
Hurricane Hill, **6**
Nelson Museum, **4**

Nelson Spring, **7**
St. John's Church, **3**
St. Thomas Anglican
Church, **8**

Dining
Cooperage, **17**
Golden Rock, **21**
Hermitage, **12**
Montpelier Plantation
Inn, **14**
Nisbet Plantation
Inn, **19**
Unella's Restaurant, **11**

Lodging
Croney's Old Manor
Estate, **18**
Golden Rock, **22**
Hermitage, **13**
Montpelier Plantation
Inn, **15**

Nisbet Plantation
Inn, **20**
Pinney's Beach Hotel, **9**
Rest Haven Inn, **10**
Zetland Plantation
Inn, **16**

*White
Bay*

*Red
Cliff*

Zion

Gingerland

Charlestown

Morning
Star

*Saddle
Hill*

Fig Tree

*Dogwood
Pt.*

Long Pt.

Caribbean Sea

N

0   5 miles

0   5 km

run fiery articles advocating independence from St. Kitts, and the sister islands may separate someday. However, it's not likely that a shot will be fired, let alone one that will be heard around the world.

Before You Go

Tourist Information You can get information about the island through the **St. Kitts & Nevis Tourist Board** (414 E. 75th St., New York, NY 10021, tel. 212/535–1234), **St. Kitts & Nevis Tourist Office** (33 Niagara St., Toronto M5V 1C2, Canada, tel. 416/362–9930), and **Rosamund Bern Assoc.** (15 Wardour Mews, d'Arblay St., London W1V 3FF, United Kingdom, tel. 437/9475–7445).

Arriving and Departing
By Plane Most visitors from the United States and Canada fly into St. Kitts and connect with **LIAT** (tel. 809/462–0700), which has two daily flights to **Newcastle Airport** on Nevis. LIAT also flies in from neighboring islands, as does **Windward Islands Airways** (tel. 599/5–44230 or 559/5–44237). Many hotels on the island make arrangements with **Air Caribe** to bring guests over from Antigua, which avoids a lot of hassle. You can book through your hotel or contact **Carib Aviation** (Box 318, St. Johns, Antigua, tel. 809/462–3147).

From the Airport Taxis meet every flight and ferry. The cabs are unmetered, but fares are regulated by the government and rates are posted at the airport and the ferry slip. Some sample posted fares are: from the ferry slip to Nisbet Plantation, U.S.$10; to Zetland Plantation, U.S.$6; and to Golden Rock, U.S.$7. The fare from the airport to Zetland Plantation is U.S.$12; to Montpelier Plantation, U.S.$13. Be sure that you and your driver understand whether the rate he quotes you is in Eastern Caribbean (E.C.) or U.S. dollars.

By Boat The MV *Caribe Queen* is the Staten Island ferry of the Caribbean. Nevisians board the government-operated 150-passenger ferry to get to and from work on St. Kitts, and tourists take it to sightsee. It makes the 45-minute trip across the channel from St. Kitts daily except Thursday, which is maintenance day, and Sunday. Its schedule is as varied as a Chinese menu, so rather than trying to pick a departure hour from column B, just call the Tourist Office (tel. 809/469–5521) and ask for schedule information.

Passports and Visas U.S. and Canadian citizens need only proof of citizenship, such as a voter's registration card or a birth certificate. (A driver's license *won't* suffice.) British citizens need a passport, but a visa is not required. All visitors must have a return or ongoing ticket.

Customs and Duties The government will allow you to bring in items for your personal use, plus 200 cigarettes or 50 cigars or a half pound of tobacco. There are no customs or immigration formalities if you arrive by ferry.

Language English is spoken here with a West Indian lilt.

Staying in Nevis

Important Addresses **Tourist Information:** The **Tourism Office** (tel. 809/469–5521, ext. 2049) is on Main Street in Charlestown. The office is open Monday and Tuesday 8–4:30 and Wednesday–Friday 8–4.

Emergencies	**Police:** Call 809/469–5391.

Hospitals: There is a 24-hour emergency room at **Alexandra Hospital** (Charlestown, tel. 809/469–5473).

Pharmacies: Evelyn's Drugstore (Charlestown, tel. 809/469–5278) is open Monday–Saturday 8–5:30, Sunday 7 AM–8 PM; on Thursday it closes at 12:30 PM.

Currency Legal tender is the Eastern Caribbean dollar. The rate of exchange fluctuates but hovers around E.C.$2.65 or E.C.$2.70 to U.S.$1. The U.S. dollar is accepted everywhere, but you'll almost always get change in E.C.s. Prices quoted here are in U.S. dollars unless noted otherwise. Credit cards are not widely accepted on the island, though some of the inns will, inexplicably, take personal checks.

Taxes and Service Charges Hotels collect a 7% government tax. The departure tax is $5. Most hotels add a 10% service charge to your bill. For a job well done, a 10%–15% gratuity should be left in addition. Taxi drivers should be given a 10% tip.

Guided Tours The **taxi driver** who picks you up will offer to act as your guide to the island. Each driver is knowledgeable and does a 3½-hour tour for $35. He'll probably ask if you'd like him to make lunch reservations for you at one of the plantations, and you should say "Yes."

Another tour option is **Jan's Travel Agency** (Arcade, Charlestown, tel. 809/469–5878), which arranges half- and full-day tours of the island.

Getting Around
Rental Cars Arrive in Nevis with a valid driver's license and your car rental agency will help you obtain a local license at the police station. The cost is E.C. $30 (U.S. $12.).

Beware: The island's roads are pocked with crater-size potholes; driving is on the left; goats and cattle crop up out of nowhere to amble along the road; and if you deviate from Main Street you're likely to have trouble finding your way around. For all of the above reasons, we recommend that you take a taxi from point to point. Having said that, we won't withhold from you the information that **Skeete's Car Rental** (Newcastle Village, at the airport, tel. 809/469–9458) has Honda Civics, Toyota Corollas, Suzuki Jeeps, and minimokes; doesn't charge for mileage or gas; and accepts major credit cards. **Budget** has a branch in Charlestown (tel. 809/469–5390; or, to reserve a car before you leave home, tel. 800/527–0700).

Taxis Taxi service is readily available at the airport. Some of the island's fleet include Curtley Maynard (tel. 809/469–1973), Ralph Hutton (tel. 809/469–1767), and Luther Morton (tel. 809/469–1858).

Telephones and Mail To call Nevis from the United States, dial area code 809, followed by 469 and the local number. Communications are excellent, both on the island and with the United States, and direct-dial long distance is in effect.

Airmail letters to the United States and Canada require E.C.60¢ per half ounce; postcards E.C.35¢. It'll take at least a week to 10 days for mail to reach home. Nevis and St. Kitts have separate stamp-issuing policies, but each honors the other's stamps.

Opening and Closing Times Shops are open Monday–Saturday 8–noon and 1–4. Most shops close earlier on Thursday. Banking hours are Monday–Thursday 8–1; Friday 8–1 and 3–5. St. **Kitts & Nevis National Bank** is open Saturday 8:30–11 AM.

Beaches

All of the beaches on the island are free to the public. There are no changing facilities, so you'll have to wear a swimsuit under your clothes. If you're doing a cab tour, you may arrange with your driver to drop you off at the beach and pick you up later.

Pinney's Beach is the island's showpiece beach. It's almost 4 miles of soft, white sand backed by a cyclorama of palm trees, and it's on the calm Caribbean Sea. The palm-shaded lagoon is a scene right out of *South Pacific*. Several of the mountain inns have private cabanas and pavilions on the beach, but it is, nevertheless, a public beach.

Oualie Beach, at Mosquito Bay, just north of Pinney's, is a black-sand beach where Oualie's Beach Pub (tel. 809/469–5329) can mix you a drink and fix you up with water-sports equipment.

Newcastle Bay is the beach location of Nisbet Plantation. It's a broad beach of soft, white sand shaded by coconut palms on the northernmost tip of the island, on the channel between St. Kitts and Nevis, popular among snorkelers.

Exploring Nevis

Numbers in the margin correspond with points of interest on the Nevis map.

Charlestown ❶ About 1,200 of the island's 9,300 inhabitants live in Charlestown, the capital of Nevis. It faces the Caribbean, about 12½ miles south of Basseterre in St. Kitts. If you arrive by ferry, as most people do, you'll walk smack onto Main Street from the pier.

Turn right on Main Street and look for the **Nevis Tourist Office** (on your right as you enter the main square). Pick up a copy of the Nevis Historical Society's self-guided tour of the island, and stroll back onto Main Street.

While it is true that Charlestown has seen better days—it was founded in 1660—it's easy to imagine how it must have looked in its heyday. The buildings may be weathered and a bit worse for wear now, but there are still evidences of past glory in their fanciful galleries, elaborate gingerbread, wood shutters, and colorful hanging plants.

The **Philatelic Bureau** is next door to the Tourist Board, just across a narrow alley. The stamps of St. Kitts and Nevis are lovely and make inexpensive souvenirs and gifts.

The stonework building with the clock tower at the corner of Main and Prince William streets houses the **courthouse and library.** A fire in 1873 severely damaged the building and destroyed valuable records. The current building dates from the turn of the century. You're welcome to poke around the second-floor library (open Mon.–Sat. 9–6), which is one of the coolest places on the island.

If you intend to rent a car, the **police station** across from the courthouse is the place to get your local driver's license.

Follow Prince William Street from the courthouse to **Memorial Square,** dedicated to the fallen of World Wars I and II.

Time Out Drop into **Caribbean Confections** (across the street from the Tourist Office, no phone) for coffee and homemade pastries. There are also sandwiches, peanut-butter cookies, and popcorn.

When you return to Main Street from Prince William Street, turn right and go past the pier. Main Street curves and becomes Craddock Road, but keep going straight and you'll be on Low Street. The **Alexander Hamilton Birthplace,** which contains the **Museum of Nevis History,** is on the waterfront, covered in bougainvillea and hibiscus. This Georgian-style house is a reconstruction of the statesman's original home, which was built in 1680 and is thought to have been destroyed during an earthquake in the mid-19th century. Hamilton was born here in 1755. He left for the American Colonies 17 years later to contrive his education; he became secretary to George Washington, and died in a duel with political rival Aaron Burr. The **Nevis House of Assembly** sits on the second floor of this building, and the museum downstairs contains Hamilton memorabilia and documents pertaining to the island's history. *Low St., no phone. Admission free. Open weekdays 8–4.*

Elsewhere on the Island You'll have to resort to wheels to see the other sights and sites. The main road makes a 20-mile circuit, with various offshoots bumping and winding into the mountains. Take the road south out of Charlestown, passing **Grove Park** along the way, where soccer and cricket matches are played.

❷ About ¼ mile along you'll come to the ruins of the **Bath Hotel** (built by John Huggins in 1778) and **Bath Springs.** The springs, some icy cold, others with temperatures of 108 degrees Fahrenheit, emanate from the hillside and spill into the "great poole" that John Smith mentioned in 1607. Huggins's hotel was adjacent to the waters, with the Spring House built over the springs. The swanky hotel, which charged an outrageous price of sixpence, accommodated 50 guests. Eighteenth-century accounts reported that a stay of a few days, bathing in and imbibing the waters, resulted in miraculous cures. It would take a minor miracle to restore the decayed hotel to anything like grandeur—it closed down in the late 19th century—but the Spring House has been partially restored and some of the springs are still hot as ever. *Bathing costs 50¢. Open daily 9–4.*

❸ About 2 miles from Charlestown, in the village of Fig Tree, is **St. John's Church,** which dates from 1680. Among its records is a tattered, prominently displayed marriage certificate that reads: "Horatio Nelson, Esquire, to Frances Nisbet, Widow, on March 11, 1787."

❹ At nearby Morning Star Plantation, the **Nelson Museum** contains memorabilia pertaining to the life and times of Admiral Lord Nelson, including letters, documents, paintings, and even furniture from his flagship. Nelson was based in Antigua, but returned often to court—and eventually marry—Frances Nisbet, who lived on a 64-acre plantation here. The museum's owner, Robert Abrahams, restored the plantation and collected the Nelson memorabilia. He lives on the estate, and when he is not home, the museum is closed. It's a good idea to check with the Tourist Office to see if it's open before making the trip to see it. *Morning Star, no phone. Admission free. Open Mon.–Sat. 9–1.*

⑤ At the island's east coast, you'll come to the government-owned **Eden Brown Estate,** built around 1740 and known as Nevis's haunted house, or, rather, haunted ruins. In 1822, apparently, a Miss Julia Huggins was to marry a fellow named Maynard. However, on the day of the wedding the groom and his best man had a duel and killed each other. The bride-to-be became a recluse, and the mansion was closed down. Local residents claim they can feel the presence of . . . someone . . . whenever they go near the old house. You're welcome to drop by. It's free.

⑥ Rounding the top of the island, west of Newcastle Airport, you'll arrive at **Hurricane Hill,** from which there is a splendid view of St. Kitts.

Time Out At **Oualie's Beach Club** (Mosquito Bay, tel. 809/469–5329), you can have a rum punch, a swim in the sea, and sign up for a snorkeling or scuba-diving trip.

About 1½ miles along the Main Road, **Fort Ashby,** overgrown with tropical vegetation, overlooks the place where the settlement of Jamestown fell into the sea after a tidal wave hit the coast in 1680. Needless to say, this is a favored target of scuba divers.

⑦ At nearby **Nelson Spring,** the waters have considerably decreased since the 1780s, when young Captain Horatio Nelson periodically filled his ships with fresh water here.

⑧ Before driving back into Charlestown, a little over a mile down the road, stop to see the island's oldest church, **St. Thomas Anglican Church.** The church was built in 1643 and has been altered many times over the years. The gravestones in the old churchyard have stories to tell, and the church itself contains memorials to the early settlers of Nevis.

Participant Sports

Boating Hobie Cats and Sunfish can be rented from **Oualie Beach Club** (tel. 809/469–5329).

Deep-Sea Fishing The game here is kingfish, wahoo, grouper, and yellowtail snapper. **Jans Travel Agency** (tel. 809/469–5878) arranges deep-sea fishing trips.

Hiking The center of the island is Nevis peak, which soars up to 3,232 feet, flanked by Hurricane Hill on the north and Saddle Hill on the south. If you plan to scale Mt. Nevis, a daylong affair, it is highly recommended that you go with a guide. Your hotel can arrange it for you; you can also ask the hotel to pack you a picnic lunch.

Horseback Riding You can arrange for mountain-trail and beach rides through **Cane Gardens** (tel. 809/469–5464) and **Nisbet Plantation** (tel. 809/469–5325).

Tennis There are two tennis courts at **Pinney's Beach Hotel** and one court each at **Nisbet, Montpelier, Golden Rock,** and **Zetland** (*see* Lodging, below).

Water Sports The village of **Jamestown** was washed into the sea around Fort Ashby; the area is a popular spot for snorkeling and diving. Reef-protected **Pinney's Beach** offers especially good snorkeling. **Montpelier Plantation** (tel. 809/469–5462) has a 17-foot Boston whaler for scuba and snorkeling trips. Snorkeling and waterskiing trips can also be arranged through **Oualie Beach Club** (tel. 809/469–5329). Windsurfers can also be rented here.

Spectator Sports

Cricket and Soccer **Grove Park** is the venue for cricket (Jan.–July) and soccer (July–Dec.). Your hotel or the Tourist Board can fill you in on dates, times, and grudge matches of particular interest between Kittitians and Nevisians.

Shopping

Rare is the traveler who heads for Nevis on a shopping spree. However, there are some surprises here, notably the island's stamps, batik and hand-embroidered clothing, and the artwork of Dame Eva Wilkins.

For more than 50 years Wilkins has been painting island people, flowers, and landscapes. An Eva Wilkins mural hangs over the bar at the Golden Rock (*see* Dining, below). Her originals sell for $100 and up, and prints are available in some of the local shops. Her studio is in Gingerland (near Montpelier), and if she's not off the island, your hotel or your taxi driver can arrange a visit for you.

Stamp collectors should head for the **Philatelic Bureau,** just off Main Street opposite the Tourist Office. St. Kitts and Nevis are famous for their decorative, and sometimes lucrative, stamps. An early Kittitian stamp recently brought in $7,000.

Other local items of note are the batik caftans, scarves, and fabrics found in the Nevis branch of **Caribelle Batik** (in the Arcade of downtown Charlestown, no phone). **Caribee Clothes** (off Main St., tel. 809/469–5217) has resort clothing with hand-embroidered designs that have been praised by *Vogue*.

Dining

All of the plantation guest houses serve meals. Most of them have informal lobster bakes on the beach as well as romantic candlelit dinners in elegant dining rooms. (For more detailed descriptions of the plantations, *see* Lodging, below.) Meals in the plantations are prix fixe and run from about $25 to $35, including wine. In each case the menu changes daily.

The most highly recommended restaurants are indicated by a star ★.

Category	Cost*
Expensive	$25–$35
Moderate	$15–$25

Inexpensive	under $15

*per person, excluding drinks and service

★ **Cooperage.** An old stone dining room with high raftered ceilings provides an elegantly rustic setting. Among the specialties here are green-pepper soup, curried chicken breasts, seafood, and sorbets. *Croney's Old Manor, tel. 809/469–5445. Reservations required. AE. Expensive.*

Golden Rock. Dinner is in an opulent dining room with handsome tablecloths and soft candlelight. West Indian and Continental dishes are served. *Golden Rock, tel. 809/469–5346. Reservations required. No credit cards. Closed Sun. Expensive.*

Hermitage. The atmosphere here is subdued with white cloths, candlelight, and a backdrop of white latticework on the porch. Begin your meal with carrot and tarragon soup, then follow it with West Indian red snapper in ginger sauce, and finish off with a rum soufflé. *Hermitage Plantation, tel. 809/469–5477. Reservations required. No credit cards. Expensive.*

Montpelier Plantation Inn. Dinner is served by candlelight on the veranda; your feast might include lobster, red snapper, or even roast beef and Yorkshire pudding. *Montpelier Plantation, tel. 809/469–5462. Reservations required. No credit cards. Expensive.*

★ **Nisbet Plantation Inn.** The hardwood floors and antique-filled dining room offset the simple luncheon offerings of conch fritters and conch chowder, lobster or Greek salad, soups, and West Indian curry. West Indian and Continental cuisines are featured at dinner. *Nisbet Plantation, tel. 809/469–5325. Reservations required. No credit cards. Expensive.*

Unella's Restaurant. Sit on the plain terrace overlooking the Charlestown harbor and take your pick of lobster bisque, fish chowder, filet mignon with mushroom sauce, barbecued ribs, and Caribbean lobster grilled and served with lemon butter. *Charlestown Harbour, tel. 809/469–5574. No reservations. No credit cards. Inexpensive.*

Lodging

The island is filled with restored sugar plantations that are now guest houses and inns. Most of them operate on the MAP (Modified American Plan: breakfast and dinner included in the room rate).

The most highly recommended lodgings are indicated by a star ★.

Category	Cost*
Very Expensive	over $200
Expensive	$150–$200
Moderate	$90–$150
Inexpensive	under $90

*All prices are for a standard double room for two, MAP, excluding 7% tax and a 10% service charge.

Montpelier Plantation Inn. This old West Indian–style manor house is set in 650 beautifully landscaped acres. Neat brick paths lead through tropical gardens, and accommodations are in individual cottages, each with a patio and private bath. Transportation is provided to Pinney's Beach, where the estate has a cabana. There is a huge pool with a poolside bar, and the estate has a 17-foot Boston whaler for waterskiing, snorkeling, and fishing. *Box 474, Charlestown, tel. 809/469–5462 or 800/ 243–9420. 16 rooms. Facilities: restaurant, bar, pool, horseback riding, water-sports center. No credit cards. Very Expensive.*

★ **Nisbet Plantation Inn.** From the manor house of this 18th-century plantation you can see the beach at the end of a long avenue of coconut palms, and from the bar, you look out over an old sugar mill covered with hibiscus, cassia, frangipani, and flamboyants. There are a few rooms in the main house, but the best are those in the cottages on Nisbet's long beach of white sand. Each of the cottages is different and elegant, with hardwood floors and rattan furniture, a private bath, and a screened porch. On the beach there are volleyball nets, a bar and restaurant, and a freshwater shower. Nisbet does not accept children under 12. *Newcastle Beach, tel. 809/469–5325 or 800/344–2049 in USA. 33 rooms. Facilities: beach, 2 restaurants, 2 bars, free laundry, boutique, free snorkeling gear. No credit cards. Very Expensive.*

Croney's Old Manor Estate. Vast tropical gardens surround this restored sugar plantation, which is set 800 feet above the sea on the slopes of Mt. Nevis. Many guest rooms have high ceilings and hardwood floors, king-size canopy beds, and colonial reproductions. The outbuildings, such as the smokehouse and jail, have been imaginatively restored, and the old cistern is now the pool. This is the home of The Cooperage, one of the island's best restaurants *(see* Dining, above). There's transportation to and from the beach. The hotel is not recommended for children under 12. *Box 70, Charlestown, tel. 809/469–5445, 800/223–9815 in USA, 800/468–0023 in Canada. 10 rooms. Facilities: pool, 2 restaurants, 2 bars. AE. Expensive.*

★ **Golden Rock.** The present owner, Pam Barry, is a direct descendant of the original owner of this 200-year-old estate. She has decorated the five cottages in a style befitting a once-flourishing plantation. There are handsome four-poster beds of mahogany or bamboo, hooked rugs, rocking chairs, and island-made fabrics of floral prints. All rooms have private baths and a patio. The restored sugar mill is a large suite for honeymooners or families, and the old cistern is now a spring-fed swimming pool. The estate covers 150 mountainous acres and is surrounded by 25 acres of lavish tropical gardens, including a sunken garden. The hotel has facilities on two beaches, and a shuttle bus that makes two trips daily to them. *Box 493, Gingerland, tel. 809/469–5346, 800/223–9815 in USA, 800/468–0023 in Canada. 16 rooms. Facilities: 2 beaches, 2 restaurants, bar, pool, bike rentals, tennis court, windsurfing. No credit cards, but personal checks are accepted. Expensive.*

★ **Hermitage.** This is a wonderful 250-year-old great house with modern facilities in the restored carriage house and cottages. Each cottage sleeps two, in twin beds or magnificent king-size canopy beds, and most have a small kitchenette. There are verandas and hammocks for loafing and enjoying the tropical gardens, and an antique-filled dining room for elegant dinners. *St. Johns, Fig Tree Parish, tel. 809/469–5477, 800/223–9815 in*

USA, 800/468–0023 in Canada. 9 suites. Facilities: pool, restaurant. No credit cards. Expensive.

Pinney's Beach Hotel. These bungalows are smack on Pinney's Beach, which is so spectacular you probably won't mind that the rooms are somewhat modest (though they have colorful bedspreads, carpeting, and private terraces). Some are air-conditioned, all have private baths, and some of the cottages are set around a garden. You'll be more comfortable in one that opens directly onto the beach. *Pinney's Beach, tel. 809/469–5207. 48 rooms. Facilities: beach, 2 restaurants, 3 bars, 2 tennis courts, pool. AE, MC, V. Moderate.*

Zetland Plantation Inn. The big peach-colored great house and pastel cottages are set on 750 acres, 1,500 feet up the slope of Mt. Nevis. The restored sugar mill, with handsome brass beds and oriental rugs, can sleep up to six. Rooms and suites, all in contemporary tropical decor, are in seven double cottages. The suites have a bedroom, combination living room/dining room, and fully equipped kitchenette. The four deluxe suites have plunge pools as an extra added attraction. A shuttle bus takes guests to Charlestown and to Pinney's Beach. *Box 448, Gingerland, tel. 809/469–5454 or 800/243–2654 in USA. 22 suites. Facilities: pool, 2 restaurants, 2 bars, boutique, snorkeling and windsurfing equipment, tennis court. AE, MC, V. Moderate.*

Rest Haven Inn. This is a motelish facility on the outskirts of Charlestown. All rooms have two double beds, terrace, bath with tub and shower, and kitchenette. It's on the water, but not on the beach; however, there's a small free-form pool. The hotel is air-conditioned and well maintained. *Box 209, Charlestown, tel. 809/469–5208. 40 rooms. Facilities: restaurant, snack bar, lounge, pool, tennis court. AE. Inexpensive.*

Nightlife

The hotels usually bring in local calypso singers and steel or string bands one night a week. On Friday night the Shell All-Stars steel band entertains in the gardens at **Croney's Old Manor** (tel. 809/469–5445). The **Golden Rock** (tel. 809/469–5346) brings in the Honeybees String Band to jazz things up for the Saturday-night buffet, and **Zetlands** (tel. 809/469–5454) has a beach barbecue every Tuesday, complete with string band. You can have dinner and a dance on Wednesday nights at **Pinney's Beach Hotel** (tel. 809/469–5207).

Apart from the hotel scene, there are a few places where young locals go on weekends for hi-fi calypso, reggae, and other island music; **Mariner's Pub & Bar** (tel. 809/469–1993) near Fort Ashby and **Dick's Bar** (no phone) in Brickiln are two such places.

18 Puerto Rico

by Honey Naylor

No city in the Caribbean is as steeped in Spanish tradition as Puerto Rico's Old San Juan. Old San Juan's attractions are myriad: restored 16th-century buildings, museums, art galleries, bookstores, 200-year-old houses with balustraded balconies of filigreed wrought iron overlooking quaint, narrow, cobblestone streets. This Spanish tradition also spills over into the island's countryside, from its festivals celebrated in honor of various patron saints in the little towns, to the *paradores*, those homey, inexpensive inns whose concept originated in Spain.

Puerto Rico has, in San Juan's sophisticated Condado and Isla Verde areas, glittering hotels, flashy, Las Vegas–style shows, casinos, and frenetic discos. It has the ambience of the Old World in the seven-square-block area of the old city and in its quiet colonial towns. Out in the countryside lies its natural attractions—the extraordinary, 28,000-acre Caribbean National Forest, known more familiarly as the El Yunque rain forest, with its 100-foot-high trees, more than 200 species of them, and its dramatic mountain ranges, forest reserves with trails to satisfy the most dedicated hiker, vast caves to tempt spelunkers, coffee plantations, old sugar mills, and hundreds of beaches.

Puerto Rico, 110 miles long and 35 miles wide, was populated by several tribes of Indians when Columbus landed on the island on his second voyage in 1493. In 1508, Juan Ponce de Léon, the frustrated searcher of the Fountain of Youth, established a settlement on the island and became its first governor, and in 1521, founded Old San Juan. For three centuries, the Dutch and the English tried unsuccessfully to wrest the island from Spain. In 1897, Spain granted the island dominion status. Two years later, Spain ceded the island to the United States, and in 1917 Puerto Ricans became U.S. citizens, part of the Commonwealth.

And so, if you're a U.S. citizen, you need neither passport nor visa when you land at the bustling Luis Muñoz Marín Airport, outside San Juan. You don't have to clear customs, and you don't have to explain yourself to an immigration official. English is widely spoken, though the official language is Spanish.

Puerto Rico also boasts hundreds of beaches with every imaginable water sport available, acres of golf courses and miles of tennis courts, and small colonial towns where you can quietly savor the Spanish flavor. If it's festivals you seek, every town honors its individual patron saint with an annual festival, which is usually held in the central plaza, and can last from one to 10 days. In San Juan, *LeLoLai* is a year-round festival celebrating Puerto Rican dance and folklore, with changing programs presented in major San Juan hotels. Having seen every sight on the island, you can then do further exploring on the offshore islands of Culebra, Vieques, Icacos, and Mona, where more aquatic activities, such as snorkeling and scuba diving, prevail.

Before You Go

Tourist Information Contact the **Puerto Rico Tourism Company** at the following addresses: 575 5th Ave., 23rd floor, New York, NY 10017, tel. 212/599–6262 or 800/223–6530; 3228–I Quails Lake Village

La., Norcross, GA 30093, tel. 404/564–9362; 11 E. Adams St., Chicago, IL 60603, tel. 312/922–9701; 3386 Van Horn 106, Trenton, MI 48183, tel. 313/676–2190; 3575 W. Cahuenga Blvd., Suite 248, Los Angeles, CA 90068, tel. 213/874–5991; Peninsula Bldg., Suite 903, 200 S.E. First St., Miami, FL 33131, tel. 305/381–8915; 2504 Marilyn Cir., Petaluma, CA 94952, tel. 707/762–3468; Box 2662, St. Louis, MO 63116, tel. 314/481–8216; Box 8053, Falls Church, VA 22041–8053, tel. 703/671–0930; or 11 Yorkville Ave., Suite 1003, Toronto, Ontario, M4W IL3, Canada, tel. 416/925–5587.

Arriving and Departing By Plane The Luis Muñoz Marín International Airport east of downtown San Juan is the Caribbean hub for **American Airline** (tel. 800/433–7300). American has daily nonstop flights from New York and Dallas, and flies from Chicago via New York. **Delta** (tel. 800/221–1212) has direct service from Atlanta, and **TWA** (tel. 800/892–4141) from New York and St. Louis. Foreign carriers include **Air France** (tel. 800/237–2747), **British Airways** (tel. 800/247–9297), **BWIA** (tel. 800/327–7401), **Iberia** (tel. 800/772–4642), **LACSA** (tel. 800/225–2272), **LIAT** (tel. 800/462–0701), **Lufthansa** (tel. 800/645–3880), and **VIASA** (tel. 800/327–5454).

From the Airport **Airport Limousine Service** (tel. 809/791–4745) provides minibus service to hotels in the Isla Verde, Condado, and Old San Juan areas at basic fares of $1, $1.50, and $1.75, respectively; the fares, which are set by the Public Service Commission, can vary, depending upon time of day and number of passengers. Limousines of **Dorado Transport Service** (tel. 809/796–1214) serve hotels and villas in the Dorado area for $12 per person with a minimum of four passengers. Taxi fare from the airport to Isla Verde is about $5; to the Condado area, $8–$10; and to Old San Juan, $10–$12.

By Boat Daily hydrofoil service (tel. 809/793–7159 or 809/793–7153) runs between San Juan and Crown Bay in St. Thomas. The two-hour ride is $65 for adults, $32.50 for children.

Passports and Visas Puerto Rico is a Commonwealth of the United States and U.S. citizens do not need passports to visit the island. British citizens must have a passport and visa. Canadian citizens need proof of citizenship (preferably a passport).

Customs and Duties U.S. citizens need not clear customs or immigration when traveling to or from Puerto Rico. However, when you depart, your luggage will be inspected by the U.S. Agriculture Department as there are prohibitions against taking certain fruits and plants into the United States.

Language The official language is Spanish, but almost everyone in and around San Juan speaks English. If you plan to rent a car and travel around the island, take along a Spanish phrase book.

Precautions San Juan, like any other big city and major tourist destination, has its share of crime, so guard your wallet or purse on the city streets. Puerto Rico's beaches are open to the public, and muggings occur at night even on the beaches of the posh Condado and Isla Verde tourist hotels. Don't leave anything unattended on the beach. Leave your valuables in the hotel safe, and stick to the fenced-in beach areas of your hotel. Always lock your car and stash valuables and luggage out of sight. Avoid deserted beaches day or night.

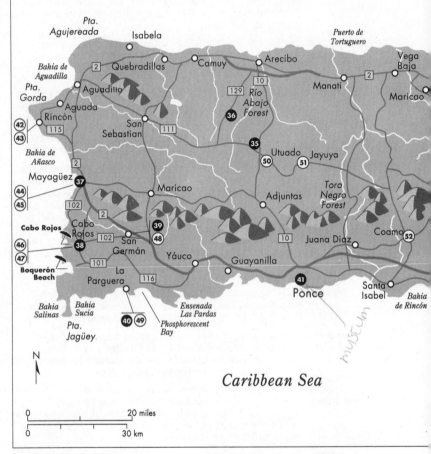

Pta.
Agujereada
Isabela
Puerto de
Tortuguero
Bahía de
Aguadilla
Quebradillas   Camuy   Arecibo   Vega
Baja
Pta.
Gorda   Aguadilla   Manatí   2
Aguada   129   Río   Maricao
Rincón   115   San   Abajo
Sebastián   111   Forest
42
43   36
Bahía de   Utuado   Jayuya
Añasco   35
Mayagüez   37   Maricao   50   51
44   Adjuntas   Toro
45   102   Negro
2   Forest
Cabo Rojos   Cabo   39   10
Rojos   102   San   48   Juana Díaz   Coamo
46   38   Germán   52
47   101   Yáuco   Guayanilla   Santa
Boquerón   La   116   Isabel   Bahía
Beach   Parguera   41   de Rincón
Ensenada   Ponce
Bahía   Bahía   40   49   Las Pardas
Salinas   Sucia   Phosphorescent
Pta.   Bay
Jagüey

museum

N

Caribbean Sea

0 ———————— 20 miles
0 ———————— 30 km

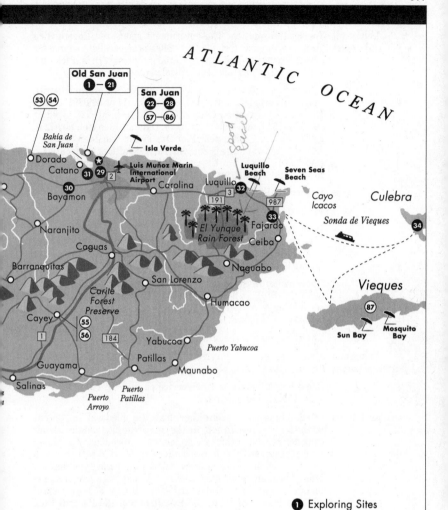

1 Exploring Sites

42 Hotels and Restaurants

Lodging

Hilton International Mayagüez, **45**

Hyatt Dorado Beach, **54**

Hyatt Regency Cerromar Beach, **53**

Parador Baños de Coamo, **52**

Parador Boquemer, **47**

Parador Casa Grande, **50**

Parador Hacienda Gripinas, **51**

Parador Oasis, **48**

Parador Villa Parquera, **49**

Sea Gate (Vieques), **87**

Staying in Puerto Rico

Important Addresses

Tourist Information: The government-sponsored **Puerto Rico Tourism Company** (tel. 809/721–2400) is an excellent source for maps, brochures, and other printed guide materials. Pick up a free copy of *¿Qué Pasa?* the official visitors guide.

Information offices are located at **Luis Muñoz Marín International Airport,** Isla Verde (tel. 809/791–1014 or 809/791–3443); **El Centro Convention Center,** Condado (tel. 809/723–3135 or 809/722–1513); **301 Calle San Justo,** Old San Juan (tel. 809/721–2400), and **La Casita,** near Pier One in Old San Juan (tel. 809/722–1709). Out on the island, information offices are located in each town's city hall on the main plaza, open weekdays from 8 AM to noon and 1 to 4:30 PM.

Emergencies

Police: Call 809/343–2020.

Medical Emergency: Call 809/343–2550.

Hospitals: Hospitals in the Condado/Santurce area with 24-hour emergency rooms are **Ashford Memorial Community Hospital** (1451 Ashford Ave., tel. 809/721–2160) and **San Juan Health Center** (200 De Diego Ave., tel. 809/725–0202).

Pharmacies: In San Juan, **Walgreen's** (1130 Ashford Ave., tel. 809/725–1510) is a 24-hour pharmacy. In Mayagüez there is another Walgreen's (16 Calle McKinley, tel. 809/833–6742), but it is not open 24 hours.

Currency

The U.S. dollar is the official currency of Puerto Rico.

Taxes and Service Charges

Hotels collect a 6% government tax on room charges. There is no departure tax.

Some hotels impose a 10% service charge. In restaurants, a 10%–15% tip is expected.

Guided Tours

Old San Juan can be seen either on a self-guided walking tour or on the free trolley. To explore the rest of the city and the island, consider renting a car. (We do, however, recommend a guided tour of the vast El Yunque rain forest.) If you'd rather not do your own driving, there are several tour companies you can call. Most San Juan hotels have a tour desk that can make arrangements for you. The standard half-day tours (at $10–$15) are of Old and New San Juan, Old San Juan and the Bacardi Rum Plant, Luquillo Beach and El Yunque rain forest. All-day tours ($15–$30) include a trip to Ponce, a day at El Comandante Racetrack, or a combined tour of the city and El Yunque rain forest.

Some of the leading tour operators are **Borinquén Tours, Inc.** (tel. 809/725–4990), **Gray Line of Puerto Rico** (tel. 809/727–8080), **Normandie Tours, Inc.** (tel. 809/725–6990 or 809/722–6308), **Rico Suntours** (tel. 809/722–2080 or 809/722–6090), and **United Tour Guides** (tel. 809/725–7605 or 809/723–5578). **Cordero Caribbean Tours** (tel. 809/799–6002) does tours (at hourly rates) out on the island in air-conditioned limousines.

Hop in a helicopter with **M & W Sky Rides** (tel. 809/724–4585) to get a gull's-eye view of the city. A 7-mile flight over Old San Juan costs $25 per person; the 18-mile Grand Tour is $50 per person. Takeoffs are from the roof of Covadonga parking lot across the street from Pier 6. *Tel. 809/724–4585. Open daily 10–6.*

Getting Around
Taxis Metered cabs authorized by the Public Service Commission (tel. 809/751–5050) charge an 80¢ drop and 10¢ for each additional ⅛ mile. There is a 50¢ charge per suitcase. Waiting time is $8 per hour.

Buses The **Metropolitan Bus Authority** (tel. 809/767–7979) operates the buses (or *guaguas*) that thread through San Juan. The fare is 25¢, and the buses run in exclusive lanes, *against the traffic* on major thoroughfares, stopping at upright yellow posts marked *Parada* or *Parada de Guaguas*. The main terminals downtown are at Plaza Colón and the Catano Ferry Terminal.

Públicos Public cars *(públicos)* with license plates ending with "P" or "PD" scoot to towns throughout the island, stopping in each town's main plaza. The five-passenger cars operate primarily during the day, with routes and fares fixed by the Public Service Commission. In San Juan, the main terminals are at the airport and on the waterfront in Old San Juan.

Trolleys If your feet fail you in Old San Juan, climb aboard the free open-air trolleys that rumble and roller-coast through the narrow streets. Departures are from La Puntilla and from the marina, but you can board them anywhere along the route.

Motor Coaches The **Puerto Rico Motor Coach Co.** (tel. 809/725–2460) makes daily runs between San Juan and Mayagüez, with stops at Arecibo and Aguadilla. A bus leaves San Juan every two hours, from 6 to 6, for a one-way fare of $6. Be sure to reserve in advance.

Ferries A round-trip ride between Old San Juan and Catano costs a mere 20¢. The ferry runs every half hour from 6:15 AM to 10 PM. The 400-passenger ferries of the **Puerto Rico Port Authority** (tel. 809/863–0705 or 809/863–0852) make the 80-minute trip twice daily between Fajardo and Vieques (one way $2 adults, $1 children), the two-hour run between Fajardo and Culebra daily (one way $2.25 adults, $1 children), and the two-hour trip between Vieques and Culebra on Saturday, Sunday, Monday, and holidays (one way $2 adults, $1 children).

Rental Cars U.S. driver's licenses are valid in Puerto Rico for three months. All major U.S. car-rental agencies are represented on the island, including **Avis** (tel. 809/791–5121), **Hertz** (tel. 809/791–0840), **Budget** (tel. 809/791–3685), and **Thrifty** (tel. 809/791–4241). Prices start at $19.95 (plus insurance), with unlimited mileage. Most car rentals have shuttle service to or from the airport and the pickup point. If you plan to drive across the island, arm yourself with a good map and be aware that there are many unmarked roads up in the mountains. Many service stations in the central mountains do not take credit cards. Speed limits are posted in miles, distances in kilometers, and gas prices in liters.

Planes **Crown Air** (tel. 809/728–2828) flies from Luis Muñoz Marín International Airport to Mayagüez (about $35 one way) to the Dorado resorts (about $30 one way) and Palmas del Mar (about $33 one way). **Vieques Air-Link** (tel. 809/722–3736) flies from the Isla Grande Airport to Vieques and to Culebra, with each trip costing about $25 one way.

Telephones and Mail The area code for Puerto Rico is 809.

Since Puerto Rico uses U.S. postage stamps and has the same mail rates (17¢ for a postcard, 25¢ for a first-class letter), you can save time by bringing stamps with you. Post offices in major Puerto Rico cities offer Express Mail next-day service to the U.S. mainland and to Puerto Rico destinations.

Opening and Closing Times Shops are open from 9 to 6 (from 9 to 9 during Christmas holidays). Banks are open weekdays from 8:30 to 2:30 and Saturday from 9:45 to noon.

Beaches

By law, all of Puerto Rico's beaches are open to the public (except for the Caribe Hilton's man-made beach in San Juan). The government runs 13 public beaches *(balnearios)*, which have lockers, showers, picnic tables, and in some cases playgrounds and overnight facilities. Admission is 25¢, parking is $1. Balnearios are open Tuesday–Sunday 9–5 in the winter, 8–5 in the summer. (When Monday is a holiday the balnearios are closed on Monday and open Tuesday.) Listed below are some of the major balnearios.

A white sandy beach bordered by resort hotels, **Isla Verde** offers picnic tables and good snorkeling, with equipment rentals nearby. *Near metropolitan San Juan, Rte. 187, Km 3.9, Isla Verde.*

Boquerón Beach is a broad beach of hard-packed sand, fringed with coconut palms. It has picnic tables, cabin rentals, bike rentals, basketball court, minimarket, scuba diving, and snorkeling. *On the southeast coast, south of Mayagüez, Rte. 101, Boquerón.*

Luquillo Beach, a crescent-shape beach, comes complete with coconut palms, picnic tables, and tent sites. Coral reefs protect its crystal-clear lagoon from the Atlantic waters, making it ideal for swimming. *30 mi east of San Juan, Rte. 3, Km 35.4.*

A recently opened beach of hard-packed sand, **Seven Seas** is already popular with bathers. It has picnic tables and tent and trailer sites; snorkeling, scuba diving, and boat rentals are nearby. *Rte. 987, Fajardo.*

Sun Bay, a white-sand beach on the offshore island of Vieques, has picnic tables, tent sites, and offers such water sports as snorkeling and scuba diving. Boat rentals are nearby. *Rte. 997, Vieques.*

Surfing Beaches. The best surfing beaches are along the Atlantic coastline from Borinquén Point to Rincón, where the surfing is best from October through April. There are several surf shops in Rincón. Aviones and La Concha beaches in San Juan, and Casa de Pesca in Arecibo, are summer surfing spots; all have nearby surf shops.

Caution for snorkelers and scuba divers: Puerto Rico's coral-reef waters and mangrove areas can be dangerous to novices. Unless you're an expert, or have an experienced guide, avoid unsupervised areas, and stick to the water-sport centers of major hotels (*see* Participant Sports, below).

Exploring Puerto Rico

Numbers in the margin correspond with points of interest on the Old San Juan map.

Old San Juan
❶ Old San Juan, the original city founded in 1521, contains authentic and carefully preserved examples of 16th- and 17th-century Spanish colonial architecture, some of the best in the New World. More than 400 buildings have been beautifully restored. Graceful wrought-iron balconies, decorated with lush green hanging plants, extend over narrow streets paved with blue-gray stones (*adequines*, originally used as ballast for Spanish ships). The old city is partially enclosed by the old walls, dating from 1630, that once completely surrounded it. Designated a U.S. National Historic Zone in 1950, Old San Juan is chock-a-block with shops, open-air cafés, private homes, tree-shaded squares, monuments, plaques, pigeons, and people. The traffic is awful. Get an overview of the inner city on a morning's stroll (bearing in mind that "stroll" includes some steep climbs). However, if you plan to immerse yourself in history, or to shop, you'll need two or three days.

El Morro and Fort San Cristóbal are described in our walking tour: You may want to set aside extra time to see them, especially if you're an aficionado of military history. UNESCO has designated each fortress a World Heritage Site; each is also a National Historic Site. Both are looked after by the National Park Service; you can take one of their tours or wander around on your own.

Sitting on a rocky promontory on the northwestern tip of the
❷ old city is **San Felipe del Morro** ("El Morro"), a fortress built by the Spaniards between 1540 and 1783. Rising 140 feet above the sea, the massive six-level fortress covers enough territory to accommodate a nine-hole golf course. It is a labyrinth of dungeons, ramps and barracks, turrets, towers, and tunnels. Built to protect the port, El Morro has a commanding view of the harbor. Its small, air-conditioned museum traces the history of the fortress. *Calle Norzagaray, tel. 809/724–1974. Admission: $1 adults, children free. Open daily 8–6:15.*

San José Plaza is two short blocks from the entrance to El
❸ Morro, but for the moment we'll bypass it and head for the **San Juan Museum of Arts and History,** which is a block east of the tour's path but a must. A bustling marketplace in 1850, this handsome building is now a modern cultural center that houses exhibits of Puerto Rican art. Multi-image audiovisual shows present the history of the island; concerts and other cultural events take place in the huge courtyard. *Calle Norzagaray, at the corner of Calle MacArthur, tel. 809/724–1875. Donation requested: $1 adults, 50¢ children. Open weekdays 9–noon and 1–5, weekends 10–noon and 1–5. Audiovisual shows Fri. at 11.*

❹ Turn back west toward San José Plaza to **La Casa de los Contrafuertes,** on Calle San Sebastián. This building is also known as the Buttress House because wide exterior buttresses support the wall next to the plaza. The house is one of the oldest remaining private residences in Old San Juan. Inside is the Pharmacy Museum, a re-creation of an 18th-century apothecary shop. The building was closed for renovation at press time.

*101 Calle San Sebastián, Plaza de San José, tel. 809/724–5949.
Admission free. Open Wed.–Sun. 9–noon and 1–4.*

⑤ The **Pablo Casals Museum,** a bit farther down the block, contains memorabilia of the famed cellist, who made his home in Puerto Rico for the last 20 years of his life. The museum holds manuscripts, photographs, and his favorite cellos, in addition to recordings and videotapes of Casals Festival concerts (the latter shown on request). *101 Calle San Sebastián, Plaza de San José, tel. 809/723–9185. Admission free. Open Tues.–Sat. 9–5; Sun. noon–5; closed Mon.*

⑥ In the center of the plaza, next to the museum, is the **San José Church.** With its series of vaulted ceilings, it is a splendid example of 16th-century Spanish Gothic architecture. The church, which is one of the oldest Christian houses of worship in the Western Hemisphere, was built in 1523 under the supervision of the Dominican friars. The body of Ponce de León, the Spanish explorer who came to the New World seeking the Fountain of Youth, was buried here for almost three centuries before being removed in 1913 and placed in the cathedral. *Calle San Sebastián, tel. 809/725–7501. Admission free. Open daily 9–4.*

⑦ Next door is the **Dominican Convent (Institute of Puerto Rican Culture).** Also built by Dominican friars in 1523, the convent often served as a shelter during Carib Indian attacks in the past and, more recently, as headquarters for the Antilles command of the U.S. Army. Now home to the Institute of Puerto Rican Culture, the beautifully restored building contains an ornate

18th-century altar, religious manuscripts, artifacts, and art. Classical concerts are held here every Sunday at 4 PM. *98 Calle Norzagaray, tel. 809/724-0700. Admission free. Chapel museum open Wed.-Sun. 9-noon and 1-4. Popular Arts Museum open Mon.-Sat. 9:15-4:15.*

❽ From San José Plaza walk west on Calle Beneficencia to **Casa Blanca.** The original structure on this site, not far from the ramparts of El Morro, was a frame house built in 1521 as a home for Ponce de León. But Ponce de León died in Cuba, never having lived in the house, and it was virtually destroyed by a hurricane in 1523, after which Ponce de León's son-in-law had the present masonry house built. His descendants occupied it for 250 years. From the end of the Spanish-American War in 1898 to 1966, it was the home of the U.S. Army commander in Puerto Rico. It is now a museum showcasing aspects of 16th- and 17th-century Puerto Rican family life. Guided tours are conducted Tuesday-Saturday. *1 Calle San Sebastián, tel. 809/ 724-4102. Admission free. Open Tues.-Sun. 9-noon and 1-4:30.*

❾ **San Juan Cathedral.** This great Catholic shrine of Puerto Rico had humble beginnings in the early 1520s as a thatch-topped wood structure. Hurricane winds tore off the thatch and destroyed the church. It was reconstructed in 1540, when the graceful circular staircase and vaulted ceilings were added, but most of the work on the church was done in the 19th century. The remains of Ponce de León are in a marble tomb near the transept. *153 Calle Cristo. Open daily 6:30-5.*

Time Out Stop in at **María's** (204 Calle Cristo, no phone) for a papaya freeze, a chocolate frost, or a pitcher of Mexican sangría. Enchiladas and tacos are also served.

Across the street from the cathedral you'll see the Ramada Gran Hotel El Convento, which was a Carmelite convent more than 300 years ago. Go west alongside the hotel on Caleta de las **❿** Monjas toward the city wall to the **Plazuela de la Rogativa.** In the little plaza, statues of a bishop and three women commemorate a legend, according to which the British, while laying siege on the city in 1797, mistook the flaming torches of a religious procession *(rogativa)* for Spanish reinforcements, and beat a hasty retreat. The monument was donated to the city in 1971 on its 450th anniversary.

⓫ One block south on Calle Recinto Oeste you'll come to **La Fortaleza,** which sits on a hill overlooking the harbor. La Fortaleza, the Western Hemisphere's oldest executive mansion in continuous use, home of 170 governors and official residence of the present governor of Puerto Rico, was built as a fortress. The original primitive structure, built in 1540, has seen numerous changes over a period of three centuries, resulting in the present collection of marble and mahogany, medieval towers, and stained-glass galleries. Guided tours are conducted every hour on the hour in English, on the half hour in Spanish. *Tel. 809/721-7000. Admission free. Open weekdays 9-4.*

⓬ At the southern end of Cristo Street is **Cristo Chapel.** According to legend, in 1753, a young horseman, carried away during festivities in honor of the patron saint, raced down the street and plunged over the steep precipice. A witness to the tragedy promised to build a chapel if the young man's life could be saved. The man lived. Inside is a small silver altar, dedicated to the Christ of Miracles. *Open Tues. 10–4 and on most Catholic holidays.*

13 Across the street from the chapel, the 18th-century **Casa del Libro** has exhibits devoted to books and bookbinding. The museum's 5,000 books include rare volumes dating back 2,000 years; more than 200 of these books—40 of which were produced in Spain—were printed before the 16th century. *255 Calle Cristo, tel. 809/723–0354. Admission free. Open weekdays (except holidays) 11–4:30.*

14 Next door, the **Fine Arts Museum,** in a lovely colonial building, occasionally presents special exhibits. The museum usually holds the Institute of Puerto Rican Culture's collection of paintings and sculptures, but those pieces have been temporarily removed. *253 Calle Cristo, tel. 809/724–5949. Admission free. Open 9–noon and 1–4:30.*

15 Follow the wall east one block and head north on Calle San José two short blocks to **Plaza de Armas,** the original main square of Old San Juan. The plaza, bordered by Calles San Francisco, Fortaleza, San José, and Cruz, has a lovely fountain with statues representing the four seasons.

16 West of the square stands **La Intendencia,** a handsome three-story neoclassical building. From 1851 to 1898, it was home to the Spanish Treasury. Recently restored, it is now the headquarters of Puerto Rico's State Department. *Calle San José, at the corner of Calle San Francisco, tel. 809/722–2121. Admission free. Open weekdays 8–noon and 1–4:30.*

17 On the north side of the plaza is **City Hall,** called the *Alcaldía.* Built between 1604 and 1789, the alcaldía was fashioned after Madrid's city hall, with arcades, towers, balconies, and a lovely inner courtyard. A tourist information center and an art gallery are on the first floor. *Tel. 809/724–7171. Open weekdays 8–4.*

Time Out **La Bombonera** (259 Calle San Francisco, no phone), established in 1903, is known for its strong Puerto Rican coffee and *Mallorca*—a Spanish pastry made of light dough, toasted, buttered, and sprinkled with powdered sugar.

18 Four blocks east on the pedestrian mall of Calle Fortaleza you'll find **Plaza de Colón,** a bustling square with a statue of Christopher Columbus atop a high pedestal. Originally called St. James Square, it was renamed in honor of Columbus on the 400th anniversary of the discovery of Puerto Rico. Bronze plaques in the base of the statue relate various episodes in the life of the great explorer. On the north side of the plaza is a terminal for buses to and from San Juan.

19 South of Plaza de Colón is the magnificent **Tapia Theater,** (Calle Fortaleza at Plaza de Colón, tel. 809/722–0407) named after the famed Puerto Rican playwright Alejandro Tapia y Riviera. Built in 1832, remodeled in 1949 and again in 1987, the municipal theater is the site of ballets, plays, and operettas. Stop by the box office to see what's showing and if you can get tickets.

20 Walk two blocks north from Plaza de Colón to Calle Sol and turn right. Another block will take you to **San Cristóbal,** the 18th-century fortress that guarded the city from land attacks. Even larger than El Morro, San Cristóbal was known as the Gibraltar of the West Indies. *Tel. 809/724–1974. Admission: $1 adults, children free. Open daily 8–6:15.*

㉑ Stroll from Plaza de Colón down to the **Port,** where the esplanade is spruced up with flowers, trees, and street lamps. Across from Pier 3, where the cruise ships dock, local artisans display their wares at the Plazoleta del Puerto. At the marina, pay 20¢ and board a ferry for a round-trip ride to Catano.

New San Juan You'll need to resort to taxis, buses, públicos, or a rental car to ㉒ reach the points of interest in "new" San Juan.

Numbers in the margin correspond with points of interest on the San Juan map.

Avenida Muñoz Rivera, Avenida Ponce de León, and Avenida Fernández Juncos are the main thoroughfares that cross Puerta de Tierra, just east of Old San Juan, to the business and tourist districts of Santurce, Condado, and Isla Verde.

㉓ In Puerta de Tierra is Puerto Rico's **Capitol,** a lovely white marble building that dates from the 1920s. The grand rotunda, complete with mosaics and friezes, was completed only a few years ago. The seat of the island's bicameral legislature, the Capitol contains Puerto Rico's Constitution, and is flanked by the modern buildings of the Senate and the House of Representatives. There are spectacular views from the observation plaza on the sea side of the Capitol. Pick up an informative booklet about the building from the House secretariat on the second floor. Guided tours are by appointment only. *Avenida Ponce de León, tel. 809/721–6040 (ext. 253). Admission free. Open weekdays 8:30–5.*

㉔ At the eastern tip of Puerta de Tierra, behind the splashy Caribe Hilton, the tiny **Fort San Jeromino** is perched over the Atlantic like an afterthought. Added to San Juan's fortifications in the late 18th century, the structure barely survived the British attack of 1797. Restored in 1983 by the Institute of Puerto Rican Culture, it is now a military museum with displays of weapons, uniforms, and maps. *Tel. 809/724–5949. Admission free. Open Wed.–Sun. 9–noon and 1–4:30.*

Dos Hermanos Bridge connects Puerta de Tierra with Miramar, Condado, and Isla Grande. Isla Grande Airport, from which you can take short hops, is on the bay side of the bridge.

On the other side of the bridge, the Condado Lagoon is bordered by Avenida Ashford, which threads past the high-rise Condado hotels and El Centro Convention Center, and Avenida Baldorioty de Castro, which barrels all the way east to the airport and beyond. Due south of the lagoon is Miramar, a primarily residential area with fashionable, turn-of-the-century homes and a cluster of hotels and restaurants.

㉕ **Santurce,** which lies between Miramar on the west and the San José Lagoon on the east, is a busy mixture of shops, markets, and offices. Internationally acclaimed performers appear at the ㉖ **Fine Arts Center.** This completely modern facility, the largest of its kind in the Caribbean, has a full schedule of concerts, plays, and operas. *Centro de Bellas Artes, corner of De Diego Ave. and Ponce de León St., tel. 809/724–4751.*

San Juan Exploring, Dining and Lodging

386

ATLANTIC OCEAN

Laguna del Condado

Laguna Los Corozos

Laguna San José

Bahia de San Juan

Luis Muñoz Marin International Airport

Isla Grande Airport

Baldorioty de Casto Expreso

Ponce de Leon

Luis Muñoz Rivera

Caño de Martin Peña

John F. Kennedy

Luis Muñoz Rivera Expreso

Muñoz Rivera Ave. Ponce de Leon

Fernandez Juncos

Del Cristo

Sol

Marina

1 mile

1 km

N

23 Exploring Sites

57 Hotels and Restaurants

Exploring
Capitol, 23
Fine Arts Center, 26
Fort San Jeronimo, 24
Muñoz Marin Park, 27
New San Juan, 22
Santurce, 25
University of Puerto
Rico, 28

Dining
Amadeus, 60
Ambrosia, 58
Augusto's, 68
Cafeteria España, 84
The Chart House, 79
Che's, 83
Dar Tiffany, 82

El Nuevo Cafe
San Juan, 62
El Paso, 70
El Patio de Convento, 57
Il Giardino, 78

Kasalta Bakery, Inc., 81
L.K. Sweeney
& Son, Ltd., 71
La Chaumiere, 63
La Compostela, 77
La Reina de España, 75
La Rotisserie, 66
La Zaragozana, 61

Santiago, 64
Scotch & Sirloin, 73
Via Appia's Italian
Deli, 80
Yukiyu, 65

Lodging
Caribe Hilton International, 67
Condado Beach
Hotel, 74
Condado Plaza Hotel
& Casino, 72
El San Juan Hotel and
Casino, 85

Excelsior, 69
Hotel La Concha, 76
Ramada Gran Hotel El
Convento, 59
Sands Hotel and
Casino, 86

South of Santurce is the "Golden Mile"—Hato Rey, the city's bustling new financial hub. Isla Verde, with its glittering beachfront hotels, casinos, discos, and public beach, is to the east, near the airport.

Time Out **Pescadería Atlántica** (81 Loiza St., tel. 809/726–6654) is a combination seafood restaurant and retail store. Stop in for a cool drink at the bar and a side dish of calamares, lightly breaded squid in a hot, spicy sauce.

Northeast of Isla Verde, Boca de Cangrejos sits between the Atlantic and Torrecilla Lagoon—a great spot for fishing and snorkeling. This is the point of embarkation for the 30-passenger launch, *La Paseadora,* which tours the coast, the mangrove swamp, and the bird sanctuary at Torrecilla Lagoon.

Southeast of Miramar, Avenida Muñoz Rivera skirts along the northern side of **San Juan Central Park,** a convenient place for jogging, tennis, and calisthenics. The mangrove-bordered park was built for the 1979 Pan-American Games. *Cerra St. exit on Rte. 2, tel. 809/722–1646. Admission free. Open Tues.–Sat. 8–10, Mon. 2–10, Sun. 10–6.*

Las Américas Expressway, heading south, goes by Plaza Las Américas, the largest shopping mall in the Caribbean, and takes you to the new **Muñoz Marín Park,** an idyllic tree-shaded spot dotted with gardens, lakes, playgrounds, and picnic areas. Cable cars connect the park with the parking area. *Next to Las Américas Expwy., west on Piñero Ave., tel. 809/763–0568. Admission free; parking $1 per vehicle. Open Tues.–Fri., 9–6, weekends 8:30–6; closed Mon.*

28 Río Piedras, a southern suburb of San Juan, is home to the **University of Puerto Rico,** located between Ponce de León Avenue and Barbosa Avenue. The university's campus is one of two sites for performances of the Puerto Rico Symphony Orchestra. Theatrical productions and other concerts are also scheduled here throughout the year. The University Museum has permanent archaeological and historical exhibits, and occasionally mounts special art displays. *Next to the university main entrance on Ponce de León Ave., tel. 809/764–0000, ext. 2452 or 2456. Open weekdays 9–9, weekends 9–3.*

The university's main attraction is the **Botanical Garden,** a lush garden with more than 200 species of tropical and subtropical vegetation. Footpaths through the thick forests lead to a graceful lotus lagoon, a bamboo promenade, an orchid garden, and a palm garden. *Intersection of Rtes. 1 and 847 at the entrance to Barrio Venezuela, tel. 809/766–0740. Admission free. Open Tues.–Sun. 9–4:30; when Mon. is a holiday, it is open Mon. and closed Tues.*

San Juan Environs *Numbers in the margin correspond with points of interest on the Puerto Rico map.*

From San Juan, follow Route 2 west toward Bayamón and you'll spot the **Caparra Ruins,** where, in 1508, Ponce de León established the island's first settlement. The ruins are that of an ancient fort. Its small **Museum of the Conquest and Colonization of Puerto Rico** contains historical documents, exhibits, and excavated artifacts. (You can see the museum's contents in less time than it takes to say the name.) *Km 6.6 on Rte. 2, tel. 809/*

781–4795. Admission free. Open weekdays 9–5, weekends and holidays 10–6.

30 Continue on Route 2 to **Bayamón.** In the Central Park, across from Bayamón's city hall, there are some historical buildings and a 1934 sugarcane train that runs through the park (open daily 8 AM–10 PM). On the plaza, in the city's historic district, stands the 18th-century Catholic church of Santa Cruz, and the old neoclassical city hall, which now houses the **Francisco Oller Art and History Museum** (open Tues.–Sat. 9–4).

31 Along Route 5 from Bayamón to Catano, you'll see the **Barrilito Rum Plant.** On the grounds is a 200-year-old plantation home and a 150-year-old windmill, which is listed in the National Register of Historic Places.

The **Bacardi Rum Plant,** along the bay, conducts 45-minute tours of the bottling plant, museum, and distillery, which has the capacity to produce 100,000 gallons of rum a day. (Yes, you'll be offered a sample.) *Km 2.6 on Rte. 888, tel. 809/795–1560. Admission free. Tours Mon.–Sat. 9:30–3:30; closed Sun.*

Out on the Island Puerto Rico's 3,500 square miles is a lot of land to explore. While it is possible to get from town to town via público, we don't recommend traveling that way unless your Spanish is good and you know exactly where you're going. The public cars stop in each town's main square, leaving you on your own to reach the beaches, restaurants, *paradores* (hotels), and sight-seeing attractions. You do much better if you rent a car. Most of the island's roads are excellent. However, there is a tangled web of roads through the mountains, and they are not always well marked. Get a good road map.

East and South Our first excursion out on the island will take us east, down the coast to the south, and back up to San Juan. The first leg of the **32** trip—to **Luquillo Beach** and the nearby **El Yunque rain forest**—can easily be done in a day. (There'll be heavy traffic and a crowded beach on weekends, when it seems as if the whole world heads for Luquillo.) The full itinerary will take two to three days, depending upon how long you loll on the beach and linger over the mountain scenery.

To take full advantage of the 28,000-acre El Yunque rain forest, go with a tour. Dozens of trails lead through the thick jungle (it sheltered the Carib Indians for 200 years), and the tour guides take you to the best observation points. Some of the trails are slippery, and there are occasional washouts.

However, if you'd like to drive there yourself, take Route 3 east from San Juan and turn right (south) on Route 191, about 25 miles from the city. The **Sierra Palm Visitor Center** is on Route 191, Km 11.6 (open daily 9:30–5). Nature talks and programs at the center are by appointment only—another good reason to go with a tour group.

El Yunque, named after the good Indian spirit Yuquiyu, is in the Luquillo Mountain Range. The rain forest is verdant with feathery ferns, thick rope-like vines, white tuberoses and ginger, miniature orchids, and some 240 different species of trees. More than 100 billion gallons of rainwater falls on it annually. Rain-battered, wind-ravaged dwarf vegetation clings to the top peaks. (El Toro, the highest peak in the forest, is 3,532 feet.) El Yunque is also a bird sanctuary and is the base of the rare Puerto Rican parrot. Millions of tiny, inch-long tree frogs *(coquis)* can be heard singing (or squawking, depending on your sensibilities). *For further information call the Catalina Field Office, tel. 809/753-4936, or write Caribbean National Forest, Box B, Palmer, PR 00721.*

To reach Luquillo Beach, take Route 191 back to Route 3 and continue east 5 miles to Km 35.4. One of the island's best and most popular beaches, Luquillo was once a flourishing coconut plantation. Coral reefs protect its calm, pristine lagoon, making it an ideal place for a swim. The entrance fee is 25¢, parking is $1, and there are lockers, showers, and changing rooms *(see* Beaches, above).

If you want to continue exploring, get back on Route 3 and ❸❸ drive 5 miles to **Fajardo,** a major fishing and sailing center with thousands of boats tied up to its three large marinas. Boats can be rented or chartered here, and the *Spread Eagle* catamaran can take you out for a full day of snorkeling, swimming, and sunning *(see* Participant Sports, below). Fajardo is also the embarkation point for ferries to the offshore islands of Culebra (a $2.25 fare) and Vieques ($2). Culebra has lovely white-sand beaches, coral reefs, and a wildlife refuge. In the sleepy town of ❸❹ **Dewey,** on Culebra's southwestern side, check at the Visitor Information Center at city hall (tel. 809/742-2191) about boat rentals. On Vieques, Sun Bay public beach has picnic facilities; Blue Beach is superb for snorkeling; and Mosquito Bay is luminous on moonless nights. You can stay overnight at the government-sponsored Parador Villa Esperanza (tel. 809/741-8675) on Vieques, which has, among other amenities, its own marina and fleet of sailing ships.

Resume your ramble on Route 3, heading south past the U.S. Naval Base and ride through the sugarcane fields to Humacao. South of Humacao (take Route 906) is the 2,700-acre Palmas del Mar, the island's largest residential resort complex.

Stay on Route 3 through Yabucoa, tucked up in the hills, and Maunabo and Patillas, where you can pick up the routes to take you through the Cayey Mountains. Route 184 north skirts Lake Patillas and cuts smack through the Carite Forest Reserve. Stay on Route 184 until it merges with Route 763. Turn left on Route 763, then right on Route 765 to Route 1, where you'll shoot northward back to San Juan.

Western Island If you're short of time, drive the 64 miles from San Juan to Ponce in 90 minutes. Take the Las Américas Expressway, which cuts through the splendid mountains of Cordillera Central.

If time is not a major problem, take a three- or four-day tour exploring the western regions of the island. This route covers Aguadilla, Mayagüez, San Germán, and Ponce. There's much to see along the way—caves and coves, karst fields and coffee plantations, mountains and beaches, and even a zoo.

❸❺ Outside Utuado, south of Route 10, is **Caguana Indian Ceremonial Park,** used 800 years ago by the Taino tribes for recreation and worship. Mountains surround a 13-acre site planted with royal palms and guava. According to Spanish historians, the Tainos played a game similar to soccer, and in this park there are 10 courts bordered by cobbled walkways. There are also stone monoliths, some with colorful petroglyphs; a small museum; and a souvenir shop. *Rte. 111, Km 12.3. Admission free. Open daily 9-5.*

From Utuado, drive west on Route 111 and then north on Route 129 to Km 18.9, where you'll find the **Río Camuy Cave Park,** one of the world's largest cave networks. Guided tours take you on a tram down through dense tropical vegetation to the entrance of the cave, where you continue on foot over underground trails, ramps, and bridges. The caves, sinkholes, and underground rivers are all spectacular (the world's second largest underground river runs through here), but this trip is not for those with claustrophobia. Be sure to call ahead; the tours allow only a limited number of people. *Rte. 129, Km 18.9, tel. 809/898–3100 or 809/756–5555. Admission: $4 adults, $2.50 children. Open Wed.–Sun. 9–5. Last tour starts at 4.*

Route 111 twists from Utuado to **Aguadilla** on the northwest coast. In this area, somewhere between Aguadilla and Anasco, south of Rincón, Columbus dropped anchor on his second voyage in 1493. Both Aguadilla and **Aguada,** a few miles to the south, claim to have been the spot where his foot first hit ground, and both towns have plaques to commemorate the occasion.

Route 115 from Aguadilla to **Rincón** is one of the island's most scenic drives, through rolling hills dotted with pastel-colored houses. Rincón, perched on a hill, overlooks its beach, which was the site of the World Surfing Championship in 1968. Skilled surfers flock to Rincón during the winter, when the water is rough and challenging.

Pick up Route 2 for the 6-mile drive to **Mayagüez,** Puerto Rico's third largest city, with a population approaching 100,000. Mayagüez, known for its needlework, has plenty of shops to browse around in. (The Mayagüez Shopping Mall is one of the island's largest. The lounge of the hilltop Mayagüez Hilton is a popular gathering place for locals and tourists.)

North of town visit the **Mayagüez Zoo,** a 45-acre tropical compound that's home to about 500 animals. In addition to Bengal tigers, reptiles, and birds, including an Andean condor, there's a lake and a children's playground. *Rte. 108 at Barrio Miradero, tel. 809/834–8110. Admission: $1 adults, 50¢ children. Open Tues.–Sun. 9–4:30.*

Due south of Mayagüez, via the coastal Route 102, is **Cabo Rojos,** once a pirates' hangout and now a favorite resort area of Puerto Ricans. The area has long stretches of white-sand beaches on the clear, calm Caribbean Sea, as well as many seafood restaurants. There are also several paradores in the region. **Boquerón,** at the end of Route 101, has one of the best beaches on the island, as well as two-room cabins for rent.

From Cabo Rojos continue east on Route 102 to **San Germán,** a quiet Old World town that's home to the oldest intact church under the U.S. flag. Built in 1606, Porta Coeli (Gates of Heaven) overlooks one of the town's two plazas (where the townspeople continue the Spanish tradition of promenading at night). The church is now a museum of religious art, housing 18th- and 19th-century paintings and statues. *Tel. 809/892–5845. Admission free. Open Tues.–Sun. 9–noon and 1–4:30.*

The fishing village of **La Parguera,** an area of simple seafood restaurants, mangrove cays, and small islands, lies south of San Germán at the end of Route 304. This is an excellent scuba-diving area, but the main attraction is **Phosphorescent Bay.**

Boats tour the bay where microscopic dinoflagellates (marine plankton), light up like Christmas trees when disturbed by any kind of movement. The phenomenon can be seen best on moonless nights. Boats leave the pier nightly at 7:30, and the trip costs $4 per person.

From San Germán, Route 2 traverses splendid peaks and valleys; pastel houses cling to the sides of steep green hills. East of Yauco, the road dips and sweeps right along the Caribbean and into **Ponce.**

Puerto Rico's second city, with a population of about 150,000, has much to explore. You have not seen a firehouse until you've seen the red-and-black-striped **Parque de Bombas,** built in 1883 on the city's central plaza, with its bright yellow firetrucks. Stroll around the plaza, with its perfectly pruned trees, graceful fountains, gardens, and park benches. **Our Lady of Guadalupe Cathedral** would surely dominate the square, were it not for the firehouse. The white-columned **Casa Alcaldía** is the city hall, where you can stop in and pick up information.

Recent efforts to restore the city can be appreciated on the streets surrounding the plaza, where freshly painted houses with wrought-iron balconies, gas lamps, Corinthian columns, and Spanish arches may remind you of New Orleans's French Quarter.

Off the Beaten Track

The Blue Dolphin is a hangout where you can rub elbows with some offbeat locals. Located behind the Empress Oceanfront Hotel at the northern tip of Isla Verde, the Blue Dolphin offers one of the best views on the island. While strolling along the Isla Verde beach, just look for the neon blue dolphin on the roof— you can't miss it. *2 Amapola St., Isla Verde, tel. 809/791-3083. Open weekends noon-4 AM, weeknights noon-2 AM.*

Participant Sports

Bicycling   The broad beach at Boquerón makes for easy wheeling. You can rent bikes at **Boquerón Balnearios** (Rte. 101, Boquerón, Dept. of Recreation and Sports, tel. 809/722-1551). In the Dorado area on the north coast, bikes can be rented at the **Hyatt Regency Cerromar Beach Hotel** (tel. 809/796-1010) or the **Hyatt Dorado Beach Hotel** (tel. 809/796-1600).

Boating   Virtually all the resort hotels on San Juan's Condado and Isla Verde strips rent paddleboats, Sunfish, Windsurfers, and the like. Contact **Condado Plaza Hotel Watersports Center** (tel. 809/721-1000, ext. 1361), **Caribbean School of Aquatics** (La Concha Hotel, Ashford Ave., Condado, tel. 809/723-4740), or **Castillo Watersports** (ESJ Towers, Isla Verde, tel. 809/791-6195). Sailing and boat rentals are also available at **Playita Boat Rental** (1010 Ashford Ave., Condado, tel. 809/722-1607). The 600-passenger *Reina de la Bahia* (tel. 809/721-6700) departs from the waterfront in Old San Juan for sightseeing, lunch, dinner, and disco excursions.

Fishing   Half-day, full-day, split charters, and big- and small-game fishing can be arranged through **Benitez Deep-Sea Fishing** (Club Náutico de San Juan, Stop 9½, Fernández Juncos Ave., Miramar, tel. 809/723-2292), **Castillo Watersports** (ESJ Towers, Isla Verde, tel. 809/791–6195), and **San Juan Fishing Charters** (Stop 10, Fernández Juncos Ave., Miramar, tel. 809/723–0415).

Golf There are 36-hole courses at **Hyatt Dorado Beach Hotel** (Dorado, tel. 809/796–1600, ext. 3238) and **Hyatt Regency Cerromar Beach Hotel** (Dorado, tel. 809/796–1010, ext. 3013). You'll find 18-hole courses at **Palmas del Mar Resort** (Humacao, tel. 809/852–6000, ext. 2525), **Club Ríomar** (Río Grande, tel. 809/887–3964), and **Punta Borinquén** (Aquadilla, tel. 809/890–9814).

Hiking Dozens of trails lace through **El Yunque** (information is available at the Sierra Palm Visitor Center, Rte. 191, Km 11.6). You can also hit the trails in **Río Abajo Forest** (south of Arecibo) and **Toro Negro Forest** (east of Adjuntas). Each reserve has a ranger station.

Horseback Riding Beach trail rides can be arranged at **Palmas del Mar Equestrian Center** (Palmas del Mar Resort, Humacao, tel. 809/852–4785). Take to the rain forest foothills trails, as well as the beaches, through **Hacienda Carabali** (tel. 809/793–8585).

Sailing Sailing instruction and trips are offered by **Palmas Sailing Center** (Palmas del Mar Resort, Humacao, tel. 809/852–6000, ext. 4498), **Caribbean School of Aquatics** (La Concha Hotel, Ashford Ave., Condado, tel. 809/723–4740), **Caribe Aquatic Adventure** (Caribe Hilton Hotel, Puerta de Tierra, tel. 809/721–0303, ext. 3447), and **Castillo Watersports** (ESJ Towers, Isla Verde, tel. 809/791–6195).

Snorkeling and Scuba Diving Snorkeling and scuba-diving instruction and equipment rentals are available at **Caribbean School of Aquatics** *(see* Sailing, above), **Coral Head Divers** (Marina de Palmas, Palmas del Mar Resort, Humacao, tel. 809/850–7208), **Cueva Submarina Training Center** (Plaza Cooperativa, Isabela, tel. 809/872–3903), **Caribe Aquatic Adventure** *(see* Sailing, above), **Castillo Watersports** *(see* Sailing, above), **Jack Becker's Spread Eagle** (Villa Marina Yacht Harbor, Fajardo, tel. 809/863–1905), and **Parguera Divers Training Center** (Lajas, tel. 809/899–4171).

Tennis There are 17 lighted courts at **San Juan Central Park** (Cerra St. exit on Rte. 2, tel. 809/722–1646), 6 lighted courts at the **Caribe Hilton Hotel** (Puerta de Tierra, tel. 809/721–0303, ext. 1730), 8 courts, 4 lighted at **Carib Inn** (Isla Verde, tel. 809/791–3535, ext. 6), and 2 lighted courts at the **Condado Plaza Hotel** (Condado, tel. 809/721–2000, ext. 1775). Out on the island, there are 14 courts, 2 lighted, at **Hyatt Regency Cerromar Beach Hotel** (Dorado, tel. 809/796–1010, ext. 3040), 7 courts at the **Hyatt Dorado Beach Hotel** (Dorado, tel. 809/796–1600, ext. 3220), 20 courts, 2 lighted, at **Palmas del Mar Resort** (Humacao, tel. 809/852–6000, ext. 2527), 3 lighted courts at the **Mayagüez Hilton Hotel** (Mayagüez, tel. 809/834–7575, ext. 2150), and 4 lighted courts at **Punta Borinquén** (Aguadilla, tel. 809/891–8778).

Windsurfing Windsurfing rentals are available at **Caribbean School of Aquatics, Castillo Watersports, Palmas Sailing School,** and **Playita Boat Rental** *(see* Sailing, above, for all information).

Spectator Sports

Cockfighting It's the national sport of Puerto Rico, but it's not for the faint of heart. If you're curious about cockfights, head for **Club Gallístico.** *Rte. 37, Km 1.5, Isla Verde, tel. 809/791–6005. Open Sat. 1–7.*

Horse Racing Races are run year-round at **El Comandante Racetrack.** On race days the dining rooms open at 12:30 PM. *Rte. 3, Km 15.3, Canovananas, tel. 809/724–6060. Open Wed., Fri., Sun., and holidays.*

Baseball If you have a post–World Series letdown, you can fly down to the island, where the season runs October–April. Many major-league ballplayers in the United States made their start in Puerto Rico's baseball league and some return home in the off-season to hone their skills. Stadiums are in San Juan, Santurce, Ponce, Caguas, Arecibo, and Mayagüez. Contact the Tourist Office for details.

Shopping

San Juan is not a free port, and you won't find bargains on electronics and perfumes. You can, however, find excellent bargains in china, crystal, fashions, and jewelry.

Shopping for native crafts can be great fun. You'll run across a lot of tacky things you can live your whole life without, but you can also find some treasures, and in many cases you'll be able to watch the artisans at work. (For guidance, contact the Tourism Artisan Center, tel. 809/721–2400, ext. 248.)

The work of some Puerto Rican artists has brought them international acclaim: the paintings of Francisco Oller hang in the Louvre, and the portraits of Francisco Rodon are in the permanent collections of New York's Museum of Modern Art and the Metropolitan Museum. Look for their works, and those of other native artists, in San Juan's stylish galleries.

Popular souvenirs and gifts include *santos* (small, hand-carved figures of saints or religious scenes), hand-rolled cigars, handmade lace, carnival masks, and fancy men's shirts called *guayaberas.* Also, some folks swear that Puerto Rican rum is the best in the world.

Shopping Districts **Old San Juan** is full of shops, especially on Cristo, Fortaleza, and San Francisco streets. The **Las Américas Plaza** south of San Juan is the largest shopping mall in the Caribbean, with 200 shops, restaurants, and movie theaters. Other malls out on the island include **Plaza del Carmen** in Caguas, and the **Mayagüez Mall.**

Good Buys
Clothing You can get 30%–50% discounts on Hathaway shirts and clothing by Christian Dior and Ralph Lauren at **Hathaway Factory Outlet** (203 Cristo St., tel. 809/723–8946); 40% reductions on men's, women's, and children's raincoats at the **London Fog Factory Outlet** (156 Cristo St., tel. 809/722–4334).

Jewelry There is gold, gold, and more gold at **Reinhold** (201 Cristo St., tel. 809/725–6878) and brand-name watches at **El Gallo de Oro** (200 Fortaleza St., tel. 809/723–1989).

Native Crafts For one-of-a-kind buys, head for **El Centro Market** (weekends at El Centro Convention Center on Ashford Ave. in Condado),

Puerto Rican Arts & Crafts (204 Fortaleza St., Old San Juan, tel. 809/725–5596), **Plazoleta del Puerto** (marina, Old San Juan, tel. 809/725–3053), and **Don Roberto** (205 Cristo St., tel. 809/724–0194).

Paintings and Sculptures Popular galleries are **Galería Palomas** (207 Cristo St., Old San Juan, tel. 809/724–8904) and **Galería Botello** (208 Cristo St., Old San Juan, tel. 809/723–2879, and Plaza Las Américas, tel. 809/754–7430).

Dining

by Susan Fairbanks

A graduate of Cordon Bleu and Cornell Hotel School, Susan Fairbanks runs a food and beverage consulting business. She also teaches wine courses in Puerto Rico.

Over the past 10 years, phone book listings of restaurants in Puerto Rico have grown from four to 14 pages. As a result, there are many new places to try, many off the heavily beaten tourist's path. Whether you're dining at a fine restaurant or picking up fast food in a mall (be sure to visit the one in Plaza Las Américas to see the action), you'll find every place is extremely busy at lunch. Dinner is more relaxed and leisurely, with dress casual to casually elegant; few establishments require a jacket.

On weekends, it's common to see Puerto Rican families in their cars sightseeing in the hilly interior of the island and stopping for a late lunch on a beach or back up in the mountains. Visitors should do as the locals, and go out on the island for at least one meal. The drive is a curvy green adventure that is well worth the trip.

One unique aspect of Puerto Rican cooking is its generous use of local vegetables. Local vegetables include plaintains cooked a hundred different ways: fried green, *tostones;* baked ripe, *amarillos;* and fried, plaintain chips. Rice and beans with tostones or amarillos on the side are basic accompaniments to every dish. Locals cook white rice with *achiote* (annato seeds) or saffron, brown rice with *gandules* (pigeon peas), and black rice with *frijoles* (black beans). Chickpeas and white beans are served in many daily specials. A wide assortment of yams are served baked, fried, stuffed, boiled, smashed, and whole. *Sofrito*—a garlic, onion, sweet pepper, coriander, oregano, and tomato purée—is used as a base for practically everything.

Beef, chicken, pork, and seafood are all rubbed with *adobo*, a garlic-oregano marinade, before cooking. *Arroz con pollo* (chicken stew), *sancocho* (beef and tuber soup), *asopao* (a soupy rice with chicken or seafood), *empanada* (breaded cutlet), and *encebollado* (steak smothered in onions) are all typical plates.

Fritters, also popular, are served in snack places along the highways as well as served at cocktail parties. Assorted fritters include *empanadillas* (stuffed, fried turnovers), *surrullitos* (cheese stuffed corn sticks), *alcapurias* (stuffed green banana croquettes), and *bacalaitos* (codfish fritters).

Local *pan de agua* is an excellent french loaf bread, best hot out of the oven. It is also good toasted and should be tried in the *Cubano* sandwich (made with roast pork, ham, Swiss cheese, pickles, and mustard).

Local desserts include flans, puddings, and fruit pastes served with native white cheese. Home-grown mangos and papayas are sweet and *pan de azucar* (sugar bread) pineapples make the best juice on the market. Fresh *parcha* juice (passion fruit), fresh *guarapo* juice (sugarcane), and fresh *guanabana* juice (a sweet juice similar to papaya) are also sold cold from trucks along the highway.

The best frozen piña coladas are served at the Caribe Hilton Hotel and Dorado Beach Hotel. Rum can be mixed with coke, soda, tonic, juices, water, served on the rocks, or even up. Puerto Rican rums range from light white mixers to dark aged sipping liqueurs. Look for Bacardi, Don Q, Ron Rico, Palo Viejo, and Barillito. Puerto Rican coffee is excellent served espresso-black or generously cut *con leche* (with hot milk).

The most highly recommended restaurants are indicated by a star ★.

Category	Cost*
Very Expensive	over $50
Expensive	$25–$50
Moderate	$15–$25
Inexpensive	under $15

per person, excluding drinks and service

Old San Juan

★ **La Chaumiere.** Reminiscent of an inn in the French provinces, this intimate yet bright white restaurant serves a respected onion soup, oysters Rockefeller, rack of lamb, and veal Oscar in addition to daily specials. *327 Tetuan St., tel. 809/722–3330. Reservations advised. AE, DC, MC. Closed Sun. Very Expensive.*

La Rotisserie. A bright peach room at its best for Tuesday and Thursday power lunches. Unfortunately, both food and service here is uninspired. Flambée specialties include steak Diane and el pescador (rice and seafood). The menu also includes Caesar salad, roast duck, and a selection of fresh seafood. *Caribe Hilton, Puerto de Tierra, tel. 809/831–7575. Jacket required. Reservations required. AE, CB, DC, MC, V. Very Expensive.*

Santiago. A very rosy and romantic restaurant featuring nouvelle Caribbean cuisine such as grouper-salmon terrine, pumpkin-tanier-plantain soup, and fresh fish in passion fruit sauce. *313 Recinto Sur., tel. 809/723–5369. Reservations recommended on weekends. AE, MC, V. Closed Sun. Very Expensive.*

La Zaragozana. One of the oldest restaurants around, this adobe hacienda re-creates an old Spanish atmosphere especially for tourists. The ambience is pleasant with strolling musicians, murals, and vaulted archways. The food and service are tired. The menu offers the usual black bean soup, steaks, lobster, paella, and flan. *356 San Francisco St., tel. 809/723–5103. Reservations advised. AE, CB, DC, MC, V. Expensive.*

★ **Yukiyu.** This is a new restaurant serving sushi, sashimi, and Japanese-inspired specials. The soft-shell crab, shrimp and vegetable tempura, tuna teriyaki, and cod steamed with ginger and orange bearnaise are all recommended. *311 Recinto Sur., tel. 809/721–0653. Reservations advised for lunch. AE, MC, V. Closed Sun. and Mon. Expensive.*

★ **Amadeus.** Featuring nouvelle Caribbean food, the atmosphere is sleek Old San Juan with a menu of 20 changing appetizers including tostones with sour cream and caviar, marlin ceviche, and crabmeat tacos. Entrées range from grilled dolphin with coriander butter to chicken lasagna and tuna or egg salad sandwich. Sit in the front room to be seen with beautiful people. *106 San Sebastian St., tel. 809/722–8635, or 809/721–6720. Reservations required. Closed Mon. AE, MC, V. Moderate.*

El Patio de Convento. Since the inner patio was covered with a plastic bubble, El Convento has lost its charm by spoiling the original architecture. The buffet lunch is a cattle train of cruise-ship tourists. The piña coladas are watery. The place is depressing. *100 Cristo St., tel. 809/723–9020. AE, MC, V. Moderate.*

Ambrosia. At the bottom of Cristo Street, the bar serves fresh frozen fruit drinks while the menu features pastas, veal, and chicken. The daily lunch specials usually include quiche and lasagna served with large mixed salads for good value. *205 Cristo St., tel. 809/722–5206. AE, MC, V. Inexpensive.*

El Nuevo Cafe San Juan. This café, which features a deli atmosphere, is good for sandwiches and grilled sausages. *151 Cruz St., no phone. No credit cards. Inexpensive.*

San Juan **Dar Tiffany.** This restaurant, just off the lobby of the glittering
★ El San Juan Hotel, is a posh place with palm fronds etched in glass, voluptuous greenery and, yes, Tiffany lamps. Knock back a two-fisted martini from the bar before tackling superb aged prime rib, Maine lobster, or fresh Norwegian salmon. *El San Juan Hotel, Isla Verde., tel. 809/791–7272. Dress: Jackets suggested. Reservations suggested. AE, CB, DC, MC, V. Very Expensive.*

★ **La Compostela.** Contemporary Spanish food and a serious 9,000-bottle wine cellar are the draws to La Compostela. Specialties include mushroom pâté and Port *pastelillo* (meat-filled pastries), grouper fillet with scallops in salsa verde, roast lamb, and paella. This is a favorite restaurant with the local dining elite and is honored yearly in local competitions. *106 Condado Ave., tel. 809/724–6088. Reservations suggested. AE, CB, DC, MC, V. Very Expensive.*

La Reina de España. Step into a soft sea-green dining room serving imaginative Castillian cuisine. Chef-owner Jesus Ramiro has just published a new cookbook on Castillian cooking and each of his dishes is artfully arranged and decorated. Specialties include flower-shape peppers filled with fish mousse, a seafood fantasy caught under a vegetable net, roast duckling with sugarcane honey, and a kiwi dessert arranged to resemble twin palms. *1106 Magdalena Ave., tel. 809/721–9049. Reservations suggested. AE, MC, V. Very Expensive.*

Augusto's. Chef-owner Augusto Schriener and his wife Claudia run an elegantly comfortable restaurant featuring classic cooking. Menus change weekly. Specialties include salmon baked in filo, lamb tenderloin with pepper-vodka fettuccine, and veal medallions with smoked mozzarella. The walls are hung with changing watercolor shows. *Excelsior Hotel, Miramar, tel. 809/725–7700. Reservations suggested. AE, MC, V. Expensive.*

The Chart House. Set in a restored Ashford mansion laced with graceful tropical verandas perfect for cocktails, the bar offers good drinks to a lively mix of people. Open-air dining rooms are upstairs, set at different levels. The menu includes prime rib, shrimp teriyaki, Hawaiian chicken, and the signature dessert: mud pie. *1214 Ashford Ave., tel. 809/728–0110. Reservations required. AE, CB, DC, MC, V. Expensive.*

★ **Il Giardino.** Overlooking Condado from atop the Dutch Inn, this roof-garden restaurant's Italian food and attentive service get rave reviews from the locals. Fresh pasta, a selection of veal dishes, and good wines make a moderate meal a pleasure. All ladies leave with a long-stemmed rose from maitre d'/owner Silverio Díaz. *Dutch Inn, 55 Condado Ave., tel. 809/722–1822. AE, MC, V. Expensive.*

L. K. Sweeney & Son Ltd. Brothers Larry and Tim Sweeney have opened a comfortable, casual, and Continental restaurant that overlooks the lagoon lights at night. You have your choice of live Maine or Caribbean lobster, beluga caviar, Norwegian salmon, and Florida stone crab. Thursdays feature a clambake (reservations are a must!). *Condado Plaza and Casino, 999 Ashford Ave., tel. 809/722–7977. AE, DC, MC, V. Expensive.*

Che's. The most established and casual of three Argentinian restaurants within a few blocks of each other, Che's features juicy churrasco steaks, lemon chicken, and grilled sweetbreads. The hamburgers are huge and the french fries are fresh. The Chilean and Argentinian wine list is also decent. *35 Caoba St., Punta Las Marias, tel. 809/721–7202. AE, CB, DC, MC, V. Moderate.*

★ **Scotch & Sirloin.** Tucked back among the tropical overgrowth overlooking the lagoon, the Scotch & Sirloin has been San Juan's most consistently fine steakhouse. Aquariums light up the bar and the fresh salad bar serves moist banana bread. Steaks are aged in-house and cooked precisely to order. *La Rada Hotel, 1020 Ashford Ave., Condado, tel. 809/722–2640. Reservations required. AE, DC, MC, V. Moderate.*

Cafeteria España. This is a busy Spanish cafeteria serving strong coffee, assorted croquettes, toasted sandwiches, soups, and a large selection of pastries. Spanish candies, canned goods, and other gourmet items for sale are packed into floor-to-ceiling shelves for a cozy, full feeling. *Centro Commercial Villamar, Baldorioty de Castro Marginal, Isla Verde, tel. 809/727–4517. No credit cards. Inexpensive.*

El Paso. Another family-run restaurant serving genuine criollo food seasoned for a local following. Specialties include asopaos, pork chops, and breaded empanadas. Daily specials include tripe on Saturday and arroz con pollo on Sunday. *405 De Diego Ave., Puerto Nuevo, tel. 809/781–3399. AE, CB, DC, MC, V. Inexpensive.*

★ **Kasalta Bakery, Inc.** Walk up to the counter and order an assortment of sandwiches, cold drinks, strong café con leche, and pastries. Try the Cubano sandwich. There are plenty of stools for sitting, reading, or just looking out the window. *1966 McLeary St., Ocean Park, tel. 809/727–7340. No credit cards. Inexpensive.*

Via Appia's Italian Deli. The only true sidewalk café in San Juan serves pizzas, sandwiches, cold beer, and pitchers of sangria. It is a good place to people-watch and get something easy to eat. *1350 Ashford Ave., Condado, tel. 809/725–8711. AE, MC, V. Inexpensive.*

Out on the Island **The Horned Dorset Primavera.** Lunch, served in a comfortable wicker room, is casual and à la carte. A fixed-price gourmet dinner is served in the upstairs dining room. Enjoy luxurious tropical architecture at its best as you feast on both food and ocean view. No children under age 12 are allowed. *Hwy. 429, Km 3, Rincón, tel. 809/823–4030. Reservations required. AE, MC, V. Expensive.*

La Rotisserie. An institution in Mayagüez, this fine dining room offers the best value for the money in town with its lavish breakfast and lunch buffets. The restaurant is known for grilled steaks and fresh seafood. A different food festival is featured Wednesday through Friday: Wednesday, Italian; Thursday, Latin American; and Friday, seafood. *Hwy. 2, Km 152.5, Mayagüez, tel. 809/834–7575. Reservations suggested. AE, CB, DC, MC, V. Moderate–Expensive.*

★ **El Batey de Tonita.** Set up in the mountains for dining in the cool country air, this restaurant serves local *criollo* cooking with unique specials such as guinea hen fricassee, rabbit in garlic sauce, and crispy "aranita" plantains. *Hwy. 7737, Km 2.1, Cayey, tel. 809/745–6312. MC, V. Moderate.*

The Black Eagle. Literally on the water's edge, you dine outside on the restaurant's veranda listening to the lapping waves under the stars. Specialties of the house include breaded conch fritters, fresh fish of the day, lobster, and prime meats that are imported by the owner. *Hwy. 413, Km 1, Barrio Ensenada, Rincón, tel. 809/823–3510. AE, MC, V. Moderate.*

★ **Goñzalez Seafood.** Nobody in Puerto Rico makes better crunchy tostones than Rosa Goñzalez. House specialties include fresh shark fillet in wine sauce, mofongo plantain stuffed with seafood, shrimp as big as lobster, and grilled porterhouse steaks. *Hwy. 102, Km 9.8, Joyuda, Cabo Rojos, tel. 809/851–9000. AE, CB, DC, MC, V. Moderate.*

Sand and the Sea. Looking down onto Guayama and out across the sea, this mountain cottage is a retreat into Caribbean living with Kentucky host Hal Hester cooking, playing piano, and singing up a storm. The menu leans toward steaks and barbecues with a good carrot vichyssoise and excellent baked beans. Bring a sweater—it cools down to 50°F at night. *Hwy. 715, Km 5.2, Cayey, tel. 809/745–6317. AE, CB, DC, MC, V. Moderate.*

Lodging

Accommodations on Puerto Rico come in all shapes and sizes. Self-contained luxury resorts cover hundreds of acres. San Juan's high-rise beachfront hotels likewise cater to the epicurean; several target the business traveler. Out on the island, the government-sponsored *paradores* are country inns modeled after Spain's paradores. They are required to meet certain standards, such as proximity to a sightseeing attraction or beach and a kitchen serving native cuisine. (Parador prices range from $35 to $76 for a double room. Reservations for all paradores can be made by calling 800/443–0266 or 809/721–2884 in Puerto Rico.)

The most highly recommended lodgings are indicated by a star ★.

Category	Cost*
Very Expensive	over $200
Expensive	$125–$200
Moderate	$50–$125
Inexpensive	under $50

All prices are for a standard double room for two, excluding 6% tax and a 10% service charge.

San Juan **El San Juan Hotel and Casino.** An immense chandelier shines
★ over the hand-carved wood paneling and rose-color marble of
the lobby in this sprawling 22-acre resort on the Isla Verde
beach. You'll be hard pressed to decide if you want a spa suite in
the main tower with whirlpool and wet bar; a garden lanai
room, with private patio and spa; or a custom-designed casita
with sunken Roman bath. (Some of the tower rooms have no
view; your best bet is an oceanside lanai, with or without spa.)
In any case, all rooms are air-conditioned, with three phones,
remote-control TV with VCR, hair dryer, minibar, and many
other amenities. *Box 2872, Isla Verde, 00902, tel. 809/791–1000
or 800/468–2818. 392 rooms. Facilities: pool, children's pool, 4
restaurants, 5 cocktail lounges, supper club, disco, casino, 3
lighted tennis courts with pro shop, activity center, water-
sports center, shopping arcade, health club, nonsmoking floor,
facilities for handicapped, complimentary shuttle bus to
Condado Plaza Hotel, courtyard Jacuzzi, concierge, valet
parking. AE, CB, DC, MC, V. Very Expensive.*

Hotel La Concha. Looking like a large pink seashell, the hotel
has individually air-conditioned rooms, all facing the ocean,
furnished in contemporary tropical decor. In the main building
and the 12 poolside cabanas there are 18 junior suites and 17
one- or two-bedroom corner suites. The VIP suites are on the
top three floors. The ritzy Club Mykonos disco is perched right
over the water. *Box 4195, 00905, tel. 809/721–6090 or 800/468–
2822. 234 oceanfront rooms. Facilities: activity center, water-
sports center, volleyball court on the beach, pool, poolside bar,
2 restaurants and lounges, disco, facilities for the handicapped, shopping arcade. AE, CB, DC, MC, V. Expensive.*

★ **Condado Beach Hotel.** Built in 1919 by Cornelius Vanderbilt,
the hotel has a pale pink lobby adorned with bouquets of flowers, a sweeping double staircase, and Victorian furnishings.
Guest rooms, each decorated in the Spanish colonial style of the
1920s, have either an ocean, lagoon, or city view. The Vanderbilt Club, floors, accessed by private elevator, provide all
manner of pampering. *Box 41266, Minillas Station, 00940, tel.
809/721–6090 or 800/468–2775. 245 rooms, including 18 junior
suites and 2 1- and 2-bedroom suites. Facilities: cable TV, 3rd-
level pool, 2 restaurants and lounges, facilities for the handicapped, water-sports center. AE, CB, DC, MC, V. Expensive.*

Condado Plaza Hotel and Casino. Nestled between the Atlantic
Ocean and the Condado Lagoon, this stunning resort is two hotels in one, with a Lagoon Wing and an Ocean Wing. Standard
rooms have walk-in closets, separate dressing areas, and amenity packages. There are a variety of suites (including spa suites
with whirlpools) and a fully equipped executive service center.
If that isn't posh enough, you can check into the Plaza Club,
which has 24-hour concierge service and a dazzling display of
pleasantries. The hotel's Isadora's Disco is a very hot nightclub. *999 Ashford Ave., 00907, tel. 809/721–1000 or 800/468–
8588. 585 rooms and suites. Facilities: 4 pools (1 saltwater), casino, disco, 2 lighted tennis courts, 5 restaurants, 7 bars and
lounges; fitness, water-sports, and business centers. AE, CB,
DC, MC, V. Expensive.*

★ **Sands Hotel and Casino.** Puerto Rico's largest casino glitters
just off the lobby, and a huge free-form pool lies between the
hotel and its beach. The air-conditioned hotel has rooms with
private balconies (ask for one with an ocean view), minibars,
and many frills. The exclusive Plaza Club section offers a mas-
seuse, private spas, and other enticements. Like its Atlantic

City sister, the Sands books top entertainers—the Club Calypso is the top-name night spot here. *Isla Verde Rd. 187, Box 6676 Loiza Sta., Santurce 00914, tel. 809/791–6100 or 800/443–2009. 420 rooms. Facilities: pool, 4 restaurants, lounge, casino, disco, concierge, 24-hr room service, facilities for handicapped, nightclub, water-sports center, business center, valet parking. AE, CB, DC, MC, V. Expensive.*

★ **Excelsior.** Recently spruced up with English carpets in the corridors and new sculptures in the lobby, this hotel is home to the estimable, award-winning Ali-Oli restaurant, which also operates the new poolside El Gazebo restaurant. Each room has a private bath with phone and hair dryer. Complimentary coffee, newspaper, and shoeshine each morning. *801 Ponce de León Ave., 00907, tel. 809/721–7400, 800/223–9815 in U.S. or 800/468–0023 in Canada. 140 rooms, 60 with kitchenettes. Facilities: pool, cocktail lounge, 2 restaurants, free parking and free transportation to the beach. AE, MC, V. Moderate.*

Old San Juan **Caribe Hilton International.** Built in 1949, this superb property
★ occupies 17 acres on Puerta de Tierra and has been further enhanced by a $25 million face-lift in 1988. The spacious lobby is decorated with rose-color marble, waterfalls, and lavish tropical plants. The hotel boasts San Juan's only private, palm-fringed swimming cove. The airy guest rooms have balconies with ocean or lagoon views. The eighth and ninth floors provide VIP treatment. *Box 1872, 00903, tel. 809/721–0303 or 800/445–8667. 636 rooms, including 31 suites. Facilities: private beach, 2 pools, 6 lighted tennis courts, health club, 4 restaurants, disco, outdoor Jacuzzi, executive business center. AE, CB, DC, MC, V. Very Expensive.*

★ **Ramada Gran Hotel El Convento.** Puerto Rico's most famous hotel, on Calle Cristo right across from the San Juan Cathedral. The pink stucco building, with its dark wood paneling and arcades, was a Carmelite convent in the 17th century. All of the rooms are air-conditioned, with twin beds and wall-to-wall carpeting. Fourteen rooms have balconies (ask for one with a view of the bay). This is a very romantic hotel and an architectural masterpiece. *100 Cristo St., 00902, tel. 809/723–9020 or 800/468–2779. 94 rooms. Facilities: pool, 2 restaurants and bar, free transport to beach. AE, CB, DC, MC, V. Moderate–Expensive.*

Out on the Island **Parador Boquemer.** Located on Route 101 near the beach in a
Cabo Rojos small, unpretentious fishing village, the parador has air-conditioned rooms, all with minifridges and private bath. In the summer of 1988, 24 rooms were added. *Box 133, 00622, tel. 809/851–2158. 64 rooms. Facilities: pool, restaurant. AE, CB, DC, MC, V. Inexpensive.*

Coamo **Parador Baños de Coamo.** On Route 546, Km 1, northeast of Ponce, this mountain inn is located at the hot sulfur springs that are said to be the Fountain of Youth of Ponce de León's dreams. The springs were known to the earliest Taino Indians, as well as to Franklin D. Roosevelt, Thomas Edison, Alexander Graham Bell, and Frank Lloyd Wright. *Box 540, 00640, tel. 809/825–2186. 48 rooms. Facilities: pool, restaurant, lounge. AE, CB, DC, MC, V. Moderate.*

Dorado **Hyatt Regency Cerromar Beach.** Located 22 miles west of San Juan at Route 693, Km 11.8, smack on the Atlantic, the Cerromar not only has a lovely reef-protected beach, it also claims its $3 million river pool—with 14 waterfalls, an underwater Jacuzzi, grottoes, and all manner of flumes—is the world's longest freshwater pool. The completely modern seven-story hotel, done up in tropical style, has tile floors, marble baths, air-conditioning, and rooms with a king-size or two double beds. (You'll find somewhat quieter rooms on the west side, away from the pool activity.) Guests at the Cerromar and its sister facility, the Hyatt Dorado Beach a mile down the road, have access to facilities of both resorts, and colorful red trolleys (free, of course) make frequent runs between the two. *Dorado 00646, tel. 809/796–1234 or 800/228–9000. 504 rooms. Facilities: airport limo, casino, disco, 4 restaurants, 3 bars, 2 18-hole Robert Trent Jones golf courses, 14 tennis courts (2 lighted), pool, sauna, horseback riding, bike rentals, jogging and hiking trails, airport for private planes. AE, CB, DC, MC, V. Very Expensive.*

★ **Hyatt Dorado Beach.** The ambience is a bit more subdued and family-oriented at the Cerromar's sophisticated sister, where a variety of elegant accommodations are in low-rise buildings scattered over 1,000 lavishly landscaped acres. Most rooms have private patios or balconies, and all have polished terra-cotta floors, marble baths, air-conditioning, and many frills. Upper-level rooms in the Oceanview Houses have handsome king-size bamboo four-poster beds, in addition to a view of the two half-moon beaches. *Dorado 00646, tel. 809/796–1234 or 800/228–9000. 300 rooms. Facilities: 2 18-hole Robert Trent Jones golf courses, 7 tennis courts, horse-drawn carriage rides, horseback riding, hiking and jogging trails, 2 pools, wading pool, casino, 3 restaurants, 2 lounges, water-sports center, airport for private planes. AE, CB, DC, MC, V. Very Expensive.*

Jayuya
★ **Parador Hacienda Gripinas.** It's a bit difficult to look for on winding mountain roads, but in due time you'll find this treasure: a white hacienda with polished wood, beam ceilings, a spacious lounge with rocking chairs, and splendid gardens. The large airy rooms are decorated with native crafts—a very romantic hideaway. *Rte. 527, Km 2.5, Box 387, 00664, tel. 809/721–2400. 19 rooms. Facilities: restaurant, lounge, pool, hiking and horseback-riding trails. MC, V. Inexpensive.*

La Parguera
Parador Villa Parguera. This parador is a stylish modern place on Phosphorescent Bay, with large colorfully decorated air-conditioned rooms. A spacious dining room, overlooking the swimming pool and the bay beyond, serves excellent native and international dishes. *Rte. 304, Box 273, Lajas 00667, tel. 809/899–3975. 50 rooms. Facilities: saltwater pool, restaurant, lounge, facilities for handicapped. AE, CB, DC, MC. Moderate.*

Mayagüez
Hilton International Mayagüez. Built on 20 acres overlooking the Mayagüez Harbor, this resort on the island's west coast is about a 2½-hour drive from San Juan. All the rooms have a view of the sea. A recent $6 million renovation resulted in completely redecorated rooms, a new casino, and two executive floors. The hotel is 2 miles from the town of Mayagüez. Also close by are the Boquerón swimming beach, Punta Higuero surfing beach, the Mayagüez Marina for deep-sea fishing, seven excellent skindiving spots, and two golf courses. *Rte. 2, Km 152.5, Box 3629, 00709, tel. 809/831–7575 or 800/445–8667 on the island. 150 air-conditioned rooms and suites. Facilities: Olympic-size pool, 3 lighted tennis courts, casino, disco, restaurant, lounge. AE, CB, DC, MC, V. Expensive.*

San Germán **Parador Oasis.** The Oasis, not far from the town's two plazas, was a family mansion 200 years ago. You'll get a better taste for its history in the older front rooms; rooms in the new section in the rear are small and somewhat motelish. *2 Luna St., Box 144, 00753, tel. 809/892–1175. 50 rooms. Facilities: restaurant, pool, Jacuzzi, lounge, gym, sauna. AE, CB, DC, MC, V. Inexpensive–Moderate.*

Utuado **Parador Casa Grande.** The restored hacienda is on 107 acres of a former coffee plantation, with wood walkways leading to cottages snuggled among the lush green hills. Each unit has four spacious balconied rooms (No. 9 is way in the back, quiet, with a lovely mountain view). There are trails for hikers, hammocks for loafers, and occasional music for romantics. *Box 616, 00761, tel. 809/894–3939. 20 rooms. Facilities: pool, restaurant, lounge. AE, MC, V. Inexpensive.*

Vieques **Sea Gate.** Occupying 2 acres of a hilltop, this whitewashed hotel is a family-run operation. Proprietors John and Ruthye Miller will meet you at the airport or ferry, drive you to the beaches, arrange scuba-diving and snorkeling trips, and give you a complete rundown on their adopted home. Accommodations include three-room efficiencies with full kitchen and terrace. *Box 747, 00765, tel. 809/741–4661. 16 rooms. No credit cards. Inexpensive.*

The Arts and Nightlife

¿Qué Pasa? the official visitors guide, has current listings of events in San Juan and out on the island. Also, pick up a copy of the *San Juan Star,* and check with the local tourist offices to find out what's doing.

Music, Dance, and Theater **LeLoLai** is a year-round festival that celebrates Puerto Rico's Indian, Spanish, and African heritage. Performances take place each week, moving from hotel to hotel, showcasing the island's music, folklore, and culture. Sponsored by the Puerto Rico Tourist Company and major San Juan hotels, the festivities are free to visitors staying in a participating hotel for at least five nights. *Tickets can be purchased at the Condado Convention Center, tel. 809/723–3135. Admission: $8 for performances, $15–$35 for performances including dinner.*

Casinos By law, all casinos are in hotels, primarily in San Juan. The government keeps a close eye on them. Alcoholic drinks are not permitted at the gaming tables, although free soft drinks, coffee, and sandwiches are available. Dress for casinos tends to be on the formal side, and the atmosphere is refined. The law permits casinos to operate noon–4 AM, but individual casinos set their own hours, which change with the season.

Casinos are located in the following San Juan hotels (*see* Lodging, above): **Condado Plaza Hotel, Condado Beach Hotel, Caribe Hilton, Carib-Inn, Clarion Hotel, Ramada, Dutch Inn, Sands,** and **El San Juan.** Elsewhere on the island, there are casinos at the **Hyatt Regency Cerromar** and **Hyatt Dorado Beach hotels,** at **Palmas del Mar,** and at the **Hilton International Mayagüez.**

Discos In Old San Juan, young people flock to **Neon's** (203 Tanca St., tel. 723–6448) and to **Lazers** (251 Cruz St., tel. 725–7581).

In Puerta de Tierra, Condado, and Isla Verde, the 30-something crowd heads for **Juliana's** (Caribe Hilton Hotel, tel. 809/

721–0303), **Isadora's** (Condado Plaza Hotel, tel. 809/722–5430), **Mykonos** (La Concha Hotel, tel. 809/721–6090), and **Amadeus** (El San Juan Hotel, tel. 809/791–1000).

Nightclubs The Caribe Hilton's **Club Caribe** books headliners like Tony-award-winner Chita Rivera. The Sands Hotel's **Club Calypso** brings in big names like Joan Rivers, Jay Leno, and Rita Moreno. El San Juan's **Tropicoro** presents international revues and top-name entertainers. (Young locals gather in the El San Juan's **El Chico** to dance to Latin music in a western saloon setting.) The Condado Plaza Hotel's **Copa Room** does a laser revue, and its **La Fiesta** sizzles with steamy Latin shows. In Old San Juan, the Ramada Gran Hotel El Convento's **El Patio del Convento** occasionally puts on flamenco shows and water ballets.

19 Saba

by Honey Naylor

This 5-square-mile fairy-tale isle is not for everybody. If you're looking for exciting nightlife or lots of shopping, forget Saba, or take the one-day trip from St. Maarten. There are only a handful of shops, even fewer inns and eateries, and only 1,100 friendly, but shy, inhabitants. Beach lovers should also take note that Saba is a virtually beachless volcanic island, ringed with steep cliffs that fall straight down to the sea.

So, why Saba? Saba is a perfect hideaway, a challenge for adventurous hikers (Mt. Scenery rises above it all to a height of 2,855 feet), a longtime haven for divers, and, for Sabans, heaven on water. It's no wonder that they call their island the "Unspoiled Caribbean Queen."

The capital of Saba (pronounced *say*ba) is The Bottom, which is at the top, not the bottom, of a hill. Meandering goats have the right of way on The Road (there's only one); chickens cross at their own risk. In tiny, toy-like villages, narrow paths are bordered by flower-draped walls and neat picket fences. Tidy houses with red roofs and gingerbread trim are planted in the mountainside among the bromeliads, palms, hibiscus, orchids, and Norwegian pines.

Saba is part of the Netherlands Antilles Leeward Islands, located 28 miles—a 15-minute flight—from St. Maarten. The island is a volcano, extinct for 5,000 years (no one even knows where the crater was). Carib Indians may have hung out here around AD 800; Columbus spotted the little speck in 1493, but somehow Saba remained uninhabited until the first Dutch settlers arrived from Statia in 1640. Having established a foothold—no mean feat—they nestled into a bowl-shape valley and were soon joined by a handful of Scotch, English, and Irish settlers. *Botte* is Dutch for "bowl," but almost at the outset the word was Anglicized to "bottom."

In the 17th, 18th, and early 19th centuries the French, Dutch, English, and Spanish vied for control of the island. Saba changed hands 12 times before permanently raising the Dutch flag.

Sabans are a hardy lot. To get from Windwardside to The Bottom, the early Sabans carved 900 steps out of the mountainside. Everything that arrived on the island, from a banana to a piano, had to be hauled up. Those rugged steps remained the only way to get about the island until The Road was built by Josephus Lambert Hassell (a carpenter who took correspondence courses in engineering) in the 1940s. The handmade road took 20 years to build, and if you like roller coasters you'll love The Road. The 6½-mile, white-knuckle route begins at sea level in Fort Bay, zigs up to 1,968 feet, and zags down to 131 feet above sea level at the airport.

After the success of the road venture, the Sabans, in 1963, constructed an airport on a flat point of land called (what else?) Flat Point. In 1965, the first television set arrived, and on Christmas Eve, 1970, Sabans received the gift of electricity, 24 hours a day! In spite of these modern conveniences, the island's uncomplicated lifestyle has persevered: Saban ladies still hand embroider the very special and delicate Saba lace, a reminder of Saban gentility that has continued to flourish since the 1870s, and brew the potent rum-based liquor, Saba Spice, sweetened with secret herbs and spices.

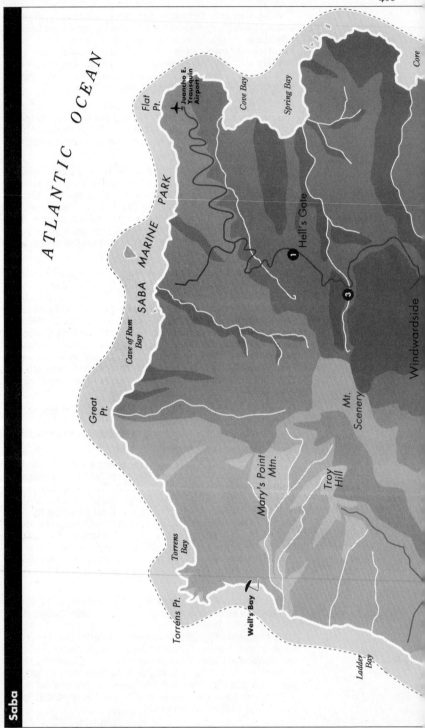

ATLANTIC OCEAN

Flat Pt.

Juancho E. Yrausquin Airport

Cove Bay

Spring Bay

SABA MARINE PARK

Cave of Rum Bay

Great Pt.

Hell's Gate

Windwardside

Mary's Point Mtn.

Mt. Scenery

Troy Hill

Torrens Bay

Torrens Pt.

Well's Bay

Ladder Bay

Saba

N

● Exploring Sites

⑥ Hotels and Restaurants

Exploring
The Bottom, **4**
Fort Bay, **5**
Holy Rosary Church, **1**
Mt. Scenery, **3**
Windwardside, **2**

Dining
Captain's Quarters, **7**
Saba Chinese Bar &
Restaurant, **8**
Scout's Place, **9**
The Serving Spoon, **6**

Lodging
Captain's Quarters, **10**
Juliana's
Apartments, **11**
Scout's Place, **12**

Before You Go

Tourist
Information

For help planning your trip, contact the public relations firm **Medhurst & Associates** (271 Main St., Northport, NY 11768, tel. 516/261–7474, 212/936–0050, or 800/344–4606) or, in Canada, **New Concepts in Travel** (410 Queens Quai W, Suite 303, Toronto, Ont., tel. 416/362–7707).

Book reservations through a travel agent or over the telephone, because mail can take from a week to a couple of months to reach the island.

Arriving and
Departing
By Plane

Unless you parachute in, you'll arrive from St. Maarten via **Windward Islands Airways** (tel. 599/5–44230 or 599/5–44237). The approach to Saba's tiny airstrip is the stuff that nightmares are made of. The strip is only 1,312 feet long, but the STOL (Short Takeoff and Landing) aircrafts are built for it, and the pilot only needs half of it. Try not to panic; remember that the pilot knows what he is doing and wants to live just as much as you do. Once you've touched down on the Band-Aid–like airstrip, the pilot taxis an inch or two, turns, and deposits you just outside a little shoebox called the Juancho E. Yrausquin Airport.

By Boat

Style, an open-air vessel with an open bar, departs St. Maarten's Great Bay Marina, Phillipsburg, Tuesday–Saturday at 9 AM and returns at 5 PM. The trip takes an hour and round-trip fare costs $45 (tel. 599/5–22167). If you take the watery way, however, you'll have lost more than an hour of sightseeing time on Saba.

Passports
and Visas

U.S. citizens need proof of citizenship. A passport is preferred, but a birth certificate or voter's registration card will do (a driver's license will *not* do). British citizens must have a "British Visitors" Passport. All visitors must have an ongoing or return ticket.

Customs
and Duties

This is a free port, with no customs to clear, so you don't have to worry about bringing in receipts for expensive possessions.

Language

Saba's official language is Dutch, but everyone on the island speaks English.

Precautions

Everyone knows everyone else on the island, and crime is virtually nonexistent. Take along insect repellent, sunscreen, and sturdy no-nonsense shoes that get a good grip on the ground.

Further Reading

Tales From My Grandmother's Pipe, by Senator Will Johnson, Saba's unofficial historian, is a treasure trove of Saba lore. *Saba, the First Guidebook,* by Natalie and Paul Pfanstiehl, takes you on a delightful exploration of the island, and even includes recipes. Dr. J. Hartog's *History of Saba* is filled with facts, figures, and fascinating photographs. All books are available at the **Saba Tourist Office,** Windwardside *(see* Tourist Information, below).

Staying in Saba

Important
Addresses

Tourist Information: The amiable Glenn Holm is at the helm of the **Saba Tourist Office** (Windwardside, tel. 599/4–2231) weekdays 8–noon and 1–5.

Emergencies **Police:** call 599/4–3237.

Hospitals: The **A. M. Edwards Medical Center** (The Bottom, tel. 599/4–3288) is a 10-bed hospital with a full-time physician and various clinics.

Pharmacies: The **Pharmacy** (The Bottom, tel. 599/4–3289) .

Currency U.S. dollars are accepted everywhere, but Saba's official currency is the Netherlands Antilles florin (also called guilder). The exchange rate fluctuates, but is around NAf1.80 to U.S.$1. Prices quoted here are in U.S. dollars unless noted otherwise. **Barclays Bank** is the island's only bank; it's open weekdays 8:30–1:30.

Taxes and Service Charges Hotels collect a 5% government tax. The departure tax is $1 from Saba to St. Maarten or St. Eustatius.

Most hotels and restaurants add a 10%–15% service charge to your bill.

Guided Tours All 10 of the taxi drivers who meet the planes at Yrausquin Airport also conduct tours of the island. The cost for a full-day tour is $30, which includes up to four people; there is a charge of $7 per person for more than four. If you're just in from St. Maarten for a day trip, have your driver make lunch reservations for you at **The Serving Spoon** or the **Captain's Quarters** *(see* Dining, below) before starting the tour. After a full morning of sightseeing, your driver will drop you off for lunch, complete the tour after, and return you to Yrausquin in time to make the last flight back to St. Maarten.

Getting Around *Rental Cars* Saba's one and only road—The Road—is a serpentine affair with many a hairpin (read hair-raising) curve. However, if you dare to make your way about by car, there are nine rental cars at the **Avis** outlet (Windwardside, tel. 599/4–2289). Cars can also be rented at **Scout's Place** (Windwardside, tel. 599/4–2205). A car rents for about $30 per day, with a full tank of gas and unlimited mileage. (If you run out of gas, call the island's only gas station, down at Fort Bay, tel. 599/4–3272).

Hitchhiking Carless Sabans get around the old-fashioned ways—walking and hitchhiking (very popular and safe). If you choose to get around by thumbing rides, you'll need to know the rules of The Road. To go from The Bottom (which actually is near the top of the island), sit on the wall opposite the Anglican Church; to go from Fort Bay, sit on the wall opposite Saba Deep dive center in Captain's Quarters, where the road begins to twist upward.

Telephones and Mail To call Saba from the United States, dial 011/599/4, followed by the four-digit number. On the island, it is only necessary to dial the four-digit number. Telephone communications are excellent on the island, and direct-dial long distance is in effect.

To airmail a letter to the United States costs NAf1.30; a postcard, NAf.60.

Opening and Closing Times Businesses and government offices on Sabas are open weekdays 8–5.

Exploring Saba

Numbers in the margin correspond with points of interest on the Saba map.

Begin your driving tour with a trip from Flat Point, at the airport, up to Hell's Gate. Because there is only one road, we'll continue along its hairpin curves up to Windwardside, and then on to The Bottom and down to Fort Bay. This cross-island tour will give you a quick overview of tiny Saba, its limited cultural sights and varied natural settings.

There are 20 sharp curves on The Road between the airport and Hell's Gate. On one of these curves, poised on Hell's Gate's hill, **①** is the stone **Holy Rosary Church,** which looks medieval but was built in 1962. In the **Community Center** behind the church, village ladies sell blouses, handkerchiefs, tablecloths, and tea towels embellished with the very special and unique Saba lace. These same ladies also turn out innocent-sounding Saba Spice, a rum-based liqueur that will knock your proverbial socks off.

The Road spirals past banana plantations, oleander bushes, **②** and stunning views of the ocean below. In **Windwardside,** the island's second largest village, teetering at 1,968 feet, you'll see rambling lanes and narrow alleyways winding through the hills, and a cluster of tiny, neat houses and shops.

On your right as you enter the village is the **Church of St. Paul's Conversion,** a colonial building with a red-and-white steeple. Your next stop should be the **Saba Tourist Office** (next door to the post office), where you can pick up brochures and books about Saba. You may then want to spend some time browsing through the **Square Nickel,** the **Saba Shop,** and the **Island Craft Shop** (*see* Shopping, below).

The **Saba Museum,** surrounded by lemongrass and clover, lies just behind the Captain's Quarters. There are small signs marking the way to the 150-year-old house that has been set up to look much as it did when it was a sea captain's home. Its furnishings include a handsome mahogany four-poster bed with pineapple design, an antique organ, and, in the kitchen, a rock oven and a hearth. Among the old documents on display is a letter a Saban wrote after the hurricane of 1772, in which he sadly says, "We have lost our little all." *Windwardside, no phone. Admission: $1 donation requested. Open weekdays 10–3.*

Near the museum are the stone and concrete steps—1,064 of **③** them—that rise to **Mt. Scenery.** The steps lead past giant elephant ears, ferns, begonias, mangos, palms, and orchids, up to a mahogany grove at the summit. On a cloudless day the view is spectacular. For a breathtaking journey, have your hotel pack a picnic lunch, wear nonslip shoes, take along a jacket and a canteen of water, and hike away. The round-trip excursion will take about a half day and is best begun in the early morning.

On the way from Windwardside to The Bottom, you'll pass through the small settlement of **St. John's.** As you round one of those many curves, look down on **Giles Quarter** by the ocean, where the Netherlands is funding a new airport to be built over a 10-year period.

④ You'll be zigzagging downhill from Windwardside to **The Bottom,** which sits in its bowl-shape valley 820 feet above the sea. The Bottom is the seat of government and the home of the lieutenant-governor. The large house next to Wilhelmina Park has fancy fretwork, a high pitched roof, and wraparound double galleries.

Time Out	**Earl's Snack Bar** is the place to get grilled-cheese sandwiches, burgers, beer, ice-cream cones, and Eskimo pie. *The Bottom, no phone. Open daily 8:30–12:30, 3–4, and 7–9:30.*

On the other side of town is the **Wesleyan Holiness Church,** a small stone building with bright white fretwork, and dating from 1919. Stroll by the church, beyond a place called The Gap, and you'll come to a **lookout point** where you can see the rough-hewn steps leading down to Ladder Bay. Ladder Bay, with 524 steps, and Fort Bay, with its 200 steps, were the two landing sites from which Saba's first settlers had to haul themselves and their possessions. Sabans sometimes walk down to Ladder Bay to picnic. Think long and hard before you do, bearing in mind that it's 524 steps back *up* to The Road. (Hitchhiking from down there will get you nowhere!)

⑤ Last stop on The Road is **Fort Bay,** which is the jumping-off place for the island's two dive operations *(see* Scuba Diving and Snorkeling, below). There's also a gas station, a 277-foot deep-water pier that accommodates the tenders from ships that call here, and the information center for the **Saba Marine Park** *(see* Scuba Diving and Snorkeling, below).

Off the Beaten Track

It wasn't easy, but we found the only beach on Saba! Each April, a 20-foot strip of what's known as black (but is actually gray) sand appears at **Well's Bay,** down below Mary's Point. The beach is good for swimming and sticks around all summer and into early November. It used to take six hours to hike down there, but a new road, an extension of The Road, has shortened the travel time to 15 minutes from Windwardside.

Participant Sports

Boating	**Saba Deep** (tel. 599/4–3347 or 599/4–2201) conducts one-hour, round-island cruises that include cocktails, hors d'oeuvres, and a sunset you won't soon forget.
Deep-Sea Fishing	**Saba Deep** runs half- and full-day charters that include lunch, drinks, bait, and tackle.
Hiking	You can't avoid some hiking, even if you just go to mail a post-card. The big deal, of course, is Mt. Scenery, with 1,064 crude, slippery steps leading up to the top *(see* Exploring, above).
	For information about Saba's 18 botanical hiking trails through the rain forest and up Mt. Scenery, check with Glenn Holm at the Tourist Office *(see* Tourist Information, above).
Scuba Diving and Snorkeling	The island's first settlers probably found the **Saba Bank** (a fertile fishing ground 3 miles southwest of Saba) a crucial point in their decision to set up house here. In more recent times, divers have enjoyed Saba's coral gardens and undersea mountains. **Saba Marine Park** was established in 1987 to preserve and manage Saba's marine resources. The park circles the entire island, dipping down to 200 feet, and is zoned for diving, swimming, fishing, boating, and anchorage. At press time, a snorkeling trail was in the planning stage and a guidebook on diving in Saba was scheduled for publication in late 1989. The park also offers talks and slide shows for divers and snorkelers, and provides brochures and literature on marine life. *Harbor Office,*

Fort Bay, tel. 599/4–3295. Open weekdays 8–5. Call first to see if anyone's around.

Saba Deep and **Sea Saba** (tel. 599/4–2246) will take you to explore Saba's 25 diving spots. Both offer rental equipment and certified instructors.

Shopping

Gift Ideas The island's most popular purchases are Saba lace and Saba Spice. The history of Saba lace (also called Spanish lace) goes back more than a century to Saban Gertrude Johnson, who attended a Caracas convent school where she learned the art of drawing and tying threads to adorn fine linens. When she returned home in the 1870s, she taught lacemaking to other Saban ladies, and the art has endured ever since. Collars, tea towels, napkins, and other small items are relatively inexpensive, but larger items, such as tablecloths, can be pricey. You should also know that the fabric requires some care—it is not drip-dry.

Saba Spice may *sound* as delicate as Saba lace, and the aroma is sweet as can be. However, the base for the liqueur is 151-proof rum, and all the rest is window dressing.

Shops Saba's famed souvenirs can be found in almost every shop. In Windwardside, stop in at **The Square Nickel, Island Craft Shop,** and **Saba Shop.** In The Bottom, the **Saba Artisan Foundation** (tel. 599/4–3260) turns out hand-screened fabrics, which you can buy by the yard or already made into resort clothing for men, women, and children.

Dining

In most of Saba's restaurants you pretty much have to take potluck. If you don't like what's cooking in one place, you can check out the other restaurants. However, it won't take you long to run out of options.

The most highly recommended restaurants are indicated by a star ★.

Category	Cost*
Expensive	$25–$30
Moderate	$20–$25
Inexpensive	under $20

per person, excluding drinks and service

★ **Captain's Quarters.** Dining is comfortable on a cool porch surrounded by flowers and mango trees. There's usually a homemade soup and a choice of two entrees: the catch of the day, served with Creole sauce, and T-bone or sirloin steak. *Windwardside, tel. 599/4–2201. Lunch is served at 12:30, dinner at 7:30. Reservations required. MC, V. Closed Sept. Expensive.*

Saba Chinese Bar & Restaurant. A plain house with plastic tablecloths, where you can get, among other things, sweet-and-sour pork or chicken, cashew chicken, and some curried dishes.

Windwardside, tel. 599/4–2268. Reservations advised. No credit cards. Closed Mon. Inexpensive.

Scout's Place. Chef Diana Medero turns out chicken cordon bleu, braised steak with mushrooms, and lobster (broiled or Newburg). You can get sandwiches all day long. *Windwardside, tel. 599/4–2295. Dinner is at 7:30. Reservations required. No credit cards. Inexpensive.*

★ **The Serving Spoon.** Queenie Simmons's chicken with peanut-butter sauce is famous throughout the islands. Her house adjoins her eight-table restaurant, where plates come heaped with huge portions. Stop by and ask her what she's preparing for the day. It might be meatballs with rice, seafood, french fries, steamed vegetables, or curried goat with butter. *The Bottom, tel. 599/4–3225. Reservations required. No credit cards. Inexpensive.*

Lodging

Like everything else on Saba, the guest houses are tiny and tucked into tropical gardens. The selection is limited and because most restaurants are located in the guest houses, you would do well to take advantage of meal plans.

The most highly recommended lodgings are indicated by a star ★.

Category	Cost*
Expensive	over $180
Moderate	$50–$65
Inexpensive	under $50

*All prices are for a standard double room for two with breakfast and dinner, excluding 5% tax and a 10%–15% service charge.

Hotels **Captain's Quarters.** All the rooms here are spacious and airy,
★ with antique Victorian furnishings (including four-poster beds) and views of the tiny pool that's perched 1,500 feet above the sea. Four choice bedrooms are in a small house that was built by a Saban sea captain in 1832. Dining is in a shaded garden pavilion surrounded by hibiscus, poinsettia and papaya trees. *Windwardside, tel. 599/4–2201 or 800/468–0023. 10 rooms with bath. Facilities: pool, restaurant, gift shop, bar and lounge. MC, V. Expensive.*

Juliana's Apartments. Near the Captain's Quarters, Mrs. Juliana Johnson offers eight studio apartments and a 2½-room apartment with private bath, balcony, kitchenette, living/dining room, bedroom, and a large porch facing the sea. Guests have the use of facilities at the CQ, whose manager, Steve Hassell, is Mrs. Johnson's brother. *Windwardside, tel. 599/4–2269. AE, MC, V. Moderate–Expensive.*

★ **Scout's Place.** Billed as "Bed 'n Board, Cheap 'n Cheerful," Scout's Place, near the post office and within walking distance of Sea Saba Dive Center, was originally the Government Guest House. "Scout" is retired owner Scout Thirkield, who turned his place over to his longtime cook Diana Medero and who is still very much in evidence. Ten new rooms, all with four-poster beds, reproductions of antiques, private balconies, and private baths with hot water, have been added to the original four rooms, which have *no* hot water. There's a small breakfast room where you can have cheese omelets, bacon, and coffee. *Windwardside, tel. 599/4–2205. 14 rooms, 12 with private bath. Facilities: restaurant, pool, bar. No credit cards. Inexpensive.*

Apartments Twenty apartments and wood cottages, all with hot water and modern conveniences, are available for weekly and monthly rentals. For information, check with Glenn Holm, **Saba Tourist Office** *(see* Tourist Information, above).

The Arts and Nightlife

The arts can be summed up in two words: **Royal Cinema** (Windwardside, tel. 599/4–3263), which gets films about two weeks after they're released. If you're in a movie mood, ask around to find out what's showing.

As for nightlife, you can dance till 2 AM on Sunday at **Guido's** (Windwardside, tel. 599/4–2330), do the nightclub scene at **The Lime Tree Bar & Restaurant** (The Bottom, tel. 599/4–3256), or just hang out at **Scout's Place** or the **Captain's Quarters.**

20 St. Barthélemy

by Regina McGee

Regina McGee is a freelance writer living in New York City. She writes frequently on business and leisure travel.

Scale is a big part of St. Barthélemy's charm: a lilliputian harbor; red-roof bungalows dotting the hillsides; minimokes, not much bigger than golf carts, buzzing up narrow roads or through the neat-as-a-pin streets of Gustavia; exquisite coves and beaches, most undeveloped, all with pristine stretches of white sand. Just 8 square miles, St. Barts is for people who like things small and perfectly done. It's for Francophiles, too. The French cuisine here is tops in the Caribbean, and gourmet lunches and dinners are rallying points of island life. A French *savoir vivre* pervades, and the island is definitely for the style conscious—casual but always chic. This is no place for the beach-bum set.

Rothschild and Rockefeller built estates here, and for a long time the island, 15 miles from St. Maarten in the French West Indies, was the haunt of the privileged and the well-informed. In the past eight years, the tourist base has expanded, and last year more than 100,000 visitors stopped by, including day-trippers from nearby islands and passengers from the cruise ships that now anchor just outside the harbor.

Longtime visitors speak wistfully of the old, quiet St. Barts. While development *has* quickened the pace, the island has not been overrun with prefab condos or glitzy resorts. The largest hotel has only 80 rooms, and the remaining 550 rooms are scattered in cottages and villas around the island; no high rises are allowed. The tiny airport accommodates nothing bigger than 19-passenger planes, and there aren't any casinos or flashy late-night attractions. Moreover, St. Barts is generally not a destination for the budget-minded. Development has largely been in luxury lodgings and gourmet restaurants, and as the dollar continues to decline, island-wide prices have increased sharply in recent years.

When Christopher Columbus "discovered" the island in 1493, he named it after his brother, Bartholomeo. A small group of French colonists arrived from nearby St. Kitts in 1656 but were wiped out by the fierce Carib Indians that dominated the area. A new group from Normandy and Brittany arrived in 1694. This time the settlers prospered —with the help of French buccaneers, who took full advantage of the island's strategic location and well-protected harbor. In 1784 the French traded the island to King Gustav III of Sweden in exchange for port rights in Göteborg. He dubbed the capital Gustavia, laid out and paved streets, built three forts, and turned the capital into a prosperous free port. The island thrived as a major shipping and commercial center until the 19th century, when earthquakes, fire, and hurricanes brought financial ruin. Many residents fled for newer lands of opportunity, and in 1878 France agreed to repurchase its beleaguered former colony.

Today the island is still a free port, and, as a dependency of Guadeloupe, is part of an overseas department of France. Dry, sunny, and stony, St. Barts was never one of the Caribbean's "sugar islands," and thus never developed an industrial slave base. Most natives are descendants of those tough Norman and Breton settlers of three centuries ago. They are feisty, industrious, and friendly but insular.

You may hear some speak the old Norman patois of their ancestors or see the older women dressed in the traditional garb of provincial France. They have prospered with the tourist boom, but some are worried the upward swing of prices may threaten business, especially tour groups and families. So far, though, this gem of an island continues to draw an ever-widening circle of fans.

Before You Go

Tourist Information Contact the **French West Indies Tourist Board** (610 5th Ave., New York, NY 10020, tel. 212/757–1125). The **French Government Tourist Office** can supply information in Canada (1981 Ave., McGill College, Suite 49D, Montreal, P.Q. H3A 2W9, tel. 514/288–4264, or 1 Dundas St. W., Suite 2405, Toronto, Ont. M56 1Z3, tel. 416/593–4717) or in the United Kingdom (178 Piccadilly, London W1V 0AL, tel. 01/499–6911).

Arriving and Departing
By Plane The principal gateway from North America is St. Maarten's Juliana Airport, where several times a day you can catch a 10-minute flight to St. Barts on either **Windward Islands Airways** (tel. 590/27–61–01) or **Air St. Barthélemy** (tel. 590/27–71–90). **Air Guadeloupe** (tel. 590/27–61–90) offers daily service from Espérance Airport in St. Martin, the French side of the same island. Air Guadeloupe also has direct flights to St. Barts from Guadeloupe and Antigua, while **Virgin Air** (tel. 590/27–71–76) operates daily flights between St. Barts and both St. Thomas and San Juan. Reconfirmation on all return interisland flights, even during off-peak seasons, is strongly recommended. Windward, Air St. Barthélemy, and Virgin Air also offer charter service.

From the Airport Airport taxi service costs $3 to $15 (to the farthest hotel). Since the cabs are unmetered, you may be charged more if you make stops on the way. Cabs meet all flights, and a taxi dispatcher (tel. 590/27–66–31) operates from 8:30 AM to 10 PM.

By Boat Catamarans leave Philipsburg in St. Maarten at 9 AM daily, arriving in Gustavia's harbor around 11 AM. These are one-day, round-trip excursions (about $45, including open bar), with departures from St. Barts at 3:30 PM. If there's room, one-way passengers ($25) are often taken as well. Contact **Bobby's Marina** in Philipsburg (tel. 5995/2–3170) for reservations. *St. Barth Express*, a 12-seat open powerboat, leaves Gustavia at 8:15 AM on Monday, Wednesday, and Friday, arriving at Philipsburg at 9 AM and in Marigot (St. Martin) at 9:30 AM. The boat departs from Marigot at 3:30 PM on the same days and goes directly to St. Barts. One-way fare is about $25 and round-trip $45. The **Yacht Charter Service** (tel. 590/27–62–38) in Gustavia handles reservations. The *Princess* motorboat makes the same run every Wednesday and can be booked through **La Marine Service** (tel. 590/27–70–34) in Gustavia.

Passports and Visas U.S. and Canadian citizens need either a passport (one that is no more than five years expired will suffice) or other proof of citizenship, such as a notarized birth certificate with a raised seal or a voter's registration card, both accompanied by photo identification. A visa is required for stays of more than three months.

Customs and Duties Items for personal use, including tobacco, film, and cameras, are admitted.

St. Barthélemy

Ile Chevreau

Ile Frégate

Pt. à
Colombier

Colombier

*La Petite
Anse*

⑪ ⑫ ⑬

Flamands

*Anse à
Galets*

Anse de
Petit Jean

⑧

❸ Colombier

Corossol

❷

Corossol Beach

⑨ ⑩

⑭

❹ St. Jean

㉑ — ㉘

**St. Jean
Airport**

**Baie de
St. Jean**

Public Beach

*Les Islettes
La Baleine*

TO ST. MARTIN

Les Saintes

Gustavia ❶

⑮ ⑯ ⑰ ⑱ ⑲ ⑳

**Petit Anse
de Galet**

Lurin

Mt. Lurin

Caribbean Sea

㉙ ㉚

**Anse
du
Gouverneur**

❶ Exploring Sites

⑧ Hotels and Restaurants

Grande Pt.

↑
Ile Toc Vers

ATLANTIC OCEAN

Les Grenadiers

La Tortue

Pt. Milou

③④ ③⑤ ③⑥

Grand Cul de Sac

③⑦ — ④③

③① ③② ③③

Lorient

Marigot

④④

Lorient

Marigot

⑤

④⑤ ④⑥

Petit Cul de Sac

Vitet

Toiny

Mt. du Grand Fond

Morne du Vitet

⑥

Morne de Grand Fond

Pt. à Toiny

Grande Saline

Anse du Grand Fond

N

⑦

Grand Saline

0 _____ 1 mile

0 _____ 1 km

ur *Pt. du Gouverneur*

Lodging

Auberge de la
Petite Anse, **8**

Baie des Flamands, **12**

Castalets, **30**

Club la Banne, **31**

El Sereno Beach
Hotel, **42**

Filao Beach, **26**

François Plantation, **9**

Grand Cul de Sac
Beach Hotel and St.
Bart's Beach Hotel, **43**

Guanahani, **41**

Hostellerie des Trois
Forces, **46**

Hotel Manapany
Cottages, **14**

L'Hibiscus, **20**

La Normandie, **33**

Le Petit Morne, **10**

Les Mouettes, **32**

Marigot Bay Club, **35**

Marigot Sea Club, **36**

Tropical Hotel, **27**

Village St. Jeane, **28**

White Sand Beach
Cottages, **13**

Language French is the official language, though a Norman dialect is spoken by some longtime islanders. Many hotel and restaurant employees speak English, but not all.

Precautions Roads are narrow and sometimes very steep, so check the brakes and gears of your rental car *before* you leave the lot. Some hillside restaurants and hotels require a bit of climbing, so if that's a problem, inquire ahead of time.

Staying in St. Barthélemy

Important Addresses **Tourist Information:** The **Office du Tourisme** (tel. 590/27–60–08) is in the Mairie de St. Barth (town hall), rue August Nyman, Gustavia. Hours are weekdays 7:30–noon and 2–6. The office is closed on weekends and Wednesday afternoons.

Emergencies **Hospitals: Gustavia Clinic** (tel. 590/27–60–35) is on the corner of rue Jean Bart and rue Sadi Carnot.

Pharmacies: There is a pharmacy in Gustavia on rue de la République (tel. 590/27–61–82).

Currency The French franc is legal tender. Figure about 6.30F to the U.S. dollar. U.S. dollars are accepted everywhere; credit cards are accepted mainly at the more expensive shops, hotels, and restaurants. Note: Prices quoted here are in U.S. dollars unless indicated otherwise.

Taxes and Service Charges Hotels add a 7% government tax. A 10F departure tax is charged if you are headed for St. Martin; 15F for other destinations.

Some hotels add a 10%–15% service charge to bills; others include it in their tariffs. All restaurants are required to include a 15% service charge in their published prices. It is especially important to remember this when your credit card receipt is presented to be signed with the tip space blank, or you could end up paying a 30% service charge.

Most taxi drivers own their vehicles and do not expect a tip.

Guided Tours Tours are by minibus or taxi. An hour-long tour costs about $30 for one–two people and $40 for up to eight people. A five-hour island tours cost about $87 per vehicle. Itineraries are negotiable. Tours can be arranged at hotel desks, through the Tourist Office, or by calling any of the island's taxi operators, including **Hugo Cagan** (tel. 590/27–61–28) and **Constant Gumbs** (tel. 590/27–61–93).

Getting Around *Taxis* You may arrange cab service by calling tel. 590/27–66–31, 590/27–60–59, or 590/27–63–12. Note: Fares double from 8 PM to 6 AM and on Sundays and holidays.

Rental Cars It's more fun to have your own car, though the steep, curvy roads require careful driving. **Avis** (tel. 590/27–71–43), **Budget** (tel. 590/27–66–30), and **Europcar** (tel. 590/27–64–87) are represented at the airport, among others. All accept credit cards. You must be 25 years old, and in high season there may be a three-day minimum. VW Beetles, open-sided Gurgels (VW jeep), and Mini Mokes—all with stick shift only—rent in season for $40–$45 a day, with unlimited mileage and limited collision insurance. Car-rental reservations are advised, especially during February and around Christmas. Some hotels have their own car fleets, and a car should be rented at the time you make your room reservation. The choice of vehicles may be limited, but many hotels offer 24-hour emergency road service, which most rental companies do not.

Motorbikes Motorbike companies rent bikes for $25 per day and require a $100 deposit. Call **Topolino's** (tel. 590/27–70–92) or **Rent Some Fun** (tel. 590/27–70–59).

Telephones To phone St. Barts from the United States dial 011–590 and the **and Mail** local number. To call the United States from St. Barts, dial 19–1, the area code, and the local number. For local information, dial 12. Automatic telephone booths around the island require "pay-in-advance" credit cards, which can be purchased at the post office. To dial a local number on the island, dial six digits; no area code is required.

Mail is slow. It can take up to three weeks for correspondence between the United States and the island. Post offices are in Gustavia and Lorient.

Opening and Businesses and offices close from noon to 2 during the week and **Closing Times** all day Sunday. Shops in Gustavia are open weekdays 8:30–noon and 2–5, and until noon on Saturday. Shops across from the airport and in St. Jean also open Saturday afternoons and until 7 PM on weekdays. The two banks, both in Gustavia, are open weekdays 8–noon and 2–3:30.

Beaches

There are nearly 20 plages (beaches), each with a distinctive personality and all of them public. Topless sunbathing is common but nudism is forbidden. Here are the main attractions:

St. Jean is like a mini Côte d'Azur—beachside bistros, bungalow hotels, bronze beauties, and lots of day-trippers. The reef-protected strip is divided by Eden Rock promontory, and there's good snorkeling west of the rock. **Lorient** is popular with St. Barts's families and surfers, who like its rolling waves. **Marigot** is a quiet fishing beach with good snorkeling along the rocky far end. Shallow, reef-protected **Grand Cul de Sac** is especially nice for small children and windsurfers; it has excellent lunch spots and lots of pelicans. Secluded **Saline** is just about everyone's favorite beach and is great for swimmers. **Anse du Gouverneur** is equally spectacular, with good views of St. Kitts, Saba, and Statia.

A five-minute walk from Gustavia is **Petit Anse de Galet,** named after the tiny shells on its shore. Both **Public Beach** and **Corossol Beach** are best for boat- and sunset-watching. The beach at **Colombier** is the least accessible but the most private; you'll have to take either a rocky footpath from La Petite Anse, or climb for 30 minutes down a cacti-bordered trail from the top. **Flamands** is the best of the hotel beaches—a roomy strip of palm-shaded sand.

Exploring St. Barthélemy

Numbers in the margin correspond to points of interest on the St. Barthélemy map.

Gustavia and With just a few streets on three sides of its tiny harbor, **the West** Gustavia is easily explored in a two-hour stroll, including time **❶** to browse through shops or visit a café. This will leave you the rest of the afternoon for a trip to the west coast to enjoy a picnic and a swim.

Park your car harborside on the rue de la République, and head to the **Tourist Office** in the *Mairie* (town hall) on rue August Nyman. Here you should pick up an island map and free copy of *St. Barth Magazine*, a monthly publication on island happenings. Then settle in at either **Brasserie L'Oubli** or **Le Select** (*see* Dining, below), two cafés at the corner of rue de la France and rue de la République, for coffee and croissants and a quick leaf through the magazine's listings of the week's events.

One block west is the island's principal quay, where flashy catamarans, yachts, and sailboats are moored. For boating or diving information, stop by **La Marine** (*see* Participant Sports, below) on the far side of the harbor directly across from the quay.

As you stroll through the little streets, you will notice that plaques sometimes spell out names in both French and Swedish, a reminder of the days when the island was a Swedish colony. Small shops along **rue Roi Oscar II** and **rue de Général de Gaulle** sell French perfumes, resort wear, crystal, gold jewelry, and other luxury items.

On the other side of the harbor, next door to the Trois Gourmands restaurant, a **market** has been set up where ladies from Guadeloupe and Dominica have arranged colorful displays of tropical fruit and vegetables. You might want to stop by **La Rotisserie** (rue de Lafayette and rue de Roi Oscar II) or **Taste Unlimited** (rue de Général de Gaulle) to pick up the makings for a picnic. And, if you feel like a swim, drive around the end of the harbor to **Anse de Galet.** This quiet little plage is also known as Shell Beach for the tiny shells heaped ankle-deep in some places.

Head back the way you came and turn off at the sign for Lurin. The views up the winding road overlooking the harbor are spectacular. A small rocky route off to the right will take you bumping and grinding down a steep incline to **Anse du Gouverneur,** one of St. Barts's most beautiful beaches, where pirate's treasure is said to be buried. If the weather is clear, you will be able to see the islands of Saba, St. Eustatius, and St. Kitts.

Time Out The hilltop **Sante Fe Restaurant** (Morne Lorne, tel. 590/27–61–04) is a favorite spot for sundowners, watching sunsets, and the island's best hamburgers.

Corossol, Colombier, Flamands ❷ ❸ Starting at the airport intersection, take the road to Public Beach and on to **Corossol,** a two-street fishing village with a little beach. Corossol is where the island's French provincial origins are most evident. Residents speak an old Norman dialect, and some of the barefoot older women still wear traditional garb—ankle-length dresses and starched white sunbonnets called *quichenottes* (kiss-me-not hats). The women are shy and don't like to be photographed. However, they are pleased when you buy some of their handmade straw work—handbags, baskets, broad-brim hats, and delicate strings of birds—made from lantania palms. The palms were introduced to the island 100 years ago by foresighted Father Morvan, who planted a grove in Corossol and Flamands, thus providing the country folk with a living that is still pursued today. Here, too, is the

Inter Oceans Museum (tel. 590/27–62–97), which features a small but excellent collection of marine shells from around the world. *Tel. 590/27–62–97. Admission: 20F. Open daily 10–5.*

Return to the main road and turn left for **Colombier.** Follow the signs illustrated with hummingbirds to reach island artist **Jean-Yves Froment's Studio** (tel. 590/27–61–72). Visitors are welcome, but call ahead to reserve a personalized demonstration in which the artist shows how his popular hand-blocked fabrics are created. Tropical fabrics and fashions are sold in his shop next door to the studio.

From Colombier, head down the main road about a mile to **Baie des Flamands,** a wide beach with a few small hotels. From here, take a brisk hike to the top of what is believed to be the now extinct volcano that gave birth to St. Barts. From the peak you can take in the gorgeous view of the offshore islands.

Time Out Chef Solange Gréaux serves a delicious fish soup and home cooking at the **Baie des Flamands Hotel** (Anse des Flamands, tel. 590/27–64–85).

A drive to the end of Flamands Road brings you to a rocky footpath that leads to the island's most remote beach, **Anse de Colombier.**

St. Jean, Grand Cul de Sac, Saline Brimming with bungalows, bistros, sunbathers, and windsurfing sails, the half-mile crescent of sand at **St. Jean** is the ❹ island's most famous beach. Lunch at a beachside bistro such as **Le Pelican** or **Chez Francine** (*see* Dining, below), perhaps interrupted by a swim in the surf, is de rigueur, followed by a stroll through nearby boutiques.

❺ Leaving St. Jean, take the main road about a mile to **Lorient.** On your left are the royal palms and rolling waves of Lorient Beach. Lorient, site of the first French settlement, is one of the island's two parishes, and a newly restored church, historic headstones, a school, post office, and gas station mark the spot.

Bear left and continue along the coast. Your route rolls around the island's pretty windward coves, past **Pointe Milou,** an elegant residential colony, and on to **Marigot,** where you can pick up a bottle of fine wine at **La Cave.** The bargain prices may surprise you (*see* Shopping, below).

The winding road passes through the mangroves, ponds, and beach of **Grand Cul de Sac,** where there are plenty of excellent beachside restaurants and water-sport concessions. Tucked beside the Lafayette Club is **Paulette Blardat's Magnolia Coiffure** (no phone), a beauty salon set right on the beach.

❻ Just beyond Grand Cul de Sac is the much-photographed **Toiny coast.** Drystone fences crisscross the steep slopes of Morne Vite along a rocky shoreline that resembles the rugged coast of Normandy. The road turns inland and up the slopes of Morne de Grande Fond. At the first fork (less than a mile), the road to the right leads back to Lorient. A left-hand turn at the next intersection will bring you within a few minutes to a dead end at ❼ **Grande Saline.** Ten years ago the big salt ponds of Grande Saline were shut down after a half-century of operation. The place looks desolate, but climb the short hillock behind the ponds for a surprise—the long arc of **Anse de Grande Saline.**

Time Out Stop for lunch, dinner, or drinks at **Le Tamarind** (Saline, tel. 590/27–72–12), a delightful spot by a huge tamarind tree. Paco the pet parrot greets guests. You may want to try your hand at archery between sipping drinks and ordering from the excellent specials listed on a blackboard.

Participant Sports

Boating St. Barts is a popular yachting and sailing center, thanks to its location midway between Antigua and St. Thomas. Gustavia's harbor, 13 to 16 feet deep, has mooring and docking facilities for 40 yachts, with good anchorages available at Public, Corossol, and Colombier. **Loulou's Marine** (tel. 590/27–62–74) is the place for yachting information and supplies. **La Marine Service** (tel. 590/27–70–34) and the **Yacht Charter Agency** (tel. 590/27–62–38) offer sunset and half- and full-day sails. La Marine also has unskippered motor rentals for about $220 a day.

Diving and Deep-sea fishing can be arranged through **Yacht Charter Agen-**
Deep-Sea Fishing **cy** (tel. 590/27–62–38), **La Marine** (tel. 590/27–70–34), or with **Pierre Choisy** (tel. 590/27–61–22) on his boat *Bertram*. La Marine also operates a PADI diving center, with scuba-diving trips for about $45 per person, gear included. **Club La Bulle** (tel. 590/27–68–93) and PADI-certified **Dive with Dan** (tel. 590/27–64–78) are other scuba options.

Tennis There are two tennis courts at the **Gaunahani** (tel. 590/27–66–60), **Le Flamboyant Tennis Club** (tel. 590/27–75–65), and two at the **Sports Club of Colombier** (tel. 590/27–61–07). The Manapany (tel. 590/27–66–55) and the **St. Barths Beach Hotel** (tel. 590/27–62–75) each have one court.

Windsurfing Windsurfing fever has definitely caught on here. Boards can be rented for about $11 an hour at water-sports centers along Flamands, St. Jean, and Grand Cul de Sac beaches. Lessons are offered for about $35 an hour at **St. Barts Wind School** (St. Jean, tel. 590/27–70–96), **Wind Wave Power** (St. Barths Beach Hotel, tel. 590/27–62–73), and **Grand Bay Watersports** (Guanahani, tel. 590/27–66–60).

Shopping

St. Barts is a duty-free port and there are especially good bargains in jewelry, porcelain, imported liquors, and French perfumes, cosmetics, and designer resort wear.

Shopping Areas Shops are clustered in **Gustavia, St. Jean's Commercial Center,** and the **Village Creole,** a cottage complex also in St. Jean. More shops and a gourmet supermarket are located across from the airport.

Good Buys Stop in Corossol to pick up some of the intricate straw work
Island Crafts (wide-brim beach hats, mobiles, handbags) that the ladies of Corossol create by hand (*see* Exploring, above). In Gustavia, look for hand-turned pottery at **St. Barth's Pottery** (tel. 590/27–62–74) and exotic coral and shell jewelry at the **Shell Shop** (no phone). In Colombier you'll find one of the best buys on the island, the hand-blocked prints of local artist **Jean-Yves Froment** (*see* Exploring, above).

Wine and Wine lovers will enjoy **La Cave** (Marigot, tel. 590/27–63–21),
Gourmet Shops where an excellent collection of French vintages are stored in

temperature-controlled cellars. Also check out **La Cave du Port Franc** (tel. 590/27–65–27) on the far side of the harbor for vintage wines, contemporary paintings, and objets d'art.

For exotic groceries or picnic fixings, stop by St. Barts's fabulous gourmet delis—**La Rotisserie** (tel. 590/27–63–13) on rue Oscar II (branches in Villa Creole and Pointe Milou) and **Taste Unlimited** (tel. 590/27–70–42) on rue de Général de Gaulle.

Dining

Dining out is a ritual on St. Barts. The quality of fare is generally high and so are the prices, which are reputed to be some of the steepest in the Caribbean. Many places offer prix fixe menus, which are usually a recommended choice. Creole and French/Creole restaurants tend to be the least expensive alternative. *Acras* (salt cod fritters) with Creole sauce (minced hot peppers in oil), spiced *christophene* (a kind of squash), *boudin Créole* (a very spicy blood sausage), and a lusty *soupe de poissons* are some of the delicious and ubiquitous Creole dishes.

The most highly recommended restaurants are indicated by a star ★.

Category	Cost*
Expensive	over $45
Moderate	$25–$45
Inexpensive	under $25

per person, excluding drinks, service, and sales tax (4%)

L'Ananas. Two small porches hold 14 tables outside a lovely old house overlooking Gustavia. The chef's specialty is fish; the sashimi and salmon dishes are little masterpieces. The chocolate truffle with moka sauce is a recommended finish. *Rue Sadi Carnot, Gustavia, tel. 590/27–63–77. Reservations required. AE, MC, V. Expensive.*

Bartolomeo. There's a small bar as you enter, and at the rear is a pretty dining room that seats 35. The eclectic menu includes such pleasant surprises as lobster-stuffed ravioli and chicken breasts with ratatouille. For dessert, don't miss the luscious crème brûlée. *Hotel Guanahani, Grand Cul de Sac, tel. 590/27–66–60. Reservations required. AE, MC, V. Closed Wed. Expensive.*

★ **Castelets.** The romantic mountaintop setting, the first-class cooking of Marseilles-born Michel Viali, exceptional wines, and the soigné service make a meal at this classy *auberge* a St. Barts experience to savor. The cuisine is classic French and the tables are few and much in demand. *Morne Lurin, tel. 590/27–61–73. Reservations required. AE, MC, V. Closed Tues., Wed. for dinner. Expensive.*

L'Hibiscus. This popular in-town spot has a romantic terrace overlooking the harbor and a jazz trio playing nightly until 11:30. The food is just a tad disappointing for the price, but if you're looking for cozy, lively atmosphere this is the place. *Rue Thiers, Gustavia, tel. 590/27–64–82. Dinner reservations required. AE, MC, V. Expensive.*

Lafayette Club. This "in" beach bistro offers simple but tasty lunch fare to a casually chic crowd. Grilled (barbecued in local parlance) lobster or crispy duck, followed by a fruit sherbet or *tarte tatin,* is the way to go. *Grand Cul de Sac, tel. 590/27–62–51. Closed the end of May–mid-Nov. Reservations suggested. No credit cards. Expensive.*

Le Pelican. This popular lunchtime terrace serves good seafood brochettes, salads, and grilled meats. Decor in the evening dining room is nothing special, but the food is generously portioned and tasty. *St. Jean, tel. 590/27–64–64. Dinner reservations required. AE. Expensive.*

Taiwana. A casual but exclusive beach club/hotel, this out-of-the-way lunch spot serves salads, lobsters, and grilled fish. Overnight patrons include a few celebrities and other folks invited by the owner. *Baie des Flamands, tel. 590/27–64–76. Reservations suggested. No credit cards. Expensive.*

★ **Gloriette.** This beachside bistro serves delicious local dishes such as crunchy *acras* and grilled red snapper with Creole sauce. Light salads and Creole dishes are served at lunch and the house wine is always good. *Grand Cul de Sac, tel. 590/27–75–66. No credit cards. Moderate.*

Hostellerie des Trois Forces. Fermented fruit juices, New Age chitchat, and a swim-up bar set the tone at this rustic mountaintop inn. A tasty Niçoise salad and omelet are excellent lunch choices, priced under $15. Dinner is served in a pretty country dining room. Especially good is the veal with cream butter and Calvados. Vegetarian dishes are also served. *Vitet, tel. 590/27–61–25. AE, MC, V. Moderate.*

La Langouste. Reserve a harborside table and order freely from the Creole and French menu, but save some room for the coconut flan dessert. The food is hearty and reasonably priced and the airy pink dining rooms draw an eclectic crowd. *Rue Bord de la Mer, Gustavia 590/27–69–47. Reservations suggested. No credit cards. Closed for dinner Thurs. Moderate.*

★ **Le Patio.** Gourmet pizzas, salads, pastas, brochettes, and hamburgers are offered for lunch. In the evening there's all that plus fancier Italian fare—all reasonably priced. You'll like the breezy outdoor and indoor dining rooms, the views of the bay, and the friendly family service. *St. Jean, tel. 590/27–61–39. No credit cards. Closed Wed. Moderate.*

Marigot Bay Club. Generous portions and consistent quality help make this 16-table beachside place a favored lunch and dinner spot. Lightly spiced Creole dishes and simple fish and seafood entrées are featured. *Marigot, tel. 590/27–75–45. Reservations required. AE, V. Closed Sun. and for lunch on Mon. Moderate.*

Le Relais. On a spacious hilltop porch overlooking the cove, Le Relais has friendly proprietors who serve up large portions of spicy Creole food (some French entrées). Try the thick fish soup and the grouper in mild curry sauce. Lunch is especially reasonable. *Petit Cul de Sac, tel. 590/27–73–00. Reservations suggested. No credit cards. Moderate–Inexpensive.*

Brasserie La Créole. Good breakfast omelets, croissants, and fresh fruit juices are served at open-air tables at this restaurant in the St. Jean shopping complex. For lunch and dinner there are salads, grilled dishes, and sandwiches. *St. Jean, tel. 590/27–68–09. AE. Inexpensive.*

Chez Francine. Swimsuit-clad patrons lunch on the terrace or at wood tables set in the sand. The lunch-only menu features grilled chicken, beef, and lobster, all served with crispy french fries for $15. *St. Jean Bay, tel. 590/27–60–49. MC, V. Inexpensive.*

Chez Pompi. Locals count on the simple but reliable French and Creole cooking found at this hillside outpost. *Grand Cul de Sac, tel. 590/27–75–67. Closed Sun. No credit cards. Inexpensive.*

★ **Le Marine.** Mussels from France arrive on Thursday and in-the-know islanders are there to eat them at dockside picnic tables. The menu always includes fresh fish, hamburgers, and omelets. *Rue Jeanne d'Arc, Gustavia, tel. 590/27–64–50. No credit cards. Inexpensive.*

Topolino. Popular with families, Topolino's offerings range from hearty Italian dishes to pizza. Trap your own lobster in the pond. *St. Jean, tel. 590/27–70–92. MC, V. Inexpensive.*

Lodging

The most highly recommended lodgings are indicated by a star ★.

Category	Cost*
Very Expensive	over $300
Expensive	$200–$300
Moderate	$125–$200
Inexpensive	under $125

* All prices are for a standard double room for two, excluding a 10%–15% service charge; there is no government room tax.

Hotels **Castelets.** Artists and dancers frequent this elegant hilltop inn with stunning views. Mme. Geneviève Jouany graciously presides over antiques-furnished rooms that are always in demand. You will need a car to go to the beach. *Box 60, Mt. Lurin, 97133, tel. 590/27–61–73. 10 rooms and 2 duplex villas. Facilities: small pool, restaurant. AE, MC, V. Very Expensive.*

Filao Beach. Comfortable duplex cottages surround a flower-filled garden on one of the island's most popular beaches. Service is very good and St. Jean's attractions are within easy walking distance. *Box 167, St. Jean, 97133, tel. 590/27–64–84. 30 rooms. Facilities: pool, terrace restaurant/bar. Very Expensive.*

★ **Guanahani.** This 7-acre resort adjoining the Rothschild estate is the island's largest. Red-roof bungalows nestle in the hillside and some have lovely private pools. Beachside suites are much in demand. This is a full-service resort that knows how to pamper, pamper. *Box 109, Grand Cul de Sac, 97133, tel. 590/27–66–60. 30 doubles with ocean views, 20 oceanfront doubles, plus junior and 1-bedroom suites, 10 with private pools and full kitchens. Facilities: 2 restaurants, 2 lighted tennis courts, pool with Jacuzzi, beach, water-sport center. AE, MC, V. Very Expensive.*

Hotel Manapany Cottages. A ramshackle entry road ends at this luxury enclave, which is built around Anse des Cayes. Accommodations vary from St. Barts–style cottages and suites tucked into the hillside to much-in-demand beachfront suites with marble baths and four-poster beds. Bronze jet-setters line the pretty pool. The small beach sometimes has a strong undercurrent. *Box 114, tel. 590/27–66–59; 212/757–0225 in the U.S. 20 cottages and 12 club suites. Facilities: 2 restaurants, 2 bars, pool, Jacuzzi, beach, bocci-ball court, exercise room, boutique, lighted tennis court, water-sport center. AE, MC, V. Very Expensive.*

Club La Banne. Rustic luxury is the style of these romantic bungalows just off the beach. Rooms are tastefully decorated and especially popular with owner Jean Marie Rivière's celebrity friends. *Quartier Lorient, 97133, tel. 590/27–68–25. Facilities: restaurant, 2 pools, Jacuzzi. AE. Expensive.*

★ **François Plantation.** A colonial-era graciousness pervades this four-star complex of hilltop bungalows managed by longtime island habitués Françoise and François Beret. Everything is designed to take full advantage of the terrain, vegetation, and location high above Flamands. Rooms are air-conditioned and have refrigerators and satellite TV. You'll need a car for the beach and reservations for the elegant restaurant. *Colombier, 97133, tel. 590/27–78–82; 800/932–3222 in the U.S. 4 garden and 8 sea-view rooms. Facilities: pool, restaurant. AE, V. Expensive.*

L'Hibiscus. Air-conditioned bungalow rooms overlook Gustavia, though some of the patios look out on nearby buildings, too. A beach is within walking distance and the nightlife is always lively in the hotel's jazz lounge. *Rue Thiers, B. P. 86, Gustavia, 97133, tel. 590/27–64–82. 11 rooms with kitchenettes. Facilities: restaurant, pool, lounge. AE, DC, MC, V. Expensive.*

El Sereno Beach Hotel. A quiet, casually chic ambience pervades, and managers Chistine and Marc Llepez are perfect hosts. Small but comfortable rooms with high-walled patios surround a central garden. The restaurant food is outstanding, and the clientele includes many repeats. *Box 19, Grand Cul de Sac, 97133, tel. 590/27–64–80. 20 rooms (3 sea-view). Facilities: restaurant, bar, pool, beach with water-sports center, boutique. DC, MC, V. Expensive.*

Grand Cul De Sac Beach Hotel and **St. Barths Beach Hotel.** These side-by-side properties owned by Guy Turbé stretch out on a narrow peninsula between lagoon and sea. Both are comfortable, unpretentious, and popular with families and tour groups who take advantage of the full range of sports available on the hotels' beach. Upper-level rooms are best at the two-story St. Barths Beach Hotel; the best rooms at Grand Cul de Sac Beach Hotel, a group of small air-conditioned bungalow units with kitchenettes, are right on the beach. The windows are screenless and if left open, mosquitoes can be a problem. There's limited parking for cars not rented through Turbé's agency. *Box 81, Grand Cul de Sac, 97133, tel. 590/27–62–73. 35 rooms; 16 bungalows. Facilities: 2 restaurants, bar, saltwater pool, tennis court, windsurfing school and water-sports center, TV/library room. AE, MC, V. Moderate–Expensive.*

Baie des Flamands. Upper-level rooms have balconies and lower-level ones have terrace kitchenette units in this newly refurbished motel-style hotel. One of the first hotels on the island, it is still run by a St. Barts family and is popular with families and tour groups. It has a good restaurant and an outstanding beach location. *Box 68, Anse des Flamands, 97133, tel. 590/27–64–85. 24 rooms with baths. Facilities: restaurant, bar, beach, saltwater pool, TV/library room, rental cars. AE, MC, V. Moderate.*

Marigot Bay Club. Jean Michel Ledee's pleasant apartments across from his popular seaside restaurant feature comfortable furniture, louvered doors and windows, air-conditioning, twin beds, kitchen/living areas, and large terraces with good views. *Marigot, 97133, tel. 590/27-75-45. 6 apartments. Facilities: restaurant, nearby beach. AE, V. Moderate.*

Marigot Sea Club. The Marigot Bay Club's sister property has spacious suites and a beautifully landscaped garden. All rooms have living room, kitchen, terrace, shower/bath. *Marigot, 97133, tel. 590/27-75-36. 10 suites. Facilities: restaurant, beach within walking distance. No credit cards. Moderate.*

Le Petit Morne. Families like these mountainside studios, each with a private balcony, air-conditioning, and good views. A snack bar serving breakfast and light lunches recently opened. *Box 14, Colombier, 97133, tel. 590/27-62-64. 14 rooms with kitchens. Facilities: pool, snack bar, reading room. AE, MC, V. Moderate.*

Tropical Hotel. Up the hill from St. Jean's Beach, this cozy gingerbread complex encircles a lush garden and small pool. The ambience is friendly; accommodations are air-conditioned. *Box 147, St. Jean, 97133, tel. 590/27-64-87. 20 rooms. Facilities: restaurant, reception bungalow with bar and wide-screen video lounge, pool. AE, MC, V. Moderate.*

★ **Village St. Jean.** This stone and redwood resort, up a short, steep hill from St. Jean's Beach, is now run by the second generation of the Charneau family. It has acquired a strong following over the years. The accent is on service, privacy, and wholesomeness. There are a variety of accommodations with air-conditioning and fine views of the town. Rounding out the picture will be a pool, which is scheduled for completion in 1990. This is a good value. *Box 23, St. Jean, 97133, tel. 590/27-61-39. 25 rooms. Facilities: restaurant, bar, small grocery, boutique, game and reading room. V. Moderate.*

★ **White Sand Beach Cottages.** The road in front of the place is a little ramshackle but these cottages are pleasant, air-conditioned, and well equipped. The cottage on the beach is the best. *Anse des Flamands, 97133, tel. 590/27-63-66. 4 cottages with kitchenettes. Facilities: beach, sun deck, MC, V. Inexpensive-Moderate.*

Auberge de la Petite Anse. Minimal decor but comfortable rooms with terraces and air-conditioning are offered in eight bungalows just above the beach. A grocery, bar, and restaurant are within walking distance. *Box 117, Anse des Flamands, tel. 590/27-64-60. 16 rooms with kitchenettes. AE, V. Inexpensive.*

La Normandie. This small inn offers reasonably priced rooms, a restaurant, and dancing in the evening on a glass floor set over the pool. Ask for one of the two air-conditioned rooms. *Lorient, 97133, tel. 590/27-61-66. 8 rooms. Facilities: pool, restaurant. V. Inexpensive.*

★ **Les Mouettes.** Good family accommodations are provided in bungalows overlooking the island's best surfing beach. *Lorient, 97133, tel. 590/27-60-74. 6 rooms. Each room has a shower, patio, and kitchenette. Facilities: car rental. Inexpensive.*

Apartment Rentals Villas, apartments, and condos can be rented through SIBARTH (tel. 590/27-62-38), which handles about 200 properties. WIMCO (800/932-3222) is the agency's representative in the United States. Rents average $1,000 per week for one-bedroom villas, $3,500 for three-bedroom villas, and more for houses with pools.

Nightlife

St. Barts is a mostly in-bed-by-midnight island. However, some of the hotels and restaurants provide some late-night fun. Cocktail hour finds the barefoot boating set gathered in the garden of **Gustavia's Le Select;** the more sophisticated up at **L'Hibiscus's** jazz bar; the French at **Brasserie l'Oubli.** Sunset-watchers head up to **Santa Fe** in Lurin or to **Chez Mayas's** terrace in Public. Then it's a long, leisurely meal, followed by an after-dinner drink on a breezy terrace—possibly **Castelets** in Lurin or your own. Roger Parat holds forth in **Manapany's** piano bar nightly, and there's a talented pianist at the **Guanahani** till midnight. The young and the hip gather after 10 at **Autour du Rocher** (tel. 590/27–60–73) in Lorient, a disco with billiards and backgammon. **La Licorne,** a newer disco also in Lorient, can be lively on weekends.

21 St. Eustatius

by Honey Naylor

The flight approach to this tiny Dutch island of St. Eustatius, commonly known as Statia (pronounced Staysha) in the Netherlands Antilles, is almost worth the visit itself. The plane circles The Quill, a 1,968-foot-high extinct volcano, which has an inviting rain forest within its crater. Here are giant elephant ears, ferns, flowers, wild orchids, fruit trees, wildlife, and birds hiding in the trees. The whole island is alive with untended greenery—bougainvillea, oleander, hibiscus, and alemanda.

During the American Revolutionary War, when the British blockaded the North American coast, food, arms, and other supplies for the American revolutionaries were diverted through the West Indies, notably through neutral Statia. (Benjamin Franklin had his mail routed through Statia to ensure its safe arrival in Europe.) On November 16, 1776, the brig-of-war *Andrew Doria*, commanded by Captain Isaiah Robinson of the Continental Navy, sailed into Statia's port flying the Stars and Stripes and fired a 13-gun salute to the Royal Netherlands standard. Governor Johannes de Graaff ordered the cannons of Fort Oranje to return the salute, and that first official acknowledgment of the new American flag by a foreign power earned Statia the nickname "America's Childhood Friend." Each year on November 16, Statian dignitaries in colonial-style garb participate in a colorful reenactment of the occasion at Fort Oranje; the festivities include parades, bands, picnics, and speeches.

Little 8-square-mile Statia, past which Columbus sailed in 1493, had prospered almost from the day the Dutch Zeelanders colonized it in 1636. In the 1700s, a double row of warehouses crammed with goods stretched for a mile along the bay, and there were sometimes as many as 200 ships tied up at the duty-free port. The island was called the "Emporium of the Western World" and "Golden Rock." There were almost 8,000 Statians on the island in the 1790s (today, there are about 1,700). Holland, England, and France fought one another for possession of the island, which changed hands 22 times. In 1816 it became a Dutch possession and has remained so to this day.

Four months after Statia's salute to the new American flag, Britain declared war on Holland, and on February 3, 1781, British Admiral George Rodney captured Dranjestad and proceeded to rob the island blind. Statia had aided, abetted, and acknowledged Britain's rebellious colony, and in revenge Rodney closed its shops, sealed its warehouses, auctioned off goods, and even confiscated the personal possessions of the islanders. For a month he kept the Dutch flag flying, thus luring and entrapping as many as 150 ships and confiscating their cargos. Less than a year later, having fattened his personal purse with about 4 million pounds sterling, Rodney departed. Statia bounced back, and flourished for another 10 years. Ironically, Statia's prosperity ended partly due to the success of the American Revolution. The island was no longer needed as a transshipment port, and its bustling economy gradually came to a stop.

Statia is in the Dutch Windward Triangle, 178 miles east of Puerto Rico and 35 miles south of St. Maarten. Oranjestad, the capital and only "city" (note quotes), is on the western side facing the Caribbean. The island is anchored at the north and the south by extinct volcanoes, like the Quill, which are separated by a central plain.

Statia is a wonderful playground for hikers and divers. There's as much to see underwater as on the island. Myriad ancient ships rest on the ocean floor alongside 18th-century warehouses that were slowly buried in the sea by storms. Much of the aboveground activity has to do with archaeology and restoration. Students from William and Mary's College of Archaeology converge on the island each summer; the University of Leyden in the Netherlands has a pre-Columbian program that includes the study of Statian Indian sites and artifacts; and the island's Historical Foundation is actively engaged in restoring Statian landmarks.

Most visitors will be content with a day visit from nearby St. Maarten, exploring some of the historical sights and enjoying a relaxed meal at the Old Gin House. Those who stay longer tend to be collectors of unspoiled islands with a need to relax and a taste for history.

Before You Go

Tourist Information
Contact the **Saba and St. Eustatius Tourist Information Office** (c/o Medhurst & Assoc., 271 Main St., Northport, NY 11768, tel. 516/261–7474, 212/936–0050, or 800/344–4606). You may also contact the **Tourist Board** on the island (Oranjestad, St. Eustatius, Netherlands Antilles, tel. 599/3–2433.) While telephone communications are good, it can take anywhere from a week to two months for mail to get through.

Arriving and Departing
By Plane
Windward Islands Airways (tel. 599/5–44230 or 599/5–44237) makes the 20-minute flight from St. Maarten four times a day, the 10-minute flight from Saba daily, and the 15-minute flight from St. Kitts daily. **LIAT** (tel. 809/462–0700) has twice-weekly flights from St. Kitts.

From the Airport
Planes put down at the **Franklin Delano Roosevelt Airport,** where taxis meet all flights and charge about $3 for the drive into town.

Passports and Visas
All visitors must have proof of citizenship. A passport is preferred, but a birth certificate or voter registration card will do. (A drivers license will *not* do). British citizens need a "British Visitors" passport. All visitors need a return or ongoing ticket.

Customs and Duties
There is no customs, as Statia is a free port, so you don't have to worry about documentation for expensive possessions.

Language
Statia's official language is Dutch; it's used on government documents. However, everyone speaks English and Dutch is taught as a second language in the schools, and street signs are in both Dutch and English.

Further Reading
St. Maarten bookstores carry Dr. J. Hartog's book *St. Maarten, Saba and St. Eustatius*. At the Statia Historical Foundation you can get a copy of *St. Eustatius—A Short History,* by Ypie Attema.

Staying in St. Eustatius

Important Addresses
Tourist Office: The **St. Eustatius Tourist Office** is at the entrance to Fort Oranje (3 Fort Oranjestraat, tel. 599/3–2433). Office hours are weekdays 8–noon and 1–5.

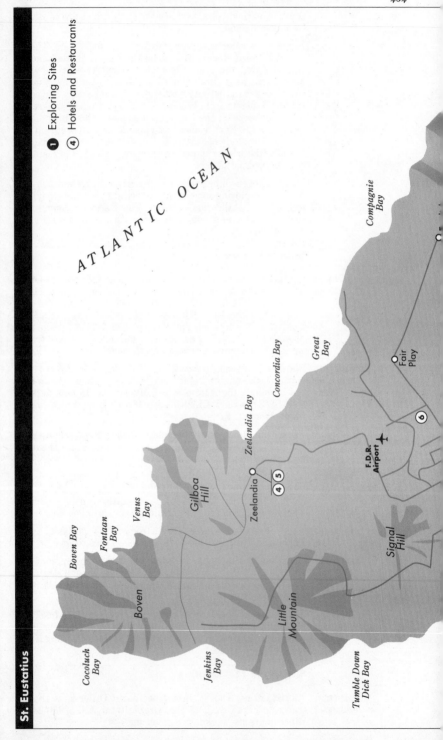

● Exploring Sites

④ Hotels and Restaurants

ATLANTIC OCEAN

Boven Bay

Cocoluch
Bay

Boven

Fontaan
Bay

Venus
Bay

Jenkins
Bay

Gilboa
Hill

Little
Mountain

Zeelandia

Zeelandia Bay

④ ⑤

F.D.R.
Airport

Signal
Hill

Tumble Down
Dick Bay

Concordia Bay

Great
Bay

⑥

Fair
Play

Compagnie
Bay

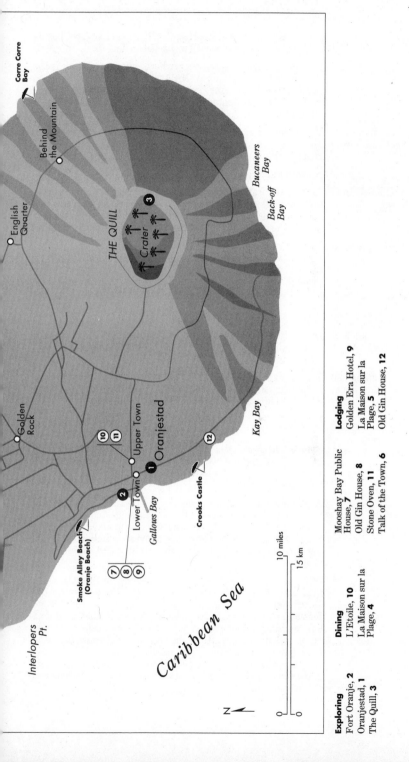

Caribbean Sea

Interlopers Pt.

Corre Corre Bay

Behind the Mountain

English Quarter

Golden Rock

THE QUILL

Crater

Bucaneers Bay

Back-off Bay

Kay Bay

Crooks Castle

Oranjestad

Upper Town

Lower Town

Gallows Bay

Smoke Alley Beach (Oranje Beach)

N

0   10 miles

0   15 km

Exploring
Fort Oranje, **2**
Oranjestad, **1**
The Quill, **3**

Dining
L'Etoile, **10**
La Maison sur la Plage, **4**

Mooshay Bay Public House, **7**
Old Gin House, **8**
Stone Oven, **11**
Talk of the Town, **6**

Lodging
Golden Era Hotel, **9**
La Maison sur la Plage, **5**
Old Gin House, **12**

Emergencies	**Police:** call 599/3–2333.
	Hospitals: Princess Beatrix Hospital (25 Prinsesweg, tel. 599/3–2211) has a full-time licensed physician on duty.
Currency	U.S. dollars are accepted everywhere, but legal tender is the Netherlands Antilles florin (NAf). Florins are also referred to as guilders. The exchange rate fluctuates, but is about NAf1.80 to U.S.$1. Prices quoted here are in U.S. dollars unless noted otherwise.
Taxes and Service Charges	Hotels collect a 5% government tax and a 5% electricity tax. The departure tax is $5 for destinations outside the Netherlands Antilles.
	All hotels and restaurants add a 10%–15% service charge.
Guided Tours	All seven of Statia's taxis are available for island tours. Some of them provide an audiocassette tape, which is otherwise available from the Tourist Office or from the Historical Foundation (*see* Exploring, below). A full day's outing costs $30 per vehicle.
Getting Around	To explore the island (and there isn't very much), car rentals are available through the **Avis** outlet at the airport (tel. 599/3–2421) at a cost of about $30 per day. Rentals are also available through the island's seven taxi drivers. Statia's roads are pocked with potholes and the going is slow and bumpy. Cattle have the right of way.
Telephones and Mail	Statia has microwave telephone service to all parts of the world. To dial Statia from the United States, dial 011–599/3 + local number. Airmail letters to the United States are NAf1.30; postcards NAf.60.
Opening and Closing Times	Most offices are open weekdays 8–noon and 1–4 or 5. **Barclays Bank** (the only bank on the island) is open Monday–Thursday 8:30–1; Friday 8:30–1 and 4–5.

Beaches

Smoke Alley Beach (also called Oranje Beach) is a favorite with locals. The beige and black-sand beach is on the Caribbean, off Lower Town, and is relatively deserted until late afternoon when the locals arrive.

A 30-minute hike down an easy marked trail off Mountain Road will bring you to **Corre Corre Bay** and its gold-sand cove. On the Atlantic side, especially around Concordia Bay, the surf is rough and there is sometimes a dangerous undertow, making beaches in this area better for strolling and sunning than swimming.

A big deal on the beaches here is searching for Statia's famed blue glass beads. Manufactured in the 17th century by the Dutch West Indies Company, the blue glass beads were traded for rum, slaves, cotton, and tobacco. Although they are found only on Statia, some researchers believe that beads like these were traded for Manhattan. The area around **Crooks Castle** on the leeward side, north of Oranjestad, seems to yield the most treasure, although they are getting harder to find. (Glass beads in the sand should tell you something about running barefoot on the beach.)

Exploring St. Eustatius

Numbers in the margin correspond with points of interest on the St. Eustatius map.

Oranjestad, Statia's capital and only town, sits on the western coast facing the Caribbean. It's a split-level town: Upper Town and Lower Town. History buffs will enjoy poking around the ancient Dutch colonial buildings, which are being restored by the Historical Foundation, while hikers will want to head for the hills of The Quill. Both Oranjestad and Lower Town are easily explored on foot.

Oranjestad First stop is the **Tourist Office,** which is right at the entrance to
① Fort Oranje. You can pick up maps, brochures, and friendly advice, as well as a copy of the Historical Foundation's eight-page *Walking Tour* (50¢) and a listing of 12 marked hiking trails. You can also pick up the audiocassette tour, produced by the Historical Foundation in five languages, and available free on loan.

When you leave the Tourist Office, you will be at the entrance
② to **Fort Oranje.** With its three bastions, the fort has clutched these cliffs since 1636. In 1976, Statia participated in the U.S. Bicentennial celebration by restoring the old fort, and now there are gleaming black cannons pointing out over the ramparts. In the parade grounds a plaque, presented in 1939 by Franklin D. Roosevelt, reads, "Here the sovereignty of the United States of America was first formally acknowledged to a national vessel by a foreign official." Various government buildings, including the post office, are within the fort, and restoration continues.

From the fort, cross over to Wilhelminaweg (Wilhelmina Way) in the center of Upper Town. The **St. Eustatius Historical Foundation Museum** is in the Doncker/de Graaff house, a lovely building with slim columns and a high gallery. British Admiral Rodney is believed to have lived here while he was stealing everything in sight. The house, acquired by the foundation in 1983 and completely restored, is Statia's most important intact 18th-century dwelling. Exhibits trace the island's history from the 6th century to the present and among the displays are Indian artifacts and a complete Amerindian skeleton. The eight-page *Walking Tour*, postcards, souvenirs, and books about Statia are sold here, and the foundation's audiocassette tour is available here also. *12 Van Tonningen weg, no phone. Admission: $1 adults, 50¢ children. Open weekdays 9–5.*

Return to Fort Oranjestraat (Fort Orange St.) and turn left. Continue to 4 **Fort Oranjestraat,** at the corner of Kerkweg (Church Way). The big yellow house, with a stone foundation, shingled walls, and gingerbread trim, is typical of the houses built in the West Indies around the turn of the century. Just behind it is **Three Widows Corner**, a tropical courtyard where you'll see two more examples of Statian architecture in a town house and another gingerbread house.

Now head west down Kerkweg to the edge of the cliff, where you'll find the **Dutch Reformed Church,** built in 1775. Once a ship's landmark, its square tower now houses a Historical Foundation information center. Ancient tales can be read on the gravestones in the 18th-century cemetery adjacent to the church.

Continue on Kerkweg and take the next two left turns onto Synagogepad (Synagogue Path) to **Honen Dalim** ("She Who Is Charitable to the Poor"), one of the Caribbean's oldest synagogues. It dates from 1738 and is now in ruins but slated for restoration.

❸ The Quill, the volcanic cone rising in the northern sector, is 3 miles south of Oranjestad on the main road *(see* Hiking, below).

Time Out The **Kool Corner,** directly opposite the Tourist Office, is a cool spot to have a beer and shoot the breeze. It's also the place where locals pick up daily fresh-baked bread. *Fort Oranjestraat, no phone. Open daily 8:30 AM–10 PM.*

Follow Prinsesweg back to the main square and zigzag down the cobblestone Fort Road to Lower Town. Warehouses and shops that in the 18th century were piled high with European imports are now either abandoned or simply used to store local fishermen's equipment, but the restoration of the 18th-century cotton mill on the land side of Bay Road is impressive. The palms, flowering shrubs, and park benches along the water's edge are the work of the Historical Foundation members. As you walk along the water, imagine the time when this town was the center of commerce in the Caribbean.

Time Out **Old Gin House** (Lower Town, tel. 599/3–2319) is one of the nicest places on the island to rest, have a drink, or lunch.

Participant Sports

Hiking Trails range from the easy to the "Watch out!" The big thrill here is The Quill, the 1,968-foot extinct volcano with its craterful of rain forest. The Tourist Office has a list of 12 marked trails and can put you in touch with a guide (whose fee will be about $20).

Scuba Diving If you've never gone to an undersea supermarket, here's your chance. The "supermarket" is actually two parallel shipwrecks less than 50 yards apart. It's but one of the many wrecks and 18th-century submerged seaports you can see. **Surfside Statia,** (tel. 800/468–1708), a fully equipped dive shop offering certification courses, is operated by Americans Mike Guderian and Joe Donahue out of a warehouse next to the Old Gin House.

Snorkeling Crooks Point has several stands of pillar coral, giant yellow seafans, and seawhips. Jenkins Bay is another favorite with snorkelers. For equipment rental, contact **Surfside Statia** *(see* Scuba Diving, above).

Tennis There's a lone tennis court at the **Community Center** that's even lighted at night. There are changing rooms, but you'll have to bring your own racquets and balls. Cost is $2 (check with the Tourist Office for more information).

Dining

The variety of cuisine here is surprising, given the size of the island. Besides the traditional West Indian fare, you can find French and Italian cuisine.

The most highly recommended restaurants are indicated by a star ★.

Category	Cost*
Expensive	$25–$35
Moderate	$15–$25
Inexpensive	under $15

per person, excluding drinks and service

★ **La Maison sur la Plage.** The view is of the Atlantic, the cloths are crisp and white, and the fare is French. For dinner, openers include fish soup and quiche Lorraine. Among the entrees are duck breast with green-peppercorn sauce and entrecôte forestière (sirloin with mushrooms, cream, and red wine). Try the crepes à l'orange for dessert. *Zeelandia, tel. 599/3–2256. Reservations required. AE. Expensive.*

★ **Mooshay Bay Public House.** Co-owner Marty Scofield's recipes have been praised by *Gourmet* magazine, and with justification. Your four-course, fixed-price feast likely will begin with warm grapefruit soup or a salad of smoked red snapper. The main course could be chateaubriand Dijonnaise, roast duck with sweet-and-sour sauce, or lobster mousse with caviar and horseradish. Two wines are included with the dinner. The setting is elegantly rustic, with old-brick walls, candlelight, pewter, and gleaming crystal. *Old Gin House, Lower Town, Oranjestad, tel. 599/3–2319. Reservations required. AE, DC, MC, V. Expensive.*

★ **Old Gin House.** Dining is delightful on the oceanside terrace of this hotel. The menu includes lobster Antillean (lobster chunks stewed with onions, red wine, pernod, and a dash of hot pepper), plain burgers and dillyburgers (with sour cream and dill sauce), lobster salad, and sandwiches. *Old Gin House, Lower Town, tel. 599/3–2319. Reservations advised. AE, DC, MC, V. Moderate.*

Talk of the Town. The cuisine here is West Indian with a touch of Dutch, a soupçon of French, and a smattering of Italian. Have the fish soup for starters, then choose from Caribbean red snapper, spaghetti Bolognese, or beef Stroganoff. *On the airport road, Golden Rock, tel. 599/3–2236. Reservations required. No credit cards. Moderate.*

★ **L'Etoile.** West Indian dishes such as spicy stuffed land crab and deep-fried meat turnovers are prepared by Caren Henriquez in a simple snack bar/restaurant. You can also get hot dogs, hamburgers, and spareribs. *Prinsesweg, Upper Town, Oranjestad, tel. 599/3–2299. No credit cards. Inexpensive.*

Stone Oven. West Indian specialties such as "goat water" (stew) are featured here. You can eat either indoors in the little house or outside on the palm-fringed patio. *16A Feaschweb, Upper Town, Oranjestad, tel. 599/3–2247. Reservations required. No credit cards. Inexpensive.*

Lodging

There are only three full-service hotels on the island, and a few apartment rentals.

The most highly recommended lodgings are indicated by a star ★.

Category	Cost*
Very Expensive	over $100
Expensive	$80–$100
Moderate	$60–$80
Inexpensive	under $60

All prices are for a standard double room for two, excluding 10% tax and a 15% service charge.

Hotels
★

Old Gin House. American expatriates Marty Scofield and John May have fashioned a comfortable inn out of the ruins of an 18th-century cotton-gin factory and warehouse. The cluster of buildings includes one that is two stories high, its bougainvillea-swathed double balconies overlooking a secluded tropical courtyard and pool; the highly acclaimed Mooshay Bay Publick House; a terrace restaurant and bar by the sea; and an additional six rooms in a two-story building with high ceilings, custom-made furnishings, and balconies that jut out over the ocean. The rooms are spacious and individually decorated with antique furnishings. There's a gallery with a library and lounge for cards and backgammon, and a cozy pub with beam ceilings and an 18th-century Bristol clock. *Box 172, Oranjestad, tel. 599/3–2319 or 800/223–5581 in USA. 20 rooms with bath. Facilities: pool, 2 restaurants, bar, lounge, library, boutique. AE, DC, MC, V. Very Expensive.*

Golden Era Hotel. This is a harborfront hotel whose rooms are neat, small, air-conditioned, and motel-modern. All have little terraces, but only half have a full or partial view of the sea. The other rooms look out over concrete or down on the roof of the restaurant. In the coffee-shop-style restaurant, fluorescent lights shine on curried dishes, fried chicken, spareribs, and conch and dumplings—all reasonably priced. Things pick up on Sundays, when a live band holds forth. *Box 109, Oranjestad, tel. 599/3–2345 or 800/223–6510. 19 rooms, 1 suite; all with private bath. Facilities: restaurant and bar. MC, V. Moderate–Expensive.*

La Maison sur la Plage. The plage is a 2-mile crescent of gray sand slapped by the wild waters of the Atlantic. The undertow here can be dangerous, so you should do your swimming in the pool. A cozy lobby has rattan furnishings, a checkerboard on the coffee table, and shelves filled with books. There's a stone-and-wood bar, and a *très* French dining room bordered by a trellis and greenery. French-born Michelle Greca's *maison* (house) is actually eight Spartan cottages, where you've a choice of twin, double, or king-size beds. Each cottage has a bath and a private veranda, where a Continental breakfast is served. The most active thing in this isolated area is the Atlantic. *Box 157, Zeelandia, tel. 599/3–2256 or 800/845–9504. 10 rooms with bath. Facilities: pool, restaurant, bar, and lounge. AE. Moderate.*

Apartment Rentals

Statia has only a handful of apartments, and the only luxury accommodation is **Cherry Tree Villa** (tel. 800/325–2222 or 813/787–2579), which sprawls over 17 lush acres. The moderately priced, two-bedroom villa sleeps four, and its luxe touches include a Cuisinart, dishwasher, microwave oven, outdoor Jacuzzi facing the sea, and use of a car. A Hobie Cat and a 32-foot skippered yacht are available for an extra charge.

The **Henriquez Apartments** (tel. 599/3–2299), near the airport, are inexpensive studios with carpeted floors, small refrigerators, TVs, fans, coffeemakers, private baths, and either two double or twin beds. There's an outdoor patio with a barbecue pit and a meeting room that can accommodate 12. Check with the Tourist Office for information about these and other apartment rentals in Oranjestad.

Nightlife

Statia's three local bands divide their time between gigs at the occasional Saturday-night dances at the **Community Center** *(see* Exploring, above); for alfresco soirees at the **Chinese Bar and Restaurant** *(see* Dining, above); and on Sunday nights at the **Golden Era** *(see* Lodging, above). An alternative to all that activity is to just hang out at the **Kool Corner** till it closes *(see* Exploring, above).

22 St. Kitts

by Honey Naylor

Tiny though it is, St. Kitts, the first English settlement in the Leeward Islands, crams some stunning scenery into its 65 square miles. St. Kitts is fertile and lush with tropical flora and has some fascinating natural and historical attractions: a rain forest, replete with waterfalls, thick vines, and secret trails; a central mountain range dominated by the 3,792-foot Mt. Liamuiga whose crater has been long dormant; and Brimstone Hill, the Caribbean's most impressive fortress, which was known in the 17th century as the Gibraltar of the West Indies. The island is home to 35,000 people and hosts some 60,000 visitors annually.

Until 1988, the island's official name was St. Christopher (Columbus named it after his patron saint), and its nickname was St. Kitts. Since everybody called it by its nickname anyway, the island officially changed its name to St. Kitts. The island is known as the Mother Colony of the West Indies, because it was from here that the English settlers sailed to Antigua, Barbuda, Tortola, and Montserrat, and the French dispatched colonizing parties to Martinique, Guadeloupe, St. Martin, St. Barts, Desirade, and Les Saintes. The French, who, inexplicably, brought a bunch of monkeys with them, arrived on St. Kitts a few years after the British.

As was the case on many Caribbean islands during the 17th and 18th centuries, the British and the French fell to squabbling. They joined forces long enough to massacre the cannibalistic Carib Indians and to reach an agreement by which the French held the north and south of the island and the British controlled the midsection, after which everybody (except the Caribs) set about growing tobacco, ginger, indigo, cotton, and, later, sugar. Slaves were brought in from Africa, magnificent plantation homes were built, and sugar became the island's main export.

Things never were that friendly between the English and the French, and in the late 18th century, the French lay siege to Brimstone Hill and took it. Ultimately, the terms of the Treaty of Versailles in 1783 gave the British full control of the island. In 1967, St. Kitts and Nevis—together with Anguilla—became a self-governing state, from which Anguilla seceded later in the same year. St. Kitts-Nevis gained full independence from Britain in 1983.

The shape of St. Kitts has been variously compared to a whale, a cricket bat, and a guitar. It's roughly oval shape, 19 miles long and 6 miles wide, with a narrow peninsula trailing off toward Nevis, 2 miles across the strait. It's one of the Leeward Islands of the Lesser Antilles, in the eastern Caribbean.

As rich in history as it is fertile and lush with tropical flora, St. Kitts is just beginning to develop its tourism industry, and this quiet member of the Leeward group has that rare combination of natural and historic attractions and fine sailing, island hopping, and water-sports options offshore.

Before You Go

Tourist Information
Contact the **St. Kitts & Nevis Tourist Board** (414 E. 75th St., New York, NY 10021, tel. 212/535–1234), **St. Kitts & Nevis Tourist Office** (33 Niagara St., Toronto M5V 1C2, Canada, tel. 416/362–9930), and **Rosamunde Bern Association** (15 Wardour

St. Kitts

① Exploring Sites

⑧ Hotels and Restaurants

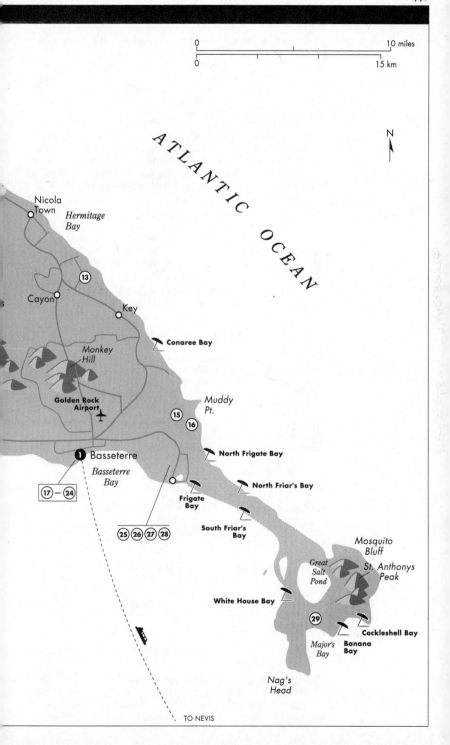

0   10 miles

0   15 km

N

ATLANTIC OCEAN

Nicola
Town

*Hermitage
Bay*

(13)

Cayon

Key

Monkey
Hill

Conaree Bay

**Golden Rock
Airport**

*Muddy
Pt.*

(15)

(16)

(1) Basseterre

North Frigate Bay

*Basseterre
Bay*

North Friar's Bay

(17) — (24)

**Frigate
Bay**

(25)(26)(27)(28)

**South Friar's
Bay**

*Mosquito
Bluff*

*Great
Salt
Pond*

*St. Anthonys
Peak*

White House Bay

(29)

Cockleshell Bay

*Major's
Bay*

**Banana
Bay**

*Nag's
Head*

TO NEVIS

Mews, d'Arblay St., London W1V, 3FF, United Kingdom, tel. 01/437–9475).

| **Arriving and Departing** *By Plane* | At press time, the only international carrier with direct service from the United States was **BWIA** (tel. 800/327–7401), flying nonstop from New York, Miami, and, during high season only, from Toronto. **American** (tel. 800/433–7300), **Delta**, (tel. 800/221–1212) and **Pan Am** (tel. 800/221–1111) fly from the United States to Antigua, St. Croix, St. Thomas, St. Maarten, and San Juan, Puerto Rico, where connections can be made on regional car-riers such as **American Eagle** (tel. 800/433–7300), **LIAT** (tel. 809/462–0701), **Windward Island Airways** (tel. 809/465–0810), and **Air BVI** (tel. 800/468–2485). LIAT has two flights daily to and from Nevis. **British Airways** (tel. 800/247–9297) flies from London to Antigua, **Air Canada** (tel. 800/422–6232) from Toronto to Antigua, and American from Montreal to San Juan. |

From the Airport You'll arrive at Golden Rock Airport, where taxis meet every flight. The taxis are unmetered, but fixed rates are posted at the airport and at the jetty. The fare from the airport to the closest hotel in Basseterre is E.C.$10 (U.S. $3.70); to the farthest point, E.C.$474 (U.S. $17.40). Be sure to clarify whether the rate quoted is in E.C. or U.S. dollars.

By Boat The 150-passenger government-operated ferry MV *Caribe Queen* makes the 45-minute crossing to Nevis daily except Thursday, which is maintenance day, and Sunday. The schedule is a bit erratic, so confirm departure times with the tourist office. Round-trip fare is U.S.$7.

Passports and Visas U.S. and Canadian citizens need only produce proof of citizenship (voter registration card or birth certificate; a driver's license will not suffice). British citizens must have a passport; visas are not required. All visitors must have a return or ongoing ticket.

Customs and Duties This is a duty-free port, and you can bring in any items of a personal nature, including 200 cigarettes or 50 cigars or ½ pound of tobacco. Stern-faced customs officials will look through your luggage to ascertain if your personal items include coke or crack.

Language English is spoken here with a West Indian lilt.

Precautions Visitors, especially women, are warned not to go jogging on long, lonely roads.

Staying in St. Kitts

Important Addresses Tourist Information: The **St. Kitts Tourist Board** (Church St., Basseterre, tel. 809/465–4040 or 2620) is open Monday–Saturday 8 AM–noon and 1–5 PM. The **St. Kitts–Nevis Hotel Association** (tel. 809/465–2380) is in the same building and keeps the same hours.

Emergencies **Police:** Call 809/465–99.

Hospitals: There is a 24-hour emergency room at the **Joseph N. France General Hospital** (Basseterre, tel. 809/465–2551).

Pharmacies: In Basseterre, **Skerritt's Drug Store** (Fort St., tel. 809/465–2083) is open Monday–Saturday 8–5 and can provide 24-hour prescription service. **City Drug** (locations on Fort St., Basseterre, and at Sun 'n' Sand, Frigate Bay, tel. 809/465–

2156) is open Monday–Wednesday and Friday 8–7; Thursday 8–5, Saturday 8–8, Sunday and holidays 8 AM–10 AM.

Currency Legal tender is the Eastern Caribbean (E.C.) dollar (often called "beewees.") At press time, the rate of exchange was E.C.$2.65 or E.C.$2.70 to U.S.$1. U.S. dollars are accepted practically everywhere, but you'll almost always get change in E.C. Prices quoted here are in U.S. dollars unless noted otherwise. Most large hotels, restaurants, and shops accept major credit cards, but small inns and shops usually do not. It's always a good idea to check current credit-card policies before turning up with only plastic in your pocket.

Taxes and Service Charges Hotels collect a 7% government tax. The departure tax is $5. (There is no departure tax from St. Kitts to Nevis.)

All hotels add a 10% service charge to your bill. In restaurants, a tip of 10%–15% is appropriate.

Guided Tours **Tropical Tours** (tel. 809/465–4167) can run you around the island and take you to the rain forest. **Delise Walwyn** (tel. 809/465–2631) also offers a variety of island tours. **Kriss Tours** specializes in half- and full-day treks into the rain forest (tel. 809/465–4042).

Getting Around
Taxis Taxi tours of the island take about three hours and cost about U.S.$35.

Buses A privately owned minibus circles the island. Check with the tourist office about schedules.

Rental Cars and Scooters You'll need a local driver's license, which you can get by presenting yourself, your valid driver's license, and E.C.$30 (U.S.$12) at the police station, Cayon Street, Basseterre. Rentals are available at **Budget** (tel. 809/465–4020) and **Caines** (tel. 809/465–2366). Delise Walwyn (tel. 809/465–2631) operates **Economy Car,** which also rents scooter bikes. **TDC Rentals** (tel. 809/465–2991) can put you in minimokes, as well as cars. Car rentals run about U.S.$35 per day. At press time, the price of gas was U.S.$1.72 per gallon. Remember to drive on the left!

Telephones and Mail To call St. Kitts from the United States, dial area code 809, then access code 465 and the local number. Telephone communications, both on the island and with the United States, are as clear as a bell, and you can dial long distance direct. To make an intraisland call, simply dial the seven-digit number.

Airmail letters to the United States and Canada cost E.C.$.60 per half ounce; postcards require E.C.$.35. Mail takes at least 7–10 days to reach the United States. St. Kitts and Nevis each issues its own stamps, but each also honors the other's. The beautiful stamps are collector's items, and you may have a hard time pasting them on postcards.

Opening and Closing Times Shops are open Monday–Saturday 8 AM–noon and 1–4 PM. Some shops close earlier on Thursday. Banking hours are Monday–Thursday 8 AM–1 PM; Friday 8 AM–1 PM and 3–5 PM. **St. Kitts & Nevis National Bank** is also open Saturday 8:30 AM–11 AM.

Beaches

All beaches on the island are free and open to the public, even those occupied by hotels. The powdery white-sand beaches are all at the southern end of the island and on the peninsula.

The beaches on the peninsula, accessible only by boat, are secluded, do not have facilities, and are used primarily by locals. Few tourists know about them, but they are among the best on the island.

The twin beaches of **Banana Bay** and **Cockleshell Bay,** which together cover almost 2 miles, are anything but deserted. The OTI Banana Bay Beach Hotel, a fine cooling-off place, sits between the two. Other good peninsula beaches are **Friars Bay** (on both the Atlantic and the Caribbean sides) and **White House Bay.**

North of Banana Bay, the beaches of **Frigate Bay** are talcum-fine. **North Frigate Bay,** on the Atlantic, is 4 miles wide and a favorite with horseback riders *(see* Participant Sports, below).

Beaches elsewhere on the island are of gray-black volcanic sand. **Conaree Bay** on the Atlantic side is a narrow strip of gray-black sand, where the water is good for body surfing (no facilities). Snorkeling and windsurfing are good at **Dieppe Bay,** a black sand beach on the north coast, where the Golden Lemon Hotel is located *(see* Participant Sports, below, for equipment rental).

Exploring St. Kitts

Numbers in the margin correspond with points of interest on the St. Kitts map.

The capital city of Basseterre, set in the southern part of the island, was once held by the French, hence its French name. It's an easily walkable town, graced with tall palms and small, beautifully maintained houses and buildings of stone and pastel-colored wood.

Basseterre
❶ Your first stop is at the **St. Kitts Tourist Board** (Church St.) to pick up maps. Turn left when you leave there and walk past the colonial building that houses Government Headquarters and turn right on Princes Street. A two-block walk will bring you to the octagonal **Circus,** which contains a fanciful memorial to Thomas Berkeley, a former president of the Legislative Assembly. Duty-free shops fill the streets and courtyards leading off from around the Circus. The **St. Kitts Philatelic Bureau** (open weekdays 8–4) is nearby on the second floor of the Social Security Building (Bay St.).

The colorful **Bay Street produce** market is open on weekends only. On the waterfront, next to the Treasury Building, is the air-conditioned **Shoreline Plaza,** with its tax-free shops, and nearby is the landing for the ferries to Nevis.

Time Out **Q. T.'s Delis** (Shoreline Plaza, tel. 809/465–3424) is a delightful spot for a drink and a light snack right on the waterfront.

From the Circus, Bank Street leads to **Independence Square,** with lovely gardens on the site of a former slave market. The square is surrounded on three sides by Georgian buildings, including the popular **Georgian House** restaurant *(see* Dining, below).

Walk up West Square Street, away from the bay, to Cayon Street, turn left, and walk one block to **St. George's Anglican Church.** This handsome stone building with crenelated tower was built by the French in 1670 and called Nôtre Dame. The British burned it down in 1706 and rebuilt it four years later, naming it after the patron saint of England. Since then, it has suffered fire, earthquake, and hurricanes and was once again rebuilt in 1859.

Elsewhere on the Island Main Road traces the perimeter of the island, circling the central mountain ranges. Head west on it out of Basseterre to explore the rest of St. Kitts. For the first few miles, you'll be driving through gently rolling hills, past old sugar plantations and ancient stone fences covered with vines, and through tiny villages with tiny houses of stone and weathered wood.

You won't have any trouble identifying the villages as you come across them; small white welcome signs are posted outside each village, placed by members of the 4-H Club. Just outside Challengers is **Bloody Point,** where in 1629, French and British soldiers joined forces to repel a mass attack by the Caribs. The scenery on the drive into **Old Road Town** is spectacular.

From Old Road Town, take the road through the rain forest to visit **Romney Manor,** where batik fabrics are printed at **Caribelle Batik.** (*see* Shopping, below). The house is set in 6 acres of gardens, with exotic flowers, an old bell tower, and a 350-year-old Saman tree (sometimes called a rain tree). Inside, you can watch artisans hand-printing fabrics by the 2,500-year-old Indonesian process known as *batik.*

The village after Old Road Town is **Middle Island,** where Thomas Warner, the "gentleman of London" who brought the first settlers here, died in 1648 and is buried beneath a green gazebo in the churchyard of **St. Thomas Church.**

The road continues through the village of Halfway Tree to **Brimstone Hill,** the most important historic site on St. Kitts. From the parking area, it's a long walk to the 38-acre fortress, but the exercise is well worth it if military history and spectacular views interest you. After routing the French in 1689, the English erected a battery on top of Brimstone Hill, and by 1736, there were 49 guns in the fortress. In 1782, the French lay siege to the fortress, which was defended by 350 militia and 600 regular troops of the Royal Scots and East Yorkshires. A plaque in the old stone wall marks the place where the fort was breached. When the English finally surrendered, the French allowed them to march from the fort in full formation out of respect for their bravery. (The English afforded the French the same honor when they surrendered the fort a mere year later.) A hurricane did extensive damage to the fortress in 1843, and in 1852 it was evacuated and dismantled.

The citadel has been partially reconstructed and its guns remounted. You can see what remains of the officers' quarters, the redoubts, barracks, the ordnance store, and the cemetery. Its museums display, among other things, weaponry, uniforms, photographs, and old newspapers. In 1985, Queen Elizabeth visited Brimstone Hill and officially opened it as part of a national park. There's a splendid view from here that includes Montserrat and Nevis to the southeast, Saba and Statia to the northwest, and St. Barts and St. Maarten to the north. *Main Rd., Brimstone Hill. Admission: $2. Open Mon.–Sat. 9–6, Sun. 9–4.*

Time Out	**J's Place** (tel. 809/465–6264) across from the entrance to the fort is ideal for a drink, a sandwich, or a full meal.

Continuing on through seas of sugarcane, past breadfruit trees **❻** and old stone walls, you'll come to the town of **Sandy Point Town.** The houses here are West Indian–style raised cottages. The **Roman Catholic Church** has lovely stained-glass windows.

Farther along, just outside the village of **Newton Ground,** are the remains of an old sugar mill and some ancient coconut palms. Outside the village of **St. Paul's** is a road that leads to **Rawlins Plantation,** a restored sugar plantation that's popular for dining and lodging. The fishing town of **Dieppe Bay** is at the northernmost point of the island. Its tiny black-sand beach is backed by the **Golden Lemon,** one of the Caribbean's most fa-**❼** mous inns (*see* Lodging, below). The **Black Rocks** on the Atlantic coast just outside the town of Sadlers, in Sandy Bay, are lava deposits, spat into the sea ages ago when the island's volcano erupted. They have since been molded into fanciful shapes by centuries of pounding surf. The drive back to Basseterre around the other side of the island is a pleasant one, through small, neat villages with centuries-old stone churches and pastel-colored cottages.

Participant Sports

Boating	Hobie Cats can be rented at **Pelican Cove Marina** (tel. 809/465–2754 or 465–2380).
Deep-Sea Fishing	Angle for yellowtail snapper, wahoo, mackerel, dolphin, and barracuda, with **Tropical Tours** (tel. 809/465–4167) or **Pelican Cove Marina.**
Golf	There is an 18-hole championship course in the Frigate Bay area (Tourist Board, tel. 809/465–4040).
Hiking	Trails in the central mountains vary from easy to don't-try-it-by-yourself. Monkey Hill and Verchild's Mountain are not difficult, although the Verchild's climb will take the better part of a day. Don't attempt Mt. Liamuiga without a guide. You'll start at Belmont Estates on horseback, then proceed on foot to the lip of the crater at 2,600 feet. You can go down into the crater, clinging to vines and roots. **Kriss Tours** (tel. 809/465–4042) takes small groups into the crater and to Dos d'Anse Pond on Verchild's Mountain.
Horseback Riding	Frigate Bay and Conaree Beach are great for riding. Guides from **The Stable** (tel. 809/465–3226) will lead you at a more leisurely gait into the hills.
Scuba Diving and Snorkeling	Kenneth Samuel of **Kenneth's Dive Centre** (tel. 809/465–2670) is an independent dive operator who takes small groups of divers with C cards to nearby reefs. Equipment, rentals, and trips are also available through **Caribbean Watersports** (tel. 809/465–8050) and **Fisherman's Wharf** (tel. 809/465–2754).
Sea Excursions	**Tropical Tours** (tel. 809/465–4167) offers moonlight cruises on the 52-foot catamaran *Cileca III* and glass-bottom-boat tours. The **OTI** (tel. 809/465–2754) has a fleet of boats, based at Fisherman's Wharf, which run daily shuttles to Banana Bay on the peninsula. **Kantours** (tel. 809/465–2098) takes you on a Banana Bay Beach Safari for a day of snorkeling and swimming and an evening barbecue.

Tennis There are three lighted courts at **Jack Tar Village/Royal St. Kitts** (tel. 809/465–2651) and a lighted grass court at **Rawlins Plantation** (tel. 809/465–6221).

Waterskiing and Windsurfing Rentals are available at **Fisherman's Wharf** (tel. 809/465–2754).

Spectator Sports

Cricket matches are played in Warner Park from January to July; **soccer** from July to December, **softball** from January to August. Contact the Tourist Board (tel. 809/465–4040) for schedules.

Shopping

St. Kitts has limited shopping, but there are a few duty-free shops where you can find some good buys in jewelry, watches, perfume, china, and crystal. Among the island crafts, the best known are the batik fabrics, scarves, caftans, and wall hangings of Caribelle Batik. There are also locally produced jams, jellies, herb teas, and handicrafts of local shell, straw, and coconut.

Shopping Districts Most shopping plazas are near The Circus in downtown Basseterre. Some shops have outlets in other areas, particularly in Dieppe Bay. **T.D.C. Plaza** is just off The Circus in downtown Basseterre. **Shoreline Plaza** is next to the Treasury Building, right on the waterfront in Basseterre. **Palms Arcade** is on Fort Street, also near The Circus.

Good Buys **T.D.C.** (T.D.C. Plaza, on bank St., tel. 809/465–2511) carries fine china and crystal, along with cameras and other imports.

Slice of the Lemon (Palms Arcade and Dieppe Bay, tel. 809/465–2889) carries fine perfumes but is better known for its elegant jewelry.

Caribelle Batik (Romney Manor, tel. 809/465–6253), **The Kittitian Kitchen** (Palms Arcade, Basseterre, and at the Golden Lemon, Dieppe Bay, no phone), and **Palms Crafts** (also in Palms Arcade, no phone) all sell that special something (island crafts, jams and jellies, batik) to take home as gifts and souvenirs.

Dining

St. Kitts restaurants range from funky little beachfront bistros to elegant plantation dining rooms.

The most highly recommended restaurants are indicated by a star ★.

Category	Cost*
Expensive	over $25
Moderate	$15–$25
Inexpensive	under $15

Per person, excluding drinks and service. There is no sales tax on St. Kitts.

The Georgian House. Dining is by candlelight in a restored, antiques-filled British manor house. There is a changing à la carte menu that might include cucumber soup, roast leg of lamb, and lobster Thermidor. *S. Independence Sq., Basseterre, tel. 809/465–4049. Dress: casually elegant. Reservations advised. No credit cards. Closed Sun. Expensive.*

★ **Frigate Bay Beach Hotel.** The piña coladas are sensational in this split-level restaurant overlooking the hotel pool. Candlelit dinners are romantic and dishes are beautifully presented. The à la carte menu includes curried chicken with rice, lobster with lemon butter, and shrimp Creole. *Frigate Bay Beach Hotel, tel. 809/465–8935. Reservations suggested. AE, MC, V. Expensive.*

The Patio. Owner Peter Mallalieu prepares six-course meals, by reservation only, in his flower-filled home. The fixed-price feast includes wine and liqueurs. Fresh seafood and vegetables are prepared to order, and the menu changes nightly. *Frigate Bay Beach, tel. 809/465–8666. Reservations required. No credit cards. Expensive.*

★ **The Golden Lemon.** Owner Arthur Leaman creates the recipes himself for the West Indian, Continental, and American cuisine served in his hotel, and he never repeats them more than once in a two-week period. The patio, lush with bougainvillea and ferns, is a popular spot for Sunday brunch, which can include banana pancakes, rum beef stew, and spaghetti with white clam sauce. *Dieppe Bay, tel. 809/465–7260. Dress: casually elegant. Reservations required. No credit cards. Moderate–Expensive.*

The Anchorage. This is an informal beachside eatery where lobster is king, but burgers, steaks, salads, and sandwiches are also offered. *Frigate Bay Beach, no phone. Reservations not required. No credit cards. Moderate.*

★ **Ballahoo.** Curried conch, beef Stroganoff, salads, and sandwiches are served in a delightful upstairs gallery overlooking Pelican Gardens and The Circus. *Bay Rd., Basseterre, tel. 809/465–4197. Reservations not required. AE, MC, V. Closed Sun. Moderate.*

★ **Fisherman's Wharf.** At the Ocean Terrace Inn, this waterfront eatery serves the island's best Friday-night buffet. Steak barbecue alternates with West Indian specialties, grilled lobster, and fish. Dinner is followed by dancing and entertainment. *Fortlands, Basseterre, tel. 809/465–2754. Reservations not required. No credit cards. Moderate.*

Ocean Terrace Inn. This is a popular place with locals and visitors, where you can dine by candlelight inside or on a balcony overlooking the bay. Lobster is the specialty here—grilled, broiled, and Thermidor. Curried chicken, conch chowder, and other West Indian dishes are served, as well as Continental offerings. *Fortlands, Basseterre, tel. 809/465–2754. Reservations required. AE, MC, V. Moderate.*

★ **Rawlins Plantation Sou Tai.** Cantonese cuisine is served in the great house of an erstwhile estate on a hill overlooking the Atlantic. *Canada Estate, tel. 809/465–8456. Reservations advised. No credit cards. Moderate.*

Jong's Oriental Restaurant. It's pronounced *yong's*, it's on the sands at Conaree Beach, and it's got a spectacular view of the Atlantic. *Conaree Beach, tel. 809/465–2062. Reservations advised. No credit cards. Closed Sun. and Mon. Inexpensive.*

Paradise Pizza. You'll find excellent pizza right next to the Island Paradise Condominiums. Other Italian dishes are also served, as well as sandwiches. *Frigate Bay, no phone. No credit cards. Closed Sun. and Mon. Inexpensive.*

★ **Victor's Hideaway.** Hidden behind the Church of the Immaculate Conception, this friendly dinner spot has some of the best food in the capital. Stew—mutton, curried goat, or lobster—is the specialty, but deep-fried fish and beef and chicken dishes are also on the menu. It gets crowded, and you may have to stand in line unless you ask your taxi driver to stop by and book a table before picking you up. *9 Stainforth St., no phone. No credit cards. Closed Sun. Inexpensive.*

Lodging

Choices run from guest houses to full-service hotels to elegant inns in restored plantation homes. Some of the inns include breakfast and dinner in their rates, which will be indicated in the descriptions that follow.

The most highly recommended lodgings are indicated by a star ★.

Category	Cost*
Very Expensive	over $250
Expensive	$175–$250
Moderate	$125–$175
Inexpensive	under $125

*All prices are for a standard double room for two, excluding 7% tax and a 10% service charge.

Hotels **The Golden Lemon.** Arthur Leaman, a former editor of *House* ★ *and Garden,* has created a hotel that is internationally famous, and with good reason. The four original rooms have high ceilings, hardwood floors, and galleries overlooking the black-sand beach, palm trees, and the ocean. Each room in the hotel is different; there are wonderful white-iron four-posters, carved armoires, chaises lounges, ceiling fans, mosquito nets, rocking chairs, and a fine collection of Meissen china in a display case. Solar-heated water guarantees that showers (there are no tubs) are always hot. Rates include breakfast (served in your room or on the veranda), afternoon tea, and elegant dinner. There's a staff of 38, and the maximum stay is two weeks. **The Lemon Court Condominiums** are sleek, secluded studios and one- and two-bedroom, two-story units that surround manicured gardens. Some have private Grecian pools, and all are decorated with a collection of antiques and Caribbean art. The 10 latest additions were opened in December 1988. *Box 17, Dieppe Bay, tel. 809/465–7260 or 800/845–9504. 27 rooms and suites. Facilities: beach, pool, restaurant, duty-free shop, free laundry service, one tennis court. AE. Very Expensive.*

Jack Tar Village/Royal St. Kitts. Once you've registered and had your picture taken for the ID card you'll have to wear at all times, you're all set for the island's most action-packed hotel. The schedule of daily activities includes horseshoe pitching, volleyball, shuffleboard, horseback riding, biking, and hiking. This is also the home of the island's only casino. Entertainment often includes folkloric shows and steel bands. This is an all-inclusive resort, which means that everything is included in the room rate—meals, taxes, snacks, greens fees, drinks,—everything. *Box 406, Frigate Bay, tel. 809/465-8651 in USA 214/670-9888 or 800/527-9299. 250 rooms. Facilities: casino, 2 pools, 2 restaurants, bars and lounges, horseback riding, 3 lighted tennis courts, facilities for handicapped, water-sports center. AE, DC, MC, V. Very Expensive.*

★ **Rawlins Plantation.** This lovely inn is set 350 feet above sea level in 25 acres of a once-flourishing sugar plantation. The view from the veranda is splendid, and there is a cozy parlor, done in stylish tropical decor, with bookshelves lining the walls. Guests take dinner in a formal dining room (breakfast, afternoon tea, and dinner with wine are included in the rate). Accommodations (with double, queen-size, or king-size beds), are in the main house and in cottages tucked in the hillside. All are individually decorated with delicate prints and come equipped with mosquito nets on four-poster beds. A 17th-century stone windmill contains the split-level honeymoon suite with sunken bathroom. The property is owned and operated by Philip and Frances Walwyn, who can arrange crater trips and picnic lunches for guests at an extra charge. In season, the minimum stay is four days. *Box 340, Mt. Pleasant, tel. 809/465-6221 (617/367-8959 in USA). 9 rooms. Facilities: pool, restaurant, lighted tennis court, croquet. No credit cards. Very Expensive.*

★ **OTI Banana Bay Beach Hotel.** If you want to get away from it all in style, this is the place to do it. Set on the secluded peninsula and between the island's two best beaches (Banana Bay and Cockleshell Bay), the hotel is accessible only by boat. (The hotel runs shuttle boats daily from Pelican Cove Marina.) It belongs to the owners of the Ocean Terrace Inn, hence the prefix OTI, and Banana Bay guests can avail themselves of the facilities there. The fan-cooled rooms here are spacious, with double or king-size beds, minibars, and balconies facing Nevis. No children under 16. *Box 65, Basseterre, tel. 809/465-2754 or 800/ 223-5695. 20 rooms with bath. Facilities: 2 beaches, restaurant, water-sports center. AE, MC, V. Expensive.*

Frigate Bay Beach Hotel. The third fairway of the island's golf course adjoins the property, but the beach is about a mile away, and reached by complimentary shuttle buses. The cluster of white-washed, air-conditioned buildings contain standard rooms as well as condominium units with fully equipped kitchens. There are hillside and poolside units, the latter preferable. Standard rooms are large but simply furnished, with tile floors, and sliding glass doors leading to a terrace or balcony. There's a pool with swim-up bar and a friendly staff. *Box 137, Basseterre, tel. 809/465-8936, 809/465-8935, or 800/622-7836. 64 rooms. Facilities: pool, restaurant, bar. Moderate-Expensive.*

★ **Ocean Terrace Inn.** Affectionately called OTI, this is one of the island's most luxurious hotels, offering an assortment of rooms, all of which are air-conditioned, with cable TV and radio. There are rooms with kitchenettes and condominium units with private terraces overlooking one of the inn's two pools. In a section called Fisherman's Village are luxury one-bedroom and two-bedroom split-level suites overlooking Basseterre's harbor. Fisherman's Wharf restaurant is famed island-wide for its buffets, and the hotel's Pelican Cove Marina has its own fleet of boats that take you to the OTI's secluded sister hotel on Banana Bay. Modified American Plan available. *Box 65, Basseterre, tel. 809/465–2754 or 800/223–5695. 52 rooms. Facilities: beach, 2 pools, outdoor Jacuzzi, 2 restaurants, 2 bars, cable TV, fleet of boats, water-sports center. AE, MC, V. Moderate.*

Fairview Inn. This hotel celebrated its 20th anniversary in 1988. The main building is an 18th-century great house, with graceful white verandas and Oriental rugs on hardwood floors. Rooms are in cottages sprinkled around the backyard, which happens to be a mountain of considerable size. The rooms have functional furnishings, with either twin or double beds, private patios, and radios. All have private baths with showers or bath tubs. Some have air-conditioning, some fans, some neither. *Box 212, Basseterre, tel. 809/465–2472 or 800/223–9815; 212/840–6636 in NY; 800/468–0023 in Canada. 30 rooms. Facilities: 2 restaurants, bar, pool. AE, DC, MC, V. Inexpensive.*

Fort Thomas Hotel. This hotel is on the site of an old fort. Popular with tour groups, it's set in 8 acres on a hillside at the outskirts of Basseterre. Rooms are spacious, and all have private baths, air-conditioning, radio, and phone; TVs can be rented. There's a free shuttle bus to the beach. *Box 407, Basseterre, tel. 809/465–2695, 800/223–9815 in USA, 800/468–0023 in Canada. 64 rooms. Facilities: pool, game room, restaurant, bar. AE, CB, DC, MC, V. Inexpensive.*

★ **Sun 'n Sand Beach Village.** These studio and two-bedroom, self-catering cottages are immaculately clean and right on the beach on the Atlantic side of the island. Furnishings are simple and tropical, with tile floors, terraces, twin or queen-size beds, and private baths (shower only). Studios are air-conditioned; apartments have window air-conditioners in bedrooms, and ceiling fans in living rooms. Bedroom apartments have convertible sofas in living rooms and fully equipped kitchens with microwave ovens and full-size refrigerators. Taped Glenn Miller-type music plays nightly in the low-key restaurant. *Box 341, Frigate Bay, tel. 809/465–1021 or 800/621–1270. 32 studios, 18 2-bedroom cottages. Facilities: beach, restaurant, pool, children's pool, 2 lighted tennis courts, grocery store, drugstore, gift shop. No credit cards. Inexpensive.*

Condos and Guest Houses This little island has a number of condominiums and guest houses available to visitors. For information, contact the St. Kitts Tourist Board (Box 132, Basseterre, St. Kitts, tel. 809/465–4040).

Nightlife

Most of the Kittitian nightlife revolves around the hotels, which host folkloric shows, calypso music, steel bands, and such.

Casinos The only game in town is at the **Royal St. Kitts Casino** in Jack Tar Village (*see* Lodging, above), where you'll find blackjack tables, roulette wheels, craps tables, and one-armed bandits. Dress is casual, and play continues till the last player leaves.

Discos Kittitian and Italian dishes are served in **The Lighthouse** (Deepwater Port Rd., tel. 809/465–8914), but come after 11 PM Thursday–Saturday when the place spins into a disco, attracting a mostly local crowd. At **J's Place** (across from Brimstone Hill, tel. 809/465–6264), you and the locals can dance the night away Friday and Saturday.

23 St. Lucia

by Honey Naylor

Oval, lush St. Lucia, 27 miles long and 14 miles wide, sits at the southern end of the Windward Islands. It has two topographical features, apart from its beaches, that earn it a special place in the Caribbean tableaux of islands: the twin peaks of the Pitons (Petit and Gros), which rise to more than 2,400 feet, and the bubbling sulfur springs in the town of Soufrière, part of a low-lying volcano that erupted thousands of years ago, which now attracts visitors for the springs' curative waters.

This is a ruggedly beautiful island, with towering mountains, lush green valleys, and acres of banana plantations. Yachtsmen put in at Marigot Bay, one of the Caribbean's most beautiful secluded bays. The diving is good, and so is the liming—the St. Lucian term for "hanging out."

Generations of St. Lucians have long celebrated December 13 as Discovery Day, believing Columbus came upon the island on that date in 1502. But in recent years doubts have been cast on the theory. Some historians think St. Lucia (pronounced *loo*-sha) was found in 1499 by Juan de la Cosa, Columbus's navigator.

The first inhabitants were the Arawaks, who paddled up from South America some time before AD 200. The ferocious Caribs followed them, killed them off, and were still living on the island when the first Europeans began to arrive.

In 1605, 67 English settlers bound for Guiana were blown off course and landed near Vieux Fort. Within a few weeks the cannibalistic Caribs had devoured all but 19, who escaped in a canoe. Another group of English settlers arrived 30 years later, but their attempt at colonization was also unsuccessful. It was the French who, in 1660, managed to sign a treaty with the Caribs and gain control of the island.

Thus began a 150-year period of battles between the French and the English for control of the 238-square-mile island. In the late 18th century, English Admiral George Rodney had his headquarters on St. Lucia. The island changed hands 14 times before the British took permanent possession in 1814.

During those battle-filled years, Europeans colonized the island. They developed sugar plantations, using slaves from West Africa to work the fields. Most of today's 140,000 St. Lucians are descendants of those West Africans. The coal industry was begun on the island in 1883, and by the turn of the century Castries, the capital, had become the leading coal port in the West Indies. In 1960, banana plantations began to flourish, and bananas are now the island's leading export.

On February 22, 1979, St. Lucia became an independent state within the British Commonwealth of Nations, with a resident governor-general appointed by the Queen. Still, there are many relics of the French occupation, notably in the island patois, the Creole cuisine, and the names of the places and the people.

Before You Go

Tourist Information Contact the **St. Lucia Tourist Board** (820 2nd Ave., 9th floor, New York, NY 10017, tel. 212/867–2950. In Canada: 151 Bloor St. W, Suite 425, Toronto, M5S 1S4, tel. 416/961–5606. In the United Kingdom: 1 Collingham Gardens, London, tel. 01/370–0926).

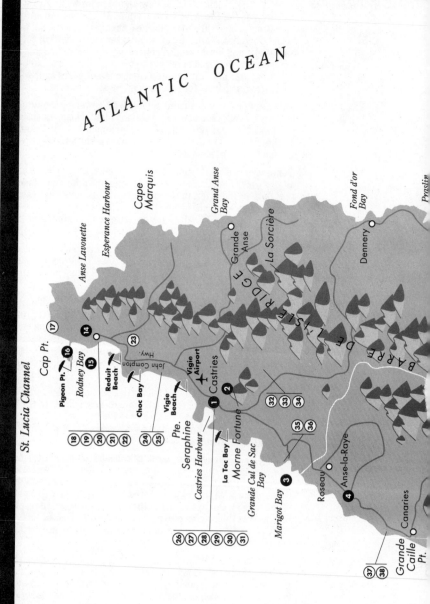

St. Lucia

ATLANTIC OCEAN

St. Lucia Channel

Cap Pt.

Cape Marquis

Esperance Harbour

Anse Lavourette

Pigeon Pt. ⑯ ⑰

Rodney Bay ⑮

⑭

㉓

Reduit Beach

John Compton Hwy.

Vigie Airport

Castries ①

② ㉜ ㉝ ㉞

Choc Bay

Vigie Beach

⑱ ⑲ ⑳ ㉑ ㉒ ㉔ ㉕

Pte. Seraphine

Castries Harbour

La Toc Bay

Morne Fortune

Grande Cul de Sac Bay

Marigot Bay ③

㉖ ㉗ ㉘ ㉙ ㉚ ㉛

Grand Anse Bay

Grande Anse ○

La Sorcière

BARRE DE L'ISLE RIDGE

Fond d'or Bay

Denney ○

Praslin

㉟ ㊱

Roseau ○

Anse-la-Raye ○

④

Canaries ○

Grande Caille Pt.

㊲ ㊳

● Exploring Sites

⑰ Hotels and Restaurants

Exploring
Anse-la-Raye, 4
Castries, 1
Choiseul, 10
Diamond Falls and
Mineral Baths, 6

Fort Charlotte, 2
Gros Islets, 14
La Soufrière Volcano, 9
Laborie, 11
Maria Islands Interpre-
tive Centre, 13
Marigot Bay, 3

Pigeon Point, 16
Pitons, 8
Rain forest, 7
Rodney Bay, 15
Soufrière, 5
Vieux Fort, 12

Dining
Capone's, 18
Coal Pot, 26
DoLittle's, 35
Green Parrot, 32
Jimmie's, 27
The Lime, 19
Rain, 28

San Antoine's, 33
The Still, 37
Sweet Dreams, 20

Lodging
Anse Chastanet
Hotel, 38

Club Med St. Lucia, 40
Club St. Lucia, 29
Couples, 24
Cunard Hotel La Toc
and La Toc Suites, 30
Green Parrot, 34
Halcyon Beach Club, 25
Harmony Apartel, 22

Islander, 23
Kimatrai, 39
Le Sport, 17
Marigot Bay
Resort, 36
St. Lucian, 21
Vigie Beach Hotel, 31

Arriving and Departing
By Plane There are two airports on the island. Wide-body planes land at Hewanorra International Airport on the southern tip of the island. Vigie Airport, near Castries, handles interisland and charter flights. **BWIA** (tel. 800/327–7401) has direct service from Miami and New York. **American** (tel. 800/433–7300) has daily service from New York, Dallas, and other major U.S. cities, with a stopover in San Juan. **Air Canada** (tel. 800/422–6232) flies from Toronto to Barbados and Antigua, connecting with flights to St. Lucia. **LIAT's** (tel. 809/462–0701) small island hoppers fly into Vigie Airport, linking St. Lucia with Barbados, Trinidad, Antigua, and other islands.

From the Airport **Taxis** are unmetered, and although the government has issued a list of suggested fares, these are not regulated. You should negotiate with the driver *before* you get in the car, and be sure that you both understand whether the price you've agreed upon is in E.C. or U.S. dollars. The drive from Hewanorra to Castries takes about 90 minutes and should cost about U.S. $35.

Passports and Visas U.S., Canadian, and British citizens must produce some proof of identity. A passport is best, but a notorized birth certificate accompanied by a photo ID will suffice. A driver's license alone will *not* do. In addition, all visitors must have a return or ongoing ticket.

Customs and Duties In addition to personal items, 200 cigarettes or 50 cigars or 8 ounces of tobacco, 40 ounces of liquor, and gifts and souvenirs not exceeding E.C.$50 (about U.S. $18.50) in value are allowed in. Visitors under 18 are not entitled to the tobacco and alcohol allowances.

Language The official language is English, but you'll also hear some French and patois.

Precautions Bring along industrial-strength insect repellent to ward off the mosquitoes and sand flies. Centipede bites, while rare and not lethal, can be painful and cause swelling. If you're bitten, you should see a doctor. If you happen to step on a sea urchin, its long black spines may lodge under the skin; don't try to pull them out as you could cause infection. Apply ammonia, or an ammonia-based liquid, as quickly as possible.

Manchineel trees have poisonous fruit and leaves that can cause skin blisters on contact. Even raindrops falling off the trees can cause blisters, so you shouldn't sit beneath the trees.

The waters on the Atlantic (east) coast can be rough, with dangerous undertows, so you shouldn't swim on that side of the island.

Vendors and self-employed guides in places like Sulphur Springs (where your entrance fee includes a guided tour) can be tenacious. If you do hire a guide, be sure the fee is clearly fixed up front.

As a courtesy rather than a precaution, you should always ask before taking an islander's picture and be prepared to part with a few coins.

Staying in St. Lucia

Important Addresses **Tourist Information: St. Lucia Tourist Board** is based at the Pointe Seraphine duty-free complex on Castries Harbor (tel.

809/452–4094 or 809/452–5968). There is also a tourist information center on Jeremies Street in Castries (same telephone number). Both offices are open weekdays 8–5.

Emergencies   **Police:** Call 999.

Hospitals: Hospitals with 24-hour emergency rooms are **Victoria Hospital** (Hospital Rd., Castries, tel. 809/452–2421) and **St. Jude's Hospital** (Vieux Fort, tel. 809/454–6041).

Pharmacies: The largest pharmacy is **Williams Pharmacy** (Williams Bldg., Bridge St., Castries, tel. 809/452–2797).

Currency   The official currency is the Eastern Caribbean dollar (E.C.$). Figure about E.C.$2.70 = U.S. $1.00. U.S. dollars are readily accepted, but you'll usually get change in E.C. dollars. Major credit cards are widely accepted, as are traveler's checks. Prices quoted here are in U.S. dollars, unless indicated otherwise.

Taxes and Service Charges   Hotels collect an 8% government tax.

The departure tax is $8; $4 if you're headed to another Caribbean destination.

Hotels add a 10% service charge to your bill; most restaurants add 10%. Taxi drivers expect a 10% tip.

Guided Tours   **Taxi drivers** take special guide courses and offer the most personalized way to see the island. A tour around the island costs about $14 an hour, not including tip.

The **Carib Touring Company** (tel. 809/452–2689) offers a variety of half- and full-day tours.

Barnard's Travel (Bridge St., Castries, tel. 809/452–2214) also offers a full range of half- and full-day island tours, as well as excursions to Dominica, Martinique, St. Vincent, and the Grenadines.

Island Helicopters (tel. 809/452–8216) gives you a gull's-eye view of Castries and the Pitons.

Getting Around   This is a cheap means of transportation. There's no organized
Buses   service, but minivans cruise the island and, like a taxi, will stop when hailed. You can also catch a minivan in Castries by hanging around outside Clarke Cinema (corner Micoud and Bridge Sts.).

Taxis   Taxis are always available at the airport, the harbor, and in front of the major hotels. Most hotels post the names and phone numbers of drivers.

Rental Cars   To rent a car you have to be 25 years old and hold a valid driver's license. You must buy a temporary St. Lucian license at the airports or police headquarters (Bridge St., Castries) for $11. Rental agencies include **Avis** (tel. 809/452–2700 or 800/331–2112), **Hertz** (tel. 809/452–4777 or 800/654–3131), **National** (tel. 809/452–8028 or 800/328–4567), and **Carib Touring Ltd.** (tel. 809/452–3184).

Telephones and Mail   To call St. Lucia from the United States, dial area code 809, access code 45, and the local five-digit number. You can make direct-dial long-distance calls from the island, and the connections are excellent. To place intraisland calls, dial the local five-digit number.

Postage for airmail letters to foreign countries is E.C.$.65 for up to one ounce; postcard postage is E.C.$.15.

Opening and Closing Times	Shops are open weekdays 8–12:30 and 1:30–4 Saturday 8–noon. Banks are open Monday–Thursday 8–noon, Friday 8–noon and 3–5.

Beaches

All of St. Lucia's beaches are public, and many are flanked by hotels where you can rent water-sport equipment and have a rum punch. There are also secluded beaches, accessible only by water, to which hotels can arrange boat trips. It is not advisable to swim along the windward (east) coast because the Atlantic waters are rough and sometimes dangerous.

Anse Chastanet is a white-sand beach just north of Soufrière with a backdrop of green hills and the island's best reefs for snorkeling and diving. The wooden gazebos of the Anse Chastanet Hotel are nestled among the palms, with a dive shop and bar on the beach (*see* Lodging, below).

Anse Cochon, on the Caribbean coast, is a white-sand beach accessible only by boat. The waters are superb for swimming and snorkeling.

Vigie Beach and **Choc Bay,** north of Castries Harbour, have fine beige sand and calm waters (*see* Lodging, below).

Reduit Beach is a long stretch of beige sand between Choc Bay and Pigeon Point and is home to the St. Lucian Hotel, which offers numerous water sports.

Pigeon Point off the northern shore has secluded white-sand beaches, fine for picnicking and swimming.

Jalousie Bay, south of Soufrière, is a bay several miles deep between the Pitons. Accessible only by boat, it offers great snorkeling and diving.

La Toc Bay to the south is Soufrière's beach. The sand here is gray.

Vieux Fort, at the southernmost tip, has a long secluded stretch of gray volcanic sand and waters protected by reefs. **Honeymoon Beach** is another sandy escape just west of Vieux Fort.

Exploring St. Lucia

Numbers in the margin correspond with points of interest on the St. Lucia map.

Castries
❶

Castries, on the northwest coast, is a busy city with a population of about 60,000. It lies in a sheltered bay surrounded by green hills. Ships carrying bananas, coconut, cocoa, mace, nutmeg, and citrus fruits for export leave from **Castries Harbour,** one of the busiest ports in the Caribbean. Cruise ships dock here, too.

Take a cab or drive to **Pointe Seraphine,** the Spanish-style complex of 23 duty-free shops by Castries Harbour. Pick up maps, arrange tours, and find out anything you want to know about St. Lucia at the information desk of the **Tourist Board** just inside the main terminal. This is the starting point for many of the island tours.

The John Compton Highway connects the duty-free complex to downtown Castries. To reach the downtown center from Pointe Seraphine's transportation terminal, you can stroll for 20 minutes, or you can drive, take a cab, or hop on a double-decker shuttle bus.

Castries, with Morne Fortune (the Hill of Good Luck) rising behind it, has had more than its share of bad luck over the years, including two hurricanes and four fires. As a result, Castries lacks the colorful colonial buildings found in other island capitals. Most of Castries's buildings are modern, and the town has only a few sights of historical note.

Head first to **Columbus Square,** a green oasis ringed by Brazil, Laborie, Micoud, and Bourbon streets. At the corner of Laborie and Micoud streets there is a 400-year-old saman tree. A favorite local story is of the English botanist who came to St. Lucia many years ago to catalogue the flora. Awestruck by this huge old tree, she asked a passer-by what it was. "Massav," he replied, and she gratefully jotted that down in her notebook, unaware that "massav" is patois for "I don't know."

Directly across the street is the Roman Catholic **Cathedral of the Immaculate Conception,** which was built in 1897.

Some of the 19th-century buildings that managed to survive fire, winds, and rains can be seen on Brazil Street, the southern border of the square.

Time Out In the courtyard of the Victorian building that houses Rain Restaurant, the **Pizza Park** (Columbus Sq., tel. 809/452–3022) sells takeout or eat-in pizza all day.

Head north on Laborie Street and walk past the government buildings on your right. On the left, William Peter Boulevard is one of Castries's shopping areas. "The Boulevard" connects Laborie Street with Bridge Street, which is another shopping street.

Continue north for one more block on Laborie Street and you'll come to Jeremie Street. Turn right, and you'll see the **market** on the corner of Jeremie and Peynier streets. The market is a busy place, especially on Saturday mornings when farmers bring their produce to town.

Elsewhere on To reach **Morne Fortune,** head due east on Bridge Street. The
the Island drive will take you past the **Government House,** the official resi-
Morne Fortune dence of the governor-general of St. Lucia. If you want to take a picture of the house, ask the guard on duty before focusing your camera. You cannot take pictures when the governor-general is in residence.

Driving up the Hill of Good Fortune, you'll see some of the Caribbean's most beautiful tropical plants—frangipani, lilies, bougainvillea, hibiscus, and oleander—along the road.

Two hundred years ago the Vigie Peninsula had the island's heaviest concentration of fortifications. That former battleground and the area to the north of it now have the island's greatest concentration of resort playgrounds. The island rising on the horizon is Martinique. To the south you'll see the twin peaks of the Pitons.

2 Fort Charlotte on the Morne was begun in 1764 by the French as the *Citadelle du Morne Fortune.* It was completed 20 years later, but during those years many battles were fought here, and the fortress changed hands a number of times. The

Inniskilling Monument is a tribute to one of the most famous battles, fought in 1796, when the 27th Foot Royal Inniskilling Fusiliers wrested the Hill of Good Fortune from the French. Admission to Fort Charlotte is free, and you can wander at will to see the Four Apostles Battery; the Combermere Barracks, which are now part of an educational complex; the redoubts, guard room, stables, and cells. Stop in the Military Cemetery. It was first used in 1782, and the faint inscriptions on the tombstones tell the tales of the French and English soldiers who died here. Six former governors of the island are buried in this cemetery.

South of Castries   The road from Castries to Soufrière travels through beautiful country. Keep in mind though that the many hairpin curves make this road a difficult drive. You'll also be handling a right-hand drive vehicle on the left side of a curving road.

3 In the village of Roseau, make a detour and drive to **Marigot Bay.** In 1778, British Admiral Samuel Barrington took his ships into this secluded bay within a bay and covered them with palm fronds to hide them from the French. The resort community today is a great favorite of yachtspeople. You can arrange to charter a yacht, swim, snorkel, or lime with the yachting crowd at one of the bars on the bay. A 24-hour water taxi connects the various points on the bay.

Time Out   Stop for rum punch, lunch, and atmosphere at the **Rusty Anchor** (Hurricane Hotel, tel. 809/453–4230), a happy haunt of boaters.

If you continue south, you'll be in the vicinity of one of the island's two rum distilleries. Major production of sugar ceased here in about 1960, and distilleries now make rum with imported molasses. You're still in banana country, with acres of banana trees covering the hills and valleys. More than 127 different varieties of bananas are grown on the island.

In the mountainous region ahead you'll see **Mt. Parasol,** and if you look hard enough through the mists, you may be able to make out **Mt. Gimie,** St. Lucia's highest peak, rising to 3,117 feet.

4 The next village you'll come to is **Anse-la-Raye.** The beach here is a colorful sight, with fishing nets hanging on poles to dry and brightly painted fishing boats bobbing in the water. The fishermen of Anse-la-Raye still make canoes the old-fashioned way, by burning out the center of a log.

Soufrière   As you approach the town of **Soufrière,** you'll be in the island's
5   breadbasket, where most of the mangoes, breadfruit, tomatoes, limes, and oranges are grown.

The town of Soufrière, which dates from the mid-18th century, was named after the nearby volcano and has a population of about 6,000 people. The Soufrière Harbour is the deepest harbor on the island, accommodating cruise ships that nose right up to the wharf. The government and the Soufrière Development Committee are working to give the town a face-lift and boost tourism in the area. In April 1988 the **Soufrière Tourist Information Centre** (Bay St., tel. 809/454–7419) was opened; you should stop in their offices to get information about the attractions in the area, which, in addition to the Pitons, include La Soufrière, billed as the world's only drive-in volcano, and sulphur springs; the Diamond Mineral Baths; and the rain forest. You can also ask at the Tourism Centre about Soufrière Estate, on the east side of town, where construction of botanical gardens and a zoo is under way.

6 Adjoining Soufrière Estate are the **Diamond Falls and Mineral Baths,** which are fed by an underground flow of water from the sulphur springs. Louis XVI provided funds for the construction of these baths for his troops to "fortify them against the St. Lucian climate." During the Brigand's War, just after the French Revolution, the baths were destroyed. They were restored in 1966, and you can see the waterfalls and the gardens before slipping into your swimsuit for a dip in the steaming curative waters. *Soufrière. Admission: E.C.$5. Open daily 9–5.*

7 The island's dense tropical **rain forest** is to the east of Soufrière on the road to Fond St. Jacques. The trek through the lush landscape takes three hours, and you'll need a guide. Mt. Gimie (St. Lucia's highest peak), Piton Canaries, Mt. Houlom, and Piton Tromasse are all part of this immense forest reserve. The views of the mountains and valleys are spectacular.

8 For the best land view of the **Pitons,** take the road south out of Soufrière. The road is awful and leads up a steep hill, but if you persevere, you'll be rewarded by the sight of the twin peaks. The perfectly shaped pyramidal cones, covered with tropical greenery, were formed of lava from a volcanic eruption 30 million to 40 million years ago. The tallest is Petit Piton (2,619 feet) and its twin, Gros Piton (2,461 feet). Gros Piton is so named because, although it is shorter, it is fatter than its twin.

9 To the south of Soufrière, your nose will note the left turn that takes you to **La Soufrière,** the drive-in volcano, and its **sulfur springs.** There are more than 20 pools of black, belching, smelly sulfurous waters, and yellow-green sulfur baking and steaming. Take the guided tour offered by the Tourist Board. *La Soufrière. Admission: E.C.$5 (including guided tour). Open daily 9–5.*

10 Follow the road farther south and you'll come next to the coastal town of **Choiseul,** home to wood-carving and pottery shops. At the turn of the road past the Anglican Church, built in 1846, a bridge crosses the River Doree, so named because the riverbed is blanketed with fool's gold.

11 The next stop is **Laborie,** a little fishing village, where you can buy cheese, bread, and fish. There is also an underground passage that leads from an old fort at Saphire, up the coast, to an opening at the sea.

12 Drive now along the southern coast of the island to **Vieux Fort,** St. Lucia's second largest city and home of the Hewanorra International Airport. Drive out on the **Moule-à-Chique Peninsula,** the southernmost tip of the island. If you look to the north, you can see all of St. Lucia and, if the day is especially clear, you can spot the island of St. Vincent 21 miles to the south. Looking straight down, you can see where the waters of the Caribbean blend with the bluer Atlantic waters.

Time Out **Chak Chak** (Beanfield Rd., Vieux Fort, tel. 809/454–6260) is a casual, airy restaurant that serves Creole dishes.

⓭ At the **Maria Islands Interpretive Centre** you can find out all there is to know about the Maria Islands Nature Reserve. The reserve consists of two tiny islands in the Atlantic off the southeast coast of St. Lucia. The 25-acre Maria Major and its little sister, 4-acre Maria Minor, are inhabited by rare species of lizards and snakes that share their home with frigate birds, terns, doves, and other wildlife. *Moule-à-Chique, no phone. Admission: Wed.–Sat. E.C.$3, Sun. E.C.$.50. Open Wed.– Sun. 9:30–5.*

A good road leads from Vieux Fort through the towns on the Atlantic coast. The road will take you past **Honeymoon Beach,** a wide, grassy, flat Anse l'Islet peninsula jutting into the ocean. Drive through Micoud and, a few miles farther north, Dennery, both of which are residential towns overlooking the Atlantic. At Dennery the road turns west and climbs across the Barre de l'Isle Ridge through a tiny rain forest with dense vegetation. There are trails along the way that lead to lookout points where you can get a view of the National Forest Preserve. This bumpy road will take you all the way back to Castries.

The North End and Gros Islet For another tour up the coast north of Castries, take the John Compton Highway north out of town for about five minutes to the Vigie Airport. This whole northwest stretch of the Caribbean coast is of far more interest to the hedonist than to the historian. This area features some of the island's best beaches and it's loaded with resort hotels.

⓮ The little village of **Gros Islets** to the north is a quiet fishing village, not unlike Anse-la-Raye to the south. But on Friday nights, Gros Islet hosts a street festival to which everyone is invited.

⓯ **Rodney Bay,** named after Admiral Rodney, is an 80-acre manmade lagoon that boasts a host of hotels and restaurants. The St. Lucian Hotel and Club St. Lucia are in this area, as are Capone's, Lime, and other popular restaurants.

Pigeon Point **⓰** **Pigeon Point,** jutting out on the northwest coast, was Pigeon Island until a causeway was built to connect it to the mainland. Tales are told of the pirate Jambe de Bois (wooden leg), who used to hide out here. This 40-acre area, a strategic point during the struggles for control of the island, is now a national park, with long sandy beaches, calm waters for swimming, and areas for picnicking.

The **Pigeon Point Museum** includes the ruins of barracks, batteries, and garrisons dating from the French and English battles. *Pigeon Point, no phone. Admission: E.C.$3. Open Mon.–Sat. 9–4.*

Off the Beaten Track

If you want a close-up look at a working banana plantation, and are willing to get a little wet and muddy in the process, you can tour the island's largest, the **Marquis Plantation.** St. Lucia Plantation Tours (tel. 809/542–8658) will pick you up at your hotel in an air-conditioned bus. Wear your most casual clothes, and be prepared to rough it.

Participant Sports

Most hotels have Hobie Cats, Sunfish, water skis, fins, masks, and other water-sport equipment offered free to guests and for a fee to nonguests.

Boating Captain Mike's (tel. 809/452–0217) has a fleet of Bertram's charter boats for snorkeling and swimming cruises and private charter parties. Bare-boat or skippered yacht charters are available through **Stevens Yachts** (tel. 800/638–7044), which has a fleet of 39- to 56-foot sailing yachts; **Trade Wind Yacht Charters** (Rodney Bay, tel. 809/452–8424 or 800/222–6656); and the **Moorings Yacht Charter** (Marigot Bay, tel. 809/453–4357 or 800/535–7289).

Deep-Sea Fishing Among the sea creatures in these waters are dolphin, Spanish mackerel, barracuda, and white marlin. Contact **Captain Mike's** (tel. 809/452–0217) to steer you in the right direction.

Golf There is a nine-hole course at **Cunard La Toc Hotel** (tel. 809/452 –3081) and a nine-plus-nine course at **Cap Estate Golf Club** (tel. 809/452–8523). Greens fees at both are about E.C.$15, and clubs are available for rental.

Hiking The island is laced with trails, but you should not attempt the challenging peaks on your own. Your hotel or the Tourist Board can provide you with a guide.

Horseback Riding For trail rides on the beach, contact **Trim's Riding Stables** (Cas-En-Bah and Cap Estate, tel. 809/452–8273) and **Sunset Riding School** (Cap Estate, tel. 809/452–8628).

Jogging You can jog on the beach by yourself or team up with the **Roadbusters** (tel. Jimmie at 809/452–5142 or evenings at 809/452–4790).

Parasailing Contact **Jacob's Watersports** (tel. 809/452–8281).

Scuba Diving Scuba St. Lucia (tel. 809/454–7355) is a PADI five-star training facility that offers daily beach and boat dives, resort courses, underwater photography, and day trips. **Marigot Bay Resort** (tel. 809/453–4357) offers a full scuba program. Dive trips are also arranged through most of the hotels.

Sea and Snorkeling Excursions The 140-foot square-rigger *Brig Unicorn* (tel. 809/452–6811) sails to Soufrière, with steel bands, a swim stop, rum punch, and soda. Its sister schooner, the *Buccaneer,* also does outings. **Captain Mike's** (tel. 809/452–0216) does swimming and snorkeling cruises; the *Sailing Bus* (tel. 809/452–8725) offers a full-day sail from Rodney Bay to Marigot; and **Jacob's Watersports** (tel. 809/452–8281) features speedboat and snorkeling cruises.

Squash There is one squash court at **Cap Estate Golf Course** (tel. 809/452–8523; open 8–4).

Tennis The largest tennis center is at **Cunard La Toc Hotel** (tel. 809/452–3081), where there are five lighted courts and bookings are essential. Additional courts are available at most major hotels for a fee.

Waterskiing Contact **Jacob's Watersports** (tel. 809/452–8281). Rentals are also available at most of the hotels.

Windsurfing The **St. Lucian Hotel** is the local agent for Mistral Windsurfers (tel. 809/452–8351). Also contact **Marigot Bay Resort** (tel. 809/

453–4357) and **Jacob's Watersports** (tel. 809/452–8281). Most hotels rent Windsurfers to nonguests.

Spectator Sports

Contact the Tourist Board (tel. 809/452–4094) for specific information regarding schedules.

Cricket and **soccer,** the two national pastimes, are played at **Mindoo Philip Park** in Marchand, 2 miles east of Castries.

Shopping

Shopping on St. Lucia is low key, but the island's best-known products are the unique hand-silk-screened and hand-printed designs of Bagshaw Studios. Bagshaw products are designed, printed, and sold only on St. Lucia. The island is also home to Windjammer Clothing, which is sold on virtually every Caribbean island. Apart from those indigenous products, there are native-made wood carvings, pottery, and straw hats and baskets.

Shopping Areas St. Lucia entered the duty-free market with the opening of **Pointe Seraphine,** a Spanish-style complex by the harbor, where 23 shops sell designer perfume, china and crystal, jewelry, watches, leather goods, liquor, and cigarettes. Native crafts are also sold in the shopping center. Castries has a number of shops, mostly on **Bridge Street** and **William Peter Boulevard,** selling locally made souvenirs. There are also shopping arcades at the **La Toc** and **St. Lucian hotels.**

Good Buys In Pointe Seraphine, look for designer perfumes at **Images** (tel.
Duty-Free 809/452–6883). **J. Q. Charles** (tel. 809/452–2721) carries fine china and crystal, as does **Touch of Class** (tel. 809/452–7443). **Mano's** (tel. 809/452–7442) has liquor, cigars, and cigarettes. Leather handbags, jewelry, crystal, and perfumes can be found at **Meli** (tel. 809/452–7587).

Fabrics and Bagshaw's silk screen fabrics and clothing can be found at
Clothing Pointe Seraphine and at the **La Toc** shop (tel. 809/452–2139). **Windjammer Clothing Company** (tel. 809/452–1040) has its main store at Vigie Cove and an outlet at Pointe Seraphine. **Caribelle Batik** (Old Victoria Rd., The Morne, Castries, tel. 809/452–3785) creates batik clothing and wall hangings. Visitors are welcome to watch the craftspeople at work.

Native Crafts Trays, masks, and figures are carved from mahogany, red cedar, and eucalyptus trees in the studio adjacent to **Eudovic's** (Morne Fortune, 15 min south of Castries, tel. 809/452–2747). Hammocks, straw mats, baskets and hats, carvings, as well as books and maps of St. Lucia are at **Noah's Arkade** (Bridge St., Castries, and Pte. Seraphine, tel. 809/452–2523).

Dining

If you stop by the Castries market (*see* Exploring St. Lucia, above) on a Saturday, you'll see the riches produced in this fertile volcanic soil. Mangoes, plantains, breadfruit, limes, pumpkins, cucumbers, pawpaw (pronounced poh-poh here, known as papaya elsewhere), green figs, yams, christophene (a green vegetable), and coconuts are among the fruits and vegetables that appear on menus throughout the island. Every menu lists the catch of the day (especially flying fish), along with the ever-popular lobster. Chicken, pork, and barbecues are also big-time here. Most of the meats are imported—beef from Argentina and Iowa, lamb from New Zealand. The French influence is strong in St. Lucian restaurants, and most chefs cook with a Creole flair.

The most highly recommended restaurants are indicated by a star ★.

Category	Cost*
Expensive	$15–$20
Moderate	$10–$15
Inexpensive	under $10

*per person, excluding drinks, service

Coal Pot. A breezy, romantic waterside setting favored by boaters, the Coal Pot serves superb piña coladas and a selection of Creole-style seafood dishes. The house specialty is a pepper-pot meat dish served in a coal pot. Lobster is always available. *Lunar Park, Gantner's Bay, tel. 809/452–5643. Reservations suggested. AE, MC, V. Closed Sun. Expensive.*

Green Parrot. The Green Parrot Inn comes complete with sommelier and crisp white napery. The Continental menu includes poached fish fillet with mushroom cream and white-wine sauce glaze; tournedos cordon rouge (steak fillet topped with foie gras and Madeira sauce); and entrecote sautéed in butter and embellished with pineapple and cherries in red-wine sauce. There is lively entertainment on Wednesday and Saturday nights, with limbo and belly dancers. *Red Tape La., Morne Fortune, tel. 809/452–3399. Jacket required. Reservations essential. AE, MC, V. Expensive.*

Capone's. The gang here does a skillful job of blending the tropics, the Jazz Age, and Art Deco touches. There are black-and-white tile floors, a polished wood bar, and a player piano. Waiters and waitresses dressed like gangsters serve rum drinks called Valentine's Day Massacre and Mafia Mai Tai and bring your check in a violin case. The pasta is fresh, and the meat dishes include *osso buco alla Milanese* and chicken rotisserie. The **Pizza Parlour** turns out burgers and sandwiches, as well as pizza. *Rodney Bay, across from the St. Lucian Hotel, tel. 809/452–0284. Reservations suggested. AE, MC, V. No lunch; closed Mon. Moderate–Expensive.*

★ **San Antoine's.** High on the Morne, with splendid views of Castries below and Martinique in the distance, this restored historic building was originally the great house of the San Antoine Hotel, built in the mid-1800s and destroyed by fire in 1970. Now there is fine china and crystal on the tables and a superb wine list. Guests must choose from a 60-page menu, which contains specialties such as escargots in pastry, smoked-salmon mousse, and hazelnut meringue cake. After coffee and liqueurs, stroll down the nature trail through the bamboo forest. *Morne Fortune, tel. 809/452–4660. Jacket required. Reservations suggested. AE, V. No lunch; closed Sun. Moderate–Expensive.*

Dolittle's. Take the ferry across from the Hurricane Hotel to this waterside eatery, named after the Rex Harrison movie shot here. Callaloo soup is among the openers. Main dishes include marinated red snapper; ask about the daily specials. *Marigot de Roseau on Marigot Bay, tel. 809/453–4246. Reservations suggested. AE, MC, V. Moderate.*

Jimmie's. The bar here is a popular meeting place and the restaurant is a romantic spot for dinner. Specialties include Madras fish and seafood risotto, but there's also a wide choice of seafood, meat, chicken, and vegetable dishes. *Vigie Cove, Castries, tel. 809/452–5142. No reservations. No credit cards. Moderate.*

The Lime. Across the street from Capone's, the Lime is a favorite place to lime. A casual place with lime-colored gingham curtains, straw hats decorating the ceiling, and hanging plants, it offers a fixed-price three-course dinner. Starters might include homemade pâté or stuffed crab back. Entrée choices might be medallions of pork fillet with chef's special orange-and-ginger sauce or fish fillet poached in white wine and mushroom sauce. There's an extensive wine list. *Rodney Bay, tel. 809/452–0761. Reservations suggested for dinner. MC, V. Closed Tues. Moderate.*

★ **Rain.** This is one of the island's stellar attractions. The restaurant is in a Victorian building, and the balcony overlooking Columbus Square is a favored spot. It's usually crowded and the tables are a tad too close together, but you can still soak up the atmosphere. Lunchtime offerings include Creole soup, crab farci, rainburgers, quiches, and salads; Creole chicken is a specialty. At night, the "Champagne Buffet of 1885" is a lavish but moderately priced seven-course feast. For dessert there's old-fashioned hand-cranked ice cream. *Columbus Sq., Castries, tel. 809/452–3022. Reservations advised. AE, MC, V. Moderate.*

The Still. Converted from an old rum distillery, this restaurant is on the grounds of a working plantation, which supplies most of the meats and produce served. The emphasis is on local foods—christophene, breadfruit, yams, and callaloo, as well as seafood, pork chops, and beef dishes. A popular Creole buffet is served at lunch. *Soufrière, tel. 809/454–7224. Reservations suggested. MC, V. Moderate.*

Sweet Dreams. Sweet, indeed. More than 150 kinds of sweets are offered here, including soft ice cream, 30 varieties of milk shakes, muffins, cookies, candies, and doughnuts. There's a children's playground where children can play while parents enjoy an uninterrupted sundae. *Rodney Bay, no phone. No reservations. No credit cards. Closed Mon. Inexpensive–Moderate.*

Lodging

St. Lucia's Caribbean coast is splashed with hotels, most of them along the strip from Castries to Cap Estate. There are hotels with social directors who will have you doing calisthenics on the beach at dawn, and West Indian guest houses where hanging out is the day's only scheduled activity. You should reserve four months in advance for a room during the winter season.

The most highly recommended lodgings are indicated by a star ★.

Category	Cost*
Very Expensive	over $150
Expensive	$100–$150
Moderate	$50–$100
Inexpensive	under $50

All prices are for a standard double room for two, excluding 8% tax and a 10% service charge.

Hotels **Club St. Lucia.** Everything is included in the price here, which means meals and unlimited drinks, golf greens fees and clubs, horseback riding, a full-day boat cruise, and a supervised children's miniclub. The resort sits on 12 acres, with rooms and suites in bungalows scattered over the hillside, and has two beaches. The accommodations are spacious, with king-size beds (twins on request), tile floors, patio, bath with tub and shower, and air-conditioning in all but the standard rooms, which have ceiling fans only. There are clock radios in all of the rooms, but no phones. Live entertainment is scheduled nightly. *Box 915, Smugglers Village, Castries, tel. 809/452–0551 or 800/223–9868 in Britain, 154 rooms and suites. Facilities: restaurant, 2 bars, pool, 2 tennis courts, disco, minimart, water-sports center, transport to stables, golf club, squash court. AE, DC, MC, V. Very Expensive.*

Couples. Exactly as the name suggests, this all-inclusive resort is for couples only. Things tend to be quite active, with volleyball in the pool and on the beach, aerobics, and water exercises. The activities desk can arrange anything, including a wedding. Rooms and suites are on the chic side, with king-size four-poster beds and marble baths. There is an oceanfront wing with 24 air-conditioned rooms and 12 fan-cooled rooms. Other accommodations are in the three-story air-conditioned main building. There is nightly live music for dancing, and a piano bar that closes when the last couple leaves. Once you've paid the up-front fee, your hands need not touch money again during your stay. *Box 190, Malabar Beach, tel. 809/452–4211 or 800/221–1831. 100 rooms. Facilities: restaurant, 2 bars, pool, 2 lighted tennis courts, sauna, Jacuzzi, exercise room, bicycles, horseback riding, water-sports center. MC, V. Very Expensive.*

★ **Cunard Hotel La Toc and La Toc Suites.** In a secluded 110-acre valley, this posh air-conditioned resort's reception area is done in rose colors with fresh flowers, statuary, Oriental rugs, and artwork. Spacious standard rooms in the hotel section, furnished with artwork and upscale rattan and pine, have king-size or twin beds, clock radios, and bath with amenity packages, tub, and shower. The La Toc Suites, adjacent to the hotel, originally intended to be sold as condominiums but used as the hotel's suites, are now being operated as a separate hotel. A resident host and hostess are on hand, as are 24-hour attendants who help you unpack, turn your bed down and serve you breakfast in it, and pamper you throughout your stay. The two-bedroom suites have private plunge pools, wet bars, refrigerators, TVs and VCRs, plus all of the facilities of the sister hotel. When you call to reserve ask about Cunard's land-and-sea packages. *Box 399, Castries, tel. 809/452–3081 or Cunard 800/222–0939. 192 rooms in the hotel; 54 La Toc Suites. Facilities: 3 restaurants, 3 bars, 2 pools, 6 lighted tennis courts, fitness center,* beauty salon, boutiques, 9-hole golf course, water-sports center. AE, DC, MC, V. Very Expensive.

Halcyon Beach Club. You register in a wood-paneled breezeway, and a path leads from there to the small sandy beach. Located on Choc Bay, 3 miles north of Castries, this hotel has accommodations in chalet-style buildings with simple tropical furnishings, two double beds, air-conditioning, clock radios, and patios or balconies. Standard rooms are in the gardens and superior rooms line the beach. The Chanticleer Wharf Restaurant sits out on a jetty, where there is also a disco. There's a children's playground (children under 12 stay for free with their parents), and a pool just off the beach. There's plenty of entertainment. By noon the music is revved up and going strong. *Box 388, Castries, tel. 809/452-5331 or 800/223-9815. 140 rooms. Facilities: 2 restaurants, 2 bars, disco, 2 lighted tennis courts, pool, horseback riding and golf nearby, children's playground, water-sports center. AE, DC, MC, V. Very Expensive.*

Le Sport. A $15 million investment transformed the Cariblue Hotel into this resort, which bills itself as the Body Holiday. If you've been dying to dip into thalassotherapy (seawater massages, thermal jet baths, and such), this is the place to do it. In addition to the beauty treatments, eucalyptus inhalations, and seaweed nutrient wraps, the all-inclusive resort offers a daily program involving everything from aerobics to yoga. Cushy air-conditioned rooms are done in luscious pastels, all with twin beds, marble baths, hair dryers, and fridges. A band plays nightly, and there's a piano bar. *Box 437, Cariblue Beach, tel. 809/452-0368 or 800/221-1831. 128 rooms and suites. Facilities: restaurant, 2 bars, 2 pools, bicycles, 2 lighted tennis courts, water-sports center, thalassotherapy, beauty and rejuvenation treatments, Jacuzzi, Turkish baths, exercise rooms, health shop, boutique, bank, medical facilities. AE, DC, MC, V. Very Expensive.*

★ **Marigot Bay Resort.** Villas, an inn, and a hotel comprise this village, which is located on a lovely bay, surrounded by green hills with lush tropical trees and flowers. A little trolley edges up the hill from Dolittle's Restaurant and the market to the one-, two-, and three-bedroom villas with wide plank verandas and fully equipped kitchens. The West Indian–style Marigot Inn next to the restaurant has lanai studios, each with kitchenette and balcony overlooking the marina. Fan-cooled stone cottages with wicker, bamboo, and rattan furnishings, king-size beds, and kitchenettes comprise the harborside Hurricane Hole Hotel, which has the ambience of a hunting lodge. A 24-hour water taxi connects the resort's facilities. *Box 101, Castries, tel. 809/453-4357 or 800/535-7289. 47 rooms. Facilities: 2 restaurants, 2 bars, market, dive shop, yacht charters, sailing, water-sports center. AE, DC, MC, V. Very Expensive.*

★ **St. Lucian.** The lobby is broad and white, with Oriental rugs and upholstered sofas. This was once two hotels and the rooms are spread out over considerable acreage, some on Reduit Beach, some in gardens. All have individually controlled air conditioners, two double beds, clock radios, direct-dial phones, and patios or terraces. This is the home of Splash, one of the island's hottest discos, and the local agent for Mistral Windsurfers. Water sports, including windsurfing lessons, are free to hotel guests. *Box 512, Castries, tel. 809/452-8351 or 800/221-1831. 192 rooms. Facilities: 2 restaurants, 4 bars, disco, pool, laundry/dry cleaning, 2 lighted tennis courts, dive* *shop, boutiques, ice-cream parlor, beauty salon, minimarket, water-sports center. AE, DC, MC, V. Expensive–Very Expensive.*

Vigie Beach Hotel. A glassed-in bar sits on the mile-long Vigie Beach, and a path leads through gardens up to the hotel. Rooms are spacious with modern decor, double beds, balconies with garden or beach view, and individually controlled air conditioners. Meals are served buffet style, and there is nightly entertainment. TVs are available for rent, and guests can use the tennis courts at the Halcyon Beach Hotel. You'll be sunning to the sound of small planes, as the hotel is located adjacent to Vigie Airport. *Box 395, Castries, tel. 809/452–5211 or 800/468–0023. 49 rooms. Facilities: restaurant, 2 bars, pool, Jacuzzi. AE, DC, MC, V. Expensive–Very Expensive.*

★ **Anse Chastanet Hotel.** Rooms are in a cluster of octagonal gazebos planted in a tropical hillside forest. In addition to the gazebos, there are 12 suites, some with plunge pools. All have ceiling fans and verandas. The hotel is on a 400-acre estate near Soufrière and the Pitons. From the main restaurant, 125 steps lead to a lovely white-sand crescent where there is another restaurant, a thatch-roof bar, and a dive shop. Sunfish and Windsurfers are gratis to guests. The restaurants serve fine West Indian fare. The hotel is quiet, peaceful, and secluded. *Box 216, Soufrière, tel. 809/454–7355. 37 rooms and suites. Facilities: 2 restaurants, 2 bars, tennis court, dive shop, water-sports center. AE, DC, MC, V. Expensive.*

Club Med St. Lucia. The four-story air-conditioned hotel is on a 95-acre beachfront property on the southeast coast, where the rough Atlantic waters are not recommended for swimming. All of the usual Club Med activities are here, including nightly entertainment. Hewanorra International Airport is five minutes away. *Vieux Fort, tel. 809/455–6001 or 800/CLUBMED. 256 rooms. Facilities: restaurant, bar, boutique, fitness center, 8 tennis courts, pool, horseback riding, water-sports center. AE, DC, MC, V. Expensive.*

Harmony Apartel. On Rodney Bay Marina, this two-story apartment hotel has accommodations ranging from small studios to two-bedroom apartments with fully equipped electric kitchens. All have wall-to-wall carpeting, twin beds, showers, TVs with VCRs, balconies or patios, and token-operated air conditioners. The two-bedroom apartments sleep up to six, and you've a choice of one or two baths. Poolside rooms, away from the marina, are quieter. Windsurfing is free; other water sports are available. There's a manager's rum-punch party every Tuesday. The Mortar and Pestle restaurant serves fine Caribbean food. *Box 155, Castries, tel. 809/452–8756 or 800/223–6510. 21 units. Facilities: restaurant, minimarket, maid service, pool, water-sports center, VCR library and books library. AE, MC, V. Moderate–Expensive.*

★ **Green Parrot.** There are green velvet chairs in the small reception room, a popular sunken bar, and a formal wood-paneled dining room. The stone and stucco inn sits high up in the Morne above Castries, and the view is spectacular. A free bus scoots you to town and the beach. Large rooms have patio, phone, air-conditioning, and bath with tub/shower and vanity. The hotel arranges boat trips to Jambette Beach for barbecue and snorkeling for about $30. *Box 648, Castries, tel. 809/452–3399. 30 rooms. Facilities: 2 restaurants, bar, game room, nightclub. AE, MC, V. Moderate.*

★ **Islander.** An upscale motel just 300 yards from Reduit Beach, the Islander offers standard air-conditioned rooms with clock radios, wall-to-wall carpeting, king-size beds, refrigerators, balconies, and phones. There are also suites with kitchenettes. The Islander is in the Rodney Bay area. Supermarkets, restaurants, and nightlife are a few steps away. *Box 907, Castries, tel. 809/452–8757 or 800/223–9815. 60 units. Facilities: restaurant, bar, pool, movie room. AE, MC, V. Moderate.*

Kimatrai. This is a clean, family-owned and -operated hotel on the southeast coast, just above Vieux Fort. The Hewanorra International Airport is five minutes away. Accommodations include double rooms, self-contained apartments and bungalows. All are air-conditioned with private shower. The hotel operates only on the European Plan (no meals included). *Box 238, Vieux Fort, tel. 809/454–6328. 25 units. Facilities: restaurant, bar. No credit cards. Inexpensive–Moderate.*

Home and Apartment Rentals For private-home rentals, contact **Carribbean Home Rentals** (Box 710, Palm Beach, FL 33480) or **Happy Homes** (Box 12, Castries, St. Lucia).

Nightlife

Most of the action is in the hotels, which offer entertainment of the island variety, such as limbo dancers, fire-eaters, calypso singers, and steel band jump-ups.

Splash (St. Lucian Hotel, tel. 809/452–8351) is a sophisticated place with a good dance floor and splashy lighting effects. Open Monday–Saturday from 9 PM. At the **Halcyon Wharf Disco** (Halcyon Beach Club, tel. 809/452–5331), you can dance on the jetty under the stars every night. If you're looking for local flavor, **Monroe's** (Rodney Bay, no phone) is a strictly local place that welcomes visitors.

On weekends, locals usually hang out at **The Lime** (Rodney Bay, tel. 809/452–0761) before heading to the discos. If you're a nostalgia buff, you'll have a hard time leaving **Rain** (Columbus Sq., Castries, tel. 809/452–3022), where locals and tourists hang out nightly. **Capone's** (Rodney Bay, tel. 809/452–0284) is an Art Deco place right out of the Roaring Twenties, with a player piano and rum drinks. **The Charthouse** (Rodney Bay, tel. 452–8115) has a popular bar, jazz on stereo, and live music on Saturday. **San Antoine's** (Morne Fortune, tel. 809/452–4660), overlooking Castries Harbor, is a slightly formal place for after-dinner liqueurs and small talk. The **Rusty Anchor** (Marigot Bay, tel. 809/453–4357) is an informal hangout for the yachting crowd. Young boaters tie up at the **A-Frame** (Rodney Bay, tel. 809/452–8725) for drinks, chess, darts, and backgammon. (You can take the ferry for E.C.$2, which leaves every hour across the road from The Islander Hotel.) The **Green Parrot** (The Morne, tel. 809/452–3399) is in a class all by itself. Chef Harry Edwards hosts the floor show, which features limbo dancers. Harry has been known to shimmy under the pole himself. There are also belly dancers. Great fun; formal attire.

24 St. Martin
St. Maarten

by Honey Naylor What are the pros and cons of a visit to St. Maarten/St. Martin?

On the positive side, there are frequent nonstop flights from the United States, so you don't have to spend half your vacation getting here—a critical advantage if you have only a few days to enjoy the sun. The 37-square-mile island is home to two sovereign nations, St. Maarten (Dutch) and St. Martin (French), so you can experience two cultures for the price of one.

The island, particularly the Dutch side, is ideal for people who like lots of things to do. Whatever can be done in or on the water—snorkeling, windsurfing, water-skiing—is available here; and there is golf and tennis as well. There are enough quality restaurants for serious diners to try a different one each night, even on a two-week stay. The duty-free shopping is as good as anywhere in the Caribbean, except perhaps in the U.S. Virgin Islands. There's an active nightlife, with discos and casinos. Water-sports enthusiasts will love Simpson Bay Lagoon, the largest inland body of water in the Caribbean. Day trips can be taken by ship or plane to the nearby islands of Anguilla, Saba, St. Eustatius, and St. Barthélemy. There are hotels for every taste and budget—from motel-type units for the package tour trade to some of the most exclusive resorts in the Caribbean. The standard of living is one of the highest in the Caribbean, so the islanders can afford to be honest and to treat visitors as welcome guests.

On the negative side, the island is not one of the most beautiful the Caribbean has to offer, and there is little indigenous art, architecture, or culture. St. Maarten/St. Martin has been thoroughly discovered; unless you stay in an exclusive resort, you are likely to be sharing beachfronts with tour groups or conventioneers. Yes, there is gambling, but the table limits are so low that hard-core gamblers will have a better time gamboling on the beach. It can be fun to shop, and there's an occasional bargain, but many goods, particularly electronics, are cheaper in the United States.

Perhaps what makes this island unique is the opportunity it affords the visitor to lead an active life one moment, and to come to a complete halt the next. For all its bustle, St. Martin/St. Maarten is still a Caribbean island brushed by gentle trade winds. You can do nothing at all and enjoy yourself immensely.

Before You Go

Tourist Information For information about the Dutch side, contact the **St. Maarten Tourist Office** (275 7th Ave., New York, NY 10001, tel. 212/989–0000) or the **St. Maarten Information Office** (243 Ellerslie Ave., Willowdale, Toronto, Ont. M2N 1Y5, tel. 416/223–3501). Information about French St. Martin can be obtained through the **French West Indies Tourist Board** (610 5th Ave., New York, NY 10020, tel. 212/757–1125). **In Canada:** 1981 Ave. McGill College, Montreal, Quebec H3A 2W9, tel. 514/288–4264. **In the United Kingdom:** 178 Piccadilly, London W1Z OAL, tel. 01/493–6594.

Arriving and Departing
By Plane There are two airports on the island. L'Esperance on the French side is small and handles only island-hoppers. Bigger planes fly into Juliana International Airport on the Dutch side. **American Airlines** (tel. 800/433–7300) has daily nonstop flights from New York and excellent connections from more than 100

U. S. cities via its San Juan hub. **Pan Am** (tel. 800/221–1111) has daily nonstop service from New York. **BWIA** (tel. 800/327–7401) flies in via Antigua from Toronto, Jamaica, San Juan, Trinidad, and Miami. **LIAT** (tel. 809/462–0701) flies from Antigua; **ALM** (tel. 800/327–7230) from Aruba, Bonaire, Curaçao, the Dominican Republic, and four times a week from New York. **Air Martinique** (tel. 596/51–08–09) connects the island with Martinique twice a week. **Windward Islands Airways (Winair,** tel. 599/54–42–30), which is based on St. Maarten, has daily scheduled service to Saba, St. Eustatius, St. Barts, Anguilla, St. Thomas, and St. Kitts/Nevis. **Air Guadeloupe** (tel. 590/90–37–37) has several flights daily to St. Barts and Guadeloupe from both sides of the island. **Air St. Barthélemy** (tel. 590/27–71–90) has frequent service from Juliana. Tour and Charter services are available from Winair and **St. Martin Helicopters** (Dutch side, tel. 599/4–4287).

By Boat   Motorboats zip several times a day from Anguilla to the French side; three times a week from St. Barts. Catamaran service is available daily from the Dutch side to St. Barts. The 50-passenger *Style* (tel. 599/5–22167) slaps across from Saba four times a week.

Passports   U.S. citizens need proof of citizenship. A passport (valid or not
and Visas   expired more than five years) is preferred. An original birth certificate with raised seal (or a photocopy with notary seal), or a voter's registration card are also acceptable. All visitors must have a confirmed room reservation and an ongoing or return ticket. British and Canadian citizens need valid passports.

Customs and   There are no customs as St. Martin/St. Maarten is a free
Duties   port.

Language   Dutch is the official language of St. Maarten and French is the official language of St. Martin, but almost everyone speaks English. If you hear a language you can't quite place, it's Papiamento, a Spanish-based Creole of the Netherlands Antilles.

Further Reading   Dr. J. Hartog's *St. Maarten, Saba, and St. Eustatius,* usually available in paperback in the island's bookstores, gives you a rundown on the islands' history and includes interesting photographs.

Staying in St. Martin/St. Maarten

Important   **Tourist Information:** On the Dutch side the **Tourist Information**
Addresses   **Bureau** is on Cyrus Wathey (pronounced watty) Square in the heart of Philipsburg, at the pier where the cruise ships send their tenders. *Tel. 599/5–22337. Open weekdays 8–noon and 1–5, except holidays.*

On the French side, there is a small **Tourist Information Office** on the Marigot pier. *Tel. 590/87–53–26. Open weekdays 9–noon and 2–3:30; closed holidays and the afternoon preceding a holiday.*

Emergencies   **Police:** Dutch side (tel. 599/5–22222), French side (tel. 590/85–50–10).

Ambulance: Dutch side (tel. 599/5–22111), French side (tel. 590/87–54–14).

Hospitals: St. Rose Hospital (Front St., Philipsburg, tel. 599/5–22300) is a fully equipped 55-bed hospital.

St. Martin / St. Maarten

TO ANGUILLA

Pt. Arago

Pte. du Bluff

Baie de la Potence

Pt. du Plum

Baie Rouge

Pte. des Pierres a Chaux

Baie de Marigot

Plum Baie

Marigot

Baie Longue

Simpson Bay Lagoon

Cupecoy Beach

Sentry Hill

Mullet Bay

S T.

Juliana International Airport

Maho Bay

Simpson Bay

Koolbaai

Cole Bay

Caribbean Sea

N

0   2 miles
0   3 km

1 Exploring Sites

8 Hotels and Restaurants

Pharmacies: Pharmacies are open Monday–Saturday 7–5. **Central Drug Store** (Philipsburg, tel. 599/5–22321), **Mullet Bay Drug Store** (tel. 599/5–42801, ext. 342), and **Pharmacie** (Marigot, tel. 590/87–50–79).

Currency Legal tender on the Dutch side is the Netherlands Antilles florin (guilder), written NAf; on the French side, the French franc (F). The exchange rate fluctuates, but in general is about 1.80 NAf to U.S. $1 and 5.5F to U.S. $1. On the Dutch side, prices are usually given in both NAf and U.S. dollars, which are accepted all over the island, as are credit cards. Note: Prices quoted here are in U.S. dollars unless otherwise noted.

Taxes and Service Charges On the Dutch side, there is a 5% government tax added to hotel bills. On the French side, a *taxe de sejour* (visitor's tax) is tacked onto hotel bills (the amount differs from hotel to hotel, but the maximum is $1 per day, per person). All visitors pay a $5 departure tax from Juliana Airport. It will cost you 10 French francs to depart by plane from l'Esperance Airport or by ferry to Anguilla from Marigot's pier.

In lieu of tipping, service charges are added to hotel bills all over the island, and, by law, are included in all menu prices on the French side. On the Dutch side, most restaurants add 10%–15% to the bill.

Hotels on the Dutch side add a 15% service/energy charge to the bill. Hotels on the French side add 10%–15% for service.

Taxi drivers expect a 10% tip.

Guided Tours A 2½-hour taxi tour of the island costs $30 for one or two people, $7 for each additional person. Your hotel or the Tourist Office can arrange it for you. Best bet is the 20-passenger vans of **St. Maarten Sightseeing Tours** (Philipsburg, tel. 599/5–22753), which offer, among other options, a 2½-hour island tour for $6 per person. You can tour in deluxe comfort with **St. Maarten Limousine Service** (tel. 599/5–24698 or 599/5–22698) for $40–$50 per hour with a three-hour minimum. Fully equipped Lincoln Continentals accommodate up to six people and are furnished with stereo, fully stocked bar, and air-conditioning. The limo service also offers transportation to and from Juliana Airport at rates ranging from $30 to $65 one way. (They include one hour of waiting time free of charge for late arrivals.)

Getting Around **Taxis** Taxi rates are government regulated and authorized taxis display stickers of the St. Maarten Taxi Association. There is a taxi service, headed by Raymond Helligar, at the Marigot port near the Tourist Information Bureau. Fixed fares apply from Juliana Airport and the Marigot ferry to the various hotels and around the island. Fares are 25% higher between 10 PM and midnight; 50% higher between midnight and 6 AM.

Buses One of the island's best bargains at 85¢, buses operate frequently between 7 AM and 7 PM and run from Philipsburg through Cole Bay to Marigot.

Rental Cars You can book a car at Juliana Airport, but a strong taxi union makes it impossible for you to drive it away from there. You'll have to take a taxi to your hotel where your car will be delivered without additional cost. (You can drive the car to the airport and leave it when you depart.) All foreign driver's licenses are honored, and major credit cards are accepted. The cost is about $30 a day, plus collision insurance, with unlimited mileage. **Avis** (tel. 800/331–1212), **Budget** (tel. 800/527–0700), **Dollar** (tel. 800/421–6868), **Hertz** (tel. 800/223–6472), and **National** (tel. 800/328–4567) all have offices on the island. Most hotels will reserve a car for guests in advance, an offer that you should take advantage of, especially during the height of the winter season.

Telephones and Mail To call the Dutch side from the United States, dial 011–599 + local number; for the French side, 011–590 + local number. To phone from the Dutch side to the French, dial 06 + local number; from the French side to the Dutch, 3 + local number. Keep in mind that a call from one side to another is an overseas call, not a local call. Telephone communications, especially on the Dutch side, leave something to be desired. On the French side, it is not possible to make collect or credit card calls to the United States, and there are no coin phones. If you think you'll need to use public phones on the French side, go to the special desk at Marigot's post office and buy a Telecarte (it looks like a credit card), which gives you 40 units for around 31F or 120 units for 93F.

Letters from the Dutch side to the United States and Canada cost NAf 1.30; postcards, NAf .60. From the French side, letters up to 20 grams, 4.10F; postcards, 2.80F.

Opening and Closing Times Shops on the Dutch side are open Monday–Saturday, 8–noon and 2–6; on the French side, Monday–Saturday 9–noon or 12:30, and 2–6. Some of the larger shops on both sides of the island open Sunday and holidays when the cruise ships are in port. Some of the small Dutch and French shops set their own capricious hours.

Banks on the Dutch side are open Monday–Thursday 8–1 and Friday 4–5. French banks open weekdays 9–noon and 2–3 and close afternoons preceding holidays.

Beaches

The island's 10 miles of beaches are all open to the public. Beaches occupied by resort properties charge a small fee (about $3) for changing facilities, and water-sport equipment can be rented in most of the hotels. The island has as many beaches as it has square miles. Some of the 37 beaches are secluded, some are located in the thick of things. Topless bathing is virtually de rigueur on the French side. If you take a cab to a remote beach, be sure to arrange a specific, clearly understood time for your driver to return to pick you up, and don't leave valuables unattended on the beach.

Hands down, **Baie Longue** is the best beach on the island. It's a beautiful, mile-long curve of white sand on the westernmost tip of the island. This is a good place for snorkeling and swimming, but beware of a strong undertow when the waters are rough. You can sunbathe in the buff. Pack a lunch. There are no facilities.

Cupecoy Beach is a narrower, more secluded strip of white sand with a backdrop of cliffs and caves. It's just south of Baie Longue on the western side of the island, near the Dutch-French border. There are no facilities.

You can sunbathe au naturel at **Baie Rouge,** one of the most secluded and quietest beaches on the island. This little patch of sand is located at the base of high cliffs and backed by private homes rather than hotels. No facilities.

You have to approach the **Dawn Beach–Oyster Pond** area through the Dawn Beach Hotel. This long white-sand beach is partly protected by reefs (good for snorkeling), but the waters are not always calm. When the waves come rolling in, this is the best spot on the island for bodysurfing. There are water-sports rentals at **Red Ensign Watersports** (*see* Participant Sports, below), a snack bar, and facilities.

Ecru-color sand, palm and sea grape trees, calm waters, and the roar of jets lowering to nearby Juliana Airport distinguish the beach at **Maho Bay.** Concession stand, beach chairs, and facilities are available.

At **Mullet Bay,** the powdery white-sand beach is crowded with guests of the Mullet Bay Resort, where you can get refreshments. Rentals are available at the hotel through Maho Watersports (*see* Participant Sports, below).

Simpson Bay is a long half-moon of white sand near Simpson Bay Village, one of the last undiscovered hamlets on the island. In this small fishing village you'll find refreshments, the **Ocean Explorers** (*see* Participant Sports, below) for water-sports rentals, and the opportunity to take a small tour of the neat little ultra-Caribbean town homes.

Orient Beach is the island's best known "clothes optional" beach. It's a fairly deserted Atlantic beach where you can rent equipment at Club Orient (*see* Lodging, below).

Ilet Pinel is a little speck off the northeast coast, with about 500 yards of beach, where you can have picnics and privacy. There are no facilities.

Exploring St. Martin/St. Maarten

Numbers in the margin correspond with points of interest on the St. Martin/St. Maarten map.

Philipsburg The Dutch capital of Philipsburg, which stretches about a mile
❶ along an isthmus between Great Bay and the Salt Pond, has three more or less parallel streets: Front Street, Back Street, and Pond Fill. Your first stop should be the **Tourist Office** on **Wathey Square.** After arming yourself with maps, brochures, and friendly advice, stroll out on the pier. **Great Bay** is rolled out before you, and the beach stretches alongside it for about a mile. The square bustles with vendors, souvenir shops, and tourists. There's a taxi stand where you can arrange for a driver to take you around, if you'd rather not rent a car. Philipsburg should be explored on foot, but you'll need wheels to get around the island.

Directly across the street from Wathey Square you'll see a striking white building with a cupola. It was built in 1793, and has served since then as the commander's home, a fire station, and a jail. It now serves as Town Hall and the post office.

The square is in the middle of the isthmus on which Philipsburg sits. To your right and left the streets are lined with hotels, duty-free shops, fine restaurants, and cafés, most of them in pastel-colored West Indian cottages gussied up with gingerbread trim. Narrow alleyways lead to arcades and flower-filled courtyards where there are yet more boutiques and eateries.

Little lanes called *steegjes* connect Front Street with Back Street, which is considerably less congested because it has fewer shops.

Time Out Behind a filigree facade you can get a Haagen Dazs "fix" at **Donchee's Ice Cream Parlor.** (Back St., tel. 599/5–22452). There are oven-warm pastries, too.

Our drive begins at the western end of Front Street. The road (it will become Sucker Garden Rd.) leads north along Salt Pond and begins to climb and curve just outside of town. Take the **2** first right to **Guana Bay Point,** from which there is a splendid view of the island's east coast, tiny deserted islands, and small St. Barts, which is anything but deserted.

Sucker Garden Road continues north through spectacular scenery. Continue along a paved roller-coaster road down to **Dawn Beach,** one of the island's best snorkeling beaches.

3 **Oyster Pond** is the legendary point where two early settlers, a Frenchman and a Dutchman, allegedly began to pace in opposite directions around the island, to divide it between their respective countries. (The official boundary marker is on the other side of the island.)

Elsewhere on From Oyster Pond, follow the road along the bay and around
the Island Etang aux Poissons (Fish Lake), all the way to **Orléans.** This
4 settlement, which is also known as the French Quarter, is the oldest on the island. Noted local artist and activist Roland Richardson makes his home here. He holds open studio on Thursdays from 10 to 6 to sell his art. He's a proud islander ready to share his wealth of knowledge about the island's cultural history.

A rough dirt road leads eastward to **Orient Beach,** the island's best-known nudist beach. Offshore, little Ilet Pinel is an uninhabited island, fine for picnicking, sunning, and swimming.

5 North of Orleans you'll come to **French Cul de Sac,** where you'll see the French colonial mansion of St. Martin's mayor nestled in the hills. Little red-roof houses look like open umbrellas tumbling down the green hillside. The scenery here is glorious, and the area is great for hiking. There is a lot of construction, however, as the surroundings are slowly being developed. The descent to L'Habitation, the elegant resort at Anse Marcel on the north coast, may turn your knuckles white.

The road swirls south through green hills and pastures, past flower-entwined stone fences. Past Esperance Airport is the **6** town of **Grand Case.** Though it has only one mile-long main street, it's known as the "Restaurant Capital of the Caribbean": More than 20 restaurants serve French, Italian, Indonesian, and Vietnamese fare, as well as the freshest seafood. At press time the street was completely torn up, with construction underway on a bypass road that will eventually unclog the traffic that can build up around dinnertime. **Grand Case Beach Hotel** is at the end of this road and has two beaches to choose from for a short dip.

7 Follow the signs south from Grand Case to Rue de la République, which brings you to the French capital of **Marigot.** If you're a shopper, a gourmand, or just a Francophile, you'll want to tarry here a while. Marina Port La Royale is the shopping complex at the port, but Rue de la République and Rue de la Liberté, which border the bay, are also filled with duty-free shops, boutiques, and bistros.

One road from Marigot leads west and circles **Simpson Bay Lagoon,** where there is a concentration of fine beaches and luxury resorts. The Mediterranean-style village of **La Belle Creole** commands Point du Bluff. The beaches of **Plum Bay, Baie Rouge,** and **Baie Longue** cling to the westernmost point of the island. They are all accessible down bumpy but short dirt roads, and are perfect for swimming and picnicking.

From here, the road continues eastward along the south coast and on to Juliana Airport.

Time Out **Stop & Shop** (Airport Rd., tel. 599/5–42626) is a little convenience market across from the airport. There's porch seating on the lagoon and seafood heroes to consume.

The road due south of Marigot to Philipsburg passes the official boundary, where a simple border marker, erected by the Dutch and French citizenry to commemorate 300 years of peaceful coexistence, bears the dates "1648 to 1948." The only formality at the border is an occasional pause to allow a herd of cows to meander across the road.

At the airport, the road from Marigot to the north and Simpson Bay to the west join together and lead to Philipsburg, passing the cut-off to Divi Little Bay Beach Resort.

What to See and Do with Children

Live Eagle Spectacular (*see* Off the Beaten Track, below).

Fun City. An entertainment center with local limbo and fire dancers, Caribbean folkloric dancers, and steel drum players. Shows daily at 11 AM and 2 PM. For further information call The Caribbean Entertainment Center (Philipsburg, tel. 599/5–22261 or 599/5–23194).

Off the Beaten Track

No doubt about it, Jean-Pierre Bordes has a way with birds. For more than 20 years he's been talking to them, listening to them, and teaching them to straighten up and fly right. What kinds of birds? Oh, vultures, falcons, eagles—your basic birds of prey. And why? You can see for yourself high on a hilltop overlooking St. Maarten, where Bordes presents his **Live Eagle Spectacular.** This is one of only six places in the world where falconry is performed publicly. Bordes's hooded peregrine falcon rises high in the sky and dives toward Earth at a speed of 200 miles an hour. Each of his four griffin vultures has a wing span of nine feet. There's no show unless the weather's right, so ask at your hotel or at the Tourist Office before you drive up the narrow dirt road that leads to it. *In Maho Bay on the road to Pointe Pirouette, just past Casino Royale (follow the yellow signs). Admission: $8 adults, $4 children. Shows daily, weather permitting, at 10:30, 2:30, and 4.*

Participant Sports

All the resort hotels have activities desks that can arrange virtually any type of water sport.

Boating Motorboats, speedboats, Dolphins, pedal boats, sailboats, and canoes can be rented at **Lagoon Cruises & Watersports** (tel. 599/5–42801, ext. 337) and **Caribbean Watersports** (tel. 599/5–44387).

Sun Charters (tel. 800/772–3500) has a fleet of 30 Centurion sailboats for hire. A new yacht charter company is **Dynasty** (Marigot's Port La Royale Marina, tel. 590/87–85–21).

Deep-Sea Fishing Angle for yellowtail, snapper, grouper, marlin, tuna, and wahoo on half-day deep-sea excursions, including bait and tackle, instruction for novices, and open bar. Contact **Wampum** (Bobby's Marina, Philipsburg, tel. 599/5–22366).

Golf **Mullet Bay Resort** (tel. 599/5–42081) has an 18-hole championship course.

Horseback Riding Contact **Crazy Acres Riding Center** (Wathey Estate, Cole Bay, tel. 599/5–22061) or **Caid & Isa** (Anse Marcel, tel. 590/87–32–92).

Jet- and Waterskiing Rent equipment through **Caribbean Watersports** (tel. 599/5–42801 or 599/5–44363) and **Maho Watersports** (tel. 599/5–44387).

Parasailing A great high can be arranged through **Lagoon Cruises & Watersports** (tel. 599/5–42801).

Running The **Road Runners Club** (Pelican Resort Activities Desk, tel. 599/5–42503) meets weekly for its 5K or 10K run.

Scuba Diving On the Dutch side is Proselyte Reef, named for the British frigate H. M. S. *Proselyte* which sank south of Great Bay in 1802. In addition to wreck dives, reef, night, cave, and drift dives are popular. Off the northeast coast of the French side, dive sites include Ilet Pinel, for good shallow diving; Green Key, a prolific barrier reef; and Flat Island (also known as Ile Tintamarre) for sheltered coves and subsea geologic faults. NAUI and PADI certified dive centers offer instruction, rentals, and trips at **Tradewinds Dive Center** (tel. 599/5–22167), **Maho Watersports** (tel. 599/5–44387), **St. Maarten Divers** (tel. 599/5–23008, ext. 536), **Under the Waves Watersports** (tel. 590/87–51–87), **Watersports Unlimited** (tel. 599/5–23434), and **Little Bay Watersports** (tel. 599/5–22333).

Sea Excursions You can take a day-long picnic sail (wine, beer, soft drinks, lunch, and snorkeling equipment are included) to offshore islands or secluded coves aboard the 45-foot ketch *Gabrielle* (tel. 599/5–23170); the 41-foot ketch *Pretty Penny* (tel. 599/5–2167); or the 60-foot schooner *Gandalf.* The catamaran *Bluebeard II* (tel. 599/5–42801 or 599/5–42898), moored in Marigot, sails around Anguilla's south and northwest coasts to Prickley Pear, where there are excellent coral reefs for snorkeling and powdery white sands for sunning. Included in the deal are mixed drinks, snacks, beer, the use of underwater cameras, and a chicken and seafood barbecue.

The luxurious 75-foot motor catamaran *White Octopus* (tel. 599/5–23170) does full-moon and cocktail cruises, complete with calypso music. In St. Martin, sailing, snorkeling, and picnic excursions to offshore islands can be arranged through **Pat Turner Watersports** (Le Galion, tel. 590/87–51–77), **Papagayo**

(Club Orient, tel. 590/87-33-85), **L'Habitation** (tel. 590/87-33-33), **La Belle Creole** (tel. 590/87-58-66), and **La Samanna** (tel. 590/87-51-22).

Snorkeling Coral reefs teem with marine life, and clear water allows visibility of up to 200 feet. Some of the best snorkeling on the Dutch side can be had around the rocks below Fort Amsterdam off Little Bay Beach, the west end of Maho Bay, Pelican Key and the rocks near the Caravanserai Hotel, and the reefs off Dawn Beach and Oyster Pond. On the French side, the area around Orient Bay, Green Key, Ilet Pinel, and Flat Island (or Tintamarre) is especially lovely for snorkeling, and has been officially classified a regional underwater nature reserve. Arrange rentals and trips through **Watersports Unlimited** (tel. 599/5-23434), **Red Ensign Watersports** (tel. 599/5-22929), **Ocean Explorers** (tel. 599/5-45252), and **Little Bay Watersports** (tel. 599/5-22333).

Tennis There are two lighted courts at **Dawn Beach Hotel** (tel. 599/5-22944), two lighted courts at **Pelican Resort** (tel. 599/5-42503), three asphalt courts at **Little Bay and Belair Beach Resorts** (tel. 599/5-22333 or 599/5-23362), four courts at **Maho Reef & Beach** (tel. 599/5-42115), four lighted courts at **Le Privilege** (Anse Marcel, 590/87-59-28), and 16 all-weather courts at **Mullet Bay Resort** (tel. 599/5-42081).

Windsurfing Rental and instruction are available at **Little Bay Beach Hotel** (tel. 599/5-22333, ext. 186), **Maho Watersports** (tel. 599/5-44387), and **Red Ensign Watersports** (tel. 599/5-22929).

Shopping

About 180 cruise ships call at St. Maarten each year, and they do so for about 500 reasons. That's roughly the number of duty-free shops on the island.

Prices can be 25%-50% below those in the United States and Canada on French perfumes, liquor, cognac and fine liqueurs, cigarettes and cigars, Swedish crystal and Finnish stoneware, Irish linen, Italian leather, German cameras, European designer fashions, plus thousands of other things you never knew you wanted. But check prices before you leave home, especially if you live in the New York City area—Manhattan's prices for cameras and electronic equipment are hard to beat anywhere.

St. Maarten's best-known "craft" is its guavaberry liqueur, made from rum and the wild local berries (not to be confused with guavas) that grow only on this island's central mountains.

Prices are quoted in florins, francs, and dollars; shops take credit cards and traveler's checks. Most shopkeepers, especially on the Dutch side, speak English. (If more than one cruise ship is in port, avoid Front Street. It's so crowded you won't be able to move.)

Shopping Areas In St. Maarten: **Front Street,** Philipsburg, is one long strip lined with sleek boutiques and cozy shops gift wrapped in gingerbread. **Old Town,** near the end of Front Street, has 22 stores, boutiques, and open-air cafés. The newest addition, just outside of Philipsburg, is **Amsterdam Shopping Center,** with 22 pastel West Indian–style shops and restaurants on cobblestone streets. And there are almost 100 boutiques in **Mullet, Mayo,** and **Treasure Island Cupecoy Piazza.**

In St. Martin: Wrought-iron balconies, colorful awnings, and gingerbread trim decorate Marigot's smart shops, tiny boutiques, and bistros in the **Marina Port La Royale, Galerie Perigourdine,** and on the main streets, **Rue de la Liberté** and **Rue de la République.**

Good Buys   Little Switzerland (Marigot and Philipsburg, tel. 800/524–2010) and **Spritzer and Fuhrmann** (Marigot, tel. 590/87–59–62; Philipsburg, tel. 599/5–44381) handle the finest in crystal and china.

Jewelry and watches can be found at **Oro del Sol** (Marigot, tel. 590/87–57–02; Treasure Island Cupecoy Piazza, tel. 599/5–22602), **Carat** (Marigot, tel. 590/87–73–40; Philipsburg, tel. 599/5–22180), **Little Switzerland** (Marigot and Philipsburg, tel. 800/524–2010), and **Little Europe** (Philipsburg, tel. 599/5–23062).

Pick up a bottle of wine for your picnic at **La Cave du Savour Club** (Marigot, tel. 590/87–58–51).

Lipstick (Marigot, tel. 590/87–73–24) and **Oro del Sol** (Marigot, tel. 590/87–57–02) carry perfumes and cosmetics.

For designer fashions head to **La Romana** (2 locations on Front St., tel. 599/5–22181) and **Havane** (Marigot, tel. 590/87–70–39).

New Amsterdam Store (Philipsburg, tel. 599/5–22787) and **The Yellow House** (Philipsburg, tel. 599/5–23438) handle fine linens and porcelain.

The Lil' Shoppe (Philipsburg, tel. 599/5–2177) carries eel-skin wallets, handbags, perfumes, and a large selection of swimwear. Shoes, belts, and handbags are also sold at **Maximoflorence** (Philipsburg, tel. 599/5–23735).

Island Specialties   Caribelle Batik, hammocks, handmade jewelry, herbs and spices are stashed at **The Shipwreck Shop** (Philipsburg, tel. 599/5–22962); sculpture, oils, and watercolors, plus "a few of a kind of attire and sundries" are on display at American mystery writer De Forbes's **Pierre Lapin** (Grand Case, tel. 590/87–52–10); and T-shirts, beach towels, native dolls, Indian glass bangles, and hand-painted Delft souvenirs can all be found at **Sasha's** (Philipsburg, tel. 599/5–24331).

K-Dis (Marigot, tel. 590/87–52–23) is a supermarket with French wines, and liqueurs, and cheeses, pâtés, heat-and-serve dishes, salads, and cold cuts.

Dining

It may seem that this island has no monuments. Au contraire, there are many of them, all dedicated to gastronomy. You'll scarcely find a touch of Dutch; the major influences are French and Italian. This season's "in" eatery may be next season's remembrance of things past, as things do have a way of changing rapidly. In high season, unless otherwise noted in our text, be sure to make reservations, and call to cancel if you can't make it. Many restaurants close during August and/or September.

The most highly recommended restaurants are indicated by a star ★.

Category	Cost*
Very Expensive	over $50
Expensive	$40–$50
Moderate	$25–$40
Inexpensive	under $25

per person, excluding drinks and service

Dutch Side **Antoine's.** This is an elegant, airy terrace overlooking Great Bay. You might start your meal, which is served by candlelight, with French onion soup, then move on to steak au poivre, veal sweetbreads in vermouth sauce, or lobster Thermidor. For dessert, try cheesecake with raspberry melba sauce. *Front St., Philipsburg, tel. 599/5–22964. AE, MC, V. Very Expensive.*

La Rosa. An intimate dining room with piano music, where Italian specialties begin with a mixed antipasto or *prosciutto e melone*. Pasta offerings include rigatoni la Rosa (young fennels done up with fresh sardines, onions, tomato sauce, raisins and Parmesan cheese). Among the best meat dishes are broiled veal rolls. Save room for the tartufo. *Sea Palace Hotel, Front St., Philipsburg, tel. 599/5–23832. AE, MC, V. Very Expensive.*

★ **Le Bec Fin.** To reach the well-known upstairs restaurant, you stroll through a flowery courtyard where La Coupole's croissants and cakes are baked daily (a nice thing to bear in mind come breakfast time). Le Bec Fin's starters include chilled tomato soufflé and snails baked in mushroom caps with hazelnut sauce. Try the fresh red snapper fillet with mussel sauce, or the duck breast in cranberry sauce. The meringue swan with mint ice cream is as delightful to the eye as to the palate. *Front St., Philipsburg, tel. 599/5–22976. AE. Very Expensive.*

Le Bilboquet. A tiny hillside terrace of the home of Bob Donn and Bill Ahlstrom is the setting for a prix-fixe dinner (about $40), which is served to a maximum of 20 people. You must make your reservations 24 hours in advance. The menu is posted on a board out in front, along with the reservation list. Each night Bob, the chef, choreographs two five-course meals that might include Cuban bean soup, caviar torte Romanoff, fish grilled with herbs, or roast beef. *Pointe Blanche, no phone. No parties of more than 4. Closed Mon. No credit cards or checks. Very Expensive.*

★ **Oyster Pond Yacht Club.** Reopened in September 1988 after renovation, the hotel and its dining room are even more elegant than before. You'll find fine linens and china, fresh flowers, and a delightful terrace. Chef Paul Souchette, originally from Martinique, cooks with an island flair. His specialties include cucumber soup, coquilles St. Jacques, fillet of red snapper in sauce piquante, and sweet, billowy soufflés for dessert. The hotel's guests have priority in this romantic dining room, so you should reserve well in advance. *Oyster Pond, tel. 599/5–22206 or 599/5–23206. AE, MC, V. Very Expensive.*

Red Snapper. A breezy terrace restaurant on Great Bay with white rattan chairs, salmon-color cloths, fine china, and a splendid view. Try goat cheese in pastry shells for openers. Chef Lionel's specials include baked red snapper fillet served with thinly sliced potatoes, and sea scallops on a bed of braised endive. For dessert, chocolate amaretto cake is a must. *93 Front St., Philipsburg, tel. 599/5–23834. AE, MC, V. Very Expensive.*

Spartaco. Northern Italian cuisine is served in a 200-year-old stone plantation house. Everything here is either homemade or imported from Italy. Some of the specialties are black angel-hair pasta with shrimp and garlic, tagliata of swordfish baked with pink pepper and rosemary, and veal Vesuviana, with mozzarella, oregano, and tomato sauce. *Almond Grove, Cole Bay, tel. 599/5–45379. No lunch. MC, V. Very Expensive.*

Felix. This classy little beachside eatery serves dinner by candlelight. At lunchtime, take a dip before feasting on salad Felix (an imaginative concoction of bananas, sweet potatoes, and avocado), rack of lamb Provençale, or steak au poivre. The restaurant is on the road to Pelican Resort. *Pelican Key, tel. 599/5–45237. AE. Closed Tues. Expensive.*

L'Escargot. A lovely 19th-century house wrapped in verandas is home to one of St. Maarten's oldest French restaurants. Starters include homemade pâté with pink peppercorns. For an entrée, try the duck in pineapple-banana sauce or the poached yellowtail in cream sauce with fresh mint. *76 Front St., Philipsburg, tel. 599/5–22483. AE, MC, V. Expensive.*

Le Perroquet. In a cool green-and-white West Indian–style house on the peaceful lagoon, chef Pierre Castagna turns out such exotic specialties as breast of ostrich. *Airport Rd., Simpson Bay, tel. 599/5–44339. Closed Mon. AE, V. Expensive.*

★ **West Indian Tavern.** A local favorite, famous for its guavaberry drinks, this is a casual tavern with gingerbread frill, verandas, and hanging plants. For starters, try crisp fried local cristophene (a vegetable fruit) or coconut fried prawns. Entrées include grouper sautéed with bacon, chopped hazlenuts, and light cream, and curried chicken with homemade mango-and-bamboo chutney and fresh coconut. Don't miss the Key-lime pie. If you're on the island on St. Patrick's Day, this is the place to be (the owner's Irish). *Front St., Philipsburg, tel. 599/5–22965. No lunch. AE, MC, V. Expensive.*

★ **Cafe Royal.** Owner Rene Florijn once coordinated a little lunch for Princess Margaret and a few (400) friends. The café's few tables sprinkle the sidewalk, and inside brass ceiling fans whir over a pink and green garden set in the atrium. The menu includes smoked Norwegian salmon, snails in garlic butter, fresh lobster salad, and hamburgers. Breakfasts range from simple to sumptuous, and afternoon tea is refreshing. For picnics, have the deli in the back pack a basket for you. *Palm Plaza, Front St., Philipsburg, tel. 599/5–23443. AE, MC, V. Moderate.*

Chesterfield's. Burgers and salads are served at lunch, but menus are more elaborate for dinner on this indoor/outdoor terrace overlooking the marina. Menu offerings include French onion soup, roast duckling with fresh pineapple and banana sauce, and chicken cordon bleu. The Mermaid Bar is a popular spot with yachtsmen. *Great Bay Marina, Philipsburg, tel. 599/5–23484. AE, MC, V. Moderate.*

Le Pavillon. Creole and French specialties, such as Assiette Tricolore (lobster, snapper, and shrimp with three sauces) and duckling in pineapple sauce, are served in this little beachside bistro. *Simpson Bay Village, tel. 599/5–44254. No lunch. AE, MC, V. Moderate.*

Callaloo. You can find a little bit of everything except callaloo. There's a pizza piazza, the lively Gazebo Bar, and a little air-conditioned café where you can get quiche, burgers, oversize sandwiches, barbecued chicken, and charbroiled steaks. *Prom-*

enade, Front St., Philipsburg, no phone. Reservations not required. No credit cards. Inexpensive.

Fandango. In this tropical rainforest setting, complete with chattering parrot, macaw, and cockatoo, West Indian specialties, along with burgers, omelets, oversize sandwiches, exotic drinks, and hearty breakfasts are served. *St. Maarten Beach Club Hotel, tel. 599/5–23434. AE, MC, V. Inexpensive.*

★ **Sam's Restaurant and Pub.** Sam's is enormously popular with a motley crowd of locals, tourists, the boating crowd, and especially American expatriates. Featured are thick-cut onion rings, charbroiled shrimp and steak kebab, pork chops and apple sauce, and big burgers. Come here for a huge American breakfast. Also, the downstairs bar is one of *the* places to be at night for live music. *Front St., Philipsburg, tel. 599/5–22989. AE, MC, V. Inexpensive.*

Wajang Doll. Indonesian dishes are served in the garden of this West Indian–style house. The specialty is *ryjsttafel*—the Indonesian rice table that offers 14 or 19 dishes in a complete dinner. *Front St., Philipsburg, tel. 599/5–22687. AE, MC, V. Inexpensive.*

French Side **L'Aventure.** This is a handsome restaurant with a veranda
★ smothered in bougainvillea and a gull's-eye view of the harbor. This is the fourth restaurant brothers Roger Petit and Ray Peterson have presented to the island. Favorites here are chilled cauliflower soup with diced smoked salmon, hot lobster and sweetbread terrine, smoked breast of duck with pears, and lobster tails grilled with orange cream. Lunch is served Sundays only in high season. *On the port, Marigot, tel. 590/87–72–89. AE, MC, V. Very Expensive.*

La Belle France. The gourmet restaurant of the stunning L'Habitation resort offers a spicy lobster pâté served with an assortment of island fish, homemade foie gras, sliced monkfish in a light sauce of green leeks, and, for dessert, mano delight in sweet pineapple sauce. *Anse Marcel, tel. 590/87–32–32. No lunch. AE, MC, V. Very Expensive.*

La Nadaillac. On a quiet terrace overlooking Marigot Bay, chef Gernand Malard presents rich dishes involving foie gras and truffles. Other offerings include bouillabaisse for two and red snapper flamed in pernod on a bed of fennel branches. Baked Alaska is made with a mixture of fruit, and the after-dinner digestif is served in a brandy snifter nestled in a bed of ice and hibiscus. *Galerie Perigourdine, rue d'Anguille, Marigot, tel. 590/87–53–77. No lunch. AE. Very Expensive.*

Le Poisson d'Or. Posh and popular, this restaurant is in a restored stone house with a 15-table terrace. You can feast on home-smoked lobster, lobster salad with fresh fruit, and terrine of leek and foie gras with fruit vinegar. Closed for lunch during off-season. *Off rue d'Anguille on the sea, Marigot, tel. 590/87–72–45. Closed Tues. for lunch in high season. AE, MC, V. Very Expensive.*

La Provence. Dining is on an upscale terra-cotta terrace that abuts the stone plaza of La Belle Creole. Chef Jacques François Benoit's selections include sweet peppers and wild mushrooms terrine, fresh pasta with crabmeat and truffles, roast rack of lamb garnished with zucchini, eggplant and garlic puree, and grilled lobster with butter and parsley. *Pointe des Pierres a Chaux, tel. 590/87–58–66. AE, CB, DC, MC, V. Very Expensive.*

La Rhumerie. The chef turns out Creole and traditional French fare, with specialties including crab farci, curried goat, herbed conch, boudin, frogs' legs, snails, and duck à l'orange. *Colombier, no phone. No credit cards. Very Expensive.*

★ **La Samanna.** This restaurant has an exquisite setting in the celebrated hotel. A brilliantly colored Indian wedding tent billows over the octagonal bar, and you can dine by candlelight on a tented terrace surrounded by bougainvillea. Chef Jean-Pierre Jury's à la carte menu might include Beluga caviar, broccoli terrine with carrots and chives, sautéed filet mignon with walnuts, or grilled red snapper with Creole sauce (the latter a low-calorie offering). The clientele is chic, international, and often famous. *Baie Longue, tel. 590/87-51-22. Jackets suggested. AE, DC, MC, V. Very Expensive.*

La Vie En Rose. This is a popular second-floor restaurant. Try to reserve a table on the balcony. The menu rewards adventurous eaters with mint-flavored vichyssoise with mussels, lobster salad with kiwis and basil, and sliced breast of duck in lemon/ginger sauce. Save room for chocolate mousse cake topped with vanilla sauce. The ground-floor tearoom and pastry shop serve an excellent luncheon with wine for $7. *Blvd. de France, Marigot, tel. 590/87-54-42. AE, MC, V. Very Expensive.*

Auberge Gourmande. A cozy setting on the main street of Grand Case. Chef Daniel Passeri, a native of Burgundy, is also in charge of Le Tastevin across the street. For openers, try the escargots de bourgogne or frogs' legs in puff pastry, then move on to beef tenderloin in Roquefort sauce or duck breast with three-berry sauce. Reservations can be made across the street at Le Tastevin. *Grand Case, no phone. Closed Aug., Sept., and Wed. MC, V. Expensive.*

★ **La Residence.** An intimate setting with soft lighting, a tinkling fountain, and such specialties as fresh snapper baked in foil with olive oil and spices, bouillabaisse, and fresh lobster in a cognac sauce. The soufflés are sensational. *Marigot, tel. 590/87-70-37. AE, MC, V. Expensive.*

Le Privilege. High on a hill, with a commanding view, Le Privilege is a sports and entertainment complex that is open 24 hours a day. Its various restaurants serve everything from burgers and fries to lobster cannelloni in truffle sauce. The pool is available for day or night dips; the disco is one of the island's hot boîtes on weekends. *Anse Marcel, tel. 590/87-37-37. AE, V. Expensive.*

Le Tastevin. The setting here is elegant: a chic pavilion, with tropical plants and ceiling fans, overlooks the water. Dine on lobster soup with basil, snails in white wine sauce, medallions of pork in black currant sauce, or duck breast with apples and cider. *Grand Case, tel. 590/87-55-45. MC, V. Expensive.*

Bistrot Nu. A friendly and enormously popular late-night spot that serves fish soup, snails, pizza, and seafood until 2 AM. *Rue de Hollande, Marigot, no phone. No credit cards. Moderate.*

Cas' Anny. Creole cooking is the specialty of Anne-Marie Boissard's seaside terrace restaurant. She turns out Creole boudin, crabe farci, and lambi (conch) Provençale. *Rue d'Anguille, tel. 599/87-53-38. AE, MC, V. Moderate.*

Chez Martine. This is a small guest house whose restaurant is a pink and blue gingerbread-frilled terrace. Frogs' legs in puff pastry, homemade sea stew, Maine lobster, and saffron-flavored lamb chops are among the choices. *Grand Case, tel. 590/87-51-59. AE, MC, V. Moderate.*

★ **Don Camillo da Enzo.** Country-style decor and excellent service distinguish this small eatery. Both northern and southern Italian specialties are featured. Some favorites are the carpaccio, green gnocchi in Gorgonzola cream sauce, and veal medallions in marsala sauce. *Port La Royale, Marigot, tel. 590/87-52-88. AE, MC, V. Moderate.*

Jean DuPont. You can expect high-quality preparation and presentation at gentle prices. Lobster soufflé and duck with peaches are worth a try. *Marina Port La Royale. Marigot, tel. 590/87-71-13. No credit cards. Moderate.*

Maison sur le Port. Watching the sunset from the palm-fringed terrace is not the least of the pleasures in this old West Indian house. The meat of the matter has to do with duck (a house specialty), *trois filets* (lamb, veal, or steak in a light sauce), and poached lobster in pink pepper sauce. Chef Christian Verdeau's imaginative salads are lunchtime treats. *On the port, Marigot, tel. 590/87-56-38. AE. Moderate.*

Mini Club. The popular upstairs terrace is virtually a treehouse nestled in the coconut palms. A pleasant eatery anytime, but especially Wednesday and Saturday, when there is a sumptuous buffet of almost 30 dishes—salads, roast pork, suckling pig, beef, fish, lobster—all for $30 per person, with wine. *Rue d'Anguille, Marigot, tel. 590/87-50-69. AE. Moderate.*

Chez Max. Pure island Creole fare put before you on a plain formica table, where a bowl of red-hot Bello pepper and piquant vinegar dare you to use them. *Rue Felix Eboue, Marigot, no phone. No decor, no reservations, no credit cards. Inexpensive.*

Lodging

Until very recently, the Dutch side commanded all of the big, splashy resorts. The casinos are still to be found exclusively on the Dutch side—gambling is illegal on the French side. However, St. Martin is having something of a building boom, especially in the area around Nettle Bay. There are also small inns and Mediterranean-style facilities on both sides of the island. Many of the hotels offer enticing packages that are worth investigating. You'll also save substantially if you travel off-season; the downside of that is that many hotels and restaurants are closed for refurbishing or just plain recovering from the winter onslaught.

As a rule, rooms that are on the beach command the highest prices.

The most highly recommended lodgings are indicated by a star ★.

Category	Cost*
Very Expensive	over $300
Expensive	$140–$300
Moderate	$80–$140
Inexpensive	under $80

*All prices are for a standard double room for two, excluding 5% tax (Dutch side), a taxe de sejour (set by individual hotels on the French side), and a 10%–15% service charge.

Hotels
Dutch Side

Belair Beach Hotel. On Little Bay beach, this air-conditioned, all-suites oceanfront hotel is done in tropical decor with soft island prints. All suites are identical, with living and dining room, master bedroom with king-size bed, small guest room, two baths, color TV, two direct-dial phones, full kitchen, serve-through bar, and sliding glass doors opening onto a terrace that overlooks the sea. *Box 140, Philipsburg, tel. 599/5–23362 or 800/622–7836. 72 suites. Facilities: beach, 2 restaurants, 2 bars, boutique, gift shop, food and liquor store, laundry service, car rental desk, water-sports center. AE, CB, DC, MC, V. Very Expensive.*

Caravanserai. The lobby, which is decorated with artwork, oriental rugs, potted palms, and peacock chairs, opens onto a breezeway with a view of the reefs of Maho Bay. Choose from a variety of accommodations: spacious rooms, villas, suites, or studios. Rooms are individually furnished and some have private lagoons. Water sports are available at sister facility Mullet Bay Resort, and a shuttle bus runs nightly to the casino there. High tea is served each afternoon in the Palm Court. *Box 113, Philipsburg, tel. 599/5–42510 or 800/223–9815; 800/468–0023 in Canada. 84 rooms. Facilities: 2 restaurants, 2 pools (1 saltwater). AE, DC, MC. V, Very Expensive.*

La Vista. All of the accommodations are air-conditioned suites with cable TV, direct-dial phones, balconies, and lovely white iron queen-size beds. A junior suite in low season is less than $100, but the seven-day minimum stay catapults this facility into the most expensive category. *Box 40, Pelican Key, tel. 599/5–43005, 800/223–9815, 212/840–6636 in NY, or 800/468–0023 in Canada. 24 suites. Facilities: horseback riding, pool, restaurant, tennis. AE, MC, V. Very Expensive.*

Maho Beach Hotel & Casino. A variety of accommodations are available at this facility. All have two double beds or a king-size bed, and a private balcony. The Casino Royale is the island's largest casino, and Studio 7, atop the casino, is currently the rage. The trick here is to get a room far enough away from the airport's landing strip (those in the tennis complex are the quietest). *Maho Bay, tel. 599/5–42115 or 800/223–9815. 247 rooms. Facilities: beach, casino, 4 restaurants, 3 bars, disco, pool, boutiques, 4 lighted tennis courts, shopping arcade, all water sports. AE, DC, MC, V. Very Expensive.*

★ **Oyster Pond Yacht Club.** The hotel, which had a facelift in 1988, is built around a courtyard. Each of the two towers has two split-level suites and individually decorated rooms with terracotta floors, white wicker, ceiling fans, and pastel French cottons. All rooms have a secluded balcony or terrace and a view of the ocean, the courtyard, or the pond. Rooms have screened louvers for those who prefer sea breezes to air-conditioning. The hotel is on a mile-long beach that's excellent for snorkeling. The dining room opens onto the Atlantic Ocean; the pool perches right on the ocean's edge. You'll find hammocks instead of TVs, and the hotel's only phone is manned by a staff member at the front desk. *Box 239 Philipsburg, tel. 599/5–22206, 599/5–23206, or 800/372–1323. 20 rooms. Facilities: restaurant, bar, saltwater pool, 2 tennis courts, water-sports center. AE, MC, V. Very Expensive.*

★ **Pointe Pirouette Villa Hotels.** If you're willing to pay the price for ultimate privacy (including your own pool), consider this complex of four Mediterranean-style villas located on a privately owned peninsula. Point Pirouette, Point Petite, Venezia, and the newest, Punta Venezia, contain ultramodern accommodations, ranging from studios to penthouses. A rental car is included with each rental. There are no casinos, supper clubs, or discos—just peace and quiet. *Box 484, Philipsburg, tel. 599/ 5–44207. 25 units. Facilities: private boat dock, tennis court, commissary, 24-hr security, rental cars. AE, MC, V. Very Expensive.*

Treasure Island Hotel & Casino at Cupecoy. Accommodations in this 17-acre Mediterranean-style village are in villas in a hilltop complex and suites in the Beach Club, which offers garden or ocean views. Lovely Cupecoy Beach lies at the foot of the sandstone cliffs. *Box 14, Philipsburg, tel. 599/5–43219 or 800/535– 2929. 260 rooms and suites, some with TV and radio. Facilities: bank, beauty salon, boutiques, casino, convention center, 2 tennis courts, 3 pools, water-sports center. AE, CB, DC, MC, V. Very Expensive.*

Dawn Beach Hotel. Rooms are air-conditioned and are located on the hillside or on the beach. All are spacious, with handsome rattan furnishings, combination living room/bedroom with king-size bed, kitchenettes, closed-circuit color TV, radio, and private patio. (If you prefer tubs to showers, opt for the hillside villa.) The pool has a waterfall, and the white-sand beach is one of the island's best for snorkeling. There's bus service to town twice daily. *Box 389, Philipsburg, tel. 599/5–22929, 800/351– 5656 in U.S., or 800/468–0023 in Canada. 155 rooms. Facilities: restaurant, 2 beach bars, pool, 2 lighted tennis courts, car-rental desk, water-sports center. AE, CB, DC, MC, V. Expensive.*

Divi Little Bay Beach Resort & Casino. Air-conditioned one-, two-, and three-bedroom casitas and villas stretch along the 1,000-foot beach, surround the pool, and nestle in tropical gardens. The rooms are large, with king-size beds, minifridges, satellite color TV, radios, terraces, modern rattan furniture, and carpeted or tile floors. There's live entertainment nightly and a pricey New York–style deli. The Little Bay Beach & Racquet Club, a time-share resort, completes the picture. *Box 61, Philipsburg, tel. 599/5–22333 or 800/367–3484. 120 rooms (plus 40 time-shares). Facilities: beauty salon, casino, 2 restaurants, 2 bars, shopping arcade, car-rental desk, pool, 3 lighted tennis courts, water-sport center. AE, DC, MC, V. Expensive.*

Pelican Resort & Casino. An assortment of white stucco buildings house the resort's air-conditioned apartments, suites, and deluxe studios, all of which have a sweeping view of the Caribbean. Each has a fully equipped kitchen (including hibatchi and microwave), satellite TV, king-size beds, rattan furniture, and many frills (some have hot tubs). The resort has 1,400 feet of ocean frontage, and its own 60-foot catamaran, *El Tigre*, which is available for charters. *Simpson Bay, tel. 599/5–44309, 800/ 451–5510, or 212/354–5510 in NY. 342 suites and studios. Facilities: casino, 2 restaurants, 2 bars, 5 pools, health spa, Jacuzzi, 4 lighted tennis courts, children's playground, grocery store and shopping area, water-sport center. AE, DC, MC, V. Expensive.*

Holland House. This is an ideally situated hotel, with the shops of Front Street at its doorstep and a mile-long backyard called Great Bay Beach. (Rooms 104 through 107 open directly onto the beach.) Each room has contemporary tropical furnishings, balcony, kitchenette, satellite cable TV, and air-conditioning.

Its delightful open-air restaurant overlooking the water serves reasonably priced dinners. *Box 393, Philipsburg, tel. 599/5–22572, 800/223–9815, or 212/840–6636 in NY. 52 rooms, 2 suites. Facilities: beach, restaurant, lounge, gift shop. AE, DC, MC, V. Moderate.*

Mary's Boon. This informal inn has enormous rooms with kitchenettes, seaside patios, and ceiling fans. Meals are served family style, and there is an honor bar. Pets are welcome. The inn is on Simpson Bay's big beach. The many repeat guests don't seem fazed by the roar of the jets landing at the nearby airport. *Box 2078, Philipsburg, tel. 599/5–44235 or 212/986–4373 in U.S. 12 studios. Facilities: beach, restaurant, bar. No credit cards. Moderate.*

★ **Passangrahan Royal Guest House.** It's entirely appropriate that the bar here is named Sidney Greenstreet. This is the island's oldest inn, and it looks like a set for an old Bogie-Greenstreet film. The building was once Queen Wilhelmina's residence (there's a picture of her in the lobby) and the government guest house. Wicker peacock chairs, slowly revolving ceiling fans, balconies shaded by tropical greenery, king-size mahogany four-poster beds, and a broad tile veranda are some of the hallmarks of this guest house. Afternoon tea is served. There are no TVs or phones in the guest house. *Box 151, Philipsburg, tel. 599/5–23588 or 800/622–7836. 30 rooms and suites. Facilities: Great Bay Beach, rental bikes, bar, restaurant. AE, MC, V. Moderate.*

Seaview Hotel & Casino. Another good buy on Front Street and Great Bay Beach. The air-conditioned, twin-bed rooms are modest, cheerful, and clean. All rooms have baths (some with showers only), satellite TV, and phones. The four rooms above the sea have the best views. *Box 65, Philipsburg, tel. 599/5–22323, 800/223–9815, 212/840–6636 in NY, or 800/468–0023 in Canada. 45 rooms. Facilities: beach, breakfast room, casino. AE, MC, V. Moderate.*

★ **Caribbean Hotel.** You expect Sadie Thompson to vamp through those beaded glass curtains any minute. Frankly, this hotel is recommended more for its atmosphere, which is funky, almost campy, than for its facilities, which are passable and clean. It's on a second floor above Front Street, across the street from the beach. Rooms have tile floors, air-conditioning, TV, kitchenettes, private baths. *Box 236, Philipsburg, tel. 599/5–22028. 34 rooms. Facilities: restaurant, bar. AE, MC, V. Inexpensive.*

French Side **La Samanna.** This luxurious, secluded hotel looks as if it had
★ been transported to St. Martin from Morocco. The hotel is set in a tropical garden on a slope overlooking Baie Longue. Red hibiscus is everywhere. There is a rich (the word is used advisedly) variety of accommodations from which to choose. There are nine rooms and two suites in the air-conditioned main building, all with private terraces. You can choose an apartment, a two-story beachfront villa, or a secluded three-bedroom villa with private patio, private beach, or split-level terrace. *Box 159, Marigot 97150, tel. 590/87–51–22 or 212/696–1323. 85 rooms. Facilities: restaurant, lounge, pool, 3 lighted tennis courts. AE. Very Expensive.*

★ **La Belle Creole.** This 25-acre re-creation of an old Mediterranean village is replete with a stone central plaza. Completed in 1988, the enormous rooms and 17 suites have every modern convenience, including air-conditioning, direct-dial phones, and minibars. Accommodations (king-size or two double beds) are in 27 one- to three-story villas linked by stone-paved streets and graceful courtyards. Most villas have private balconies with a view of the ocean, the island, or Marigot Bay. Grand as it is, La Belle Creole has a casual, relaxed atmosphere. *Box 118, Marigot 97150, tel. 590/87–58–66 or 800–HILTONS. 156 rooms and suites. Facilities: 3 beaches, activities desk, shopping arcade, free-form pool, 4 lighted tennis courts, restaurant, 2 bars, 5 rooms with facilities for the disabled. AE, CB, DC, MC, V. Expensive–Very Expensive.*

Grand Case Beach Club. This informal condo complex is situated on Grand Case's crescent-shape beach. Air-conditioned studios and one- and two-bedroom apartments all have balconies or patios and kitchenettes. The 62 oceanfront units are much in demand. There's satellite TV in the lounge, and complimentary Continental breakfast is included in the rate. There are lots of repeat guests, so reserve well in advance. Attractive packages are offered. *Box 339, Grand Case 97150, tel. 590/87–51–87 or 800/223–1588. 75 studios and apartments. Facilities: 2 beaches, restaurant, lounge, 1 lighted tennis court, billiards, car rental, catamaran. AE, MC, V. Expensive–Very Expensive.*

★ **Hevea.** This is a small, white guest house with smart awnings in the heart of Grand Case. Rooms are dollhouse small but will appeal to romantics. There are beam ceilings, washstands, carved wood beds with lovely white coverlets and mosquito nets. The air-conditioned rooms, studios, and apartment are on the terrace level; fan-cooled studios and apartments are on the garden level. *Grand Case 97150, tel. 590/87–56–85. 8 units. Facilities: restaurant. MC, V. Expensive.*

L'Habitation. A white-knuckle road leads down to this resort, which is set in a 150-acre nature reserve with 1,600 feet of white-sand beach. The two-story main building is a white-column structure with red-tile roof and graceful galleries. All of the air-conditioned rooms, suites, and apartments have spacious baths, balconies, wall safes, TV, and fridges. One-bedroom apartments have fully equipped kitchens and private patios. Guests have complimentary access to the facilities of Le Privilege, a sports and entertainment complex on the hill (a minibus makes frequent trips to it). *Box 581, Marcel Cove 97150, tel. 590/87–33–33, 87–78–80, 800/847–4249 in U.S. and Canada, 212/747–0225 in NY 200 rooms, 50 apartments. Facilities (including Le Privilege): beach, boutiques, aerobics, car rental, disco, 3 restaurants, 3 bars, 6 lighted tennis courts, 2 pools, 2 squash courts, 1 racquetball court, 100-slip marina, water-sport center. AE, CB, DC, MC, V. Expensive.*

La Residence. Located in Marigot and popular with business travelers, this soundproof hotel is an excellent choice. All of the accommodations have baths (with showers only), phones, and air-conditioning. You've a choice among double rooms, studios, mezzanine loft beds, and apartments with or without kitchenettes. You'll have to take a cab to get to the beach. *Rue du Général de Gaulle, Marigot 97150, tel. 590/87–70–37. 20 rooms. Facilities: restaurant, lounge. AE, MC, V. Moderate.*

★ **La Royale Louisiana.** This upstairs hotel is as fresh as a spring breeze. White and pale green galleries overlook the flower-filled courtyard. There's a selection of twin, double, and triple air-conditioned duplexes, all with private bath (tub and shower), TV, VCR, and phone. *Rue du Général de Gaulle, Marigot*

97150, tel. 590/87–86–51. 75 rooms. Facilities: restaurant, snack bar. AE, DC, MC, V. Moderate.

Bertine's. This is a simple, isolated guest house on a hilltop near La Savane. Christine and Bernard Piticha have many repeat guests who gather for cocktails, conversation, and dinner in the excellent restaurant. *La Savane, Grand Case 97150, tel. 590/87–58–39. 4 rooms, 1 bedroom apartment. Facilities: lounge, restaurant. No credit cards. Inexpensive.*

Palm Plaza Hotel. Right in the center of Marigot, this hotel is upstairs above a patio. All rooms have air-conditioning, white wicker furniture, and private baths (with either shower or tub). Rooms are rather small. *Rue de la République, Marigot 97150, tel. 590/87–51–96. 21 rooms. AE, MC, V. Inexpensive.*

Home and Apartment Rentals
Both sides of the island offer a wide variety of homes, villas, condominiums, and housekeeping apartments. Information in the United States can be obtained through **Caribbean Home Rentals** (Box 710, Palm Beach, FL 33480, tel. 407/833–4454), **Jane Condon Corp.** (211 E. 43rd St., New York, NY 10017, tel. 212/986–4373), or **St. Maarten Villas** (707 Broad Hollow Rd., Farmingdale, NY 11735, tel. 516/249–4940). On the island, contact **Carimo** (tel. 590/87–57–58), **Ausar** (tel. 590/87–51–07), or **St. Maarten Rentals** (tel. 599/5–44330).

Nightlife

To find out what's doing on the island, pick up any of the following publications: *St. Maarten Nights, What to Do in St. Maarten, St. Maarten Events,* or *St. Maarten Holiday,* all distributed free in the tourist office and hotels. *Discover St. Martin/St. Maarten,* also free, is a glossy magazine, put together by artist Roland Richardson and friends, that includes articles about the island's history and the latest on shops, discos, restaurants, and even archaeological digs.

Each of the resort hotels has a Caribbean spectacular one night a week, replete with limbo and fire dancers and steel bands. Often the same group of entertainers moves from hotel to hotel, so if you happen to miss it in your resort, you can catch the act elsewhere.

Casinos are the main focus on the Dutch side but there are discos that usually start late and keep on till the fat lady sings. Discos here have a high turnover rate; one season's hottest spot can burn out and almost literally disappear by dawn's early light. There are a lot of bars, some with live music.

Casinos
All eight of the casinos have craps, blackjack, roulette, and slot machines. You must be 18 years old to gamble. The casinos are located at the **Great Bay Beach Hotel, Divi Little Bay Beach Hotel, Pelican Resort, Mullet Bay Hotel, Seaview Hotel, St. Maarten Beach Club, Treasure Island at Cupecoy,** and (the largest) **Casino Royal at Maho Beach.**

Discos
New in 1988, **The Tropics** is a hot disco that draws a mixed crowd of locals (by Madame Estate in Royal Inn Motel). **Studio 7** (tel. 599/5–42115) attracts a young crowd in its ultramodern digs atop Casino Royale across from Maho Beach Resort. **Le Club** (Mullet Bay, tel. 599/5–42801) draws a mixed crowd of locals and tourists, and features a floor show, "Les Folies de Sint Maarten." French nationals and locals flock to **L'Atmosphere** (no phone) on the second floor of L'Auberge de Mer in Marigot.

Le Privilege (Anse Marcel, tel. 590/87–38–38) caters to the young and hip French. Night Fever (Colombier, outside Marigot, no phone) attracts a young crowd of locals.

Bars and Nightclubs A boating crowd seems to favor **Sam's Place,** (Front St., Philipsburg, tel. 599/5–22989), for live jazz, R&R, and island music nightly *(see* Dining, above). **The Blue Note,** (Front St., Philipsburg, tel. 599/5–22166) in Pinocchio's Arcade, pulls young people in nightly for live jazz, R&R, and pop. A mixed crowd of locals and tourists, all ages, hangs out at the **Heartbreak Bar** (St. Maarten Beach Club Hotel, tel. 599/5–23434).

25 St. Vincent and the Grenadines

by Joan Iaconetti   St. Vincent and the Grenadines form a necklace of volcanic islands that beckon the traveler, sailor, and day-tripper who are more intrigued by blooming flowers than by Bloomingdale's. The fertile volcanic soil has helped to create the oldest botanic gardens in the Western Hemisphere, and a rich assortment of aromatic valleys covered with bananas, coconuts, and arrowroot form a welcome vacation spot for those more accustomed to smog-choked cities.

St. Vincent, with a population of about 117,000, is only 18 miles long and 11 miles wide, but it has managed to please those who enjoy the picturesque, both below and above its crystal seas. Equipped with little more than a snorkel and a sense of adventure, the explorer of St. Vincent can discover unrivaled underwater landscapes. In contrast to St. Vincent's beaches of black volcanic sand, the Grenadines offer numerous powdery white bays and coves on both calm leeward and surfy windward shores.

The Grenadines' peaceful, laid-back atmosphere is due to its residents' hospitality rather than to five-star amenities or designer shopping. Hotels are small, food is simple, and the islands appeal to adventurous singles and couples who prefer active sports to glitz and gambling.

While the islands have their share of the poor and unemployed, the superfertile volcanic soil allows everyone to grow enough food to eat and trade for necessities. Since the locals haven't come to regard tourists as meal tickets, beggars and hawkers are few.

The history of the island dates back to at least 4300 BC when it is believed that the Ciboney Indians first inhabited St. Vincent. Unhampered by passports and political unrest, the Ciboney made their way to Cuba and Haiti, leaving St. Vincent to the Arawaks. Columbus sailed by in 1492, while the Arawaks were involved in intermittent skirmishes with the bellicose Caribs; his arrival, named Discovery Day (or St. Vincent and the Grenadine's Day), is still commemorated on January 22.

Declared a neutral island by French and British agreement in 1748, St. Vincent became something of a political football in the years that followed. Ceded to the British in 1763, it was captured by the French in 1779 and restored to the British by the Treaty of Versailles in 1783. By the 19th century, St. Vincent was quite sure it was more British than French.

On October 27, 1979, St. Vincent gained independence from Great Britain. The current prime minister of St. Vincent is James "Son" Mitchell, whose New Democratic Party replaced the Labor Party. Mitchell won another landslide victory in May 1989.

In contrast to its colorful history, the 32 islands and cays that make up the Grenadines seem timeless, as free from politics as the beaches are free from debris. Nine miles south of St. Vincent is Bequia, the second-largest Grenadine. Admiralty Bay offers one of the finest anchorages in the Grenadines. With superb views, snorkeling, hiking, and swimming, the island has much to offer the international mix of backpackers and luxury yacht owners who frequent its shores.

A 90-minute sail south is Mustique, equipped with a small airstrip. More arid than Bequia, Mustique does not seek tourists, least of all those hoping for a glimpse of the famous people (Princess Margaret, Mick Jagger) who own houses here. The appeal of Mustique is seclusion and privacy: Here you can rent an elegant villa all to yourself.

Just over 3 square miles, Canouan is an unspoiled island that offers travelers an opportunity to relax, snorkel, and hike.

Numerous yachts and catamarans can be chartered for day sails from any of these islands to the tiny uninhabited islets known as The Tobago Cays (pronounced toe-bay-go keys). For those especially interested in snorkeling, Tobago Cays has some of the best hard and soft coral formations you'll find outside the Pacific Ocean. The beaches here are perfect for secluded picnics.

The tiny island of Mayreau (pronounced my-ro) has 150 residents, no phones, and one of the area's most beautiful beaches. The Caribbean is often mirror-calm, yet just yards away on the southern end of this narrow island is the rolling Atlantic surf. The Tobays Cays are just 30 minutes away by sailboat.

John Caldwell has spent 20 years turning Palm Island from a mosquito-infested mangrove swamp into a small island paradise for couples and families. The Caldwell family also hosts day-tripping cruise passengers who come to lounge on the wide white beaches, which are dotted and fringed with hundreds of palm trees that Caldwell has planted over the years.

Petit St. Vincent is another private luxury resort island, reclaimed from the jungle by manager Haze Richardson. It's actually possible to spend your entire vacation in one of the resort's widely spaced stone houses without ever seeing another human being. Those who enjoy socializing and activities might be happier at Palm, Mayreau, or Young Island.

Union Island isn't really a place for landlubbers: The island caters almost completely to French sailors, who keep very much to themselves. Surface transport is limited, and to see the island you need a boat. You won't find the laid-back friendliness of the other Grenadines here.

Before You Go

Tourist Information
The **St. Vincent and the Grenadines Tourist Office** (801 2nd Avenue, 21st floor, New York, NY 10017, tel. 212/687–4981; in Canada: 100 University Ave., Suite 504, Toronto, Ont. M5J 1V6, tel. 416/971–9666 or 416/971–9667; in the United Kingdom: 10 Kensington Court, London W8 5DL, tel. 01/937–6570) can supply information.

Arriving and Departing
By Plane
Most U.S. visitors fly via **American** (tel. 800/433–7300) or **Pan Am** (tel. 800/221–1111) into Barbados or St. Lucia, then take a small plane to St. Vincent's E.T. Joshua Airport (formerly Arnos Vale Airport) or to Mustique, Canouan, Union, or Palm, the only islands with airstrips. (Other destinations require a boat ride on either a scheduled ferry, a chartered boat, or your hotel's launch.) Other airlines that connect with interisland flights are **BWIA** (tel. 800/327–7401), **British Airways** (tel. 800/247–9297), **Air Canada** (tel. 800/422–6232), **VIASA** (tel. 800/327–5454), and **Air France** (tel. 800/237–2747).

LIAT (Leeward Islands Air Transport, tel. 809/458–4841), **Air Martinique** (tel. 596/51–0809 or 596/51–0990), and **St. Vincent Airways** (tel. 809/456–4176) (also known as Air Mustique) fly interisland. Delays are common but usually not outrageous. A surer way to go is with Air St. Vincent's six- or eight-seat charter flights, which meet and wait for your major carrier's arrival, even if it's delayed (bring earplugs if you're supersensitive to noise).

From the Airport Taxis and/or buses are readily available at the airport on every island. A taxi from the airport to Kingstown will cost $5–$7 (E.C. $15–$20); bus fare is less than 40¢. If you have a lot of luggage, it might be best to take a taxi—buses are very short on space.

Passports and Visas U.S. and Canadian citizens must have a passport; a voter registration card, birth certificate, or driver's license will *not* do. All visitors must hold return or ongoing tickets. Visas are not required.

Language English is spoken everywhere in the Grenadines, often with a Vincentian patois or dialect.

Precautions Insects are a minor problem on the beach during the day, but when hiking and just sitting on your veranda, you'll be glad you brought industrial-strength mosquito repellent.

Plants to watch out for include the manchineel tree, whose little green apples look tempting but are toxic. Even touching the sap of the leaves will cause an uncomfortable rash. Most trees on hotel grounds are marked with signs; on more remote islands, the bark may be painted red. Hikers should watch for Brazil wood trees/bushes, which are similar to poison ivy.

When taking photos of market vendors, private citizens, or homes, be sure to get permission first and expect to give a gratuity for the favor.

Further Reading *Exploring the Windward Islands*, by Chris Doyle, is available on the islands at most large hotels and shops. Doyle covers off-the-beaten-track sites, recipes, and island lore.

Staying in St. Vincent and the Grenadines

Important Addresses **Tourist Information:** The **St. Vincent Board of Tourism** (tel. 809/457–1502) is located in a marked building on Egmont Street, on the second floor.

Emergencies **Police:** (tel. 809/457–1211).

Hospitals: (tel. 809/456–1185).

Pharmacies: Deane's (tel. 809/457–1522), **Reliance** (tel. 809/456–1734), both in Kingstown.

Currency Although U.S. and Canadian dollars are taken at all but the smallest shops, Eastern Caribbean currency (E.C.$) is accepted and preferred everywhere. At press time, the exchange rate was U.S.$1 = E.C.$2.65; banks give a slightly better rate of exchange.

Price quotes are normally given in E.C. dollars; however, when you negotiate taxi fares and such, be sure you know which type of dollar you're agreeing on. All prices here are in U.S. dollars unless noted otherwise.

Taxes and Service Charges The departure tax from St. Vincent and the Grenadines is $6 (E.C.$15). Restaurants charge a 5% government tax, and if a

10% service charge is included in your bill, no additional tips are necessary.

Guided Tours Tours can be informally arranged through taxi drivers who double as informal but knowledgeable guides. Your hotel or the Tourism Board will recommend a driver. When choosing a driver/guide, look for the Taxi Driver's Association decal on the windshield and talk with the driver long enough to be sure you'll be able to understand his patois over the noise of the engine. Settle the fare first ($30–$40 is normal for a two- or three-hour tour). To prearrange a taxi tour, contact the Taxi Driver's Association (tel. 809/457–1807).

Grenadine Tours (St. Vincent, tel. 809/458–4818 or 809/458–3577 in Bequia) arranges air, sea, and land excursions throughout the islands.

Getting Around Many of the roads in the Grenadines are not in the best repair,
Taxis so you may prefer taxis to a rented car.

Minivans Public buses come in the form of brightly painted minivans with names like "Struggling Man" and "Who to Blame." Bus fares run E.C.$1–$5 in St. Vincent, with the route direction indicated on a sign in the windshield. Just wave from the road, and the driver will stop for you.

Smaller islands also have taxi-vans and pickup trucks with benches in the back and canvas covers for when it rains.

Rental Cars Rental cars cost an average of $35 per day; driving is on the left. Although major improvements are being made, St. Vincent's roads are not well marked or maintained. To orient yourself, consider taking a half-day taxi tour (*see* Guided Tours, above).

To rent a car you'll need a temporary Vincentian license (unless you already have an International Driver's License), which costs E.C.$10. Among the rental firms are **Johnson's U-Drive** (tel. 809/458–4864) at the airport and **Kim's Auto Rentals** (tel. 809/457–2797), which has a larger selection of slightly more expensive rental cars that must be rented by the week.

Telephones The area code for St. Vincent and the Grenadines is 809. If you
and Mail use Sprint or MCI in the United States, you may need to access an AT&T line to dial direct to St. Vincent and the Grenadines. From St. Vincent, you can direct-dial to other countries; ask the hotel operator for the proper country code and for the probable charge, surcharge, and government tax on the call. Local information is 118; international is 115.

When you dial a local number from your hotel in the Grenadines, you can drop the 45-prefix. Only Mayreau has no telephones; on other islands, few hotels have phones in the rooms.

Mail between St. Vincent and the United States takes two–three weeks. Airmail postcards cost 45¢; airmail letters cost 65¢ an ounce.

Bic-Pac, an overnight courier service that's part of Federal Express, is located on Bay Street in Kingstown.

Opening and Stores and shops in Kingstown are open weekdays 8–4. Many
Closing Times close for lunch from noon to 1 or so. Saturday hours are 8–noon. Banks are open weekdays 8–noon, Fridays from 2 or 3–5. The post office is open weekdays 9–3, Saturdays 9–11:30.

St. Vincent

Beaches

Most of the hotels and white-sand beaches are near Kingstown; black-sand beaches ring the rest of the island. The placid west coast, site of **Villa Beach** (white sand), **Questelle's Bay** (black sand), and **Buccament Bay** (black sand), are good for swimming; the beaches at Villa and the CSY Yacht Club are small but safe, with dive shops nearby. The exposed Atlantic coast is dramatic, but the water is rough and unpredictable. No beach has lifeguards, so even experienced swimmers are taking a risk. There are no beach facilities on the windward side of the island.

Exploring St. Vincent

Numbers in the margin correspond with points of interest on the St. Vincent map.

Kingstown's shopping/business district, cathedrals, and sights can easily be seen in a half-day tour. Outlying areas, botanical gardens, and the Falls of Baleine will each require a full day of touring.

Kingstown Kingstown, the capital and port of St. Vincent's, is located at *Tour 1* the southeastern end of the island.

① Begin your tour on **Bay Street,** near Egmont Street, a shopping mecca. Kingstown's boutiques feature such local crafts as cotton batik hangings and clothing, floor mats, baskets, and black coral jewelry.

Saturday's **fish/vegetable market** on Bay Street is a hectic, lively place. Arrive before 11 AM to catch all the action. Note: Keep a tight grip on your valuables in the market.

Unusual gifts for stamp collectors are at the **post office** on Granby Street east of Egmont. St. Vincent is known worldwide for its particularly beautiful and colorful issues, which commemorate flowers, undersea creatures, and architecture.

Follow Back Street (also called Granby Street) west past the Methodist Church to **St. George's Cathedral,** a yellow Anglican church built in the early 19th century. The dignified Georgian architecture includes simple wood pews, an ornate hanging candelabra, and stained glass windows. The gravestones tell the history of the island.

Across the street is **St. Mary's Roman Catholic Cathedral,** built in 1823 and renovated in the 1930s. The renovations resulted in a strangely appealing blend of Moorish, Georgian, and Romanesque styles. When the adjacent school lets out between 2 and 3, local children are eager to pose for photos.

A few minutes away by taxi or bus is St. Vincent's famous **Botanical Gardens.** Founded in 1765, it is the oldest botanical garden in the Western Hemisphere. Captain Bligh brought the first breadfruit tree to this island, a direct descendant of which is in the gardens. St. Vincent parrots and green monkeys are housed in cages, and unusual trees and bushes cover the well-kept grounds. Local guides offer their services for a few dollars an hour. *Information: c/o Minister of Agriculture, Kingstown,* *tel. 809/457–1003. Tours: 75¢ for 1 person, $1.10 for 2. Open weekdays 7–4, Sat. 7–11AM, Sun. 7–6.*

The tiny **National Museum** houses ancient Indian clay pottery found by Dr. Earle Kirby, St. Vincent's resident archaeologist. Dr. Kirby's historical knowledge is as entertaining as it is extensive. Contact him for a guided tour, as the labels in the museum offer little information. *Tel. 809/456–1787. Open Wed. 9:45–11:45AM, Sat. 4–6.*

2 Flag another taxi for the 10-minute ride to **Fort Charlotte,** built in 1806 to keep Napoleon at bay. The fort sits 636 feet above sea level, with cannons and battlements perched on a dramatic promontory overlooking the city and the Grenadines to the south, Lowman's Beach and the calm east coast to the north. The fort saw little military action; it was used mainly to house paupers and lepers.

Outside Kingstown The coastal roads of St. Vincent offer panoramic views and insights into the island way of life. Life in the tiny villages has changed little in centuries. This full-day driving tour includes Layou, Montreal Gardens, Mesopotamia Valley, and the Windward coast. Make sure to keep your eyes on the narrow road and to honk your horn before you enter the blind curves.

3 Beginning in Kingstown, take the Leeward Highway about 45 minutes north through hills and valleys to **Layou,** a small fishing village. Just north of the village are **petroglyphs** (rock carvings) left by the Caribs 13 centuries ago. If you're seriously interested in archaeological mysteries, you will want to stop here. Phone the Tourism Board to arrange a visit with Victor Hendrickson, who owns the land. For E.C.$5, Hendrickson or his wife will meet you and escort you to the site.

4 Half an hour farther north is **Barrouallie** (pronounced Barrelly), a whaling village where whaling boats are built and repaired year-round.

Time Out Ten minutes away from Barrouille is **Wallilabou** (wally-la-boo), a particularly beautiful bay where you can stop for a bring-your-own picnic, sunbathe, and swim (there are no showers, though).

Tour 2 Backtrack to Kingstown and continue toward Mesapotamia to **5** the **Montreal Gardens,** another extensive collection of exotic flowers, trees, and spice plants. It's not as well-maintained as the Botanical Gardens, but the aroma of cocoa and nutmeg wafting on the cool breeze is enticing. Spend an hour with well-informed guides or wander on your own along the narrow paths. Vincentian newlyweds often spend their honeymoons in the Garden's tiny cottage appropriately named "Romance." *Tel. 809/458–5452. Open daily.*

6 Now drive southeast (roads and signs aren't the best, so ask directions at Montreal Gardens) to the **Mesopotamia region.** The rugged, ocean-lashed scenery along St. Vincent's windward coast is the perfect counterpoint to the lush, calm west coast. Mesopotamia is full of dense forests, streams, and bananas, which are St. Vincent's major export. The blue plastic bags on the trees protect the fruit from damage in high winds. Coconut, breadfruit, sweet corn, peanuts, and arrowroot grow here in the rich soil. St. Vincent is the world's largest supplier of arrowroot, which is used to coat computer paper.

Exploring
Barrouille, **4**
Colonaire, **7**
Falls of Baleine, **9**
Fort Charlotte, **2**
Fort Duvernette, **10**
Kingstown, **1**
Mesopotamia region, **6**
Montreal Gardens, **5**
Petroglyphs, **3**
Rabacca Dry River, **8**

Dining
Basil's Bar and Restaurant, **12**
Chicken Roost, **16**
Dano's, **13**
The Dolphin, **22**
French Restaurant, **20**
Mariner's Inn, **21**
Tail of the Whale, **26**
Young Island, **19**

Lodging
CSY Yacht Club, **27**
Cobblestone Inn, **15**
Emerald Valley Resort, **11**
Grand View Beach Hotel, **17**
Heron Hotel, **14**
Mariner's Inn, **24**
Sunset Shores, **23**
Umbrella Beach Hotel, **25**
Young Island, **18**

- Exploring Sites
- Hotels and Restaurants

⑦ Turn north on the Windward Highway up the jagged coast road toward Georgetown, St. Vincent's second-largest city. You'll pass Argyle, many small villages, and the town of **Colonarie.** In the hills behind the town are hiking trails. Locals are helpful with directions as signs are limited.

⑧ Continue north to **Georgetown,** amid coconut groves and the long-defunct Mount Bentinck Sugar factory. A few miles north is the **Rabacca Dry River,** a rocky gulch carved out by the lava flow from the 1902 eruption of La Soufrière. Here hikers begin the two-hour ascent to the volcano. Return south to Kingstown via the Windward Highway.

The Falls of **⑨** Nearly impossible to get to by car, the **Falls of Baleine** are an
Baleine and absolute must to see on an escorted all-day boat trip or by char-
Fort Duvernette tered boat from Kingstown (*see* Participant Sports, below). The ride offers scenic island views. When you arrive, be prepared to climb from the boat into shallow water to get to the beach. Local guides help visitors make the 15-minute sneakers-and-swimsuit trek over the boulders in the stream leading to the falls; the government recently built a walkway so children, the handicapped, and photo buffs can enjoy them as well. Swim in the freshwater pool, climb under the 63-foot falls (they're chilly), and relax in a hidden environment. Most boat trips include a stop at a calm bay for lunch, snorkeling, and swimming.

⑩ On your return to Villa Beach, catch sunset at **Fort Duvernette,** the tiny island that juts up like a loaf of pumpernickel behind Young Island Resort. Take the *African Queen*–style ferry for a few dollars from the dock at Villa Beach near Kingstown (call the boatman from the phone on the dock) and set a time for your return (60–90 minutes is plenty). When you arrive at the island, climb the 100 or more steps carved into the mountain. Views from the 195-foot summit are terrific, but avoid the overgrown house near the top where you'll encounter (harmless) bats. Rusting cannons from the early 1800s are still here, aimed not at seagoing invaders but at the marauding Caribs.

Participant Sports

Water Sports The constant trade winds are perfect for windsurfing, and 80-foot visibility on numerous reefs means superior diving. Many experienced divers prefer the Grenadines to Bonaire and the Caymans; the sites are nearly as spectacular and far less crowded. Bequia and St. Vincent have the best diving, and snorkeling is among the world's best in the Tobago Cays.

Dive operations are small, often less luxurious than on other islands, but competent and professional. Many offer three-hour beginner "resort" courses, full certification courses, and excursions to nearby reefs, walls, and wrecks. Dive shops are on St. Vincent, Bequia, Mustique, Union, and Palm Islands; individual island listings have full information. Most dive shops and larger hotels also rent Sunfish, Windsurfers, and snorkel gear.

Dive St. Vincent (tel. 809/457–4714) on Villa Beach, just across the Young Island, is where NAUI instructor Bill Tewes and his staff offer beginner and certification courses. A single-tank dive is about $40.

Mariner's Watersports (tel. 807/457–4228) on Villa Beach, offers complete scuba trips and gear as well as beginner's resort courses and full certification. They also rent waterskis and Windsurfers and offer full instruction on the use of this gear.

Young Island has some of the most colorful snorkeling in the Caribbean. If you're not a guest on this private island, phone the resort for permission to take the ferry and rent equipment from their water-sport center (*see* Lodging, below).

Hiking Dorsetshire Hill, about 3 miles from Kingstown, rewards you with a sweeping view of city and harbor; picturesque Queen's Drive is nearby. Mt. St. Andrew, on the outskirts of the city, is a pleasant climb through a rain forest on a well-marked trail.

But the queen of climbs is La Soufrière, St. Vincent's active volcano (which last erupted, appropriately enough, on Friday the 13th in 1979). Approachable from both windward and leeward coasts, this is *not* a casual excursion for inexperienced walkers; you'll need stamina and sturdy shoes for this climb of just over 4,000 feet. Be sure to check the weather before you leave; hikers have been sorely disappointed to reach the top only to find the view completely obscured by enveloping clouds.

Climbs are all-day affairs; a LandRover and guide can be arranged through your hotel or a knowledgeable taxi driver. The four-wheel-drive vehicle takes you past Rabacca Dry River through the Bamboo Forest. From there it's a two-hour hike to the summit, and you can arrange in advance to come down the other side of the mountain to the Chateaubelair area.

Sailing and Charter Yachting Unless you're plagued with motion sickness, the Grenadines are the perfect place to charter a sailboat or catamaran (bareboat or complete with captain, crew, and cook) to weave you around the islands for a day or a week. Boats of all sizes and degrees of luxury are available; we recommend CSY Yacht Club (Caribbean Sailing Yachts, tel. 809/458–4308) in the Blue Lagoon area of St. Vincent.

Shopping

Noah's Arkade (tel. 809/457–1513), on Bay Street, features such local crafts as batiks and baskets. The best batiks are at **Batik Carib** (tel. 809/456–1666) and **Sprotties** (tel. 809/456–1647) also on Bay Street. The **St. Vincent Craftsmen Center** (tel. 809/457–1288), in the northwest end of Kingstown on James Street above Granby Street, sells grass floor mats and other woven items. Swiss watches and clocks, perfumes, crystal, bone china, and gold and silver jewelry can be found at **Stecher's** (tel. 809/457–1422) on Bay Street in the Cobblestone Arcade (a branch is at the airport). Across the way is **Giggles** (tel. 809/457–1174), a boutique with a wide selection of contemporary clothing and accessories for men and women.

Dining

The most highly recommended restaurants are indicated by a star ★.

Category	Cost*
Expensive	over $20
Moderate	$10–$20

Inexpensive	under $10

per person, excluding drinks and sales tax (5% on credit card purchases only)

★ **Basil's Bar and Restaurant.** This air-conditioned restaurant, downstairs in the Cobblestone Inn, opens at 8 AM for Kingstown's version of the power breakfast. Basil's also serves a buffet lunch with hearty callaloo soup, lobster, and barbecued conch, plus seafood pasta and chicken in fresh ginger and coconut milk. *Bay St., Kingstown, tel. 809/457–2713. Reservations recommended. AE, MC, V. Expensive.*

★ **French Restaurant.** Referred to as "The French," this open-air place has what is unanimously acclaimed to be the best food in the Grenadines. A nearby lobster pool assures freshness, and the chef does wonders with locally available ingredients (garlic soup instead of onion soup, for example). Choose from crepes, lobster bisque, and grilled lamb chops; the lunch menu includes quiche and sandwiches. There's also a varied wine list and a bar inside. *Villa Beach, tel. 809/458–4972. Dinner reservations recommended. AE, V. Expensive.*

Tail of the Whale. The tail serves excellent soups and delectably spicy West Indian lobster, probably the island's best. The bar is lively and sociable. *CSY Yacht Club, Blue Lagoon, tel. 809/458–4308. V. Expensive.*

Young Island. Five-course chef's-choice dinners include seafood, whole roast pig, beef, and chicken. A barbecue with a steel band is featured on Saturday night. *Young Island, tel. 809/458–4826. Reservations required. AE, MC, V. Expensive.*

Mariner's Inn. Hearty, homemade West Indian food is served on a veranda with a view of Young Island. The Friday night barbecue and jump-up is among the best for quality, quantity, and desserts. *Villa Beach, tel. 809/458–4287. AE, MC, V. Moderate.*

Chicken Roost. This eatery is handy if you're waiting at the airport across the street, and worth a visit even if you're not. The *rotis* (Caribbean burritos), sandwiches (including shark), pizzas, and ice cream can't be beat. Open daily till midnight. *Opposite airport, tel. 809/457–1032. No credit cards. Inexpensive.*

Dano's. Stop in while you're strolling Kingstown for good, cheap Caribbean burritos and lots of local color. *Middle St., Kingstown, tel. 809/457–2020. No credit cards. Inexpensive.*

★ **The Dolphin.** The restaurant's inviting garden, open-air dining areas, and bar create a friendly and unpretentious atmosphere that is great for socializing with fellow travelers. The pizza is your best bet, but the menu also includes fish- or chicken-and-chips, burgers, soups, and salads. *Villa Beach, tel. 809/458–4238. No credit cards. Inexpensive.*

Lodging

Luxury resorts require booking about six months in advance, but most St. Vincent hotels can squeeze you in with far less notice. There's a bit of a lull in January, between the Christmas week and February rush, when rooms are sometimes available on a day's notice. Many hotels offer MAP (Modified American Plan, with breakfast and dinner included).

The most highly recommended lodgings are indicated by a star ★.

Category	Cost*
Very Expensive	over $200
Expensive	$115–$200
Moderate	$60–$115
Inexpensive	under $60

All prices are for a standard double room for two, excluding 5% tax and a 10% service charge.

Young Island

★ **Young Island.** A 36-acre privately owned island just 200 yards off the Villa Beach dock in St. Vincent, Young Island is an upscale resort that attracts mostly over-35 couples who prefer casual elegance to the glitzy atmosphere of traditional luxury resorts. Airy rooms are set in the hills amid flowering almond and hibiscus trees. Each room has lovely views, though cottages No. 30 and 17 near the summit have the most dramatic vistas (also the longest walk uphill). Sail-hotel packages and day sails are available on Young Island's two yachts, and snorkeling around Young Island is superior. Dive St. Vincent is just across the channel. All meals are included. *Box 211, Young Island, tel. 809/458–4826; U.S. agent: Ralph Locke Associates, Box 800, Waccabuc, NY 10597, tel. 914/763–5526 or 800/223–1108. 29 rooms. Facilities: scuba diving saltwater pool, watersports center, lighted tennis court. AE, MC, V. Very Expensive.*

Emerald Valley

Emerald Valley Resort. About 30 minutes from Kingstown, up in the hills, Emerald Valley is the one place in the Grenadines where you can gamble—but don't expect Las Vegas glitz. New management is downplaying gaming in favor of family activities that take advantage of the natural beauty of the site. Hikers will enjoy the nature trail in the surrounding hills. Simple accommodations are in chalets with kitchens. *Box 1081, St. Vincent, tel. 809/458–7421. 12 chalets. Facilities: casino, restaurant, 2 tennis courts, grass volleyball court, croquet, pool. AE, MC, V. Expensive.*

Villa Beach

★ **Grand View Beach Hotel.** The original plantation house of the Sardine family is still run by managers Tony and Heather Sardine. A charmingly homey hotel with fantastic views, it sits on eight secluded acres about five minutes from the airport. There's a trail down to the beach, good snorkeling, and the picture-perfect pool sits atop Villa Point. *Box 173, St. Vincent, tel. 809/458–4811. 12 rooms. Facilities: tennis and squash courts, pool, reading room, restaurant, water-sports center nearby. AE, MC, V. Expensive.*

Sunset Shores. Everything in this very simple but livable hotel is arranged around the pool. Business travelers appreciate the clipboard in the central sitting area that carries daily Caribbean, financial, sports, and international news from the wire services. The better rooms have patios. *Box 849, across from Young Island on Villa Beach, St. Vincent, tel. 809/458–4411. 27 air-conditioned rooms. Facilities: restaurant, pool, water-sports center nearby. AE, MC, V. Expensive.*

Mariner's Inn. A bit scruffy around the edges, the mariner is a sprawling, multibuilding hotel at the end of Villa Beach. Popular with old salts and adventurous younger couples, it's getting a much-needed renovation by new management. Lots of socializing goes on around the outdoor bar that is fashioned from a lifeboat of the *Antilles*, which sank off Mustique 20 years ago. The dining room's cuisine is on the upswing. The beach is a 10-minute stroll away. *Box 839, St. Vincent, tel. 809/458-4287. 25 rooms. Facilities: bar, restaurant. AE, MC, V. Moderate.*

Umbrella Beach Hotel. The hotel's small, simple, and charming rooms with kitchenettes are set in a garden on Villa Beach. The three best rooms face the water. Excellent breakfast is served outdoors in a garden overlooking the beach. Here you'll find superior value and location for the price. Next door is The French, St. Vincent's best restaurant. *Box 530, St. Vincent, tel. 809/458-4651. 9 rooms. Facilities: bar, restaurant. MC, V. Inexpensive.*

Blue Lagoon
★

CSY Yacht Club. Located in Blue Lagoon, about 15 minutes from the airport, this is the place to charter a sailboat or trade stories with the yacht owners and former charter-yacht-owner-turned-manager Mike O'Brien. The spacious, modern rooms have cathedral ceilings and private patios. The long shallow-water beach that curves around Blue Lagoon offers a view of anchored sailboats. A beach bar has music and dancing on weekends. The secluded swimming pool is up a circuitous stone walk, set among flowering bushes. *Box 133, St. Vincent, tel. 809/458-4308 or 800/631-1593; U.S. agent: Anchor Reservations, 795 Franklin Ave., Franklin Lakes, NJ 07417, tel. 800/526-4789. 19 air-conditioned rooms. Facilities: pool, bar, restaurant, conference room. MC, V. Moderate.*

Kingstown

Heron Hotel. In Kingstown, this West Indian inn is located on the second floor of a converted Georgian plantation's warehouse and is preferred by pleasantly eccentric travelers, young and old, who want to be near the dock for the early boat. Rooms are faded but atmospheric, and Room 15 is large and has a sitting area. *Box 226, St. Vincent, tel. 809/457-1631. 15 air-conditioned rooms. Facilities: courtyard, dining room. AE, MC, V. Moderate.*

Cobblestone Inn. This pre-1814 stone building used to be a sugar warehouse. Wicker fills its large, airy rooms. Room 5 overlooks the street and is sunny but a bit noisy. The nearest beach is 3 miles away. The plant-filled courtyard leads to a rooftop bar that's popular for breakfast and lunch. Rates include breakfast. *Box 862, St. Vincent, tel. 809/456-1937. 19 rooms. Facilities: bar, restaurant. AE, V. Inexpensive.*

Nightlife

Don't look for fire-eaters and limbo demonstrations on St. Vincent. Nightlife here consists mostly of hotel barbecue buffets and jump-ups, so called because the lively steel-band music makes listeners jump up and dance.

The Attic (on Grenville St., tel. 809/457-2558), a new jazz club with modern decor, offers international artists and steel bands. There is a small cover charge, and you should call ahead for hours and schedules.

Vidal Browne, manager of **Young Island** (tel. 809/458-4826), hosts sunset cocktails and hor d'oeuvres each Thursday on Fort Duvernette, the tiny island behind the resort. On that night

100 steps up the hill are lit by flaming torches and a string band plays. Reservations are necessary for nonguests.

The Friday night barbecue and jump-up at **Mariner's Inn** (tel. 809/458–4287) draws both tourists and locals.

The Grenadines

The Grenadines are wonderful islands to visit for fine diving and snorkeling opportunities, good beaches, and unlimited chances to laze on the beach with a picnic waiting for the sun to set so you can go to dinner. For travelers seeking privacy, peace and quiet, or an undisturbed holiday, these are the islands of choice.

For price information on restaurants and hotels, see the charts in the Dining and Lodging sections of St. Vincent, above.

Bequia

Arriving and Departing Your flight may arrive in St. Vincent too late in the day to make the *Admiral* ferry's last departure from Kingstown to Bequia at 4:15 PM. This means either an overnight stay in St. Vincent or chartering a sail or speedboat. Take a taxi to the Villa Beach Dock or the CSY Yacht Club. Charters cost about $80 and up.

All scheduled transportation departs from the main dock in Kingstown. The SS *Admiral* motor ferry leaves Monday–Saturday at 10:30 AM, 12:30, and 4:15 PM. The trip takes 70–90 minutes and costs less than $3. The SS *Snapper* mail boat travels south on Mondays and Thursdays at about 10 AM, stopping at Bequia, Canouan, Mayreau, and Union, and returns north on Tuesdays and Fridays. Cost is under $10, and you can stay in a cabin aboard the *Snapper* for E.C.$20 if you're worried about missing its 6 AM departure from Union. Weekday service between St. Vincent and Bequia is also available on the island schooner *Friendship Rose*, which leaves about 12:30 PM. The "St. Vincent and the Grenadines Visitor's Guide" available in hotels and at the airport, has complete interisland schedules.

Important Addresses **Tourist Information:** The **Bequia Tourism Board** (tel. 809/458–3286) is located on the main dock.

Emergencies **Police:** (tel. 809/456–1955).
Medical Emergencies: (tel. 999).

Guided Tours To see the views, villages, and boat-building around the island, hire a taxi and negotiate the fare in advance. Water taxis, available from any dock, will also take you by Moonhole, a private community of stone homes with glassless windows, some decorated with bleached whale bones. The fare is about $11.

For those who prefer sailboats to motorboats, Arne Hansen and his catamaran *Toien* can be booked through the **Sunsports Dive Shop** (tel. 809/458–3577). Day sails to Mustique run $35–$40 per person, including drinks. An overnight snorkel/sail trip to the Tobago Cays costs about $150 for two people, which includes breakfast and drinks. Longer custom charters can also be arranged.

Those in search of the picturesque will want to try a rum-punch sunset cruise aboard the hand-built, wood Scandinavian sailboat *Fredag*. Reserve through your hotel.

TO ST. VINCENT

Bequia

Industry Bay

Hope Bay

Port Elizabeth

1

2 — 9

Friendship Bay

13

Admiralty Bay

Princess Margaret Beach

Lower Bay

10

Derrick

11 12

Isle a Quatre

Battowia Island

Baliceaux Island

Mustique

Macaroni Beach

Dovers

14

Britannia Bay

15

Airport

Petit Mustique Island

Savan Island

Caribbean Sea

Petit Cannouan

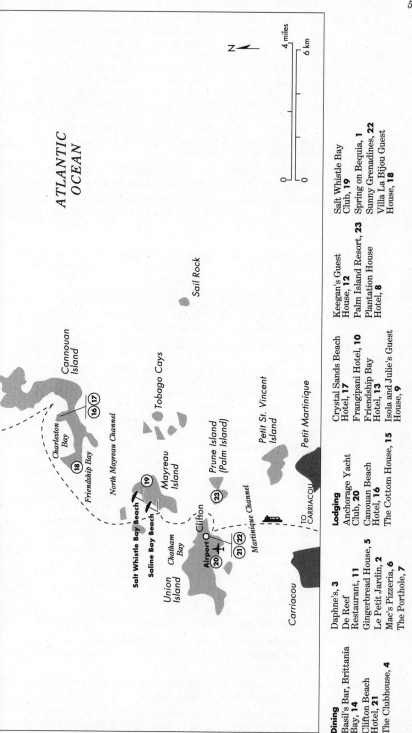

Dining
Basil's Bar, Brittania Bay, **14**
Clifton Beach Hotel, **21**
The Clubhouse, **4**
Daphne's, **3**
De Reef Restaurant, **11**
Gingerbread House, **5**
Le Petit Jardin, **2**
Mac's Pizzeria, **6**
The Porthole, **7**

Lodging
Anchorage Yacht Club, **20**
Canouan Beach Hotel, **16**
The Cottom House, **15**
Crystal Sands Beach Hotel, **17**
Frangipani Hotel, **10**
Friendship Bay Hotel, **13**
Isola and Julie's Guest House, **9**
Keegan's Guest House, **12**
Palm Island Resort, **23**
Plantation House Hotel, **8**
Salt Whistle Bay Club, **19**
Spring on Bequia, **1**
Sunny Grenadines, **22**
Villa La Bijou Guest House, **18**

Beaches A half-hour walk from the Plantation House Hotel will lead you over rocky bluffs to **Princess Margaret Beach,** which is quiet and wide, with a natural stone arch at one end. Though it has no facilities, it is a popular spot for swimming, snorkeling, or simply relaxing under palms and sea-grape trees. Snorkeling and swimming are also excellent at **Lower Bay,** a wide, palm-fringed beach, that can be reached by taxi or by hiking beyond Princess Margaret Beach; wear sneakers, not flipflops. Facilities for windsurfing and snorkeling are here, and the De Reef restaurant features waiters who will find you on the sand when your lunch is ready. Enjoy a beer with fish-and-chips but don't expect to be served right away.

Friendship Bay can be reached by land taxi and is well equipped with windsurfing and snorkeling, rentals and an outdoor bar.

Industry Bay boasts towering palm groves, a nearly secluded beach, and a memorable view of several uninhabited islands. The Crescent Bay Lodge is here; its huge bar offers drinks and late lunches.

Hope Beach, on the rougher Atlantic side, is accessible by a long taxi ride (about E.C.$20—every driver knows how to get there) and a mile-long walk downhill on a semipaved path. Your reward is a magnificent beach and total seclusion and—if you prefer—nude bathing. Be sure to ask your taxi driver to return at a prearranged time. Bring your own lunch and drinks; there are no facilities and swimming can be dangerous.

Participant Sports
Water Sports Bequia's two dozen uncrowded dive sites are just being recognized as some of the Caribbean's finest. The best are Devil's Table, a shallow dive rich in fish and coral; a sailboat wreck nearby at 90 feet; the 90-foot drop at The Wall, off West Cay; the Bullet, off Bequia's north point for rays, barracuda, and the occasional nurse shark; the Boulders for soft corals, tunnel-forming rocks, thousands of fish; and Moonhole, shallow enough in places for snorkelers to enjoy.

Sunsports (tel. 809/453–3577) is the new addition to Bequia diving, located in the Clubhouse complex on Admiralty Bay. Enthusiastic NAUI instructor Nancy Boake and her staff lead dives in a comfortable covered boat. Equipment sales and rental, personal instruction, air fills, and night dives are available. A two-dive excursion includes lunch on a nearby uninhabited island. Sunsports also offer excellent windsurfing instruction, plus Sunfish, floats, and snorkel gear for rent.

Dive Bequia (tel. 809/458–3504), at the Plantation House Hotel, offers one- and two-tank dives, night dives, and certified instruction. A special package allows vacationers who want to become certified divers but don't want to be stuck on one island all week to spread the five-day course out among any of three participating shops: **Dive Bequia, Dive Mustique** (tel. 809/456–4777), and **Dive St. Vincent** (tel. 809/457–4714 or 809/457–4948).

For snorkeling, take a water taxi to the bay at Moon Hole or contact **Sunsports** (tel. 809/458–3577) for snorkel excursions and equipment rental.

Shopping All Bequia's shops are along the beach and are open weekdays 10:30–5 or 6, Saturdays 10:30–noon.

Best Buys Handmade model boats (you can special order a replica of your own yacht) are at **Mauvin's** (a ¼-mile down the road to the left of the main dock, no phone). Along Admiralty Bay, handprinted and batik fabric, clothing, and household items are sold at the **Crab Hole** (no phone). You can watch the fabrics being made in the workshop out back. **Solana's** (tel. 809/458–3554) offers attractive beachwear, sarong-like pareos, and handy plastic beach shoes. **Local Color** (tel. 809/458–3202), above the Porthole restaurant in town, has an excellent and unusual selection of handmade jewelry, wood carvings, resort clothing, and scrimshaw (ink drawings on ivory). **Wearable Art** (above the Frangipani Hotel, (tel. 809/458–3368) offers hand-painted Egyptian cotton beachwear and jewelry. The **Bequia Bookstore** (tel. 809/458–3258) has novels, books on island lore, postcards, and decorative maps.

Dining   Dining on Bequia ranges from West Indian to gourmet cuisine, and it's consistently good. Barbecues at Bequia's hotels mean spicy West Indian seafood, chicken, or beef, plus a buffet of spicy side dishes and sweet desserts. Restaurants are occasionally closed on Sundays; phone to check.

★ **Le Petit Jardin.** This new chalet-style French restaurant offers gourmet lobster and fish prepared with West Indian touches and ingredients. The elegant style and service here is welcome in this part of the world. *Port Elizabeth, tel. 809/458–3318. Reservations necessary. No credit cards. Expensive.*

Daphne's. For a special West Indian meal, go two streets east of Knight's Supermarket on the bay where you'll see a sign that reads DAPHNE COOKSIT. Daphne Grant cooks hearty West Indian curries and spicy Creole seafood. Drop by a day in advance— Daphne prepares custom meals only. *Port Elizabeth, tel. 809/458–3271. Reservations a must. No credit cards. Moderate–Expensive.*

★ **The Clubhouse.** The newly completed Clubhouse, under a peaked roof with gingerbread trim, offers light lunches of sandwiches and curries plus mulligatawny and carrot-pumpkin soup, plus full dinners. Home-baked cakes, muffins, and espresso are served at the adjacent **Gingerbread House,** which also sells gourmet yacht provisions, island-made sauces, and marmalades. *Port Elizabeth, tel. 809/458–3577. Dinner reservations suggested. AE, V. Moderate.*

De Reef Restaurant. On Lower Bay Beach, De Reef serves casual lunches and exceptional dinners including gingered lamb and seafood. *Lower Bay, tel. 809/458–3203. No credit cards. Inexpensive–Moderate.*

★ **Mac's Pizzeria.** The island's best lunches and casual dinners are enjoyed amid fuschia bougainvillea on the covered outdoor terrace overlooking the harbor. Choose from mouthwatering lobster pizza, quiche, pita sandwiches, lasagna, home-baked cookies, and muffins. Friendly cats and amiable service add to the pleasurable experience. *On the beach, Port Elizabeth, tel. 809/458–3475. Dinner reservations necessary. No credit cards. Inexpensive–Moderate.*

The Porthole. Located in town, this is where sailors gather for drinks, chicken and rice, or rotis (Caribbean burritos). *Port Elizabeth, tel. 809/458–3458. No credit cards. Inexpensive.*

Lodging   **Plantation House Hotel.** A 1988 fire destroyed the main house ★ but left the pink cottages intact; manager Jaques Ducau has sped rebuilding, adding a new beach cottage and a bigger Dive Bequia scuba shop. The new building, which resembles the original but has modern conveniences, should be completed before the 1990 winter season and five more rooms should be added. The cottages are being completely refurbished. The Plantation House attracts mostly older couples who enjoy its relatively secluded, spacious, palm-filled grounds. The restaurant serves good French-accented food and a room-size cage of parakeets near the bar keeps imbibers entertained. *Box 16, Admiralty Bay, Bequia, St. Vincent, W.I., tel. 809/458-3425. 17 cottages. Facilities: diving, pool, bar, restaurant. AE, MC, V. Very Expensive.*

Spring on Bequia. The only Bequia hotel not on the water, Spring is nestled in green hills overlooking groves of tall palms and grazing goats. The hotel is about a mile above town (a pretty walk, though you may want to take a taxi back uphill), and the nearest beach, lovely but too shallow and occasionally seaweedy for serious swimming, is a 10-minute stroll away. The large wood and stone rooms attract upscale travelers who want serenity and seclusion. The airy veranda bar is the site of manager Candy Leslie's deservedly famous Sunday curry lunch (reservations necessary). *Bequia, St. Vincent, W.I. tel. 809/458-3414; U.S. agent: Spring on Bequia, Box 19251, Minneapolis, MN 55419, tel. 612/823-1202 or 612/823-9925. 11 rooms. Facilities: pool, bar, restaurant, tennis. AE, MC, V. Expensive.*

Friendship Bay Hotel. This 27-unit white hotel on the hill features rooms with large terraces and sweeping views and rooms built of coral stone closer to the beach. While the service has been wildly uneven on recent visits, Friendship offers a long white-sand beach and improved food by a new Argentine chef. On Saturday nights owners Joanne and Eduardo Guadagnino still hold the liveliest beachside barbecue/jump-up in the Grenadines. Enjoy a rum punch at the MauMau Beach Bar, a cozy establishment equipped with swings instead of seats. Since the swings have backs and armrests, you don't have to worry about falling off. *Box 9, Bequia, St. Vincent, W.I., tel. 809/458-3222; U.S. agent: Ralph Locke, Box 800, Waccabuc, NY 10957, tel. 800/223-1108. 27 rooms. Facilities: water-sports center, restaurant, 2 bars; boutique. AE, MC, V. Moderate-Expensive.*

★ **The Frangipani Hotel.** The Frangi has long since gained the status of venerable institution, that rare combination of comfortable hotel and local gossip center where absolutely everyone ends up to share drinks and stories. Managed by Marie Kingston and Lou Keane, the main building used to be Prime Minister Son Mitchell's family home. Surrounded by tropical trees and flowering bushes, the garden units are built of stone, and the rooms, with private verandas and baths, are some of the nicest obtainable. Four simple, less expensive rooms are in the main house, although only one has a private bath. A two-bedroom, two-bath house with a patio overlooks the tennis court and another apartment with a large bedroom and kitchen is in the nearby Clubhouse. Several more garden units and two-bedroom dwellings are planned. At the beachside terrace bar and dining area, string bands appear on Mondays with folk songs on Friday nights during tourist season. The Thursday night steel-band jump-up, which draws throngs of visitors and locals, is a must. *Box 1, Bequia, St. Vincent, W.I. tel. 809/458-3255. 11 rooms. Facilities: tennis, bar, restaurant, water-sports center; yacht services. AE, MC, V. Inexpensive-Moderate.*

Keegan's Guest House. This is the place for budget-minded beach lovers who want quiet, friendly surroundings. Located on Lower Bay, John Keegan's house offers family-style West Indian breakfasts and dinners for its guests. Rooms 3, 4, and 5 have a shared bath and are cheaper, although there is no hot water to be found (you really do get used to it). *Bequia, St. Vincent, W.I., tel. 809/458-3530. 7 rooms. Facilities: dining room. No credit cards. Inexpensive.*

Isola and Julie's Guest House. Right on the water in Port Elizabeth, these two separate buildings share a small restaurant and bar. Furnishings (which are few) run to early Salvation Army, but the rooms are airy and light with private baths; some have hot water. *Box 12, Isola's Guest House, Bequia, St. Vincent, W.I., tel. 809/458-3304, 809/458-3323, or 809/458-3220. 25 rooms. Facilities: bar, restaurant. No credit cards. Inexpensive.*

Nightlife Each night but Sunday there's a jump-up at a different place: **Mac's** on Tuesday, the **Frangipani** on Thursday, **Plantation House** on Friday, **Friendship Bay** on Saturday. Big-screen videos are shown evenings twice a week at the **Clubhouse** (the small charge goes to the Bequia Museum), where string or steel bands play for dancing Monday and Wednesday.

Canouan

This is an island where goatherding is still a career option and organized activities are nil. Walk, loaf, swim, or snorkel; Canouan still lives in the 18th century.

Dining and Lodging **Canouan Beach Hotel.** In Charlestown Bay on a golden-sand beach, the CBH recently completed a marina. Airy little cottages with brightly colored decor are available and windsurfing and snorkeling are best at Friendship Point. Day sails on the hotel's catamaran leave Monday–Saturday for a different destination to nearby islands and the Cays. Steel bands perform on Mondays and Thursdays. From April to October scuba-diving instruction and rentals are available. *Charlestown, St. Vincent, W.I., tel. 809/458-8888. 35 rooms. Facilities: air-conditioning, bar, restaurant, marina, windsurfing, snorkeling. AE, V. Very Expensive.*

Crystal Sands Beach Hotel. Locally run and extremely simple, Crystal Sands is located on Charleston Bay and has a veranda bar and dining area. Cottages share a connecting door for larger groups and are equipped with private baths and patios. Fishing, sailing, and great snorkeling can be found off the fine beach. Phone the managers to arrange for air pickup in St. Vincent. If you take the mail boat from Kingstown *(see* Getting Around, above), pack light and be prepared to climb from the large ferry into a small rowboat to get to shore. *Canouan, St. Vincent, W.I., tel. 809/458-8015. 20 beds in rooms and cottages. Facilities: bar, dining area, snorkeling, fishing. No credit cards. Moderate.*

Villa La Bijou Guest House. Up the hill and only a 10-minute walk from Friendship Bay (15 minutes from the airstrip; pack light—taxis are rarely available), La Bijou is the mosaic-stone "dream house" of the de Roche family, who treat their guests more like friends than paying customers. A great view of the Cays and good French food make for a pleasant stay. *M. de Roche, Villa La Bijou, Canouan, St. Vincent, W.I., tel. 809/458-8025. 6 rooms. No hot water in the shared baths. Facilities:*

snorkeling, Sunfish, windsurfing, dining room. No credit cards. Inexpensive–Moderate.

Nightlife Surprise: There's a bar/disco at **La Bijou.**

Mayreau

Farm animals outnumber citizens on tiny Mayreau (pronounced *my-ro*). Except for water sports and hiking, there's nothing to do, and visitors like it that way. This is the perfect place for a meditative or vegetative vacation.

Guided Tours You can swim and snorkel in the Cays or nearby islands on day trips with Chuck Burghard on his spacious, rainbow-striped catamaran *Carnival*. Contact Chuck through **Undine Potter** at the Salt Whistle Bay Resort (from the U.S., tel. 800/387–1752; in the Grenadines, marine radio VHF channel 68 or 16). Note that the Salt Whistle Bay's snorkel equipment has seen better days. Buy or rent your own before you arrive.

Beaches Top honors go to **Salt Whistle Bay Beach**—the Caribbean's prettiest. The beach is an exquisite half moon of powdery white sand, shaded by perfectly spaced palms and flowering bushes, with the rolling Atlantic a stroll away. Hike 25 minutes over Mayreau's mountain (wear shoes; bare feet or flip-flops are a big mistake) to a good photo opportunity at the stone church atop the hill. Once you've put your camera away, you can investigate Mayreau's one tiny town or enjoy the swimming on beautiful, swimmable **Saline Bay Beach** (no facilities here).

Participant Sports NAUI instructor Bill Tewes of Dive St. Vincent is opening a new scuba shop on Salt Whistle Bay in late 1989.

Dining and Lodging Set far back from the water, the roomy stone cottages at the **Salt Whistle Bay Club,** Mayreau's one hotel, are so cleverly hidden that sailors need binoculars to be sure a hotel is there at all. With names like "Oleander" and "Ivora," the cottages sport round-stone showers (no hot water) that look like large, medieval telephone booths. You can dry your hair on the breezy, shared second-story veranda atop each two-room building. The outdoor dining area has stone tables covered with thatched palms. On top of these tables, duck, fish-and-chips, and coconut cake are served while music from the bar drifts in. There used to be a jump-up, but guests preferred peace and quiet. *Salt Whistle Bay Club, 610 Reynolds St., Toronto, Ont., L1N 6H8, Canada, tel. 416/430–1275, FAX 416/430–8988; in the Caribbean, marine radio channel 16 or 68. 14 units, 5 double cottages, 8 smaller rooms, 1 suite. Facilities: windsurfing, snorkeling, catamaran charter, bar, restaurant. No credit cards. Very Expensive.*

Mustique

This island has no town and no activities, though horseback riding is available and motorbikes can be rented from **TechServe** (tel. 809/458–4621; ask for TechServe). If you're not a hotel or villa guest, it's easiest to arrange for these via marine radio from Basil's Bar when you arrive.

Beaches **Macaroni Beach** is Mustique's most famous stretch of sand, offering surfy swimming (no lifeguards, so be careful) with trees and mountains rising behind you. There's not much shade, and no facilities, which also describes Mustique's smaller, nameless beaches. Daytrippers can also swim near **Basil's Bar.**

Dining **Basil's Bar, Britannia Bay.** Day sailors are welcome for lunch at the famous if exorbitantly priced Basil's, another Grenadines institution. Homemade ice cream, lobster, and occasional glimpses of the rich and famous provide gastronomic and visual distractions. Wednesday features a jump-up and barbecue; Monday night, live music. The restaurant also has a boutique with designer batiks and Basil's T-shirts. *Tel. 809/458–4621. Reservations suggested. AE, MC, V. Moderate.*

Lodging **The Cotton House.** This restored 18th-century stone and coral Georgian house accommodates half the guest rooms, while three guest cottages near the "Roman ruin" pool and a two-story wing houses eight other rooms. Custom-designed furnishings accent the light, breezy rooms, all of which have patios or balconies. Manager Cristophe Lajus continues the Cotton House's tradition of excellent food. Full water sports, tennis, and horseback riding are available here, and shopping can be found at the Treasure Boutique, which features chic international designer resort wear and accessories. *Mustique, St. Vincent, W.I., tel. 809/456–4777. U.S. agent: Ralph Locke Associates, Box 800, Waccabuc, NY 10597, tel. 914/763–5526 or 212/696–1323. 30 rooms. Facilities: pool, bar, restaurant, boutique, diving, windsurfing, tennis, horseback riding. AE, V. Very Expensive.*

Villa Rentals. Leasing an elegant villa of your own (complete with maid and cook) can be expensive, but sharing the cost with another couple makes the price more reasonable. Where else can you vacation in the house Princess Margaret owns? Contact the Manager of the Mustique Company (Mustique, St. Vincent, W.I., tel. 809/458–4621) for listings and information.

Palm Island

One of the area's most beautiful islands, this private resort offers many activities. **Palm Island Resort's** new fitness walk circles past private homes, hills, and deserted Atlantic beach. The 12 stone cottages with outdoor showers all have a beach view, verandas, and newly refurbished pastel/rattan interiors. Recently added solar power now provides hot water, and a full health spa with indoor/outdoor exercise area is planned. Tea is served on your terrace every day at 4 PM, and West Indian meals in the refurbished outdoor dining/bar area are good. *Palm Island, St. Vincent, W.I., tel. 809/458–4804. U.S. Agent: Scott Calder, 152 Madison Ave., NY 10016, tel. 212/535–9530. 12 cottages, 24 rooms. Facilities: minifridge, bar, ceiling fans, mosquito netting; diving, snorkeling, windsurfing, Zodiac and Sunfish rentals, fitness course; fishing, catered day sails or extended trips, yacht provisioning. AE, MC, V. Very Expensive.*

Petit St. Vincent

Many upscale travelers consider Petit St. Vincent the finest private island in the Grenadines, and the privacy is as perfect as the food: The imported duck and game hen are worthy of any four-star Manhattan restaurant. Here the clientele communicates with flags. A yellow flag hoisted outside your stone and wood house means that you want room service. If you have food delivered, make sure you don't confuse your Jeep-driving waiter by raising the red "leave me alone" flag.

Meals are served the old-fashioned way in the Pavilion (without the aid of flags). You can play table tennis and listen to occasional live piano music in the outdoor bar, while manager Haze Richardson's six Labradors stroll the grounds.

Beaches Small, secluded beaches surround the island, now hidden from the jogging/fitness trail by skillful new landscaping. The hotel will drop you for the day at Mopion, a tiny sandbar with one thatch-roof shelter for shade. There is good swimming all over.

Participant Sports Activities include tennis, croquet, windsurfing, waterskiing (small extra charge), snorkeling, sailing trips, and jogging on a new 20-stop, 32-exercise fitness trail that runs along the beaches and around a wooded area. Shaded hammocks are strung up every 100 feet along the trail. *PSV, Box 12506, Cincinnati, OH 45212, tel. 513/242–1333 or 809/458–4801. 22 houses. No credit cards. Closed Sept. and Oct. Very Expensive.*

Union

Union's airstrip is right behind the Anchorage Yacht Club.

Beaches The beach around Clifton Harbour is narrow, unattractive, rocky, and shadeless. Other beaches have no facilities and are virtually inaccessible without a boat; the desolate but lovely Chatham Bay offers good swimming.

Participant Sports **Dive Anchorage,** run by NAUI instructor Glenroy Adams and his brother Rick on the grounds of the Anchorage Yacht Club, offers reef dives at Mayreau and in the Tobago Cays and wreck dives at the *Purina,* a sunken WWI English gunship. Resort courses, certification courses, glass-bottom boat trip, and snorkel trips are offered. *Tel. 809/458–8221. Cost: about U.S.$40 per dive. No credit cards.*

Dining **Clifton Beach Hotel.** Excellent West Indian food is served here, thanks to new chefs who formerly worked on Mustique. The outdoor bar-restaurant area is pleasant and faces the harbor. *Tel. 809/458–8235. AE, V. Inexpensive–Moderate.*

Lodging **Anchorage Yacht Club.** Sprawling between the airstrip and what little beach there is are rooms and bungalows with concealed outdoor showers and terraces facing the water, all comfortably refurbished and full of French yachtsmen. Scuba, fishing, windsurfing, and Hobie Cats are available, plus yacht charters to nearby islands and provisioning for visiting boats. The expensive boutique offers French fashions and accessories not found on other islands, and new manager Charlotte Honnart has improved the restaurant's French and Creole cuisine. The enormous bar area is fronted by a pool inhabited by dozens of nurse sharks so docile that a sign warns, PLEASE DO NOT TOUCH THE SHARKS. *Union, St. Vincent, W.I., tel. 809/458–8221. 15 rooms, 6 bungalows. Facilities: water-sports center, restaurant, bar, boutique, air-conditioning, yacht provisioning and charters. AE, MC, V. Expensive.*

Sunny Grenadines. Simply furnished, airy, and appealing, the dozen rooms are in several two-story stone buildings arranged around a plant-filled garden. A few rooms have kitchens, some are big enough for four or five people, and all have small porches and twin beds. The harbor view is pleasant if not spectacular. Hospitable manager Augustus Mitchell arranges boat trips to the Cays. *Union, St. Vincent, W.I., tel. 809/458-8327. 10 rooms, some with kitchens. Facilities: bar and restaurant. MC, V. Inexpensive–Moderate.*

Nightlife A steel band plays Monday and Friday nights at the **Anchorage Yacht Club.**

26 Trinidad and Tobago

by Mark Rowland

Mark Rowland is Pacific Editor of Musician magazine. His feature articles have appeared in Esquire, American Film, Americas, and other publications.

Trinidad and Tobago, the southernmost islands in the West Indies chain, could not be more dissimilar. Trinidad's cosmopolitan capital, Port of Spain, bustles with shopping centers, modern hotels, sophisticated restaurants, and an active nightlife. It is also home of Carnival, the birth place of steelband music, and a busy port. The 1.2 million Trinidadians know prosperity from oil (it is one of the biggest producers in this hemisphere), a steel plant, natural gas, and a multiplicity of small businesses. More than half of them—Indians, Africans, Europeans, Asians, and Americans, each with its own language and customs—live in Port of Spain. The Trinidadians are heavy on cricket and horse racing. But you have to leave the capital to find a good beach. And because it is one of the most active commercial cities in the West Indies, most visitors are business travelers.

Tobago, 22 miles away, offers the lazier life most tourists seek. The Robinson Crusoe island is more laid-back, the pace slower, with beautiful, near-deserted beaches, secluded bays, small hotels, and little fishing villages. Goats outnumber cars. Tobago is popular with snorkelers and divers; its Buccoo Reef is an underwater wonderland.

Columbus reached these islands on his third voyage in 1498. Three prominent peaks around the southern bay where he anchored prompted him to name the land La Trinidad, after the Holy Trinity. Trinidad was formally ceded to England in 1802, ending 300 years of Spanish rule.

Tobago's history was more complicated. It was "discovered" by the British in 1508. The Spanish, Dutch, French, and British all fought for it until it was ceded to England under the Treaty of Paris in 1814. In 1962, both islands—T & T, as they're commonly called—gained their independence within the British Commonwealth, finally becoming a republic in 1976.

In 1986, the National Alliance for Reconstruction (NAR) won a landslide victory, toppling the People's National Movement (PNM), which had been in power for 30 years but had brought the country to the brink of economic ruin. The NAR is now in the process of reconstruction and development.

Trinidad's capital may be noisy and its way of life somewhat frenetic, but its countryside is rich in flora and fauna, home to more than 400 species of birds and 700 varieties of orchids.

Before You Go

Tourist Information

Contact the **Trinidad and Tobago Tourist Board** (In the United States: Forest Hills Tower, 118–35 Queens Blvd., Queens, NY 11375, tel. 718/575–3909; 330 Biscayne Blvd., Suite 310, Miami, FL 33122, tel. 305/374–2056 or 800/325–1337, ext. 700. In the United Kingdom: 48 Leichester Sq., London WC2H 7QD, tel. 01/930–6566. In Canada: 40 Holly St., Suite 102, Toronto, Ont. M4S 3C3, tel. 416/486–4470 or 800/268–8986).

Arriving and Departing By Plane

There are daily direct flights to Piarco Airport, about 30 miles east of Port of Spain, from New York, Miami, and Toronto on **BWIA** (tel. 800/327–7401), Trinidad and Tobago's national airline. You can also fly from one or more of these cities on **Pan Am** (tel. 800/221–1111), **American** (tel. 800/433–7300), and **Air Canada** (tel. 800/422–6232). BWIA has flights three times a week from London and serves Boston and Baltimore once a week.

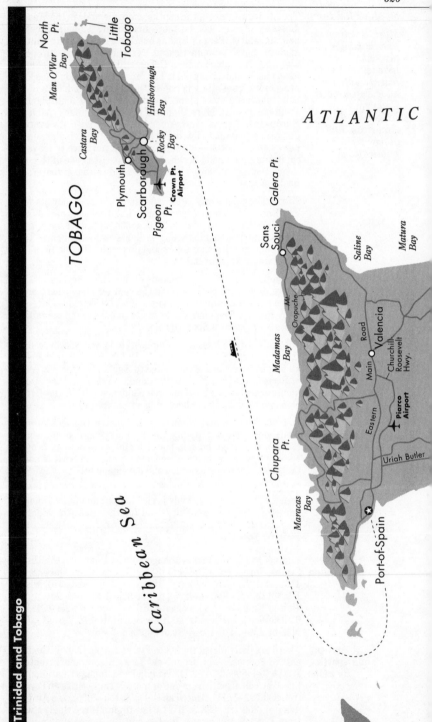

Trinidad and Tobago

ATLANTIC

Caribbean Sea

TOBAGO

North Pt.
Man O'War Bay
Little Tobago
Castara Bay
Hillsborough Bay
Plymouth
Scarborough
Rocky Bay
Pigeon Pt. Crown Pt. Airport

Galera Pt.
Sans Souci
Saline Bay
Matura Bay
Madamas Bay
Mt. Oropuche
Valencia
Main Road
Churchill Roosevelt Hwy.
Piarco Airport
Eastern
Uriah Butler
Chupara Pt.
Maracas Bay
Port-of-Spain

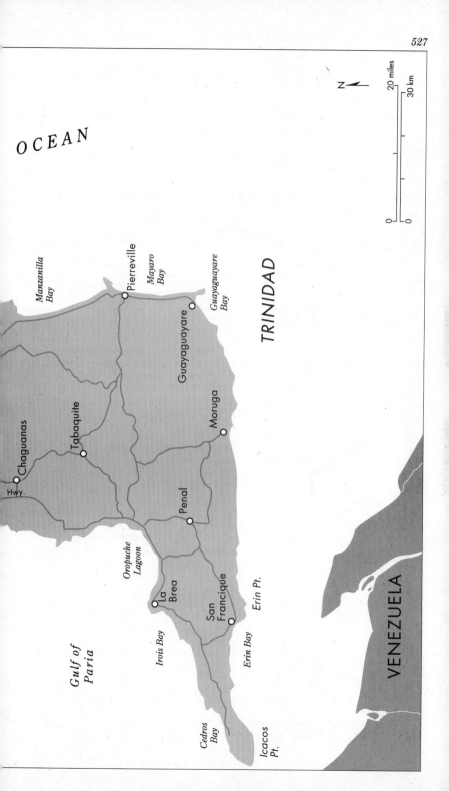

There are flights from Amsterdam and Paramaribo via **KLM Royal Dutch Airlines** (tel. 800/777–5553). **ALM** (tel. 800/327–7230) and Pan Am have flights from New York via Curaçao, the latter at a lower cost than most standard fares. There are numerous interisland flights in the Caribbean by BWIA and **LIAT** (tel. 809/462–0701). All flights to Trinidad alight at Piarco Airport. Most round-trip fares include a free round-trip ticket to Tobago from Piarco, a $25 value, so be sure to check with your agent. BWIA flights from Trinidad to Crown Point Airport in Tobago take about 15 minutes and depart about six to 10 times a day.

Package tours aren't generally touted as heavily as they are for other Caribbean islands, but there are bargains to be had, especially around Carnival. One particularly good agency in this regard is **Pan Caribe Tours** (Box 46, El Paso, TX 79940, tel. 915/542–3370).

By Boat The Port Authority runs a ferry service between Trinidad and Tobago; the ferries leave twice a day. The trip takes about six hours (flying is more preferable); return fare is $7, cabin fare $19 (one-way double occupancy), with an extra charge for vehicles. Tickets are sold at offices in Port of Spain (tel. 809/625–4906) and at Scarborough, in Tobago (tel. 809/639–2181).

Passports and Visas Citizens of the United States, United Kingdom, and Canada who expect to stay for less than two months may enter the country with an original birth certificate (not a photocopy) and some other identification with a photograph. Citizens of other countries need passports. A visa is required for a stay of more than two months.

Customs and Duties Adult visitors may carry out 50 cigars or 200 cigarettes and one quart of spirits without paying a duty.

Language The official language is English, although there is no end of idiomatic expressions used by the loquacious Trinis *(see* Further Reading, below). You will also hear smatterings of French, Spanish, Chinese, and Hindi.

Precautions Insect repellent is a must during the rainy season (June–December) and is worth having around anytime. If you're prone to carsickness, bring your preferred remedy. Trinidad is only 11 degrees north of the equator, and the sun here can be intense. Even if you tan well, it's a good idea to use a strong sun block, at least for the first few days.

Further Reading *Trinidad and Tobago Dialect (Plus)*, by Dr. Martin Haynes, is an entertaining dictionary of Trinidadian expressions with the cumulative effect of an anthropological study. *The Dragon Can't Dance*, by Earl Lovelace, is an engaging novel about Carnival set in Laventille and based on the generally accepted folk history of the steel bands. *The Middle Passage* contains an insightful—if rather unsparing—portrait of Trinidad by its most famous writer, V. S. Naipaul. Also recommended is *Sea Grapes* by the Trinidadian poet Derek Walcott.

Staying in Trinidad and Tobago

Important Addresses **Tourist Information:** Information is available from the **Trinidad Tourist Board** (122–24 Frederick St., Port of Spain, tel. 809/623–1932 or 809/623–1933; Piarco Airport, tel. 809/664–5196). For Tobago, write to the **Tobago Division of Tourism** (Tobago

House of Assembly, Scarborough Hall, Scarborough, tel. 809/ 639–2125).

Emergencies   **Police:** Call 999.

Fire and Ambulance: Call 990.

Hospitals: Port of Spain General Hospital is on Charlotte Street (tel. 809/625–7869). **Tobago County Hospital** is on Fort Street in Scarborough (tel. 809/639–2551).

Pharmacies: Oxford Pharmacy (tel. 809/627–4657) is at Charlotte and Oxford streets near the Port of Spain General Hospital. **Ross Drugs** (tel. 809/639–2658) is in Scarborough. For a complete list of other pharmacies, check the T&T Yellow Pages.

Currency   The Trinidadian dollar (TT$) has been devalued twice in recent years. The current exchange rate is about U.S.$1 to TT$4.20. The major hotels in Port of Spain have exchange facilities whose rates are comparable to official bank rates. Most businesses on the island will accept U.S. currency if you're in a pinch. Note: All prices quoted here are in U.S. dollars unless indicated otherwise.

Taxes and Service Charges   Hotels add a 10% government tax; restaurants add a 3% tax. The airport departure tax is TT$20 (about U.S.$5).

Many hotels and restaurants add a 10% service charge to your bill. If the service charge is not added, you should tip 10%–15% of the bill for a job well done.

Guided Tours   **Trinidad and Tobago Sightseeing Tours** (Galleria Shopping Centre, Western Main Rd., St. James, Port of Spain, tel. 809/628–1051) has a variety of sightseeing packages, from a tour of the city to an all-day drive to the other side of the island. Another reputable agency is **Hub Travel Limited** (Hilton Hotel lobby, tel. 809/625–3155; Piarco Airport, tel. 809/664–4359). Almost any **taxi driver** in Port of Spain will be willing to take you around the town and to the beaches on the north coast, and you can haggle for a cheaper rate. For a complete list of tour operators and sea cruises, contact the Tourist Board. For nature guides *see* Participant Sports, below.

Getting Around   Taxis in Trinidad are easily identified by their license plates,
Taxis   which begin with the letter *H*. Passenger cars and vans called Maxi Taxis pick up and drop off passengers as they travel. They are easily hailed day or night along most of the main roads near Port of Spain. For longer trips you will need to hire a private taxi. There are set rates, though they are not always observed, particularly at Carnival. To be sure, pick up a rate sheet from the Tourist Board. On the whole, the drivers are honest, friendly, and informative, and the experience of riding in a Maxi Taxi with a souped-up sound system during Carnival is worth whatever fare you pay.

Buses   Buses cover the island and are inexpensive, but they are very old and very crowded.

Rental Cars/ Scooters   If you are a first-time visitor to Port of Spain, where the streets are often jammed with traffic and drivers who routinely play "chicken" with one another, taxis are your best bet. But if you're set on wheels and not prone to headaches, you can call on several car-rental services around town. Try **Premier Auto Rental Limited** (10 Nook Ave., St. Ann's, Port of Spain, tel.

809/624–7265) or **Bacchus Taxi Service** (37 Tragerete Rd., Port of Spain, tel. 809/622–5588). All agencies require a large deposit and you must make reservations well in advance of your arrival. Figure on paying about $30–$45 per day.

In Tobago you will be better off renting a car or jeep than relying on taxi service, which is less frequent and ultimately much more expensive. Try **Sweet Jeeps** (Sandy Point, tel. 809/639–8533) or **Tobago Travel** (Box 163, Tobago, tel. 809/639–8778). You can also rent **motor scooters** from **Banana Rentals** (c/o Kariwak Village, Crown Point, tel. 809/639–8441). Rentals average $25–$35 a day.

As befits one of the world's largest exporters of asphalt, Trinidad's roads are fairly well paved. In the outback, however, they are often narrow, twisting, and prone to washouts in the rainy season. Inquire about conditions before you take off, particularly if you're heading toward the north coast. Never drive into downtown Port of Spain during afternoon rush hour. Don't forget to drive on the left.

Telephones and Mail The area code throughout the two islands is 809. For telegraph, telefax, teletype, and telex, contact **Textel** (1 Edward St., Port of Spain, tel. 809/625–4431). Cables can be sent from the Tourist Board and major hotels. **Postage** for first-class letters to the United States is TT$25; postcards, TT$.80.

To place an intraisland call, dial the local seven-digit number. To reach the United States by phone, dial 1, the appropriate area code, and the local number.

Opening and Closing Times Most shops open weekdays 8–6:30 and Saturday 8–noon. Banking hours are Monday–Thursday 9–2 and Friday 9–1 and 3–5.

Carnival

Trinidad always seems to be either anticipating, celebrating, or recovering from a festival, the biggest of which is **Carnival.** It occurs each year between February and early March. Trinidad's version of the pre-Lenten bacchanal is reputedly the oldest in the Western Hemisphere; there are festivities all over the country but the most lavish is in Port of Spain.

Carnival officially lasts only two days (from *J'ouvert* at sunrise on Monday through the *las lap* to midnight the following day). If you're planning to go, it's a good idea to arrive in Trinidad a week or two early to enjoy the events leading up to Carnival. Not as overwhelming as its rival in Rio, or as debauched as Mardi Gras in New Orleans, Trinidad's fest has the warmth and character of a massive family reunion.

Carnival is about extravagant costumes: Individuals prance around in imaginative outfits. Colorfully attired troupes— called *mas*—that sometimes number in the thousands march to the beat set by the steel bands. You can visit the various mas "camps" around the city where these elaborate costumes are put together—the addresses are listed in the newspapers— and perhaps join one that strikes your fancy. Fees run anywhere from $35 to $100; you get to keep the costume. Children can also parade in a Kiddie Carnival that takes place on Saturday morning a few days before the real thing.

Throwing a party is not the only purpose for Carnival; it's also a showcase for calypso performers. Calypso is music that mixes dance rhythms with social commentary, sung by characters with such evocative names as Shadow, the Mighty Sparrow, and Black Stalin. As Carnival approaches, many of these singers perform nightly in Calypso tents, which are scattered around the city. You can also visit the pan yards of Port of Spain, where steel orchestras, such as the Renegades, Desperadoes, Catelli All-Stars, Invaders, and Phase II, rehearse their arrangements of calypso.

For several nights before Carnival, costume makers display their talents, and the steel bands and calypso singers perform in spirited competitions in the grandstands of the racetrack in Queen's Park, where the Calypso Monarch is crowned. At sunrise, or J'Ouvert, the city starts filling up with metal-frame carts carrying steel bands, flatbed trucks hauling sound systems, and thousands of revelers who squeeze into the narrow streets. Finally, at the stroke of midnight on "Mas Tuesday," Port of Spain's exhausted merrymakers go to bed. The next day everybody settles back to business.

Beaches

Trinidad Contrary to popular notion, Trinidad has far more beaches than Tobago; the catch is that Tobago's beaches are close to hotels, and Trinidad's are not. There are, however, four worthy sites within an hour's drive of Port of Spain, spread out along the north coast road.

Tyrico Bay is a small beach lively with surfers who flock here to enjoy the excellent surfing. The strong undertow may cow some swimmers. **Maracas Bay** is a long stretch of sand with a cove and a fishing village at one end. It's a local favorite, so it can get crowded on weekends. Parking sites are ample, and there's a snack bar and rest facilities.

A few miles up the north coast road is **Las Cuevas Bay,** a narrow, picturesque strip of sand fanned by palms. A stand offers tasty snacks, and vendors hawk fresh fruit across the road. It's less crowded here, and seemingly serene, although, like Maracas, the current can be treacherous. About 8 miles east, along the north coast road, is another narrow beach. **Blanchisseuse Bay** is palm-fringed and the most deserted of the lot. Facilities are nonexistent, but the beach is ideal for a romantic picnic.

The drive along the northeast coast toward Toco takes several hours, but does reward the persistent traveler with gorgeous vistas and secluded beaches. **Balandra Bay,** sheltered by a rocky outcropping, is popular among bodysurfers. **Salibea Bay,** just past Galera Point, which juts toward Tobago, is a gentle beach with shallows and plenty of shade, perfect for swimming. Snack vendors abound in the vicinity. The road to **Manzanilla Beach** and **Cocos Bay** to the south is lined by stately coconut palms and the longest continuous stretch of beach in the country. Manzanilla has picnic facilities, and a postcard-pretty view of the Atlantic, though its water is occasionally muddied by the Orinoco River, which flows in from South America.

Tobago Traveling to Tobago without sampling the beaches is like touring the south of France without drinking the wine. So, starting from the town of Plymouth and gravitating—slowly—counterclockwise, we'll explore a dozen of the island's more memorable sand spots.

Great Courland Bay, near Fort Bennett, is a long stretch of clear, tranquil water, bordered on one end by **Turtle Beach,** so named for the turtles that lay their eggs here at night between April and May. (You can watch; the turtles don't seem to mind.) A short distance west, there's a side road that runs along **Stone Haven Bay,** a gorgeous beach that's virtually unspoiled save for local fishing boats (at least for now; a hotel is under construction nearby).

Mt. Irvine Beach, across the street from the Mt. Irvine Beach Hotel, is an unremarkable setting that has the best surfing in July and August. It's also ideal for windsurfing in January and April. There are picnic tables surrounded by painted concrete pagodas and a snack bar.

Pigeon Point is the locale inevitably displayed on Tobago travel brochures. It's the only privately owned beach on the island, part of what was once a large coconut estate, and you must pay a token admission (about $1) to enter the grounds. The beach is lined by royal palms, and there's a food stand, gift shop, and paddleboats for rent. The waters are calm.

Store Bay, where boats depart for Buccoo Reef, is probably the most socially convivial setting in the area. Next to the bustling Crown Reef Hotel, the beach is little more than a small sandy cove between two rocky breakwaters. Farther west along Crown Point, **Sandy Beach** is abutted by several hotels, including the Tropikist, Crown Point, and Sandy Point Beach Club. You won't lack for amenities around here.

Just west of Scarborough, take Milford Road off the main highway to the shores of **Little Rockly Bay.** The beach is craggy and not much good for swimming, but it is quiet and offers a pleasing view of Tobago's capital across the water.

After driving through Scarborough, continue south on Bacolet Street 4 miles to **Bacolet Beach,** a dark-sand beach that was the setting for the film *Swiss Family Robinson.*

The road from Scarborough to Speyside has plenty of swimming sites of which **King's Beach,** surrounded by steep green hills, is the most visually satisfying—the bay hooks around so severely you feel like you're swimming in a lake. It's easy to find as it's marked by a sign about halfway between Roxborough and Speyside.

Man of War Bay in Charlotteville is flanked by one of the prettiest fishing villages in the Caribbean. You can lounge on the sand and purchase the day's catch for your dinner. Farther west across the bay is **Lovers Beach,** so-called because of its pink sand and because it can be reached only by boat. You can hire one of the locals to take you across.

Parlatuvier, on the north side of the island, is best approached via the road from Roxborough. The beach here is a classic Caribbean crescent, a scene peopled by villagers and local fishermen.

Exploring Trinidad

Numbers in the margin correspond with points of interest on the Trinidad map.

Port of Spain
❶

It is not really surprising that a sightseeing tour of Port of Spain begins at the port. (If you're planning to explore by foot, start early in the day; by mid-afternoon Port of Spain can be hot.) Though it is no longer as frenetic as during the oil boom of the 1970s, **King's Wharf** entertains a steady parade of cruise and cargo ships, a reminder that the city started from this strategic harbor. Across Wrightson Road is **Independence Square,** which is not a square at all: It's a wide, dusty thoroughfare crammed with pedestrians, car traffic, taxi stands, and peddlers of everything from shoes to coconuts. Flanked by government buildings and the familiar towers of the Financial Complex (familiar because its facade also adorns one side of all TT dollar bills), the square is representative of this city's chaotic charm.

Near the east end of Wrightson Road stands the Roman Catholic **Cathedral of the Immaculate Conception,** built in 1832 under the aegis of an Anglican governor, Sir Ralph Woodford. Its treasures consist of a Florentine-marble altar, iron framework from England, and stained glass from Ireland.

Up Picton Road are **Fort Chacon** and **Fort Picton,** erected to ward off invaders by the Spanish and British regimes, respectively. The latter is a striking martello tower with a fine view of the gulf.

At the corner of Prince and Frederick streets, look across **Woodford Square** toward the magnificent **Red House,** a Renaissance designed building that takes up an entire city block. Trinidad's House of Parliament takes its name from a paint job done in anticipation of Queen Victoria's Diamond Jubilee in 1897. Woodford Square has served as the site of political meetings, speeches, public protests, and occasional violence. The original Red House, in fact, was burned to the ground in a 1903 riot. The present structure was built four years later. The chambers are open to the public.

The view of the south side of the square is framed by the Gothic spires of **Trinity,** the city's other cathedral, and by the impressive **public library** building. *Tel. 809/623–6142. Open weekdays 7–3.*

Continue north along Pembroke Street and note the odd mix of modern and colonial architecture, gingerbread and graceful estate houses, and stucco storefronts. Pembroke crosses Keate Street at **Memorial Park.** A short walk north leads to the greater green expanse of **Queen's Park,** more popularly called the **Savannah.**

Time Out **The Paddock** (2 Queen's Park W., across from the racetrack, no phone), a dim pub with red tablecloths and calypso on the stereo, is a pleasant spot for a cold Carib beer and a sandwich.

Proceeding west along the Savannah, you'll come to a garden of architectural delights: the elegant lantern-roof **George Brown House;** what remains of the **Old Queen's Park Hotel;** and a series of astonishing buildings constructed in a variety of 19th-century styles, known as the **Magnificent Seven.**

Notable among these are **Killarney,** patterned after Balmoral Castle in Scotland, with an Italian-marble gallery surrounding the ground floor; **Whitehall,** constructed in the style of a Venetian palace by a cacao-plantation magnate and currently the

Trinidad

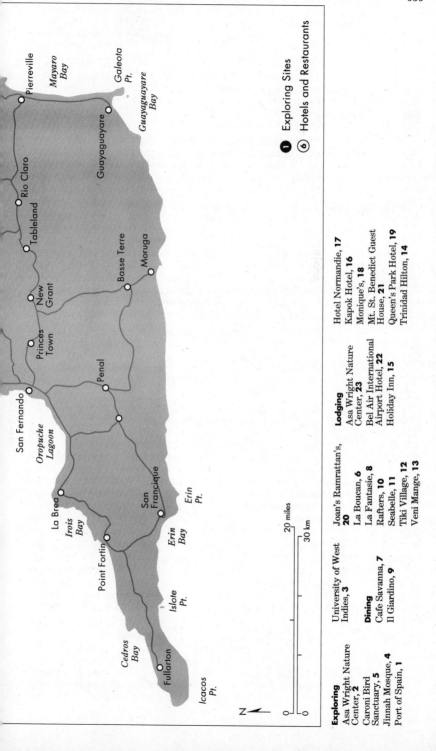

● Exploring Sites

⑥ Hotels and Restaurants

Exploring
Asa Wright Nature
Center, **2**
Caroni Bird
Sanctuary, **5**
Jinnah Mosque, **4**
Port of Spain, **1**

University of West
Indies, **3**

Dining
Cafe Savanna, **7**
Il Giardino, **9**

Joan's Ramrattan's,
20
La Boucan, **6**
La Fantasie, **8**
Rafters, **10**
Seabelle, **11**
Tiki Village, **12**
Veni Mange, **13**

Lodging
Asa Wright Nature
Center, **23**
Bel Air International
Airport Hotel, **22**
Holiday Inn, **15**

Hotel Normandie, **17**
Kapok Hotel, **16**
Monique's, **18**
Mt. St. Benedict Guest
House, **21**
Queen's Park Hotel, **19**
Trinidad Hilton, **14**

0 ___ 20 miles
0 ___ 30 km

office of the prime minister; **Roomor,** a flamboyantly baroque colonial-period house with a preponderance of towers, pinnacles, and wrought-iron trim that suggests an elaborate French pastry; and the **Queen's Royal College,** in German Renaissance style, with a prominent tower clock that chimes on the hour.

The **racetrack** at the southern end of the Savannah serves as more than just a venue for horse racing. It is the setting for music and costume competitions during Carnival, and, when not jammed with calypso performers, costumes, or horses, tends toward quietude.

The northern end of the Savannah is devoted to plants. A rock garden, known as the **Hollow,** and a fish pond add to the rusticity. The **Botanic Gardens,** across the street, date from 1820. The official residences of the president and prime minister are on these grounds.

Out on the Island   The intensely urban atmosphere of Port of Spain belies the tropical beauty of the countryside surrounding it. It's there, but you will need a car to find it. Begin by circling the Savannah—seemingly obligatory to get almost anywhere around here— to Saddle Road, the residential district of **Maraval.** After a few miles the road begins to narrow and curve sharply as it climbs into the Northern Range. Here are undulating hills of lush, jungle-like foliage. An hour through this hilly terrain will lead you to the beaches at **Tyrico Bay** and **Maracas Bay;** a few miles past that is **Las Cuevas Beach.**

Follow the road past Las Cuevas for several miles, then climb into the hills again into the tiny village of **Blanchisseuse.** Here the road narrows again, winding through canyons of moist, verdant foliage and mossy grottoes. As you painstakingly execute the hairpin turns, you'll begin to think you've entered a tropical rain forest. You have.

In the midst of this greenery lies a bird-watcher's paradise, the ❷ **Asa Wright Nature Center.** The grounds are festooned with delicate orange orchids and yellow tube flowers. The surrounding acreage is atwitter with more than 100 species of birds from the hummingbird to the rare nocturnal oilbird. The oilbirds' breeding grounds in Dunston Cave are included among the sights along the center's guided hiking trails. If you're not feeling too energetic, lounge on the veranda of the handsome estate house, which offers a panorama of the Arima Valley. You can also make reservations for lunch. *No phone. Admission: $5 adults, $3 children. Open daily 9–5.*

The descent to **Arima,** about 7 miles, is equally pastoral; the Eastern Main Road connecting Arima to Port of Spain is anything but: It's a busy, bumpy, and densely populated corridor full of roadside stands and businesses. Along the way, you'll ❸ pass the **University of West Indies** campus in Curepe and the ma-❹ jestic turrets and arches of the **Jinnah Mosque** in St. Joseph.

Proceed east from Arima along the Churchill-Roosevelt Highway, a limited-access freeway that runs parallel to the Eastern Main Road a few miles to the south. Both avenues cross the Uriah Butler Highway just outside Port of Spain; a few miles south ❺ on Butler Highway, take the turnoff for the **Caroni Bird Sanctuary.** Across from the sanctuary's parking lot is a sleepy canal with several boats and guides for hire; the smaller boats are best.

The Caroni is a large swamp with maze-like waterways bordered by mangrove trees, some plumed with huge nests of termites. In the middle of the sanctuary are several islets that are home to Trinidad's national bird, the scarlet ibis. Just before sunset they arrive by the thousands, their richly colored feathers brilliant in the gathering dusk, and, as more flocks alight, they turn their little tufts of land into bright Christmas trees. It's not something you see every day. Bring a sweater and insect repellent for your return trip. The boat fee is usually about $6–$10. Advance reservations can be made with boat operators Winston Nanan (tel. 809/645–1305) or David Ramsahai (tel. 809/663–2207).

Exploring Tobago

Numbers in the margin correspond with points of interest on the Tobago map.

❶ **Scarborough** is as pretty as a picture, and just about as alive. It is nestled around the aptly named **Rockly Bay,** and it gives the feeling that not much here has changed since it was settled two centuries ago. This is its charm.

❷ The road east from Scarborough soon narrows as it twists through **Mt. St. George,** a village that clings to a cliff high above the ocean. There's an overlook where you can eye the black-sand beach of **Fort Granby.** The sea dips in and out of view as you pass through a series of small settlements and the town of ❸ **Roxborough.** About an hour's drive will bring you to **King's Bay,** an attractive crescent-shape beach. Just before you reach the bay is a bridge with an unmarked turnoff that leads to a gravel parking lot; beyond that, a landscaped path leads to a waterfall with a rocky pool where you can refresh yourself. You may meet enterprising locals who'll offer to guide you to the top of the falls, a climb that you may find not worth the effort.

❹ After King's Bay the road rises dramatically; just before it dips again there's a marked lookout with a vista of **Speyside,** a small fishing village.

Time Out **Jemma's Sea View Kitchen** (tel. 809/660–4066), a stand along the main road in Speyside, offers tasty West Indian lunches served on a picnic table by the ocean.

❺ Past Speyside the road cuts across a ridge of mountains that separates the Atlantic side of Tobago from the Caribbean. On the far side is **Charlotteville,** a remote fishing community, albeit the largest village on the island. Fishermen here announce the day's catch (usually flying fish, red fish, or bonito) by sounding their conch shells.

❻ The paved road ends a few miles outside Charlotteville, in Camberton; Returning to Speyside, take a left at the sign for **Flagstaff Hill.** Follow a well-traveled dirt road for about 1½ miles to a radio tower. It's one of the highest points in Tobago, surrounded by ocean on three sides and with a view of the hills, Charlotteville, and Bird of Paradise Island in the bay.

Participant Sports

Bird-Watching Bird-watchers can fill up their books with notes on the variety of species to be found in Trinidad at the **Asa Wright Nature Cen-**

Tobago

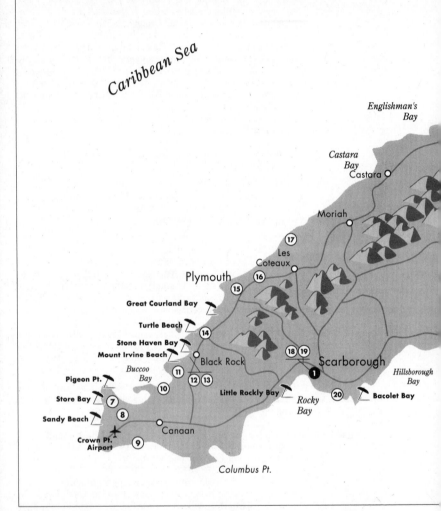

Caribbean Sea

Englishman's
Bay

Castara
Bay
Castara ○

Moriah ○

⑰

Les
Coteaux ○

Plymouth

⑯

⑮

Great Courland Bay

Turtle Beach

⑭

Stone Haven Bay

Mount Irvine Beach

Black Rock

Buccoo
Bay

⑱ ⑲

Scarborough

Hillsborough
Bay

Pigeon Pt.

⑪

⑫ ⑬

Store Bay

⑩

⑦

Little Rockly Bay

Rocky
Bay

⑳

Bacolet Bay

Sandy Beach

⑧

Canaan

Crown Pt.
Airport

⑨

Columbus Pt.

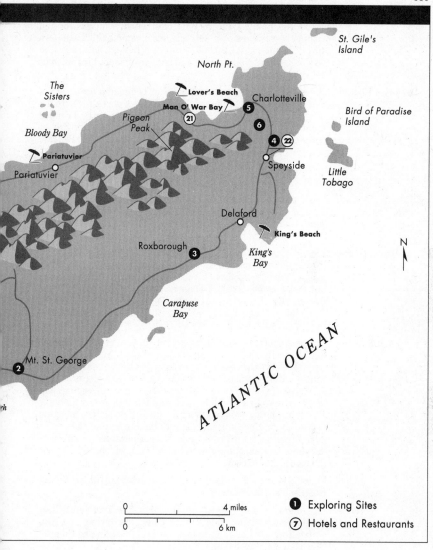

St. Gile's
Island

North Pt.

The
Sisters

Lover's Beach

Man O' War Bay

Charlotteville

Bird of Paradise
Island

Pigeon
Peak

⑤

Bloody Bay

㉑

⑥

④ ㉒

Pariatuvier

Speyside

Little
Tobago

Pariatuvier

Delaford

King's Beach

Roxborough

③

King's
Bay

Carapuse
Bay

N

Mt. St. George

②

ATLANTIC OCEAN

rh

0   4 miles

0   6 km

❶ Exploring Sites

⑦ Hotels and Restaurants

ter, the **Caroni Bird Sanctuary** (*see* Exploring Trinidad, above), and at the **Pointe-à-Pierre Wild Foul Trust,** which is located within the confines of a petrochemical complex (42 Sandown Rd., Pt. Cumana, tel. 809/637–5145). In Tobago, naturalist **David Rooks** offers walks inland and trips to offshore bird colonies (tel. 809/639–9408).

Deep-Sea Fishing The islands off the northwest coast of Trinidad offer excellent waters for deep-sea fishing; the ocean here was a favorite angling spot of Franklin D. Roosevelt. Members of the **Trinidad Yacht Club** (Bayshore, tel. 809/637–4260) may be willing to arrange a tour. The Tourist Board also recommends **Mr. Pouchet** (tel. 809/622–8974).

In Tobago, contact **Dillon Tours and Charters** (tel. 809/639–8765). Dillon's the most expensive, about $350 per day.

Golf There are nine golf courses in the country, the best of which are the **Mt. Irvine Golf Club** (tel. 809/639–8871) in Tobago, and **Moka Golf Course** in Maraval (tel. 809/629–2314), just outside Port of Spain.

Scuba Diving Tobago draws scuba diving aficionados from around the world. You can get information, supplies, and instruction at **Dive Tobago** (tel. 809/639–2266 or 809/639–3695), **Tobago Marine Sports Ltd.** (tel. 809/639–0291), **Tobago Scuba** (tel. 809/660–4327), and **Tobago Dive Experience** (Crown Point, tel. 809/639–0343; in Trinidad, tel. 809/639–1263). Also in Trinidad is **Scuba Shop Ltd.** (Mirabella, tel. 809/658–2183).

Snorkeling The best spots for snorkeling are on Tobago, of which **Buccoo Reef** is easily the most popular—perhaps a bit too popular. Over the years the reef has been damaged by the ceaseless boat traffic and by the thoughtless visitors who take pieces of coral for souvenirs. Even so, it's still a trip worth experiencing, particularly if you have children. For $8 (tickets are available in almost any hotel), you board a Plexiglass-bottom boat at either Store Bay or Buccoo Beach; the 15-minute trip to the reef, 2 miles offshore, is made only at low tide. Operators provide rubber shoes, masks, and snorkels but not fins, which are helpful in the moderate current.

There is also good snorkeling by the beach near the **Arnos Vale Hotel** and at **Blue Waters.**

Tennis The following hotels have tennis courts: **The Trinidad Hilton, Turtle Beach, Arnos Vale, Crown Point, Mt. Irvine,** and **Blue Waters Inn** (*see* Lodging, below); so does the **Trinidad Country Club** (tel. 809/622–3470).

Shopping

Thanks in large part to Carnival costumery, there's no shortage of fabric shops on the islands. The best bargains for Oriental and East Indian silks and cottons can be found downtown on **Frederick Street** and around **Independence Square.** Other good buys are such duty-free items as Angostura Bitters and Old Oak or Vat 19 rum, all widely available throughout the country.

Good Buys
Boutiques Upscale boutiques at the **Hilton** and in the **Long Circular Mall** make for more relaxed browsing. Luxury items are available at **Y. de Lima,** with branches on High Street and at the West Mall,

and at **Stecher's** at the Hilton and Crown Reef hotels and in the Long Circular Mall.

Local Crafts The Tourist Board can provide an extensive list of local artisans who specialize in everything from straw and cane work to miniature steel pans. **St. Ann's Village** (Nook St., next to the Hotel Normandie) has several shops that specialize in indigenous fashions, crafts, and a gallery of contemporary Trinidadian art.

Records For the best selection of calypso and soca music, check out **Rhyner's Record Shop** (54 Prince St., 809/623–5673) or **Metronome** (2 Madras St., 809/622–4157), both in Port of Spain.

Dining

Trinidad Port of Spain doesn't lack for variety when it comes to eateries. Two devaluations of the Trinidad dollar in recent years have persuaded some of the more expensive dining establishments to trim their prices, resulting in more reasonable rates as well as imaginative hybrids of European and Caribbean cuisines. In addition to the establishments listed below, there is also no shortage of East Indian and Chinese restaurants and pizzerias (but don't expect New York–style pizza).

Trinidadians are particularly fond of *callaloo*, a soup or stew of dasheen leaves (similar to spinach) and okra, flavored with anything from pork to coconut, pureed and served at every restaurant in the country. It's hard to believe anything this green and swampy looking can taste so delicious. Other items in a Trinidadian menu worth sampling are *coocoo*, a dumpling of cornbread and okra; *roti*, a sandwich of East Indian origin, on flat bread or in a pocket pita, usually filled with curried chicken and potatoes; *pelau*, a rice-and-peas dish inspired by Chinese cuisine; *tamarind ball*, a dessert made from the sweet-sour tamarind; and *peanut shake*, a peanut butter–flavor milk shake that really does taste better than it sounds.

No Trinidadian dining experience can be complete, of course, without a rum punch with fresh fruit, and the legendary Angostura Bitters, made by the same company that produces the excellent Old Oak rum. Carib beer and Stag are recommended for washing down the spicier concoctions.

Tobago With few exceptions, the restaurants in Tobago are located in hotels and guest houses; several of the large resort complexes also feature some form of nightly entertainment. The food isn't as eclectic as on Trinidad, generally favoring local styles, but in terms of quality and service Tobagonian "home cooking" more than holds its own.

For grabbing a quick bite, the main streets in Port of Spain's downtown abound in beef and rice joints, homemade ice cream shops, and chicken roti stands. At the Savannah, day or night, are vendors selling cold coconut drinks called cold nut. For about 50¢, the vendor will lop off a green coconut with a deft swing of his machete and provide you with a straw.

The most highly recommended restaurants are indicated by a star ★.

Category	Cost*
Expensive	over $25

Moderate	$15–$25
Inexpensive	under $15

per person, excluding drinks, service, and sales tax (3%)

Trinidad **La Boucan.** This place has long been considered the best restaurant in town, in part because of its sophisticated decor. A large mural of a social idyll in the Savannah dominates one wall of a room. The restaurant strives for elegance: silver service, uniformed waiters, candlelight, pink tablecloths, and the soft tinkling of a grand piano. The chef has an imaginative touch that extends to presenting some of his culinary creations in fantastic shapes. Specialties run from smoked duck breast to Creole dishes and French crepes. The meals here tend toward good-but-not-really-gourmet, suggesting an Anglicized French restaurant. In a setting this civilized, you probably won't mind. *Trinidad Hilton, Lady Young Rd., Port of Spain, tel. 809/624–3211. Jackets recommended. Reservations recommended. AE, DC, MC, V. Expensive.*

★ **Cafe Savanna.** Caribbean style, with bare wood walls and Sade on the sound system, this cozy den consistently serves the best fare on the island. The menu specializes in Trinidadian dishes with a distinctive flair: coconut curried shrimp and fillet of grouper marinated in fresh herbs. The callaloo soup here sets the standard for other island delicacies. The three-course lunch special for about $9 is a bargain. *Kapok Hotel, 16–18 Cotton Hill, Port of Spain, tel. 809/622–6441. AE, DC, MC, V. Expensive.*

La Fantasie. A pastel dining room with high ceilings seeks to mix postmodern design with a sense of fun. The menu calls itself Cuisine Créole Nouvelle and tends toward Trinidadian dishes of fresh fish and poultry, seasoned and presented in the French manner. Customers are invited to name dishes. The selections change often; if you happen to dine here on a night when fresh homemade ice cream is offered, you're in luck. *Normandie Hotel, 10 Nook Ave., St. Ann's, Port of Spain, tel. 809/624–1181. AE, DC, MC, V. Expensive.*

Il Giardino. This restaurant is run by an Italian chef in a setting that resembles a greenhouse; potted plants of all varieties fill display shelves and trellises support orchids. Chef Luciano holds forth in the kitchen, creating pasta specialties to the sounds of opera. *6 Nook Ave., St. Ann's, Port of Spain, tel. 809/624–1459. AE, DC, MC, V. Moderate.*

Rafters. Behind a stone facade with green rafters is a pub that has become an urban institution. Once it was a rum shop; currently under the proprietorship of Paul Mowser, it's a bar and a restaurant. The pub is the center of activity. In late afternoons the place begins to swell with Port-of-Spainers ordering from the tasty selection of burgers and barbecue and generally loosening up. On Fridays the place is packed; a more convivial introduction to the city would be difficult to replicate. *6A Warner St., Port of Spain, tel. 809/628–9258. AE, DC, MC, V. Moderate.*

Seabelle. This restaurant is hard to find—there's no sign or street number. The entrance looks like the door to a private home—which is part of its charm. The ambience is beatnik with 1950s jazz on the stereo, a pool in the back, and a darkened bar where time almost stands still. The accent is on seafood. It has only seven tables so you must call for reservations—and directions. *27 Mucurapo Rd., St. James, Port of Spain, tel. 809/622–3594. No credit cards. Moderate.*

Tiki Village. The rooftop restaurant of the Kapok Hotel affords a romantic view of the city and the Gulf of Paria. Its elevator entrance is flanked by two colorful wood totems; its walls are adorned with native crafts, including copper masks. It's a pleasant setting for fine Polynesian meals, including tasty egg rolls. *16–18 Cotton Hill St., St. Clair, Port of Spain, tel. 809/622–6441. Reservations recommended. AE, DC, MC, V. Moderate.*

★ **Veni Mange.** The best lunches in town are served inside this small stucco house. Credit Allyson Hennessy, a Cordon Bleu-trained cook who has become a celebrity of sorts because of a TV talk show she hosts, and her sister/partner Rosemary Hezekiah. The cuisine here is Creole. It is open for lunch only, unfortunately, and it is often crowded, especially on Fridays when no one wants to leave. *13 Lucknow St., St. James, Port of Spain, no phone. No credit cards. No dinner. Moderate.*

Joan Ramrattan's. Although it looks like a roadside bar there's delicious home cooking inside, courtesy of the proprietress. A good place to waft the flavors of city living, it is well off the tourist beat. *164 Eastern Main Rd., corner of Hammersmith St., Port of Spain, tel. 809/623–0168. No credit cards. No Dinner. Inexpensive.*

Tobago **Blue Crab.** Perched on a wide porch above a busy corner of
★ downtown Scarborough, this is the spot for lunch. Best bets here are the fresh kingfish or flying fish with callaloo and vegetables, prepared with élan by cook Ken Sardinha. While nominally closed for dinner, the proprietors will open the restaurant and serve a supper upon the request of even one couple. *Corner of Main and Fort Sts., Scarborough, tel. 809/639–2737. No credit cards. Moderate.*

Cocrico Inn. A café with a bar against one wall, the Cocrico offers Southern-style home cooking. The chefs frequently use fresh fruits and vegetables grown in the neighborhood. There is nothing fancy here, just warm and delicious food. *Corner of North and Commissioner Sts., Plymouth, tel. 809/639–2691. AE, V. Moderate.*

★ **Papillon.** Named after one of the proprietor's favorite books, this restaurant is a homey room with an adjoining patio. The menu is the most varied on the island, with such unusual items as banana-vichyssoise soup. There's also an astute selection of wines. *Bucco Bay Rd., Mt. Irvine, tel. 809/639–0275. AE, DC, MC, V. Moderate.*

The Old Donkey Cart House. The name is something of a curiosity, since this attractive restaurant is set in and around a green and white colonial house, about a 2-mile drive south of Scarborough. There's an outdoor dining in a garden with twinkling lights. The cuisine is a mélange of German and Caribbean delights, including a cheese board, an extensive selection of imported wines, and rich desserts. *Bacolet St., Scarborough, tel. 809/639–3551. No credit cards. Moderate.*

Sugar Mill Restaurant. This restaurant is housed in a converted 18th-century mill with walls constructed from sea coral; a conical, shingle roof descends like an enormous hat over an expansive outdoor patio. The prix fixe dinner is usually a choice of grilled meats or the catch of the day, expertly prepared, with extras including a tasty pâté. Dining is by candlelight, sometimes to the accompaniment of a steel band, while the refreshing Caribbean breeze wafts in. *Mt. Irvine Bay Hotel, tel. 809/639–8871. AE, DC, MC, V. Moderate.*

Lodging

Accommodations in Trinidad and Tobago comprise all sizes, shapes, and standards: There are large and small hotels, guest houses, and private homes. On Trinidad most lodging establishments are located within the vicinity of Port of Spain, far from any beach. On Tobago, it's the opposite; every establishment listed here, with one exception, is either on or within walking distance of the ocean. Carnival week is one of two times in the year (the other is Christmas) you should book reservations far in advance; expect to pay twice the price charged during the rest of the year.

Most places do offer breakfast and dinner for an additional flat rate (MAP), but on the whole these offer less variety than if you strike out for meals on your own. If you're lodging on the east side of Tobago, however, MAP is almost essential because of the dearth of restaurants.

The most highly recommended lodgings are indicated by a star ★.

Category	Cost*
Very Expensive	over $150
Expensive	$90–$150
Moderate	$55–$90
Inexpensive	under $55

All prices are for a standard double room for 2, excluding 3% tax and a 10% service charge.

Trinidad Hotels ★

Trinidad Hilton. Perched over Port of Spain, the Hilton radiates an air of luxury. Each room either has a balcony, which opens to a fine view and the distant murmur of the city below, or overlooks the equally inviting Olympic-size pool, shaded by trees harboring brightly crested cornbirds. This is easily Port of Spain's most elegant hotel, with prices to match. It frequently bustles with conventioneers, which may be its only drawback. The good news is that it's usually available for last-minute Carnival bookings. The Aviary bar serves the creamiest drinks in town. *Lady Young Rd., Box 442, Port of Spain, tel. 809/624–3211. 442 rooms. Facilities: 2 restaurants, bar, conference rooms, satellite TV, pool, health club, tennis courts, drugstore, gift shops, car rental, taxi service. AE, DC, MC, V. Expensive.*

Holiday Inn. Located at the port and close to Independence Square, which affords the hotel a pastel panorama of the old town and of ships idling in the Gulf of Paria. There's not a whole lot to do within walking distance, and traffic during rush hour is not a pretty sight. (An exception is during Carnival; then you're in the middle of all the festivities.) The hotel's rooftop restaurant was closed at press time, which leaves a humdrum coffee shop as the lone eatery in the area. The place is dependable but, true to its name, it's still short on charm. *Wrightson Rd., Box 1017, Port of Spain, tel. 809/625–3361. 235 rooms. Fa-*

cilities: satellite TV, pool, health spa, conference rooms, beauty salon, taxi service. AE, DC, MC, V. Expensive.

Asa Wright Nature Center. Set in a lush rain forest about 90 minutes east of Port of Spain, this handsome lodge, constructed in 1908 by a tycoon for his young bride, attracts international legions of bird-watchers and nature photographers. There are impressive views of the verdant Arima Valley and the Northern Range from the veranda, where tea is served each afternoon. The rooms are uncomplicated and comfortably furnished; some of the beds have hand-carved frames cut from trees from the surrounding forest, which is now protected by a private trust. Three meals a day and an evening rum punch are included in the rates. Reservations at least six months in advance are recommended. (For more information about the center, see Exploring, above.) *Bag 10, Port of Spain; write: Caligo Ventures, Box 21, Armonk, NY 10504, tel. 914/273–6333. No credit cards. Moderate.*

Bel Air International Airport Hotel. The Bel Air's big selling point is that it is situated three minutes from the airport; after sleeping here you'll swear it's on the runway. The noise is stupendous; accommodations, by contrast, are so tiny you barely have room to think. The catch is that the next closest hotel is in Port of Spain, 30 miles away. If you do get marooned here, your silver lining is a good restaurant with a well-stocked bar. Start by ordering a double. *Piarco Airport, Piarco, tel. 809/664–4771. 56 rooms. Facilities: bar and restaurant, pool, car rental, light-airplane flying school. AE, DC, MC, V. Moderate.*

★ **Hotel Normandie.** Built in the 1930s by French Creoles on the ruins of an old coconut plantation, the Normandie has touches of Spanish, English-colonial, and even postmodern architecture, giving the place an agreeably artsy patina. Fittingly, it has become the linchpin of a complex in St. Ann's that includes a gallery, a café, and an array of shops. *10 Nook Ave., St. Ann's Village, Port of Spain, tel. 809/624–1181. 61 rooms. Facilities: restaurant and bar, pool, meeting rooms, gallery, café, shops, car rental, taxi service. AE, DC, MC, V. Moderate.*

★ **Kapok Hotel.** This hotel has been run by the Chan family for years and all but gleams with cheerful efficiency. It's a great location, just off the north end of the park, near the zoo and Presidential Palace, and away from the worst traffic. Its two distinctive restaurants, the *Savanna* and *Tiki Village*, are among the best in town. Rooms are comfortably furnished in a wicker motif and command a pleasing view on the park side. The Kapok is a good bargain for your buck. *16–18 Cotton Hill, Port of Spain, tel. 809/622–6441. 71 rooms. Facilities: TV, pool, 2 restaurants, taxi service. AE, DC, MC, V. Moderate.*

★ **Monique's.** This homey lodging is a nest of congeniality only minutes from downtown. Mike and Monique Charbonne have been running their home as a guest house for 10 years. They have recently expanded the place to 12 rooms, one specifically designed for the disabled. All rooms have private baths. Their philosophy is to make their house your own, and it's not unusual for hosts and lodgers to be found fraternizing in the living room. Meals are available on request, and Mike will occasionally organize a picnic to the couple's 100-acre plantation near Blanchisseuse. *114 Saddle Rd., Maraval, tel. 809/628–3334. 12 rooms. Facilities: common-room area with TV. AE. Inexpensive.*

Mt. St. Benedict Guest House. A country-style guest house that feels like a retreat, this nonsectarian lodging is situated on a hill overlooking the valley about 10 miles east of Port of Spain. The flat fee of $45 a day per person includes three meals, mostly local cuisine. Rooms are tidy, with shared baths. There is a steady breeze along the hillside that negates the need for air-conditioning. A good getaway while visiting the city, but a car is necessary. *Tunapuna, tel. 809/662–4084. 20 rooms. Facilities: TV room. AE, DC, MC, V. Inexpensive.*

Queen's Park Hotel. Constructed in 1895 and once the belle of Port of Spain, what beauty remains here is awaiting renovation; the section of the hotel that is open was built in the 1950s, and suggests a cross between art deco and a housing project. The rooms are cozy and include refrigerators, though the halls feel more like a dormitory; a few rooms have balconies that overlook the southern end of the Savanna. The service here is gracious and attentive, and the location is ideal. *5 Queen's Park W, Port of Spain, tel. 809/625–1061. 74 rooms. Facilities: pool, open-air dining, lounge. AE, DC, MC, V. Inexpensive.*

Bed-and-Breakfasts The number of private homes in Trinidad offering bed-and-breakfast accommodations is growing each year. For a complete listing of homes in Trinidad approved for guest accommodation by the **Trinidad and Tobago Bed and Breakfast Association** (Box 3231, Diego Martin, Trinidad).

Tobago **Arnos Vale Hotel.** The hotel is an attractive hideaway that
Hotels crosses Tobago horticulture with Mediterranean design. White stucco cottages are set on a hill that descends through a series of winding paths to a secluded beach, a newly constructed pool, and a handy bar. The hilltop restaurant, with iron lattice tables, a chandelier, and a hand-painted piano, leads to a crescent-shape patio that offers a sweeping view of the sea. The grounds are getting a face-lift, which will include a disco and several new rooms. *Arnos Vale, tel. 809/639–2881; for reservations contact: M.G. Benati, Vacanze SRL, Via Rastrelli-2, 20122 Milan, tel. 02–85391. 32 rooms. Facilities: pool, bar, restaurant, tennis, beach, snorkeling. AE, DC, MC, V. Expensive.*

★ **Mt. Irvine Bay Hotel.** Once the site of a 17th-century sugar plantation, the mill has been deftly recast as a restaurant. There's open-air dining on the surrounding patio, which overlooks a magnificent pool, a cabana bar, and the quiet water of the Caribbean. The balcony rooms of this rambling, two-story complex afford the same view as the restaurant with broader horizons, or else survey the adjacent Mt. Irvine golf course, considered among the finest in the world. The Mt. Irvine gently pampers guests with a panache that puts its own brochures to shame. Rates are steep by Tobago standards. Candlelit suppers to the sounds of a steel band, however, soon put the cost in context. *Mt. Irvine Bay, Box 222, Tobago, tel. 809/639–8871. 64 rooms, 42 cottages. Facilities: pool, 2 bars, 2 restaurants (1 formal), tennis courts, convention facilities, beach across the street, beauty parlor, shops, taxi service. AE, DC, MC, V. Expensive.*

Turtle Beach Hotel. The ranch-style lobby of this hotel leads to a seemingly endless bar, which in turn empties onto a wide beach peppered with thatch cabanas. The rooms have easy access to the beach. The restaurant is expanding its menu, which boasts a reputable Creole buffet on Sundays. There are two bars (one on the beach) and a tiny pool that is a good place to watch the sun set. *Great Courland Bay, tel. 809/639–2851;*

write: Box 201, Scarborough, Tobago. 125 rooms. Facilities: restaurant, 2 bars, beach, pool, tennis court, water-sport center, bike rentals, gift shop. AE, DC, MC, V. Expensive.

★ **Blue Waters Inn.** It's easy to miss the sign for this gem of a hotel nestled on the shore of Batteaux Bay; the entrance road appears to drop over a cliff. It's all part of the charm of this rustic retreat, where birds fly through a dining room ornamented with driftwood. A variety of beamed rooms and cabins include new apartments with kitchenettes. The beach here is free of currents; nature walks are popular along the 48 acres of grounds. Anyone craving peace and quiet will welcome the news that the place doesn't have a pool, air-conditioning, TV, or phone. The home cooking is dependably delicious. *Batteaux Bay, Speyside, Tobago, tel. 809/660–4341. 20 rooms. Facilities: tennis, beach, dive instruction. No credit cards or personal checks. Moderate.*

Cocrico Inn. Named after the national bird of Tobago, this comfortable inn is set on a quiet side street in the village of Plymouth, a short walk from a local bird sanctuary as well as a beach. The accent here is on native culture; the café-style restaurant prepares Tobagonian dishes using homegrown fruits and vegetables (including a delicious guava punch). *North and Commissioner Sts., Box 287, Plymouth, Tobago, tel. 809/639–2961. 16 rooms. Facilities: restaurant, bar, pool. AE, V. Moderate.*

★ **Kariwak Village.** The resort's motif attempts to recapture the spirit of the Carib and Arawak Indians who originally lived here, without diminishing creature comforts. There's a suitably tropical bar, highly touted Caribbean cooking, and open-air dining. The gift shop features a thoughtful selection of local crafts and books; there are often shows on the premises by Tobago artists. Nine cabanas, which resemble equatorial igloos, have been divided into 18 cozy apartments, all of which look onto the pool. *Crown Point, tel. 809/639–8545; write: Box 27, Scarborough, Tobago. 18 rooms. Facilities: shuttle service to beach, pool, restaurant, bar, scooter rentals. AE, V. Moderate.*

Man O' War Bay Cottages. Seven separate apartments are set along the sleepy shoreline of an overgrown cacao plantation. The clientele runs to scientists and travelers who want to escape the rigors of urban living. The local amenities include fishermen who will take you out fishing for a fee and nature guides. Watch for the flocks of wild parrots that fly by in the late afternoon. *Charlotteville, tel. 809/639–4327. 7 cottages with kitchens. Facilities: beach, snorkeling and fishing nearby, access to Marine Institue lab. No credit cards. Moderate.*

Della Mira Guest House. Proprietor Neville Miranda built this establishment in 1954, and he's still running the place. The restaurant off the main lobby has a marvelous view of Rockly Bay. A walk lined with mango and banana trees leads to *La Tropicale*, a dance club along the water that's very romantic; unfortunately, it's rarely open. The bedrooms are clean but far from fancy. The beach is a short drive from the hotel. The Della Mira is very economical, and Mr. Miranda is a warm and ingratiating host. *Box 203, Scarborough, Tobago, tel. 809/639–2531. 14 rooms. Facilities: restaurant, lounge, pool, nightclub, beauty salon. No private phones or TV. No credit cards. Inexpensive.*

The Golden Thistle Hotel. The look here is that of a respectable 1950s motel. There's a surprisingly huge auditorium in the back that's a popular site with locals for weekend entertain-

ment. Several of the rooms include kitchenettes, making this
spot particularly attractive to travelers on a budget. Proprietor Clyde St. Louis is attentive to all requests, even driving
elderly guests to the beach at nearby Pidgeon Point (it's a 10-
minute walk). It's that kind of place. *Store Bay Rd., Crown
Point, Tobago, tel. 809/639-8521. Facilities: pool, bar, TV
room, restaurant, kitchenette. No credit cards. Inexpensive.*

The Arts and Nightlife

Trinidad   Trinidadian culture doesn't end with music, but it definitely
begins here. While both calypso and steel bands are best displayed during Carnival, the steel bands play at clubs, dances,
and fetes throughout the year. There's no lack of nightlife in
Port of Spain.

Mas Camp Pub (corner of Ariapata and French Sts., Wood-
brook, tel. 809/627-8449) is Port of Spain's most comfortable
and dependable night spot. There are tables, a bar, an ample
stage in one room, and an open-air patio with more tables and a
bar with a TV. There's a kitchen if you're hungry and **Hush,**
which makes delicious fruit-flavor ice cream, is right next door.

Cricket Wicket (149 Tragarete Rd., tel. 809/622-1808), a popular watering hole with a cupola-shape bar in the center, is a fine
place to hear top bands, dance, or just sit and enjoy the nocturnal scenery.

In the late afternoons the locals come to **Rafters** (6A Warner
St., tel. 809/628-9258) to wind down and wind up.

Tobago   Nightlife on Tobago is generally confined to hotel-sponsored
entertainment, which runs the gamut from steel band performances to limbo dancers. In addition, **Kariwak Village** features
a melange of calypso and jazz. There are nightclubs at the **Della
Mira Guest House** in Scarborough and at the **Golden Thistle
Guest House** in Crown Point, both of which feature dancing on
weekends and occasional live performances, usually during
Carnival season.

27 Turks and Caicos Islands

by Honey Naylor

The Turks and Caicos Islands are relatively unknown except to collectors of beautiful beaches and scuba divers, who religiously return to these waters year after year.

First settled by the English more than 200 years ago, the British Crown Colony of Turks and Caicos (population 8,000) is renowned in two respects: Its booming banking and insurance institutions lure investors from the United States and elsewhere, and its offshore reef formation entices divers to a world of colorful marine life surrounding its 40 islands, only eight of which are inhabited.

The Turks and Caicos are two groups of islands in an archipelago lying 575 miles southeast of Miami and about 90 miles north of Haiti. Some 8,000 people live on the eight large islands and over 40 small cays (pronounced "keys"), which have a total land mass of 193 square miles. The Turks Islands include Grand Turk, which is the capital and seat of government, and Salt Cay, with a population of about 400. According to local legend these islands were named by early settlers who thought the scarlet blossoms on the local cactus resembled the Turkish fez.

Some 22 miles west of Grand Turk, across the 7,000-foot-deep Turks Island Passage, is the Caicos group, which includes South, East, West, Middle, and North Caicos, and Providenciales. South Caicos, Middle Caicos, North Caicos, and Providenciales (nicknamed Provo) are the only inhabited islands in this group; Pine Cay and Parrot Cay are the only inhabited cays. "Caicos" is derived from *cayos*, the Spanish word for cay.

In the years following Ponce de León's landing in 1515, a band of pirates also established communities in the archipelago. Around 1678, Bermudians, lured by the wealth of salt in these islands, began raking salt from the flats and returning to Bermuda to sell their crop. Despite French and Spanish attacks and pirate raids, the Bermudians persisted and established a trade that became the bedrock of the Bermudian economy. In 1766, Andrew Symmers settled here to hold the islands for England. Later, Loyalists from Georgia obtained land grants in the Caicos Islands, imported slaves, and continued the lifestyle of the pre–Civil War American South.

With an eye toward tourism dollars to create jobs and increase the standard of living, the government has devised a long-term development plan to improve the Turks and Caicos' visibility in the Caribbean tourism market. Providenciales, in particular, is slated not only for tourism development, but also for development of banking, registration of business companies, and offshore insurance.

Before You Go

Tourist Information

Contact the **Caribbean Tourist Organization** (20 E. 46th St., New York, NY 10017, tel. 212/682–0435) or the **Turks and Caicos Tourist Board** (c/o Medhurst & Assoc., Inc., 271 Main St., Northport, NY 11768, tel. 516/261–7474 or 212/936–0050). You can also reach the **Turks and Caicos Tourist Board** on Grand Turk toll-free at 800/441–4419. They can provide more complete and up-to-date information.

Arriving and Departing By Plane

Pan Am (tel. 800/221–1111) has several weekly flights from Miami to Provo and Grand Turk. **Bahamasair** (tel. 809/327–8451) offers turbo-prop service from Nassau to South Caicos weekly.

The **Turks & Caicos National Airlines** (TCNA) (tel. 809/946–2082) makes several flights weekly to Grand Turk from Puerto Plata in the Dominican Republic. Interisland air service is provided by TCNA on a regularly scheduled daily basis.

From the Airport Taxis are available at the airports; expect to share a ride. Rates are fixed. A typical fare from the airport to the Island Reef hotel might be around $5.

By Boat Because of the superb diving, two live-aboard dive boats call regularly. Contact the ***Aquanaut*** (c/o See & Sea, tel. 800/DIV–XPRT) or Peter Hughes's ***Sea Dancer*** (tel. 800/333–3484).

Passports and Visas U.S. citizens need some proof of citizenship such as a voter's registration card, birth certificate, or passport. British subjects require a current passport. All visitors must have an ongoing or return ticket.

Customs and Duties There is no restriction on the import of cameras, film, sports equipment, or other personal items so long as they are not for resale.

Language The official language of the Turks and Caicos is English.

Precautions Petty crime does occur here, and you're advised to leave your valuables in the hotel safe-deposit box. Bring along a can of insect repellent. Deer flies and sand flies are ubiquitous and sadistic critters.

If you plan to explore the uninhabited island of West Caicos, be advised that the interior is overgrown with dense shrubs that include manchineel, which has a milky, poisonous sap that can cause painful, scarring blisters.

On Grand Turk, Salt Cay, and South Caicos, signs are posted reading, "Please help us conserve our precious water." Those islands have no freshwater supply other than rainwater collected in cisterns, and rainfall is scant. Drink only from the decanter of fresh water your hotel provides, and avoid even rinsing your mouth with the tap water.

Staying in Turks and Caicos Islands

Important Addresses **Tourist Information:** The **Government Tourist Office** (Front St., Cockburn Town, Grand Turk, tel. 809/946–2321) is open Monday–Thursday 8–4:30 and Friday 8–4.

Emergencies **Police:** Grand Turk, tel. 809/946–2299. Providenciales, tel. 809/946–4259. South Caicos, tel. 809/946–3299.

Hospitals: There is a 24-hour emergency room at **Grand Turk Hospital** (Hospital Rd., tel. 809/946–2333) and the **Providenciales Health-Medical Center** (Leeward Hwy. and Airport Rd., tel. 809/946–4201).

Pharmacies: Prescriptions can be filled at the **Government Clinic** (Grand Turk Hospital, tel. 809/946–2040) and in Provo, at the **Providenciales Health-Medical Center** (Leeward Hwy. and Airport Rd., tel. 809/946–4201).

Currency The unit of currency is U.S. dollars.

Taxes and Service Charges Hotels collect a 7% government tax. The departure tax is $10.

Hotels add a 10% service charge to your bill. In restaurants, a tip of 10%-15% is appropriate. Taxi drivers expect a 10% tip.

Guided Tours A taxi tour of any one of the islands costs $20 an hour. The driv-

Turks and Caicos

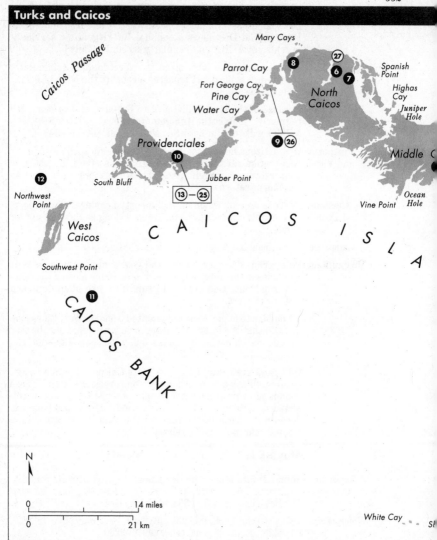

Caicos Passage

Mary Cays

Parrot Cay

Fort George Cay
Pine Cay
Water Cay

North
Caicos

Spanish
Point

Highas
Cay

Juniper
Hole

Providenciales

South Bluff

Jubber Point

Northwest
Point

West
Caicos

Southwest Point

C A I C O S   I S L A

Middle C

Ocean
Hole

Vine Point

CAICOS BANK

N

0   14 miles
0   21 km

White Cay

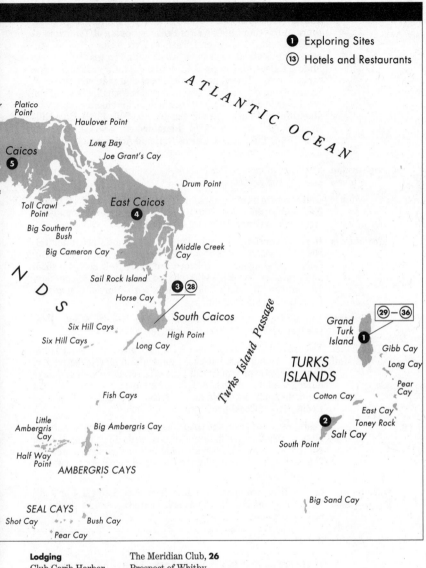

● Exploring Sites

⑬ Hotels and Restaurants

ATLANTIC OCEAN

Platico Point

Haulover Point

Long Bay

Joe Grant's Cay

Caicos ❺

Drum Point

Toll Crawl Point

East Caicos ❹

Big Southern Bush

Big Cameron Cay

Middle Creek Cay

N D S

Sail Rock Island

③ ㉘

Horse Cay

South Caicos

Six Hill Cays

Six Hill Cays

High Point

Long Cay

Turks Island Passage

Grand Turk Island ❶

㉙ — ㊱

Gibb Cay

Long Cay

TURKS ISLANDS

Pear Cay

Cotton Cay

Fish Cays

East Cay

Toney Rock

Little Ambergris Cay

Big Ambergris Cay

❷ Salt Cay

South Point

Half Way Point

AMBERGRIS CAYS

Big Sand Cay

SEAL CAYS

Shot Cay   Bush Cay

Pear Cay

Lodging

Club Carib Harbor Hotel, **28**

Club Med Turkoise, **19**

Erebus Inn, **20**

Evan's Inn, **33**

Hotel Kittina, **34**

Island Princess, **21**

Island Reef, **35**

Mariner's Hotel, **22**

The Meridian Club, **26**

Prospect of Whitby Hotel, **27**

Salt Raker Inn, **36**

Third Turtle Inn, **23**

Treasure Beach Villas, **24**

Turtle Cove Yacht and Tennis Resort, **25**

ers are friendly and know everything and everybody. **Executive Tours** (tel. 809/946–4524) offers a variety of bus and small-plane tours. A bus tour takes in all of Provo, stopping off for drinks at Le Deck and at the Seven Dwarfs at Turtle Cove Marina. Another tour is of the conch farm. The Flying Pirates airlift you to Middle Caicos, the largest of the islands, for a visit to its mysterious caves. They'll put you in a boat and take you to Parrot Cay, and in a donkey cart to tour one of the smaller isles. If you want to island-hop on your own schedule, air charters are available through **Charles Air Service** (tel. 809/946–4352), **Blue Hills Aviation** (tel. 809/946–4226), **Flamingo Air Services** (tel. 809/946–2109), and **Turks & Caicos National Airlines** (tel. 809/946–2350).

Getting Around *Taxis*	Taxis are unmetered, and rates, posted in the taxis, are regulated by the government.
Planes	Daily hops to all of the inhabited islands are via **Turks & Caicos National Airlines'** (tel. 809/946–2082) five-seaters. Round-trip airfare from Grand Turk costs from $20 to $90.
Rental Cars	**Hertz** has outlets on Grand Turk at the **Island Reef Hotel** (tel. 809/946–2055) and on Provo in **BCP Plaza** (tel. 809/946–4475). Local rental agencies on Provo are **Pride** (tel. 809/946–4325) and **Provo** (tel. 809/946–4404). Rates average $25–$35 per day. To rent cars on South Caicos, check with your hotel manager for rates and information.
Scooters	You can scoot around Provo by contacting **Holiday Scooter Rentals** (tel. 809/946–4422) or **Scooter** (tel. 809/946–4684.)
Telephones and Mail	You can call the islands direct from the United States by dialing 809 and the number, but the volume of commercial activity in the business capital of Grand Turk often creates lengthy delays during weekday office hours. International credit card calls can be made from the **Cable and Wireless (WI) Ltd.** exchange on Front Street, Cockburn Town, Grand Turk.

Postal rates for letters to the United States, Bahamas, and Caribbean are 25¢ per half ounce; postcards 15¢; letters to the United Kingdom and Europe, 40¢ per half ounce; postcards, 20¢; letters to Canada, Puerto Rico, and South America, 30¢; postcards, 15¢.

Opening and Closing Times — Most offices are open weekdays from 8 or 8:30 till 4 or 4:30. Banks are open Monday, Tuesday, Thursday, and Friday 8:30–noon and 2–4:30.

Beaches

There are more than 230 miles of beaches in the Turks and Caicos Islands, ranging from secluded coves to mile-long stretches. Most beaches are soft coralline sand. Tiny uninhabited cays offer complete isolation for nude sunbathing and skinny-dipping. Many are accessible only by boat.

Governor's Beach is a long white strip on the west coast of **Grand Turk.** Hotel Kittina/Omega Divers and the Salt Raker Inn/Blue Waters Divers are located on this beach.

East Caicos, an uninhabited island accessible only by boat, boasts a magnificent 17-mile beach.

A fine white-sand beach stretches 12 miles along the northeast coast of **Providenciales.** Other splendid beaches are at **Sapodilla Bay,** and rounding the tip of the northwest point of the island.

The north end of **South Caicos** is only a few hundred yards wide and is fringed with fine white sand.

The entire island of **North Caicos** is bordered by great beaches for swimming, scuba diving, snorkeling, and fishing.

Big Ambergris Cay, an uninhabited cay about 14 miles beyond the **Fish Cays,** has a magnificent beach at Long Bay.

There are superb beaches on the north coast of **Salt Cay,** as well as at **Big Sand Cay** 7 miles to the south.

Pine Cay, an upscale retreat, has a 2½-mile strip of beach—the most beautiful in the archipelago.

Exploring Turks and Caicos Islands

Numbers in the margin correspond to points of interest on the Turks and Caicos Islands map.

Grand Turk Chickens skitter across the road, horses and cattle wander around as if they owned the place, and the occasional donkey cart clatters by, carrying a load of water or freight. Front Street, the main drag, lazes along the western side of the island **❶** and eases through **Cockburn Town,** the colony's capital and seat of government. Buildings in the capital reflect the 19th-century Bermudian style of architecture, and the narrow streets are lined with low stone walls and old street lamps, now powered by electricity.

Time Out The **Pepper Pot** (no phone) is a little blue shack at the end of Front Street, where Peanuts Butterfield is famous for conch fritters.

About half of the colony's 8,000 residents live on this 7-square-mile island. Diving is definitely the big deal here. Grand Turk's Wall, with a sheer drop to 7,000 feet, is well known to divers.

Salt Cay This tiny 2½-square-mile dot in the water is home to about 400 **❷** people. The island boasts one telephone, a few stores in **Balfour Town,** and splendid beaches on the north coast. Old windmills, salt sheds, and salt ponds are silent reminders of the days when the island was a leading producer of salt.

South Caicos **Cockburn Harbour,** the best natural harbor in the Caicos chain, **❸** is home to the Commonwealth Regatta, held each year in May. This 8½-square-mile island was once an important salt producer; today it's the heart of the fishing industry. Spiny lobster and queen conch may be found in the shallow Caicos bank to the west and are harvested for export by local plants. Bonefishing here is some of the best in the West Indies.

At the northern end of the island there are fine, white-sand beaches; the south coast is great for scuba diving along the drop-off; and the windward (east) side is excellent for snorkeling, where large stands of elkhorn and staghorn coral shelter a variety of small tropical fish.

East Caicos Uninhabited and accessible only by boat, this island has on its **❹** north coast a magnificent 17-mile beach. It was once a cattle range and the site of a major sisal-growing industry.

Middle Caicos The largest (48 square miles) and least-developed of the inhabited Turks and Caicos Islands, Middle Caicos is home to **❺** limestone **Conch Bar Caves,** with their eerie underground salt lakes and milky-white stalactites and stalagmites. Archaeologists have discovered Arawak and Lucayan Indian artifacts in the caves and the surrounding area. The boats that dock here and the planes that land on the island's little airstrip provide the island's 500 residents with their only connection to the outside world. **Executive Tours** can fly you over and take you through the mysterious caves (*see* Guided Tours, above).

North Caicos The **Prospect of Whitby Hotel** is on the north end of this 41-square-mile island. To the south of Whitby is **Flamingo Pond,** a nesting place for the beautiful pink birds. If you take a taxi tour of the island, you'll see the ruins of the old plantations and, in the little settlements of **Kew** and **Sandy Point,** a profusion of tropical trees bearing limes, papayas, and custard apples. The beaches here are superb for shelling, snorkeling, scuba diving, swimming and fishing, as well as for lolling.

Pine Cay One of a chain of small cays connecting North Caicos and Provo, 800-acre Pine Cay is privately owned and under development as a planned community. It's home to the exclusive **Meridian Club** resort, playground of jet-setters, and its 2½-mile beach is the most beautiful in the archipelago. The island has a 3,800-foot airstrip, and electric carts for getting around.

Providenciales In the mid-18th century, so the story goes, a French ship was wrecked near here and the survivors were washed ashore on an island they gratefully christened La Providentielle. Under the Spanish, the name was changed to Providenciales.

Provo's 37½-square miles are by far the most developed in the Turks and Caicos. With its rolling green hills and 12-mile beach, the island is a prime target for developers. More than 15 years ago a group of U.S. investors, including the DuPonts, Ludingtons, and Roosevelts, opened up this island for visitors and those seeking homesites in the Caribbean. A new Sheraton and a new Ramada are under construction and work on Frenchman Pierre Gely's Leeward Development of villas and condominiums is proceeding. Provo is also the home of Club Mediteranée's showpiece, Club Med Turkoise, which was built in 1984.

Downtown Provo, located near Ludington International Airport, is a cluster of stone and stucco buildings that house car-rental agencies, law offices, boutiques, banks, and businesses.

Time Out Stop in **Fast Eddie's** (Airport Rd., no phone) for a relaxing drink and a platter of seafood.

Provo is home to the **Caicos Conch Farm,** a major mariculture operation where the mollusks are farmed commercially. You can tour the farm's facilities and geodesic dome, watch a slide show, and browse in the gift shop.

About 1,700 people live on Provo, a considerable number of which are expatriate U.S. and Canadian business people and retirees.

West Caicos Over the past few centuries numerous wrecks occurred in the area between West Caicos and Provo, and author Peter Benchley is among the treasure-seekers who have been lured to this island. **Molasses Reef** is now a restricted area currently being surveyed by an underwater marine-archaeology group who believe they may have located the *Pinta*, which is thought to have been wrecked in the early 1500s.

Charter planes can put down on a 3,000-foot dirt airstrip, but this island is uninhabited, untamed, and there are no facilities whatsoever. A glorious white beach stretches for a mile along the northwest point, and offshore diving is the most exotic in the islands. A wall inhabited by every kind of large marine life ⓬ begins a quarter-mile offshore, and the **Northwest Reef** offers great stands of elkhorn coral and acres of staghorn brambles. But this area is only for experienced divers. The wall starts deep, the currents are strong—and there are sharks in the waters.

If you do tour West Caicos, take along several vats of insect repellent. It won't help with the sharks much, but it should fend off the mosquitoes, deer flies, and sand flies. Be advised, too, that the interior is overgrown with dense shrubs including manchineel.

Participant Sports

Bicycling
Provo has a few steep grades to conquer, but very little traffic. Bikes can be rented at **Sun Cycles** (Airport Rd., next to **Touch of Class** boutique, tel. 809/946–4612).

Boat Rentals
You can rent a boat with private pilot for a half or full day of sportsfishing through **Executive Tours** (Provo, tel. 809/946–4524). Catamarans and power boats can be rented at the **Hotel Kittina** (Grand Turk, tel. 809/946–2232).

Fishing
Executive Tours (Provo, tel. 809/946–4524) will take a maximum of four people out for half- or full-day fishing expeditions, bait and tackle included. The same outfit will arrange half- or full-day deep-sea fishing trips in search of shark, marlin, kingfish, sawfish, wahoo, and tuna, with all equipment furnished. Deep-sea, bonefishing, and bottom fishing are also available aboard the *Sandbox* (Third Turtle Inn, tel. 809/946–4683), **Seatopia** (tel. 305/442–1396), and the *Sakitumi* or the *Safari* (tel. 809/946–4684).

Horseback Riding
Horses roam lazily around the main roads on Grand Turk. If you see one that appeals to you, find out who owns it, get permission to ride it, and hop on.

Scuba Diving
Diving is the top attraction here. (All divers must carry and present a valid certification card before they'll be allowed to dive.) These islands are surrounded by a reef system of more than 200 square miles, and much of it is unexplored. Grand Turk's famed wall drops more than 7,000 feet. There are undersea cathedrals, coral gardens, and countless tunnels. Among the operations that provide instruction, equipment rentals, underwater video equipment, and trips are **Omega Divers** (Hotel Kittina, Grand Turk, tel. 809/946–2232 or 800/255–1966), **Blue Water Divers** (Salt Raker Inn, Grand Turk, tel. 809/946–2432), **Dolphin Cay Divers** (Prospect of Whitby Hotel, North Caicos, tel. 800/346–4295), **Provo Turtle Divers** (Provo, tel. 809/946–4232 or 800/328–5285), and **Seatopia** (tel. 305/442–1396).

Sea Excursions
Seatopia (tel. 305/442–1396) does glass-bottom boat excursions, and sails to uninhabited islands. The 56-foot trimaran *Tao* (tel. 809/946–4393) runs sunset cruises, as well as sailing and snorkeling outings. The Provo Turtle Divers' 20-foot glass-

bottom *Grouper Snooper* (Provo, tel. 809/946–4232) offers sightseeing and snorkeling excursions.

Snorkeling **Wet Pleasures** (Provo, tel. 809/946–4455), **Blue Water Divers** (tel. 809/946–2432), **Omega Divers** (Grand Turk, tel. 809/946–2232), and **Provo Turtle Divers** (Provo, tel. 809/946–4232) all provide rentals and trips.

Tennis There are two lighted courts at **Turtle Cove Yacht & Tennis Club** (Provo, tel. 809/946–4203), eight courts (four lighted) at **Club Med Turkoise** (Provo, tel. 809/946–4491), one court at the **Meridian Club** (Pine Cay, tel. 800/225–4255), and two courts at the **Erebus Inn** (Grand Turk, tel. 809/946–4240).

Waterskiing/ Jet-skiing Equipment is available at the **Island Princess** (Provo, tel. 809/946–4260), **Third Turtle Inn** (Provo, tel. 809/946–4230), and **Wet Pleasures** (Provo, tel. 809/946–4455).

Windsurfing Rental and instruction are available through **Dolphin Cay Divers** (Prospect of Whitby Hotel, North Caicos, tel. 800/346–4295), **Seatopia** (tel. 305/442–1396), **Salt Raker Inn** (Grand Turk, tel. 809/946–2260), and **Wet Pleasures** (Provo, tel. 809/946–4455).

Spectator Sports

The only game in town is cricket. The season runs from June to November.

Dining

Like everything else on these islands, dining out is a very laid-back affair, which is not to say that it is cheap. Because of the high cost of importing all edibles, entrees in all of the restaurants are more expensive than on other islands, and all of the menus are à la carte. A 7% government tax and a 10% service charge are added to your check. Reservations are not required, and dress is casual.

The most highly recommended restaurants are indicated by a star ★.

Category	Cost*
Very Expensive	over $35
Expensive	$25–$35
Moderate	$20–$25
Inexpensive	under $20

per person, excluding drinks, service, and sales tax (7%)

Grand Turk **Island Reef.** This stone and glass building with beam ceilings
★ sits right on the water's edge. The owner is a transplanted Texan, and you know it the minute you bite into the country-fried steak. Other offerings are lobster, panfried grouper, seafood platter, burgers, and sandwiches. *Island Reef Hotel, tel. 809/946–2055. AE, MC, V. Expensive.*

★ **Papillon's Rendezvous.** This is a rustic French restaurant overlooking the water. Begin with onion soup or escargots, then try grilled quail, snapper filet, or fillet mignon. *Front St., tel. 809/946–2088. No credit cards. Closed Sun. and Mon. Expensive.*

Sandpiper. Candles flicker on the Sandpiper's terrace beside a flower-filled courtyard. Its blackboard specialties might include pork chops with applesauce, lobster, filet mignon, or seafood platter. *Hotel Kittina, tel. 809/946-2232. AE, MC, V. Moderate.*

Salt Raker Inn. In this informal open dining pavilion, you might start with tomato and mozzarella salad or melon and ginger. Popular entrees include lobster in cream and sherry sauce, barbecue steak, and seafood curry. For dessert, try oranges in caramel or banana splits. *Salt Raker Inn, tel. 809/946-2260. AE, MC, V. Moderate.*

Providenciales   **Erebus Inn.** The inn's starters include snails in garlic and parsley butter. Among the main dishes are duck à l'orange, grilled steak, broiled lobster tail, cracked conch, and veal cutlet with mustard sauce. *Erebus Inn, tel. 809/946-4240. MC, V. Very Expensive.*

★ **Island Princess.** This is a very special place, with crisp pink napery, a sweeping view of the beach and the sea, and a friendly staff. The grouper cordon bleu is special—so are the lobster and the turtle steak. *Island Princess Hotel, The Bight, tel. 809/946-4260. MC, V. Expensive.*

Banana Boat. This casual spot has a varied menu including chicken français, spaghetti and meatballs, chicken cutlet parmigiana, meatball hoagies, cracked conch, lemon chicken, hamburgers, and hot dogs. *Turtle Cove Marina, tel. 809/946-4312. AE, MC, V. Moderate-Expensive.*

Hong Kong Restaurant. A no-frills place with plain wood tables and chairs, the Hong Kong offers lobster with ginger and green onions, chicken with black-bean sauce, sliced duck with salted mustard greens, and sweet-and-sour chicken. *Leeward Rd., tel. 809/946-4695. AE, MC, V. Closed Sun. Moderate.*

★ **Hey, Jose.** This canopied outdoor restaurant is popular for Tex-Mex treats like tacos, tostados, nachos, burritos, and margaritas. You can build your own pizza. *Leeward Rd., no phone. No credit cards. Inexpensive-Expensive.*

Dora's. Small vases of hibiscus sit on blue plastic cloths in Dora's cheerful white room. Appetizers include conch fritters and fish chowder, and among the main dishes are pork chops, fish and chips, lobster salad, and turtle steak. *Leeward Hwy., no phone. No credit cards. Closed weekends. Inexpensive-Moderate.*

Lodging

Hotel accommodations are available on Grand Turk, South Caicos, Pine Cay, and Provo. There are also some small guest houses on Salt Cay. Accommodations range from small island inns to the splashy Club Med Turkoise. Because of the popularity of scuba diving here, virtually all the hotels have dive shops and offer very attractive dive packages.

The most highly recommended lodgings are indicated by a star ★.

Category	Cost*
Expensive	$85–$140
Moderate	$55–$85

Inexpensive	under $55

*All prices are for a standard double room for two, excluding 7% tax and a 10% service charge.

Grand Turk **Hotel Kittina.** Choose between the sleek, balconied, air-
★ conditioned suites with kitchens, which sit on a gleaming
white-sand beach, or the older main house across the street,
which oozes island atmosphere. Rooms in the latter are simple;
strong winds blow through the rooms and keep things so cool
you don't need the ceiling fans. *Box 42, tel. 809/946–2232 or
800/548–8462. 54 rooms and suites. Facilities: restaurant, 2
bars, pool, boutique, Omega Dive Shop, T&C Travel Agency.
AE, MC, V. Expensive.*

★ **Island Reef.** These modern air-conditioned efficiency and one-
bedroom units sit on a ridge on the eastern coast, where you can
stroll out of your room and onto the beach. Furnishings are contemporary, and each unit has a complete electric kitchen. *Box
10, tel. 809/946–2055 or 800/243–4954. 20 rooms. Facilities: restaurant, bar, tennis, pool, boutique, water sports arranged
with dive operations. AE, MC, V. Moderate.*

Evan's Inn. These rooms and apartments are situated on a
ridge overlooking the ocean inlet of North Creek. Some rooms
are air-conditioned. There is a patio for outdoor barbecues, and
free transportation to the beach and into town. *Box 65, tel. 809/
946–2098. 16 rooms. Facilities: restaurant, bar, saltwater
pool. AE, DC, MC, V. Moderate.*

Salt Raker Inn. Across the street from the beach, this renovated, galleried house was the home of a Bermudian ship-
wright 150 years ago. The rooms and suites are not elegant, but
are individually decorated and have a home-like atmosphere.
Accommodations include a garden house with screened
porches and three one-bedroom suites, some with air-conditioning. *Box 1, tel. 809/946–2260. In U.K., 44 Birchington Rd.,
London NW6 4LJ, tel. 01/328–6474. 9 rooms and suites. Facilities: restaurant, bar, dive packages. AE, MC, V. Moderate.*

Pine Cay **The Meridian Club.** High-rollers get away from it all in high
★ style on this privately owned 800-acre island. Club guests enjoy, among other things, an unspoiled cay with 2½ miles of soft
white sand and a 500-acre nature reserve, with tropical landscaping, freshwater ponds, and nature trails that lure bird-
watchers and botanists. There are seaside cottages, each with
twin beds and a patio fronting on the beach, and a round cottage with two ocean-view atrium units. *Pine Cay, tel. 800/225–
4255. Drawer 114; Box 52–6002, Miami, FL 33152, tel. 212/
696–4566 in U.S. 15 rooms and cottages. Facilities: restaurant,
bar, pool, tennis court, dive packages, water-sports center. No
credit cards. Expensive.*

Providenciales **Club Med Turkoise.** This lavish $23 million resort is one of the
most sumptuous of all of Club Med's villages. One-, two-, and
three-story bungalows line a mile-long beach, and all of the usual sybaritic pleasures are here. *Providenciales, tel. 809/946–
4491 or 800–CLUBMED; 212/750–1687 in NY. 306 rooms. Facilities: restaurant, bar, disco, boutique, 8 tennis courts (4
lighted), bicycles, Jacuzzis, TV/video room, library, fishing,
water-sports center. AE, MC, V. Expensive.*

★ **Erebus Inn.** All units in this stylish resort have two double beds
and modern wicker furnishings. Some rooms are in the older
chalet; units in the newer section are air-conditioned, with 13-

channel cable TV and phones. The hotel sits on a cliff overlooking Turtle Cove, which affords a wonderful view of the marina and the Caribbean beyond. The excellent French restaurant and lively bar make this a popular gathering spot. *Turtle Cove, Box 238, Providenciales, tel. 809/946–4240. 30 rooms. Facilities: restaurant, bar, 2 pools (1 saltwater), 2 tennis courts, miniature golf, dive packages. MC, V. Expensive.*

★ **Third Turtle Inn.** Wood walkways lace around the limestone hillside upon which this small, serene resort sits. One of Provo's oldest resorts, it is a long-time haunt of the rich and famous. It's also a favorite hangout of a colorful cast of pilots, yachtsmen, and local characters, and many a tall tale is told in the famous Seven Dwarfs Bar. Rooms have minibars and many amenities, and there is a heavy emphasis on water sports. *Providenciales, tel. 809/946–4230 or 800/323–7600. Box 526002, Miami, FL 33151. 15 rooms. Facilities: restaurant, bar, tennis court, boutique, marina, dive shop/dive packages. AE, MC, V. Expensive.*

Treasure Beach Villas. These one- and two-bedroom self-catering apartments have fully equipped kitchens, fans, and Provo's 12 miles of white sandy beach for beachcombing and snorkeling. *The Bight, tel. 809/946–4211 or 800/227–2157. Box 8409, Hialeah, FL 33012. 8 single, 10 double rooms. Facilities: pool, tennis court. AE. Expensive.*

★ **Island Princess.** Wood walkways at the hotel lead up to and around the rooms, which are situated in two wings. All rooms have cable TV and private balconies. There is an excellent restaurant overlooking the beach and the sea. *The Bight, tel. 809/946–4260. 80 rooms. Facilities: restaurant, bar, 2 pools, game room, children's playground, dive packages, boat rentals, water-sports center. MC, V. Moderate.*

Mariner's Hotel. A gravel road leads to the hotel, which has contemporary tropical furnishings in fan-cooled rooms and baths with showers. The hotel is on the south end of the island, with easy access to a white-sand beach; there's a dive shop on the premises. *Sapodilla Point, tel. 809/946–4488. 25 rooms. Facilities: restaurant, bar, pool, bakery and pastry shop, dive shop. AE, MC, V. Moderate.*

★ **Turtle Cove Yacht and Tennis Resort.** Occupying 1½ acres, this air-conditioned recreation facility has rooms and condominium units facing the marina. All rooms have TVs and phones. *Providenciales, tel. 809/946–4203. 12 rooms and condominiums. Facilities: restaurant, 2 bars, 2 lighted tennis courts, pool, marina. AE, MC, V. Moderate.*

South Caicos **Club Carib Harbor Hotel.** Within walking distance of the township, this small resort overlooking Cockburn Harbour and the fishing district has simple, functional rooms. *Box 1, South Caicos, tel. 809/946–3251. 12 rooms. Facilities: restaurant, bar. AE, MC, V. Moderate.*

North Caicos **Prospect of Whitby Hotel.** This is a secluded retreat with a pool
★ near a 7-mile-long beach. Some rooms are air-conditioned, some have kitchenettes, but the focus here is on diving. The hotel is home to Dolphin Cay Diving, whose 40-foot catamaran *Surfbreaker* and 28-foot *Formula* spirit guests out to the reefs. *Box 21, Grand Turk, tel. 809/946–4250 or 800/346–4295. 28 rooms. Facilities: restaurant, bar, pool, dive shop. MC, V. Expensive.*

Nightlife

On Grand Turk, check out **The Ladies** (Hospital Rd., no phone), where there are dart boards and dancing to live island music on weekends. Another island favorite is the **Uprising** (Lighthouse Rd., no phone), which also has live music and dancing on weekends.

On Provo, the **Banana Boat** (tel. 809/946–4312) has live Top 40s, reggae, and soca on Thursday, Friday, and Saturday nights. On Tuesday nights you can hear live calypso at the **Erebus Inn** (tel. 809/946–4240), and on Thursday nights **The Third Turtle** (tel. 809/946–4230) has live island music. **Le Deck** (tel. 809/946–4547) offers varied evening entertainment, from open-air dancing every night and live bands to one-armed bandits.

28 The U.S. Virgin Islands

by David Grambs

Your destination here will be either St. Thomas (13 miles long); its neighbor St. John (9 miles long); or, 40 miles to the south, St. Croix (23 miles long). These are the big three of some 75 bits and pieces of volcanic land that make up the northern hook of the Lesser Antilles, just east of Puerto Rico. Whichever you visit, there are bracing breezes, courtesy of the trade winds.

A pro/con thumbnail sketch of the three main U.S. Virgin Islands might put it that St. Thomas is bustling (hustling) and the place for shopping and discos (commercial glitz and overdevelopment); St. Croix is more Danish, picturesque, and rural (more provincial and duller, particularly after dark); and St. John is matchless in the beauty of its National Park Service–protected land and beaches (a one-village island mostly for the rich or for campers).

St. Thomas may be building too much and too quickly and have oppressive cruise-ship crowds (Wednesdays, notably) and even some sewage problems, but it also has a lively nightlife scene, secluded beach resorts, and frequent 20-minute ferries to St. John. St. Croix, for all its slower and steadier pace, has elegant resort dining, horseback riding, and three golf courses, Buck Island and its reef, and a more small-town atmosphere. St. John, though small and relatively upscale, has a tasteful new harborside mall and reasonable restaurants in one village, which is cozy and lively; 20 hiking trails; and lustrous beaches.

The United States bought its half of the Virgin Islands in 1917. English, seasoned with Creole, is the language; the U.S. dollar is the currency. Even Cable TV with HBO and fast-food outlets will make you feel at home here.

Long before the Virgin Islands were Americanized, they had to be "discovered"—by Columbus, of course, in 1493, the beginning of a colorfully hybrid and unimaginably complicated history that turned out to be a round dance (after the Arawak, Taino, and Carib Indians left) among the European powers, along with the Knights of Malta. It is a history of slave trading, pirates and privateers, sugar plantations, and slave revolt and liberation. Through it all, the Danes had the staying power; from the 17th to the 19th centuries, they oversaw a plantation economy that produced molasses, rum, cotton, and tobacco.

Remnants and whiffs of this history are everywhere in the U.S. Virgin Islands today, from the ruins of the stone sugar-mill right next to the St. Croix airport runway to the graceful Danish architecture and arcades of Christiansted and Charlotte Amalie. Many of the stones that you see in buildings or tread on in the streets were once used as ballast on sailing ships. Pirate watchtowers grace the grounds of two popular hotels overlooking the St. Thomas harbor, and there are forts or ruins of forts on all three islands. St. John has a partially restored sugar-mill and petroglyphs left by slaves—or are they pre-Columbian? Old plantation names, such as Sally's Fancy, Bonne Esperance, Sweet Bottom, and Parasol, are alive and well in St. Croix.

Before You Go

Tourist Information Information about the U.S. Virgin Islands is available through the **U.S. Virgin Islands Government Tourist Office** (1270 Ave. of the Americas, New York, NY 10020, tel. 212/582–4520) and at the **U.S. Virgin Islands Division of Tourism** offices in Atlanta

(235 Peachtree Center, Suite 1420, Gaslight Tower, Atlanta, GA 30303, tel. 404/688–0906), Chicago (122 S. Michigan Ave., Suite 1270, Chicago, IL 60603, tel. 312/461–0180), Los Angeles (3460 Wilshire Blvd., Suite 412, Los Angeles, CA 90010, tel. 213/739–0138), Miami (2655 Le Jeune Rd., Suite 907, Coral Gables, FL 33134, tel. 305/442–7200), and Washington, DC (1667 K St., NW, Suite 270, Washington, DC 20006, tel. 202/293–3707). British travelers can write or visit the **U.S. Virgin Islands Division of Tourism** office in London (16 Bedford Sq., London WC1B 3JA, tel. 01/637–8481).

Arriving and Departing **American Airlines** (tel. 800/433–7300) offers direct flights to St. Thomas/St. Croix from New York, Boston, and Raleigh/
By Plane Durham. **Pan Am** (tel. 800/221–1111) also has nonstop service from New York and Miami. **Midway** (tel. 800/621–5700) flies from Chicago to St. Thomas/St. Croix. (Note that St. John, a popular destination and a short ferry ride from St. Thomas, has no airport.)

Most flights to the U.S. Virgin Islands from other U.S. cities—including Baltimore, Chicago, Hartford, Los Angeles, Minneapolis/St. Paul, Philadelphia, and Washington, DC—are via San Juan, Puerto Rico, where connections can be made with intra-island commuter service on **Air BVI** (tel. 800/468–2485), **American Eagle** (tel. 800/433–7300), **Crownair** (tel. 809/723–1212), **Leeward Islands Air Transport (LIAT)** (tel. 809/462–0701,) **Virgin Air** (tel. 809/791–4898) and **Virgin Islands Seaplane Shuttle** (TWA's link) (tel. 800/524–2050).

Passengers leaving from Albany, Buffalo, New Orleans, Pittsburgh, Rochester, St. Louis, and Syracuse can make the connecting service at Maimi. **Delta** offers connecting service to San Juan via Atlanta from Charleston, Cincinnati, Dallas, Denver, Detroit, Houston, and New Orleans and flies direct to San Juan from Chicago and Los Angeles.

Virgin Islands Seaplane Shuttle, in addition to the intra-island flights already mentioned, flies several times daily from St. Croix to St. Thomas, St. John, and San Juan.

By Boat Some 20 cruise-ship lines stop at St. Thomas or St. Croix throughout the year; a number of ships from the West Coast make regular runs to St. Thomas/St. Croix via the Panama Canal.

Among the cruise-ship lines that offer stopovers at St. Thomas or St. Croix are **Holland American Line** (300 Elliott Ave. W, Seattle, WA 98119, tel. 206/281–3535), **Princess Cruises** (2029 Century Park E, Suite 3000, Los Angeles, CA 90067, tel. 800/421–0522 or 213/553–1770), **Royal Caribbean Cruises** (903 South America Way, Miami, FL 33132, tel. 800/327–6700, or, in Canada, 800/245–7225), **Royal Viking Line** (1 Embarcadero Center, San Francisco, CA 94111, tel. 800/422–8000), **Cunard Line** (555 Fifth Ave., New York, NY 10017, tel. 800/528–6273, 800/458–9000, or 212/661–7777), and **Home Lines** (1 World Trade Center, Suite 3939, New York, NY 10048, tel. 212/432–1414, or, in Canada, 514/842–1441).

There is a regular ferry service from Charlotte Amalie and Red Hook Harbor on St. Thomas to St. John.

Passports and Visas U.S. and Canadian citizens are required to present some proof of citizenship, if not a passport then a birth certificate or voter's registration card. If you are arriving from the U.S.

United States Virgin Islands

Caribbean Sea

Buck Island Channel

Buck Island

N

4 miles
6 km

ST. CROIX

East Pt.

Grapetree Bay

Great Pond Bay

Christiansted Harbour

Long Reef

Christiansted

Canegarden Bay

Krause Pt.

CHARLOTTE AMALIE TO CHRISTIANSTED
APPROXIMATELY 40 MILES

(DISTANCE ON MAP IS COMPRESSED)

Cane Bay

Davis Bay

Alexander Hamilton Airport

Long Pt.

Hams Bay

West End Salt Pond

Long Pt. Bay

Frederiksted

Sandy Pt.

mainland or Puerto Rico, you need no inoculation or health certificate.

Customs and Duties Before you leave the U.S. Virgin Islands to return to the U.S. mainland, your baggage will be subject to inspection by U.S. Customs in St. Thomas or St. Croix; however, if you are making a connecting flight in San Juan, you will go through Customs in Puerto Rico. A U.S. resident may bring back up to $800 worth of duty-free imports (goods not made in the U.S. Virgin Islands or United States) every 30 days, twice the limit allowed those coming from other Caribbean islands. This includes an allowance of 200 cigarettes and 100 cigars (non-Cuban). Residents 21 years or older may bring back five bottles of liquor duty-free, or six bottles if one was produced in the U.S. Virgin Islands. If you exceed your $800 exemption in foreign-made goods brought home, you will pay a duty of 5% for the next $1,000; thereafter, the duty changes somewhat, up to your maximum "take-home" of $2,000 worth. Apart from the $800 exemption, you may mail home up to $50 worth of gifts to friends or relatives on any one day. Keep your sales slips conveniently handy, just in case any questions arise at Customs.

Language English, often with a Creole or West Indian lilt, is the medium of communication in these islands.

Precautions Crime exists here, but not to the same degree that it does in larger cities on the U.S. mainland. In Charlotte Amalie, pickpockets recognize a big spender when they see one, and it's best to stick to well-lit streets at night. If you plan on carrying things around, rent a car, not a jeep, and lock possessions up in the trunk. Keep your rental car locked wherever you park.

Aside from an ornery donkey or two, there are no dangerous animals or snakes in the U.S. Virgin Islands. Tap water is quite safe. The trade winds prevent insects from becoming a major problem in these climes, though mosquitoes and no-see-ums are not yet extinct.

Further Reading The word-of-mouth classic about life in the Virgin Islands is Herman Wouk's novel *Don't Stop the Carnival*.

Staying in the U.S. Virgin Islands

Important Addresses **Tourist Information:** The **U.S. Virgin Islands Division of Tourism** has an office in St. Thomas (Box 6400, Charlotte Amalie, U.S. Virgin Islands 00804, tel. 809/774–8784), St. Croix (Box 4538, Christiansted, U.S. Virgin Islands 00822, tel. 809/773–0495, and at the Customs House Bldg. Strand St., Frederiksted, U.S. Virgin Islands 00840, tel. 809/772–0357), and St. John (Box 200, Cruz Bay, U.S. Virgin Islands 00830, tel. 809/776–6450).

There is a **Visitors Center** in Charlotte Amalie, across from Emancipation Square and at Havensight Mall. In St. Croix, go to the Old Scalehouse at the waterfront, across from Fort Christiansvaern. The **National Park Service** also has visitor centers at the ferry areas on St. Thomas (Red Hook) and St. John (Cruz Bay).

Emergencies **Police:** Call 915. The number is the same for all three islands.

Hospitals: The emergency room of **St. Thomas Hospital and Community Center** in Charlotte Amalie (tel. 809/776–8311) is open 24 hours a day. On St. Croix there is the **St. Croix Hospital and Community Health Center** in Christiansted (tel. 809/778–6311 or 809/778–5895) and the **Ingeborg Nesbett Clinic** (tel. 809/772–0260) in Frederiksted. For medical emergencies on St. John, contact the **De Castro Clinic** (tel. 809/776–6222) or the **Myrah Keating Smith Clinic** (St. John Clinic) (tel. 809/776–6400).

Pharmacies: St. Thomas has numerous pharmacies, among them **Cathedral Pharmacy** (tel. 809/776–4080), **Sunrise Pharmacy** (tel. 809/774–5333), and **St. Thomas Apothecary Hall** (tel. 809/774–5432).

Currency The U.S. dollar is the medium of exchange here.

Taxes and Service Charges A 7.5% tax is added to hotel rates. There is no departure tax for the U.S. Virgin Islands.

Some hotels and restaurants add a 10% to 15% service charge to your bill.

Guided Tours Hotels can provide information about group tours or about private taxi guides. (On St. Thomas and St. Croix, group tours in open safari vehicles are popular among cruise-ship passengers; on St. John, the passengers are mainly visitors from St. Thomas who come over by ferry.)

Bus tours on St. Thomas are offered by **Grayline** (tel. 809/776–1515) and **Tropic Tours** (tel. 809/774–1855). On St. Croix, contact **St. Croix Safari Tours** (tel. 809/773–5922 or 809/778–3727), **St. Croix Sun Tours** (tel. 809/773–9661), and **Travelers Tours** (tel. 809/778–1636). On St. John, you can book an extensive safari bus tour through the **National Park Service** (tel. 809/776–6201) or **Cool Breeze** (tel. 809/776–6588).

If you want to leave the driving to a knowledgeable local and are willing to pay a bit more not to be part of a camera-laden tourist herd on a safari bus, a personal taxi tour is the answer. Plenty of drivers offer this service, for a half day or a full day, for a prearranged price. Ask the management at your hotel for a recommendation (or, better yet, ask a fellow guest who has just taken such a tour).

One recommended private limousine van service on St. Thomas, for personalized island tours or airport pickups, is **Executive Transportation, Inc.** (or **Extra, Inc.**, tel. 809/775–6974 or 809/775–5204), run by Bob Kirkpatrick, a former New Yorker who knows this island as few others do. On St. John, the one-woman operation called **Miss Lucy's Taxi** (tel. 809/776–6804) is a delightful service. Lucy is something of a mellow philosopher who wears a flower in her hair. Her taxi is the van with the blossom-bedecked goat horns. Don't take too long to make up your mind—she may retire soon.

Getting Around **Taxis** Taxis of all shapes and sizes are available at various ferry, shopping, resort, and airport areas on St. Thomas and St. Croix and respond quickly to a call. U.S. Virgin Islands taxis do not have meters, but you need not worry about fare gouging if you (1) check a list of standard rates to popular destinations, often posted in hotel and airport lobbies and printed in free tourist brochures and periodicals, such as *St. Thomas This Week;* (2) ask a resident or someone at your hotel what it should cost (roughly) to where you want to go; and (3) settle the final fare with your driver before you start. Remember, too, that you can signal to a taxi that is already occupied. The drivers take multiple fares and sometimes even trade passengers at midpoints: This can can keep your fare low.

Buses Public buses are not the best or quickest way to get around on the islands, and the service is minimal. (There is no service on St. John.) On St. Thomas, the **Manassah Country Bus** makes hourly trips (75¢) between Charlotte Amalie and Red Hook, site of the main ferry dock.

Mopeds For two-wheel motoring on St. Thomas, call **A-1 Scooter and Jeep Rental** (tel. 809/776–4872) or **Paradise Scooter Rentals** (tel. 809/775–2724). On St. Croix, call **American Scooter** (tel. 809/773–3278) or **Island Scooters** (tel. 809/778–7470). On St. John, call **Cruz Bay Scooter Rental** (tel. 809/776–6493). You must be at least 15 years old to rent a scooter.

Rental Cars Any U.S. driver's license is good for 90 days here; the minimum age for drivers is 18.

Driving is on the *left* side of the road (although your steering wheel will be on the left side of the car). Many of the roads are narrow and the islands are dotted with hills, so there is ample reason to drive carefully. Even at the sedate speed of 20 miles per hour, driving can be an adventure—for example, you may find yourself in a stick-shift jeep slogging behind a slow tourist-packed safari bus at a steep hairpin turn on St. John. Give a little beep at blind turns. Note that the general speed limit on these islands is only 25 to 35 mph, which will seem fast enough for you on most roads.

On St. Thomas, you can rent a car from **ABC Rentals** (tel. 809/776–1222 or 800/524–2080), **Anchorage E-Z Car** (tel. 809/775–6255), **Aristocrat** (tel. 809/776–0021), **Avis** (tel. 809/774–4616), **Budget** (tel. 809/776–5774), **Caribbean Jeep & Car** (tel. 809/776–6811), **Cowpet Car Rental** (tel. 809/775–7376 or 800/524–2072), **Dependable** (tel. 809/774–2253 or 800/522–3076), **Discount** (tel. 809/776–4858), **Dollar** (tel. 809/776–0850), **Econo-car St. Thomas** (tel. 809/775–6763), **Hertz** (tel. 809/774–1879), **Paradise** (tel. 809/775–2724), **Sea Breeze** (tel. 809/774–7200), **Sun Island** (tel. 809/774–3333 or 800/233–7941), Thrifty (tel. 809/776–3500), and **V.I. Auto Rental** (tel. 809/776–3616 or 800/843–3571).

On St. Croix, call **Avis** (tel. 809/778–9365), **Budget** (tel. 809/778–4663), **Caribbean Jeep & Car** (tel. 809/773–4399 or 809/778–1000), **Charlie's** (tel. 809/778–8200 or 809/773–1678), **Hertz** (tel. 809/778–1402), **Olympic** (tel. 809/773–2208), and **St. Croix Jeep & Honda** (tel. 809/773–0161, 809/773–8370, or 809/773–1351).

On St. John, call **Cool Breeze** (tel. 809/776–6588), **Dalmidia by the Sea** (DBS) (tel. 809/776–6374), **Delbert Hill Jeep & Auto** (tel. 809/776–6637 or 809/776–7947), **O'Connor Jeep** (tel. 809/776–6343), **Roosevelt Jeep Rental** (tel. 809/776–6628), **St. John Car Rental** (tel. 809/776–6103), or **Spencer's Jeep** (tel. 809/776–6628).

Telephones and Mail The area code for the U.S. Virgin Islands is 809, and there is direct dialing to the mainland. Local calls from a public phone cost 25¢ for each five minutes. On St. John, the place to go to for *any* telephone or message needs is **Connections** (tel. 809/776–6922).

Postal rates are the same as they are elsewhere in the United States: 25¢ for a letter, 15¢ for a postcard. **Post offices** on St. Thomas are located near Emancipation Square and Frenchtown; on St. Croix, at the King's Wharf area of Christiansted and within walking distance of the pier in Frederiksted; and on St. John, near the ferry dock in Cruz Bay.

Opening and Closing Times On St. Thomas, Charlotte Amalie's Main Street area shops are open from 9 A.M. to 5 P.M. Monday through Saturday, and the same applies to shops at Havensight Mall. Cruise-ship arrivals, however, also dictate shop hours. Shops at hotels—notably the two-story arcade of 24 shops at Frenchman's Reef—are usually open evenings as well. St. Croix store hours are usually 9 or 9:30 to 5 or 5:30 Monday through Friday, but you will definitely find some shops in Christiansted open in the evening. On St. John, like everything else, store hours are "casual."

Beaches

All beaches in the U.S. Virgin Islands are open to the public, including those in front of hotels. (This means the *beaches only*, not the resort's beach chairs, sailboards, etc.) Each island also has some beaches with picnic facilities and rest rooms. You can always find truly remote and untrammeled beaches if you are willing to drive on some unpaved roads (four-wheel drive is recommended) and do a little walking. Exercise caution in swimming or snorkeling, since there are few lifeguards. Among the three islands, there are more than 50 recognized and commonly visited beaches areas you can consider for a visit.

Buck Island and its reef, which is under environmental protection, is not listed below because it can be reached only by boat; nonetheless, it is a must outing on any visit to St. Croix. Its beach is beautiful, but its finest treasures are those you can see when you plop off the boat and adjust your face mask, snorkel, and flippers.

St. Thomas Government-run **Magens Bay** is usually crowded and busy because of its spectacular loop of white beach, more than a half-mile long, and its calm waters—two peninsulas protect it. The bottom is flat and sandy, so this is a place for sunning and swimming rather than snorkeling. Food, changing facilities, and rest rooms are available.

The condo resort at **Secret Harbour** doesn't at all detract from the attractiveness of this covelike East End beach. Not only is it pretty, it is also superb for snorkeling—go out to the left, near the rocks.

At **Morningstar Beach,** close to Charlotte Amalie, many young residents show up for body surfing or volleyball or less. The sandy-bottom water is in the shadow of the huge, cliffside Frenchman's Reef Hotel. Snorkeling is good here when the current doesn't affect visibility.

From **Sapphire Beach,** there is a fine view of St. John and other islands. Snorkeling is excellent at the reef to the right or east, near Pettyklip Point. All kinds of water-sports gear are for rent. Be careful when you enter the water, since the bottom is not all sandy.

Hull Bay, on the north shore, has a rugged beach that faces Inner and Outer Brass cays and attracts fishermen and beachcombers. Surfing and snorkeling are good.

St. Croix   The waters are not always gentle at **Cane Bay,** a breezy north-shore beach, but the scuba diving and snorkeling are wondrous, and there are never many people around. Just swim straight out to see elkhorn and brain corals. Less than 200 yards out is the dropoff or so-called Cane Bay Wall.

Tamarind Reef Beach is a small but attractive hotel beach east of Christiansted. Both Green Cay and Buck Island seem smack in front of you and make the view arresting. Snorkeling is good.

Sandy Point, the largest beach in the U.S. Virgin Islands, is a must on your itinerary. The shallow, calm water makes for wonderful swimming, and you won't see that many people around. Also here are the mangroves and birds of West End Salt Pond, prized by bird-watchers and environmentalists.

Isaac Bay, at St. Croix's east end, is tricky to get to but worth it if you want some seclusion and calm swimming plus a barrier reef for snorkeling. You can get here via footpaths from Jacks Bay.

St. John   **Trunk Bay** is the main beach draw on the island because of its underwater snorkeling trail. Crowds or not, it's still beautiful. Though veteran snorkelers pooh-pooh the "picked clean" trail reef, the reef fish are definitely still there. Lifeguards are on duty here.

Hawksnest Bay has a narrow but lovely beach. The water seems especially clear, and both swimming and snorkeling are good. Scenes for the movie *The Four Seasons* were shot here.

Cinnamon Bay beach, at a campground site, has some wide parts and looks out on several green cays. There is a snack bar here.

Salt Pond Bay, on the southeastern coast of St. John, is a scenic area to explore, being next to Coral Bay and rugged Drunk Bay. There is shade if you want it, as well as picnic tables and charcoal grills and few people. Swimming and snorkeling are good.

Exploring St. Thomas

Numbers in the margins correspond with points of interest on the St. Thomas and Charlotte Amalie maps.

Our first suggested itinerary, of town and on foot, does entail a bit of uphill walking, but it mixes sights of historic buildings related to both church and state affairs with duty-free shopping and one spectacular view of the island's most important town. The second tour—north and east of Charlotte Amalie—is to be made in a car.

Charlotte Amalie   Start by enjoying the good harbor breeze at **Frenchtown,** where the Frenchies, descendants of immigrants from St. Barthélemy (or St. Barts), pull up their boats and slap down yellowtail, squirrelfish, old wife, and other fish for sale. The island you see out there is **Hassel Island,** now a Virgin Island National Park, where you can view military ruins; you can reach it by ferry ($3 round-trip). You may see a number of people cleaning fish on the wood-roof jetty or bending elbows at the Maison Noel bar. Take a moment to walk west to some of Frenchtown's winding streets.

Turning north, cross Veterans Drive, also known as Waterfront Highway (watch the traffic!), and walk east before turning left on Strand Gade to see the open-air stalls of **Market Square.** This busy produce bazaar was an infamous slave market two centuries ago. You'll begin to see vendors here, as you're now at the western end of Charlotte Amalie's feverish duty-free shopping district along both **Main Street** (Dronnigens Gade) and **Back Street** (Vimmelskaft Gade).

Among the retail and discount stores are numerous historic churches. A few blocks to the west is **St. Peter and St. Paul Church,** built in 1844, and right off Market Square is **Christ Church Methodist,** dating back to 1700.

Stroll east on Back Street and enjoy a little window shopping before turning left and up Raadet's Gade. Up here on Denmark Hill, you will see the old Greek Revival **Danish Consulate** building (1830)—look for the red-and-white flag—and Villa Santana (1858). Two more notable St. Thomas churches are here: **All Saints Anglican Church** (1848) and the 1844 **Dutch Reform Church,** whose congregation goes back to at least 1660. Perhaps more singular, however, is the **Synagogue** nearby on Crystal Gade. The second oldest temple in the Western Hemisphere (the oldest is in Curaçao), it was rebuilt several times—Jews have lived on St. Thomas since at least 1665. The sand on the floor commemorates the biblical Exodus.

Once you've caught your breath from this hilly, interdenominational adventure head back down Raadet's Gade to Main Street.

Time Out Nothing refreshes a hard-touring American like a glass of lemonade. Stop on Main Street at the cart of **Mr. Lemonade,** a slow-talking Coloradan who will "custom-make" your drink —honey? sugar?—to your wishes. Drink up. There's some more uphill walking ahead!

While you're on Main Street, don't let the shopping crowds keep you from the **Pissarro Building** in the block between Storetvaer Gade and Trompeter Gade (the plaque is around the block on Back Street). The famed French Impressionist painter was born here and lived upstairs (now the Tropicana Perfume Shop).

After browsing at Bakery Square (off of Back Street between Nye Gade and Garden Street), go back down to Main Street and turn left. Just past Garden Street turn left again and go up some steps to the beautiful Spanish-style **Hotel 1829,** whose restaurant is one of the best on St. Thomas. You may want to take a peek into its cool, dark bar and picturesque courtyard. Now walk to the right and you'll find yourself at the foot of the **99 Steps,** on Government Hill, a staircase "street" built by the Danes in the 1700s. If you're feeling energetic, go for it and start up—they're low steps and you can lean on the railing while you catch your breath. Now that you're at the top, we can tell you that there are a few more than 99 steps. Continue ahead on the street to the right and U-turn up the drive to **Blackbeard's Castle,** originally Fort Skytsborg and now a small hotel. The massive five-story stone watchtower here was built in 1679 and possibly was used by the notorious pirate Edward Teach. If you walk past it to the other end of the hotel's pool,

St. Thomas

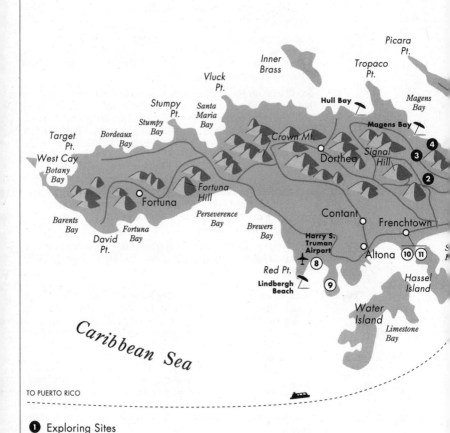

Picara Pt.

Tropaco Pt.

Inner Brass

Vluck Pt.

Hull Bay

Magens Bay

Stumpy Pt.

Santa Maria Bay

Magens Bay

Stumpy Bay

Crown Mt.

Dorthea

Signal Hill

4

3

2

Target Pt.

Bordeaux Bay

West Cay

Botany Bay

Fortuna Hill

Fortuna

Perseverence Bay

Contant

Frenchtown

Barents Bay

Fortuna Bay

Brewers Bay

Harry S. Truman Airport

8

Altona

10 11

David Pt.

Red Pt.

Lindbergh Beach

9

Hassel Island

Water Island

Limestone Bay

Caribbean Sea

TO PUERTO RICO

1 Exploring Sites

8 Hotels and Restaurants

you'll get your reward for taking on those 99-plus steps: an unsurpassed view of Charlotte Amalie and its impressive harbor.

With gravity now on your side, head back down the steps. To the right, down Kongen's Gade, you'll come to **Government House** (1867), the official residence of the governor of the U.S. Virgin Islands. (The first two floors are open to the public.) Inside you'll find murals and paintings with a historical motif by Camille Pissarro, whose birthplace you passed on Main Street. Continue down to Norre Gade, where you'll see the **Frederik Lutheran Church,** the second-oldest Lutheran church in the Western Hemisphere. Its walls date back to 1793.

You can mail letters and postcards across the way at the **Post Office,** which is worth entering to see the early murals of Stephen Dohanos, who once did covers for the *Saturday Evening Post.* Walk down Tolbod Gade toward the water, and you'll find yourself at historic **Emancipation Park** (or Garden or Square), so called because it honors the freeing of the slaves in 1848. Various official ceremonies are still held here. You'll also find a smaller version of the Liberty Bell here. Sit on a bench near the gazebo and relax a bit. On the north side of the park is the 19th-century **Grand Hotel** building, now housing offices, shops, and a visitors' hospitality lounge. In the large corner shop, you'll find souvenirs, ranging from exotic seashells and Haitian wood carvings to message (tropical) T-shirts.

Closer yet to the harborfront is **Fort Christian,** St. Thomas's oldest standing structure (1672–87) and a U.S. national landmark. The clock tower was added in the 19th century. This remarkable redoubt has, over time, seen use as a jail, governor's residence, town hall, courthouse, and church. Its dungeons now house a museum featuring artifacts of Virgin Islands history.

From outside the fort you can see the waters of the harbor and if you now cross back over Veterans Drive, you'll be at **Kings Wharf.** Also situated near the pier is the lime-green **Legislature Building** (1874), since 1957 the seat of the 15-member USVI Senate. Built originally by the Danish as a police barracks, the building was later used to billet U.S. Marines and, much later, housed a public school. Look across the harbor and you'll see Frenchtown, where this tour began.

North and East of Charlotte Amalie Having explored Charlotte Amalie, you may want to rent a car and explore the north side of the island, far more beautiful, the northsiders will tell you, than anything on the Caribbean side. Head northwest out of Charlotte Amalie—it's all uphill!—on Mafolie Road (Route 34) to Route 35, turn left onto Route 33, ❷ and bear west to **Fairchild Park,** which was a gift to the people of this island from philanthropist Arthur Fairchild. Wind ❸ around to **Mountain Top,** where you will be afforded a splendid view of the northern side of St. Thomas: Magens Bay, Tortola, and, if the sky is clear, some 18 other islands. You're at 1,547 feet elevation here. There's a full-service restaurant at Mountain Top, as well as souvenirs and clothing to buy. If it isn't too early for you, you can drink one of the half-million banana daiquiris served here annually.

From Mountain Top, drive east; Route 40 or Route 37 brings ❹ you to an overlook called **Drake's Seat** and another spectacular vista of the island's Atlantic coastline, Magen's Bay, and out-lying islands. Sir Francis Drake, who was one of Queen

Elizabeth's privateers, used this place as a vantage point over his anchored fleet, and you will even find an actual chair ensconced here to symbolize the idea (you may sit in it).

Take Route 35 east to Route 42 and the lovely scenery of **Mahogany Run** and its championship golf course. Proceed east on Route 42 and left on Route 38 until you come to a fork and the ❺ sign for **Coki Beach** and **Coral World Marine Park.** The snorkeling is excellent at Coki, with reefs at its eastern and western ends, and you may want to dash in for a swim (you'll find shower facilities here) or just do some people watching while nibbling on a meat pâté snack from one of the vendors. Just down from the beach, you will find the entrance to Coral World, an experience not to be missed. The domed tower you see at the end of the pier is a three-level underwater observatory. If you arrive by 11 AM, you'll be lucky enough to see divers feeding barracudas, sharks, and other sea creatures. Yet some of the most colorful fish to be seen here are those in the smaller tanks surrounding you. (The lowest level is the real thing, the sea bottom, not a tank.) You can take a break upstairs at the restaurant and bar before you walk outside to the nature path, museum, and Marine Gardens Aquarium. There are rest rooms, lockers, showers, and changing rooms here.

❻ Going back the way you came, west on Route 38, stop at **Jim Tillett's Art Gallery and Boutique,** an old sugar-mill site on Estate Tutu, where you can watch crafts people working at silkscreening, ceramics, and painting. You can buy fabrics or articles of clothing with artful prints.

Time Out At the Tillett's Mexican restaurant, **El Papagayo** (at the entrance to Tillett's, tel. 809/775–1550), relax near the fountain on the patio and enjoy a taco, burrito, hamburger, or some chicken wings. A strawberry Margarita is a good liquid option.

Drive east again on Route 38 and take the right hand of the fork, the continuation of Route 38. This road loops around the eastern end of St. Thomas and takes you past many of the island's best hotels and beaches, including the Stouffer Grand Beach Resort (Water Bay), Point Pleasant (Smith Bay), and Sapphire Beach Resort. You'll also pass, on the right side of the road, Pavilions & Pools, where each room has its own private swimming pool. At **Red Hook Harbor,** you can get a quick ferry to St. John (20 minutes each way, departures on the hour).

From here, Route 32 brings you west toward Charlotte Amalie and past turnoffs for other fine hotels and beaches, among them Secret Harbour Beach Resort, Bolongo Bay Beach and Tennis Club (Bovoni Bay), and Limetree Beach Hotel (Frenchman's Cove). Proceeding west, you will also pass the road to the spectacular and huge Frenchman's Reef–Morningstar hotel complex, which looks like a cross between a promontory fortress and a mammoth cruise ship and has, among other things, a cliffside elevator tower.

Speaking of cruise ships, you may now see one or two ahead as ❼ you approach the **West Indian Dock** at the eastern edge of Charlotte Amalie. Pull in to **Havensight Mall** for some major dutyfree shopping with an ambience that is a little spiffier than that in town around Main Street. Also here is the headquarters for the *Atlantis* submarine, on which you can book an unforgettable underwater ride (it's best to call ahead for reservations, tel. 809/776–5650).

Time Out Drop into the cool **Cafe Havensight** (next to the Atlantis Submarine office, tel. 809/774–5818). Behind the high bar are six metal dispensers, each of which holds a first-rate frozen tropical drink. Which shall it be, the fuzzy navel, virgin peach, piña colada, white Russian, mad mongoose, or lime squeeze?

Exploring St. Croix

Numbers in the margin correspond with points of interest on the St. Croix map.

This tour will take you to many worthwhile St. Croix sights except for those of downtown Christiansted (which is easily explored on foot—pick up a copy of the *Walking Tour Guide)* and the more remote eastern end of the island. You'll visit historic plantation settings; a botanical garden; a rum distillery; the largest and one of the most beautiful beaches in the West Indies; Frederiksted; and, in addition, you'll enjoy some scenic coastal driving.

If you're trying to escape the tight-squeeze traffic of Christiansted, head from the main waterfront area up Company Street and right out to Route 75, Northside Road. A few miles up the road, you can make a detour by turning right onto Route 751, which leads you to **St. Croix by the Sea**, a beautifully landscaped hotel with one of the most spectacular sea views on St. Croix. Have breakfast at the room off the majestic pink-and-white lobby and feast on the view, to the east, of Christiansted and Buck Island. Before you leave, be sure to walk outside for a look at the 154-foot ocean-fed swimming pool, the largest saltwater pool in the Caribbean.

❶ A bit farther down Route 75 is **Judith's Fancy**, where you can see the ruins of an old great house and the tower left from a 17th-century chateau. This was once home to the governor of the Knights of Malta. The "Judith" comes from the first name of a woman buried on the property. Here, too, you have a good view of **Salt River Bay**, where Christopher Columbus landed in 1493. The Salt River estuary draws many scuba divers and a few years ago had an operational Hydrolab 50 feet down.

After driving back to Route 75, continue west and then north on Route 80 toward the coast and pull over at windy **Cane Bay**. This is one of St. Croix's best beaches for scuba diving, and near the small stone jetty you may see a few wet-suited, tank-backed figures making their way out to the "drop-off" (a bit farther out there is steeper drop-off to 12,000 feet). Other than divers, you won't see too many people here.

❷ Rising behind you is **Mt. Eagle**, St. Croix's highest peak, at 1,165 feet. Leaving Cane Bay and passing North Star beach, follow the beautiful coastal road to **Davis Bay**. First, you will enjoy the panoramic views of the sea along this winding corniche. Second, it's worth getting a glimpse of the strikingly beautiful setting of Carambola, a luxurious new Rockresort hotel.

The road comes to an end here. Drive back about a mile and follow Route 69, River Road, to the right, inland, continuing on it all the way to Centerline Road (Route 70, or Queen Mary Highway). This is the island's central superhighway, the quickest route between Christiansted and Frederiksted. After driving about 1½ miles, you can turn off to the right for a visit to the **St.**

❸ **George Village Botanical Gardens,** 17 acres of lush and fragrant flora amid the ruins of a 19th-century sugarcane plantation village.

Just across the Centerline Road, off of Route 64, you'll find the

❹ **Cruzan Distillery,** which is, well, a rum business. The rum is made with pure rain water. Visitors are welcome for a tour and a free piña colada. If you hear a whoosh in your head, it's not the rum but the sky traffic at nearby Alexander Hamilton Airport.

Return to Centerline Road and drive west to Frederiksted. On

❺ the way, the **Whim Greathouse** is a must stop. The lovingly restored estate, with a windmill, cookhouse, and other buildings, will give you a true sense of what life was like on St. Croix's sugar plantations in the 1800s. The singular oval-shape and high-ceiling great house has antique furniture, decor, and utensils well worth seeing. Notice that it has a fresh and airy atmosphere. (The waterless moat around the great house was used not for defense but for gathering cooling air.) It is built of stone, coral, lime, and molasses. Its apothecary exhibit is the largest in all the West Indies. You will also find a museum gift shop.

Now let's head for the beach—the largest in all the U.S. Virgin Islands. **Sandy Point,** a National Natural Landmark site at St.

❻ Croix's southwestern tip, has a splendid beach and the **West End Salt Pond,** rife with mangroves and little blue herons. In the spring, large leatherback sea turtles clamber up the white sand to lay their eggs here. You will also find seashells and brown pelicans.

A short drive up the placid western coast of the island brings

❼ you to correspondingly placid **Frederiksted,** founded in 1751. A single long cruise-ship pier juts into the sparkling sea from this historic coastal town, noted less for its Danish than for its Victorian architecture (dating from after the uprising of former slaves and the great fire of 1878). A stroll around will take you no more than an hour.

Restored **Fort Frederik,** next to the pier, was completed late in the 18th century. Here, in 1848, the slaves of the Danish West Indies were freed by Governor General Peter van Scholten. Right at the end of the pier, you can stop at the **Customs House,** which has a Division of Tourism Visitors Bureau. Walk down Market Street to the **Market Place,** where you can buy fresh fruits and vegetables early in the morning, and around the corner on Prince Street to the **Old Danish School,** designed in the 1830s by a Danish architect named Hingleberg and now part of Frederiksted's Ingeborg Nesbett Clinic. **St. Paul's Episcopal Church,** a mixture of classic and Gothic Revival architecture, is two blocks south on Prince Street; it survived several hurricanes after its construction in 1812 and became Episcopal when the United States purchased the island in 1917. A few steps away, on King Cross Street, you'll come to **Apothecary Hall,** which survived the fire of 1878. Walk south and turn right on Queen Cross Street to the **Old Public Library,** or **Bell House,**

St. Croix

Caribbean Sea

① Exploring Sites

⑩ Hotels and Restaurants

Exploring
Cruzan Distillery, **4**
Davis Bay. **2**
Frederiksted, **7**
Judith's Fancy, **1**
St. Croix Leap, **8**

St. George Village
Botanical Gardens, **3**
Scenic Road West, **9**
West End Salt Pond, **6**
Whim Greathouse, **5**

Dining
Captain's Table, **14**
Club Comanche, **15**
Cormorant Beach
Club, **13**
King's Alley, **16**
Ritz Cafe, **18**
Serendipity, **17**

Lodging
Anchor Inn, **26**
The Buccaneer, **21**
Carambola Beach
Resort and Golf Club, **12**
Cathy's Fancy
Beach Hotel, **32**
Club Comanche, **30**

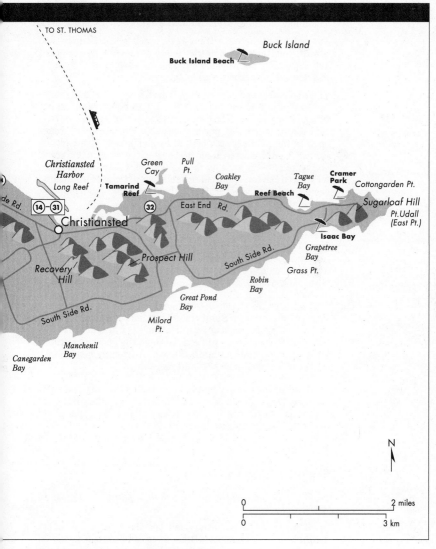

TO ST. THOMAS

Buck Island

Buck Island Beach

Christiansted
Harbor

Green
Cay

Pull
Pt.

Coakley
Bay

Tague
Bay

Cramer
Park

Cottongarden Pt.

Long Reef

**Tamarind
Reef**

Reef Beach

Sugarloaf Hill

de Rd.

⑭—㉛

32

East End Rd.

Pt. Udall
(East Pt.)

Christiansted

Isaac Bay

Prospect Hill

South Side Rd.

Grapetree
Bay

Recovery
Hill

Grass Pt.

Robin
Bay

South Side Rd.

Great Pond
Bay

Milord
Pt.

Manchenil
Bay

Canegarden
Bay

N

0   2 miles

0   3 km

Cormorant Beach
Club, **22**
Divi St. Croix, **24**
The Frederiksted, **10**
Hotel Caravelle, **19**
Hotel on the Cay, **25**
King's Alley Hotel, **31**
Moonraker Hotel, **20**
The Pink Fancy, **28**

Queen's Quarter
Hotel, **27**
St. Croix by the Sea, **23**
Sprat Hall, **11**
Tamarind Reef
Beachside Inn, **29**

which now houses an arts and crafts center and, in a more recent addition, the **Dorsch Cultural Center** for performing arts.

You're back at the waterfront again and if you walk up Strand Street, you'll come to **Victoria House,** once a private residence and now a landmark that is Frederiksted's best-known example of Victorian gingerbread architecture.

The whole west end of the island, from Sandy Point on the south to Ham's Bluff on the north, is lined with one inviting empty beach after another. The area north and east of Frederiksted is **rain forest,** much of it private property but laced with roads open to the public. Just north of Frederiksted, turn right on **❽** Route 76, or **Mahogany Road** (the best of the roads in this area), and watch for the sign on the right to **St. Croix Leap,** a place where you can see or purchase handsome articles of mahogany, saman, or thibet wood crafted by local artisans. You'll find that the rain-forest air is surprisingly cool.

Return west to the coast road (Route 63) and head north to **Sprat Hall Plantation,** owned and run for generations by the Hurd family and famed for its home-cooked food (you can stay here as a guest). The beautiful great house is the oldest in the Virgin Islands. This is also the place to arrange a few hours of horseback riding.

Time Out Pull up a chair at the breezy **Sprat Hall Beach Restaurant** (across the road from Sprat Hall Plantation, tel. 809/772–0305) and have a cooling soda or rum drink and an order of its famous pumpkin fritters while you gaze through the beach sea grapes at the calm and glistening Caribbean. A friendly banana quit with a sweet tooth may hop onto your table.

From here, you can return to Christiansted the easy and swift way, south on Route 63 to Frederiksted and then left onto Centerline Road. But if time allows and you have four-wheel drive, zip north toward Hams Bluff and take the marvelous **❾** **Scenic Road West** to its end at Route 69, near North Star Beach and Cane Bay.

Exploring St. John

Numbers in the margin correspond with points of interest on the St. John map.

St. John is a conveniently small island. While many of its southern-coast beaches and other sites can be reached only on foot, most of the island's famed beaches are easily accessible by car or jeep. This suggested itinerary takes you along much of the scenic northern coast before a return trip over a paved road on the central, mountainous ridge of St. John.

❶ **Cruz Bay** is the starting point for just about everything on St. John. Stop first at the northern side of the ferry dock at the **National Park Service Visitors Center.** Pick up a handy guide to St. John's hiking trails or see various large maps of the island, which you can buy for a few dollars.

Turn left, past Mongoose Junction, and head north on North Shore Road, Route 20. A half mile ahead, you'll come to the well-groomed gardens and beaches of **Caneel Bay,** purchased and developed in the 1950s by Laurance Rockefeller (who turned over much of the rest of the island to the U.S. government as parkland) and one of the Caribbean's best-known and most ecologically conscious resorts. Visitors are welcome at designated areas.

Continue east on North Shore Road with all the sense of anticipation that you can muster: you are about to see, one after the other, four of the most beautiful beaches in all the Caribbean. But the road is narrow and hilly, so drive carefully (and no more than 20 mph). **Hawksnest,** the first beach you will come to, is where Alan Alda shot scenes for his film *The Four Seasons*. Though it is closer to Cruz Bay, you'll usually find fewer people here than at the beaches farther ahead. Just past Hawksnest, swing left to Peace Hill (sometimes called Sugarloaf Hill)
❷ to the *Christ of the Caribbean* statue and an old sugar-mill tower. The area is grassy, and views do not get much better than this.

Your next stop—and that of quite a few tourist-filled safari buses—is **Trunk Bay,** whose famed beach has an underwater snorkeling trail (those red, white, and blue markers you see out there) and lifeguards on duty. This beach is worth a return visit. **Cinnamon Bay,** after Trunk, has a wider and more sweeping beach and is also a campground site, as is **Maho Bay,** after Cinnamon. Beware of a few major potholes on the level strip of road between Cinnamon and Maho.

Past Maho Bay, keep to the left and head north to the area of **Mary Point** and **Mary Creek,** where there are mangrove swamps and the mountainous island of Tortola is only about a mile away to the northeast of Leinster Bay. At Mary Point is
❸ historic **Minna Neger Ghut,** a rocky ravine, where in 1733, rebelling slaves are said to have jumped to their deaths rather than capitulate to French troops brought in by the Danes.

❹ The partially restored **Annaberg Plantation,** built in the 1780s and once an important sugar mill, is just ahead on North Shore Road. Pick up a guide pamphlet and stroll around. Slaves, Danes, and Dutchmen toiled here for years to produce crude sugar, molasses, and rum for export. If you want to get your feet literally wet, be here on Monday at 2 PM for a 1½-hour guided seashore walk along beaches and mangrove lagoons.

From Annaberg, keep to the left and swing south; then go east,
❺ on Route 10 to the lovely, sleepy area of **Coral Bay,** where St. John's first sugar plantations were established. This being the dry end of the island, you'll see quite a few cacti. If you wish, detour here past Hurricane Hole to the remote and pristine
❻ **East End,** only a 15- or 20-minute ride from Coral Bay, where two millennia ago there were Indian settlements. At Haulover Bay, only a couple of hundred yards separate the Atlantic Ocean from the Caribbean.

❼ South of the ball field at Coral Bay is **Fortsberg.** This is the site of Fort Frederik, which was taken by oppressed slaves during a bloody revolt in 1733.

From Coral Bay, Route 107 takes you south to the peninsula of
❽ **Salt Pond,** which is only about a foot above sea level. If you're weary of driving, you can hike a trail south to the spectacular cliffs of **Ram Head.** In any case, you—or your rented car—can't proceed much farther on 107 without venturing onto a truly rocky road west. But be sure to get at least a view of beautiful

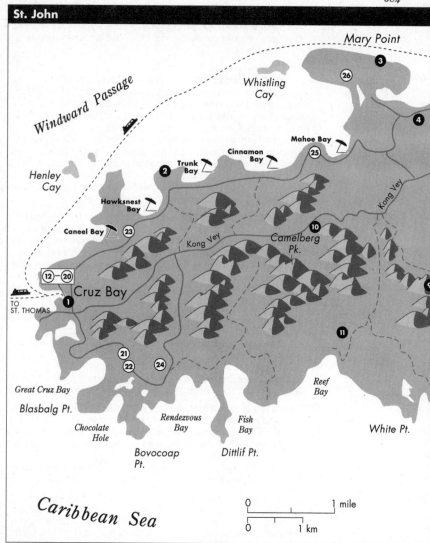

St. John

Mary Point

Whistling
Cay

Windward Passage

Henley
Cay

Mahoe Bay
25

Cinnamon
Bay

Trunk
Bay
2

Hawksnest
Bay

Caneel Bay 23

Kong Vey

Kong Vey

Camelberg
Pk.

10

Kong Vey

12 — 20

Cruz Bay
1

TO
ST. THOMAS

9

11

21
22 24

Great Cruz Bay

Blasbalg Pt.

Chocolate
Hole

Rendezvous
Bay

Fish
Bay

Reef
Bay

White Pt.

Bovocoap
Pt.

Dittlif Pt.

Caribbean Sea

0   1 mile

0   1 km

Exploring
Annaberg Plantation, **4**
Bordeaux Mountain, **9**
Christ of the Caribbean
Statue, **2**
Coral Bay, **5**
Cruz Bay, **1**
East End, **6**

Fortsberg, **7**
Kong Vey, **10**
Minna Neger Ghut, **3**
Reef Bay Trail, **11**
Salt Pond, **8**

Dining
The Back Yard, **14**
Fred's, **15**
Frond's, **21**
Lime Inn, **13**

Pusser's, **12**
Shipwreck Landing, **27**
The Upper Deck, **24**

Lodging
Caneel Bay, **23**
Cinnamon Bay
Campground, **25**

The Cruz Inn, **19**
Cruz Views, **17**
Gallows Point, **16**
The Inn at Tamarind
Court, **20**
Maho Bay Camp, **26**
Raintree Inn, **18**
Virgin Grand Beach
Hotel, **22**

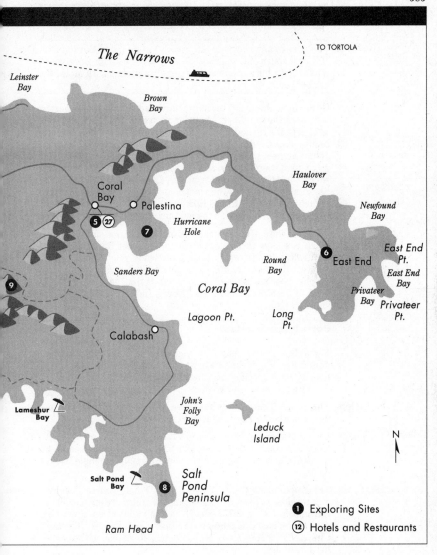

TO TORTOLA

The Narrows

Leinster Bay

Brown Bay

Coral Bay

○ Palestina

5 **27**

7

Hurricane Hole

Haulover Bay

Newfound Bay

6 East End

East End Pt.

East End Bay

Sanders Bay

Round Bay

9

Coral Bay

Privateer Bay

Privateer Pt.

Lagoon Pt.

Long Pt.

Calabash ○

John's Folly Bay

Leduck Island

Lameshur Bay

N

Salt Pond Bay

8

Salt Pond Peninsula

Ram Head

1 Exploring Sites

12 Hotels and Restaurants

Lameshur Bay, one of the best snorkeling places on St. John and an area used for underwater training by the U.S. Navy.

Time Out Pull over to airy and tidy **Shipwreck Landing and Bar** (on Rte. 107, just south of Coral Bay, tel. 809/776–8540) for some conch fritters or a burger and some friendly chitchat with Mike, the affable young owner.

Go north on Route 107 to Centerline Road, Route 10. Go west or left, over the heights of the island toward Cruz Bay. On your left, past the turnoff for the North Shore Road, you'll pass the **9** bumpy road leading to **Bordeaux Mountain,** at 1,277 feet St. John's highest peak. This is also an area of rain forest. Stop for a moment hereabouts and you'll find bay trees (*Pimenta racemosa*). Crackle a leaf from one and you'll get a whiff of the bay rum for which St. John is famous. A mile ahead, stop on the **10** right at **Kong Vey** ("King's Road") for a good view of some of the British Virgin Islands to the northeast.

To appreciate the Bordeaux Mountain region fully, return **11** when you have time and hike down the **Reef Bay Trail** (off of Centerline Road), which ultimately leads you to some sugar-estate ruins and St. John's renowned and mysterious petro-glyphs, pool-surrounded rock carvings that have been attrib-uted to both pre-Columbian Arawak Indians and later island slaves.

Participant Sports

For water sports, especially, you've come to the right islands. Your hotel, if it doesn't have its own boats, dive shop, etc., will usually have arrangements with sailing, scuba, and other en-terprises to meet your wishes.

Golf The U.S. Virgin Islands has three 18-hole golf courses and one 9-hole course, none of them on St. John.

St. Thomas Scenic **Mahogany Run** (tel. 809/775–5000), with a par-70 18-hole course and a view of the British Virgin Islands, lies to the north of Charlotte Amalie and has one "Devil's Triangle" trio of holes.

St. Croix **The Buccaneer's** (tel. 809/773–2100) 18-hole course is conve-niently close to (east of) Christiansted. Yet more spectacular is **Carambola** (tel. 809/778–0747), in the valleyed northwestern part of the island, designed by Robert Trent Jones. **The Reef Club** (tel. 809/773–9250), at the northeastern part of the island, has nine holes.

Horseback Riding St. Thomas has little to offer the equestrian, but St. Croix and St. John both have stables and beautiful countryside to trot through.

St. Croix At Sprat Hall, near Frederiksted, Jill Hurd runs **Jill's Eques-trian Stables** (tel. 809/772–2880 or 809/772–2627) and will take you clip-clopping through the rain forest, along the coast, or on moonlit rides. Sunday-morning brunch rides are one of the op-tions offered by **Hidden Valley Equestrian Center** (tel. 809/778–8670), just east of The Buccaneer.

St. John | **Pony Express Riding Stables** (tel. 809/776–6922 or 809/776–6494), rides out on scenic trails around Bordeaux Mountain and along beaches.

Sailboarding | Most of the major water-sports centers on the three islands can accommodate the Windsurfer.

St. Thomas | The **St. Thomas Diving Club** (tel. 809/776–2381 or 809/775–1800, ext. 185), at Bolongo Bay, caters to sail-boarders as well as scuba divers.

St. Croix | Call either **Caribbean Sea Adventures,** at Kings Wharf in Christiansted (tel. 809/773–5922), or **Sea Shadows,** at Cane Bay (809/778–3850).

St. John | Contact **St. John Watersports,** in Cruz Bay (tel. 809/776–6256).

Sailing/Boating | The U.S. Virgin Islands constitutes the biggest charter-boat fleet base in the Western Hemisphere, and you can choose among ketches, yawls, schooners, sloops, cutters, catamarans, power boats, and trimarans. More than 175 professionally crewed charter yachts are associated with the **Virgin Islands Charteryacht League,** at Homeport, St. Thomas (tel. 809/774–3944 or 800/524–2061).

St. Thomas | Most boats operate out of Red Hook, at the eastern end of the island. **Watersports Center** (Sapphire Bay, tel. 809/775–6755) will book you a full-day or half-day sail; so will **Sea Adventures** (Frenchman's Reef Hotel, tel. 809/774–9652; 809/776–8500, ext. 625; or 800/524–2096). **Coconut Cruises** (at Stouffer Grand Beach Resort, tel. 809/775–5959) has half-day, full-day, and sunset cruises aboard a 51-foot trimaran, with an open bar. Snorkeling, fishing gear, and underwater cameras are pro- Snorkeling, fishing gear, and underwater cameras are provided.

St. Croix | **Mile-Mark Charters** (tel. 809/773–2285) has both a sloop and a trimaran for full- or half-day sails. **Caribbean Sea Adventures** (tel. 809/773–5922) arranges bareboat and crewed charters and rents small boats as well.

St. John | **St. John Watersports** (Mongoose Junction, Cruz Bay, tel. 809/776–6256) handles both day sails and charters.

Scuba Diving and Snorkeling | There are more than 20 dive operators on the three islands, and many of the hotels on St. Thomas and St. Croix offer dive packages. For drop-offs or walls, St. Croix, where 18 hotels have scuba packages, is the place.

St. Thomas | **Joe Vogel Diving Co.** (tel. 809/775–7610), the oldest scuba certification school in the U.S. Virgin Islands, is run by an ex-navy frogman who personally conducts all classes and dives and is something of a legend on St. Thomas; among Joe's offerings is a sunrise shore dive to an airplane wreck. Other reliable scuba and snorkel operators are **Aqua Action** (Secret Harbour, tel. 809/775–6285), **Underwater Safaris** (Ramada Yacht Haven Motel and Marina, tel. 809/774–1350 and 809/774–9700), and **St. Thomas Diving Club** (Bolongo Bay, tel. 809/775–1800 and 800/524–4746).

St. Croix | **Caribbean Sea Adventures** has year-round dive packages for 6, 10, or 14 boat dives and is headquartered at The Buccaneer (tel. 809/773–6011 or 809/773–5922). You are also in good hands with Steve Fordyce and **Sea Shadows** (tel. 809/778–3850 or 809/773–1441) right at Cane Bay and its splendid wall. **The Belangers Virgin Dive** (tel. 809/778–9764) headquarters is at Salt River

Marina, near where Columbus once landed. If you're a beginning snorkeler, try Dick Mooney's **Snorkeling Safari** (Tamarind Reef, tel. 809/773–0951).

St. John   **Low Key Watersports** (Wharfside Village, (tel. 809/776–6042) dives three different wrecks, including that of the *Rhone*. Other scuba operators are **Cruz Bay Watersports** (tel. 809/776–6234) and **St. John Watersports** (tel. 809/776–6256).

If you'd like to get introduced to the feel of scuba diving but would rather stay in shallow water and have an air-hose tether to a "buoyant flotation unit," try **Snuba** (tel. 809/775–4063 or 809/776–6922).

Sportfishing   In the past quarter-century, some 20 world records—many for blue marlin—have been set in these waters. Sailfish, skipjack, bonito, tuna (allison, blackfin, and yellowfin), and wahoo are abundant. On St. Thomas and St. John, there are also more than a hundred government-listed spots for shoreline fishing where you may hook up with tarpon, crevalle, snook, bonefish, snapper, or even barracuda.

St. Thomas   Call **American Yacht Harbor** at Red Hook (tel. 809/775–6454) if you're interested in some serious angling. Or you may join **Captain Spike** (tel. 809/775–6582 or 809/775–6465) on an air-conditioned 46-foot Bertram any day of the week.

St. Croix   **Caribbean Sea Adventures,** at Kings Wharf (tel. 809/773–5922), has deep-sea fishing charters. **Ruffian Enterprises,** also at Kings Wharf (tel. 809/773–6011 or 809/773–0917), will take you out on a 41-foot Hatteras. Or join Captain Bunny Jones aboard the *Catch 22* (tel. 809/773–0576, 809/773–4482, or 809/778–6987). At Kings Alley Dock, you will find the *Lady Mac K* (tel. 809/778–6118 or 809/778–0487), a custom-rigged Hatteras Fisherman.

St. John   **Caneel Bay** (tel. 809/776–6111), at the edge of Cruz Bay, will arrange fishing outings.

Tennis   Numerous hotels on St. Thomas and St. Croix have tennis courts for both day and night play, and there are a few public courts on all three islands.

St. Thomas   Among the hotels having tennis courts are **Bluebeard's Castle, Bolongo Bay Beach, Frenchman's Reef, Limetree Beach, Sapphire Beach, Secret Harbour, Stouffer Grand Beach,** and **Virgin Isle.** There are also two public courts at Long Bay and two at Sub Base.

St. Croix   There are courts at **The Buccaneer, Carambola Beach, Divi St. Croix, Hotel on the Cay, St. Croix by the Sea, Cormorant Beach Club,** and **Queen's Quarter** hotels. Public courts can be found at Conegata Park (two) and Fort Frederik (two), on the western side of St. Croix.

St. John   Resorts having courts are **Caneel Bay, Cruz Inn, Edie's Eden,** and **Virgin Grand.** There are also four public courts in Cruz Bay.

Shopping

St. Thomas: Charlotte Amalie   There are well over 400 shops in Charlotte Amalie alone, and in the Havensight area, where the cruise ships dock, there are at least 50 more clustered in converted warehouses. Even diehard

Charlotte Amalie Shopping

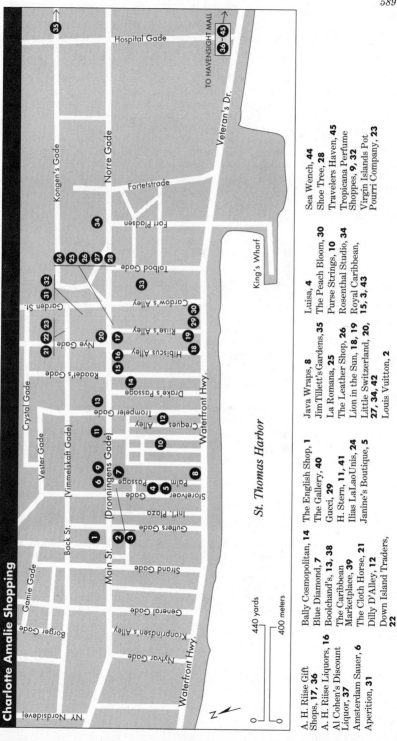

St. Thomas Harbor

Hospital Gade

Kongen's Gade

Norre Gade

Fortetstrade

Fort Pladsen

Tolbod Gade

Cardow's Alley

Riise's Alley

Garden St.

Nye Gade

Hibiscus Alley

Raadet's Gade

Drake's Passage

Crystal Gade

Trompeter Gade

Creque's Alley

Vester Gade

Back St. (Vimmelskaft Gade)

Main St. (Dronningens Gade)

Palm Passage

Storvaer Gade

Int'l. Plaza

Gutters Gade

Strand Gade

Veteran's Dr.

King's Wharf

TO HAVENSIGHT MALL

Waterfront Hwy.

General Gade

Kronprindsen's Alley

Nyvar Gade

Borger Gade

Gamle Gade

Ny Nordsidevej

440 yards

400 meters

A. H. Riise Gift Shops, **17, 36**
A. H. Riise Liquors, **16**
Al Cohen's Discount Liquor, **37**
Amsterdam Sauer, **6**
Aperition, **31**

Bally Cosmopolitan, **14**
Blue Diamond, **7**
Boolchand's, **13, 38**
The Caribbean Marketplace, **39**
The Cloth Horse, **21**
Dilly D'Alley, **12**
Down Island Traders, **22**

The English Shop, **1**
The Gallery, **40**
Gucci, **29**
H. Stern, **11, 41**
Ilias LaLaoUnis, **24**
Janine's Boutique, **5**

Java Wraps, **8**
Jim Tillett's Gardens, **35**
La Romana, **25**
The Leather Shop, **26**
Lion in the Sun, **18, 19**
Little Switzerland, **20, 27, 34, 42**
Louis Vuitton, **2**

Luisa, **4**
The Peach Bloom, **30**
Purse Strings, **10**
Rosenthal Studio, **34**
Royal Caribbean, **15, 3, 43**

Sea Wench, **44**
Shoe Tree, **28**
Travelers Haven, **45**
Tropicana Perfume Shoppes, **9, 32**
Virgin Islands Pot Pourri Company, **23**

shoppers won't want to cover all the boutiques, since a large percentage peddle the same T-shirts and togs. Many visitors devote their shopping time on St. Thomas to the stores that sell handicrafts and luxury items. Even if you don't intend to buy a fur coat, it's fun to say you tried one on in St. Thomas, and there are now several furriers where you can do just that.

Although those famous "give away" prices no longer abound, shoppers on St. Thomas can still save money. Today, a realistic appraisal puts prices on many items at about 20% off stateside prices. What's more, there is no sales tax in the U.S. Virgin Islands, and visitors can take advantage of the $800 duty-free allowance and the additional 5% discount on the next $800 worth of goods. Remember to save receipts.

You won't need to spend a lot of time comparison shopping since some luxury items—perfumes, cosmetics, liquor—are uniformly priced throughout the U.S. Virgin Islands. Prices on almost everything else, from leather goods to leisure wear, vary very little from shop to shop. The prices on jewelry do vary quite a bit, however, and it's here that you'll still run across some real "finds."

Shopping Districts. The major shopping area is in downtown Charlotte Amalie in centuries-old buildings that once served as merchants' warehouses and that for the most part, have been converted to retail establishments. Both sides of **Main Street** are lined with shops, as are the side streets and walkways between Main Street and the Waterfront. These narrow lanes and arcades have names like Drake's Passage, Royal Dane Mall, Palm Passage, Trompeter Gade, Hibiscus Alley, and Raadet's Gade.

The **Bakery Square Shopping Mall** (one block north of Main St. off of Nye Gade) has about 15 boutiques. The streets adjacent to Bakery Square, notably Back Street, Nye Gade, Garden Street, Kongens Gade, and Norre Gade, are also very good areas for browsing. At **Havensight Mall,** which is close to the deep-water port where the cruise ships dock, you'll find many branches of downtown stores as well as specialty shops and boutiques.

Listed here are many of the major shops and the types of merchandise they carry. Virtually all stores accept MasterCard and Visa, and most accept American Express and other major credit cards.

Cameras and Electronics **Boolchand's** (31 Main St., tel. 809/776–0794; Havensight Mall, tel. 809/776–0302) carries all kinds of cameras and audio-video equipment.

Royal Caribbean (33 Main St., tel. 809/776–4110; Havensight Mall, tel. 809/776–8890) has attractive prices on some cameras and accessories; Sony Walkmans are usually good buys here.

China and Crystal **A.H. Riise Gift Shops** (37 Main St. and Havensight Mall, tel. 809/776–2303) carries Waterford and Wedgwood, Royal Crown and Royal Doulton at good prices. For example, a five-piece place setting of Royal Crown Derby's Old Imari goes for under $350.

The English Shop (Main St. at Market Square and Havensight Mall, tel. 809/774–3495) offers china and crystal from major European and Japanese manufacturers. Spode, Limoges, Royal Doulton, Royal Crafton, Royal Worcester, and Villeroy & Boch are featured.

Little Switzerland (3 locations on Main St., 1 at Havensight Mall, tel. 809/776–2010) has crystal pieces from Lalique, Baccarat, Waterford, Swarovski, Riedel, and Orrefors and china from Villeroy & Boch, Aynsley, Wedgwood, Royal Doulton, and Wedgwood.

Clothing **Janine's Boutique** (8A-2 Palm Passage, tel. 809/774–8243) features women's and men's dressy and casual apparel from European designers and manufacturers, including the Louis Feraud collection. They also carry accessories. A men's-only corner has select finds from Valentino, Christian Dior, and Pierre Cardin.

La Romana (Main St., tel. 809/774–8135; Havensight Mall, tel. 809/776–8555; Barclays Bank Annex Bldg., tel. 809/774–2620; Frenchman's Reef Hotel, tel. 809/774–8135) stocks very expensive and upscale Italian designs.

Lion in the Sun (Riise's Alley, tel. 809/776–4203) is another place to shop for designer fashions for men and women. Some items are available for about 25% less than stateside prices. The Riise's Alley location is bigger and usually has the better buys.

Galleries **The Gallery** (Veteran's Dr., tel. 809/776–4641) carries some very good Haitian art along with works by a number of Virgin Islands artists. Items on display include oil paintings, metal sculpture, wood carvings, painted screens and boxes, figures carved from stone, and oversize papier-mâché figures. Prices range from $100 to $5,000.

Gifts and Crafts **The Caribbean Marketplace** (Havensight Mall, Bldg. III, tel. 809/776–5400) is the place to look for Caribbean handicrafts, including Caribelle batiks from St. Lucia; bikinis from the Cayman Islands; and Sunny Caribee spices, soaps, teas, and coffees from Tortola. Visitors can make an appointment to tour the adjacent fragrance factory (tel. 809/774–2166).

The Cloth Horse (Bakery Square, tel. 809/774–4761) has signed pottery from the Dominican Republic; wicker and rattan furniture and household goods from the island of Hispañola; and pottery, rugs, and bedspreads from all over the world.

Down Island Traders (Bakery Square and Frenchman's Reef, tel. 809/774–3419) offers hand-painted calabash bowls ($5); jams, jellies, spices, and herbs; herbal teas made of rum, passion fruit, and mango; high mountain coffee from Jamaica; and a variety of handicrafts from throughout the Caribbean.

Jim Tillett's Gardens (Estate Tutu, tel. 809/775–1405) is more than worth the cab fare to reach the complex. Tillett's artwork is on display, and you can watch craftsmen and artisans produce silk-screened fabrics, pottery, candles, watercolors, and other handicrafts.

Java Wraps (24 Palm Passage, tel. 809/774–3700) has Indonesian batik creations. This store offers a complete line of beach cover-ups, swimwear, and leisure wear for women, men, and children. The most interesting items are the signed sarongs ($35–$120) and the ceremonial puppets from Java ($60).

The **Virgin Islands Pot Pourri Company** (Bakery Square, tel. 809/776–1038) displays the owner's own snazzy batik and tie-dye creations as well as the work of other Virgin Islands fabric artists.

Jewelry **A.H. Riise Gift Shops** (37 Main St. and Havensight Mall, tel. 809/776–2303), St. Thomas's oldest and largest shop for luxury items, offers jewelry, pearls, ceramics, china, crystal, flatwear, perfume, and watches, as well as an unusual collection of artwork, books, and historic prints.

Amsterdam Sauer (14 Main St., tel. 809/774–2222) displays many fine, one-of-a-kind designs.

Aperition (3A Main St., tel. 809/776–0780) is a good spot for lovely jewelry made by Greek and Italian designers.

Blue Diamond (25A Main St., tel. 809/776–4340) is favored by many locals; this store shows many of its own 14K and 18K designs crafted by European goldsmiths.

H. Stern (12 Main St., Havensight Mall, Frenchman's Reef, Stouffer Grand Beach Resort, and Bluebeard's, tel. 809/776–1939) is one of the most respected names in gems. The boutique at the Havensight Mall has one of the best collections of tennis bracelets available anywhere.

Ilias LaLaoUnis (37 Main St., tel. 809/774–5294) includes collections of 18K- and 22K-gold pieces designed by its Greek owner.

Little Switzerland (2 locations on Main St., 1 on Emancipation Sq., tel. 809/776–2010) is the sole distributor for Rolex watches. The store also does a booming mail-order business; ask for a catalogue.

The **Peach Bloom** boutique (Post Office Alley, tel. 809/776–2788) shows select pieces of antique jewelry and one-of-a-kind pieces from the United States and Europe ranging in price from $50 into the thousands. The selection includes bracelets, rings, pendants, lockets, pins, watches, fobs, and Victorian silver baby spoons and teething rings.

Leather Goods **Gucci** (A.H.Riise Gift Alley, 37 Main St., tel. 809/774–7841) offers traditional Gucci insignia designs in wallets, bags, briefcases, totes, walking shoes, and loafers for men and women.

The Leather Shop (Main St. at Dronningens Gade, tel. 809/776–3995; Havensight Mall, Bldg. II, tel. 809/776–0040) has some big names at big prices: Fendi and Bottega Veneta are prevalent.

Louis Vuitton (24 Main St. in Palm Passage, tel. 809/774–3644) is an example of St. Thomas shopping at its most elegant. From scarves and umbrellas to briefcases and steamer trunks, all Vuitton workmanship is the finest.

Luisa (Palm Passage, tel. 809/776–1085) has shoes and bags exclusively from Italy.

At **Purse Strings** (2A-1 Royal Dane Mall, tel. 809/774–1219) handbags ranging from designs by Christian Dior, Carlo Fiori, and Lesandro Saraso to straw and canvas Caribbean creations hang from the walls, counters, and ceiling. There is also a large selection of eelskin and snakeskin bags and accessories; eelskin attaches are a good buy for $160.

The **Shoe Tree** (37 Main St., tel. 809/774–3900) carries women's shoe styles under a top price of $70—one of the Caribbean's best kept shopping secrets. Designers include Bandolino, Pierre Cardin, Evan Picone, and Liz Claiborne.

Travelers Haven (Havensight Mall, tel. 809/775–1798) has leather bags, backpacks, vests, and money belts.

Liquor   Liquor prices are standard throughout all the Virgin Islands, and U.S. citizens can carry back a gallon of liquor or five "fifths" duty free.

A.H. Riise Liquors (34 Main St. and Havensight Mall, tel. 809/ 774–6900) has a large selection of liquors, cordials, wines, and tobacco, including rare vintage cognacs, Armagnacs, ports, and Madeiras; they also stock imported cigars, fruits in brandy, and barware from England.

Al Cohen's Discount Liquor (across from Havensight Mall, Long Bay Rd., tel. 809/774–3690), a warehouse-style store with a large wine department, is open seven days a week.

Perfumes   Fine fragrances from France waft around every bend in the cobblestoned roads; where you buy hardly matters, since prices are the same in all shops.

The **Tropicana Perfume Shoppes** (2 Dronningen Gade, tel. 809/ 774–0010; 14 Dronningen Gade, tel. 809/774–1834) offers the largest selection of fragrances for men and women in the Virgin Islands; both shops give small free samples to customers.

A.H. Riise Gift Shop (tel. 809/774–6900) is the best bet for perfumes in the Havensight Mall.

Sportswear   **Bally Cosmopolitan** (Drake's Passage, tel. 809/776–2040) may have the largest collection of Gortex swimsuits outside Israel: the inventory includes about 300 different styles of bikinis, maillots, and "constructed" one-piece suits. For men, this store offers one of the best selections of knit sport shirts from Italy (Fila, Ellesse) and the finest sea-island cotton shirts from the London firm of Smedley.

At the **Dilly D'Alley** boutique (Trompeter Gade, tel. 809/776– 5006) shoppers can select from over 20 lines of swimwear. Definitely a best buy are the unusually comfortable, tie-dyed cotton wrap-around dresses.

Sea Wench, at the Havensight Mall (Building III, tel. 809/776– 1088), mixes known names in swimwear (Cacharel, Roxanne, Jantzen) with California-casual designs and Brazilian briefs. They also import some very lacy lingerie from France, Austria, and the U.S.

St. Croix   While St. Croix does not have nearly as many shops as St. Thomas does, the selection of duty-free goods is still fairly large. Many of St. Thomas's leading shops have branches in St. Croix, but there are also plenty of independent merchants that have items you may not be able to find in Charlotte Amalie. In Christiansted, most of the shops are clustered in the historic district near the harbor. **King Street, Strand Street,** and the arcades that lead off them comprise the major shopping district. The longest arcade is **Caravelle Arcade,** located in the hotel of the same name.

St. John The opportunities for duty-free shopping are more limited—and the prices a bit higher—on St. John compared to the other islands. One spot popular with visitors is **Wharfside Village,** an attractive, compact mall of some 30 shops overlooking Cruz Bay Harbor. **Mongoose Junction,** a shopping center just north of Cruz Bay across from the Park Service Visitor Center, has a number of shops that sell handicrafts designed and fashioned by resident artisans.

Dining

Just about every kind of cuisine you can imagine is available in the U.S. Virgin Islands, and the price range is broad enough to match any visitor's pocketbook. With so much air traffic between the mainland and the islands, supplies are as fresh as they are in most major cities of the United States. Beef, pork, and poultry are as good as you will find them at home; the unusual and delicious variety of local fruits, vegetables, and seafood is a culinary bonus here.

St. Thomas is the most cosmopolitan of the islands and has the most visitors, so it is not surprising that the island also has the largest number and greatest variety of restaurants. St. Croix restaurants are both more relaxed, and, in some ways, more elegant. Dining on St. John is, in general, more casual; the emphasis is on simple food prepared to order in an informal setting at a reasonable price.

The most highly recommended restaurants are indicated by a star ★ .

Category	Cost*
Very Expensive	over $35
Expensive	$25–$35
Moderate	$15–$25
Inexpensive	under $15

average cost of a three-course dinner, per person, excluding drinks, service, and sales tax

St. Thomas **Fiddle Leaf.** American and French nouvelle cuisine is featured at this elegant Art Deco restaurant. Selections range from New Orleans blackened fish and Wisconsin veal to more embellished, sauce-rich fare. The desserts are highly praised. *Watergate Villas, tel. 809/775–2810. Reservations required. AE, MC, V. Very Expensive.*

★ **Hotel 1829.** The seafood, prime ribs, and venison dishes at Hotel 1829 make dining here one of the best experiences to be had on St. Thomas. The chef's soufflés have won awards. *Government Hill, a few steps up from Main St., Charlotte Amalie, tel. 809/776–1829. Reservations required. AE, MC, V. Very Expensive.*

Bird of Paradise. At this lovely terrace restaurant in a sheltered cove, you will dine seated in majestic peacock chairs. The cuisine is French Caribbean. Lobster, veal, and fresh fish dishes are featured, as is duckling flambéed by your table. *Secret Harbour Resort, east end of the island, tel. 809/775-6198. Reservations required. AE, MC, V. Expensive.*

Entre Nous. The view here, high over Charlotte Amalie's harbor, is exhilarating, and the dining is elegant. The Caesar salad is outstanding, and the entrées include rack of lamb, Caribbean lobster, veal, and Chateaubriand. Try Grand Marnier–flamed baked Alaska for dessert. *Bluebeard's Castle, Charlotte Amalie, tel. 809/776-4050. Reservations required. AE, MC, V. Expensive.*

Tonga Reef. Here you can enjoy American, Polynesian, or West Indian dishes by torchlight next to a waterfall. A boardwalk leads you past boulders and over pools, and you can have drinks on tiny "Mermaid Island." *Carib Beach Hotel, Charlotte Amalie, tel. 809/774-2525. Reservations advised. AE, DC, MC, V. Expensive.*

The Chart House. On the premises of an old great house called Villa Olga, this restaurant features kabob and teriyaki dishes, lobster, Hawaiian chicken, and a large salad bar. Mud pie is a favorite dessert. *Villa Olga, Frenchtown, tel. 809/774-4262. No reservations except for 10 or more. AE, MC, V. Moderate.*

For the Birds. The beer is served in Mason jars and the Margaritas are available in 46-ounce servings at this beach restaurant with a disco dance floor. You can have sizzling fajitas, barbecued baby back ribs, seafood, or steaks. *Scott Beach, near Compass Point on the east end of the island, tel. 809/775-6431. Reservations only for a party of 6 or more. AE, MC, V. Moderate.*

★ **Gregerie East.** Candlelight and night breezes are featured in this restaurant located on a marina. Its French Caribbean menu includes seafood, lamb, beef, veal, and pasta dishes. Don's Hole in the Wall Bar is convivial and popular with the yachting crowd. *Leeward Islands Sailing Complex (Frenchtown), tel. 809/774-2432. AE, MC, V. Closed Mon. Moderate.*

Harbourfront. Here, right at the waterfront, you can sit next to saltwater aquariums and feast on Caribbean seafood or prime ribs. If you bypass the dolphin (the food fish) or mako shark and choose the prime ribs, you'll soon know the Godzilla-size portion will feed three and then some. *72 Kronprindsens Gade, Charlotte Amalie, tel. 809/776-0200. Reservations advised. AE, MC, V. Moderate.*

Hunan Restaurant. This spot is distinctly Chinese in decor and air-conditioned, and the cuisine is Hunan and Szechwan, although you may dine on Peking duck if you order it when you make reservations. *Wheatley II Shopping Plaza, at the foot of Raphune Hill, Charlotte Amalie, tel. 809/776-3939. AE, MC, V. Moderate.*

Zorba's. A waterfall punctuates your conversation at this courtyard Greek restaurant. Souvlaki and moussaka are on the lunch menu, and fish dishes and roast leg of lamb are among the dinner selections. *Government Hill, Charlotte Amalie, tel. 809/776-0444. AE, DC, MC, V. Moderate.*

Eunice's Terrace. The West Indian menu at this lively, porch-like bar and restaurant includes conch strips sautéed in butter-and-garlic sauce, snapper or grouper fillet, and a seafood combination plate. For dessert there is rum cake, Key lime pie, or sweet potato pie. *Rte. 38, near the Coral World turnoff, tel. 809/775-3975. AE. Moderate-Inexpensive.*

Little Bo Peep. The French West Indian fare at this restaurant includes curried beef, goat, or chicken; conch Creole, callaloo, and, of course, rice and peas, fungi, fried plantain, or potato stuffing as side dishes. *7B Back St., Charlotte Amalie, tel. 809/ 774–1959. AE, DC, V. Closed Mon. Inexpensive.*

Sparky's Waterfront Saloon. This is a lively and inexpensive place for chili, burgers, or fish 'n' chips at lunchtime or steak, fresh fish, or pasta at dinner. *Waterfront, Charlotte Amalie, tel. 809/774–8015. MC, V. Inexpensive.*

St. Croix   **Captain's Table.** Seafood is the forte at this pleasant courtyard restaurant, from shellfish appetizers to island conch, wahoo with white wine, shrimp done Indonesian style, and bouillabaisse. You can also have steak or surf and turf. *Company St., Christiansted, tel. 809/773–4532. Reservations required. AE, MC, V. Expensive.*

★ **Cormorant Beach Club.** Candlelight and the sounds of the night surf create the atmosphere here, where a California chef brings her own touch to Continental and Cruzan dishes. The boneless breast of chicken is blackened with Creole spices and served with black beans and avocado *salsa*. Among the appetizers are conch fritters and carrot orange soup. *La Grande Princesse, west of Christiansted, tel. 809/778–8920. Reservations suggested. AE, MC, V. Expensive.*

Club Comanche. The atmosphere is very friendly and casual at this upstairs terrace restaurant, where the decor includes an outrigger canoe hanging from the ceiling. The curry of beef fillet is a popular dish, as is the stuffed shrimp Savannah. There are some 15 appetizers on the varied menu. *Strand St., Christiansted, tel. 809/773–2665. Reservations advised. AE, MC, V. Moderate.*

King's Alley. Some nice shrubbery and trees surround this open-air place at the waterfront, where you can get chicken wings, stuffed potato skins, sandwiches, burgers, barbecued ribs or chicken, steak, and even a few Mexican and Japanese selections. *King's Alley, Christiansted, tel. 809/773–0468. AE, MC, V. Moderate.*

★ **Serendipity.** This cozy, iron-gated beach restaurant has brick walls and a front-and-center bar with high rattan arm-stools. The house specialty is a shrimp-stocked pasta delight, but you can also have Barbadian flying fish, filet mignon, or a special, such as chicken breast sautéed with a cranberry–Grand Marnier sauce. Friday-night barbecues and Sunday brunches are very popular. *Mill Harbour, Christiansted, tel. 809/773– 5762. Reservations advised. AE, MC, V. Moderate.*

Ritz Cafe. If you just want a burger or some good bar food, this polished-wood nook is special. There are seven tables and one booth. John Courage beer is on draft. *53-B Company, Christiansted, tel. 809/773–2985. No credit cards. Inexpensive.*

St. John   **Fronds.** If you have to ask how much, don't come. At this gourmet restaurant at the Virgin Grand Beach Hotel, a five-course meal is served on Fitz and Lloyd china. The chefs' masterpieces include Swedish rainbow trout Laplandia sauté meunière with cream chives and dill sauce. Live classical guitar or piano music accompanies the dining "experience." *Virgin Grand Beach Hotel, tel. 809/776–7171. Reservations advised. Jacket required. AE, DC, MC, V. Very Expensive.* **Pusser's.** On an upper level and overlooking the Cruz Bay harbor, this is a lovely place to dine in the cool of an evening.

British lunch specialties are shepherd's pie and steak and ale pie. For dinner, there is steak, chicken, lamb or pork chops, lobster tail, or a chef's special, such as skewers of fillet chicken with curry sauce, beef with peanut sauce, and monkfish with barbecue sauce. *Wharfside Village, Cruz Bay, tel. 809/774–5489. Reservations advised for 6 or more. AE, MC, V. Expensive.*

★ **Lime Inn.** This busy, roofed open-air restaurant has a nice ornamental garden and beach-furniture chairs. There are several shrimp and steak dishes and such specials as sautéed chicken with artichoke hearts in lemon sauce. On Wednesday nights, there is an all-you-can-eat shrimp feast. *Downtown, Cruz Bay, tel. 809/776–6425. Reservations advised. AE, MC, V. Moderate.*

The Upper Deck. It *is* like a deck, and the view from here at sunset is excellent. Herring and New England fish chowder are appetizers, and besides steak or chops you can have fried scallops, clams, or shrimp, as well as baked local fish or pan-fried liver with bacon and onions. *Up in the hills off South Shore Rd., tel. 809/776–6318. Closed Mon. and Tues. MC, V. Moderate.*

The Back Yard. This open-air, down-to-earth bar/restaurant has a limited menu: burgers, barbecued ribs, kingfish, and sometimes Miss Maggie's West Indian stewed conch. Many locals hang out here. *Downtown, Cruz Bay, tel. 809/776–8553. No credit cards. Inexpensive.*

Fred's. This simple place, offering West Indian dishes, is in the center of town. Chicken and fish dishes are complemented by johnnycake and fungi. *Downtown, Cruz Bay, tel. 809/776–6363. No credit cards. Inexpensive.*

★ **Shipwreck Landing.** If you're tooling around St. John east of Cruz Bay, this is a pleasant oasis to stop in for food or refreshment. Burgers, chicken teriyaki, sandwiches, taco salad, and conch fritters are choices for lunch. There is a regular dinner special, along with Cajun dishes and a chicken cordon bleu that comes with banana cream sauce. *Rte. 107, Coral Bay, tel. 809/776–8540. Dress: informal. No credit cards. Inexpensive.*

Lodging

The U.S. Virgin Islands win the numbers game. They have more hotels per square inch than any other area in the Caribbean. The concentration is at Charlotte Amalie, St. Thomas, and Christiansted, St. Croix, but almost every beach has its hotel as well. The government rate sheet, published twice yearly (for low summer and high winter rates) lists 52 choices on St. Thomas, 37 on St. Croix, and about a dozen on St. John. Places range from luxury hotels to small guest houses, apartments, and campsites.

St. Thomas leads in the field of smaller accommodations, with more inns than any other island in the Caribbean; St. Croix has beach resorts and places scattered around the countryside; St. John has Caneel Bay and the Virgin Grand for elegance and comfort and, at the opposite end of the spectrum, Cinnamon Bay and Maho Bay offer campsites and cabins in the national park if you want to "rough it."

High-season rates are generally in effect from December 15 to April 15. Rates are from 25% to 50% lower the rest of the year.

The most highly recommended lodgings are indicated by a star ★.

Category	Cost*
Very Expensive	over $200
Expensive	$125–$200
Moderate	$65–$125
Inexpensive	under $65

All prices are for a standard double room, excluding 7.5% accommodations tax.

Hotels
St. Thomas

★ **Frenchman's Reef** (and **Morning Star Beach Club**). Sprawling, luxurious, and situated on a prime harbor promontory east of Charlotte Amalie, Frenchman's Reef is St. Thomas's American superhotel par excellence. There are cavernous restaurants and ballrooms, 23 duty-free shops, a helicopter pad, and an elevator to the beach. Most rooms have sea views, and Morning Star offers on-the-beach villas. There are guest activities and live entertainment galore. *Box 7100, Charlotte Amalie, 00801, tel. 809/776–8500 or 800/524–2000. 518 rooms. Facilities: beach, 7 restaurants, 6 bars, 2 Olympic-size pools, 4 tennis courts, water sports, aerial tours by helicopter. AE, DC, MC, V. Very Expensive.*

★ **Sapphire Beach.** This resort is on one of St. Thomas's prettiest beaches. There is a marina for boating enthusiasts and, for divers, good snorkeling. An interesting bonus is the opportunity to watch sea turtles feed at an area set aside for the purpose. All villas and suites have beachfront balconies and come with fully equipped kitchens, air-conditioning, telephones, and cable TV. Children under 12 are welcome. They eat free and can join the Little Gems Kids Klub. *Box 8088, Red Hook, 00801, tel. 809/775–6100 or 800/524–2090. 141 rooms. Facilities: beach, restaurant, bar, 4 tennis courts, water sports, nearby golf. AE, MC, V. Very Expensive.*

Stouffer Grand Beach Resort. The resort's zigzag architectural angles spell luxury, from the marble atrium lobby to the one-bedroom suites with private whirlpool bath. The beach is excellent, and there is a new health club with Nautilus machines. The Ultimate Lifestyle Package includes a private secluded-island picnic and a flight to San Juan for a dinner-and-casino evening. The 34-acre resort is diligently managed. *Smith Bay Rd., Box 8267, 00801, tel. 809/775–1510 or 800/468–3571. 290 rooms. Facilities: beach, 6 lit tennis courts, 2 pools, water sports, nearby golf. AE, DC, MC, V. Very Expensive.*

★ **Point Pleasant Resort.** Perched high over Smith Bay, affording a great view of St. John and Drake Passage to the east and north, this resort offers a wide range of accommodations—from simple bedrooms to multiroom suites scattered in several hillside units. The air-conditioned rooms have balconies and most have kitchens. Every guest gets four hours' free use of a car daily. There are monthly full-moon jazz concerts at the main pool. *Estate Smith Bay, 00802, tel. 809/775–2000, 800/524–2300, or 800/645–5306. 148 rooms. Facilities: 2 beaches, restau-*

rant, bar, 3 pools, tennis court (lit), water sports. AE, MC, V. Expensive–Very Expensive.

Bluebeard's Castle. Though not exactly a castle, this large, red-roof complex offers kingly modern comforts and is on a steep hill overlooking the town, which from here glistens at night like a Christmas tree. All rooms are air-conditioned and equipped with cable TV and a refrigerator; most have terraces. Haven-sight Mall, where the cruise ships come in, is not far. The hotel offers free transportation to Magens Bay Beach. *Box 7480, Charlotte Amalie, 00801, tel. 809/774–1600 or 800/524–6599. 167 rooms. Facilities: 2 restaurants, bar, pool, 2 tennis courts, nearby golf. AE, DC, MC, V. Expensive.*

Bolongo Bay Beach and Tennis Club. A mecca for water-sports enthusiasts and the headquarters of the St. Thomas Diving Club, Bolongo has oceanfront and garden-view rooms with efficiency kitchens, cable TV, telephones, air-conditioning, and balconies. At the shaded poolside patio, you can watch breakers dashing against the promontory to the left while you rest your feet and discuss life's vicissitudes with amiable bar manager Tony Hunt. *Box 7337, 00801, tel. 809/775–1800 or 800/524–4746. 78 rooms. Facilities: beach, restaurant, 4 tennis courts (2 lit), pool, water sports. AE, DC, MC, V. Expensive.*

Fairway Village. The villas, banked on a lush, green hillside, are right at the Fazio-designed Mahogany Run 18-hole golf course. Studios and one-bedroom apartments have fully equipped kitchens. This is a golfer's heaven; for swimmers, there is a wooden-decked swimming pool and Magen Bay Beach is nearby. *Property Management Caribbean, Inc., Rte. 6, 00802, tel. 809/775–1220 or 800/524–2038. 25 rooms. Facilities: golf, pool. AE. Expensive.*

Hotel 1829. This historic Spanish-style hillside inn has a lovely courtyard and, outside, a handsome bar and a terrace shaded by a green awning. The less expensive rooms are near the terrace; the suites and deluxe rooms come with cable TV, wet bars, and balconies. All rooms are air-conditioned. No children under 12 are admitted. *Box 1567, Charlotte Amalie, 00801, tel. 809/776–1829 or 800/524–2002. 15 rooms. Facilities: pool, restaurant. AE, MC, V. Expensive.*

Limetree Beach Hotel. The surf is gentle at the quiet inlet of Limetree Beach, and the hotel is known for the stone-faced but friendly vegetarian iguanas on its tropically landscaped grounds. Standard (first-floor), superior, and deluxe rooms have air-conditioning, cable TV, telephone, Servi-bars, and electronic safes; most have an ocean view. All guests receive a complimentary scuba lesson. *Box 7337, 00801, tel. 809/775–1800, or 800/524–4746. 84 rooms. Facilities: beach, restaurant, 2 tennis courts, volleyball, shuffleboard, water sports. AE, DC, MC, V. Expensive.*

Pavilions & Pools. Simple, tropical-cool decor and immured privacy are ambient here, where each island-style room has its own 20-foot-by-14-foot or 18-foot-by-16-foot pool. The unpretentious accommodations include air-conditioning, telephone, full kitchen, and VCR. Water sports are available at Sapphire Beach on the adjacent property. The management is particularly attentive to your wishes and does everything to preserve the general quiet. *Rte. 6, 00802, tel. 809/775–6110 or 800/524–2001. 25 rooms, each with a private pool. AE, DC, MC, V. Expensive.*

★ **Secret Harbour.** The white buildings, with air-conditioned studios and suites, are nestled around an inviting, perfectly framed cove on Nazareth Bay, where you can watch the marvelous sunsets. In the one-bedroom suites, equipped with a kitchenette, the decor consists of pastel-hued fabric art on the walls and a chandelier. You'll find hardcover fiction on the bookshelves. The restaurant has majestic peacock chairs. The beach is no secret to local residents who appreciate good snorkeling. Children under 12 can stay for free. *Box 7576, 00801, tel. 809/775-6550 or 800/524-2250 (10 AM-4 PM). 60 rooms. Facilities: beach, restaurant, bar, tennis court, water sports. No credit cards. Expensive.*

Watergate Villas. The air-conditioned villas, east of Charlotte Amalie at Bolongo Bay, have modern studios and suites with one, two, or three bedrooms, all with a large living–dining room and fully equipped kitchen. *Estate Bolongo Bay, Property Management Caribbean, Inc., Rte. 6, 00802, tel. 809/775-2270 or 800/524-2038. 140 rooms. Facilities: restaurant, bar, beach, 2 pools, tennis, water sports. AE. Expensive.*

★ **Blackbeard's Castle.** This small inn on Government Hill has a tiptop view of Charlotte Amalie and the harbor and an intimate atmosphere. All the rooms, many with handsome wall hangings, have air-conditioning, new telephones, and cable TV. The picturesque piratical lookout tower is the oldest structure on the island. Continental breakfast is complimentary and transportation to the beach is free as well. The restaurant is excellent. Order a tropical cocktail and sip it while listening to romantic piano music. *Box 6041, Charlotte Amalie, 00801, tel. 809/776-1234. 16 rooms. Facilities: pool, restaurant, bar. AE, MC, V. Moderate.*

★ **Heritage Manor.** This regally immaculate, air-conditioned European-style guest house has gleaming 1837 tile floors, brass beds, wall-mounted hair dryers, and city-theme prints. The Tokyo room is coziness incarnate. Suites have refrigerators. Continental breakfast is complimentary. The house has its own parking strip, and it is a short walk downhill to the shops. Children under 10 are not admitted. *Box 90, Charlotte Amalie, 00804-0090, tel. 809/774-3003. 7 rooms, 3 with private bath. Facilities: pool. AE, DC, MC, V. Moderate.*

Island Beachcomber Hotel. This hotel, whose air-conditioned rooms have refrigerators and patios or balconies, is close to the airport but right on Lindbergh Beach. (Unlike most hotels on St. Thomas, it is west of Charlotte Amalie.) It is especially casual: you can live here in your swimsuit—but do put on a cover-up at the garden restaurant. The restaurant cuisine is Caribbean. *Box 1618, Charlotte Amalie, 00801, tel. 809/774-5250 or 800/982-9898. 50 rooms. Facilities: beach, restaurant, water sports. MC, V. Moderate.*

Sea Horse Cottages. These simple cottages, located at the eastern end of the island, look across to St. John. There is a rocky, irregular beach and a pool that overlooks a marina. All rooms have kitchens and ceiling fans. *Box 2312, 00801, tel. 809/775-9231. 25 rooms. Facilities: beach, pool. No credit cards. Moderate.*

Villa Blanca Hotel. Located above Charlotte Amalie on Raphune Hill, the hotel is surrounded by an attractive garden and has modern, balconied rooms with rattan furniture, kitchenettes, cable TV, and ceiling fans. The eastern rooms face the Charlotte Amalie harbor; the western ones look out on rolling hills and a partial view of Drake's Channel and the British Virgin Islands. *Box 7505, Charlotte Amalie, 00801, tel. 809/ 776-0749. 12 rooms. Facilities: pool. AE, DC, MC, V. Moderate.*

Maison Greaux. Up the hill and not far from Frenchtown, this guest house has reasonable rates and a harbor view. The rooms are air-conditioned. *Box 1856, Charlotte Amalie, 00801, tel. 809/774-0063. 10 rooms. No credit cards. Inexpensive-Moderate.*

Galleon House. This small hotel has a panoramic view of St. Thomas and offers a variety of accommodations, some with private verandas; similarly, some have air-conditioning and cable TV, and some do not. A Continental breakfast is served, and there is a player piano on the main veranda. *Box 6577, Charlotte Amalie, 00801, tel. 809/774-6952 or 800/524-2052. 14 rooms. Facilities: pool, restaurant. AE, MC, V (plus 5% service charge). Inexpensive.*

St. Croix **The Buccaneer.** If you like tropical golf or a 240-acre self-contained beach resort offering all water sports, tennis, basketball, a nature/jogging trail, shopping arcade, health spa, and several restaurants, this is the place for you. All rooms have refrigerators and safes. The hotel's newsletter informs guests of scheduled island tours, pig roasts, terrace jazz concerts, and bartender "drink demos." *Box 218, Christiansted, 00820-0218, tel. 809/773-2100 or 800/223-1108. 148 rooms. Facilities: beach, 4 restaurants, golf, health spa, pool, tennis, basketball, horseback riding, jogging trail, water sports, shopping arcade. AE, DC, MC, V. Very Expensive.*

Carambola Beach Resort and Golf Club. This horticulturally lush Rockresorts property looks like a red-roof village in a green valley next to the sea. (It's between Christiansted and Frederiksted.) The air is redolent of exotic gardens and of the beautiful wood of which everything seems to be made. The villa rooms—three upstairs, three downstairs—are spacious and elegant in an island way, with bench showers and screened porches. *Box 3031, Kingshill, 00850, tel. 809/778-3800 or 800/ 223-7637. 156 rooms plus 1 suite. Facilities: beach, 5 tennis courts (2 lighted), golf course, pool, water sports, 2 Jacuzzis, 2 restaurants. AE, DC, MC, V. Very Expensive.*

★ **Cormorant Beach Club.** Breeze-bent palm trees, hammocks, the thrum of the north-shore waves, and a blissful sense of respected privacy rule here. All beachfront villa rooms have a patio or balcony, air-conditioning, telephone, and double-sink bath. Coffee is set out daily in the building breezeways, and you have a "CBC" terry-cloth robe to wear when you walk to the beautifully ledged polygonal pool. The airy, high-ceiling restaurant is one of St. Croix's best. *108 LaGrande Princesse, Christiansted, 00820, tel. 809/778-8920 or 800/548-4460. 38 rooms. Facilities: beach, pool, restaurant, bar, water sports, 2 tennis courts. AE, MC, V. Very Expensive.*

St. Croix by the Sea. The hotel's coastal landscape and view east to Christiansted and Buck Island are spectacular, as is its huge, curved seawater pool. Standard, superior, and ocean-view rooms all have air-conditioning, cable TV, telephone, and shower-massage heads. *Box 248, Christiansted, 00820, tel. 809/ 778-8600, 800/524-5006, or 800/223-5695. 62 rooms. Facilities: 2 restaurants, saltwater pool, 4 tennis courts. AE, DC, MC, V. Expensive-Very Expensive.*

Divi St. Croix. Being on the less traveled southeastern coast, busy Divi caters comprehensively to its guests. Name your water-sports vehicle. Pool-view and ocean-front rooms have been completely renovated with new archways for canopy beds and brown pedestal sinks. Spinnakers Restaurant has dazzling stage shows. *Box 4289, Christiansted, 00820, tel. 809/773–9700 or 800/367–3484. 86 rooms. Facilities: beach, 2 restaurants, bar, pool, water sports, 2 tennis courts. AE, DC, MC, V. Expensive.*

Hotel on the Cay. This resort on Protestant Cay is the visual centerpiece of Christiansted's harbor and has two fine beach areas that guests at other hotels boat to. Canal-like garden "ponds" flow outside the rooms, which have air-conditioning, telephone, and cable TV and have just been redone. Ferry service is incredibly frequent. *Box 4020, Christiansted, 00820, tel. 809/773–2035 or 800/524–2035. 55 rooms. Facilities: restaurant, pool, 4 tennis courts, water sports. AE, MC, V. Expensive.*

★ **The Pink Fancy.** This is a homey, restful place right in town. The oldest of the four buildings here is a 1780 Danish town house, and old stone walls and foundations enhance the setting. The inn's efficiency rooms are very clean and well-tended; four have air-conditioning. Articulate host Wendall Snyder may reveal to you why St. Croix scuba diving is the Caribbean's best-kept secret. *27 Prince St., Christiansted, 00820, tel. 809/773–8460 or 800/524–2045. 13 rooms. Facilities: pool, bar. MC, V. Expensive.*

Anchor Inn. Here stairs and porchways lead to motel-like rooms with small balconies, air-conditioning, cable TV, small refrigerators, and bedspreads in orange-brown shades. Your harbor window may overlook a corrugated roof, but bathrooms have tubs and showers and the inn is right at the heart of the Christiansted waterfront. *58 King St., Christiansted, 00820, tel. 809/773–4000 or 800/524–2030. 30 rooms. Facilities: restaurant, bar, pool, water sports nearby. AE, DC, MC, V. Moderate.*

Cathy's Fancy Beach Hotel. Don't misunderstand the "Fancy" part of the old plantation-estate name. The surf is always audible at this hideaway in the sands, which has wooden paths to its efficiency apartments and three-bedroom villas; all rooms have kitchens. Near the wire-fenced pool is a funky beach bar. On Sunday, there is a beach barbecue. This, management notes, is the way the Caribbean was 25 years ago "and we mean to keep it that way." *Box 400, Pelican Cove, west of Christiansted, 00820, tel. 809/773–5595 or 800/524–5004. 21 rooms. Facilities: beach, bar, snorkeling. MC, V. Moderate.*

Queen's Quarter Hotel. Like a serene hilltop campus, the hotel lies above a verdant valley in central St. Croix. Guest units, from studios to villas, have such old-sugar-plantation names as Work 'n Rest, Fanny's Fancy, and Solitude. For beach access, buses take guests to the Hotel on the Cay or Cathy's Fancy. If you don't much care about water sports, you will find this a special and especially peaceful lodging. *Box 770, Christiansted, 00820, tel. 809/778–3784 or 800/524–2033. 37 rooms. Facilities: restaurant, pool, bar. Moderate.*

★ **Sprat Hall.** This seaside Frederiksted establishment is a restored plantation estate, the oldest in the U.S. Virgin Islands. The Hurd family serves stylish meals in the homey, antique-furnished great house (no smoking, please). You can stay at a family cottage or modern duplex suite on the extensive grounds. This is the place for horseback riding; across the road is a beach restaurant dappled with sunlight. *Box 695, Frederiksted, 00840, tel. 809/772-0305 or 800/843-3584. 17 rooms. Facilities: beach, restaurant, horseback riding, water sports. No credit cards. Moderate.*

Tamarind Reef Beachside Inn. There is a superb little beach and snorkeling reef here, and Little Green Cay and Buck Island seem thrillingly close. All rooms are ground level and have sea views, kitchenettes, and patio hibachis; no telephones or TV; two rooms have air-conditioning. (There are no individual bungalows.) *Estate Southgate, Christiansted, 00820, tel. 809/773-0463. 16 rooms. Facilities: beach, pool, bar, water sports. AE, MC, V. Moderate.*

Club Comanche. The picturesque stone mill (looking like a topless lighthouse) at dockside houses only canoes, and guests' rooms are anything but uniform. A split-level suite can be had, as can a room with a fourposter or (in Room 52) a waterbed. Evenings bring the sounds of cocktail piano music from the balcony of the Comanche Restaurant. The pool is long enough for decent lap swimming. *1 Strand St., Christiansted, 00820, tel. 809/773-0210 or 800/524-2066. 36 rooms, most with private bath. Facilities: restaurant, bar, saltwater pool, water sports. AE, MC, V. Inexpensive-Moderate.*

King's Alley Hotel. This slatted, brown-painted hotel has angled, recessed balconies; some of its rooms look out on the Christiansted waterfront and marina; all have telephones, air-conditioning, and cable TV. The adjacent courtyard is lovely on a breezy morning and romantically lighted at night. *King's Alley, Christiansted, 00820, tel. 809/773-0103 or 800/843-3574. 23 rooms. Facilities: pool, restaurant, water sports, AE, DC, MC, V. Inexpensive-Moderate.*

★ **The Frederiksted.** Ask for the ocean view: traffic on the street outside is usually light, and you can gaze across to the tranquil western sea through a floor-to-ceiling window. All the inn's rooms have air-conditioning, cable TV, wet bar, and refrigerator. The Frederiksted's pool is a small splash, but the lanterned and awninged red-tile courtyard is very pretty and cozy. *20 Strand St., Frederiksted, 00840, tel. 809/772-0500 or 800/524-2025. 28 rooms. Facilities: pool. AE, DC, MC, V. Inexpensive.*

★ **Hotel Caravelle.** There is a tidy European elegance about the Caravelle. All rooms have air-conditioning, cable TV, and refrigerators (under the bathroom counter), and the matching blues, grays, and purples of the bedspreads and wall hangings are tastefully cool and summery, as a northerner might put it. Superior rooms overlook the harbor. Manager Elsie Galloway is friendly and helpful. *44A Queen Cross St., Christiansted, 00820, tel. 809/773-0687 or 800/524-0410. 43 rooms. Facilities: waterfront restaurant and bar, pool, water sports. AE, DC, MC, V. Inexpensive.*

Moonraker Hotel. Squirreled away downtown, the Moonraker has simple rooms with air-conditioning, cable TV (with free HBO), telephone, and small refrigerator; all are the same price. You'll find white bedspreads, oval mirrors, and nifty small, bureau-ledge lamps. *43A Queen Cross St., Christiansted, 00820, tel. 809/773-1535. 15 rooms. AE, MC, V. Inexpensive.*

St. John **Caneel Bay.** The beauty of St. John virtually begins here at this
★ 170-acre peninsula, developed in the 1950s by Laurance Rockefeller. It is like an ecologist's park, but one with tropical

gardens, seven beaches, three restaurants, and an 18th-century sugar mill. Rustic rooms have simple interiors of regional woods and handwoven fabrics. No telephone or TV in the rooms, since this is the prototypical Rockresort. Male guests are asked to wear jackets after 6 PM. *Caneel Bay (St. John's North Shore), 00830, tel. 809/776–6111 or 800/223–7637. 171 rooms. Facilities: beach, 3 restaurants, 11 tennis courts, water sports. AE, DC, MC, V. Very Expensive.*

Virgin Grand Beach Hotel. St. John's major new big resort, this 34-acre property has impressively landscaped suites and luxurious town houses with marble-platform whirlpool baths, a long beach and marina, and a quarter-acre pool. Some units have full kitchen facilities. The Fronds restaurant offers gourmet dining. It all has the aspect of a semi-neo-Aztec royal city. *Great Cruz Bay, 00830, tel. 809/776–7171 or 800/323–7249. 264 rooms. Facilities: beach, marina, 2 restaurants, pool, water sports, tennis. AE, DC, MC, V. Very Expensive.*

★ **Gallows Point.** These gray quadragonal-roof buildings with jalousied windows grace the peninsula south of the Cruz Bay ferry dock. Garden apartments have spacious garden showers, and upper-level apartments have loft bedrooms. The kitchen facilities are excellent. There's a fine little snorkeling beach below the pool. The entranceway is bridged by Ellington's restaurant. *Box 58, Cruz Bay, 00830, tel. 809/776–6434 or 800/323–7229. 60 rooms. Facilities: beach, pool, snorkeling. AE, DC, MC, V. Expensive.*

Cruz Views. The views are from a hill close to Cruz Bay Village. Five of the 10 one-bedroom condo units have lofts, and all have covered decks and garden showers. Sofas have pull-out beds. The rooms are island-simple and neat but, without air-conditioning, not always as cool as one would like. No telephone or TV in the rooms. *CDC Realty & Management Company, Box 458, Cruz Bay, 00830, tel. 809/776–6152, 800/524–2095, or 800/338–0987. 10 rooms. Facilities: pool. MC, V. Moderate.*

Raintree Inn. If you want to be right at the action in town and bunk at an affordable, island-style place, go no farther. The dark-wood rooms have a nicely simple, tropical-cabin feeling to them. Three efficiencies here have kitchens and—if you don't mind climbing an indoor ladder—a comfortable sleeping loft. A restaurant, The Fish Trap, is next door. *Box 566, Cruz Bay, 00830, tel. 809/776–7449. 11 rooms. MC, V. Inexpensive–Moderate.*

The Cruz Inn. The buildings here are only a few blocks away from the Cruz Bay ferry dock and have a view of Enighed Pond. One building has seven carpeted guest rooms that share two baths. There are also suites with or without cooking facilities, an air-conditioned apartment, and an efficiency with cold water only. Continental breakfast is complimentary. *Box 566, Cruz Bay, 00830, tel. 809/776–7688. 14 rooms, 5 with private bath. Facilities: restaurant, bar. MC, V, D. Inexpensive.*

The Inn at Tamarind Court. If you can only barely afford a vacation on St. John, try this inexpensive hostelry located right in town. It's especially suited to singles. There is an "inn" part, with six rooms and two shared baths, and a "hotel" part, with 11 rooms with private bath and shared-bath family rooms. The front-courtyard bar is a friendly hangout: Darts, Ping-Pong, and a horseshoe pit are provided. *350 Cruz Bay, 00830, tel. 809/776–6378. 20 rooms, 11 with private bath. AE, MC, V. Inexpensive.*

Campgrounds **Cinnamon Bay Campground.** Tents, one-room cottages, and bare sites are available at this National Park Service location on an attractive beach. The tents are 10 feet by 14 feet, with flooring, and come with living, eating, and sleeping furnishings and necessities; the 15-foot-by-15-foot cottages have twin beds. Bare sites, which come with a picnic table and a charcoal grill, must be reserved in writing no earlier than eight months prior to arrival. *Cruz Bay, 00830–0720, tel. 809/776–6330 or 800/-223–7637. Facilities: beach, commissary, bathhouses (showers and toilets), restaurant, water sports. MC, V.*

Maho Bay Camp. Eight miles from Cruz Bay, this National Park Service campground is a lush hillside community of three-room tent cottages linked by boardwalk stairs and ramps, which also lead down to the beach. The 16-foot-by-16-foot shelters have beds, dining table and chairs, electric lamps (and outlets), propane stove, ice cooler, and kitchenware and cutlery. *Box 310, Cruz Bay, 00830, tel. 809/776–6240, 809/776–6226, or 800/393–9004. 99 tent-cottages. Facilities: beach, restaurant, commissary, barbecue areas, bathhouses (showers, sinks, and toilets), water sports. No credit cards.*

Nightlife

Don't look for brassy casino shows in these isles. Nightlife in the U.S. Virgin Islands consists of a choice between town and resort, resort being one of the large or even small hotels that have local bands or limbo shows one or more nights each week.

Charlotte Amalie on St. Thomas has the biggest club scene, with the music ranging from disco and live rock to West Indian pop, steel bands, and cocktail piano. But you can also find varied entertainment, including occasional stage shows, from night to night at the luxury hotels. Call ahead to be sure when and which things are happening.

St. Thomas Among the most popular clubs in downtown Charlotte Amalie are **The Greenhouse, Yesterday's, Barnacle Bill's Club 54,** and the **Old Mill.** For a disco that's a little dressier, try **Club Z.** You can enjoy more local or island music at the **Hillside Club** or **Walter's Living Room.** St. Thomas hotels offering quite a menu of entertainment, from combos to calypso, include **Frenchman's Reef, Bluebeard's Castle, Limetree Beach,** and **Stouffer Grand Beach.** For romantic piano—and great views—head uphill to **Bluebeard's Castle** or **Blackbeard's Castle.**

In the realm of the arts, major concerts and shows on St. Thomas are held at the **Reichhold Center for the Arts,** on the campus of the College of the Virgin Islands (tel. 809/774–4482).

St. Croix Christiansted has a lively and eminently casual club scene near the waterfront (Frederiksted has considerably less to offer). **Rumors** is a disco with a decklike dance floor, while at **Hondo's Backyard,** you'll hear live guitar and vocals in an open-air courtyard with a bar and Cinzano tables. The upstairs **Moonraker Lounge** brings in lively performers for periods of several weeks, such as Gary Loyd from Nashville. Milder piano music can be enjoyed on the broad veranda of **Club Comanche.** For jazz, there is the **Bombay Club,** with Jimmy Hamilton and his band. St. Croix hotels worth checking out for nightly music and weekly shows are **The Buccaneer** and **Divi St. Croix.**

St. John For live or recorded music in the little village of Cruz Bay, try **Fred's,** which has live local sounds a couple of nights a week, or **World Headquarters,** at MonGoose Junction, which is lively pretty late on weekends. A solid late-hours hangout is **The Back Yard.** At new Wharfside Village, there is Pusser's **Crow's Nest** pub, where you might hear folk singer–entertainer Jeff Cahill, and the spacious pool-table bar **Larry's Landing.** For resort entertainment a little outside of town, try the luxurious **Virgin Grand.**

Index

Personal Itinerary

Departure *Date*

Time

Transportation

Arrival *Date* *Time*

Departure *Date* *Time*

Transportation

Accommodations

Arrival *Date* *Time*

Departure *Date* *Time*

Transportation

Accommodations

Arrival *Date* *Time*

Departure *Date* *Time*

Transportation

Accommodations

Personal Itinerary

Arrival *Date*   *Time*

Departure *Date*   *Time*

Transportation

Accommodations

Arrival *Date*   *Time*

Departure *Date*   *Time*

Transportation

Accommodations

Arrival *Date*   *Time*

Departure *Date*   *Time*

Transportation

Accommodations

Arrival *Date*   *Time*

Departure *Date*   *Time*

Transportation

Accommodations

Personal Itinerary

Arrival *Date*   *Time*

Departure *Date*   *Time*

Transportation

Accommodations

Arrival *Date*   *Time*

Departure *Date*   *Time*

Transportation

Accommodations

Arrival *Date*   *Time*

Departure *Date*   *Time*

Transportation

Accommodations

Arrival *Date*   *Time*

Departure *Date*   *Time*

Transportation

Accommodations

Personal Itinerary

Arrival *Date*   *Time*

Departure *Date*   *Time*

Transportation

Accommodations

Arrival *Date*   *Time*

Departure *Date*   *Time*

Transportation

Accommodations

Arrival *Date*   *Time*

Departure *Date*   *Time*

Transportation

Accommodations

Arrival *Date*   *Time*

Departure *Date*   *Time*

Transportation

Accommodations

Personal Itinerary

Arrival *Date*   *Time*

Departure *Date*   *Time*

Transportation

Accommodations

Arrival *Date*   *Time*

Departure *Date*   *Time*

Transportation

Accommodations

Arrival *Date*   *Time*

Departure *Date*   *Time*

Transportation

Accommodations

Arrival *Date*   *Time*

Departure *Date*   *Time*

Transportation

Accommodations

Personal Itinerary

Arrival   *Date*   *Time*

Departure   *Date*   *Time*

Transportation

Accommodations

Arrival   *Date*   *Time*

Departure   *Date*   *Time*

Transportation

Accommodations

Arrival   *Date*   *Time*

Departure   *Date*   *Time*

Transportation

Accommodations

Arrival   *Date*   *Time*

Departure   *Date*   *Time*

Transportation

Accommodations

Personal Itinerary

Arrival *Date*   *Time*

Departure *Date*   *Time*

Transportation

Accommodations

Arrival *Date*   *Time*

Departure *Date*   *Time*

Transportation

Accommodations

Arrival *Date*   *Time*

Departure *Date*   *Time*

Transportation

Accommodations

Arrival *Date*   *Time*

Departure *Date*   *Time*

Transportation

Accommodations

Addresses

Name	*Name*
Address	*Address*
Telephone	*Telephone*
Name	*Name*
Address	*Address*
Telephone	*Telephone*
Name	*Name*
Address	*Address*
Telephone	*Telephone*
Name	*Name*
Address	*Address*
Telephone	*Telephone*
Name	*Name*
Address	*Address*
Telephone	*Telephone*
Name	*Name*
Address	*Address*
Telephone	*Telephone*
Name	*Name*
Address	*Address*
Telephone	*Telephone*
Name	*Name*
Address	*Address*
Telephone	*Telephone*

Addresses

Name	*Name*
Address	*Address*
Telephone	*Telephone*
Name	*Name*
Address	*Address*
Telephone	*Telephone*
Name	*Name*
Address	*Address*
Telephone	*Telephone*
Name	*Name*
Address	*Address*
Telephone	*Telephone*
Name	*Name*
Address	*Address*
Telephone	*Telephone*
Name	*Name*
Address	*Address*
Telephone	*Telephone*
Name	*Name*
Address	*Address*
Telephone	*Telephone*
Name	*Name*
Address	*Address*
Telephone	*Telephone*

Addresses

Name	*Name*
Address	*Address*
Telephone	*Telephone*
Name	*Name*
Address	*Address*
Telephone	*Telephone*
Name	*Name*
Address	*Address*
Telephone	*Telephone*
Name	*Name*
Address	*Address*
Telephone	*Telephone*
Name	*Name*
Address	*Address*
Telephone	*Telephone*
Name	*Name*
Address	*Address*
Telephone	*Telephone*
Name	*Name*
Address	*Address*
Telephone	*Telephone*

Fodor's Travel Guides

U.S. Guides

Alaska
Arizona
Atlantic City & the
  New Jersey Shore
Boston
California
Cape Cod
Carolinas & the
  Georgia Coast
The Chesapeake Region
Chicago
Colorado
Dallas & Fort
  Worth

Disney World & the
  Orlando Area
Florida
Hawaii
Houston &
  Galveston
Las Vegas
Los Angeles, Orange
  County, Palm Springs
Maui
Miami, Fort Lauderdale,
  Palm Beach
Michigan, Wisconsin,
  Minnesota

New England
New Mexico
New Orleans
New Orleans (Pocket
  Guide)
New York City
New York City (Pocket
  Guide)
New York State
Pacific North Coast
Philadelphia
The Rockies
San Diego
San Francisco

San Francisco (Pocket
  Guide)
The South
Texas
USA
Virgin Islands
Virginia
Waikiki
Washington, DC
Williamsburg

Foreign Guides

Acapulco
Amsterdam
Australia, New Zealand,
  The South Pacific
Austria
Bahamas
Bahamas (Pocket
  Guide)
Baja & the Pacific
  Coast Resorts
Barbados
Belgium & Luxembourg
Bermuda
Brazil
Britain (Great Travel
  Values)
Budget Europe
Canada
Canada (Great Travel
  Values)
Canada's Atlantic
  Provinces
Cancún, Cozumel,
  Mérida, the
  Yucatán
Caribbean

Caribbean (Great
  Travel Values)
Central America
China
China's Great Cities
Eastern Europe
Egypt
Europe
Europe's Great Cities
Florence & Venice
France
France (Great Travel
  Values)
Germany
Germany (Great Travel
  Values)
Great Britain
Greece
The Himalayan
  Countries
Holland
Hong Kong
Hungary
India, including Nepal
Ireland
Israel

Italy
Italy (Great Travel
  Values)
Jamaica
Japan
Japan (Great Travel
  Values)
Jordan & the Holy Land
Kenya, Tanzania,
  the Seychelles
Korea
Lisbon
Loire Valley
London
London (Great Travel
  Values)
London (Pocket Guide)
Madrid & Barcelona
Mexico
Mexico City
Montreal &
  Quebec City
Munich
New Zealand
North Africa
Paris

Paris (Pocket Guide)
Portugal
Rio de Janeiro
The Riviera (Fun on)
Rome
Saint Martin &
  Sint Maarten
Scandinavia
Scandinavian Cities
Scotland
Singapore
South America
South Pacific
Southeast Asia
Soviet Union
Spain
Spain (Great Travel
  Values)
Sweden
Switzerland
Sydney
Tokyo
Toronto
Turkey
Vienna
Yugoslavia

Special-Interest Guides

Bed & Breakfast
  Guide: North America
Health & Fitness
  Vacations

Royalty Watching
Selected Hotels of
  Europe

Selected Resorts
  and Hotels of the U.S.
Shopping in Europe

Skiing in North
  America
Sunday in New York

Help us evaluate hotels and restaurants for the next edition of this guide, and we will send you a free issue of Fodor's newsletter, TravelSense.

Title of this guide:

1 Hotel ❑ **Restaurant** ❑ *(check one)*

Name

Number/Street

City/State/Country

Comments

2 Hotel ❑ **Restaurant** ❑ *(check one)*

Name

Number/Street

City/State/Country

Comments

3 Hotel ❑ **Restaurant** ❑ *(check one)*

Name

Number/Street

City/State/Country

Comments

General Comments

Please complete for a free copy of TravelSense

Name

Number/Street

City/State/Zip

Business Reply Mail

First Class   *Permit № 7775*   *New York, NY*

Postage will be paid by addressee

Fodor's Travel Publications

201 East 50th Street
New York, NY 10022